THE PRODUCTION OF BOOKS
ENGLAND 1350–1500

Between roughly 1350 and 1500, the English vernacular became established as a language of literary, bureaucratic, devotional and controversial writing; metropolitan artisans formed guilds for the production and sale of books for the first time; and Gutenberg's, and eventually Caxton's, printed books reached their first English consumers. This book gathers the best new work on manuscript books in England made during this crucial but neglected period. Its authors survey existing research, gather intensive new evidence and develop new approaches to key topics. The chapters cover the material conditions and economy of the book trade; amateur production both lay and religious; the effects of censorship; and the impact on English book production of manuscripts and artisans from elsewhere in the British Isles and Europe. A wide-ranging and innovative series of essays, this volume is a major contribution to the history of the book in medieval England.

ALEXANDRA GILLESPIE is Associate Professor of English and Medieval Studies at the University of Toronto. She is the author of *Print Culture and the Medieval Author* (2006) and editor of a special issue of *Huntington Library Quarterly* on *Tudor Literature in Manuscript and Print* and, with Ian Gadd, of *John Stow (1525–1625) and the Making of the English Past* (2004).

DANIEL WAKELIN is Lecturer in English at the University of Cambridge. He is the author of *Humanism, Reading and English Literature 1430–1530* (2007).

Cambridge Studies in Palaeography and Codicology

FOUNDING EDITORS

Albinia de la Mare
Rosamond McKitterick   *Newnham College, University of Cambridge*

GENERAL EDITORS

David Ganz   *King's College London*
Teresa Webber   *Trinity College, University of Cambridge*

This series has been established to further the study of manuscripts from the Middle Ages to the Renaissance. It includes books devoted to particular types of manuscripts, their production and circulation, to individual codices of outstanding importance, and to regions, periods, and scripts of especial interest to scholars. The series will be of interest not only to scholars and students of medieval literature and history, but also to theologians, art historians and others working with manuscript sources.

RECENT TITLES

William Noel   *The Harley Psalter*

Charles F. Briggs   *Giles of Rome's De regimine principum: Reading and Writing Politics at Court and University, c.1275 – c.1525*

Leslie Brubaker   *Vision and Meaning in Ninth-Century Byzantium: Image as Exegesis in the Homilies of Gregory of Nazianzus*

Francis Newton   *The Scriptorium and Library at Monte Cassino, 1058–1105*

Lisa Fagin Davis   *The Gottschalk Antiphonary: Music and Liturgy in Twelfth-Century Lambach*

Albert Derolez   *The Palaeography of Gothic Manuscript Books: From the Twelfth to the Early Sixteenth Century*

Alison I. Beach   *Women as Scribes: Book Production and Monastic Reform in Twelfth-Century Bavaria*

Yitzhak Hen and Rob Meens, editors   *The Bobbio Missal: Liturgy and Religious Culture in Merovingian Gaul*

Marica Tacconi   *Cathedral and Civic Ritual in Late Medieval and Renaissance Florence: The Service Books of Santa Maria del Fiore*

Anna A. Grotans   *Reading in Medieval St Gall*

THE PRODUCTION OF BOOKS
IN ENGLAND 1350–1500

Edited by

ALEXANDRA GILLESPIE AND DANIEL WAKELIN

CAMBRIDGE
UNIVERSITY PRESS

The Edinburgh Building, Cambridge CB2 8RU, UK

Published in the United States of America by Cambridge University Press, New York

Cambridge University Press is part of the University of Cambridge.

It furthers the University's mission by disseminating knowledge in the pursuit of
education, learning and research at the highest international levels of excellence.

www.cambridge.org
Information on this title: www.cambridge.org/9781107680197

© Cambridge University Press 2011

First published 2011
First paperback edition 2013

A catalogue record for this publication is available from the British Library

ISBN 978-0-521-88979-7 Hardback
ISBN 978-1-107-68019-7 Paperback

Contents

Contents

vi

Illustrations

3 MAPPING THE WORDS

4 DESIGNING THE PAGE

8 COMMERCIAL ORGANIZATION AND ECONOMIC INNOVATION

9 VERNACULAR LITERARY MANUSCRIPTS AND THEIR SCRIBES

Contributors

MARGARET CONNOLLY is an Honorary Research Fellow in the School of English, University of St Andrews; she was formerly Senior Lecturer in English at University College, Cork. She is the editor of *Contemplations of the Dread and Love of God* (1993), with T. G. Duncan of *The Middle English Mirror* (2003) and with Linne Mooney of *Design and Distribution of Late Medieval Manuscripts in England* (2008). She is the author of *John Shirley: Book Production and the Noble Household in Fifteenth-Century England* (1998) and recently published *The Index of Middle English Prose Handlist XIX: Manuscripts in the University Library, Cambridge (Dd–Oo)* (2009).

ORIETTA DA ROLD is a lecturer in Chaucer and Medieval Literature at the University of Leicester. She has published on medieval manuscripts, paper and scribes, and is particularly interested in the textual culture of the manuscripts of *The Canterbury Tales*. She held a Falconer Madan Award from the Bibliographical Society and a visiting scholarship at Wolfson College, Oxford in order to research the introduction of paper into England.

MARTHA DRIVER is Distinguished Professor of English and Women's and Gender Studies at Pace University in New York City. She is a co-founder of the Early Book Society for the study of manuscripts and printing history and writes about illustration from manuscript to print, book production and the early history of publishing. She is the author of *The Image in Print: Book Illustration in Late Medieval England* (2004) and, with Michael Orr, of *An Index of Images in English MSS* (2007) and editor, with Sid Ray, of two books: *The Medieval Hero on Screen* (2007) and *Shakespeare and the Middle Ages* (2009).

ALEXANDRA GILLESPIE is Associate Professor of English and Medieval Studies at the University of Toronto. She is the author of *Print Culture and the Medieval Author* (2006) and editor of a special issue of *Huntington Library Quarterly* on *Tudor Literature in Manuscript and Print* and, with Ian Gadd, of *John Stow*

(1525–1625) and the Making of the English Past (2004). She is currently working on a study of medieval English bookbinding.

SIMON HOROBIN is a reader in the Faculty of English and a Fellow of Magdalen College, University of Oxford. He is the author of *The Language of the Chaucer Tradition* (2003) and *Chaucer's Language* (2006), and has published widely on fifteenth-century manuscript production.

ERIK KWAKKEL teaches manuscript studies at Leiden University, The Netherlands, where he directs an NWO-funded research project on twelfth-century manuscript innovation. He has published on a variety of codicological and palaeographical topics, including the introduction of paper in vernacular book production and the physical appearance of miscellanies. He has published a book on manuscript production in Brussels, 1350–1400 (2002) and a co-edited volume on Middle Dutch bible translations and their manuscripts (2007).

LINNE R. MOONEY is Professor of Medieval English Palaeography at the University of York and Director of the Centre for Medieval Studies at York. Her research on the scribes of late medieval English literature won her international recognition when she discovered the identity of Adam Pinkhurst, the scribe who worked for Chaucer and wrote the Hengwrt and Ellesmere manuscripts of *The Canterbury Tales*. She is now Principal Investigator of an AHRC-funded project to identify more of these scribes.

MICHAEL ORR is Professor of Art History and Chair of the Department of Art and Art History at Lawrence University in Appleton, Wisconsin. He is a contributor to the Harvey Miller series *An Index of Images in English Manuscripts from the Time of Chaucer to Henry VIII* (2009) and has recently completed chapters on the hierarchies of decoration in English Books of Hours and on the iconography of St Anne teaching the Virgin to read.

STEPHEN PARTRIDGE is an Assistant Professor of English at the University of British Columbia. He was a contributor to *The Wife of Bath's Prologue on CD-ROM* (Cambridge University Press, 1996) and editor, with Siân Echard, of *The Book Unbound* (2004). He has published on Chaucer and other Middle English manuscripts and printed books in *English Manuscript Studies*, *The Chaucer Review* and elsewhere.

DEREK PEARSALL was a professor of English at the University of York and one of the founders of York's Centre for Medieval Studies; he retired as Gurney Professor of English at Harvard University. He is the author of books on Chaucer, Gower, Lydgate and Langland, and an editor and bibliographer of these and other medieval authors' works. He has recently published a complete revision of his 1978 edition of the C text of *Piers Plowman*.

JEAN-PASCAL POUZET studied at the Université de Paris IV-Sorbonne and in Cambridge and Oxford. He is a lecturer in English and teaches at the Université de Limoges and a research fellow at the Centre d'Études Supérieures de Civilisation Médiévale (Université de Poitiers). He has published various articles on manuscript production by Augustinians, on the manuscript circulation of Insular French in England and on the manuscripts of parabiblical writings in English.

DAVID RUNDLE is a member of the History Faculty at the University of Oxford and former Lyell Research Fellow in Palaeography and Manuscript Studies at Corpus Christi College, Oxford. He has published work on the uses of libraries in the late medieval and early modern period and on international aspects of humanist culture in the period before the Reformation. He has recently revised Roberto Weiss's *Medium Ævum* Monograph, *Humanism in England during the Fifteenth Century* for on-line publication and is completing his own monograph on *England and the Identity of Italian Renaissance Humanism, c.1400–c.1460.*

WENDY SCASE is Geoffrey Shepherd Professor of Medieval English Literature at the University of Birmingham. She is the author of *Piers Plowman and the New Anticlericalism* (Cambridge University Press, 1989), *Reginald Pecock* (1998) and *Literature and Complaint in England 1272–1553* (2007). She is also co-editor of *New Medieval Literatures* and director of the AHRC-funded catalogue of 'Manuscripts of the West Midlands' and of the Vernon Manuscript Project at the University of Birmingham.

FIONA SOMERSET is Associate Professor at Duke University. She is the author of *Clerical Discourse and Lay Audience in Late Medieval England* (Cambridge University Press, 1998) and editor of *Four Wycliffite Dialogues* (2009). She edits the *Yearbook of Langland Studies* with Andrew Cole and Lawrence Warner and is currently at work on a monograph about lollards, entitled *Feeling Like Saints*, and is collaborating with Stephen E. Lahey and J. Patrick Hornbeck II to produce a volume of modernized writings on *Wycliffite Spirituality*.

JOHN J. THOMPSON is Professor of English Textual Cultures at Queen's University, Belfast. He is the author of *Robert Thornton and the London Thornton Manuscript* (1987) and *The Middle English Cursor Mundi: Poem, Texts and Contexts* (1998), and has co-edited a number of collections of essays. He is currently writing a history of Anglophone Ireland from 1300 to 1660.

DANIEL WAKELIN is a lecturer in English Literature at the University of Cambridge and a Fellow of Christ's College. He has published *Humanism, Reading and English Literature 1430–1530* (2007) and is currently researching scribal corrections in Middle English and editing William Worcester's *The Boke of Noblesse*.

Foreword

DEREK PEARSALL

References in the Introduction to the present volume make it clear that it is viewed to some extent as a successor to an earlier collection of essays on the same subject, *Book Production and Publishing in Britain 1375–1475*, edited by Jeremy Griffiths and Derek Pearsall. This book had its inception in a series of conferences in York in 1981, 1983 and 1985. The first was called 'Manuscripts and Readers in Fifteenth-Century England: The Literary Implications of Manuscript Study', the conference papers being published under that title in 1983; the second was set up to discuss and prepare for the forthcoming book on book production; the third was on the editing of fifteenth-century texts, and the volume that followed was called *Manuscripts and Texts: Editorial Problems in Later Middle English Literature* (1987). The inspiration for the first conference was the presence at York of an outstanding group of graduate students working under my supervision on topics to do with later medieval manuscripts. For many of them, the impulse to work on manuscripts came from Elizabeth Salter, who died in 1980 but whose work in later years was much directed towards manuscript studies and whose example was irresistible. My own interest in manuscript studies was always and is still in their use for the literary scholar, not just as sources for editing texts, but also for their evidence of the complex nature of authorial revision, including 'rolling revision', and for the important part they played in shaping, even creating, authors' purposes. Inevitably, much of this work on manuscripts drew towards 'reception' as an essential part of our understanding of texts – how texts were transmitted by their scribes or commented on by readers, and how they gave rise to complex networks of patrons, buyers and owners. When the *Book Production* volume came out in 1989, the influence of that first conference was still strong, and some of its participants were contributors; seven of the fifteen essays were on texts or reception, while three of the four essays on production were content-dominated. Jeremy Griffiths was a codicologist more than a literary scholar, and it was he who supervised the essays on paper, decoration and binding, and most of the work on production.

The change that has taken place over twenty years is striking: the 'History of the Book' has taken over. Here the first seven chapters of thirteen progress from the beginning ('Materials') to the end ('Binding') of the production process. There are then three on larger aspects of production and two at the end on English books outside England and on the continent. The essay on 'Censorship' corresponds to the earlier Hudson essay on lollardy. The major difference from the 1989 collection – and it is fairly obvious – is that in that book the emphasis was on the contents of manuscripts, whether literary or not, and who owned and read them. In this book, the main emphasis is on the methods, circumstances and economy of production. The distinction that Partridge makes between the purposes of Parkes in his work on *ordinatio* and the purposes of his own chapter in this volume sums up admirably the different emphasis between the two books. Where Parkes treats page design as 'an intellectual project', Partridge says, here more attention is paid to it as 'a pragmatic challenge and a commercial expectation'. It is a deliberate difference of approach which produces a wholly different kind of book. Just as there is nothing in this book to compare with the marvellous work of Harris and Meale on books and owners, so there was nothing there to compare with the work here, typically, of Mooney, Kwakkel and Pouzet. The splendid essays of these scholars on the evidence of scribes working on several manuscripts and on the organization and economics of production are an index to the great change that has taken place in the approach to the subject, which in turn is part of a larger historical process, in which the individual text, whether 'literary' or not, must find its place in a complex network of historical circumstances and processes.

Other characteristics of the new work in this volume are the quality and intense, minute precision of the detail, some of it made possible by new methodologies and technologies, such as those for identifying scribes and dialects by on-line access to manuscripts and by the appearance of new scholarly tools such as the *Index of Middle English Prose* (IMEP) , whose handlists make it possible for Connolly to present an unrivalled survey of representative collections of religious and utilitarian compilations of all kinds. Also, to contrast with the readiness to move away from text-based study and standard texts, there is a deliberate attempt to press hard at the edges of the subject and leave better-known material to look after itself. This is something made possible by the existence of the earlier book, which can be trusted to 'take care', so to speak, of important genre-based work on music books, on anthologies and compilations, on religious works, and on medical and scientific books. In this respect, the new book can best be seen not as a 'successor' to the earlier one but, as the editors remark in the Introduction, as a complement to it. It is, further, in its own right a magnificent, wide-ranging, innovative and often distinguished series of essays on the English scene.

Acknowledgements

The editors would like to thank all the contributors, but especially Derek Pearsall for very early and continued encouragement of this volume. Linne Mooney also generously allowed them to discuss the rationale behind the volume in a 'round table' with Professor Pearsall at the conference 'Making the Medieval Manuscript' held at the Centre for Medieval Studies at the University of York in July 2005. They are grateful for excellent feedback, both sceptical and enthusiastic, from people present on that occasion (including many people who have turned out to be contributors) which informed the planning of this volume. Finally, thanks to Ian Doyle and the other, anonymous reader from Cambridge University Press for their very useful suggestions, and to Linda Bree and Maartje Scheltens for patient advice and assistance.

Many of the editorial tasks were made easier by the Herculean labours of Peter Buchanan, Christina da Silva, Michael Raby, Helen Marshall, Richard Nalli-Petta, Katherine Sehl, Devani Singh, Robin Sutherland-Harris, Trevor Abes, Samhita Gupta and especially Gregory Fiorini. Their work was supported by generous grants from Canada's Social Sciences and Humanities Research Council (SSHRC) and the University of Toronto, which also provided funds to subsidize photography. Cambridge University Library, Pembroke College, Trinity College and St John's College in Cambridge, the Beinecke Library in Yale University, the Rosenbach Library and the Huntington Library generously waived fees for reproduction rights for this volume.

The research of several contributors was made possible by travel grants provided by their various universities and university departments and other bodies including SSHRC; the Henry E. Huntington Library; and the Bibliographical Society, London. And their research was made enjoyable by the helpfulness of staff at the many libraries and archives whose manuscripts and rare books lie at the heart of the discussions that follow.

Abbreviations

For full titles, see the Bibliography.

Beinecke	New Haven, CT, Yale University, Beinecke Library
BL	London, British Library
ANTS	Anglo-Norman Text Society
BJRL	*Bulletin of the John Rylands Library*
BLR	*Bodleian Library Record*
BodL	Oxford, Bodleian Library
BRUC	Emden, *A Biographical Register of the University of Cambridge*
BRUO	Emden, *A Biographical Register of the University of Oxford*
CBMLC	Corpus of British Medieval Library Catalogues
CCCC	Cambridge, Corpus Christi College Library
CHBB: II	Morgan and Thomson (eds.), *The Cambridge History of the Book in Britain: Volume II, 1100–1400*
CHBB: III	Hellinga and Trapp (eds.), *The Cambridge History of the Book in Britain: Volume III, 1400–1557*
CUL	Cambridge, University Library
DMBL	Watson, *Catalogue of Dated and Datable Manuscripts … in the British Library*
DMCL	Robinson, *Catalogue of Dated and Datable Manuscripts … in Cambridge Libraries*
DMLL	Robinson, *Catalogue of Dated and Datable Manuscripts … in London Libraries*
DMOL	Watson, *Catalogue of Dated and Datable Manuscripts … in Oxford Libraries*
EEBO	Early English Books Online, http://eebo.chadwyck.com/home
EETS	Early English Text Society
	os original series
	ss supplementary series
	es extra series

EHR	*English Historical Review*
Ellesmere	HEHL, MS Ellesmere 26.C.9, *The Canterbury Tales*
ELN	*English Language Notes*
EMS	*English Manuscript Studies 1100–1700*
G&P	Griffiths and Pearsall (eds.), *Book Production and Publishing in Britain 1375–1475*
GUL	Glasgow, University Library
HEHL	San Marino, CA, Henry E. Huntington Library
Hengwrt	NLW, MS Peniarth 392.D, *The Canterbury Tales*
IPMEP	Lewis, Blake and Edwards, *Index of Printed Middle English Prose*
IMEP, I–XIX	*The Index of Middle English Prose, Handlist I–XIX*
IMEV	Brown and Robbins, *The Index of Middle English Verse*; Cutler and Robbins, *Supplement to the Index of Middle English Verse*; Boffey and Edwards, *A New Index of Middle English Verse*
JEBS	*Journal of the Early Book Society*
JRL	Manchester, John Rylands University Library
JWCI	*Journal of the Warburg and Courtauld Institutes*
LALME	McIntosh, Samuels and Beskin, *A Linguistic Atlas of Late Mediaeval English 1350–1450*
Library	*The Library: Transactions of the Bibliographical Society*
Longleat	Wiltshire, Longleat House
MÆ	*Medium Ævum*
MED	Lewis (gen. ed.), *The Middle English Dictionary*, http://quod.lib.umich.edu/m/med/
MLGB	Ker, *Medieval Libraries of Great Britain*
MLGB Suppl.	Watson, *Medieval Libraries of Great Britain: Supplement*
MMBL	Ker and Piper, *Medieval Manuscripts in British Libraries*
NA	London, National Archives (formerly PRO)
NLS	Edinburgh, National Library of Scotland
NLW	Aberystwyth, National Library of Wales
ODNB	Matthew, Harrison and Goldman (eds.), *Oxford Dictionary of National Biography*, www.oxforddnb.com/public/index.html
OED	*Oxford English Dictionary*, www.oed.com/
Pembroke, Camb.	Cambridge, Pembroke College Library
PML	New York, Pierpont Morgan Library
PRO	Kew, Public Record Office
SAC	*Studies in the Age of Chaucer*
SB	*Studies in Bibliography*

St John's, Camb.	Cambridge, St John's College Library
STC	Pollard and Redgrave, *A Short-Title Catalogue of Books Printed in England, Scotland and Wales* (2nd edn)
TCBS	*Transactions of the Cambridge Bibliographical Society*
TCC	Cambridge, Trinity College Library

Introduction

ALEXANDRA GILLESPIE AND DANIEL WAKELIN

Some time in the mid fifteenth century, an illustrator – perhaps the London stationer-limner William Abell – was commissioned to illustrate BL, MS Cotton Tiberius A.vii, a copy of an English translation of Guillaume de Guileville's *Pilgrimage of the Life of Man*, sometimes ascribed to John Lydgate.[1] One of the hundreds of unframed, pen-drawn miniatures that the limner produced appears on the cover of this book and is reproduced again here (Figure 0.1). Lady Hagiography, who has led the pilgrim-narrator on his wanderings through the poem, leads him and Lady Lesson behind him into a room filled with books: Lady Hagiography stands between the shelves and gestures to all the tomes of wisdom the pilgrim has yet to acquire.

The image has proved an evocative one for students of literary culture in the fourteenth and fifteenth centuries, and of the manuscripts which were that culture's essential tools. In 1942, Laura Hibbard Loomis took up the argument of earlier commentators and described Lady Hagiography's environs as a bookshop.[2] Loomis made this a proof of her argument that in the decades before Geoffrey Chaucer established England's vernacular canon, the production of books was organized out of shops. The wares they produced included the vernacular books that were models for Chaucer's work, such as the 1330s Auchinleck manuscript of English romances in which Loomis was especially interested. In her discussions of this manuscript and England's fourteenth-century book 'shops' generally, Loomis posed some still important, still current questions. In the century or so before the advent of printing, and the decades after the arrival of the press, how were books made in England, and by whom? What were such books like, and how did they promote, sustain or counterbalance all the many literary and historical changes of this period?

[1] See Firth Green, 'Lydgate and Deguileville'; for Abell, see Driver and Orr (Chapter 5), and Alexander, 'William Abell "Lymnour"'.

[2] 'The Auchinleck Manuscript and a Possible London Bookshop'.

I

Figure 0.1 BL, MS Cotton Tiberius A.vii, f. 91v: Lady Hagiography,
Pilgrim and Lady Lesson in a book-filled room.

Loomis's argument about Abell's miniature shop is no longer widely accepted. The furniture around Lady Hagiography is now interpreted another way: the shelves, set up in what has been called the 'lectern-system',[3] resemble those of a library. They suggest the importance of books to religious devotion, scholarship and teaching; the networks of people who shared books and their ideas; and the storing of books in the great libraries of English monasteries such as Bury St Edmunds, or in households such as that of Humfrey, Duke of Gloucester, or Sir John Fastolf.[4] Research into manuscripts has explored in depth how books such as those Lady Hagiography gestures to were owned and read – and thus illuminated these meanings of this miniature.[5]

Yet the picture still suggests something not only of the use but of the production of books. If the ascription of the work in this book to Abell is correct, then it

[3] Streeter, *The Chained Library*, 3–16.

[4] For example, Summit, *Memory's Library*; Beadle, 'Fastolf's French Books'.

[5] On the history of reading in the fourteenth and fifteenth centuries, see, for example, Brantley, *Reading in the Wilderness*; Wakelin, *Humanism, Reading, and English Literature*; Kerby-Fulton and Hilmo (eds.), *The Medieval Professional Reader*; and the seminal essays of Harris, 'Patrons, Buyers and Owners' and Meale, 'Patrons, Buyers and Owners'.

was illustrated and perhaps copied in the context of flourishing commercial book manufacture in London in this period, activities whose archival remains C. Paul Christianson has documented so usefully.[6] A London setting for the book's manufacture raises questions about the eastern dialect of the scribe who copied out its text. Did he work elsewhere, and was the book carried to the metropolis for decoration? Or did Abell work, in this as doubtless in many instances, with a scribe who was raised out of town but came to London to practise his craft? Or was the book in fact made, as Kathleen Scott has argued, outside the metropolis, in West Suffolk, and illustrated there by an artist she calls the 'Cotton Master'?[7] And, whether the book is the work of London or provincial artisans, who organized their work, and how?

In their 1978 essay on early manuscripts of the works of Geoffrey Chaucer and John Gower, A. I. Doyle and M. B. Parkes rejected the idea that vernacular books of the fourteenth or early fifteenth centuries were produced in a highly coordinated way in single 'shops', inside or outside London. Craftsmen who made books and documents in this period did occupy 'shops': the records of the Scriveners' Company in this period refer to guild members' shops; the stationer John Robert was using such a shop when he produced twelve books on hunting for Henry V in 1421.[8] Slowly, scholars are assembling a complex picture of the work that took place in such spaces in the period covered in this book. It was not conducted in uniform ways, but included both organized commissions and contracts involving patrons, stationers and artisans, as well as much more ad hoc activities. It was not simply 'commercial' in ways that we now understand that term. Nor was it always (as the debate about BL, MS Cotton Tiberius A.vii suggests) metropolitan. It involved the activities of members of religious orders, schools and households throughout England, although their activities were never wholly detached from the world of English commerce and other religious, social and economic activities, or for that matter from an international traffic in texts, books and other commodities. Nor was 'book production' a static process across this period – materials were changing; techniques of copying, decorating, illustrating and assembling, stitching and covering books were in a state of flux *before* as well as during the period in which printing was introduced. It is with these dynamic activities of book production – and with the way that these activities are described minutely by their own products, like the miniatures in BL, MS Cotton Tiberius A.vii – that this collection of essays is concerned.

---

[6] *Memorials of the Book Trade; A Directory of London Stationers*; 'The Rise of London's Book Trade'.

[7] *Later Gothic Manuscripts*, II.252.

[8] See Gillespie, 'Books', 98; Christianson, 'Evidence for the Study of London's Late Medieval Manuscript Book-Trade', 100.

The period covered by this collection of essays stretches roughly from 1350 to the first few decades after the coming of printing to England in 1476. The book's argument is that the period, somewhat neglected in recent, major treatments of the history of the book, is interesting in its own right and important for an understanding of book production and cultural life in England over the *longue durée*.

These were, for a start, years of vital importance in the history of writing in English. Despite brilliant literature in all the languages of England before these years, the late fourteenth century was a watershed for literary history, when, in the wake of plague and seemingly endless hostilities with France, a large number of Latin and French texts were newly translated, and a great many writers who might previously have composed works in Latin or French began to do so in English – the most famous of them, the well-connected Chaucer. The importance of these years is perhaps distorted by the significance of Chaucer, and of his contemporaries William Langland and John Wyclif, for later readers and historians. Nevertheless, the writers of this period asserted their innovativeness; and the assertion itself inspired or at least signalled change. English vernacular literary activity from the late fourteenth century onwards did flourish with new vigour.[9]

The changes in book production in England in this period, alluded to above, occurred alongside changes in literary activity in this period, and scholars have sometimes suggested close links between them.[10] The lengthening shelf of self-consciously 'literary' works in English was met by a sharp increase in the production of manuscripts of that literature. A. S. G. Edwards and Derek Pearsall note a twentyfold increase in the survival of books of vernacular literature from the period before the last quarter of the fourteenth century, to the century after that watershed – the decades in which Chaucer, Gower, Langland and Julian of Norwich were at work, and John Lydgate and Thomas Hoccleve were beginning to put pen to paper.[11] But there was not merely an increase in the copying of literary works; there was also a large increase in the writing and copying of all manner of texts. Pardons, personal correspondence from households other than the king's, statutes, archival records, chancery documents, prayerbooks, household manuals and works for the newly thriving universities – all these were made, or at least, survive, in more copies in the hundred or so years before printing came to England than in previous centuries.[12]

---

[9] For arguments along these lines see, for instance, Cannon, *The Making of Chaucer's English*; Wogan-Browne, Watson, Taylor and Evans (eds.), *The Idea of the Vernacular*.

[10] Pearsall, 'The Ellesmere Chaucer', 267.

[11] Edwards and Pearsall, 'The Manuscripts of the Major English Poetic Texts', 257; see also Sargent, 'What Do the Numbers Mean?', 243.

[12] It may be that book production was slower in this period in some monastic houses than it had been in previous centuries, as collections were established; but in some monasteries there is evidence of concerted efforts, especially in the fifteenth century, to consolidate, renew and refurbish existing collections

These changes reflect a growth in the use of writing, and in varieties of literacy, in fourteenth- and fifteenth-century England. By about 1400, the increasing reliance on written records in business, law and administration had come to affect a very great part of the English population. A proliferation of records produced far more need for literate work – for the creation of writs, deeds, wills – and led to a much wider familiarity with the written word.[13] In parallel, it was in the late 1300s that the ecclesiastical authorities licensed the issue of letters of confraternity and confession in place of orally conferred pardons.[14] The established church, like the Wycliffites who wanted to reform it, sought to affirm the faith of the laity in the fourteenth and fifteenth centuries by the dissemination of written works, as well as by visual artefacts and dramatic performances.[15] For every Wycliffite Bible made in the fourteenth or fifteenth centuries there survives a personal prayerbook made for the Sarum use.[16]

As we have already suggested, it is possible to overstate the case – change always has a long prehistory. Every century of England's recorded history brought the increased use of writing in the administration of the realm; the edicts of the 1215 Lateran Council on the matter of the education of the laity had a long-lasting effect; and so on. If the matter of vernacularity – the new literature heralded by the Ricardian poets; the new religious discourses promulgated by Wycliffism and its opponents – is put to one side, then it might be said that the late fourteenth and fifteenth centuries continue rather than begin many trends in the English uses of books, writing and varieties of literacy. But the contributors to this volume show that what was new about written culture in the late fourteenth and fifteenth centuries was compounded, in the same period, by re-imaginings of the book itself. In chapters on materials by Orietta da Rold, scribal hands by Daniel Wakelin and visual design by Stephen Partridge and by Martha Driver and Michael Orr this collection argues for important innovations in the production and the design of books – especially, though not exclusively, English vernacular books – in the century before the advent of printing. It was in this period that paper appeared – firstly for record-keeping in business and government, then for practical writing of various sorts and, in time, books designed to last. As Erik Kwakkel and Orietta da Rold show below, the use of paper changed the economics of book production considerably. Other writing technologies were in transition: the sort of handwriting used in documents had long been used in books, but in our period, documentary hands were used ever more widely for the copying of longer works, including longer works

(perhaps meant to match continental efforts, e.g., those associated with the Melk reform in Austria and Southern Germany). See some relevant discussion by Gillespie (Chapter 7) and Pouzet (Chapter 10).

[13] Clanchy, *From Memory to Written Record*; Firth Green, *A Crisis of Truth*.

[14] Swanson, *Indulgences in Late Medieval England*.

[15] Somerset, *Clerical Discourse and Lay Audience*.

[16] Duffy, *Marking the Hours*.

in English, and including works that extended literary culture beyond the essential, traditional texts of worship and learning. The page layouts associated with learned books (which scholars often call, somewhat loosely, their *ordinatio*) spread into books of vernacular literature, firstly in France under Charles V, then in England. Varieties of binding techniques, from the cheap to the luxurious, offered new ways of finishing books – or leaving them deliberately unfinished, better to allow for the diverse methods of distribution and book assembly described by Margaret Connolly in her chapter.

The claim made in this book for the significance of the period covered – and even its very loose start-date, around 1350 – also rests on observations about the organization of book production. Economic change in England more broadly (the rise of the guilds, especially) led to innovations in the provision of books. For example, the increasing ownership of Books of Hours, by merchants as well as by the wealthy nobility, made possible the development of systems for the mass speculative production of these books (mostly in the Low Countries). It is in this context that the question raised by Loomis in her 1942 essay, and taken up again by Parkes and Doyle in 1978, emerges. How far was English book production 'organized'? Or more broadly, what were the new sorts of social, economic and institutional conditions for book production before printing – conditions that are not unrelated to the advent and the successful management and spread of that new technology? These are matters taken up, in each case from a slightly different perspective, in the chapters here by Erik Kwakkel, Linne Mooney and Jean-Pascal Pouzet. In the 1350s, the first London records of the existence of commercial organization of the book trade – of guilds of book artisans – appear. There is evidence, from occupational surnames, from subsidy records and later shop rentals, of the work of commercial scribes, binders, parchmenters and limners in earlier periods. The decades around 1200 mark the likely inception, as Rodney M. Thomson and Nigel Morgan have noted,[17] of work done on books outside monastic houses (although in-house monastic work was never without a 'commercial' aspect, as Pouzet shows in his chapter). In the 1350s, the guilds of the Textwriters and Limners are first identified. By 1373, the Scriveners had formed their own trade organization. By 1403, a new guild of Stationers amalgamated the interests of some of these book producers. And it was the Stationers, not much less than the technology itself, whose monopoly over printing was so influential in coming centuries. Their efforts to control an expanding trade in books began in the period described here, quite independently of the invention of moveable type.[18]

[17] Morgan and Thomson, *The Cambridge History of the Book in Britain*, 'Introduction', xvii.

[18] Steer (ed.), *Scriveners' Company*, vii–ix; Blayney, *The Stationers' Company before the Charter*. On the importance of the Stationers in later centuries, see, for instance, Rose, *Authors and Owners*, on their role in the invention of copyright.

So in spite of the debate about the importance of 'shops' – and of evidence that manuscript production was typically distributed among artisans at work in their own spaces – the stationer's premises was at least one of the settings for the commissioning of books, the oversight of their production and thus their commercial distribution of books, as Kwakkel argues in his chapter. Stationers might be members of the London guild, after 1403 (although this term was not applied to that organization consistently for many decades); they might also be the men styled 'stationers' who worked around the University of Oxford in this period, and earlier. Yet stationers were not the only ones taking charge of book production. As Pouzet and Mooney stress, books in the period were the products of lay artisans in monastic settings, of 'freelancing' scriveners and of town or privy-seal clerks. They were given bindings by itinerant artisans or were sent, having been copied by the religious, to centres such as Oxford for the finishing touches of the commercial binders busy there, as Alexandra Gillespie notes. David Rundle shows us that books arrived from abroad too, in the hands of importers and humanist scholars; and John Thompson depicts similar arrivals from, and also departures to, late medieval Ireland (of books, and bookish practices as well). Book production was more organized in this period, but it was not – not even when printing made its first appearance – the massively organized commercial activity it became later.[19] It is notable that, in the picture of Lady Hagiography and her bookshelves in Cotton Tiberius A.vii, there is some coherence to the books, in size, colour and arrangement of textual material, as far as we can see in that small picture. But that picture comes from a dream-vision of a heightened, perfected world; in the production of actual manuscript books such coherence was an ideal to which the producers and purchasers of books may have aspired but never attained. Real-world conditions produced something else alongside occasional dreams of perfection: the diverse forms of manuscript books which survive, with all their inconsistencies, oddities and particularities. The contributors to this volume are aware of this diversity and particularity, even as they suggest some general hypotheses. The balance between organization and order, and particularity, improvization, chaos and disorder, is one of the key themes which recurs across several of the essays in this collection. The attempt to draw together some larger patterns with the observation of disruption of those patterns is vital – vital in showing how the books produced in England in these years fit into wider cultural history in general and the history of the book in general.

Firstly, the balance of order and disorder upsets tidy ideas about literary creativity. This has long been one of the main achievements of the conjunction of the history of the book with literary history. D. F. McKenzie, the scholar perhaps most influential in theorizing this conjunction, saw that the study of the physical forms

---

[19] On the commercialization of the book trade in the eighteenth century especially, see Johns, *The Nature of the Book*; Raven, *The Business of Books*.

of text would resist formalist idealization of the 'text itself' and would complicate the editorial habit of using bibliographical evidence to establish one final authorial text.[20] Scholars of Middle English manuscripts have uncovered rich evidence of the material conditions that produced literary texts in the fourteenth and fifteenth centuries and have argued that this evidence is a useful check on or supplement to an anachronistic or idealized concept of 'literature'.[21] Essays in this collection also point out the ways that, say, parts of *The Canterbury Tales* in a particular book may have been formed by accidents in the supply of parchment or the fit of text on a page. Others show how the forms of canonical English verse, such as Lydgate's shorter poetry, were shaped by choices over handwriting or the international traffic in books and scribes.

Secondly, the balance of the grand narratives sketched above and the chaotic particularities of the books themselves suggest ways in which the books discussed in this collection of essays fit into the wider history of the book. This collection, we hope, provides a kind of summary of manuscript culture in the years just before and just after printing began in England. We hope that, as such, it could inform comparisons of manuscript and print, of 'medieval' and 'early modern' books, comparisons which still suffer from ignorance by scholars on each side of these divides. Yet these essays also upset simple contrasts and comparisons. The 'medieval' book was as complex and diverse in its manifestations as the 'early modern' one (or the 'classical' or 'modern'). The essays below suggest trends which might seem typical of, perhaps anticipatory of, printing: patterns of commodification, or standardization of products and even mass production, of cheap as well as quality work. However, they also suggest countertrends which upset any simple model of progress: the persistence, right through the period, of the production of books in thriving religious institutions; the vital life of the bespoke trade in books; and the personal copy, the book made by a person unconnected with any craft or trade, for his or her own use. We might usefully seek analogies for these aspects of production in later periods of the history of the book – might watch out for continuity, as well as change.[22]

Nonetheless, the collection of essays here does provide a kind of background to printing: it shows that the passion for books, and the hectic production of them, did not begin with William Caxton's press. 'Print culture' did not emerge out of a vacuum; it emerged from things already known, from familiar practices and aspirations already held and shared. English people in the late fourteenth and fifteenth centuries made, used and apparently wanted, or at least were able to obtain and preserve,

[20] *Bibliography and the Sociology of Texts.*

[21] See Hanna, *Pursuing History*, 7, 63–82; and for reflection on this, see recently Meyer Lee, 'Manuscript Studies', 14–15.

[22] See McKitterick, *Print, Manuscript and the Search for Order*, esp. 31–6; Gillespie, 'Analytical Survey 9'.

more books than their forebears. Printing was developed and introduced within that culture. As Caxton writes in his *Recuyell*, his first book printed in English, books created with 'penne and ynke' are made laboriously, one at a time, whereas printed books are made all 'attones'. But they are still *books*; no new word is needed to describe them, and little further comment seems necessary (from Caxton or any other contemporary commentator).[23] The chapters in this book, though deliberately focussed on manuscripts, do mention printing: when they do, they suggest no sharp division between manuscript and print production. They argue instead that its 'revolutionary' effects stem from much longer-lived ideas about how to use and organize the various technologies of book production. The contributors thus suggest the things that we might be missing in histories of the book that do not attend to those processes of late medieval manuscript production that were changed by, and were a meaningful context for, printing.

The separation is apparent in the scholarly field of book history to which this volume belongs – for instance, in the monumental and impressive Cambridge series *The History of the Book in Britain*, which began publication in 1999 and is still underway. The division of two volumes around 1400 (volume II covers 1100–1400; volume III covers 1400–1557)[24] on the one hand registers the increase in book production in the vernacular and for the laity around the late fourteenth century (as just described). It would seem to encourage discussion of fifteenth-century manuscripts alongside printing. However, in practice, volume III attends only briefly to manuscript production.[25] Much discussion of manuscripts in the years before 1400 offered in volume II of *The Cambridge History* is of course germane to the years after 1400 too.[26] But the bookish world of England sketched above – the technological shifts in the materials, handwriting and layouts of manuscripts, the incipient commercialization of book production and the sudden and rapid expansion of textual culture – is not fully sketched in *The Cambridge History*. The burgeoning of literate activities in England and in English and the development of printing alongside developments in manuscript production need to be further explored.

Of course, the editors of *The Cambridge History of the Book in Britain* can, and do, refer readers to another collection that does cover the period of interest here: Jeremy

---

[23] Caxton, trans., *The Recuyell*, *STC* 15375, unsigned leaf 351r.

[24] Ed. Morgan and Thomson and ed. Hellinga and Trapp, respectively.

[25] Volume III does contain some very important work on the reading and storage of manuscripts, in chapters on the use of books (in royal libraries, by gentlewomen and so on) and on particular genres of book (school books, legal books and so on), but its main focus is printing: for more discussion see Gillespie, 'The History of the Book in Britain, 1400–1557'.

[26] Especially, for example, work by Parkes, 'Layout and Presentation of the Text' and 'Handwriting in English Books'; Hudson, 'Lollard Literature'; and a chapter by Boffey and Edwards, 'Middle English Literary Writings, 1150–1400' that usefully complements the chapter 'Literary Texts' that they contributed to volume III.

Griffiths and Derek Pearsall's collection of essays *Book Production and Publishing in Britain 1375–1475*, published in 1989. They are rightly confident that it still offers a magisterial survey of manuscript production in English on the eve of printing. Happily, that volume is once more available in print, but it is also over twenty years old, and the currently thriving interest in the history of the book among scholars of other periods and the interest among historians and critics of fourteenth- and fifteenth-century culture in the links between literary, devotional and social practices and material texts suggest that an overview of new work and new research opportunities is desirable. Griffiths and Pearsall's *Book Production and Publishing* remains the definitive contribution to the field: the aim of the present collection is to complement it in various ways.

Griffiths and Pearsall's *Book Production and Publishing* is partly arranged around 'genres' of writing, such as the manuscripts of medical or literary texts, or connected to particular social groups of users, such as patrons or Wycliffite readers. By contrast, the present collection brings together ideas and evidence dispersed by this arrangement. It begins with seven chapters on methods of book production, including some topics not covered in 1989, such as Simon Horobin's on dialect, Wakelin's on processes of writing, Partridge's on layouts (as distinct from illustrations), Da Rold's on parchment and ink (alongside considerable new work on the arrival of paper) and Gillespie's on bindings before the return of blind-stamping *c.*1450. Connolly and Driver and Orr approach the topics of book illustration and book assembly from new perspectives and with considerable new evidence.

This collection, then, considers books not in terms of their content, but in terms of contexts and systems for their production and distribution. The social and economic organization of book-making in England is covered by Kwakkel and Pouzet, whose chapters, like the work of the book-makers they discuss, are often focussed on Latin language materials. The circumstances in which paid scribes of various kinds made multiple copies of vernacular and literary works are described by Mooney in a chapter that brings together her extensive and important work on this topic. Rundle and Thomson write about the relationship of English book production to other countries. Fiona Somerset discusses the ways that books were made under pressure of censorship and censure, especially in the context of the Wycliffite movement.

We hope that, in this way, the collection will introduce findings, ideas and approaches to manuscript study that have emerged since 1989. And we hope that the collection will suggest some themes to animate future work on manuscripts and printed books, both in their own right and in relation to wider cultural history and literary criticism. The volume is thus not meant to be the last word on its subject, but to encourage continuing discussion, and it raises some questions for which it does not offer comprehensive answers. Firstly, what more might be said about the production of documents as distinct from books – or about distinguishing a 'book' from a document, or whether we should distinguish it thus? Usually contributors here are discussing the codex – at least, gatherings of folded pages. However, when Mooney alludes to the documents made by scribes who also copied vernacular books, such as Pinkhurst or Hoccleve, or Da Rold alludes to the materials and handwriting deployed by these scribes for both sorts of activities, they point to fruitful areas for further research. Gillespie and Rundle's brief discussions of the second-hand book trade in England suggest that this is another area open to more work. Thompson focusses his discussion of 'books beyond England' on Anglophone Ireland in order to show that 'English' manuscript production and book consumption can be understood in light of more complex geo-historical realities. His work opens the way for similar treatment of Scotland, Wales and late medieval English border cultures.

Finally, the collection points up the importance of readers, libraries and provenance study, but the use of books is not its focus. Instead, it is explicitly dedicated to discussion of the *production* of books: how they were made, by whom, and in what locales, using what resources, according to what conventions, in response to what historical circumstances and what technological, economic and political or religious constraints. Of course, the essays here show that the production and use of books are not processes that can easily be separated. As McKenzie argues, 'new readers make new texts' that themselves deserve new readings.[27] Handling, storage and reception contribute to books' 'production' in less material senses – to the way that books were conceptualized *as* books, or as luxury commodities, or junk, or ideas, and so on. As this collection describes the making of books, it thus provides new frameworks for work on the use of books as well.

At the heart of this volume, finally, is a conviction that fourteenth- and fifteenth-century books are a fascinating subject for intellectual enquiry in their own right, and that the processes of making them also reveal a lot about the ways in which people organized labour, passed on their faith, passed on useful knowledge, cured the sick, taught students, recorded their lives, expressed what they valued, impressed their friends, passed the time, created literature, became bored and precipitated cultural change. Studying the production of these books leads to an understanding – growing and changing – of the vital part they played in a society that still fascinates us.

---

[27] *Bibliography and the Sociology of Texts*, 29.

I

Materials

ORIETTA DA ROLD

Scholars working on manuscripts are increasingly aware of the importance of the evidence of writing surfaces and the technology of writing itself. Some of the most recent important studies along these lines include a miscellany on ancient and medieval writing materials; a collection of essays and a monograph on parchment, which consider its history, structure, production and conservation; a substantial monograph on paper; and another one on ink.[1] The making of ink, parchment and paper has been researched from antiquity to the modern era, and brief descriptions or discrete sections are included in introductions to many histories of the book.[2] However, most of these studies focus on continental book production, and there is still much ground to be covered on the significance of the study of materials in British books.[3] This chapter focusses on why materials matter in book production and why looking at materials at a textual, social and cultural level yields new information about manuscript production.

Material culture has recently become an important point of departure for archaeological, anthropological and sociological studies.[4] The study of material culture

I would like to thank the Bibliographical Society for the Falconer Madan Award for support. I am grateful to Michael Gullick, Estelle Stubbs and Elaine Treharne for reading an early draft of this essay: errors remain my own.

[1] Starting with the ground-breaking work by Reed, *Ancient Skins, Parchments and Leathers*. See also Doyle, 'Recent Directions in Medieval Manuscript Study'; Guineau, Dulin, Vezin and Gousset, 'Analyse, à l'aide de méthodes'; Rück (ed.), *Pergament*; Fuchs, Meinert and Schrempf, *Pergament*; Ornato et al., *La carta occidentale*; Zerdoun Bat-Yehouda, *Les Encres noires au Moyen Âge*.

[2] See for example: Lyall, 'Materials: The Paper Revolution'; Needham, 'The Customs Rolls'; Thomson et al., 'Technology of Production of the Manuscript Book' and Robinson, 'The Format of Books'; De Hamel, *Medieval Craftsmen: Scribes and Illuminators*, 8–29; Clemens and Graham, *Introduction to Manuscript Studies*, 3–17; Géhin, *Lire le manuscrit médiévale*, 15–52. For an overview and an extensive bibliography, see Maniaci, *Archeologia del manoscritto*.

[3] This approach to material culture was anticipated by Clanchy, *From Memory to Written Record*, 114–44. See also Doyle, 'Recent Directions in Medieval Manuscript Study'; Da Rold, 'Fingerprinting Paper'.

[4] See for instance: Miller, *Material Cultures*; Miller, *Materiality*; Appadurai (ed.), *The Social Life of Things*; Tilley et al., *Handbook of Material Culture*; DeMarrais, Gosden and Renfrew (eds.), *Rethinking Materiality*.

'centres on the idea of materiality [as] an integral dimension of culture, and indeed there are dimensions of social existence that cannot be fully understood without it'.[5] Useful concepts such as objectification, commodification and agency help to explain that objects – in this case writing materials – have an identity as a cultural item to be studied. The study of material culture enables scholars to consider the origins, movement and associations of these cultural items within human culture and society; it helps to define what we are and who we are. Materiality in manuscript studies and book history matters. Its study not only contributes to our knowledge of manuscript production, but also allows us to construct informed hypotheses as to who read manuscripts and why.[6] My aim in using materiality as a way to think about books goes beyond cultural history; it looks at the making of the particular codex and the particular bifolium. Focussing on such objects, we can try to answer questions about the availability of materials and the significance of such materials in books and fragments beyond accepted hierarchies of the book – which prefer the luxurious over the scrappy item.[7] Medieval manuscript production was diverse and its quality varied, but materials can tell stories which have not yet been fully explored beyond *prima facie* impressions.

The preparation of material as well as its choice is of pivotal importance for the construction of a manuscript and the mapping of the text on the writing surface. As Maniaci argues, materials and tools are essential instruments for the making of a book: 'Making a codex substantially means preparing a determinate quantity of material so that a determined quantity of text can be copied on it.'[8] This is a challenging observation for literary scholars, because it asks us to shift the focus of our enquiries from texts and scribes onto the writing surface. Not only did scribes copy texts, they also made books. Such an obvious statement has not attracted the level of consideration that it deserves; it is overshadowed by emphasis on the study of scripts and texts rather than on the making of a manuscript from a holistic perspective.[9] A full understanding of scripts and textual evidence is essential to further our knowledge of fourteenth- and fifteenth-century written culture, but this culture has to be fully contextualized. And to contextualize, we need not only to address historical or social contexts, but to consider the deep structure of the physical object, that is, the material which was chosen deliberately or *in absentia* by an individual to receive a given text.

[5] Tilley et al., *Handbook of Material Culture*, 1.

[6] See for instance Rust, *Imaginary Worlds*, in which the author convincingly demonstrates how far a study of the physical object can talk about the literary culture it served.

[7] As dictated by the type and quality of the material, scripts and the level of decorative technique: see De Hamel, *Medieval Craftsmen: Scribes and Illuminators*, 17.

[8] My translation from Maniaci, *Archeologia del manoscritto*, 101.

[9] For a balanced discussion of the making of the codex, see Brownrigg (ed.), *Making the Medieval Book*.

The chapter that follows will deal with some of the materials used in the making of the manuscript book. They include ink and parchment,[10] but the chapter will focus in particular on paper. In the case of ink and parchment, after summarizing well-known ground, I show some new ways in which these materials could contribute to our understanding of the manuscript and its production milieu. In the case of paper (in the final section), I dwell on a key material whose discovery in the west made printing possible. Printing brought about a revolution and systematization in the making of books which was unprecedented, and paper was the material which fostered this change. Unfortunately, paper tends to be overlooked in its earlier use in Britain, but given its importance it demands to be studied in its own right.

By the fourteenth century, ink was readily available for purchase,[11] but scribes usually prepared their own ink. Numerous surviving recipes bear witness to a variety of local practices, ingredients and methods of production.[12] However, inks can be generally grouped into two main classes: the carbon-based inks and the iron-gall-based inks. Both classes include gum arabic as a fixative; additional ingredients could be charcoal, wine, vinegar, vitriol and ferrous sulphate (copperas).[13] Despite this variation scribes often remark on the importance of preparing good black ink ('Si vis facere bonum atramentum'), proposing

---

[10] There is little or no consensus among scholars on how to refer to the name of the skin that scribes use as a writing material, be it made from goat, sheep or calf. Medieval accounts record 'vellum' and 'percameno' without additional qualifying information on the type of skins (Gullick (ed.), *Extracts from the Precentors' Accounts*, 11; Christianson, *Memorials of the Book Trade*, 14). In recent scholarship, *parchment* and *vellum* are used interchangeably to refer to the same material. For instance, Manly and Rickert (eds.), *The Text of The Canterbury Tales*, use *vellum* as a consistent generic term to distinguish animal-derived material from paper; see also De Hamel, *Medieval Craftsmen: Scribes and Illuminators*, 8–16. Other scholars either use the term *vellum* for superior-quality parchment (Ryder, 'The Biology and History', 28) or the generic term *membrane* (Doyle, 'Recent Directions in Medieval Manuscript Study', 7–8). As Gullick, 'From Parchmenter to Scribe', 145, has argued, etymologically the term *vellum* refers to calf-skin, but it is in practice difficult to recognize the type of skin from which the writing material is derived. It may, of course, be easier for conservators to tell the difference. This chapter uses *parchment* without distinguishing it from *vellum*. (See also pp. 17–22, and discussion by Gillespie, Chapter 7 below.)

[11] In the precentors' accounts of Ely Cathedral Priory numerous entries itemize the cost of galls, gum and copperas which are vital ingredients for the production of ink *in loco*, but in 1301–2, under the precentor Alexander, 18lbs. of ink were purchased for the sum of 2s 6d. See Gullick (ed.), *Extracts from the Precentors' Accounts*, 6. In London, Hoccleve bought ink for the Office of the Privy Seal. See Mooney, 'Some New Light on Thomas Hoccleve', 324–40.

[12] See, for numerous examples, Bat-Yehouda, *Les Encres noires au Moyen Âge*, 225–388; Ivy, 'The Bibliography of the Manuscript Book', 45; Clemens and Graham, *Introduction to Manuscript Studies*, 20; Clark, *The Art of All Colours*.

[13] Classes and composition of inks, methods of production and ingredients appear in Bat-Yehouda-Zerdoun, 'La Fabrication des encres noires', 13–21; Bat-Yehouda, *Les Encres noires*; Thomson et al., 'Technology of Production of the Manuscript Book', 81–2; Clemens and Graham, *Introduction to Manuscript Studies*, 19.

iron-gall-based ink as the best black quality ink to be used, for instance, on parchment.[14]

Despite this apparent uniformity in contemporary theory, there is a great deal of variation in ink-colour in texts written both on parchment and paper in the Middle Ages. Shifts in colour can be observed from black, to dark brown, brown, light brown and yellow across books as well as within single manuscripts.[15] This variation is interesting, albeit challenging. Why is there such a great disparity in ink-colour in manuscripts? And what might we learn from more study of the uses of ink? The reasons for these changes can be numerous: from the composition of the ink, to the scribe's working pattern and the amount of ink in the pen. Furthermore, ingredients perform differently depending on the type of material chosen for writing. Paper will absorb ink which lacks fixative (gum), causing the ink to lose colour and become very light. By contrast, parchment does not absorb ink which contains too much gum; after drying the composition of such ink breaks down and crumbles, and the ink looks much fainter.[16] Notably, ink for the printing press had to be thicker, in order to attach to the types which were used by the press; and an oil-based product was more suitable than a water-based one.[17]

However, it is precisely because of the lack of uniformity in ink-colour that there are several important lessons that can be learned by looking at ink from a scientific, technical and textual perspective. Recent research on the composition of medieval ink with non-invasive methods, such as PIXE procedure and Micro-Raman laser spectrometry, have already produced interesting results on the composition and dating of the ink in two Italian manuscripts.[18] More work in this direction on British manuscripts could exploit the data that ink can provide on dating manuscripts, and on possible correlations between the ingredients which are found in recipes and the ink being used.[19] But it is perhaps the implications for textual studies of variation in the ink-colour that represent the most exciting avenue of research for literary scholars. In the period of interest in this volume, for example, the manuscripts of Chaucer's *The Canterbury Tales* can be a useful basis on which to discuss the significance and the pitfalls of such study.

---

[14] BL, MS Sloane 416, f. 37v, published in Bat-Yehouda-Zerdoun, 'La Fabrication des encres noires', 263 with several other examples. See also Ivy, 'The Bibliography of the Manuscript Book', 45. On ink and parchment, see Clemens and Graham, *Introduction to Manuscript Studies*, 19.

[15] See, for remarks on the early medieval period, Thomson et al., 'Technology of Production of the Manuscript Book', 82; and Wakelin in his chapter, p. 37.

[16] Ivy, 'The Bibliography of the Manuscript Book', 45.

[17] Hellinga, 'Printing', 92.

[18] Maniaci, *Archeologia del manoscritto*, 60–1; Guinea, Dulin, Vezin and Gousset, 'Analyse, à l'aide de méthodes'.

[19] New and exciting research is being developed on CCCC, MS 363 to test new theoretical models to the study and significance of the colour of ink in twelfth-century manuscript production. See Gobbitt, 'Law in English Manuscripts'.

A shift in the colour of the ink represents an old crux for textual scholars, because it is not always possible to determine whether a change of ink hides a textually significant shift in the copy-text whose recognition is important for the establishment of the edited text. In their extensive work on the manuscripts of *The Canterbury Tales*, Manly and Rickert write that while ink changes often carry little textual significance, 'often such changes mark important events in the assembling of the texts and the order in which the parts of the MS were written'.[20] This observation makes the study of the ink worth undertaking in its own right and brings forward Maniaci's earlier argument about how the study of materials illuminates not only the study of texts but also the whole production of texts as artefacts.

Working with ink to investigate both the progress of copying and the textual quality of the exemplar is taxing, for some of the reasons pointed out above, but in particular because what looks like different ink now could have been very similar at the time of writing, because ink can be absorbed to a different and non-uniform degree by the writing surface.[21] BL, MS Add. 5140 is a case in point. It is a paper manuscript with inner and outer parchment bifolia, which was written around the middle of the fifteenth century by two scribes (scribe 1: ff. 2r–229r; scribe 2: ff. 229r–425v) and contains a copy of *The Canterbury Tales* (ff. 2r–359), as well as Lydgate's *The Siege of Thebes* (ff. 359v–425v).[22] *The Canterbury Tales* is written in black ink, which is 'noticeably faded on some pages', as Manly and Rickert note.[23] They do not qualify this statement, but the lightening of the ink mainly occurs on the parchment bifolia (for example: ff. 23–4, ff. 28–9, ff. 35–6) rather than on the paper portions of the quires. On these folios the ink does not 'change' colour but fades because of too much fixative in the ink. This kept the ink on the surface of the parchment and caused it to flake, thus lightening the colour. As explained above, gum is essential for the paper portion of the manuscript, but too much of it is deleterious to copying on parchment.

There are numerous examples in the corpus of manuscripts of *The Canterbury Tales* which show similar incompatibility between the writing surface and the ink that the scribe is using: for instance, BL, MS Add. 35286; BL, MS Harley 7335; and BL, MS Egerton 2726. In these manuscripts, ink cannot bear witness to significant evidence about the text, although such books do produce questions about the type of ink available in the fifteenth century and whether scribes bought or made ink with a specific material in mind. If a scribe were working mainly on paper, would he purchase or make ink suitable for that material rather than parchment? At this stage this possibility is still speculation, but it is a line of enquiry which may be worth pursuing for future research.

---

[20] Manly and Rickert (eds.), *The Text of The Canterbury Tales*, 1.24.

[21] Owen, 'A Note on the Ink in Some Chaucer Manuscripts'.

[22] Manly and Rickert (eds.), *The Text of The Canterbury Tales*, 1.29–33.

[23] Ibid., 1.30.

In spite of these problems and the lack of an accepted terminology in describing the colour of ink, it is possible to study systematically the relationship between ink, text and the making of some manuscript books. New research on early manuscripts of *The Canterbury Tales* indicates that when the evidence of the ink can be combined with other internal codicological or textual data, scholars are presented with useful evidence about the process of the making of a codex.[24] CUL, MS Dd.4.24, for instance, is a manuscript of Chaucer's *The Canterbury Tales* written on paper with inner and outer parchment bifolia, datable to the beginning of the fifteenth century. It is copied in three discernable shades of ink: light brown, brown and dark brown (almost black). These same shades are also used to correct the text. Once the ink-colour is mapped onto the text, as I have explained elsewhere, it is possible to prove that the scribe received his exemplar or exemplars piecemeal and did not copy the manuscript from the beginning to the end. In quire 5, he rearranged the *ordinatio* of *The Tales*. After relating the layers of corrections to the colour of ink in the main text, it is also possible to confirm that there is a clear association between the use of different ink, the progress of copying and the process of emendation.[25] The study of the ink, that is, allows an informed hypothesis on the early transmission of this Chaucerian text.[26]

Equally, the study of parchment has made impressive progress over recent years, contributing to a number of important discoveries on the making of the text. The making of parchment is a well-established profession as early as the twelfth century. A twelfth-century parchment maker, 'Gervase', worked in Leicester, and scholars have found evidence of the same activity in Oxford and Cambridge in the thirteenth century, in Exeter, Newcastle upon Tyne, London and York in the fourteenth century, and in Bury St Edmunds in the fifteenth century (for a fifteenth-century Italian image of parchment makers at work, see Figure 1.1).[27] A great deal is known about the method of production, cost and quality of parchment in the period.[28] The skin was usually washed, soaked in lime, washed again, dried under tension and dehaired.[29] This process applied to all types of skins, although in recipes the process

[24] See for example the evidence in Oxford, Corpus Christi College, MS 198; HEHL, MS Ellesmere 26.C.9; BL, MS Harley 7334; NLW, Peniarth 392D; and for discussion, see Stubbs (ed.), *The Hengwrt Chaucer*; Stubbs, 'A Study of the Codicology'.

[25] Da Rold, 'A Study of Cambridge University Library MS Dd.4.24'; Da Rold, 'The Quiring System in Cambridge University Library MS Dd.4.24'; Da Rold, 'The Significance of Scribal Corrections in Cambridge University Library, MS Dd.4.24'.

[26] Later manuscripts of *The Canterbury Tales* are also awaiting detailed investigations of this kind. Numerous manuscripts, such as Oxford, Christ Church College, MS 152 and BL, MS Harley 1239 have an interesting pattern in the colour of the ink. BL, MS Harley 1239, in particular, has a clear shift from brown to light brown at f. 94r, and a full textual and codicological analysis could be worth pursuing. See further discussion below.

[27] *The British Book Trade Index*.

[28] See for a recent discussion, for example, Fuchs, Meinert and Schrempf, *Pergament*; Rück (ed.), *Pergament*; Clarkson, 'Rediscovering Parchment'.

[29] For a recent introduction, see Clemens and Graham, *Introduction to Manuscript Studies*, 10–12.

Figure 1.1 Biblioteca Universitaria Bologna, MS 1456, f. 4r: a fifteenth-century Italian miniature depicting the shop of a 'cartolaio' with piles of paper or parchment.

of making parchment from calf-skin differs from the treatment of sheep-skin. Calf-skin had to be shaved on both sides before being soaked in the lime solution, but sheep-skin only on the flesh side, because the solution removed the wool on the hair side.[30] Nevertheless, the finished product is indistinguishable to the untrained eye, so that the size of a book may offer better clues as to the material which was employed for its production than the writing surface itself (calves producing larger skins than sheep or goats).[31] Typical examples of this distinction are two of the largest late medieval books, which contain French, Latin and English religious and didactic texts, BodL, MS Eng. poet. a. 1 (known as the 'Vernon manuscript') and its sister manuscript BL, MS Add. 22283 (known as the 'Simeon manuscript'), which measure 544 x 393mm. and 590 x 390mm. respectively. Their large size suggests the use of calf-parchment.[32]

There may be, however, some parameters that one can observe when considering the species used for parchment: the greasiness and yellowish colour on the hair side may suggest sheep-parchment; a more uniform white colour on both the hair and the flesh side may hint at calf-parchment; and dark spots on the hair side may be visible on goat-parchment.[33] These features are not stable, and they vary depending on the age of the animal, the production techniques and the quality of the finished product.[34] 'Quality' refers to the thickness, the 'drape', the colour and the overall appearance of the parchment, therefore good-quality parchment is usually even in weight (or thickness) and has a good 'drape', to do with its flexibility. Modern research suggests that the qualitative differences in the process of making the parchment had an impact on the production of the medieval book.[35] Little evidence of the quality of the parchment which was bought or sold is available in contemporary records. In the London Bridge accounts, there is only one entry in 1518 which records 'great vellum skins', but no further comments on size or finishing qualify what 'great' means.[36] But if the accounts do not offer any explanation of the quality of the parchment, it is possible to observe differences. Thomson argues that parchment 'used for university books in the fourteenth century is thin, dark and easily crinkled or creased'.[37] Maniaci notes that systematic analysis of the different thicknesses of parchment used in manuscript production suggests that parchment in

[30] Ivy, 'The Bibliography of the Manuscript Book', 35.

[31] Ibid., 34–5.

[32] See, for recent descriptions, Scase (ed.), *Manuscripts of the West Midlands*, www.mwm.bham.ac.uk; and the chapter by Connolly, pp. 132–3, below.

[33] Derolez, *Palaeography*, 31.

[34] For an overview of production technique with a close look at the scribe at work and the literary evidence for this process, see Gullick, 'From Parchmenter to Scribe'.

[35] Fuchs, Meinert and Schrempf, *Pergament*.

[36] Christianson, *Memorials of the Book Trade*, 20.

[37] Thomson et al., 'Technology of Production of the Manuscript Book', 77.

general became thinner over time, although such an observation still remains to be fully tested for different geographical areas.[38]

It is common to find parchment of dissimilar thickness and fill in fifteenth-century manuscripts (as also noted here by Erik Kwakkel and Jean-Pascal Pouzet in Chapters 8 and 10). BL, MS Add. 34779, a copy of the C version of *Piers Plowman* from the beginning of the fifteenth century, is made up of parchment of varying quality: some folios are thick, others are quite thin and of disparate colour. Scribes were skilful book-makers, using and repairing the pieces of parchment available to them. Holes, which form under tension if the skin is damaged, could be stitched, glued with a patch or simply avoided by writing around them. The damaged sheet could be folded in such a way that any irregularity and damage appear at the edges, where the binder might trim them off.[39] For example, BodL, MS Barlow 20, which contains a copy of *The Canterbury Tales* and is dated to the middle of the fifteenth century, is made of thin parchment with holes, cuts and stitches, and all the irregular edges, probably derived from the contour of the skin around the neck or shoulders, appear on the outer lower corners throughout the manuscript.[40]

These differences when studied in detail can offer important codicological evidence of how the text was mapped onto the page. For example, Oxford, Corpus Christi College, MS 198 is an early copy of Chaucer's *The Canterbury Tales* which lacks uniformity in the quality of its parchment. The scribe uses fine-quality parchment, which is interspersed with 'thicker and hornier' material.[41] Stubbs's analysis of this distribution has demonstrated that the scribe is not randomly using the low-quality parchment, but that the 'thick' parchment appears at textually significant points in the making of the manuscript.[42] This parchment especially marks the transition between one tale and the other: between The Cook's Tale and The Tale of Gamelyn, The Man of Law's and The Squire's Tales, The Squire's Tale and The Wife of Bath's Prologue, The Summoner's and The Merchant's Tales, The Merchant's and The Franklin's Tales, The Canon's Yeoman's and The Physician's Tales, and finally in The Nun's Priest's Tale, which is almost entirely contained in quire 33. These folios are mainly the inner or outer bifolia of the quires. The technique of planning the distribution of the text in this manner is cunning, as it allows a certain degree of flexibility in rearranging the text. In discussion of the establishment of the text

---

[38] Maniaci, *Archeologia del Manoscritto*, 42–4; see also Maniaci and Munafò (eds.), *Ancient and Medieval Book Materials*, for essays with further quantitative analyses of parchment.

[39] Clemens and Graham, *Introduction to Manuscript Studies*, 12–13.

[40] For a description of the manuscript, see Manly and Rickert (eds.), *The Text of The Canterbury Tales*, 1.55–7. Other manuscripts with similar variation in the standard of the parchment are BodL, MS Laud misc. 739; BodL, MS Rawl. poet. 141; BodL, MS Rawl. poet. 149.

[41] Manly and Rickert (eds.), *The Text of The Canterbury Tales*, 1.92.

[42] Stubbs, ' "Here's One I Prepared Earlier" ', 144.

of *The Canterbury Tales* and its transmission, the order of these textual parts is notoriously varied, and there is no firm consensus among scholars as to which one of the extant orders could firmly represent the final authorial intention.[43] Stubbs has suggested that there is a close relationship between the substituted folios and the change in the colour of the ink in Hengwrt, and thus argued that the Corpus manuscript was rearranged after a different collection was presented to the scribe.[44] Probably both manuscripts were copied in close proximity and under 'authorial' supervision, or, at least, the Corpus manuscript must have been worked upon at a time when Hengwrt was in the making. Oxford, Corpus Christi College, MS 198 could be considered 'a manuscript in the process of transformation', and the detection of this transformation is possible when a close scrutiny of the material is undertaken.[45]

More work could be done in this direction on the manuscripts of *The Canterbury Tales* written on parchment, including seemingly straightforward manuscripts. Such study can usefully go hand in hand with study of the ink. BL, MS Harley 1239 is dated to the middle of the fifteenth century. It contains a copy of Chaucer's *Troilus and Criseyde* (ff. 1r–62v) and some texts from *The Canterbury Tales*: the tales told by Knight, the Man of Law, the Wife of Bath, the Clerk and the Franklin (ff. 63r–106v), which are written by one hand. This manuscript is unique in many respects, but the part containing *The Canterbury Tales* has not been much studied, probably because the poem is fragmentary. The format of the book is extraordinary for a copy of Chaucer's poems – it is a long and thin book (340 × 135 mm.), which is shaped as an account book or a 'holster book' (usually defined as a book with pages much taller than they are wide).[46] Despite its format, its content makes it a coherent anthology of poems of a polite and mostly secular nature, which were probably chosen on grounds of their topics and tone, picked out of a specific order and transmitted to form a new sequence.[47] It is noticeable that the order of these tales is the same as that of Ellesmere, but without those stories which do not belong to the romance genre. The scribe concludes his selection with a colophon, asking the reader to pray for a 'heremita de Grenewych' (f. 106v), and then leaves the last folio and a half blank.

Codicologically, BL, MS Harley 1239 is made up of regular quires of eight, including missing leaves, whose arrangement of the hair and the flesh side of the parchment generally follows the 'Gregory Rule', that is, 'flesh side faces flesh side

---

[43] For an overview, see Benson, 'The Order of *The Canterbury Tales*'; Blake, 'Editorial Assumptions and Problems of *The Canterbury Tales*'; and Blake, *The Textual Tradition of 'The Canterbury Tales'*.

[44] Stubbs, '"Here's One I Prepared Earlier"', 151.

[45] Ibid., 139. See also Stubbs's work on Ellesmere; BL, MS Harley 7334; and Hengwrt in Stubbs, 'A Study of the Codicology of Four Early Manuscripts of *The Canterbury Tales*'.

[46] Manly and Rickert (eds.), *The Text of The Canterbury Tales*, 1.189–97.

[47] Edwards, 'Manuscripts and Readers', 91.

and hair side faces hair side'.[48] All outer sides of the quires (the first recto and last verso of each quire) show the hair side of the sheet, with the only exception of quire 8 (ff. 94–101). In this quire, the text on f. 94r is written on the flesh side of the parchment in distinctive lighter ink of almost yellowish tone. The scribe interrupted his writing after finishing quire 7 (ff. 86–93) and started again on a newly assembled quire in different ink. The transitions between f. 93v and f. 94r do not show any evident textual problems; they contain the end of the second part of The Clerk's Tale (lines 326–90 on f. 93v and 391–446 on f. 94r), but they show that there was an interruption in the progress of copying and tell the story of a scribe who was probably not familiar with the practices of preparing quires and/or making books.[49]

Similar observations can be extended to manuscripts written on paper, with the clear advantage that paper is hand-made by a mould which leaves an indelible fingerprint on the product. Paper stocks are traceable: recognizable across books and documents. They can thus be studied at several levels: the study of paper allows understanding of, and at times the reconstruction of, an irregular make-up of the quires; a problematic watermark sequence may reveal hidden textual problems; and dated paper stocks may assist in offering a range of dates for otherwise undated material.

Much has been published on the making of medieval paper.[50] Writing on paper in Britain in the late medieval period is, however, still an issue which has to be fully explored. The import of paper revolutionized the traditional way of producing books and offered to scribes an additional writing surface to choose from.[51] This choice translates into variety in the formats and overall presentation of the finished product. It also influences our understanding of its perceived use.

Paper can be found on its own in a manuscript. Paper quires can also be reinforced by inner and outer parchment bifolia, as in St John's, Camb., MS S. 35 (see Figure 1.2);[52] and paper and parchment can be separate parts of one book.[53] Size,

---

[48] On this rule, see Derolez, *Palaeography*, 33.

[49] This is further suggested by the appearance of the hand of *The Canterbury Tales*, which shows a different level of proficiency in mastering the tracing of letters and overall aspect of the hand as opposed to the copy of *Troilus and Criseyde*, on which see Wakelin, Chapter 2, p. 42, below.

[50] See recently Ornato, *La carta occidentale*. For an overview of the potential of studying the fingerprinted sheets in British paper manuscripts, see Da Rold, 'Fingerprinting Paper'.

[51] De Hamel, *Medieval Craftsmen: Scribes and Illuminators*, 17.

[52] This is not an unusual practice, although it is not universally adopted in paper manuscripts. For instance, among manuscripts of Chaucer's works, fifty-six manuscripts are written on paper, but only a few are made up of quires with inner and outer parchment bifolia: for example, CUL, MS Dd.4.24; CUL, MS Hh. 4.12; BL, MS Add. 5140; Longleat, MS 258; Manchester, Chetham's Library, MS 6709; BodL, MS Bodley 638; BodL, MS Rawl. C.86, HEHL, MS HM 114; and HEHL, MS HM 140; on which, see Manly and Rickert (eds.), *The Text of The Canterbury Tales*, 1.29–33; 82–3; 100–7; 472–5; Seymour, *A Catalogue of Chaucer Manuscripts*, 1. 27, 31, 37, 41–2, 71–2, 88, 94, 148, 151.

[53] For instance, NLW, MS Brogyntyn ii.1 is copied in several hands, but the transition from parchment to paper which occurs at f. 25r is performed by one scribe. I am indebted to Elaine Treharne for

Figure 1.2 St John's, Camb., MS S. 35, opening of f. 34v and 35r: insertion of paper quires to a book containing protective parchment leaves (partly visible in the gutter)

folding, pricking and ruling are techniques that may slightly change depending on the material being used, and paper does not present itself as a material that can receive a highly sophisticated level of decoration. The use of gold in paper manuscripts is unusual, at least in the west.[54]

Cataloguers, editors and manuscript scholars of the eighteenth, nineteenth and twentieth centuries sometimes seem to consider British paper manuscripts as poor relations to parchment productions – second-class manuscripts written by non-professional or amateur scribes, or at universities.[55] Even E. Heawood,

drawing my attention to this manuscript. Another example is Princeton, University Library, MS 100 (*olim* the 'Helmingham manuscript'), a copy of *The Canterbury Tales* which is written on two sets of different material, paper ff. 1–165; 203–15 and parchment ff. 166–202. Manly and Rickert (eds.), *The Text of The Canterbury Tales*, thought that one hand copied the parchment and another one the paper section, but recent work on these hands argues for one scribe's work: see Horobin, 'The Scribe of the Helmingham and Northumberland Manuscripts'.

[54] There are of course exceptions, for example, BodL, MS Arch. Selden. B.24, which is decorated with sophisticated borders: see Boffey and Edwards, with Barker-Benfield (eds.), *The Works*.

[55] Fenn (ed.), *Original Letters*; Denne, 'Observations on Paper-Marks'; Henderson, 'A Preliminary Note on 15th-Century Watermarks'; Blades, 'On Paper'; Lemon, 'A Collection of Water Marks'; Hunter,

G. S. Ivy and R. J. Lyall in their remarkable contributions to the study of paper tend to emphasize that paper has a low status within the accepted hierarchies of manuscript production,[56] so much so that it is routinely claimed that paper was rarely used in Britain in the fourteenth century and not fully accepted as a writing material until the end of the fifteenth century.

It is well known that paper was introduced in the west during the twelfth and thirteenth centuries,[57] but arrived in England only about the beginning of the fourteenth century. It was an imported commodity and was part of the Grocers' and the Mercers' business. Paper appears in accounts and inventories of the Grocers and the Mercers from the fourteenth century onwards, having been imported by both Genoese merchants and English tradesmen,[58] from the Mediterranean and through commercial links that merchants had with Flanders. London merchants traded in paper from Bruges and Sluis alongside cotton and linen.[59] By the 1350s, paper was being purchased in large quantities by religious institutions, governmental offices and royal households alike. In Ely, paper was bought by the quire as early as 1360–1,[60] and one 'Peter', a grocer of Lincoln, provided paper in quires to the household of King John of France when he was imprisoned in England in 1359 and 1360.[61] In 1394, Robert of Durham declared that '40 quaiers of paper real and other' were kept along with other goods by Thomas Adam.[62] Later, Hoccleve was a regular customer of William Surcestre and Walter Lucy, haberdashers of London, from whom he bought paper, as well as ink, wax and parchment.[63]

Paper was used in an administrative capacity in Britain from the beginning of the fourteenth century, and substantial evidence of this early use survives. In Norfolk, the paper register of the Hustings court of Bishop's Lynn began in 1308, and BL, MS Add. 31223, from Lyme Regis in Dorset, contains entries from 1309.[64] Towards the middle of the fourteenth century, the demands of the royal administration to

---

'Specimens of Marks'. For an overview of this early research, see Labarre, 'The Study of Watermarks in Great Britain', 97; Bower, 'The White Art', 8–11.

[56] Heawood, 'Sources of Early English Paper-Supply', 305–7; Ivy, 'The Bibliography of the Manuscript Book', 37–8; Lyall, 'Materials: The Paper Revolution', 11–13. On the status of paper manuscripts, see also De Hamel, *Medieval Craftsmen: Scribes and Illuminators*, 17.

[57] Paper is a Chinese invention. It was then adopted by the Muslims and introduced in Europe around the twelfth century. Evidence suggests that the first paper-mill is from Spain in 1150, then Italy (Genoa 1235; Fabriano 1264), France (Marseilles 1348) and Germany (Nuremberg 1390). See Pirani, *I maestri cartari*, 18, and Burns, 'Paper Comes to the West'.

[58] Nightingale, *A Medieval Mercantile Community*, 299, 329, 341–2, 395.

[59] Sutton, 'The Mercery Trade', 137–8.

[60] Gullick (ed.), *Extracts from the Precentors' Accounts*, 8–9.

[61] Putnam, *Books and Their Makers*, 312.

[62] Thomas (ed.), *Calendar of the Plea and Memoranda Rolls*, Roll A 33: 1393–4.

[63] Mooney, 'Some New Light on Thomas Hoccleve', 323–40.

[64] Ivy, 'The Bibliography of the Manuscript Book', 36. See also Robinson, 'The Format of Books', 48.

keep tabs on the London guilds and local affairs led to a growth in the need for writing materials; paper was available in large quantities and could accommodate large numbers of texts. Most of the guilds' books are on paper. In 1358, the Goldsmiths purchase 'a large paper register bought by the aforesaid three wardens in order to record all manner of matters worthy of memory'.[65] The records of the Mercers are also kept on paper from 1348,[66] and the Scriveners' Company's manuscript (London, Guildhall, MS 05370) is made of paper, as well as the archives of Old London Bridge, the Bridge House Accounts and the Expenditures of the Bridge.[67] Richard II's Chancery and Exchequer also used paper (for instance, NA, MS C81/1354).[68] Other early examples of paper use are associated with university towns and schools. CUL, MS Hh.1.5, datable 1382–1401, belonged to a grammar master who died in 1401 and is made up of thick, unmarked paper.[69] BL, MS Harley 3524 was written at Brasenose College, Oxford, and is dated 1390.[70] Oxford, Lincoln College, MS lat. 129 is a miscellany containing Latin and English sentences written by Thomas Schort at Newgate school in Bristol.[71] A cursory consideration of the fourteenth-century evidence demonstrates that paper is not just a fifteenth-century phenomenon: by the beginning of the fifteenth century it is already a popular material for copying texts.[72]

Thinking about who used paper, however, is a crucial step towards developing an understanding of the type of scribal environments that may have favoured the rise of paper in literary manuscript production. It seems that scribes who used paper in their own professions, perhaps in their everyday duties in clerical jobs, at universities or in schools, exported it into other ventures such as the production of literary texts. Recent research on the use of paper in Italian and Middle Dutch literature has pointed out that the widespread use of paper in literary manuscripts is directly related to the work of professionals such as notaries and clerks, who would mainly use paper in their everyday duties.[73] In England, once paper was considered a viable writing surface, it was employed to serve the increasing and varied demands of the makers of manuscripts in London and beyond.

---

[65] Jefferson, *Wardens' Accounts*, xiv.

[66] Sutton, *The Mercery of London*, 89.

[67] Christianson, *Memorials of the Book Trade*, 30.

[68] Additional evidence dated to the beginning of the fourteenth century includes BL, MS Harley 431, John Prophete's *Registrum epistolarum* and CCCC, MS 197A, *The Chronicle of the Monk of Westminster*. On the latter manuscript, see Hector and Harvey (eds.), *The Westminster Chronicle*, xiv–xxi.

[69] *DMCL*, 32, entry 46.

[70] *DMOL*, 136, entry 72.

[71] Orme, *Medieval Schools*, 110–11.

[72] On improvements in production techniques over the century, see Hills, 'Early Italian Papermaking' and Ornato, *La carta occidentale*, 1. 349–418.

[73] Kwakkel, 'A New Type of Book'; Petrucci, *Writers and Readers*, 153–7.

There are several examples which may illustrate this point. Scribes who are employed in an administrative capacity and had access to paper are, for example, the scribe of HEHL, MS HM 114; the so-called 'Hammond scribe'; the so-called 'Beryn scribe'; William Worcester; and John Shirley. At least three of these scribes have distinguished careers as professionals either copying administrative documents or as secretaries. The scribe of HEHL, MS HM 114 also copied parts of BL, MS Harley 3943 and London, Lambeth Palace, MS 491.[74] The HEHL and Lambeth manuscripts are both written on paper quires with inner and outer parchment bifolia. Their scribe, according to Hanna, was a professional scribe in London, and recent research has associated him with the *Liber Albus* and the administration of the city.[75] The 'Hammond scribe' is associated with thirteen manuscripts whose paper stocks have been fully described by Mosser.[76] Alongside literary works, he also copied BL, MS Add. 29901, containing tracts on state ceremonials,[77] although he still remains unlocalized. The same can be said of the 'Beryn scribe', who wrote nine manuscripts, some on paper.[78] William Worcester (1415–*c*.83) was secretary to Sir John Fastolf, and most of his notebooks are written on paper.[79] Finally, the career of John Shirley is well documented: he was a clerk to the Beauchamp family before he rented premises in London in which he seems to have produced books.[80] Paper features to a great extent in his manuscript production.[81] Paper is closely linked with those individuals who helped to establish the London literary horizon. Anne Sutton has demonstrated that the mercantile community, the scriveners, other clerks of London and people such as Richard Whittington and John Carpenter are pivotal to the establishment of that literary scene. These are also the very individuals who were involved in the importing of paper and the writing of texts on it.[82]

Additional evidence from fourteenth- and fifteenth-century literary manuscripts confirms that competent scribes employed paper, combining paper stocks in different ways and using them in large quantities. It is not uncommon to find religious and secular texts written on one paper stock by one scribe, for example *The Prick of Conscience* in BodL, MS e Musaeo 88, *c*.1400, *Speculum Sacerdotale* in BL, MS Add.

[74] See Wakelin, p. 46, below; Mooney, pp. 201–2, below.

[75] Hanna, *William Langland*, 172; Hanna, 'The Scribe of Huntington HM 114'; Bowers, 'Two Professional Readers', 131–3.

[76] Mosser, 'Dating the Manuscripts of "The Hammond Scribe"'.

[77] Mooney, 'A New Manuscript by the Hammond Scribe'.

[78] Mooney and Matheson, 'The Beryn Scribe'.

[79] Wakelin, 'William Worcester', 54–6.

[80] For example, BL, MS Add. 16165: London, Lambeth Palace, MS Sion College, Arc. L.40.2/E.44; TCC, MS R.3.20 and BL, MS Harley 78. On the manuscripts, see Lyall, 'Materials: The Paper Revolution', 16–21; Connolly, *John Shirley*, 10–26, 27–68, 69–101; and Connolly's discussion in this volume, pp. 131, 146–7.

[81] See for instance, Lyall, 'Materials: The Paper Revolution'; Boffey and Thompson, 'Anthologies and Miscellanies'.

[82] Sutton, *The Mercery of London*, 161–71.

36791, c.1425, and BodL, MS Rawl. B.166, a fifteenth-century copy of the prose *Brut*.[83] Alternatively, more than one scribe has worked on two or more paper stocks, for instance in BodL, MS Rawl. poet. F.32, which is a fifteenth-century anthology containing texts by Lydgate and other English poems. Research also shows that scribes who used paper display a varied level of proficiency in the writing skills and different training in the overall production of these manuscripts.[84] For example, the scribe who copied Langland's *Piers Plowman* in London, Society of Antiquaries, MS 687, datable to c.1425, establishes a rather interesting quiring technique, perhaps an indication of the fact that he is not used to copying books. BL, MS Add. 59678, containing the unique written copy of Malory's *Morte Darthur*, is copied in the later fifteenth century by two scribes who combine different levels of competence.

It may be useful to expand on the significance of the use of paper by looking closely at this last example. BL, MS Add. 59678, also known as 'the Winchester manuscript' of Malory's *Morte Darthur*, does not have elaborated illuminations, historiated initials or expensive gold leaves. It is written in dark-brown ink, occasionally black, corrected and rubricated in red.[85] On the surface it is a rather unpretentious manuscript, but its discovery in 1934 opened debates on the state of the text, authorial intention, authorial identity, textual unity and interpretation.[86] However, little scholarship has appeared on the paper used in the manuscript or on how scribes deployed the paper stock across the manuscript. Much of the focus has been on the dating of the manuscript from its paper, which firmly places the manuscript in the second half of the fifteenth century.[87]

The manuscript is made up of sixty quires of eight: 242 sheets (extant) of paper folded into folios, which represent three complete paper stocks, with twin marks appearing on the left and the right of the mould which made the sheets of paper.[88] An Arms of France with pendant appears in quires 1–5, 25–7, 29, 41–2 (except f. 333 and f. 340), 44–9, 55–6; an Arms of France without pendant is present in quires 12–24, 28, 30–4, 38–40, 43, 50–4, 57–60 and f. 333 and f. 340; a Gothic letter P covers quires 6–11 and 35–7.[89] By looking at the distribution of the paper stock in Figure 1.3, a number of observations can be made about the work of the scribes and the making of the manuscript. The paper stocks do not run linearly from quire to quire but cluster

---

[83] For recent descriptions, see Scase (ed.), *Manuscripts of the West Midlands*, www.mwm.bham.ac.uk.

[84] On scribal training, see Petrucci, *Writers and Readers*, 62.

[85] Ker (ed.), *The Winchester Malory*.

[86] Vinaver (ed.), *Malory*, xxxv–lvi.

[87] Ker (ed.), *The Winchester Malory*, x. See also Hellinga and Kelliher, 'The Malory Manuscript'.

[88] See, on the definition of a paper stock, Needham, 'Allan H. Stevenson'.

[89] A description and reproduction of the watermark appears in Hellinga and Kelliher, 'The Malory Manuscript', 106–8 and Kelliher, 'The Early History of the Malory Manuscript'. Kelliher does not identify the watermark twins.. Examples can be: ff. 10–15 and ff. 20–1 for the Arms of France with pendant; ff. 88–9 and ff. 80–1 for the Gothic letter P; and ff. 128–9 and ff. 256–7 for the Arms of France without pendant.

Paper stocks: *Arms of France with pendant; $ Gothic letter P; & Arms of France without pendant

First quire is missing

Quire 1 *	f. 9r signature 1	signature 2	signature 3	signature 4
Quire 2 *	f. 17r signature 1	signature 2	signature 3	signature 4
Quire 3 *	f. 25r signature 1	signature 2	signature 3	signature 4
Quire 4 *	missing folio	f. 34r signature 2 Verso blank; f. 34r Explicit	f. 35r	signature 4
Quire 5 *		f. 41r signature 1	signature 2	signature 3
Quire 6 $	f. 45r			
Quire 7 $	f. 53r			
Quire 8 $	f. 61r			
Quire 9 $	f. 69r	70v Explicit **Book 1**	Beginning **Book 2**	
Quire 10 $	f. 77r			
Quire 11 $	f. 85r			
Quire 12 &	f. 93r			f. 96 r Explicit **Book 2** and start **Book 3**
Quire 13 &	f. 101r			
Quire 14 &	f. 109r			
Quire 15 &	f.117r			
Quire 16 &	f. 125r			
Quire 17 &	f. 133r			
Quire 18 &	f. 141r			
Quire 19 &	f. 149r			
Quire 20 &	f. 157r		signature iii	
Quire 21 &	f. 165r signature i	signature ii	signature iii	
Quire 22 &	f. 173r signature i		signature iii	
Quire 23 &	f. 181r signature i		signature iii	
Quire 24 &	f. 189r signature I (?)			
Quire 25 *	f. 197r signature 1	signature 2	signature 3	signature 4
Quire 26 *	f. 205r signature 1	signature 2	signature 3	signature 4
Quire 27 *	f. 213r signature 1	signature 2	signature 3	signature 4
Quire 28 &	f. 221r			

Figure 1.3 Diagrammatic representation of BL, MS Add. 59678.

			f. 16v catchword: knyght	scribe A
			f. 24v catchword: and so þis	scribe A
		f. 31v	missing folio	scribe A
			f. 40v catchword: bothe	scribe A; but scribe B copies 24 lines of f. 35r and includes his style of signatures at the end of the page almost cropped
. 44v verso half blank	missing folio	missing folio	missing folio	scribe A
			f. 52v catchword: That he (Added also on 53r above writing frame)	scribe A to f. 45r line 6; scribe B onwards
			f. 60v catchword: Wyth Syr (Added also on 61r above writing frame)	scribe B
			f. 68v catchword: Olde damesel (Added also on 69r above writing frame)	scribe B
			f. 76v catchword: Suche fyffty	scribe B
			f. 84v catchword: Do dou3tyly	scribe B
			f. 92v catchword: Cheldrake	scribe B
			f. 100v catchword: as the	scribe B
			f. 108v catchword: a large	scribe B
. 113r explicit **Book 3**	Beginning **Book 4**		f. 116v catchword: The for	scribe B
			f. 124v catchword: Syr seide	scribe B
			f. 132v catchword: All thes lokis	scribe B
			f. 140v catchword: Anguyshanus of	scribe B
			f. 148r explicit **Book 4**, end page with space for rubric; f. 148v Beginning **Book 5**; catchword: Melyodas	scribe B
			f. 156v catchword: So she lette	scribe B
			f. 164v catchword: All the	scribe B
			f. 172v catchword: And þ<ere>for<e>	scribe B
			f. 180v catchword: Howell	scribe B
			f. 188v catchword: On the to	scribe B
			f. 196v catchword: beste þ<at> had	scribe B to f. 191r end the recto; scribe A from 191v onwards
			f. 204v catchword: hede	scribe A
			f. 212v catchword: the oþ<er> þ<at>	scribe A
			f. 220v catchword: Seyde þ<at>	scribe A
			f. 228v catchword: kynge Arthure	scribe A

Quire 29 *	f. 229r signature i	signature ii	signature iii	signature not fully visible
Quire 30 &	f. 237r signature i			
Quire 31 &	f. 245r			
Quire 32 &	f. 253r			
Quire 33 &	f. 261r	signature ii	signature not fully visible	signature iiii
Quire 34 &	f. 269r signature i	signature ii		signature iiii
Quire 35 $	f. 277r signature i			
Quire 36 $	f. 285r			
Quire 37 $	f. 293r			
Quire 38 &	f. 301r signature i	signature ii	signature iii	signature iiii
Quire 39 &	f. 309r signature i			signature iiii
Quire 40 &	f. 317r signature i	signature ii	signature iii	signature iiii
Quire 41 *	f. 325r signature i	signature ii	signature iii	
Quire 42 *	f. 333r &	signature ii	signature iii	signature iiii
Quire 43 &	f. 341r signature i	signature ii	signature not fully visible	signature iiii
Quire 44 *	f. 349r Beginning of **Book 6**; signature 1	signature 2	signature 3	signature 4
Quire 45 *	f. 357r signature 1	signature 2	signature 3	signature 4
Quire 46 *	f. 365r signature 1	signature 2	signature 3	signature 4
Quire 47 *	f. 373r signature 1	signature 2	signature 3	signature 4
Quire 48 *	f. 381r signature 1	signature 2	signature 3	signature 4
Quire 49 *	f. 389r signature 1	signature 2	signature 3	signature 4
Quire 50 &	f. 397r signature 1	signature 2	signature 3	signature 4
Quire 51 &	f. 405r signature 1	signature 2	signature 3	signature 4
Quire 52 &	f. 413r	signature 2	signature 3	signature 4
Quire 53 &	f. 421r signature 1	signature 2	signature 3	signature 4
Quire 54 &	f. 429r signature 1	signature 2	signature 3	signature 4
Quire 55 *	f. 437r signature 1	signature 2	signature 3	
Quire 56 *	f. 445r signature 1	signature 2	signature 3	signature 4
Quire 57 &	f. 453r signature 1	signature 2	signature 3	signature 4
Quire 58 &	f. 461r signature 1	signature 2	signature 3	signature 4
Quire 59 &	f. 469r signature 1	signature 2	signature 3	signature 4
Quire 60 &	f. 477r signature 1	signature 2	signature 3	signature 4
missing final quires				

Figure 1.3 (cont.)

			f. 236v catchword: Amaunte	scribe A to f. 229r end the recto; scribe B from 229v onwards; his signatures
			f. 244v catchword: Me sore	scribe B
		f. 251v	missing folio	scribe B
			f. 260v catchword: Sarezynes	scribe B
			f. 268v catchword: Syr Launcelot	scribe B
			f. 276v catchword: The felyship	scribe B
			f. 284v catchword: Tumbeled downe	scribe B
			f. 292v catchword: And as he	scribe B
			f. 300v catchword: There my	scribe B
			f. 308v catchword: To delyn	scribe B
			f. 316v catchword:and vppon	scribe B
			f. 324v catchword: Maydynhode	scribe B
			f. 332v catchword: Toke me and	scribe B
			f. 340v catchword: A knyght of	scribe B
	f. 346v ends **Book 5** and half folio is left blank	blank	blank	scribe B
			f. 356v catchword: he alygt	scribe A
			f. 364v catchword: her if	scribe A
			f. 372v catchword: Wyne	scribe A
			f. 380v catchword: all this londe	scribe A
			f. 388v catchword: ano\<ther> while foreward (ano\<ther> while added next to the first line of f. 389r)	scribe A
			f. 396v catchword: and \<th>ey harde	scribe A
			f. 404v catchword: to gydirs	scribe A
. 409r end of **Book 6** and half folio is left blank; f. 409v beginning of **Book 7**			f. 412v catchword: aidame (for madame)	scribe A
			f. 420v catchword: whych was	scribe A
			f. 428v catchword: kyng to	scribe A
			f. 436v catchword: of \<the> boldist	scribe A
			f. 444v catchword: the hede	scribe A
. 449r end of **Book 7** and beginning of **Book 8**			f. 452v catchword: quene	scribe A
			f. 460v catchword: In so much	scribe A
			f. 468v catchword: Now \<the> felyship	scribe A
			f. 476v catchword: gaff me	scribe A
			f. 476v catchword: except \<that>	scribe A

31

around certain quires seemingly at random. It is also remarkable that the scribes do not mix the paper stocks within the quires, with the exception of quire 42. This quire is constructed by paper with the Arms of France with pendant, but the outer bifolium (f. 333 and f. 340) belongs to another paper stock: the Arms of France without pendant. If we then compare the arrangement of the quires with the work of the two scribes who copied the text, there are some striking observations to be made: each scribe seems to stick to his paper stocks; Scribe A is mostly using the Arms of France with pendant, except in quires 18, 50–4 and 57–60; Scribe B is mostly using the Arms of France without pendant, except in quires 41–2. The Gothic letter P is used only by Scribe B, with one exception (the first six lines of f. 45r).

The questions that the distribution of the paper raises are: how did the scribes divide the paper stock? Did they collaborate or work independently? What does this tell us about how the manuscript was put together? The answers are not straightforward, but a few observations can be made. The paper stock with the letter P is particularly intriguing: the diagram in Figure 1.3 contains the running of quires of the manuscript, the division of work of the scribes and the main textual divisions, including signatures and catchwords. The paper stock with the letter P is used after the only irregular quire in the manuscript, a quire of six, which contains a pause in the writing of the text and a blank on half of the final verso. It contains the final part of Book 1 and the beginning of Book 2. This paper stock is then used again in Book 5 of the Book of Tristram, at the beginning of the story of Joyous Gard, finishing mid-way through 'The Tournament at Lonezep'. This paper evidence suggests, as Kelliher has argued, that the scribes were working with loose tales, coming from separate manuscripts,[90] a position which reinforces Vinaver's argument that Malory wrote a series of works rather than one story.[91]

I do not wish to enter the debate on the unity of this work in detail; but it is worth expanding the argument by considering some common assumptions on manuscript production. Manuscripts were produced in different ways: some had an exemplar from which material was copied in a linear fashion, but in many cases – including, for instance, some of the copies of Chaucer's *The Canterbury Tales* or, in earlier centuries, Ælfric's homilies – scribes did not have available complete manuscripts which contained works from beginning to end. Sometimes material was given to them in a piecemeal fashion, sometimes with no real order, and the scribes had to assemble the jigsaw.[92] This is what transpires from BL, MS Add. 59678. The scribes who copied it probably received textual units at different stages.

But what is the relationship between the two scribes? Ker, Kelliher and others have argued that Scribe A is the leading scribe and that Scribe B is collaborating

[90] Kelliher, 'The Early History of the Malory Manuscript', 146.
[91] Vinaver, 'Principles of Textual Emendation', xxxv.
[92] See Da Rold, 'Textual Copying'.

with Scribe A, by sharing the labour after initially working together on Book 1, 'The Tale of King Arthur'.[93] The evidence for this assumption is the shared work on f. 35r, f. 45r, f. 191r and f. 229r. But this evidence can be read in an alternative way. Scribe B often seems to be completing what Scribe A had left out; it is also doubtful to what extent they copied the work simultaneously, because, if one scribe is the leading scribe, surely he would check the work of the other scribe and then correct, emend or point Scribe B in the right direction. Instead, there is no sign of the hand of Scribe A on the folios written by Scribe B, but Scribe B signs those folios that he copied after completing the work by Scribe A, for example, f. 35r and f. 189r. It is likely that Scribe B finished the work of Scribe A, and further research on the relationship between text and paper stocks may lend support to this theory.

The focus of the discussion in the present chapter has been on three major materials: ink, parchment and paper, and on their importance to the study of manuscripts in a cultural framework. The discussion here suggests that there is scope for thinking about paper beyond the vexed question of dating material, and for thinking about ink and parchment with a view to extrapolating information from these materials about how books were constructed and understood. Material evidence narrates stories and suggests new areas of enquiry. Paper, in particular, offers its students layers of meaning – tells stories not just about who produced manuscripts, but also about who used them and why. The revolution that it sparked in Britain in the 1350s had a long-lasting impact on book production, including literary manuscript production, and enabled the development of printing.

---

[93] Ker (ed.), *The Winchester Malory*, xiii–xv; Kelliher, 'The Early History of the Malory Manuscript', 145.

2

Writing the words

DANIEL WAKELIN

And for as moche as in the wrytyng of the same my penne is worn / myn hande wery *and* not stedfast myn eyen di*mm*ed with ouermoche lokyng on the whit paper / and my corage not so prone and redy to laboure as hit hath ben […] I haue practysed *and* lerned at my grete charge and dispense to ordeyne this said book in prynte after the maner *and* forme as ye may here see / and is not wreton with penne and ynke as other bokes ben / to thende that euery man may haue them attones / ffor all the bookes of this storye named the recule of the historyes of troyes thus enpryntid as ye here see were begonne in oon day / and also fynyshid in oon day.[1]

In the first book printed in English, *The Recuyell of the Historyes of Troye* in 1473 or 1474, William Caxton explains why he learned the craft of printing. This might not be the only or even the true explanation, but it reveals one thing which for contemporaries seemed to distinguish printing from 'wrytyng' (the Middle English word for scribal work). Writing requires an amount of time over which the scribe's hand can change in quality (be 'not stedfast'), his eye can become less clear and his diligence or attention can become less 'prone and redy'. Caxton's description of writing suggests that he felt not only that it took more time, but that it took time differently from printing. All copies of an edition, 'all the bookes', are produced over the same span of time and 'fynyshid' in one day; by contrast, every handwritten book is the product of its own distinct period of time.

To understand the activity of writing books by hand, it helps to consider how it unfolds over time. This is difficult, because time is immaterial, whereas books leave only material evidence. To study time, then, requires both careful deduction from evidence and some imagination. Moreover, scribes seldom comment explicitly on their impressions of the time of writing, or on other aspects of their work. But they do sometimes record the weariness of writing, which is time felt as bodily

---

[1] Caxton, trans., *The Recuyell*, *STC* 15375, unsigned leaf 351r; on which see Kuskin, *Symbolic Caxton*, 95–6.

endurance.[2] And studies of some continental scribes who date both the start and end of their work have deduced some average rates for copying. The rate usually works out between two and three folios (four and six pages) per day, depending on the size and script, and thus between twelve and twenty folios a week.[3] The first essential point is the slowness. For example, when the scholar Gerard Skypwith of Pembroke Hall, Cambridge, copied some works of scholastic theology (Pembroke, Camb., MS 255), by 4 July 1459 he had reached f. 247r, but despite continuing without visible interruption he only reached f. 256v on 18 October 1460 (Figure 2.1); that is, nine folios seem to have taken fifteen months.[4] And the second essential point is that the more days that the job took overall, the lower the number of folios written in proportion to the number of days: that is, scribes wrote proportionally more folios per day over 100 days than they did over 200 days, as if their speed decreased over time.[5] That cannot only be because hands became 'wery' like Caxton's, but also because bigger projects were more likely to be interrupted by other activities. For example, the slowcoach Skypwith presumably had to fit his copying around the other activities of a scholar and cleric – the Church's time of yearly revolving rituals rather than a race to complete a job.[6] Yet Skypwith also managed to complete copying Duns Scotus's commentary on the *Sentences* some time in 1461, which suggests either that he sped up or that the copying of different texts took place in overlapping periods of time. In fact, this work finished last is now bound first in the book; the sequence of pages in manuscripts does not always reflect a linear temporal sequence in their production.[7] We cannot assume the same rates and systems of work as in modern western economies, nor assume that scribes copied only one book at a time.

The variable pace and the complex timing, although the product of one distinct academic milieu, were common across fourteenth- and fifteenth-century book production. Like other people who copied for their own devotion, delight or studies, such as Skypwith, the scribes of English literary works were seldom engaged single-mindedly on copying them.[8] The copying of Latin liturgical and other useful books may have been more concerted and organized,[9] but even for these books

---

[2] Dain, *Les Manuscrits*, 23–5.

[3] Gumbert, 'The Speed of Scribes', 61, 65. For an English example, the scribe of CUL, MS Ii.1.36, f. 230v, records working from 25 October 1423 to 28 March 1424, copying 224 folios and 13 lines in 156 days (1.4 folios per day).

[4] Pembroke, Camb., MS 255, f. 247r, f. 256v (the second work only beginning on f. 248r); on which see Clarke, with Lovatt (eds.), *The University and College Libraries of Cambridge*, no. UC47/121.

[5] Gumbert, 'The Speed of Scribes', 63; Overgaauw, 'Fast or Slow', 222, did not find this.

[6] Le Goff, *Time, Work and Culture in the Middle Ages*, 29–42, sketches different conceptions of time, and the slowness of work in thirteenth- to fifteenth-century Europe.

[7] Pembroke, Camb., MS 255, f. 208v. McKenzie, *Making Meaning*, 25–6, raises theoretical questions from overlapping projects in printing houses.

[8] Mooney, 'Locating Scribal Activity', 184–6; see also Mooney, p. 192 below.

[9] Kwakkel, pp. 177–82 below.

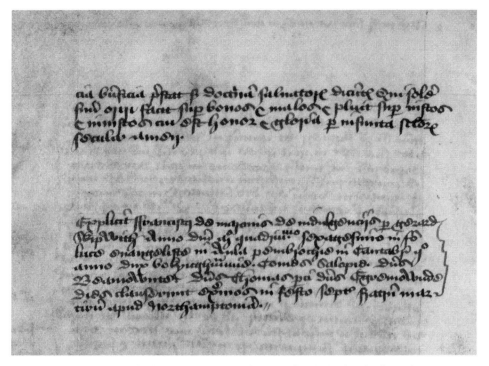

Figure 2.1 Pembroke, Camb., MS 255, f. 256v: a dated colophon by the scribe.

economic measurements – Jacques Le Goff's 'labour time' or 'merchant's time' – do not encompass all of the competing senses of time by which people might have organized the activity of writing. Economic systems of measuring time, productivity and efficiency were subject to debate alongside competing systems.[10] When scribes do record when they are working, in colophons, they sometimes measure time as 'labour time', recording the hours per page or the payment due; but they also specify when they are writing by the time of day, the monastic offices, the liturgical calendar, recent history, personal events or memorials of the dead.[11] For example, Skypwith dates his copying of one work to Pembroke Hall on the feast of St Luke in the year when several nobles – piously named – were killed at the Battle of Northampton. He suggests multiple and complex impressions of how writing takes time: as religious duty, as scholarly diligence, as an escape from the outside hurly-burly of politics – and as something arduous enough to be worth recording

---

[10] As Le Goff, *Time, Work and Culture in the Middle Ages*, 35, 37, 41, 45–7, 49, himself acknowledges; see also Strohm, *Theory and the Premodern Text*, 6, 66–7, 82; Mason Bradbury and Collette, 'Changing Times', 106.

[11] Supino Martini, 'Il libro', 6, 9–10.

when he is done.[12] These and many other possible senses of time might influence how people organize and conceive of the activity of writing.

The extended time of writing and the complex understandings of it together throw light on the inconsistencies or interruptions in manuscripts. Often, frequent changes in the colour of the ink or the aspect of the handwriting show the short stints in which a book was written. Such changes are visible in books copied on rough materials and by careless hands, and most probably for private use;[13] but they are also sometimes visible in books copied more smartly, and most probably for use by others; and these changes of ink reveal short stints, frequently and irregularly interrupted.[14] There are also many manuscripts where spelling, punctuation, layout or the exemplar used shift visibly, revealing that the time of writing, and with it the scribe's practices or intentions, changed or were interrupted.[15] Such inconsistency is one of the most distinctive features of manuscripts – the regular irregularity of them – and it is by remembering the temporal dimension that we might understand the irregularity of the hand being 'not stedfast'.

The extended time-scale also helps us to understand the scribe's most important decision about his work: the script on which he will model his hand. Scribes and readers had culturally informed notions of which genres, languages or types of book suited which scripts. These notions of script as image have recently been brilliantly recovered by Malcolm Parkes and others, and complement well the theoretical arguments that all aspects of books, including their visual and physical elements, are just as expressive as the text is.[16] But, besides image, the people writing, or paying for writing, also had to consider this: that the different degrees of speed, slowness, ease or precision with which one might write each script required different amounts of time – and so different social conditions or economic costs.[17] Paul Canart has argued that the common palaeographical procedure of describing a hand as following such-and-such a script only lets us see writing as a 'static' thing, whereas we might use such descriptions as clues to the 'dynamic aspect' of writing as a process: not only the 'expressive value', which is more often studied, but also

---

[12] Pembroke, Camb., MS 255, f. 256v.

[13] E.g., Wakelin, 'The Carol in Writing', 30, 33. On changes of ink, see Da Rold, p. 15 above.

[14] E.g., Durham, University Library, MS Cosin V.ii.15 (Walton's translation of Boethius), with changes of ink and probably therefore of stint on f. 5v, line 21, f. 8v/3, f. 11v/15, f. 12r/6, f. 16v/2, f. 20r/28, f. 21v/7, f. 22r/26, f. 25r/27, f. 31r/11. This averages three folios per stint and thus confirms the findings of Gumbert, 'The Speed of Scribes', 61, 65. Doyle, 'The Copyist of MSS Bodley 283', describes the hand.

[15] E.g., in CUL, MS Ll.4.14 the scribe marks medial caesurae in *Piers Plowman* with a *punctus elevatus* on ff. 1r–86r; unmarked caesurae (bar five lines) on ff. 86–91r; a single *punctus* after the ink-colour changes, and presumably a new stint began, on f. 91r line 21, up to f. 92r line 26; and thereafter virgules on ff. 91r–107r.

[16] Parkes, *Their Hands before Our Eyes*, 127–45, offers a magisterial overview. McGann, *The Textual Condition*, 12–13, theorizes on the cultural significances of hands or typefaces.

[17] See also Kwakkel in this volume, pp. 183–5.

the speed, direction and flow of writing, as well as for whom, and how and why, the scribe undertook this activity.[18] Careful, if necessarily tentative and interpretative, answers to these questions might reveal not just script as a visual model, but writing as a 'dynamic' process among, in competition with and as a constituent part of other social and cultural processes. Those processes include managing the household, shaping one's identity, keeping records, doing pious service, creating a luxury commodity, honouring one's patron, avoiding idleness, getting work done quickly, sparing materials and innumerable others.

Nevertheless, it is helpful to begin by identifying the 'scripts' – defined in the abstract – on which scribes modelled their hands and which allow us to describe their hands with convenience. From the thirteenth century onwards, the canonical 'Gothic' script for books was what is known now as *textualis* or textura; in fifteenth-century sheets advertising what writing-masters could teach, or in manuals of writing, it was known as 'textus', 'textura' or 'testualis'. The terms come from the Latin passive participle *textus* meaning 'woven' and refer to the visual appearance of this script.[19] It was distinguished by a dense net of thick straight vertical lines, complemented by thin lines on certain horizontal and diagonal axes, notably at the height of the top of letters *m* or *n*.[20] Although our word *text* suggests reverence for the details of language, in fact this reference to the 'weave' of the page suggests the importance of a visual impression. The impressiveness of textura is visible in books for use in church, for example, where the handwriting is often very large and very fiddly, with 'quadrata' minims, that is, squared feet at the bottom of the vertical lines for *m* and *n*, which would be cumbersome to write. For example, in two copies of bits of Scripture for reading or singing in the liturgy (CUL, MS Gg.2.8 and CUL, MS Gg.2.24 – for the latter see Figure 2.2), the large and elaborate letters modelled on textura quadrata are adorned further by being punctuated with gold initials; and red is frequently used for the 'rubrics', the textual divisions or liturgical instructions. The size and fiddliness might aid reading aloud in church, might awe the congregation or might show respect for the Lord. There is a sense of occasion recorded in the rubrics for Scripture to be read 'in tempore belli' (in time of war) and on other occasions;[21] and the act of writing itself might be an occasion of pious service.

---

[18] Canart, 'La Paléographie', 168–71, 175; and, in an outdated structuralist idiom, D'Haenens, 'Pour une sémiologie', 197. For a good statement of the opposite emphasis, on describing the morphology of graphs and refining nomenclature, see Derolez, *Palaeography*, 6, 9.

[19] Schaap, '*Scribere pulchre potes*', 51–8, 65–73; the sources specify further subdivisions. *OED*, s.v. 'text', and Hector, *The Handwriting of English Documents*, 54–5, explain the etymology.

[20] Bischoff, *Latin Palaeography*, 127–9, 134–6.

[21] CUL, MS Gg.2.8, with occasions for readings throughout (citing f. 150v, a reading from Mark 11.23); CUL, MS Gg.2.24, with a calendar ff. 3r–9v. For even more red ink, see e.g., CUL, MS Gg.5.24, ff. 7r–17r.

Scribes also imitated textura for other types of book beyond the liturgy. For example, when the Dutch scribe Theoderik Werken and an anonymous colleague copy some English religious poems by Lydgate, Maidstone and others (HEHL, MS HM 142), they both model their handwriting on a delicate textura: there is the woven effect of 'biting', or overlapping where two round letters abut each other (especially after *b* in this book), and there are unnecessary spurs sticking out of tall letters such as *l* and the top of ascending strokes – see Figure 2.3. This was a choice: Werken, at least, was also an accomplished scribe of the new humanist handwriting as well, and English verse, which was copied by the other scribe, did not usually deserve textura; but Werken and his colleague nevertheless model their handwriting here on textura, produced with care, even shifting back and forth between black and red ink and sometimes ruling pages in red. The appearance thus evokes rubricated copies of liturgy and Scripture. That is a fitting echo, for the poems here, such as Lydgate's 'Kalendare', echo and quote from these sources. One might also speculate that writing these verse prayers with lavish care was a devout act – just as, so Werken notes in a colophon, 'sayng' one of these verse prayers has the power to get one's 'desyr fulfyllyt in al godnes'.[22] Or does the visual dazzle conceal a care more for the luxury in its own right than for the text it adorns? Werken's colleague introduces several errors into the poems, some suggesting unfamiliarity with English,[23] as though the look mattered more than the content.

Compromise sometimes extended to the look of handwriting too. The busy scribes employed to copy documents – texts which addressed an urgent moment rather than eternity – sped up, relative to the scribes of books.[24] They adopted what is now known as cursive writing or *cursiva*, a name reflecting its flow or 'running' from letter to letter in simplified form: they joined letters with more hurried ties which altered the shape of individual graphs, as for example in loops on the ascenders of *b* and *d*; and they formed letters from fewer 'broken' or separate strokes, which would require lifting the pen from the writing-surface, but rather from rounder strokes, again allowing more flow.[25] The specifically English cursive is known as

---

[22] HEHL, MS HM 142, colophon on f. 60v. Evidence that the scribes provided rubric as they went along is a correction on f. 17r, where the main scribe erases his own work in red and writes over the erasure in brown. Mynors, 'A Fifteenth-Century Scribe', traces Werken's career and reproduces a page of HEHL, MS HM 142.

[23] Schulz, 'Middle English Texts', 443–4; see for example HEHL, MS HM 142, 'So ful os grace', muddling long *f* with *s* even in this common word (f. 21v), and in Werken's colophon 'whyl dey ben a sayng' (f. 60v, in which a later hand corrects 'dey' to 'they'). For other garbled English by a Netherlandish scribe who nevertheless writes a fine hand modelled on textura, see e.g., prayers in a Book of Hours in HEHL, MS HM 1344, 'folc wynge' for *following* (f. 24v), 'tus' for *thus* (f. 25r), 'dat' for *that* (f. 33r), 'de siring' (f. 104v), 'wor shypped' (f. 105r).

[24] Hector, *The Handwriting of English Documents*, 55–6; Chaplais, *English Royal Documents*, 50.

[25] Derolez, *Palaeography*, 125–8; Parkes, *Their Hands before Our Eyes*, 81–5.

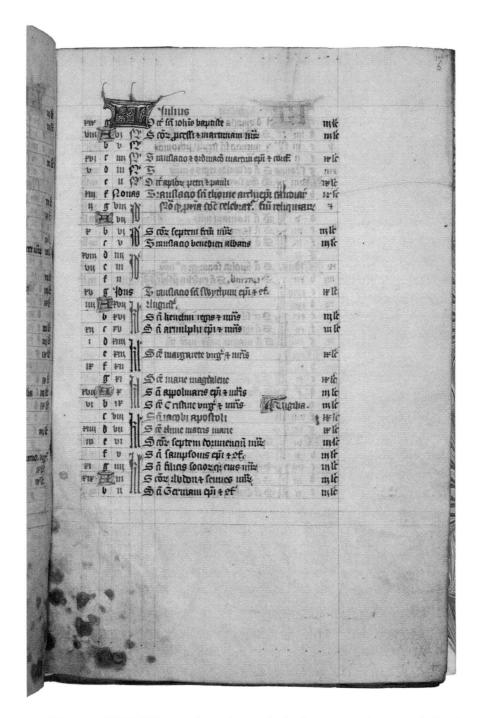

Figure 2.2 CUL, MS Gg.2.24, f. 6r: a liturgical calendar in a typical mixture of red and blue writing modelled on textura.

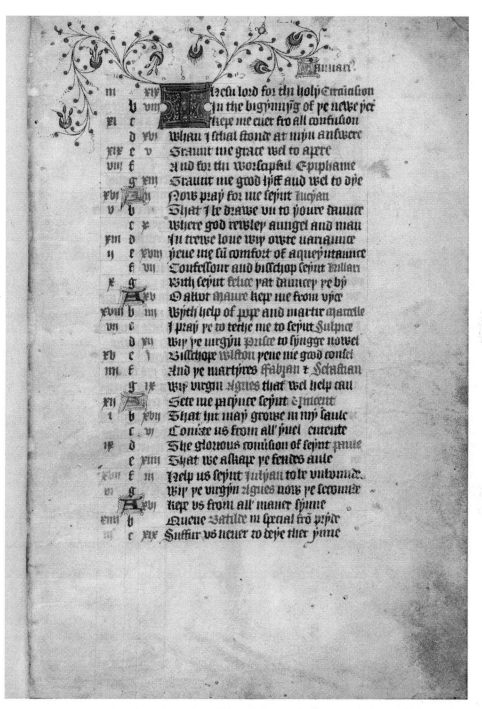

*Figure 2.3 HEHL, MS HM 142, f. 1r: Lydgate's 'Kalendar' set out to resemble
a real calendar.*

anglicana or (rarely) as *cursiva antiquior*.[26] Another slightly different cursive with a few even more simplified graphs developed on the continent, and at some time in the 1370s English scribes in contact with English-controlled Gascony began to imitate it.[27] This continental cursive when used in England is now known as secretary. The scribes themselves referred to cursive writing by the institutions in which they wrote it: they distinguished writing in 'big text hand' ('grosso texto') from writing 'in the court hand' ('sub manu curiali'), or distinguished 'textum' and 'curiam' after the courts or *curiae* which issued documents like this.[28] The asymmetric pairings – one visual term, one institutional – capture the crucial distinction between the pursuit of visual impressions in textura and the social or economic demands for speed and ease in cursive writing.

However, from the late thirteenth century onwards, scribes adopted and adapted the cursive processes of writing documents for writing books. Abandoning textura reduced the time spent writing and, when scribes were being paid, reduced their wages. This made copies of texts manageable or affordable for more people with less time, training or money.[29] Sometimes, the link between writing documents and writing books in cursive hands becomes clear, as for example when readers keep records of literary works they know in tall paper account books in very cursive hands.[30] Yet in the majority of books copied in cursive hands, there is no echo of the documentary origins of such writing. For example, one group of fifteenth-century scribes used cursive hands and the same tall thin format of account books for Chaucer's esteemed *Troilus and Criseyde* (BL, MS Harley 1239). But the scribes created this account-book format from more expensive parchment, and they evidently felt that cursive writing was compatible with their efforts to dress up the book with coloured initials and with red brackets or 'braces' to mark the artful form of the stanzas.[31] Similarly, a scribe who esteemed the lengthy English instructional poem *Speculum Vitae* enough to ascribe it, wrongly, to the revered mystic Richard Rolle nevertheless copied it in a fluent hand modelled on anglicana on an unruled page (CUL, MS Ll.1.8); even the complex two-compartment shape of *a* is formed with just two curling strokes – see Figure 2.4. The desire to copy important or canonical works more quickly and cheaply seems to have made the speed and ease of cursive handwriting more important than visual impressiveness.

[26] Derolez, *Palaeography*, 134–41; Parkes, *English Cursive*, xiv–xvi, xxii–xxiii.

[27] Hanna, *London Literature*, 225–8, 238.

[28] Chaplais, *English Royal Documents*, 50; Hanna, *London Literature*, 1.

[29] Kwakkel, 'A New Type of Book', 230, 245; Ornato, 'Les Conditions de production', 101–3.

[30] Rigg (ed.), *A Glastonbury Miscellany*, 2, 40; Wakelin, 'William Worcester', 56.

[31] BL, MS Harley 1239, ff. 1r–62v. Five of *The Canterbury Tales* were added in an even faster, rougher hand (ff. 63r–106v). See p. 22 above and p. 82 below.

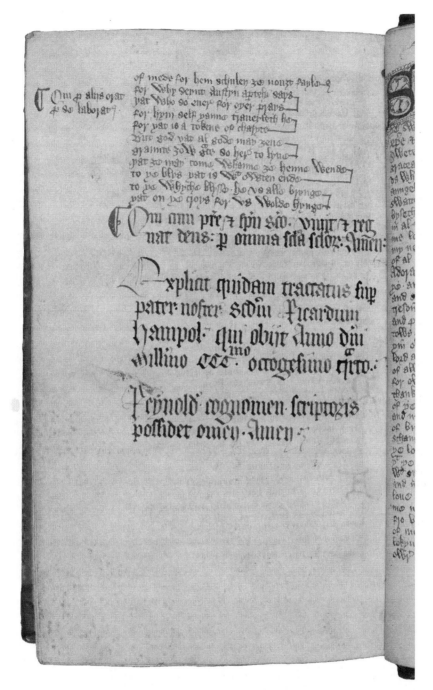

Figure 2.4 CUL, MS Ll.1.8, f. 200v: Speculum vitae *in a hand modelled on anglicana with an ascription to Richard Rolle of Hampole ('Ricardum Hampol') in a hand modelled on textura.*

Nevertheless, when scribes used cursive scripts in books, they did adapt them. A work in English seldom deserved the effort or glamour of textura, but it could deserve *some* effort. The scribe of *Speculum Vitae*, just mentioned, wrote fluently but rather neatly, so that although individual graphs are formed with one flowing movement, the graphs do not always flow into each other. Moreover, tellingly, he wrote the colophon in which he ascribes the poem to Rolle, and remembers Rolle's death, in imposing handwriting modelled on textura quadrata, and he had the book adorned with rubrication.[32] Between the extremes of service-books in handwriting modelled on textura and rough notebooks in handwriting modelled on anglicana or secretary, scribes could combine calligraphic book scripts and speedy cursive practice to different degrees. Particularly important were: spacing out the minims in *m* and *n*; avoiding too many ligatures between graphs copied currently; and adding small calligraphic spurs or horns on letters.[33] The resulting intermediary varieties are now known as anglicana formata, bastard anglicana and (with a more complex history than is sketched here) bastard secretary. Malcolm Parkes has called the range of these varieties 'the hierarchy of scripts' and shown how identifying this hierarchy might allow us to identify the different connotations of each script's 'image'.[34]

The design of this 'image' usually raises questions about the complex relationship between book production and reception, for the script is not usually identifiable as an artistic choice by the author. Rather, the image is usually formed by the scribe, as part of his reception of the text – and his image then affects the text's reception by further readers in turn: in this sense, as D. F. McKenzie argues, 'new readers make new texts'.[35] For example, in one collection of religious and moral poems, many by John Lydgate (CUL, MS Kk.1.6), the person who copied the poems, Richard Fox, modelled his handwriting on bastard anglicana, an anglicana adorned with serifs, separated minims, broken strokes and loopless straight ascenders. This choice probably does not reflect the poet's own design, for Fox records in his prefatory note that Lydgate is recently dead ('late') and prays for his soul. So how, at this moment of memorial, did Fox write? On the one hand, he made economies of time and money: he did not copy the poems in full-blown textura – unlike Werken's colleague, above – for that would be even more time-consuming; and he copied on paper, with parchment only for the outermost and innermost leaves of quires.[36] On

---

[32] CUL, MS Ll.1.8, f. 200v (colophon); on which MS, see Hanna (ed.), *Speculum Vitae*, i. xxi–xxii.

[33] Derolez, *Palaeography*, 128–30; Parkes, *English Cursive*, xiii, xvi–xvii.

[34] Parkes, *Their Hands before Our Eyes*, 106–12, 127.

[35] *Bibliography and the Sociology of Texts*, 29, traces this feedback loop.

[36] CUL, MS Kk.1.6, ff. 194r–214v. Moreover, two parchment leaves (f. 198, f. 208) have rounded corners missing, and have had since before the addition of leaf-signatures, suggesting that Fox economically used the edges of the hide in the manner described by Kwakkel, p. 187 below. Edwards, 'Fifteenth-Century Middle English Verse Author Collections', 103, suggests that the quires are simply parchment.

the other hand, he dressed up the poems in this laboured handwriting modelled on a fancier form of anglicana. The motives which shape this decision about how to spend his time need not only be financial; among other possible motives, Fox might have been paying respects to Lydgate as a member of the Benedictine order with which Fox was linked,[37] or paying respects to him as somebody recently deceased. The hand might be Fox's response to Lydgate's prestige as a poet, or it might be an attempt to create such prestige in the minds of the readers of this book. It is tempting to wonder whether the slower writing modelled on bastard anglicana might *enact* the same ponderous piety that the poems conjure. After all, the poems preach that 'Alle haste is odious' and that 'Trauel' or travail in books is good – sentiments surely shared by somebody who copied Lydgate's verse in this fiddly hand.[38] This last might or might not be the right interpretation of this book; but it illustrates how any one choice of script might suggest the complex motives and institutions – not merely one hierarchy – behind the making and use of texts.

Moreover, in fact, 'one choice of script' is not quite the right phrase. In handwriting, unlike a precast typeface, every separate graph and not merely one overall 'script' might register a single response to the text, or its occasion, readers or whatever. By reading closely the individual graphs, we can move from the abstraction of script to the dynamic processes of handwriting in real times and places. For example, it might be difficult to identify the script behind a very current hand as anglicana or secretary, say, especially in the mixed hands of the fifteenth century; but the hand might reveal something about the social world in which writing unfolded. For example, some collections of English and Latin recipes and tips for cookery, medicine and animal husbandry are copied in very current hands, with minims and short *r* so dashed that they are almost horizontal squiggles. In one such book from a provincial household the main hand oscillates haphazardly between graphs modelled on different 'scripts' – one-compartment *a* modelled on secretary and two-compartment *a* modelled on anglicana; different forms of *r* – but the informality and haste tell us lots about the occasions for copying and reading these recipes, tips and cures: private, informal, amateurish, utilitarian, urgent.[39] And if we consider the shapes of letters alongside other elements of books of practical writing – sloping lines, lack of margins or limp bindings made of rough parchment, say[40] – we might

[37] Barratt identifies Fox in her edition of Hull, *The Seven Psalms*, xiv–xxii.

[38] CUL, MS Kk.1.6, f. 205r (Lydgate, *Minor Poems*, 11.837, line 76), f. 205v (*Minor Poems*, 11.759, line 1).

[39] CUL, MS Ll.1.18, with most letters, except thorn, running into the next (f. 12r, lines 1–3: 'flessh-lynes', 'stomake' and 'strenger') and different allographs of *a* (f.12v, lines 1–4: 'Capiller', 'ways' and 'namely').

[40] E.g., CUL, MS Ii.6.33, ff. 1r–32v (sloping writing, tiny margins); CUL, MS Add. 9309 (parchment cover – on these see Gillespie's discussion in this book, pp. 165–9 below). The second half of CUL, MS Ii.6.33, is more formally copied.

deduce more about the writing process. We might reflect that although, in these practical books, individual graphs are hurried, the overall effort for one person in writing out often large collections of recipes or remedies is considerable. Even when one scribe varies from hasty and scruffy to slow and formal, revealing shifts in his motives and processes, his persistence across such shifts suggests a great investment of time and energy, nevertheless.[41] Many such texts, however roughly copied and bound, are also provided with careful textual divisions, sometimes in a more formal hand, or with finding-aids.[42] We thus learn something of domestic life and of the place of writing in it.

What is revealed, across fifteenth-century culture as a whole, is not simple: as the times and contexts of the dynamic acts of writing change, there is no neat correlation of one text or genre with one script or image. For example, other scribes might copy medical and domestic advice in grand handwriting and layouts: for example, one scribe of a set of recipes formed his letters with fiddly broken strokes and much red ink, as might befit recipes claimed to come from 'þe chef mayster of kyng Rychardes þe secunde'. Even a veterinary book could include both such formal copying and rough jotted additions.[43] A similar variety occurs in copies of other works. For example, a well-known scribe in the bureaucracy of London in the early fifteenth century twice copied Chaucer's *Troilus and Criseyde*: one time alone, on paper, in a hand that hurries from letter to letter on unruled lines, and another time collaboratively with three other scribes, on parchment, with five stanzas neatly set out to a page. In the second, slightly better-organized production his handwriting changes too, as he labours to write fiddlier serifs and broken strokes.[44] Such changes seem to reflect the differing circumstances of his writing – perhaps private pleasure and paid commission – through which he encountered Chaucer's poem.

Moreover, similar changes can also be found within one act of copying, for manuscripts are not usually the product of one moment, but of long and changing periods of time. For example, the scribe of an English translation of Christine de Pizan's *Le livre du corps de policie* (CUL, MS Kk.1.5 part 1) dresses up his handwriting, modelled on secretary, with curious calligraphic horns on his kidney-shaped

---

[41] E.g., CUL, MS Ll.1.18, in which one scribe copies ff. 3r–4v, 6r–16r, 17r–79v, 81v–130v, 131r–134v, 149v–150v, despite the varying appearance. Keiser, 'Practical Books for the Gentleman', 478–80, proposes 'several scribes' for the book.

[42] E.g., CUL, MS Add. 9309 (headings in a display handwriting); CUL, MS Ll.1.18, with finding-aids, on which see Keiser, 'Practical Books for the Gentleman', 478–80.

[43] E.g., respectively JRL, MS Eng. 7 (*The Forme of Cury* in handwriting modelled on bastard anglicana), esp. f. 4r; CUL, MS Dd.4.44, ff. 1r–22v, 23r–25v, in handwriting modelled on anglicana formata, with rough additions on f. 18v, f. 23r, ff. 25v–40v.

[44] HEHL, MS HM 114, wholly by this scribe, and BL, MS Harley 3943, ff. 2r–7v, ff. 9r–56v, ff. 63r–67v: in the latter there is an incipient serif at the foot of *h*, *l*, *m* and *n*, and broken strokes in *d* and *g*. On this much-discussed scribe, see most recently Bowers, 'Two Professional Readers'; and in the present volume, Da Rold, p. 26; Mooney, pp. 201–2.

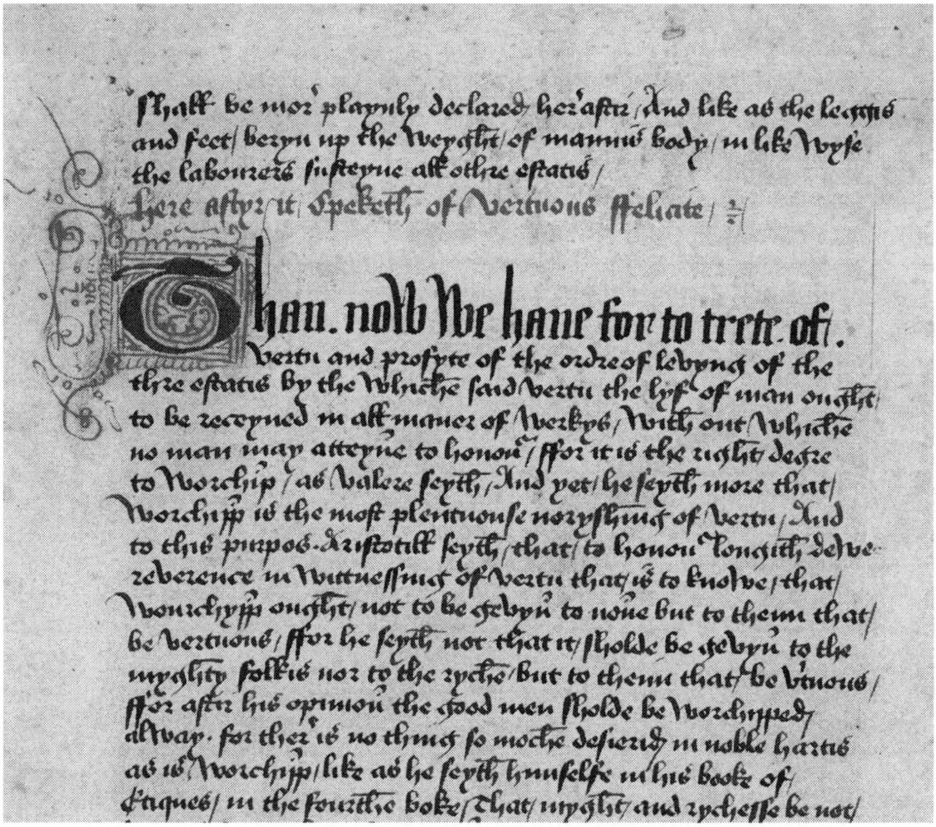
shall be mor playnly declared her after / And like as the leggis
and feet / beryn up the weyght / of mannis body / in like wyse
the labourers susteyne all other estatis /
Here aftyr it spekith of vertuous ffelicite /
Than. now we have for to trete. of.
vertu and profyte of the ordre of levyng of the
thre estatis By the whiche said vertu the lyf of man ought
to be receyued in all maner of werkys / With out whiche
no man may atteyne to honour / ffor it is the right degre
to worchip / as valere seyth / And yet / he seyth more that /
worchipp is the most plentuouse norysshing of vertu / And
to this purpos. Aristotill seyth / that / to honour longith, delyve
reverence in wittenessing of vertu that is to knowe / that /
worchyp ought / not to be gevyn to none but to them that /
be vertuous / ffor he seyth not that it / sholde be gevyn to the
myghty folkis nor to the ryche / But to them that / be vertuous /
ffor aftir his opinion the good men sholde be worchipped
alway. for ther is no thing so moche desired in noble hartis
as is worchipp / like as he seyth himselfe in his book of
Etiques / in the fourthe boke / That / myght and rychesse be not /

Figure 2.5 CUL, MS Kk.1.5 part 1, f. 2r, close-up: horns on the top of word-final letter s.

word-final *s*; but he does so only for the first two quires of the book and the start of the third, suggesting different degrees of effort at different times – see Figure 2.5.[45] Similarly, in the red chapter-titles he begins by using more separated minims and an *a* with two compartments, as if modelled on anglicana formata or textura, but stops later in the book.[46] The rest of the book shows the same blend of deliberate prettifying, but also straightened resources of time or energy, in the use of cheap paper, but with expensively wide margins, and the lack of ruling, but with a fine initial and

[45] CUL, MS Kk.1.5, part 1: horns on ff. 2r–9v (the middle of quire 1), ff. 11r–22v (quire 2), f. 23r and f. 25r (in quire 3). The outer bifolium of quire 1 (f.1r–v, f. 10r–v) also looks as though it was written at a different time from the rest of quires 1 and 2 because, besides the lack of horns on *s*, the rubrics are in a different style, the initials are three lines deep and not two lines, and there is a little blank space left on f. 1v and f. 10v.

[46] CUL, MS Kk.1.5, part 1: two-compartment *a* in grander rubrics on ff. 2r–9v, ff. 13r–28r, ff. 32r–34v. On this book, see Bornstein (ed.), *The Middle English Translation of Christine de Pisan's Livre du Corps*, 17–19.

border at the front. We can see this scribe balancing attempts to adorn a work on lofty political topics by the famous Christine for a wealthy patron, with the need to copy it more quickly and painlessly.

Sometimes the decorative elements of writing are more obviously 'added extras', as the scribe pursues penmanship for its own sake. Some scribes adorn individual graphs with decorations known as 'cadels' or 'strapwork'. Such strapwork was especially common in the grander hands modelled on secretary and bastard secretary in the late fifteenth century. One scribe, Ricardus Franciscus, has left a sheet on which he practises this elaborate strapwork to gorgeous effect.[47] Such fanciful graphs can decorate liturgical books, where – like red ink or handwriting modelled on textura – they offer a visual counterpart to the musical adornment of liturgy with anthems and carols.[48] They can decorate literary works too. For example, the scribe of the Towneley mystery cycle, probably from Wakefield (HEHL, MS HM 1), might seem to have been making a plain record of civic drama, in a hand modelled on a bureaucratic anglicana, but he adorned the first letter of most plays with spectacular strapwork.[49] One might draw analogies between the scribe's visual excess and the playwright's exceeding his didactic brief with virtuosic dialogue and stagecraft – both involve playful uses of language. Or one might compare the use of such initials at the start of civic and royal letters and charters, where they add to the sense of occasion – writing at the moment of bestowing power, or of authorizing plays. Pragmatic literacy and more ostensibly creative acts of writing blur in this example.[50]

Scribes also use much smaller flourishes or crossbars on the final few graphs or consonants of words: 'otiose' flourishes which have no clear or consistent purpose in transmitting the alphanumeric text. Such strokes occur not only in prestigious and calligraphic books but also in practical works in current handwriting. For example, one scribe of some alchemical and medical texts hurriedly copied (CUL, MS Kk.6.30) often uses a curl upwards at the end of words to abbreviate *i* in words ending '–cion', or sometimes to abbreviate *n*, but he also sometimes uses it in words in which nothing seems abbreviated.[51] We tend to call such flourishes 'otiose' strokes when they seem not to convey any linguistic information, yet they are not otiose if we consider the whole process of writing – the scribe's movement of his

[47] Drogin, *Medieval Calligraphy*, 70–2, plates 68, 142–3.

[48] E.g., HEHL, MS Ellesmere 34.B.7, f. 18v, f. 29v, ff. 43v–44r (a processional from Chester).

[49] HEHL, MS HM 1, described by Cawley and Stevens (eds.), *Towneley Cycle: A Facsimile*, ix. The initials to plays 1 and 2 are in a different style.

[50] As argued by Butcher, 'The Functions of Script', 160–1. The strapwork could also be bored doodling or could increase legibility by marking textual divisions.

[51] CUL, MS Kk.6.30, e.g. f. 15r, with a curl abbreviating *i* in fourteen words ending '–cion' (lines 25–8) and *n* in 'begynnyng' (line 10) but also abbreviating nothing consistently in 'begyn-yng-' (line 11), 'bryne- hym-' (i.e. 'burn him', line 19) and 'oon- thyng-' (line 23). The same scribe probably copied ff. 1r–45v, ff. 50r–58r and ff. 60r–61r, despite some variation in appearance.

hand, depending on what his sense of occasion or purpose might be. For example, in a copy of a herbal and other medical recipes (HEHL, MS HM 58), the scribe adds little 'horns' to the graphs *a* and *e*; but while these strokes might be otiose or needless for recording practical information, they might be important in dignifying the work of this scribe, who writes '*Christo* Gloria' (to the glory of Christ) at the top of each page.[52] The text only takes existence in such processes of writing, not prior to writing and its 'otiose' elements.[53]

However, conceiving of writing in terms of such visual, physical, ritual, economic and other processes need not entail – on the scribes' part or on ours, as critics – neglecting the text itself. After all, whatever their other concerns, scribes or their paymasters wanted to reproduce and preserve texts, or they would not have bothered to copy them. Otherwise, a painting, say, would have sufficed as a luxury commodity or pious offering as well as a liturgical book did, or remembered household dishes could have served in place of written recipes from the king's cook. On the one hand, one could argue that both the visually otiose and the rougher cursive writing reflect disregard for the text: interest in appearance over content, as with Werken and his colleague's inaccuracies in English religious poems (HEHL, MS HM 142, described above), or in hasty and rough *aide-mémoires*. But, on the other hand, one could argue that both decoration and its want reflect great care for the text: the textura of liturgical books reflects the time those holy books deserved; the hurried handwriting of medical recipes reflects the urgency with which people preserved such information.

Yet even if the scribes did care for their texts, did they care for the *details* of them? Research into scribal copying has often argued that they did not. This may be because research has tended to serve textual editing, which has often found scribes not reproducing manuscripts as well as scholarly editors do. Or it has tended to seek evidence for dialectal variation; or, more recently, tended to relish the scribes' changes to texts within theories of 'variance' or 'mouvance': theories that scribes enjoyed recasting what they copied and felt no compunction about doing so.[54] But such theories of 'variance' or 'mouvance' refer to the results of quite varied aesthetic, social and economic attitudes. For example, some people copy practical writings by including further material – but in some cases, such as the medical collection *Tabula medicinae*, such inclusions were envisaged by the original deviser. The distinction between

---

[52] HEHL, MS HM 58: '*Christo* Gloria' is trimmed off many leaves, but visible on ff. 24r–36r.

[53] Such otiose marks might also work like punctuation, whether to divide up the text linguistically or to arrange it on the page, like the otiose flourishes at the end of lines which 'justify' pages of prose and prevent any confusing interruptions in the flow of text (as in BL, MS Royal 18.B.xxii of Worcester, *The Boke of Noblesse*); this can even happen in verse (as in JRL, MS Eng. 50 of *The Prick of Conscience*). This chapter has no room for a discussion of punctuation and lineation, but they are vital elements of writing; Parkes, *Pause and Effect*, offers the best introduction.

[54] Under the influence of Zumthor, *Toward a Medieval Poetics*, 45–9; Cerquiglini, *In Praise of the Variant*, 21, 33–4.

composer, copyist and readers was never intended to hold in such texts, and the 'mouvance' reflects the circulation of knowledge in fifteenth-century medicine as much as it reflects scribal practice.[55] The scribes of poetry, too, sometimes rewrite what they copy, for example improving poems for oral performance or fabricating a style which evokes it.[56] Yet in a culture in which such changes *were* acceptable – and not only in practical or semi-oral genres – the decision *not* to change the text was important too. And indeed some groups of makers and users of books valued the accurate transmission of the text. For example, large collections of Wycliffite sermons circulated in copies which were much more accurate than they might have been, as though their scribes 'felt themselves obliged to copy without change', as has been noted by their editor, while the sermons themselves stress that any 'uaryyng of Goddis word' would have significance.[57] Copies of the Wycliffite translations of the bible are also remarkably accurate.[58] In such contexts, scribal practice in reproducing exemplars can only be understood in the context of wider intellectual histories: respect for the Word, saving souls or secret and therefore tightly controlled dissemination. It is thus difficult to generalize about 'mouvance' or 'variance' without obscuring the specificity of different influences – whether Wycliffite ones or, in other cases, potentially humanist, literary, legal and idiosyncratic influences – on writing accurately or not.

Besides directly affecting attitudes towards texts, these wider cultural attitudes indirectly affected the time spent on copying and the consequent techniques and psychology of transcription. There is room for considerably more research into these processes – research against which to test theories of scribal 'variance'. Some of the best observations have emerged so far from books for which the immediate exemplar survives, for the exemplar shows what the scribe does or does not change.[59] Further, perhaps generalizable, observations can come from comparing instances of similar date and type. For example, it is interesting to compare the following two books, both in cursive writing, in English prose and of the very late fifteenth century, for which the exemplars survive:

(i) Cambridge, Peterhouse, MS 190, an incomplete copy of *Brut* donated in 1481 to the library of Peterhouse, a college in Cambridge, after which date somebody added to it the last twenty-three lines of *Brut* and eleven folios of continuations to *Brut*, copied directly from what is now BL, MS Harley 3730;[60]

---

[55] Murray Jones, '*Tabula medicine*', 60.

[56] E.g., Horobin and Wiggins, 'Reconsidering Lincoln's Inn MS 150', 48–50; Wakelin, 'The Carol in Writing', 31.

[57] Hudson (ed.), *English Wycliffite Sermons*, 1.188, 192, and sermon E43/5–10; see also 1.139, 145, 147 on corrections.

[58] Hudson, *The Premature Reformation*, 246.

[59] Beadle, 'Geoffrey Spirleng', is the best study and notes previous studies (esp. 118–19 nn.6–7).

[60] I sampled 1,243 words from Cambridge, Peterhouse, MS 190, ff. 196v–97v, ff. 202v–203r and 208r–208v (hand B copying the last 23 lines of *Brut* on ff. 196v–97r and continuations on ff. 197r–208v), and

(ii) CUL, MS Dd.3.45, a transcription of the romance *Jason*, copied directly from Caxton's printed edition of 1477.[61]

There is no room here for a full investigation of the economic and cultural pressures which informed these two acts of writing. But in brief, the scribe of the *Brut* continuations (Peterhouse, MS 190) writes on paper in a book already in a college's library, presumably for scholarly interest among a fairly closed readership. The copy of *Jason* (CUL, MS Dd.3.45) begins with a gilded initial, as if it was paid for as a luxury commodity, as a manuscript copy from print might be;[62] but it mixes paper and parchment a lot, as if it was not being well paid for. Moreover, in these different but never lavish circumstances, both scribes used a cursive handwriting – very current in parts of CUL, MS Dd.3.45 – with graphs modelled on a mixture of anglicana and secretary, as if seeking speed and ease rather than any one 'script'. What was the influence of this cursive writing on textual reproduction?

It has long been understood that the speed of cursive handwriting would not allow the scribe to look back at the exemplar too often. The scribe could not have studied an exemplar letter by letter but must have read several words, held them in his head as sounds, and then copied what he remembered by a sort of internal dictation.[63] A few oddities in Peterhouse, MS 190, confirm this internal dictation, for they are misremembered sounds ('ʒonge chyldren' in MS Harley 3730 as 'yonke chyldren' in Peterhouse, MS 190, or 'apontment' as 'a poyngment').[64] This internal dictation by the scribes who write at speed has been identified as one of the things that prompts scribes to 'translate' an exemplar in one variety of Middle English into their own variety as they copy it (as discussed by Simon Horobin in the next chapter here). Because the scribe is writing at speed, and remembering the sound of the exemplar rather than retracing it letter by letter, he would remember the text in the sound of his own dialect, not that of the exemplar's copyist; it has been suggested that writing in cursive hands therefore almost forced dialectal 'translation'.[65] And some changes do seem to reflect differing dialects between the scribe or compositor of the exemplar and the scribe of the copy: so word-initial ʒ– and w– in MS Harley 3730 are copied as g– and wh– or qw– (for present-day English wh–) in Peterhouse, MS 190; Caxton's *hit* and *moche* are copied as *it* and *meche* in CUL, MS Dd.3.45.

their exemplar in BL, MS Harley 3730, ff. 105r–105v, 112v and 119v. On Cambridge, Peterhouse, MS 190, see Matheson (ed.), *Death and Dissent*, 77–80.

[61] I sampled 1,377 words from CUL, MS Dd.3.45, f. 1r, f. 54r, f. 106v, and their exemplar in Caxton, trans., *Jason*, *STC* 15383, unsigned leaves 4r–v, 73r–74v, 147r–148r.

[62] Although other such transcriptions could reflect a lack of money to buy printed books.

[63] Dain, *Les Manuscrits*, 41–6. Kato, 'Corrected Mistakes in Cambridge University Library MS Gg.4.27', 67–85, surveys other analyses of copying.

[64] He also improved two of his exemplar's errors ('mercy a grace' and 'the had' into 'mercy and grace' and 'thei had'), perhaps because he misheard his internal dictation in a correct form.

[65] Benskin and Laing, 'Translations and *Mischsprachen*', 90, 94; Kato, 'Corrected Mistakes in Cambridge University Library MS Gg.4.27', 85.

Such changes are fascinating to find, especially in the two copies of *Brut* continuations which were nevertheless read within one college.

Yet not all of the changes in these copies reflect spoken dialects; some reflect the visual elements of copying. So in the sample from Peterhouse, MS 190, there are two instances of eye-skip where the scribe looked back at MS Harley 3730 for the next stretch of text, remembering which word he had got to, but looked back at the wrong place, misled by the recurrence of a word.[66] That the scribes could look back very infrequently or carelessly emerges from other books with eye-skips so long that they required extra slips of parchment to be corrected later.[67] Visual misreading and the brisk pace of writing caused these errors. Moreover, other changes between exemplars and copies can only reflect changes in habits for writing rather than phonological variation in speech: for example, the scribe of Peterhouse, MS 190 turned word-initial *þ*– in his exemplar into *th*–,whereas the scribe of CUL, MS Dd.3.45 turned *th*– into *þ*–;[68] both scribes added a word-final *–e* to words and both turn the vowel *i* in their exemplars into *y*. Scribes also had different graphic and intellectual conventions about when to use abbreviation, capitalization, punctuation or word-division in otherwise identically spelled words. For example, the scribe of CUL, MS Dd.3.45, differed from Caxton's compositor in the position of punctuation, in converting upper-case letters into lower-cases ones, in using an abbreviation for *and* and in adding word-divisions (as in 'in to'). What is striking is that both copyists sampled made their changes fairly consistently, albeit with a few exceptions. The blend of consistency and a very few exceptions suggests that these changes reflect not wilful modification of the exemplar but undeliberate, almost unconscious, training, habits or conventions in quick writing. This raises questions about the significance of such minor 'variance'.

Moreover, these direct exemplars and copies reveal that one must not assume that cursive copying necessarily brings speed and error: one scribe sampled, in CUL, MS Dd.3.45, wrote cursively and sometimes even more currently, but he never in the sampled sections made eye-skips like the other. This might be because he was copying for other people's money, rather than for private study with colleagues, or because he treated a printed exemplar with more care.[69] It is important to consider the scribe's

[66] In both cases, he skipped nine words, but that does not reveal how much text he could hold in his head at one time; it merely reveals how often the text repeats a word. One other slip by sight is mistaking 'bermondesey' as 'vermondesey' in Peterhouse, MS 190.

[67] E.g., JRL, MS Eng. 3, f. 47r–v (ninety-one words skipped from Wycliffite Gospel); JRL, MS Eng. 7 (*The Forme of Cury*, discussed in n.43 above), f. 26r, with sixty-five words between the recurrences of 'aneys', of which the first eleven are added over an erasure on f. 25r–v.

[68] See Benskin, 'The Letters <þ> and <y>', 14, on variation between *þ* and *y*.

[69] The sample from CUL, MS Dd.3.45 differs from Caxton, trans., *Jason*, *STC* 15383, only in turning 'to' into 'vnto' and misunderstanding the first printed initial *A* as *N*. Elsewhere in the MS, though, the scribe omits Lefèvre's and Caxton's prologues.

very specific context when explaining his accuracy or 'variance'. Similarly, the scribe of Peterhouse, MS 190, even though he made eye-skips twice, scrutinized his exemplar by sight with care sometimes: he never changed the spelling of what seem to have been rare words, but rendered them letter by letter ('kateremas', for *quatrime*, a duty or tax; 'terment', an aphetic form of *interment*),[70] and when he did not understand 'vere' in the phrase 'of vere necessite' (*very*, meaning *true*) he conscientiously left a gap for filling later. Scribes commonly left such gaps for words which they cannot understand.[71] There is no simple or fixed correlation between quick writing and carelessness. This intermittency of precision reveals one of the most important elements of scribes' handling of their exemplars: the ways in which their attention sharpened or faded over time.

Furthermore, the intermittent precision highlights the scribe's effort, even in cursive copying, to prevent variance between exemplar and copy. Across the two sampled copies, there are few large alterations: even in Peterhouse, MS 190, including the two instances of eye-skip, the scribe only added, omitted or replaced about 2.5 per cent of words. Even if one considers every tiny difference in spelling, morphology, punctuation or the use of abbreviations, the number of changes is lower than praise of 'variance' might suggest: 31 per cent of words in Peterhouse, MS 190, and 42 per cent in CUL, MS Dd.3.45 (381 of 1,243 words; 582 of 1,377 words). Therefore, even at the most thorough comparison of differences, well over half of the copying by these two scribes is literatim, that is, identical to the exemplar letter by letter, abbreviation by abbreviation, dot by dot.[72] It is not speed but care, not 'variance' but keenness on sameness, which must explain how these scribes produce careful copies, despite the challenges of dialectal variation, time-pressures, handwriting and physical copying-processes. It is interesting that other instances yield very similar numbers: Richard Beadle's study of a copy of *The Canterbury Tales* and its exemplar found that 70 per cent was copied literatim,[73] and so was 56 per cent of an extract from Trevisa's prose *De Proprietatibus rerum*.[74] And in all these cases, under 3 per cent of the copy varied from the exemplar in the substance of the words used. This widespread feat of auditory and visual memory in keeping texts so much the same must be recognized.

Further evidence of the consistency of scribes comes from certain moments of error, paradoxically: when scribes copy the same passage twice ('double-copying').

---

[70] The exception is the omission of one *a* in the country 'vngaray', but in BL, MS Harley 3730 *a* is interlineated and tiny, easy to miss.

[71] E.g., Wakelin, 'Scholarly Scribes', 32; and JRL, MS Eng. 2, described below.

[72] For simplicity of arithmetic, I have counted punctuation marks as parts of the preceding word.

[73] Beadle, 'Geoffrey Spirleng', 145.

[74] I collated Seymour's transcription ('A Literatim Trevisa Abstract', 186–8), of a passage from BodL, MS Ashmole 1481, with its exemplar in BL, MS Add. 27944, ff. 96v–97r. I did not retranscribe BodL, MS Ashmole 1481 for myself.

It is striking how consistent the work is in passages copied twice. From a survey of such passages in nine manuscripts, some of them previously identified, some not, the table printed here shows the percentages that emerge in (a) the differences in the actual inclusion, omission or order of words, and (b) the differences in their spelling, punctuation, word-division or abbreviation.

	Passage	Words	(a)	(b)
(i)[75]	CUL, MS Gg.4.27, ff. 21r–v, f. 208r, ff. 348v–49r	347	5%	23%
(ii)[76]	CUL, MS Ii.1.36, f. 150v, f. 150*v	39	5%	18%
(iii)[77]	BL, MS Add. 21410, ff. 55v–56r	237	1%	5%
(iv)[78]	BL, MS Add. 27944, ff. 153v–154r	465	5%	14%
(v)[79]	London, Inner Temple, MS Petyt 511.17, f. 110v, flyleaf	260	10%	7%
(vi)[80]	PML, MS M. 124, f. 45r-v	698	1%	18%
(vii)[81]	PML, MS M. 249, f. 189v, f. 276r	283	0%	9%
(viii)[82]	BodL, MS Rawl. poet. 138, f. 8r–v, f. 100r, f.103r	370	2%	14%
(ix)[83]	Oxford, Trinity College, MS 49	155	8%	28%
(x)[84]	HEHL, MS HM 135, f. 48v, f. 51r	110	0%	5%

Overall, in a sample of 2,964 words, roughly half verse, half prose, in Middle English, the scribes were self-consistent letter by letter, abbreviation by abbreviation, virgule by virgule, in 82 per cent of the words they copied. In the 18 per cent of words which change, most changes concerned only the spelling, punctuation or abbreviation of the text. Only 4 per cent of words changed in the substance of lexis, grammar or being included and omitted; and most of these changes were to little details of grammar (such as 'fraunchise' / 'fraunchised',

[75] Parkes and Beadle (eds.), *Poetical Works, Geoffrey Chaucer: A Facsimile*, III.48–54, transcribe and discuss (i). All percentages are rounded to the nearest whole number. This list excludes a documentary text in Kristensson, 'Another Piece of Evidence', because it is much earlier in date (1327); it had only eight differences of spelling or abbreviation in 158 words (5 per cent).

[76] Hanna (ed.), *Speculum Vitae*, lines 10709–13.

[77] Lydgate, *Fall of Princes*, III.1282–316.

[78] Seymour, 'A Literatim Trevisa Abstract', 189, mentions but does not transcribe (iv), from Trevisa's English prose *De Proprietatibus rerum*.

[79] Smallwood, 'Another Example of the Double-Copying', transcribes from Robert Mannyng's *Chronicle*.

[80] Lydgate, *Fall of Princes*, II.1618–715.

[81] Chaucer, *The Canterbury Tales*, VI. 424–61.

[82] *The Prick of Conscience*, I, 476–88, and VII, 7678–735. Dr Richard Beadle kindly directed me to this example.

[83] Chaucer, *Canterbury Tales*, IV, 1672–90.

[84] Hoccleve, *The Regiment of Princes*, lines 2941–53.

'maner of corage' / 'maner corage').[85] And once again the more unusual words or names were rendered identically each time, even down to the seemingly interchangeable *i* and *y* or the use of abbreviation: for example, the same decisions when and when not to abbreviate *er* in 'germanye' or 'germanye' recurred in both copies of a passage in Trevisa's prose version of *De Proprietatibus rerum*. Rather than 'mouvance' and 'variance', then, the surviving exemplars and double-copying suggest sameness and consistency, at least in copying Middle English literature. (It remains to be seen whether there were similar habits in copying Latin or non-literary texts.) This sameness and consistency deserve as much study as do variation and change.

However, all of this consistency is observable only because these scribes copied a passage twice by mistake. They usually neatly deleted the error, but they did nevertheless err. Malcolm Parkes and Richard Beadle, identifying three passages of double-copying, observe both how conscientious their scribe was but also that he was prone to lapses in concentration – to changes over time.[86] The oscillating alertness of scribes often emerges from the corrections which they made to their copying: the moment of correction was a moment of sharpened attention, often after a moment of inattention. For example, one scribe of Chaucer's *Troilus and Criseyde* (Durham, University Library, MS Cosin V.ii.13) misheard his internal dictation – for example, turning 'her' into 'herte' by blurring the sounds of the line 'With subtile arte her tales to endite'; or spelling 'swoune' like the more common word 'sone' – presumably because he was writing quickly.[87] But just as he erred in haste, so he repented and corrected in haste too, *currente calamo* ('with the pen still moving'). The haste is evident in his decision to correct merely by deleting the errors with a rough horizontal line, rather than by scraping them off, which would be neat but laborious. Yet, although hasty, the correction is not stupid: he corrected at least 110 errors in 101 folios of *Troilus*, and over 85 per cent of the corrections restore what is now the received critical text of the poem (Windeatt's). He even attended to mere spellings, if they might cause confusion ('sone'/'swoune'). Similarly, a scribe writing with attention to the look of his hand might switch his attention to the verbal detail of the text sometimes. For example, one scribe of *The Fall of Princes* (JRL, MS Eng. 2) cultivated a prissy handwriting, modelled on bastard secretary, delicately written so that the descenders do not cross the stylish purple ruling; yet even he attended not only to the look of the writing but to its content when he encountered gaps or things which he

---

[85] Both from (iii), BL, MS Add. 21410, ff. 55v–56r. Smallwood, 'Another Example of the Double-Copying', does note more dramatic inconsistencies in (v), but the text and MS are earlier (1360s–90s) than the other examples. There may have been changes over the period surveyed by this book which will require further research to identify.

[86] Parkes and Beadle (eds.), *Poetical Works, Geoffrey Chaucer: A Facsimile*, III.54.

[87] Durham, University Library, MS Cosin V.ii.13, for example f. 19r, line 34 (*Troilus*, II, 257), f. 22v, line 9 (*Troilus*, II, 574). A further twenty-four corrections may be by the scribe or by somebody else.

could not comprehend in his exemplar: unfamiliar diction ('dishomme', 'suppow-aile'); classical names ('flora', 'Thebes', 'Censoryn'); or references to cows painted on the side of ships – 'In which ship þer was a // cowe // depeynt' – which he found baffling, forgivably. (The virgules // marked the gap which needed filling – see Figure 2.6.) Then, like the copyist who encountered 'vere' (above), he left gaps and added the missing word later, awkwardly spaced and in a darker ink, sacrificing tidiness to the need to make sense – at least for a moment.[88] Such corrections reveal a process of writing informed by several different attitudes to time – the value of taking time over letter-forms; the need to hurry on, leaving a hard word undecoded; the sense that it is worth meticulously checking that word later – and changes in those attitudes to time over time. Such corrections, then, reveal the inconsistency which is the only consistent feature of 'wrytyng' across time: the pen becoming 'worn', the hand and the 'corage' being sometimes stronger, sometimes not 'as hit hath ben'.

Yet Caxton was being a little disingenuous when he separated manuscripts from early printed books so sharply, for there are inconsistencies in the processes of repro-ducing text in print too. Some of these inconsistencies emerge from a comparison of an early printed book with its manuscript source. For example, the aforementioned manuscript of Lydgate's *The Fall of Princes* (JRL, MS Eng. 2) was later the copy-text for the edition of the poem printed by Richard Pynson in 1494. In a sample of the copy-text and printed version similar in size to the samples of scribal copies above, there are similar levels of closeness in reproduction: the printed book reproduces its copy-text literatim in 57 per cent of 1,326 words; only 2 per cent of words change in substance and 41 per cent in spelling, punctuation and abbreviation.[89] There are changes, though, and some might reflect changes in the English language over time, when Pynson or his compositors updated what had evidently become con-fusing since the 1430s when Lydgate wrote. The printed version of Lydgate's *Fall of Princes* expands the elisions 'tavenge' and 'atte' into 'to auenge' and 'at the', removes the plural verb inflexion –*n* and changes 'he*m*' to 'theym'.[90] However, like scribes, the compositor made many smaller changes to spelling with apparently inexplic-able randomness. For example, he often added –*e* to the end of words and updated

---

[88] JRL, MS Eng. 2, f. 3v, col. a, line 35 (*Fall*, 1.499), f. 3v/b/27 (*Fall*, 1.538), f. 9v/b/38 (*Fall*, 1.1704), f. 19v/a/38 (*Fall*, 1.3615), f. 44r/b/7 (*Fall*, II.1441), f. 66r/a/16 (*Fall*, III.1230), f. 85v/a/40 (*Fall*, IV.39). All restore what is now the edited text (Bergen's). The scribe left gaps which he could not fill on f. 9v/a/17 (*Fall*, 1.1636), f. 70r/a/17 (*Fall*, III.2239).

[89] I sampled 1,326 words from JRL, MS Eng. 2, f. 29r–v, and their reproduction in John Lydgate, *Fall of Princes* (London: Richard Pynson, 1494; *STC* 3175), sigs. e1r–e2v, using a microfilm on *EEBO*. These were Lydgate, *Fall*, 1.5474–565, 1.5846–73; the text is given in the wrong order in the manuscript here, and the printed text reproduces the misordering. Morgan, 'A Specimen of Early Printer's Copy', identi-fies this copy-text.

[90] These changes recur throughout the printed edition: e.g., sig. a2r turns 'atte commau*n*deme*n*t' and 'hem' into 'at the commau*n*deme*n*t' and 'them' (JRL, MS Eng. 2, f. 1r, col. a, lines 6 and 24). However, there are relatively few other updatings of the language; again careful reproduction seems to be the aim.

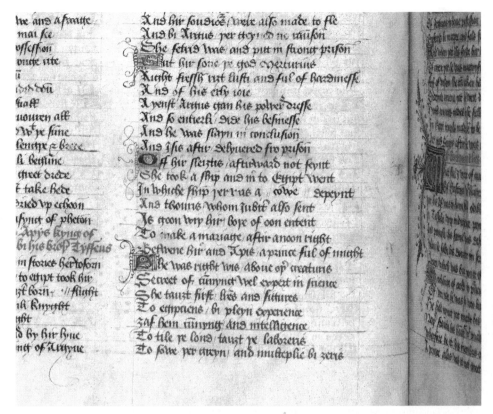

Figure 2.6 JRL, MS Eng. 2, f. 9v, close-up: the word 'cowe' written in a gap left by the scribe.

i to *y*, but he made the opposite changes too – removing final *–e* and changing *y* to *i* – about a quarter as frequently. These are the small inconsistencies which occur moment to moment during typesetting as during scribal copying.

Besides these small changes, the changes to works can be even more dramatic under the pressures of setting the text out of sequence by formes, as often occurred. For example, Caxton's compositor for Malory's *Morte Darthur* inserted spaces, paraphs and words, or sometimes cut words, in order to ensure that he had thirty-one lines of text for every printed page. De Worde's compositor for Trevisa's English *De Proprietatibus rerum* altered his text in order to justify the prose.[91] Caxton or his colleagues also made more dramatic editorial interventions: for example, by dividing Malory's text into 'books' and chapters.[92] The oscillating attention of the

[91] Kato, *Caxton's Morte Darthur*, 34, 37–9, 41–2; Mitchner, 'Wynkyn de Worde's Use of the Plimpton Manuscript', 11–18. See also Morgan, 'Pynson's Manuscript', 226–7; and in general Hellinga, 'Printing', 84–9.

[92] Kato, *Caxton's Morte Darthur*, 49–50.

compositor over time, or changes between different compositors, and the other elements of temporal disorder in the printing process could all lead to inconsistencies, just as could the time taken to write by hand.[93]

But there is one shift in the effect of time on printing as opposed to writing. No matter how quickly or slowly the compositor works, a typeface remains largely the same in shape or style throughout its period of use in any one book.[94] It was slower to model one's hand on bastard secretary than on, say, a humanistic cursive, but Caxton's Burgundian typeface, which resembles bastard secretary, was not quicker or slower to print with than the typefaces modelled on humanistic hands introduced into England in the early 1500s. What determined the choice of typeface was less the time taken to set it than the sense that different typefaces suited different subjects or readerships.[95] Time-pressure was felt instead in casting the type in the first place; and this pressure led to standardizing of founts, which became more uniform than different hands, and led to a slow decline in the use of abbreviations. Scribes often used marks of abbreviation, for they saved space, effort and time; but for printers each mark of abbreviation needed to be engraved and cast. Therefore they soon became very rare in print.[96] For example, in the aforementioned printed edition of Lydgate's *Fall of Princes*, besides eschewing the graphs þ and ȝ, the printer only uses one mark of abbreviation, and only uses it twice in the 1,326 sampled words, whereas the scribe uses many marks of abbreviation, as well as varying forms of letters page by page.[97] Time does not as often and as obviously shape the lettering of the words in print.

Of course there were inconsistencies over the time taken to set different pages, formes or quires, due to interruptions or the concurrent printing of other books. And of course stop-press corrections introduced more inconsistencies; and printed sheets needed to dry and be stored until the whole book was complete. But after all that, multiple copies of one whole book, or of the last sheet off the press, were 'fynyshid in oon day'. Compared to this simultaneity and apparent speed in printing, which dazzled Caxton, there really were differences in the ways in which time – even more particularly, more chaotically, more interruptedly, more slowly – shaped every single moment of writing.

---

[93] On which, see Tanselle, *Bibliographical Analysis*, 31–6.

[94] Of course, over the years founts got damaged, but that is not usually perceptible within one book. On damaged type, see Tanselle, *Bibliographical Analysis*, 36.

[95] Carter, *A View of Early Typography*, 29–30. Carter also suggests that some typefaces were 'troublesome to handle' (42) but he does not specify which or why.

[96] Hellinga, 'Printing', 70–1.

[97] Lydgate, *Fall of Princes*, sig. e2r, col. b, line 17 'dauɳgere' and line 39 'ruɳne' (both with a macron above *u*), here alone reproducing abbreviations in JRL, MS Eng. 2, f. 29v, col. b., line 10 'dauɳgere', line 32 'ruɳnen'.

3

Mapping the words

SIMON HOROBIN

During the period covered by this book, the English language witnessed some of the farthest-reaching changes in its entire history, including the loss of grammatical gender, the shift from a synthetic to an analytical structure and the introduction of huge numbers of loanwords into its lexicon. Perhaps the most significant change to the language during this period was the emergence of a standard variety of English, a variety which has since become so enshrined in our society that we tend to think of it as *the* English language. By contrast, during the Middle English period there was no single standard variety of English, and all regional dialects were considered to have equal status. A writer of Middle English simply employed the dialect native to the area in which he was trained to write, so that a Londoner such as Chaucer used the London dialect, while the *Gawain*-poet used his own North-West Midlands variety. This lack of a standard variety applied to writing as well as to speech, so that not only did a dialect speaker have a different accent from users of other dialects, he also had a different spelling system.

The reason for this lack of a standard spelling system is bound up with the status of the vernacular during the Middle English period and the dominance of Latin and French. Where written communication had a national function and was intended to be circulated throughout the country, it was written in either Latin or French, while English was reserved for communication at a local, parochial level. As a result there was no need for a standard variety of English, while a locally devised spelling system, reflecting regional pronunciation more closely, became desirable for communication. The result of this situation is that Middle English texts vary considerably in their spelling, such that the Middle English period is often termed the 'period of dialect variation *par excellence*'.[1] Even a very common word like 'such' survives in hundreds of different Middle English spelling forms. Some of these spellings are comparatively easy to recognize (for

---

[1] Strang, *A History of English*.

example *sech, soche, such, sych, swich, swech*), while others are rather more peculiar (*schch, sick, schut, squilk, zueche*). While such baroque variation may be unwelcome to the student of Middle English literature, for whom every text can appear to be in a different language, it presents a rich resource for the student of Middle English dialectology. This chapter considers the way that Middle English dialectologists have exploited such rich pickings and the resources they have produced. However, the uses of such resources have applications beyond the field of Middle English dialectology and affect all fields of manuscript study, enabling localization of texts, discussion of copying habits, tracing of exemplars and even the identification of scribes. This chapter will explore how this wealth of dialect evidence and the resources assembled by Middle English dialectologists can be harnessed in the study of Middle English manuscripts.

The principles that underlie the practice of historical dialectology derive from the techniques developed for the study of modern dialects. These can be traced back to nineteenth-century dialect surveys, such as the linguistic survey of France which began in 1896. Applying a method devised to map modern spoken dialects to historical texts raises a number of crucial problems. The first and most obvious point to make is that in historical dialectology we are dealing purely with written forms of the language; any inferences about the nature of the spoken language must be reconstructed from the written language. This, however, is not quite as straightforward as it sounds. Some spelling variants are of purely graphemic significance; that is, they are concerned only with spelling, such as the variation between *shall* and *schall*, where we can be pretty sure that the spelling difference does not reflect a distinction in pronunciation. Features like this can vary diatopically; that is, they can show a regional distribution. A parallel situation is found in Present Day English in the distinction between *colour* and *color*, where one spelling is British English and the other American English, even though there is no corresponding pronunciation distinction. Other written features can be assumed to have some relationship with spoken distinctions, such as differences in the spellings *stan* and *ston*, where one has an unrounded and the other a rounded vowel. These features can also be mapped geographically, but it is important to remember that we are primarily mapping the spelling of the words, not their pronunciation (even though the two clearly have some kind of relationship). A map of the different forms of *stan* and *ston* in a group of Middle English texts would simply reveal the areas in which scribes chose to use the *stan* spelling, and areas where scribes chose the *ston* form. This point becomes more evident when dealing with other forms of which the phonetic realization is much less clear. For instance, what about forms such as *xal* and *sal* for 'shall'? These appear to reflect differing pronunciations, but what exactly? The important point here is that we are studying primarily the written language, but, in some cases, this will reflect some distinction in pronunciation.

In addition to problems determining which features to consider, a further difficulty concerns the selection of texts for analysis. In carrying out a dialect survey, modern dialectologists select their informants carefully, taking into account place of birth, upbringing, education, age, gender, social class and so on. Most Middle English texts were copied by anonymous scribes and generally do not carry any indication of where and when they were written or who they were written by. Where there is information concerning provenance, it is often to do with early ownership rather than place of copying. While these two factors may be identical, they are not necessarily so, and we cannot simply assume that a text owned by the Duke of Suffolk, for example, was copied in Suffolk. Another related problem is that the scribes who copied these manuscripts were frequently very mobile, and the place of copying does not necessarily indicate the origin of the scribe who copied the manuscript, and thus his dialect. The later Middle English period experienced considerable social and geographical mobility, and scribal copyists were particularly likely to be peripatetic. The centralization of government and the emergence of professional book production centred in London meant that a large number of such scribes migrated to London from the provinces during this period. So a manuscript copied in London by a scribe trained in the West Midlands could in theory represent the dialect of the West Midlands origins of the scribe, rather than the London dialect of the place of its production. In addition to a lack of knowledge concerning the origins of the scribes and their places of training, we also lack much important information concerning the background, education, class, age and even gender of our informants.

So how do we select which texts to analyse? One solution would be to analyse them all. For the early Middle English period the evidence is comparatively sparse, and the recently completed *Linguistic Atlas of Early Middle English*, covering the period 1150–1325, is based upon an analysis of the complete corpus of early Middle English texts.[2] For the later Middle English period there is a much greater number of extant texts, and it is not possible to analyse absolutely everything, so we need to be selective. As noted above, the majority of texts from this period were written by anonymous scribes, but there is an important exception to this rule. There do survive a small number of authorial holographs: texts copied by the authors themselves. Such texts might well seem ideal candidates for dialect study, in that we know in advance something about the person who copied the texts under analysis. However, the major problem with this group of texts is that they are few in number. For the Middle English period as a whole only a handful survive. Fifteenth-century holographs include manuscript collections of his own verse by the London poet Thomas Hoccleve and copies of works by the hagiographer and Augustinian friar of Bishop's

[2] Laing and Lass, *A Linguistic Atlas*.

Lynn, Norfolk, John Capgrave.[3] While these few instances do provide evidence of different dialects, there are still large gaps in coverage: there are no Northern or Western holograph texts, for instance. Despite the problems raised by this class of evidence, the earliest Middle English dialect surveys, such as that by Moore, Meech and Whitehall, relied heavily upon scanty evidence of this kind.[4]

Another type of localized evidence used by historical dialectologists is local records. These are generally firmly localized by an explicit reference within the document, and often dated, thereby providing important information for the dialectologist. But there are problems with this kind of evidence. Even when such records are copied in the vernacular, they are still of only limited use because they tend to be short and formulaic, so that many of the items listed on a questionnaire are unlikely to be found in texts of this kind.

A revolutionary solution to the problems posed by the limitations of the surviving evidence was developed by the Middle English Dialect Project, which culminated in the publication in 1986 of the *Linguistic Atlas of Late Mediaeval English*, or *LALME*.[5] This project drew upon texts which were securely localized by internal reference, known as 'anchor texts', to localize other texts where such information was lacking. For instance, where a short formulaic document survives that is localized internally to Hereford, the *LALME* editors compared the language of this text with other longer texts to determine which of these were likely to have also been copied in Hereford. This process, known as the 'fit-technique', enabled the editors of *LALME* to supplement the forms elicited from short local documents with a much greater range of forms found in other longer texts, thereby dramatically increasing the number and range of forms which could be attributed to a particular dialect area.[6]

There is, however, a further problem that must be taken into account when applying this method to Middle English texts whose provenance is unknown. This problem concerns the way that these texts were copied. Because there was no standard spelling system in Middle English, scribes frequently 'translated' the dialect of the text they were copying into their own system. Often such translations were only partial, with the result that copied texts frequently contain a mixture of both authorial and scribal spelling forms. Traditionally, such texts have been ignored by dialectologists as representing 'corrupt' and mixed dialects, in favour of holograph manuscripts which were considered as representing 'pure' dialect usage. However, the editors of *LALME* showed that this view was overly dismissive and led to the

[3] Burrow and Doyle, *Thomas Hoccleve*; Lucas, *From Author*; Beadle 'English Autograph Writings'; discussed by Mooney in Chapter 9, pp. 197–9.

[4] Moore, Meech and Whitehall, *Middle English Dialect Characteristics*.

[5] McIntosh, Samuels and Benskin, *LALME*.

[6] For more detailed discussion of the fit-technique, see Benskin, 'The Fit-Technique'.

neglect of a considerable corpus of texts that represented consistent Middle English dialects. Rather than seeing Middle English scribal practice as random, the editors of *LALME* hypothesized that a Middle English scribe could copy a text in one of three ways:[7]

> Type 1. He could copy his exemplar exactly: carrying out a literatim, that is, letter-by-letter, transcription of the original.
>
> Type 2. He could translate the language of his exemplar into his own dialect.
>
> Type 3. He could do something in between Types 1 and 3, thereby producing a mixture of his own forms and those of his exemplar.

It is apparent that each of these different copying practices will produce different linguistic outputs. Type 1 will simply reproduce the language of the scribal exemplar, while Type 2 will result in the replacement of the language of the exemplar with a consistent scribal language. But both outputs represent consistent Middle English dialects that can be subjected to dialectological analysis. In the case of Type 1, it is the dialect of the exemplar that is being analysed, while in Type 2 it is that of the scribe. Broadly speaking, the first type of copyist is more common in the early Middle English period, while the second type is more common in the late Middle English period. The reason for this may be to do with the copying of Latin. In the early Middle English period, scribes were more used to copying Latin, a fixed language which does not permit variation in spelling. Therefore a scribe copying a Latin document would have no choice but to reproduce, letter by letter, the exact words and letters of his exemplar. A good example of a literatim scribe is found in BL, MS Cotton Caligula A.ix, an early Middle English copy of *The Owl and the Nightingale*. This text was copied by a single scribe but contains two completely distinct spelling systems, with abrupt switches from one system to the other; for example, in some sections the scribe spells Old English *eo* words with <eo>, e.g., *beoþ*, and in other places with <o>, e.g., *boþ*. The only possible explanation for this scenario is that the scribe was copying literatim an exemplar that was written by two different scribes with two different spelling systems. In the late Middle English period, scribes were more used to vernacular copying, where such variation was tolerated, and so the option to alter the spelling system of a document when copying was more readily available.

So while Types 1 and 2 are comparatively straightforward, Type 3 is more complicated, as a scribe copying in this way will produce a mixed language, containing both exemplar and scribal forms. So where scribes who copy according to Types 1 and 2 will produce outputs suitable for dialectal analysis, a text copied by a Type 3 scribe is, on the surface, unsuitable for such an analysis. But, despite the fact that texts produced by a Type 3 copyist are written in a linguistic mixture of both scribal

[7] McIntosh, 'Word Geography'.

and exemplar forms, this mixture may, in certain cases, reveal an internal consistency which enables it to be used for the purposes of Middle English dialectology.[8] Where the language of the text is a random mixture of scribal and exemplar forms, it is termed a *Mischsprache* and is unsuitable for dialectological analysis. However, where the distribution of scribal and exemplar forms is orderly and may be distinguished as separate linguistic layers, such texts are known as *pseudo-Mischsprachen* and may be subjected to dialectological analysis. Such texts may be produced when a scribe begins copying an exemplar literatim and then switches to a process of dialectal translation at an identifiable point in the text. Similarly a scribe may in theory begin by translating his text into his own dialect and then switch to a process of literatim copying, although in practice such cases are less common. However, it is common to find a period of 'working-in' in a scribal text, where a scribe gradually settles down in his copying practice and adjusts himself to the language of the exemplar from which he is working.

Another kind of scribal behaviour, which is slightly more complex than these scenarios, is known as 'constrained selection'. This term defines the work of a scribe who reproduces exemplar forms where they are familiar to him, but replaces unfamiliar forms with those from his own repertoire. The resulting linguistic mixture represents a compromise of forms, all of which are familiar to the scribe but which he would not produce as part of his spontaneous repertoire. Crucial to the concept of constraint is the distinction between active and passive repertoires. An active repertoire comprises those forms that the scribe would automatically produce when writing without any constraint from an exemplar, while a scribe's passive repertoire contains forms with which he is familiar and is willing to reproduce when confronted with them in a document which he is copying.

As if these various types of copying practice and scribal constraint were not complicated enough, there are other kinds of more restricted or specialized constraint which we must also take into account. For instance, where a scribe copies a rhyming text, his behaviour may be constrained by the use of a particular form in rhyme. In many cases this may lead to the preservation of an unusual form by a scribe who will otherwise produce a thorough translation of a text into his own dialect. However, many scribes are quite content to translate words in rhyming position without any attempt to repair the resulting damage done to the rhyme scheme. Similar situations are also true of alliterative texts, where certain scribes are constrained to reproduce unfamiliar forms in alliterating position, while others translate them with no apparent concern for the alliterative metre. So while the division of scribes into three major categories of copyists depending on their treatment of their exemplar is a fair generalization, there are a number of more specialized kinds of behaviour which must be taken into account when carrying out a dialectological analysis of a text.

---

[8] Benskin and Laing, 'Translations and *Mischsprachen*'.

The results of *LALME*'s method and its application of the fit-technique led to the localization of approximately 1,000 Middle English manuscripts: each was given a location on a map of the country and accorded a grid reference. This process of localization is inherently self-refining: the more texts one attributes to a particular area, so the dialect matrix for that area becomes more complete and thus further texts can be more accurately localized. This point also helps to highlight the essentially schematic nature of the localizations in *LALME*: it is not so much the exact geographical reference that is important, rather the relationship of a particular manuscript to other manuscripts in the matrix. This is reinforced by the fact that some manuscripts are localized to geographical locations where they simply could not have been copied, such as the top of Kinder Scout in Derbyshire or the middle of the Weald in Kent (an area of dense forest in the Middle Ages). The density of the matrix in any particular area will depend upon the amount of available data. In areas of the country where lots of texts survive, such as the South-West Midlands, the localization is considered to be accurate to a range of 10 miles, while in areas of much less dense coverage, such as the uninhabited wilds of Devon or Yorkshire, the accuracy is probably closer to 30 to 40 miles, quite a substantial difference in dialect terms.

There are various ways that these theoretical and methodological insights have been exploited by scholars working on Middle English manuscripts. One important application of *LALME* has been its use in the reconstruction of authorial dialects. As we saw above, the works of most Middle English writers survive only in scribal copies, so that we have little or no direct evidence for an author's own dialect. Application of *LALME*'s method to the earliest surviving manuscripts of writers such as Chaucer, Gower and Langland has shed considerable light on the make-up of the authors' own dialects.

In their study of Gower's dialect, M. L. Samuels and Jeremy Smith were able to discard G. C. Macaulay's association of Gower's language with that of the London court by showing that the dialect of the best and earliest copies of the *Confessio Amantis*, BodL, MS Fairfax 3 and HEHL, MS Ellesmere 26.A.17 (the 'Stafford manuscript'), show a combination of features comprising two distinct dialect strata.[9] One set of features is characteristic of the Kentish dialect, including such features as contracted third person singular present indicative verbs, spellings showing <ie> as the reflex of Old English *e*, *eo*, *selver* 'silver', *soster* 'sister'; and the other comprises features typical of the Suffolk dialect, for example *bopen* 'both', *ȝoue* 'given' and <h> for the velar fricative in words like *myhte*, *hyhe* 'high', *yhen* 'eyes'. These two dialect layers correspond closely to external evidence concerning Gower's early biography: his family owned land at Kentwell in Suffolk and had associations with Otford in Kent. Thus the language of these early copies of *Confessio Amantis*

---

[9] Samuels and Smith, 'The Language of Gower'.

was found to represent Gower's own dialect very closely. Clearly, these early regional associations were formative in establishing Gower's spelling habits, and he continued to employ this distinctive and idiosyncratic mixture while resident in London.

One of the editors of *LALME*, M. L. Samuels, has drawn upon the localizations available in *LALME* to produce an important study of the dialect of William Langland.[10] For his analysis Samuels identified a number of grammatical and phonological forms found in the earliest copies of *Piers Plowman* that can be confirmed as authorial by their presence in alliterating position. While alliterative poets commonly borrowed words from other dialects as a poetic convenience, especially such northern forms as *kirk* and *geve*, rather than the southern *chirche* and *yeve*, this is less common in the case of grammatical words. By examining the distribution of grammatical words such as pronouns and parts of the verb *be*, Samuels was able to isolate features of Langland's own dialect. Samuels showed that the alliteration of *Piers Plowman* demands a form of the third person singular feminine pronoun 'she' with initial [h], that is, *heo* or *he*. In other cases, the alliteration revealed a dialect in which more than one form was allowed, such as the spellings *are* and *beþ* as plural forms of the verb *be*. Such evidence enabled Samuels to identify a small area of South-West Worcestershire as the likely home of Langland's dialect, an area which corresponds closely with the biographical evidence and with internal references to the Malvern Hills in the poem itself. In addition to localizing the author's own dialect, Samuels also drew on *LALME*'s method to produce a localization for all surviving copies of the A, B and C texts (that is, the three identifiable versions) of the poem. This map enabled Samuels to make certain important generalizations about the dissemination of the three versions of Langland's poem which have underpinned a number of subsequent studies. Samuels's map showed that the A manuscripts were mostly geographically peripheral, none of them appearing to have been produced in London, whereas the B version survives in a large number of metropolitan copies. The manuscripts of the C text were found to cluster in two cohesive South-West Midlands groups: the textually superior i-group focussed on Malvern, while the inferior p-group radiated out from that centre into contiguous areas, such as Herefordshire, Gloucestershire and Warwickshire. The large number of copies of the C text produced in South-West Worcestershire helped to reinforce Samuels's earlier conclusions about the nature of Langland's own dialect and appeared to confirm W. W. Skeat's suggestion that Langland returned to Malvern later in his life.

More recently, I have challenged this interpretation, arguing that the consistent South-West Worcestershire dialect stratum found in the early copies of the C text is not the result of repeated copying by scribes using this dialect, but rather repeated literatim copying of a single exemplar in this dialect.[11] The professional appearance

---

[10] Samuels, 'Langland's Dialect'.
[11] Horobin, ' "In London and opelond" '.

of these early copies of C suggests that they were produced in London workshops by scribes trained to copy literatim, rather than by Worcestershire scribes working in the provinces. These findings have a number of important implications for our understanding of Langland's biography and the dissemination of the C version of *Piers Plowman*. The association of five of the earliest, and textually most important, manuscripts of the C text with London suggests that the C text was produced and released in London and only later disseminated to the West Midlands, contradicting the view that this version was only released by Langland after a return to his native West Midlands. Rather than seeing Langland's C text as primarily a provincial text, this reassessment places its earliest stage of dissemination in the same metropolitan scribal workshops as the works of Chaucer and Gower. The type of copying practice that lies behind these manuscripts, and the kinds of language employed by these London scribes, have implications for our understanding of Langlandian reception, and the development of London English during this important period in its history. These manuscripts of the C text were evidently copied by scribes who were careful to preserve many of the features of dialect and spelling associated with Langland himself, in a similar way to that found in the manuscripts of Gower discussed above. Such fidelity to the spelling of an exemplar is rare in the transmission of Middle English texts (although see Daniel Wakelin's comments above, pp. 51–5) and suggests a high regard for the integrity of Langland's text, extending to minor peculiarities of spelling and dialect, a regard accorded to other authoritative works, such as those by Chaucer and Gower, but not to many less prestigious Middle English works.

Samuels's localization of the manuscripts of the three versions of *Piers Plowman* can be paralleled in a number of similar studies which aim to map the textual transmission of works surviving in numerous copies. The foundational such study is that by Angus McIntosh and Robert E. Lewis which localizes all of the 115 surviving copies of the anonymous religious poem *The Prick of Conscience*. As well as enabling further research on questions of the provenance and readership of individual copies of the poem, McIntosh and Lewis's work helps to locate the dissemination of variant textual versions. This is best exemplified by McIntosh's identification of the 'Lichfield' group: a version of the text containing a unique prologue which survives in a number of copies dialectally linked with Lichfield. This variant version can also be linked textually with the copy of the poem found in the so-called 'Vernon manuscript', BodL, MS Eng. poet. a. 1, thereby shedding light on the channels of distribution through which the Vernon scribe sourced his exemplars.[12] More recently, Richard Beadle has drawn upon the localizations in *LALME* to map all of the surviving copies of the related northern instructional verse text, *Speculum Vitae*, as well as other devotional texts, such as Mirk's

[12] On this point, see discussion by Connolly, Chapter 6, p. 132.

Festial and the *Speculum Christiani*.[13] The maps help to identify distinctive patterns of regional distribution, such as the restricted dissemination of the *Festial*, which appears not to have been distributed north of the Humber or south of the Thames Estuary. As more maps of this kind are constructed, so we shall get a much more detailed picture of regional literary communities and their textual cultures. Despite the inevitable loss of many copies of these works, Beadle claims that there is 'an inherent likelihood in the idea that a significant proportion of our surviving manuscripts must have been copied from exemplars that lay in neighbouring places'.[14]

A different way of exploiting the data made available by *LALME* is the study of literary geography. Studies of this kind are concerned with analysis of the literary culture of particular geographical regions. Thorlac Turville-Petre's discussion of North-West Midlands reading communities represents an early gesture in this direction, while Richard Beadle's survey of the extensive literary remains associated with the county of Norfolk provides considerable resources for further research in that region, facilitated by the provision of a list of all manuscripts associated with the county through dialect evidence.[15] A new kind of resource for the study of regional literary culture also building on *LALME* is the on-line catalogue of manuscripts of the West Midlands edited by Wendy Scase.[16] This on-line database provides descriptions and images of all manuscripts localized to the six West Midlands counties of Gloucestershire, Herefordshire, Shropshire, Staffordshire, Warwickshire and Worcestershire. A volume of essays edited by Scase designed to draw upon this resource shows some of the ways that it can be tapped for further studies, both of the West Midlands as a major centre of manuscript production, but also as part of a complex system of networks through which texts could be exchanged.[17] While the essays in Scase's volume focus on manuscripts localized to the West Midlands, the numerous connections they show with other geographical areas show how this important centre can be understood only with reference to other regions. In this way, manuscript geography becomes less a study of texts within a single geographical locale and more a mapping of networks of relationships between manuscripts, or, in John Thompson's elegant formulation, 'a subtle topographical analogy that can be used to emphasize mobility, transition, and exchange rather than fixedness'.[18]

Samuels's mapping of the manuscripts of *Piers Plowman* also forms a model for Jeremy Smith's comprehensive analysis of the language of the manuscripts of

---

[13] Beadle, 'Middle English Texts and their Transmission'.

[14] Ibid., 83.

[15] Turville-Petre, 'Some Medieval English Manuscripts'; Beadle, 'Prolegomena to a Literary Geography'.

[16] Scase (ed.), *Manuscripts of the West Midlands*, www.mwm.bham.ac.uk

[17] Scase (ed.), *Essays in Manuscript Geography*.

[18] Thompson, 'Mapping', 116.

Gower's *Confessio Amantis*.[19] As well as producing localizations for manuscripts copied in provincial dialects, Smith's survey identifies a large number of scribes deliberately preserving idiosyncratic features of Gower's dialect. The identification of this phenomenon leads Smith to conclude that Gower's status as an author led scribes to consider features of his dialect to be integral to the authorial text. As a result, Gower scribes frequently demonstrated the copying behaviour described above as 'constrained selection', reproducing forms found in their exemplars in preference to those that they would use spontaneously. I observe a similar response in the manuscript tradition of Chaucer's *The Canterbury Tales*, where scribes were found to deliberately preserve features that they considered to be Chaucerian despite their increasingly archaic appearance.[20]

In addition to its use in localizing manuscript production, dialect evidence can also be used to identify the work of a single scribe copying more than one manuscript. Such identifications are, of course, primarily based upon palaeographical analysis, but dialect analysis has frequently been used to offer supplementary evidence in identifying the work of a particular scribe. The importance of dialect evidence in establishing scribal identity is emphasized by Angus McIntosh, who reports how the dialectal similarity of one of the scribes of BodL, MS Rawl. A.389, an important collection of works by Richard Rolle derived from authoritative exemplars, and that of TCC, MS R.3.8, a copy of the southern recension of *Cursor Mundi*, led him to make a comparison of their handwriting.[21] Subsequent palaeographical analysis resulted in the discovery that the two hands were in fact identical, which has in turn led to the further identification of a substantial corpus of manuscripts by this single scribe, including three copies of *The Prick of Conscience*.[22]

The large number of manuscripts attributed to this hand, including several copies of the same text, strongly implies that he was a professional scribe, supplying a ready market for copies of northern devotional works. The location of this individual and his clientele is therefore a question of considerable importance. Once again, dialect study can be used to help answer the question. Lewis and McIntosh localize the dialect of these manuscripts to the Lichfield area, a localization which fits well with the research into the provenance of these and related books. For instance, N. R. Ker identified two fifteenth-century inscriptions found in BodL, MS Rawl. A.389, as belonging to two prebendaries of Lichfield in the latter half of the fifteenth century.[23] In this example, we can see how dialect study can help in the attribution of manuscripts to a single scribe, and with the localization of that individual.

[19] Smith, 'Spelling and Tradition'.

[20] Horobin, *The Language of the Chaucer Tradition*.

[21] McIntosh, 'A New Approach to Middle English Dialectology'.

[22] For details and descriptions of manuscripts copied by this scribe, see Lewis and McIntosh, *A Descriptive Guide to the Manuscripts of the 'Prick of Conscience'*, and Doyle (ed.), *The Vernon Manuscript*.

[23] *MLGB*, 115.

Dialect evidence has also been important in helping to localize the 'Vernon manuscript' itself, the largest and most important repository of Middle English religious literature.[24] There has been much speculation about where such a vast and expensive collection may have been produced; central to such discussions are considerations of the dialect of the two scribes who copied the manuscript. The bulk of the manuscript was copied by a single copyist, known as Scribe B, who consistently imposed a Worcester dialect upon the variety of texts he copied. The consistency of this dialect across such a variety of texts strongly implies that it was the scribe's own, and would therefore appear to localize the production of the manuscript in this region. This localization is reinforced by the dialect evidence provided by the second contributor, Scribe A, who copied the table of contents and the first item in the manuscript. However, Scribe A's hand has also been identified in two copies of *The Prick of Conscience* which have been localized by *LALME* to Staffordshire (Oxford, Trinity College, MS 16B and Holkham Hall, MS 668). While this evidence strengthens the case for a West Midlands localization for the production of the Vernon manuscript, it also reminds us that scribes were mobile and that the localization of a scribal dialect is not necessarily an indication of a place of production. Itinerant professional copyists would have come across exemplars in a variety of dialects and would often have had cause to adjust their repertoires accordingly. In the case of Scribe A, it is impossible to determine from the evidence whether his native dialect was that of Staffordshire or that of Worcestershire; he was evidently familiar with both and could use either, depending upon the nature of the commission and the dialect of the exemplar from which he was copying.

In a more recent study which builds on the localizations initially carried out by both Lewis and McIntosh and by Samuels[25] and subsequently published in *LALME*, I draw on a combination of dialectal and palaeographical evidence to argue that a single scribe was responsible for a manuscript of *The Prick of Conscience* in Oxford, University College, MS 142 and a copy of the A text of *Piers Plowman* in BodL, MS Rawl. poet. 137.[26] These two manuscripts are written in a similar hand, showing an idiosyncratic mixture of anglicana and textura features, and both are copied in a similarly distinctive dialect, localized by *LALME* to South-West Sussex. Characteristic forms include 'hure' (her), 'hy' (they), 'moche' (much), 'beþ', 'beth' (are), 'or' (ere), 'ʒut' (yet), 'wordle' (world), 'guod' (good), 'hure' (hear). Drawing on the localization in *LALME* and the evidence for the scribe's name found in scribal colophons added to the two manuscripts, it is possible to identify the scribe himself as a Thomas Tilot, a member of the vicars choral at Chichester Cathedral in the early fifteenth century. This identification then forms the basis of my discussion

---

[24] Doyle (ed.), *The Vernon Manuscript*.
[25] Samuels, 'Langland's Dialect'.
[26] Horobin, 'The Scribe of Rawlinson Poetry 137'.

of the context for the production and readership of these manuscripts, as well as a consideration of the evidence they supply for the circulation of exemplars of these works. This example is a testimony to the value of *LALME* and the value of dialect study; without the Sussex localization I would have had to search records pertaining to the entire country rather than those specific to Sussex. The identification of the scribe of this manuscript sheds further light on possible connections with other copies of the A text of *Piers Plowman*. Thomas Tilot was appointed to a canonry and prebend at St David's Cathedral, an appointment which brought him into contact with Walter de Brugge, the first recorded owner of a copy of *Piers Plowman*. Connections with a benefice in Burwell, Cambridgeshire, may help to explain the close textual relationship between BodL, MS Rawl. poet. 137 and another extant copy of the poem, Oxford, University College, MS 45, written in a Cambridgeshire dialect.

These two examples also show the importance of the interaction between palaeography and dialectology for making identifications; the value of such collaboration is apparent from a number of studies that build upon pioneering work by A. I. Doyle and Malcolm Parkes in their 1978 essay on manuscripts of works by Chaucer and Gower.[27] In this article, Doyle and Parkes present palaeographical and codicological analysis of the work of five scribes who collaborated in the production of a single copy of Gower's *Confessio Amantis*, now TCC, MS R.3.2. They identify the second hand in this manuscript, termed by them Scribe B, as the copyist responsible for two of the earliest and most important manuscripts of *The Canterbury Tales*, the Hengwrt and Ellesmere manuscripts, as well as a now fragmentary copy of Chaucer's *Troilus and Criseyde*. Scribe D, the fourth contributor to the manuscript, was identified in eight copies of Gower's *Confessio Amantis*, as well as two manuscripts of *The Canterbury Tales* and single copies of Langland's *Piers Plowman* and Trevisa's translation of *De Proprietatibus rerum*. Scribe E's hand, responsible for a mere two and a half leaves, is that of the poet and clerk of the Privy Seal Thomas Hoccleve, whose hand is also found in three manuscripts containing his own poems. Since Doyle and Parkes's landmark analysis, dialectologists have built upon their identifications to analyse the linguistic outputs of individual scribes. For example, Jeremy Smith's analysis of the many manuscripts attributed to the prolific Scribe D distinguishes a series of discrete and conflicting dialectal layers within his manuscripts: forms typical of the dialects of London and the South-West Midlands.[28] A dialectal mixture of this kind may seem bewildering at first, but Smith's analysis argued that the various layers could be understood as a reflection of the various constraints that operated upon the scribe. We know from his association with Thomas Hoccleve in TCC, MS R.3.2 that Scribe D

---

[27] Doyle and Parkes, 'The Production of Copies'; and Mooney's discussion, p. 130 below.
[28] Smith, 'The Trinity Gower D-Scribe'.

was working in London, which explains the forms typical of London English; but why do all his manuscripts contain layers of South-West Midlands forms? Smith argued that the scribe must have originated in the South-West Midlands and that it was there that he learned to write, using a marked South-West Midlands dialect. When he subsequently migrated to London, as did many professional scribes in the fifteenth century, he continued to employ many of these forms throughout his career. Not only does this analysis allow us to trace the scribe's origins in the South-West Midlands, but it has also been used to determine the likely order of copying of Scribe D's many manuscripts. Smith notes that the number of South-West Midlands forms differs across the corpus of manuscripts, suggesting that Scribe D was gradually replacing these forms with London equivalents over the course of his career. This suggests that those manuscripts with the larger percentage of South-West Midlands forms were written earlier in the scribe's career than those with a smaller percentage of such forms.[29]

Dialect analysis has also proved a useful means of verifying the conclusions proposed by Doyle and Parkes on the basis of their palaeographical analysis. Roy Vance Ramsey argues against their conclusions, claiming that the Hengwrt and Ellesmere manuscripts were written by different scribes. Samuels's response to Ramsey's controversial claims draws upon a detailed analysis of the spelling of this scribe's output to show that, while there are differences between the spelling habits found across these manuscripts, the core of spellings remains stable across Hengwrt and Ellesmere, thereby indicating a single usage and single copyist.[30] Samuels argues that the differences between Hengwrt and Ellesmere may be understood to represent changes in preference over the course of the scribe's copying career, which further enables him to propose a chronology of copying. This places the Hengwrt manuscript as the earliest of the scribe's surviving output and the Ellesmere manuscript as the last of his extant copies. In a recent study of a manuscript of the B text of *Piers Plowman*, TCC, MS B.15.17, Linne Mooney and I argue that the similarities in hand and dialect between this manuscript and those written by Scribe B show that this manuscript of *Piers Plowman* should also be added to this scribe's *curriculum vitae*.[31] While this copy of *Piers Plowman* contains the same core of spellings identified by Samuels, there are certain differences between the Trinity manuscript of *Piers Plowman* and others copied by this scribe, enabling this manuscript to be placed at the beginning of Samuels's proposed sequence, before the copying of the Hengwrt manuscript. Mooney has since built upon our attribution of this manuscript of *Piers Plowman* to this scribe by identifying him as the professional London scrivener Adam Pinkhurst, whose signature is found

---

[29] For a discussion, see Owen, *The Manuscripts of the Canterbury Tales*.
[30] Samuels, 'The Scribe of the Hengwrt and Ellesmere Manuscripts'.
[31] Horobin and Mooney, 'A *Piers Plowman* Manuscript'.

accompanying his copying of the oath in the Common Paper of the Scriveners' Guild in 1392.[32]

Earlier, this chapter stressed the lack of a standard variety of Middle English. But while this is true of the period 1100–1400, the fifteenth century saw the emergence of a standard variety, which considerably complicates the localization of texts copied at the close of the Middle English period. The process by which this standard variety developed and became established was first described by Samuels in an important article of 1963. In this article, Samuels distinguishes four types of written standards in texts copied during the fourteenth and fifteenth centuries, labelled Types I–IV. Type I, also known as the Central Midlands Standard, is found in a number of texts associated with John Wycliffe and the lollard movement, including the majority of copies of the Wycliffite Bible. It is also found in manuscripts containing non-Wycliffite religious works, such as BodL, MS Laud misc. 488, a copy of Rolle's *Psalter* and BodL, MS Bodley 592, containing Hilton's *Scale of Perfection*, as well as in medical and scientific collections such as those found in BodL, MS Ashmole 1396, BL, MS Royal 17.A.iii and BL, MS Sloane 73. The language is based on the Central Midlands dialects, particularly such counties as Northamptonshire, Huntingdonshire and Bedfordshire, although texts copied in this dialect were circulated widely throughout the country.

Type II is found in a number of manuscripts copied in London in the mid fourteenth century, including the Auchinleck manuscript, three copies of the Middle English *Mirror* (CUL, MS Hunter 250; BL, MS Harley 5085; Cambridge, Magdalene College, MS Pepys 2498) and a copy of the *Early English Prose Psalter* (BL, MS Add. 17376). Type II differs from an earlier, Essex-based, London usage in that it shows a marked influence of forms from the East Anglian dialects, a result of large-scale immigration into London from those counties in the mid fourteenth century. Type III is the language of London in the late fourteenth century, recorded in the earliest manuscripts of Chaucer's works, such as the Hengwrt and Ellesmere manuscripts of *The Canterbury Tales* and the holograph manuscripts of Thomas Hoccleve's works.[33] Type III differs from Type II in containing a large number of forms derived from the Central Midlands dialects, the result of immigration into London from that region during this period. Type IV is first recorded in administrative documents copied in London from c.1430. Because of its administrative basis, Samuels termed it 'Chancery Standard', although it is not limited to the Chancery office. This language shows the influence of further waves of immigration from the Central Midlands counties, with a number of linguistic features filtered down from the northern dialects.

[32] 'Chaucer's Scribe'.
[33] Hoccleve's holograph manuscripts are HEHL, MS HM 111, HEHL, MS HM 744 part II; Durham, University Library, MS Cosin V.iii.9.

Because of the emergence of this standard variety, the survey in *LALME* covers the period up to 1450; after this point local language begins to be influenced by the forms associated with the standard language. But it is important not to assume that the existence of a standard language led to the immediate eradication of local writing systems. Chancery Standard first appeared in the administrative offices of Westminster; it took some time for it to be disseminated and adopted outside this arena. It is also important to stress a distinction made by Samuels between standardized and standard usages, or what Smith has recently termed 'focussed' and 'fixed' standards.[34] The four types of standards distinguished by Samuels are focussed standards, in that they allow a fair amount of internal variation and do not consist of a fixed set of rules. Chancery Standard was not a standard in our modern sense: it admitted variation within and between users and was not codified in the way that Present Day English spelling is. This is a distinction ignored by John Fisher in his presentation of Chancery Standard as a fixed entity and in his claim that it represented an official standard endorsed and promoted with royal approval.[35]

The process by which Chancery Standard spellings were adopted outside the Chancery and other official offices was a much more gradual process than Fisher suggests, and there is considerable tolerance of dialect usage throughout the fifteenth century. Rather than seeing local languages replaced wholesale by Chancery forms, there was an initial period in which there emerged 'colourless standards', a kind of compromise language in which the more unusual and restricted dialect forms had been replaced by forms which were accepted more widely, while dialect features that could be easily understood were retained. Recent work by Michael Benskin has helped to fill out the picture of how this process operated.[36] Benskin has argued that Chancery spellings were transmitted to the provinces by lawyers and legal clerks who came to the Inns of Court and the Inns of Chancery for their training and then returned to their provincial origins to set up practice. There was considerable social and geographical mobility during this period, and many young men of middle-class and provincial origins went to London to receive their training and then returned home. Benskin emphasizes that the process by which Chancery Standard was accepted in the provinces was by no means immediate. Many provincial dialects had their own local prestige and it took some time for Chancery Standard to establish a national prestige which ultimately overcame the local standards.

The gradual adoption of standardized forms by members of the Paston family is traced by Norman Davis in his analysis of this substantial collection of family

---

[34] Smith, *An Historical Study of English*.
[35] Fisher, *The Emergence of Standard English*.
[36] Benskin, 'Chancery Standard'.

letters.[37] But while family members who experienced social and geographical mobility, such as John II and III, show corresponding changes in their spelling habits, the Pastons who stayed at the family home in Norfolk tend to be more conservative in their linguistic habits, preserving their local, dialectal spelling system much longer.

A further important factor in the establishment of a standard variety of Middle English was of course the advent of the printing press, set up in England by William Caxton in the 1470s. The language of Caxton's printed texts was not identical to that of Chancery Standard, but he did broadly follow the same preferences adopted by the Chancery. Caxton was not a linguist concerned with standardizing the language, like Johnson or Swift in the eighteenth century; he was first and foremost a businessman keen to exploit the financial possibilities opened up by printing.[38] To do this, he needed to print books in a spelling system that could be read by the widest possible audience and so was concerned not to use spellings that would cause difficulties for his readers. Another important aspect of the advent of printing for the process of standardization was that it allowed numerous identical copies to be made of a single work, something that had never been possible in the age of manuscript-copying. When book production was the work of scribes, prone to make mistakes or to introduce their own dialect forms into a text, there was limited opportunity for a standard language to spread. Printing meant that texts could be circulated in an identical form and so removed the possibility for variation of this kind.

The mass production of books that came with printing also changed the nature of book production. The production of manuscripts was largely a bespoke trade: a client would approach a scribe or stationer and order a copy of a work which would then be produced for that single client. Printing brought with it speculative production, whereby large numbers of copies of a work were printed and then circulated to a much wider market. The cost of such books also decreased, allowing books to be owned by a wider cross-section of society. All of these factors enabled this new standardized variety to be disseminated widely both socially and geographically.

Discussion of these changes in the London dialect raises a problem associated with the dialectology of major urban centres, where rates of linguistic change are characteristically much greater than in rural areas. The techniques employed by the makers of *LALME* were developed to deal with conservative rural dialects. In cities, language change is accelerated, partly as a result of the influx of immigrants into these larger urban areas and the much greater rates of social mobility. Often the dialectal make-up of a city changes from one type to another over a short period of time, generally as a result of shifting influences from different adjacent dialect areas. As we saw above, this is precisely what happened in London during this period, as Type II (based on the East Anglian dialects) was replaced by Types III and IV

[37] Davis, 'The Language of Two Brothers'.
[38] Blake, *William Caxton*.

(based on the Central and North Midlands dialects respectively). Representing these changes on a two-dimensional map is problematic (see Figure 3.1). As *LALME* points out in discussing this issue, 'the ideal would have been a three-dimensional map in which such replacements were represented vertically'. The solution adopted by *LALME* was to map such texts in the adjacent regions which best fit the dialects of the London texts. So, for instance, a number of Type II texts which were copied in London, such as those copied by Hand A of the Auchinleck manuscript and two manuscripts of the Middle English *Mirror*, are mapped in Middlesex, despite the fact that they were probably copied in London. A number of other Type II texts are mapped in Essex, as their language is considered to fit best with the dialectal configuration characteristic of this area.

As a result of this approach there are in fact a very small number of manuscripts which are given a localization in London, despite the fact that it was one of the most densely populated cities in Western Europe in the Middle Ages, and the centre for government and book production.[39] Obviously, many more than these few manuscripts must have been copied in London during this period. Comparison of London with the much more sparsely inhabited Somerset, where seventeen texts are mapped, shows just how misleading *LALME*'s treatment of London can appear.

The reason for this problem is partly to do with immigration: many of the texts copied in London were by immigrant scribes using their own dialects or a modified version of their own dialects and not London language. Literatim copying by London scribes also testifies to the wide tolerance of provincial varieties within the capital during the fifteenth century. All of these varieties could be considered to be London English, in the sense that they represent forms of English used in London. A problem with Samuels's definition of his types is that it tends to overlook the considerable body of texts written in London that do not reflect these usages.[40] A more inclusive and more realistic representation of London English needs to take account of this diversity of different usages. To give a modern parallel: how should we define London English today? It would include local varieties such as Received Pronunciation, Cockney and Estuary English, but also numerous external varieties, such as Indian, Jamaican and Australian Englishes, reflecting centuries of immigration into the capital.

Another difficulty with the *LALME* approach to London is that it is formulated exclusively upon a model where one type of language was replaced by another. Recent work on urban dialectology and sociolinguistics has shown that different

---

[39] Manuscripts localized to London in *LALME* are BL, MS Harley 2387, the Hengwrt and Ellesmere manuscripts of *The Canterbury Tales*, Hoccleve's holographs (for details, see n.33 above), St John's, Camb., MS C. 21, Hand C of the Auchinleck manuscript (NLS, MS Advocates' 19.2.1) and Guildhall Library, Letter Books I and K.

[40] Hanna, *London Literature*.

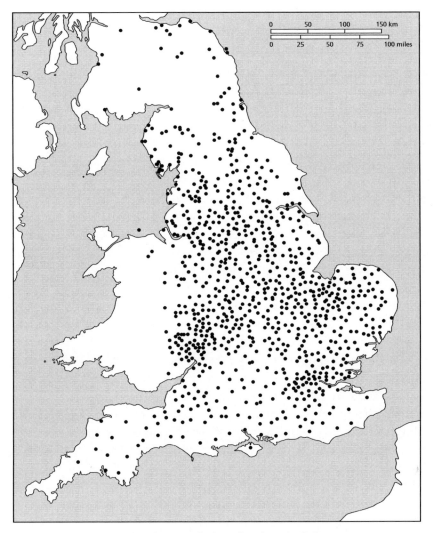

Figure 3.1 LALME, *dot map: showing distribution of all survey points.*

varieties can co-exist within urban environments and are distinguished by com-
municative or social factors, rather than by geography or chronology. It is difficult
to see how these differences could be plotted on a map, unless using the notional
three-dimensional map mentioned by the editors of *LALME*, but such factors do
need to be taken account of in a survey of the urban dialects of Middle English.

It should be clear from the preceding discussion how valuable dialect study is
for the study of Middle English manuscript books. Dialect information can play a
crucial role in identifying work by the same scribe, and in helping to localize that
scribe and his place of work. Dialect study can also draw attention to other scribes

working in the same, or nearby locales, and to other books geographically related, thereby helping to construct a network of books, texts and scribes that relate to each other in complex and illuminating ways. The resources provided by the publication of *LALME* are extremely valuable in furthering work of this kind, and scholars are only now beginning to realize the full potential of its many applications. The publication of an electronic *LALME*, already underway at the Institute for Historical Dialectology in Edinburgh, making the huge quantities of complex data fully searchable, will considerably facilitate the process of linking up the various manuscripts and scribal stints analysed in that publication.

In addition to the many uses discussed throughout this chapter, *LALME* also points the way towards some new areas of research which could be carried out using its resources. One exciting area that has hardly ever been addressed concerns the mapping of graphetic, or handwriting, features in a similar way to the mapping of graphemic, or spelling, features carried out by *LALME*. A possible methodology for a study of this kind was first sketched in an exploratory article by Angus McIntosh, who proposed compiling graphetic profiles of individual scribal hands.[41] Graphetic profiles of this kind would help in identifying the work of scribes in multiple manuscripts, as well as identifying regional palaeographical features. Profiles and maps of this kind would be extremely valuable aids in localization, and in drawing links between scribes and manuscripts. The value of this research was demonstrated in a landmark study by Benskin, who showed a clear diatopic distinction between the way that scribes write the graphemes <þ> and <y>.[42] Benskin noticed that where some scribes distinguish between the graphs for <þ> and <y>, others use a single graph for both letters. By drawing on *LALME* localizations, Benskin was able to observe a clear diatopic distinction: northern and East Anglian scribes use <y>, while southern and Midlands scribes use both <y> and <þ>. Further studies of this kind would allow us to build up a clearer picture of regional differences in handwriting and would be invaluable for studies of manuscript and scribal provenance.

[41] McIntosh, 'Towards an Inventory of Middle English Scribes'.
[42] Benskin, 'The Letters <þ> and <y>'.

4

Designing the page

STEPHEN PARTRIDGE

A scribe or printer undertaking to reproduce a text faced the task of reproducing or supplying features that would help a reader navigate that text. During the period between 1350 and 1500, readers came to expect in an English book several elements that would either facilitate reading or help a reader find particular passages or topics. These elements included headings for parts of a work such as chapters or books (headings which this essay will also refer to sometimes as rubrics or as incipits and explicits); *litterae notabiliores* or 'capital' letters; paraphs; 'running heads' at the tops of pages to identify a text or part thereof; various kinds of marginal material which identified topics, speakers, sources translated or authorities cited in the text, which simply highlighted passages of special interest or (less often) which provided direct commentary on the text; and, in more expensive books, borders which, like headings, indicated part-divisions.

In an influential essay, M. B. Parkes has shown how the origins and growing popularity of these features related to large cultural changes in the renaissance of scholarly learning in the twelfth and thirteenth centuries, such as new ways of reading, the rise of universities, the production of new kinds of books which compiled material from many sources and the composition of encyclopaedic works.[1] The page came to be designed in ways that clarified the division of a work into parts and also the relationship of several kinds of writing that might appear on the same page. In addition to the text, such writing might include passages from the work's sources, commentaries, and various kinds of headings and other finding aids. These developments in design began in Latin books intended for those in religious orders and for students but ultimately influenced the shapes of vernacular books intended for larger and more heterogeneous audiences.

I am grateful to the Huntington Library for a Mayers Fellowship, which made possible much of the research and the writing of this chapter.

[1] Parkes, 'The Influence of the Concepts of *Ordinatio* and *Compilatio* on the Development of the Book'.

These developments were essentially complete by the end of the fourteenth century.[2]

The present study, which centres on books of vernacular literature made in the fifteenth century, will therefore primarily describe the late fourteenth- and fifteenth-century reception and reproduction of such features as headings, paraphs, large *litterae notabiliores* and marginal glosses instead of exploring their origins and functions.[3] Rather than outline a single norm for scribes' management of such elements, the chapter will survey a range of behaviours by scribes which can be considered ordinary or unexceptional, and it will reflect, sometimes speculatively, on why scribes might have chosen to proceed as they did. While Parkes tends to treat page design as an intellectual project, this chapter will devote greater attention to it as a pragmatic challenge and a commercial expectation. Ideals of fidelity to exemplars and of completeness and consistency in page layout certainly influenced the appearance of fifteenth-century books, but so did accidents of production, constraints on resources and the desire for scribal convenience and speed.

To develop models of scribal behaviour, the chapter will rely primarily on the manuscript traditions of major English literary texts by Chaucer, Gower, Langland, Hoccleve and Lydgate, with a particular emphasis on *The Canterbury Tales*. These are among the Middle English works surviving in the most manuscripts, and the relationships among those manuscripts have received close attention and are well understood. These facts mean that, although instances are few in which one surviving manuscript has been copied directly from another, we can usually surmise with some confidence what kind of exemplar (or exemplars) a scribe was working with, and therefore how the scribe treated the elements of page design he inherited from that exemplar, and how far he devised new ones. Moreover, these manuscript traditions reflect significant trends in book production in fourteenth- and fifteenth-century England. As Julia Boffey and A. S. G. Edwards have observed (and as Margaret Connolly also notes in Chapter 6), the single-work book became a widespread model for English books over this period, and the rise of this model coincided with a shift in the production of English books from being primarily a regional or provincial phenomenon to being one centred in London, as the

---

[2] Parkes, 'Layout and Presentation of the Text'. This essay provides a lucid overview of the functions of the elements of page design that this chapter will consider.

[3] It will not deal with some aspects of the book treated by Parkes, such as tables of contents and indices. In addition, this chapter will devote relatively little attention to such aspects as the shape and size of the page (discussed by Da Rold, Chapter 1); borders and illustrations (discussed by Driver and Orr, Chapter 5); and the number and arrangement of columns on the page, since the number of columns tends to remain stable within the manuscript traditions on which it will focus. Moreover, this chapter will generally not be concerned with *litterae notabiliores* that appear at the beginnings of every line, stanza or sentence, but rather with those that appear less often, to mark transitions in a text; in other words, it will focus on the relationship of page design to a work's content rather than on design's function in articulating a work's form.

metropolitan taste in literature increasingly included English books in addition to French ones.[4]

Coats of arms and other marks of ownership give some of the clearest indications that English books began to be commissioned by aristocratic and other wealthy patrons, but more generally changes in the appearance of many English books testify to their rise in status. Greater white space was often allowed on their pages, and that space by itself constituted a kind of conspicuous consumption, as scribes no longer felt compelled to squeeze English texts onto as few parchment leaves as possible in order to keep down a book's cost.[5] In addition, scribes and other artisans made use of that white space for design elements which fulfilled important functions for readers and also helped to make books into prestige objects. Artisans were often asked to expend time and materials on such features as whole and partial borders and *litterae notabiliores* beyond what was needed for a reader to recognize a transition from one chapter or book to another.[6] The impression of luxury can be created both by liberal margins and by the features that sometimes occupy them, as when a manuscript's text is laid out on every page to allow for borders that appear perhaps only every ten folios.

Greater ease in planning such luxury features as borders and illustrations may have been one reason that the fundamental design of the page – the number of columns to the page, and the number of stanzas or lines per column – tended to remain quite stable within the traditions for each of the major English poetic texts.[7] Thus, as A. S. G. Edwards and Derek Pearsall observe, for example, copies of Chaucer's *Troilus and Criseyde* tend to have five rhyme-royal stanzas per page but copies of Hoccleve's *The Regiment of Princes* only four; many manuscripts of Gower's *Confessio Amantis* are laid out in two columns of forty-six lines each.[8]

[4] Boffey and Edwards, 'Literary Texts', 568. For the shift from regional to metropolitan production of English books in the late fourteenth century, see Boffey and Edwards, 'Middle English Literary Writings, 1150–1400', 388–90.

[5] Or did not *always* feel compelled to do so. Densely written English books continue to be produced through to the end of the manuscript era, and these include some copies of the literary texts which are the focus of this essay, most probably copies produced for readers beyond these works' primary audiences. See, for example, the discussion below of Longleat, MS 29, which, perhaps significantly, is devoted largely to the works of a writer from earlier in the fourteenth century, Richard Rolle.

[6] The terms *champ*, *pen-flourished initial* and *Lombard capital* refer to *litterae notabiliores*, each of these kinds being more expensive than the next in this list: see Scott, 'Limning and Book-Producing Terms' and the discussion by Driver and Orr, Chapter 5.

[7] While this chapter focusses on how scribes dealt with page design, it is likely that in at least some luxury commissions, other artisans such as illuminators supervised the scribes and that their work was responsible for more of the cost of the books than the scribes'.

[8] Edwards and Pearsall, 'The Manuscripts of the Major English Poetic Texts', 264–5. According to Parkes, 'towards the end of the fourteenth century the single column became the principal layout for verse texts' ('Layout and Presentation of the Text', 58). Gower's *Confessio* was a notable (perhaps conservative) exception. Some copies of Lydgate's longest poems, *The Fall of Princes* and *The Troy Book*, also present exceptions, presumably due to the need to accommodate more material on each page, although

These observations about consistency in page layout generally obtain also for the transmission of the specific features to be discussed here. Surveying details of design across the manuscript traditions for several of these major texts strongly suggests that the default procedure was for scribes and other artisans to reproduce their exemplars in details of layout. One major and basic piece of evidence for this inference is that manuscripts affiliated in their texts tend also to be especially alike in the form and frequency of their design. In her analysis of the Latin marginalia to Hoccleve's *The Regiment of Princes*, for example, Marcia Smith Marzec found that most often the variants in these marginalia confirmed the manuscript groups established by collating the English text of the poem itself.[9] Richard Emmerson presents data on the Latin in manuscripts of Gower's *Confessio Amantis* which reflect a correlation between a manuscript's textual group and the position, either in the margin or in the text column, and the colour, either black or red, of its Latin apparatus.[10] Although there are significant exceptions (some discussed below), one tends to find distinctive resemblances in headings, in particular, and in marginal glosses within manuscripts of *The Canterbury Tales* that are related in their texts.[11] Such scribal fidelity in reproducing exemplars can extend to what might fairly be called mistakes, so that after one early (and presumably lost) copy of Gower's *Confessio Amantis* moved its long commentaries from the margins, where they clearly belonged, into the column, where they disrupted the flow of the text, other scribes simply reproduced this arrangement.[12] Similarly, glosses to *The Canterbury Tales* were moved from the margins into the text column in a lost exemplar for two closely related manuscripts, Paris, Bibliothèque Nationale, MS anglais 39 and BL, MS Harley 1239. (See Figure 4.1, which shows f. 82r.) Some manuscripts of Chaucer's *Troilus and Criseyde* fail to identify clearly or accurately the transition from Book III to Book IV, but instead reproduce an early misplacement of the borders and headings for Book IV and its prologue, even though it seems that comparing the text at this point with the passages at similar transitions in *Troilus* would have provided an easy way to rectify the problem.[13]

Such scribal repetition, even to the point of inertia, does not represent the entire story. An analysis such as Marzec's implies, and indeed depends on, the fact that scribes introduced variants into elements of page design. Sometimes, these variants

---

because these were often large-format books, the impression of surplus white space remains, and the proportion of these manuscripts including illustration and expensive illumination is unusually high; see Edwards and Pearsall, 'The Manuscripts of the Major English Poetic Texts', 260.

[9] Marzec, 'The Latin Marginalia of the *Regiment of Princes* as an Aid to Stemmatic Analysis', 270.

[10] Emmerson, 'Reading Gower in a Manuscript Culture'; see the Appendix, 184–6.

[11] Partridge, 'The *Canterbury Tales* Glosses and the Manuscript Groups'.

[12] Pearsall describes the partial attempt by the scribe of BL, MS Add. 12043 to move these commentaries from the column back out to the margin: 'The Manuscripts and Illustrations of Gower's Works', 91.

[13] The confusion is present in, for example, PML, MS M.817 and CCCC, MS 61.

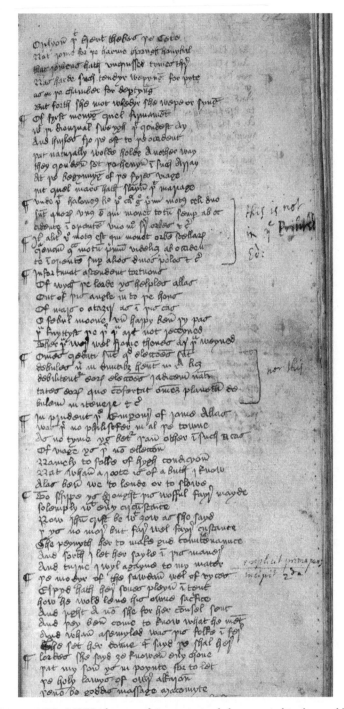

Figure 4.1 BL, MS Harley 1239, f. 82r: marginal glosses copied in the text block of The Man of Law's Tale marked with brackets by a later reader.

arose quite early in the manuscript traditions, in lost archetypes which we reconstruct only by observing similarities among groups of surviving manuscripts. Thus,
for example, the misplaced commentaries on Gower's *Confessio* in manuscripts of
the 'first recension' demonstrate the possibility of significant variation as well as
repetition. Scribes clearly selected from, expanded and modified the page layouts
they found in their exemplars. If the present chapter emphasizes how patterns are
preserved across many manuscripts, that emphasis is intended partly to balance and
provide a context for the number of valuable studies which have considered what is
distinctive about individual manuscripts.

Before considering in more detail the history of continuity with variations in
the design of fifteenth-century books, it will be helpful to outline how elements
of page design were produced or reproduced. The 'finishing' of a manuscript was
typically carried out in a separate stage of work from copying the text, or, especially in more deluxe manuscripts, in a series of stages. There were several reasons
for this practice. Working in stages would most obviously be necessary whenever
somebody other than the scribe was undertaking parts of the finishing. In the
more expensive classes of books, it would presumably have been routine to employ
one or more specialists to provide such elements as borders, large initials and
even paraphs; indeed, in such cases these specialists may sometimes have organized and overseen the production, including the work of the scribe (or scribes).
But proceeding in stages would have been simpler also for a scribe working alone.
Finishing might involve the use of red ink, and sometimes blue as well, and a scribe
could finish a book more quickly if he did all of his work with a given ink in a distinct stage. Working in stages might likewise improve efficiency when a scribe used
a different script, rather than a different ink, to distinguish such elements as page
heads, headings and glosses from his text, since the writing of such a display script
might require the use of a different pen or a different angle of approach to the page
or just work at a different pace. Finally, a scribe might improve the accuracy of his
copying by writing distinct kinds of material, such as text, headings and glosses, in
separate stages. Presumably, scribes often, though not always, sped up their work
by copying longer stretches of text – perhaps whole lines – remembered as units
of sense, rather than by copying letter by letter, and frequent interruptions to take
account of material outside the text could have limited their ability to maintain
such attention to the sense of longer passages of copy.[14]

On the other hand, scribes regularly made some preparations for the 'finishing'
stages while they were copying. As observed above, their ruling for the text increasingly allowed space on the folios for elements of page design, and ruling could
more specifically define such spaces. The ruling for some deluxe manuscripts of

---

[14] The potential for extra-textual material to disrupt a scribe's focus on his English text might have
been especially great if that extra-textual material was in French or Latin.

The Canterbury Tales, Hoccleve's *The Regiment* and Lydgate's *The Siege of Thebes*, for example, defines a column outside the text area in which glosses were written and which also helped to guide the illuminators as they provided borders – as in BL, MS Harley 4866 (see Figure 4.2, showing f. 85v). Scribes would routinely allow space for large initials and provide guide letters, and also would indicate where paraphs should appear by writing two slashes or a tiny mark. In addition, they might write versions, in cursive and light script, and perhaps abbreviated, of the incipits and explicits (see Figure 4.2 again).[15]

Sometimes these guides are still visible beneath the finished elements which followed later, but elsewhere we can see them because those finished elements were never actually provided. Such omissions can be occasional, as when a scribe or another artisan providing a series of paraphs seems simply not to have noticed a set of slashes in the sequence, or an illuminator overlooked a guide letter (perhaps more likely when the initial to be provided was smaller, and thus the space was less visible). Similarly, it is unsurprising to find rubrics occasionally absent from spaces provided for them, or running heads absent from some folios in manuscripts which generally include them.

But omissions in finishing can also be farther-reaching, in ways that tell us about how the work of finishing a manuscript could be organized. For instance, certain elements of a layout might be finished, while others remain only in rough form, or some parts of a book or work might be finished but not others. So, for example, in the copy of Chaucer's *Troilus* in CUL, MS Gg.4.27, there appears a pair of dots, rather idiosyncratically, or a pair of slashes to the left of the first line of each stanza (see Figure 4.3 showing f. 27r).[16] Red paraphs have been written over these dots and slashes to mark the first, third and fifth stanzas on each page, but blue paraphs have been supplied for the second and fourth stanzas only from f. 91v onwards, and then not on all folios. When this main scribe of MS Gg.4.27 came to copy *The Canterbury Tales* in the same book, he wrote double slashes in many tales (and similarities in their placement to other manuscripts suggest he is following his exemplar), but finished paraphs were provided only for the first few portraits in The General Prologue and then irregularly from The Pardoner's Tale to the conclusion of *The Tales*. There is also inconsistency in how fully headings have been supplied; for some tales, the headings have been provided in red, but scribbled directions for headings identifying part-divisions in The Man of Law's Tale were never followed and have been erased.

Similarly incomplete or inconsistent finishing occurs often enough in Middle English manuscripts to make it clear that scribes and others responsible for finishing

[15] Such notes for headings appear in BL, MS Harley 7335, a manuscript of *The Canterbury Tales* – to choose one example among many.

[16] It is possible that not all of these guides were written by the main scribe of CUL, MS Gg.4.27.

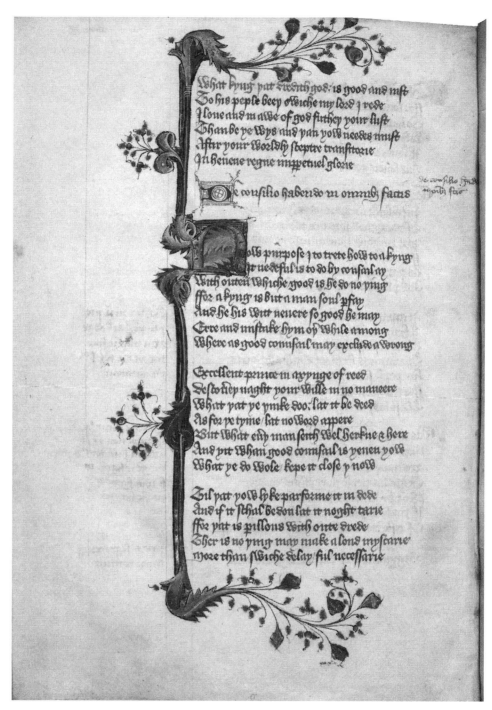

Figure 4.2 BL, MS Harley 4866, f. 85v: ruling a column for glosses.

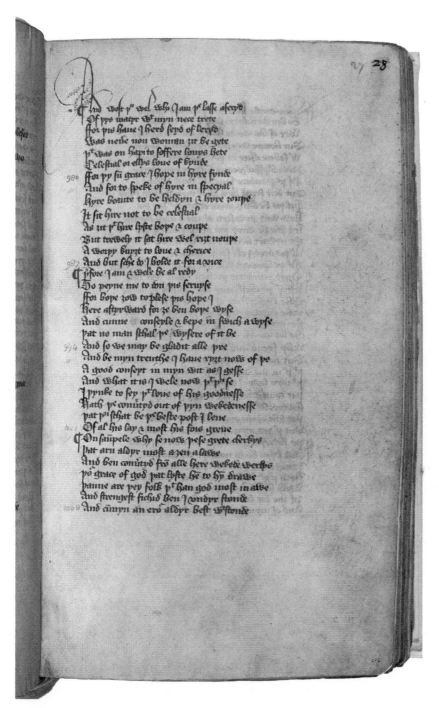

Figure 4.3 CUL, MS Gg.4.27, f. 27r: page layout and the marking of stanzas.

a book did not always work in sequence through a given work or through a book's contents but instead could finish individual quires or even bifolia in some other order. Nor should we assume that a scribe had to complete the copying of his text before he began to finish his manuscript. Without impairing his efficiency, a scribe might finish a quire or set of quires after he copied the text, and then continue with writing and finishing another portion of his book. Such an organization of work would make sense particularly if the scribe was putting together a collection of shorter texts, or was receiving in pieces his exemplars for a longer work. Moreover, the finishing of a manuscript did not necessarily proceed from the most common or simplest elements of page design to the most time-consuming and expensive. While there are incomplete paraphs and headings in CUL, MS Gg.4.27, in other respects the manuscript's design is, at least in places, quite finished. It includes a programme of illustration in *The Canterbury Tales* and several kinds of initials – champs, blue-and-red pen-flourished initials and red Lombardic capitals.[17]

There are two important corollaries to this model of finishing a book in stages. The first is that access to exemplars was not always reliable; one can imagine scenarios where an exemplar might be withdrawn after a text was copied but before all elements of page design had been finished. The second is that some aspects of page design might depend more on continued access to exemplars than others did. It would have been easiest for a scribe to provide guide letters for large initials and slashes or other indicators for paraphs as he copied his text; that scribe or another artisan, when he came to finish the manuscript, could be guided by these without needing to refer again to the exemplar.[18] Other kinds of material, such as the full versions of headings and longer marginalia, which required more writing and were less integrated with the text, seem less often to have been sketched in as the scribe wrote his text and would thus have been more vulnerable to omission if the withdrawal of an exemplar before a manuscript was finished suddenly made them unavailable.

Opportunities for inconsistency also arose when production of a manuscript involved multiple exemplars or more than one scribe. A scribe shifting, for whatever reason, from one exemplar to another might simply reproduce his differing layouts in the portions of text he copied from each. For example, the copy of Chaucer's *Troilus* in CUL, MS Gg.4.27 follows one textual tradition in Books I–II, but another in Books III–V, although it is not certain whether the scribe of MS Gg.4.27 was himself responsible for this conflation or whether he was working from a conflated exemplar.[19] Whichever is the case, that the scribe wrote running heads

---

[17] Compare Cambridge, St Catharine's College, MS 7, a copy of Gower's *Confessio Amantis* which has blue-and-gold paraphs in its top margins, presumably intended to punctuate page heads which were never supplied: see Emmerson, 'Reading Gower in a Manuscript Culture', 153, n.28.

[18] Although probably they often did, if the exemplar was still available.

[19] Root (ed.), *Troilus and Criseyde*, liii–liv; Windeatt (ed.), *Troilus and Criseyde*, 70.

in Books III–V only, and only irregularly, probably bears some relationship to the shift in textual affiliation.

A scribe might also combine exemplars in other ways. Marzec has identified instances in the tradition of Hoccleve's *The Regiment of Princes* in which a scribe drew on one manuscript for his text, but another for the Latin marginalia which appear quite consistently in the manuscripts of this work.[20] Or, a scribe could combine elements of page design from more than one exemplar. Siân Echard concludes that this was probably the case for some manuscripts of Gower's *Confessio Amantis* which place most glosses in the text column but insert into the margins others which were not available in all branches of the tradition.[21]

Such collation for elements of design could occur after production of a manuscript was essentially complete. In a very early copy of *The Canterbury Tales*, Oxford, Corpus Christi College, MS 198, the scribe appears to have obtained a second exemplar which contained many glosses, headings and paraphs not present in his first, but he appears not to have obtained the second exemplar until this fairly deluxe manuscript was largely finished.[22] In several parts of *The Tales*, the scribe copied these elements from the second exemplar, but almost always in a smaller script or even in a faint ink or drypoint; and paraphs do not precede most of the glosses drawn from his second exemplar, as they do those drawn from the first exemplar he had used for his text. This disparity suggests that he added glosses from that second source after he or another artisan had provided the manuscript's paraphs. This instance and other comparable ones illustrate scribes' interest in accumulating information about how a text could be presented, even if including it seemed somewhat to spoil the consistency and visual appeal which they had otherwise taken pains to achieve.

If more than one scribe worked on a manuscript, differing levels of interest in page design or uncertainties in supervision could lead to differing practices with layout. Such variation can be seen in TCC, MS R.3.2, a manuscript of Gower's *Confessio Amantis* produced by five scribes (the so-called 'Trinity Gower'), some of whom copied the poem's commentary and other marginal material faithfully while others essentially ignored it.[23] In BodL, MS Rawl. poet. 149, a copy of *The*

---

[20] Marzec, 'The Latin Marginalia of the *Regiment of Princes*', 272–3, 278.

[21] Echard, 'Glossing Gower', 239, n.9.

[22] Oxford, Corpus Christi College, MS 198 was produced by the prolific scribe now known as Scribe D, whose manuscripts were first identified by Doyle and Parkes in 'The Production of Copies'; see here also Mooney, Chapter 9. Joel Fredell called attention to the faint paraphs added to The Knight's Tale of Oxford, Corpus Christi College 198 in 'The Lowly Paraf', 229; the present comments are based also on my study of this manuscript.

[23] Echard remarks similar variation in other copies of Gower's *Confessio*: 'In those manuscripts which include more than one hand, the treatment of the speaker markers often changes as the hands do'; see 'Dialogues and Monologues', 74.

Canterbury Tales, as many as five scribes seem to have reproduced the page design from one exemplar until partway through The Merchant's Tale, but from that point to the work's conclusion, all copied by a further sixth scribe, different kinds of glosses were included. While the text of this portion also apparently derived from a different exemplar, the shift in glossing almost certainly owes something to the final scribe's preferences.

In the Trinity Gower and the Rawl. poet. 149 copy of *The Canterbury Tales*, each scribe was responsible for executing (or not) the layout in the section of text that he copied, but other divisions of labour were possible. In another copy of *The Canterbury Tales* in Philadelphia, Rosenbach Library, MS f. 1084/1, two scribes wrote the text, but one of these wrote virtually all the book's headings and glosses. (See Figure 4.4, showing f. 23v.) According to Susanna Fein, in BodL, MS Douce 302, which collects the poems of John Audelay along with other works, one scribe copied virtually all of the texts 'and the other has provided the rubrics and corrections'.[24]

The relationship between finishing the page design and correcting the text, which Fein observes through the division of labour in the specific case of the manuscript of Audelay's poems, was a more general phenomenon. When a scribe returned to his exemplar in order to copy such elements as glosses, headings and page heads, he would have had an opportunity for spot-checking (at least) his text. A copy of the Middle English prose *Brut* in HEHL, MS HM 133 gives some idea of how variously finishing and correction might be intertwined. The scribe has used red to 'finish' the corrections (perhaps at the same time as he was writing the chapter headings) by, for example, striking through in red words which he had subpuncted in text ink as he was writing the text. But the scribe has also apparently passed through the manuscript again with the usual ink of the text at some stage after the finishing, for in at least one place he has used text ink to correct a red chapter heading. We can also see the finishing of design and the correction of text combined in scribes' use of multiple exemplars. Marzec concludes that, in one of the copies of Hoccleve's *The Regiment of Princes*, in which different exemplars were drawn on for the text and marginalia, the scribe used the source of his marginalia also to provide some corrected readings in his text.[25] Similarly, the scribe of Oxford, Corpus Christi College, MS 198 made a few corrections to his text of *The Canterbury Tales* from his more densely designed source of additional glosses, paraphs and headings.

---

[24] Susanna Fein, 'Good Ends in the Audelay Manuscript', 98.

[25] Marzec, 'The Latin Marginalia of the *Regiment of Princes*', 278. The manuscript is BodL, MS Bodley 221.

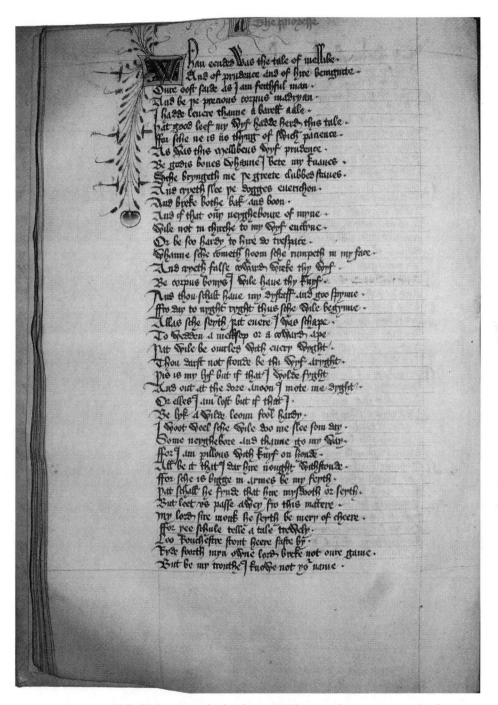

Figure 4.4 Philadelphia, Rosenbach Library, MS f. 1084/1, f. 23v: a running head, albeit an inaccurate one.

In two further manuscripts of *The Canterbury Tales*, we can see with particular clarity the scribes making use of additional exemplars when they found that those with which they apparently began lacked elements of design. These examples reveal how much importance was accorded to these elements. Both manuscripts, apparently produced by London artisans, suggest that the scribes considered attention to layout a significant part of their commission; they attest to the cultural trends outlined by Parkes by showing how a detailed page design seems to have become a routine expectation for scribes and readers. But in these instances, we can also see the scribes making choices in favour of convenience or simplicity. These choices remind us that scribes were engaged in a commercial enterprise, which demanded above all that they produce a saleable copy of a long and complex text, quite possibly to deadlines.[26]

The first of these manuscripts of *The Canterbury Tales* is BL, MS Add. 35286. Glosses, rubrics and paraphs appear to have been sparse in the main textual exemplar of this manuscript, and running heads absent, prompting the scribe to draw on, and perhaps seek out, a secondary exemplar in which these aspects of page design were plentiful.[27] The scribe combined his exemplars by discarding virtually all the glosses and rubrics in his textual exemplar, even some not available in his secondary exemplar, and taking over wholesale those in that secondary exemplar. He seems not to have made the effort to compare his two sources carefully enough to ensure that he accumulated all the rubrics and glosses available to him, choosing instead to rely on the exemplar that supplied more of these elements. The scribe of BL, MS Add. 35286 also adopted from his supplementary exemplar (although less systematically than he adopted its page design) details for the text of *The Canterbury Tales*.[28] His practice suggests that textual collation and correction may sometimes have been occasioned by a scribe's comparison of the layouts of two manuscripts. Substantial differences between the two manuscripts in their quantities of such material as headings and glosses, and thus the need to 'correct' one copy by the other, would have been more immediately obvious than differences in the details of their texts.[29]

The scribe of the second manuscript, BodL, MS Rawl. poet. 141, was relying on a textual exemplar with virtually no rubrics or paragraph marks, although it did

---

[26] The scribes' decision to seek additional exemplars to solve the need for elements of design, rather than to devise from scratch such elements, might be compared with the practice of artisans who sometimes supplied illustrations in manuscripts and early prints by taking over, perhaps with adaptations, existing programmes of illustration already used for other texts.

[27] We can make this inference partly because there survives a closely affiliated manuscript, BL, MS Harley 7335, in which design elements are sparse in most tales.

[28] Compare the behaviour of the scribe of BodL, MS Bodley 221 of Hoccleve's *The Regiment of Princes*, discussed above.

[29] See Wakelin, pp. 55–6 above, on other processes of correction.

contain a corpus of glosses.[30] Therefore he too made use of a supplemental exemplar – perhaps the same one that the scribe of BL, MS Add. 35286 had found, or a closely related one. The scribe of Rawl. poet. 141 incorporated the paraphs, rubrics and page heads of this second exemplar regularly, though less comprehensively than had the scribe of BL, MS Add. 35286. He carefully compared its glosses with those in his textual exemplar, combining these two sources and, where both offered glosses at the same line, selecting the more informative gloss – that which contained more material drawn from the text's Latin sources or a fuller description of the text's content.[31] It is rather startling that although the scribe of BodL, MS Rawl. poet. 141 appears to have collated his two exemplars for elements of design more carefully than did the scribe of BL, MS Add. 35286, he appears not to have collated the two exemplars' texts – even failing to pick up from his secondary exemplar several tales missing from his primary exemplar. Perhaps this scribe thought that the appearance of completeness created by the dense page design was more important in appealing to a patron or potential customer than a text that was actually complete.

In the sparseness of their headings, the primary exemplars of these two manuscripts were highly unusual within the tradition of *The Canterbury Tales*, and it was probably this lack specifically that pushed the scribes of BL, MS Add. 35286 and BodL, MS Rawl. poet. 141 to seek and draw on supplemental exemplars. That sparseness in their textual exemplars shows that elements of design could be lost wholesale. Headings for prologues and tales seem so fundamental that the attrition in these cases probably resulted from accidents of production, but other manuscripts which lack entire categories of design elements seem to reflect a lack of interest on the part of scribes or their patrons. Echard judges that a few manuscripts lack virtually all the marginal apparatus of Gower's *Confessio Amantis* because of scribal lack of interest.[32] In at least one manuscript of *The Canterbury Tales*, BL, MS Egerton 2726, the two scribes have similarly dropped everything which their exemplar apparently included in the margins – glosses, but also some headings within tales. The general absence from the *b* manuscripts of *The Canterbury Tales* of glosses found in all other groups argues strongly that a general stripping-away of marginal material occurred when the *b* archetype was produced. In such cases, a scribe or patron may have decided not to expend, at least for the time being, the resources that would have been required to finish a manuscript or may not have been interested in what perhaps seemed like a superfluous scholarly apparatus.

---

[30] Manly and Rickert, *The Text of The Canterbury Tales*, 1.451, concluded that the text of BodL, MS Rawl. poet. 141 was copied directly from Chicago, University Library, MS 563. Glosses shared uniquely by these manuscripts support this conclusion.

[31] The use of multiple exemplars raises any number of questions about how such work would be organized. It might be supposed that a scribe would mark up his first exemplar with additional material from his second, although Chicago, University Library, MS 563 shows no trace of such collation.

[32] 'Glossing Gower', 239–40.

Over successive generations of copying, accident and intention might combine to 'wear away' elements of page design. For example, while no copy from CUL, MS Gg.4.27 is known certainly to exist, we might wonder whether a scribe who worked from a similar manuscript which preserved only traces of a programme of paraphs might be less likely to reproduce those traces than he would to reproduce a finished array of full-sized, coloured paraphs.[33] The data on paraphs in manuscripts of the B version of Langland's *Piers Plowman* suggest that some manuscripts reproduced with considerable fidelity a programme established early in the tradition, but that in others all or nearly all of the paraphs were dropped – whether over time or in a single stage of copying it is difficult to know.[34] This deterioration of layout through multiple generations of copying might help explain why the manuscripts of *Piers Plowman* and *The Canterbury Tales* are less homogeneous in design than those of works which seem to have been copied less often.

Scribal decisions about whether to include elements of design present in their exemplars may well have been influenced by the amount and coherence of such material as well as by its degree of finish. Thus, for example, the glosses for Gower's *Confessio Amantis* and Hoccleve's *The Regiment of Princes*, both more consistent than those for *The Canterbury Tales*, are also more widespread in the manuscripts. The greater density of page design may have helped persuade scribes that this material really was an integral part of the work, and that it rewarded the additional labour needed to reproduce it. More speculatively, we might wonder whether similar thinking could lead to variations in a scribe's practice as he copied a single, longer work. In some instances, a scribe began including elements of design partway through his copying. In such scribal variation we may detect a process whereby a scribe became progressively more receptive to what he found in his exemplar. For example, to return once more to CUL, MS Gg.4.27, in the first three Books of Chaucer's *Troilus*, there are no large initials apart from those at the beginnings of Books and prologues, and the scribe has not left spaces or guide letters for any. In Books IV and V, however, there survive nineteen blue-and-red pen-flourished initials, two or three lines in height and all well prepared for by the scribe. While the shift of textual affiliation between Books II and III, discussed earlier, may help explain the shift to planning for and including large initials, other factors seem also to be at work here.[35] This instance might be compared with the copy of *The Canterbury Tales* in BL, MS Harley 7335, where the scribe

---

[33] Manly and Rickert, *The Text of The Canterbury Tales*, 1.124, speculate that the single leaf now surviving as BodL, MS Douce d.4 might have been copied from CUL, MS Gg.4.27.

[34] Benson and Blanchfield, *The Manuscripts of Piers Plowman*, 240–313; the presence of a derived programme of paraphs is especially clear beginning in Passus 3, where three composite manuscripts of *Piers Plowman* join the B version tradition.

[35] No other surviving manuscript of *Troilus* contains a comparable number in Books IV–V or anywhere else in the poem.

Robert Allen began to provide spaces and guide letters for one-line initials in The Franklin's Tale, and continued to do so in the following tales.[36]

The opposite phenomenon certainly does occur, of a scribe copying elements of design less faithfully and thoroughly as he progressed through a text. Echard observes that scribal 'fatigue or loss of interest' can be perceived in the treatment of speaker markers in some manuscripts of Gower's *Confessio Amantis*; moreover, she detects a pattern of carelessness with and omission of several kinds of glosses in the final two books of the poem.[37] This tendency to begin strongly and then taper off can also be observed when scribes are apparently devising elements of page design. In the copy of *The Canterbury Tales* in CUL, MS Ii.3.26, there appears in The Knight's Tale a unique set of glosses outlining the tale's content and also naming characters as the text introduces them. Only the latter kind continue beyond The Knight's Tale, however, and these also cease early in The Squire's Tale, not far through the manuscript. (See Figure 4.5.) In Oxford, Oriel College, MS 79, a scribe apparently lacking access to the traditional scheme of paraphs for the B text of *Piers Plowman* began to provide guide marks for his own set of paraphs, but these soon become sporadic, then very sparse, and finally disappear entirely.[38]

More systematic selection also occurred. Perhaps sometimes anticipating the audience's taste, scribes could reproduce certain kinds of glosses they apparently considered most useful or interesting, without troubling to copy others.[39] The scribe of PML, MS M.249, when copying *The Canterbury Tales* from Lichfield Cathedral, MS 29, omitted its source glosses but reproduced instead other kinds which appear at nearby lines, such as those explaining difficult words. Conflict between elements of design could provoke scribal judgements that some elements were more important than others. Echard points out that markers indicating who was speaking in Gower's *Confessio* were sometimes crowded out where borders or the long commentaries had to be fitted onto the page.[40] Limited space in the margins seems

---

[36] These are the tales of the Physician and Pardoner; the remaining tales have now been lost from this manuscript. Manly and Rickert, *The Text of The Canterbury Tales*, I. 233, do suggest a change in affiliation (and thus perhaps exemplar) for The Franklin's Tale, but in the following tales the text returns to the tradition it had been following earlier. Thus a change of exemplar on Allen's part, or somewhere in the copying that preceded his production of BL, MS Harley 7335, does not seem to explain fully the introduction of large initials in several tales.

[37] Echard, 'Dialogues and Monologues', 60–1, and 'Glossing Gower', 240–1 (see also 245, n.24, on the tendency to begin writing a programme of glosses but then abandon them).

[38] See the description by Benson and Blanchfield, *The Manuscripts of Piers Plowman*, 89.

[39] Cf. Echard, 'Glossing Gower', 240: 'the manuscripts suggest a tendency to regard the glosses as more dispensable than the verses, and some of the marginalia as more dispensable than the rest of it'.

[40] Echard, 'Dialogues and Monologues', 62. She also identifies a fascinating instance where the scribe seems to have selected speaker markers for the sake of the general appearance of his pages, so that some folios include a number of speaker markers in a balanced arrangement but others none at all, even though his exemplar probably included some speaker markers at these lines of Gower's *Confessio*.

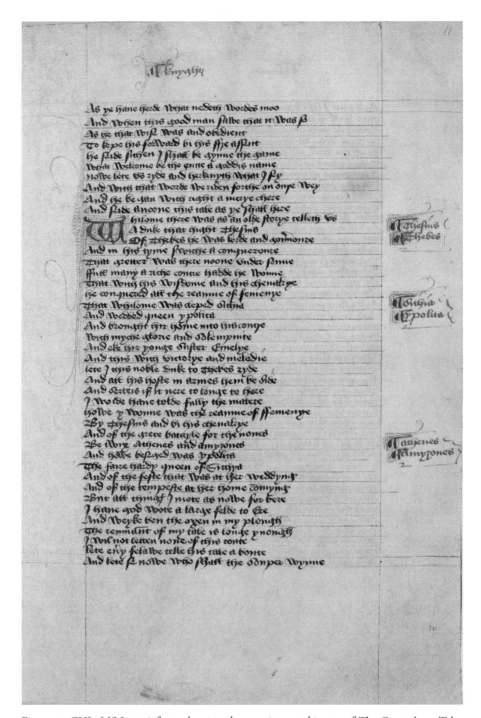

Figure 4.5 CUL, MS Ii.3.26, f. 11r, showing glosses unique to this copy of The Canterbury Tales.

to have been one factor influencing the scribe of Longleat, MS 29 when he chose to include content markers in his copy of The Parson's Tale but omitted numerous names of authorities present in the margins of his exemplar. By contrast, Adam Pinkhurst, copying The Parson's Tale in the larger and more lavish HEHL, MS Ellesmere 26.C.9, perhaps from the same exemplar as that used for Longleat, MS 29, preserved all its glosses.

Instead of, or in addition to, selecting design elements from an exemplar, book producers might modify in various ways those elements they did select for their manuscripts. One situation that required such a practice involved a manuscript produced from an exemplar of a different 'class' or level of decoration. Pearsall remarks on how the manuscripts of Gower's *Confessio* reflect a 'sliding scale' of luxury, which enabled producers to preserve a hierarchy of decoration. In what he calls the 'economy deluxe' manuscripts, the borders found in the most lavish manuscripts remain at the most important textual divisions, but pen-flourished initials replace champs elsewhere, and undecorated paraphs are substituted for decorated ones.[41] In other instances, the hierarchical distinctions between elements were lost. When printing *The Canterbury Tales*, Wynkyn de Worde made use of a manuscript that appears to have marked transitions within tales using paraphs and one or two kinds of capitals, but these have all been reproduced as paraphs in De Worde's print. This manuscript was a second exemplar for De Worde, which allowed him to add design elements to a text drawn largely from Caxton's second printing of *The Tales*, and the challenges of collating his two exemplars probably contributed to his decision to simplify the design he was adopting.[42] The scribe of TCC, MS R.3.15 seems to have made a somewhat similar set of calculations as he collated two exemplars. In Chaucer's Melibee he took from a secondary exemplar content markers and source glosses, but, while failing to copy indexing glosses and speaker markers that the exemplar included, he seems to have been prompted by them to highlight many of the names of speakers and of authorities by underlining them. Such instances of 'conversion' of design elements were probably more often a matter of the scale of decoration sliding downward, as works such as Gower's *Confessio* circulated beyond a primary audience located largely among the highest classes to a more heterogeneous readership during the fifteenth century. There are, however, also instances of deluxe manuscripts produced from modest exemplars; these suggest that a kind of consensus existed among book producers about how to mark certain divisions within

[41] Pearsall, 'The Manuscripts and Illustrations of Gower's Works', 89–90. The copying of PML, MS M.249 from Lichfield, Cathedral, MS 29, a deluxe manuscript, provides a comparable instance from the tradition of *The Canterbury Tales*.

[42] A similar 'flattening' of a hierarchy of decoration appears to have occurred somewhere in the derivation of BL, MS Add. 35286 and BodL, MS Rawl. poet. 141, discussed above.

longer texts – for example, when resources allowed, to use borders to identify the beginnings of books or tales.[43]

Such elements as running heads, rubrics (including titles) and glosses were commonly written in Latin or French, along with English, and scribes translated them with some frequency from one of these languages into another. BL, MS Lansdowne 851 belongs to a large group of manuscripts of *The Canterbury Tales* which generally record the headings for prologues and tales in English, but here they have been translated into Latin. The archetype of another group of manuscripts of *The Canterbury Tales*, Manly and Rickert's *a* family, appears to have included rubrics partly in Latin, partly in English, most probably resulting from a partial translation into Latin from some still earlier archetype. Various descendants of the *a* archetype extend this translation; in BL, MS Add. 5140, all the rubrics are in Latin, and JRL, MS 113 makes them consistently in Latin from the beginning through to the incipit to The Squire's Tale, but then, like some other members of this group, leaves the remainder in English. Incomplete programmes of translation could produce various mixtures of languages in rubrics. In BL, MS Egerton 2864, the scribe several times wrote the explicit for one part of *The Tales* in Latin or English, and then immediately wrote the incipit for the following part in the other language. More thorough mixing may be seen in a rubric for The Franklin's Tale in BL, MS Egerton 2726: 'Hic desinit [Here ends] prologus de Frankeleyne et incipit fabula sua [begins his tale] de Rokkes de Bretayne.' The polyglot wording suggests that this derives ultimately from an English incipit which has been partially translated, perhaps in distinct stages, into Latin and French. Important manuscripts of Chaucer's *Troilus* conclude with a Latin title, and copies of Chaucer's short poems provide titles in French, Latin or English. It is tempting to suppose that providing French or Latin rubrics and titles was sometimes a way of adding prestige to a text without putting off readers who could not have understood anything more substantial or less formulaic in either of those languages. But this practice was also observed by writers who presumably had less commercial motives, but may nevertheless have sought to add prestige to their books, such as Hoccleve, who provides French headings for his poems in his holograph collections. In other cases, the provision of certain extra-texual material in languages other than English may reflect its being intended only for certain readers. Such intentions might explain a widespread treatment of Nicholas Love's *Mirror of the Blessed Life of Jesus Christ*, which was to supply chapter headings in English but marginal elements in Latin. The language of some kinds of marginalia was fairly stable, but content markers such as those in many copies of The Parson's Tale seem to have been translated readily between English and Latin,

---

[43] Among manuscripts of *The Canterbury Tales*, the apparent copying of Tokyo, Takamiya MS 24 ('the Devonshire manuscript') from BL, MS Egerton 2726 is an example of a deluxe manuscript copied from a more modest one.

and even the extended commentaries of Gower's *Confessio* were occasionally translated into English.[44]

The scholarly tendency to draw sharp contrasts between the two early manuscripts of *The Canterbury Tales* made by Adam Pinkhurst, the Hengwrt and Ellesmere manuscripts, can obscure the fact that in the rubrics of both we find instances of subtle and purposeful variation, as sections of the work were identified as an 'envoi' or 'wordes' or a leave-taking (in addition to those called prologues and tales), but also of uncertainty or incompleteness, as Pinkhurst sometimes wrote 'Explicit' without specifying what, exactly, was concluding. Others among the earliest manuscripts also reflect varying kinds of inconsistency or incompleteness in rubrication. As the tradition of *The Canterbury Tales* evolved, there developed a general tendency to reduce the inconsistent organization of these earliest manuscripts to a simple alternation of prologue and tale. For example, the rubrics of BL, MS Lansdowne 851, in addition to replacing English with Latin, impose this prologue/tale structure on the work with absolute consistency. This manuscript, and others, also made rubrics more regular by including both an explicit and incipit at every transition in *The Tales*, whereas Pinkhurst and Scribe D sometimes provided only incipits in their copies. The most usual practice in the rubrics and running heads in *The Canterbury Tales* was to identify tales by teller, but the Hengwrt and Ellesmere manuscripts preserve rubrics for a few tales which also identify the tale's subject – for example, 'the Manciples tale of the crow' or 'the Merchantes tale of Januarie'. Some later manuscripts, such as BodL, MS Hatton donat. 1, show that scribes expanded this programme, modifying rubrics to other tales so that they likewise identified subject along with teller.[45]

Such efforts by scribes to expand and make more regular what they found in exemplars are witnessed also by other kinds of extra-textual material. The work of the 'Egerton glossator' of *The Canterbury Tales*, brought to scholarly attention by Susan Schibanoff, is an example of such practice.[46] This glossator worked from an exemplar which included source glosses on many tales, though none on The Wife of Bath's Prologue, and although the 'Egerton glossator' expended unique energy there, he also added and expanded source glosses and other kinds throughout *The Canterbury Tales*. BL, MS Harley 1758 was based on exemplars which included some

<hr/>

[44] Echard's 'Glossing Gower' focusses on two such manuscripts.

[45] The rubrics of BodL, MS Hatton donat. 1 do not, however, identify the topics of all tales. When tales were selected for inclusion in other anthologies or miscellanies, scribes usually substituted headings and page heads identifying subjects for those identifying tellers, presumably because the latter kind were far less useful outside the pilgrimage framework.

[46] Schibanoff, 'The New Reader and Female Textuality', considers the glossator whose work survives in BL, MS Egerton 2864 and BL, MS Add. 5140, and who presumably prepared the exemplar shared by these two manuscripts. My observations here provide a context for, but do not undermine, Schibanoff's arguments that this glossator responded strongly to what he found in the text of The Wife of Bath's Prologue.

glosses on *The Canterbury Tales*, but its producers expanded on them considerably, especially by adding in the prose tales indexing glosses and content markers which could be derived easily from the text. Echard has pointed out that the earliest manuscripts do not mark all the shifts in speaker in Gower's *Confessio*, and while the programme of speaker markers was thinned out in some later manuscripts, in others the scribes added such markers to make the programme more comprehensive.[47]

Certainly other factors also prompted scribes to add elements of design to the texts they copied. Most obviously, scribes' attention to design can sometimes be considered a measure of what they were most interested in, or expected would most interest their patrons. Thus one portion of a longer work might be given extraordinary attention, as when the 'Egerton glossator' furnished copious passages from the Vulgate in The Wife of Bath's Prologue, or the makers of TCC, MS R.3.3 supplied numerous content markers on Chaucer's Melibee but very few glosses elsewhere in *The Canterbury Tales*. Or, we can detect particular interests in annotations that run throughout a manuscript, as in the explanations of classical allusions in Chaucer's *Troilus and Criseyde* offered in BL, MS Harley 2392. Design elements also might be added where scribes or patrons supposed they were needed to clarify the structure of longer works in which the articulation of parts was somehow inadequate. The earliest manuscripts of Chaucer's *Troilus* mark prologues and books with headings and borders but very few other transitions, and later manuscripts preserve several scribal efforts to mark shifts in scene and speaker. Manuscripts of the Middle English prose *Brut* reflect a somewhat different practice. They regularly divide the chronicle into more than 200 chapters, some of them less than a page long. Initially, each king's reign generally occupies only one chapter, but particularly when the chronicle reaches the Norman and Plantaganet kings, several chapters are often devoted to a single reign. It seems that a number of scribes provided running heads identifying who was king at the period chronicled on that particular page. The scribes devised identifiers of the larger textual divisions to supplement the chapter headings which broke the text into many small pieces. A third factor prompting book producers to add design elements may have been the presence of clear markers of distinctions within a text – transitions that signalled a new speaker, episode or topic, or an inset text such as a letter or song. This factor may also help explain patterns in scribal annotation of Chaucer's *Troilus*, for example, as well as of The Knight's Tale and The Parson's Tale.

As well as these efforts by scribes and other book producers to transmit and devise aspects of page design, comparable processes also took place after primary production of a book was concluded. In some cases, readers themselves added various aids to reading, while in others they may have commissioned scribes to do so.

---

[47] Echard, 'Dialogues and Monologues', 60–1.

Sometimes such additions to a book resulted from collation, including with printed copies of the relevant texts once they had become available.[48] Elsewhere the finishing of a book's design may have had no such immediate and specific model, but was probably a simple matter of filling in elements such as page heads which had become more generally familiar, again perhaps especially through readers' experience of printed books. As books with more regular formats were produced, readers brought older books into line with the newer models.[49] The practice gives us an idea of how often reading might include collation, and that collation might inspire the ongoing 'finishing' of existing books.

This aspect of the reception of Middle English manuscripts would reward further exploration. In addition, scholarship could build on existing attempts to trace networks of influence among manuscripts of different Middle English works – to show how the format designed for one work might have been modelled on that found in copies of another.[50] We also could expand our reach in considering possible models for English practice. Parkes has magisterially surveyed precedents in the Latin tradition, especially in academic and devotional texts, but French and Italian manuscripts may sometimes have provided more immediate models for English practice in book design.[51] One can discern the broad migration of authority into English texts as they came to be laid out in the same ways as books of acknowledged authority – for example, copies of the Latin *auctores* carefully divided into parts and provided with commentary. It may, however, be possible to trace more local and specific connections between manuscripts and develop a more precise sense of how the status of English writing was negotiated with respect to other vernaculars.

In hypotheses about such networks of influence, the possible roles of authors must always be considered. There is room to develop more systematic methods for judging how far authors contributed to the page designs that survive in the manuscripts. Hoccleve's holograph copies of his poems provide unusually clear evidence

---

[48] For instance, in The General Prologue of *The Tales* in BodL, MS Laud misc. 739; or in the copy of *Confessio* in Washington DC, Folger Shakespeare Library, MS SM 1.

[49] In BL, MS Harley 7334 and Lincoln, Cathedral, MS 110, two manuscripts of *The Canterbury Tales*, multiple hands of the late fifteenth and sixteenth centuries have added running heads. In Cambridge, Magdalene College, MS Pepys 2006, a few titles for Chaucer's short poems were provided, often in explicits, by the two main scribes, but other titles have been added by later hands. In other manuscripts, later readers added titles at beginnings of works (when present, titles tended more often to appear in fifteenth-century manuscript explicits) and occasionally other elements such as tables of contents which had become standard in printed books.

[50] See Edwards and Hanna, 'Rotheley, the De Vere Circle, and the Ellesmere Chaucer' on the debt of the layout of Lydgate's *Siege of Thebes* in BL, MS Arundel 119 to Ellesmere; Doyle and Parkes, 'The Production of Copies of *The Canterbury Tales* and the *Confessio Amantis*', point out the similarity of BL, MS Arundel 38's *Regiment of Princes* to Ellesmere.

[51] Substantial beginnings have been made: for Chaucer by Kendrick, *Animating the Letter*, 217–25 and 'Linking *The Canterbury Tales*'; for Gower by Echard, 'Articulating the Author'.

for an author providing such elements as headings, paraphs and glosses as he pre-pared fair copies of his works. In addition, there is a consensus that the earliest manuscripts of *The Regiment of Princes*, production of which Hoccleve is believed to have overseen, reflect his intentions for the visual presentation of his work. Gower's authorship of the Latin commentary on *Confessio Amantis* is likewise gen-erally accepted; the grounds here seem to be its early attestation (even if scholars tend to be sceptical about Gower's direct oversight of the surviving manuscripts), its distinctive nature and its integration into a larger Latin apparatus including such elements as verse summaries of the narratives in *Confessio Amantis*.[52] About the extra-textual elements of early manuscripts of *The Canterbury Tales* there is much less scholarly agreement, no doubt because there are such sharply divergent views about that work's early publication history. For the most part, scholars have proposed only ad hoc arguments and assertions about specific aspects of those manuscripts' designs.[53]

We might consider two complementary ways of thinking about authors' involve-ment in book design when we do not have access to the kinds of evidence available for Hoccleve and Gower. On the one hand, it would be useful to recognize that in an age when the book-length work came to dominate literary production, those we classify as authors and translators – not always sharply distinct categories – must, as a matter of practical necessity, have given thought to aspects of book production which scholarship has more conventionally assigned to scribes and other artisans. While conceiving and then writing a work in which narratives were to be assigned to more than twenty pilgrims, Chaucer might well have considered how the man-uscripts would make clear which pilgrim was speaking and when. In other words, he, like other authors and translators, sometimes thought (and probably worked) like a scribe. Moreover, extrapolating from the default procedure suggested here, that scribes worked from exemplars whenever possible, would lead to the conclu-sion that whatever design an author might provide for his texts was likely to have some influence on subsequent scribal copies. Scribes also introduced variants into what they found in their exemplars, and the results of this process certainly present challenges to any attempt to distinguish the endeavours of authors thinking and acting as scribes from the work of later scribes. In at least some instances, however, book producers seem to have reduced subtleties of design to more commonplace models, in ways comparable to the practices of scribes in handling texts. In such instances we might detect conflict between authorial innovation and artisanal

---

[52] Echard does not directly address the question of Gower's possible responsibility for the speaker markers of the *Confessio* in 'Dialogues and Monologues'.

[53] For example, on the question of whether manuscript headings identifying the pilgrim-narrator of *The Canterbury Tales* as 'Chaucer' are scribal or authorial in origin, contrast Delany, *The Naked Text*, 33–4, with Bowers, *Chaucer and Langland*, 80–1.

convention. It would be rewarding to continue describing the treatment of specific design elements within textual traditions in order to develop a *usus scribendi* and determine whether it might be contrasted with the probable practices of authors. The methods of textual criticism may have much to offer book history's consideration of page design.

5

Decorating and illustrating the page

MARTHA DRIVER AND MICHAEL ORR

This chapter reviews recent research on the technical processes and identities of the artists who decorated and illustrated English books as well as the forms of illustration in them. It argues that the period between 1350 and the earliest years of printing was one in which book illustration, like other aspects of book production, gradually became a more organized and more commercial activity. Much of the illustration and decoration in manuscripts and printed books of the late fourteenth, fifteenth and sixteenth centuries was anonymous, driven by convention, instructions and models, and organized by commercial producers. Yet that work was also affected by the inconsistency and lack of centralization of processes of production that shape other aspects of book production in this period.

The lack of centralized procedures for illustrating books, or records of these, means that our knowledge of the technical processes of illustrating and decorating books must be drawn from a wide range of sources: recipe books, limning treatises and artists' handbooks; illuminated manuscripts themselves, especially unfinished books showing the stages of decoration; directions to illuminators; contemporary word lists; documentary evidence in wills and legal records; modelbooks and sketchbooks; costings for manuscripts in account books; notes in manuscripts; and images of illuminators.[1] Central to the following discussion are two key terms: 'limner' and 'shop'. A limner (from the Middle English 'limner' or the Anglo-French 'lymnour') was an individual who practised the art of illuminating manuscripts, typically as a commercial endeavour outside a monastic context: the word first appears as a trade surname in Middle English records *c.*1230.[2] From the thirteenth century onwards, records increasingly document the existence of rented spaces in

---

[1] For some recent treatments of the techniques of manuscript illumination, see De Hamel, *Medieval Craftsmen: Scribes and Illuminators*; Alexander, *Medieval Illuminators*; Lovett, *Calligraphy, Illumination and Heraldry*; Quandt and Noel, 'From Calf to Codex'; De Hamel, *British Library Guide*; Watson, *Illuminated Manuscripts*; Panayotova and Webber, 'Making an Illuminated Manuscript'; Royce-Roll, 'Materials, Preparations and Recipes'.

[2] *MED*, s.v. 'lymnour'.

which limners worked. Usually referred to as 'shops' or 'workshops', these spaces were often located in proximity to others in the book trade in urban centres such as Oxford and London.[3] By the mid fourteenth century, the London limners had formed a guild; theirs was one of those that came together with other makers and sellers of books to form the London Company of Stationers in 1403.[4] But the practices and the careers of those designated 'limner' in subsidy rolls and cartularies, the activities that took place in rented 'shops', and the commercial and social relations that dictated the shape of guilds – all these were varied and complex, as the discussion that follows shows.

In late medieval England, limners tended to work in one of three principal techniques: a fully painted style utilizing a range of opaque pigments, often combined with gold; pen-and-ink drawing; or a coloured drawing style. The fully painted style is exemplified by the famous frontispiece to Chaucer's *Troilus and Criseyde*, now CCCC, MS 61, and by the miniatures and borders in the extensively illustrated copy of John Gower's *Confessio Amantis* in PML, MS M. 126. Manuscripts illustrated in pen and ink are found frequently from the fourteenth century forward, and the style becomes increasingly popular through the fifteenth century. One of the finest examples of a manuscript illustrated in the ink-drawn style is BodL, MS Bodley 283, a copy of *The Mirroure of the World* dating from c.1470–80, with twenty-five pen-drawn illustrations. Among manuscripts illustrated in the coloured drawing style, there are four variants: tinted outline drawings, in which a dominant underlying pen line is combined with coloured tints or washes of pigment, as occurs in the Chaundler manuscript, TCC, MS R.14.5; coloured outline drawings, in which stronger colours are combined with the dominant pen line, exemplified by the de Guileville's *Pilgrimage of the Life of Man* in BL, MS Cotton Tiberius A.vii; coloured drawings, in which the pen line is subservient to pigment applied with a painterly technique, as seen, for example, in the *Gawain*, or *Pearl*, manuscript, BL, MS Cotton Nero A.x part 3 (ff. 41–2, 60, 82, 94, 129–30); and reserved pen drawings, in which figures or objects are depicted without full colour against full painted or gilded backgrounds, as, for example, in the *Privity of the Passion* in TCC, MS B.10.12, where the style occurs in conjunction with the coloured outline technique.[5] In late medieval England, individual artists tended to specialize in only one of the three major techniques, although occasionally some artists, such as William Abell (discussed further below), worked both in full pigments and coloured drawing.

As well as displaying a range of styles of illustration, English books contain a variety of illustrative and decorative formats.[6] Illustrations are usually placed within

---

[3] See the discussion below of collaboration and the location of shops.

[4] Blayney, *The Stationers' Company before the Charter*, 15.

[5] Scott, *Later Gothic Manuscripts*, 1.50–1; see also Rickert, *Painting in Britain*, 183–5.

[6] Rickert, 'Illumination'; Rickert, *Painting in Britain*; Scott, 'Design, Decoration and Illustration'; Scott, *Later Gothic Manuscripts*, 1.37–43.

books as rectangular miniatures (framed or unframed), marginal scenes or historiated initials. Rectangular miniatures typically occupy the full width of the justified text area and may range in vertical height from the full height of the text ruling to a quarter-page or less. In books with two columns of text, miniatures may be restricted in width by the vertical rulings for single columns or may extend fully across the page justification. Some manuscripts may contain miniatures that are inset within the text block but that do not extend across the full width of the justification.[7] One distinctive feature of a number of English vernacular books during this period is the placement of illustrations in the margins of the page outside the text justification. In an exceptional manuscript such as the copy of Lydgate's *Troy Book* in JRL, MS Eng. 1, multi-figured narrative scenes with landscape or architectural settings may be embedded within the border decoration (Figure 5.1).[8] More commonly, for example in the so-called 'Douce' copy of *Piers Plowman*, BodL, MS Douce 104, the 'Ellesmere' Chaucer, HEHL, MS Ellesmere 26.C.9, and a copy of *The South English Legendary* in BodL, MS Tanner 17, single unframed marginal figures occur in isolation in the vertical margins of the page (Figure 5.2).[9]

Historiated initials occur with some frequency in books throughout the period. The size of individual initials is usually based on a multiple of line widths and is determined by the scribe leaving the appropriate amount of space blank when copying the text – some representative examples from the period discussed here are the eight-line historiated initial that appears in a copy of Ranulph Higden's *Polychronicon*, BL, MS Add. 24194, f. 36r, and the five-line initial in *The Master of the Game* in BodL, MS Douce 335, f. 18v. A variety of other types of decorated initials and borders can be found in English manuscripts that are specific to this period and for which there was developed a contemporary vocabulary: sources refer to the 'champ', 'sprynget', 'vinet' and 'demi-vinet'.[10] The champ initial, probably the most widely found initial type in late medieval English manuscripts, consists of a gilded letter set against a coloured ground with penwork-flourished sprays with lobes (sometimes tinted green) and gold motifs extending into the vertical margin.[11] Champ initials may make their first named appearance in a vernacular book: the so-called 'Vernon' manuscript of English religious verse and prose,

---

[7] See, for example, Jones, 'Staying with the Programme', 209.

[8] Narrative scenes also occur in the margins of BL, MS Harley 1766 (Lydgate's *Fall of Princes*), but they are not combined with border decoration. See n.67 below on this MS.

[9] In the Ellesmere Chaucer, some figures occur adjacent to decorated borders. Scott, 'The Illustration of *Piers Plowman*', 78–80, lists late fourteenth- and fifteenth-century literary manuscripts with marginal illustrations.

[10] Rickert, 'Illumination', 562–3; Scott, 'Design, Decoration and Illustration', 48–52; Scott, 'Limning and Book-Producing Terms', 145–7, 149–50, 157–60; Craigie, ' "Champ" and "Vynet" '.

[11] Scott, 'Limning and Book-Producing Terms', 147, indicates variation in the meaning of champ during the fifteenth century but says further that 'no other term can be shown *in situ* to have so long a span of usage'.

Figure 5.1 JRL, MS Eng. 1, f. 23r: miniature in border, showing Jason and Medea departing from Colchis.

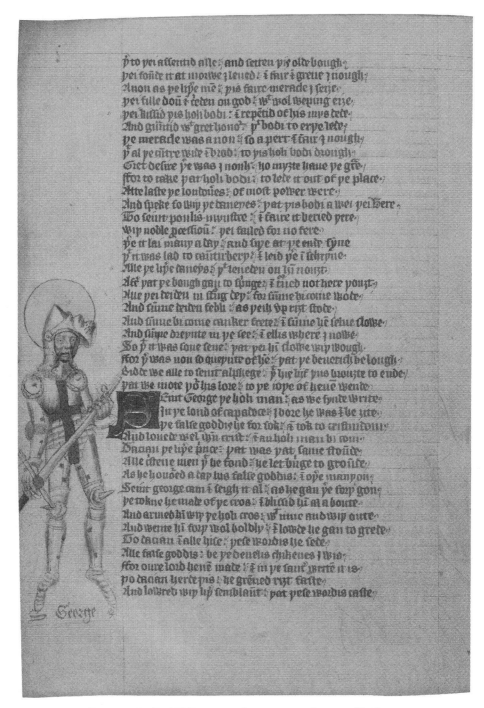

Figure 5.2 BodL, MS Tanner 17, f. 91v: marginal image of St George.

BodL, MS Eng. poet. a. 1, decorated in Western England about 1390 (Figure 5.3). Flourished initials, non-illuminated penned initials with pen flourishing extending into the margin, should be distinguished from champ initials not only because of their different appearance, but also because they would not generally have been produced by limners – they represent the work of scribes.[12] Sprynget initials, like champs, would have been produced by limners. They consist of a coloured letter set against a gold ground with sprays of coloured leaves and gold balls extending into the margin: see, for example, the copy of John Lydgate's *Life of Our Lady* in BL, MS Harley 629, f. 4v. The term 'vinet' was used in the fifteenth century to refer to a decorated letter attached to a four-sided bar-frame border, as in BL, MS Harley 1758's copy of *The Canterbury Tales*, f. 1r. If the attached bar-frame border only filled the vertical margin and coloured sprays extended horizontally into margins – as in *Confessio Amantis*, BL, MS Egerton 1991, f. 194r – the term 'demi-vinet' is used.[13]

In addition to the bar-frame design associated with vinet borders, three further types of full-page borders were commonly used in fifteenth-century English manuscripts: trellis borders, band-frame borders and mixed borders.[14] The trellis border consists of two parallel bar-frames extending around the page with the space between the bar-frames filled with leaves and vines; such a border decorates f. 1r of the copy of *The Canterbury Tales* in BL, MS Harley 7334. In the band-frame border, the bar-frame is accompanied by a monochrome decorative band, usually filled with scrolling acanthus or ribbons (as in the Hours of Richard III, Lambeth, MS 474, f. 15r) or combined with white or gold filigree work (as in Higden's *Polychronicon* in BL, MS Stowe 65, f. 166r). The mixed-border type consists of a combination of two or more of the previously identified border types. The border for f. 1r of the copy of Lydgate's *Troy Book* in BL, MS Arundel 99 is mixed: a trellis-border type is combined with bands of scrolling monochrome acanthus.

The exact sequence of steps in limning a manuscript might vary from one artisan or group of collaborating artisans to another, or from manuscript to manuscript. The general pattern of stages of illuminating is best reconstructed from examination

---

[12] Flourished initials were generally produced by scribes or by specialist flourishers (Morgan, 'Technology of Production of the Manuscript Book', 84). The York guild records distinguish tournours and flourishers, who were responsible for non-illuminated decorative initials, from limners (Doyle, 'The English Provincial Book Trade', 19; Friedman, *Northern English Books*, 208–23; Gee, 'The Printers, Stationers and Bookbinders'). Flourishers are also distinguished from limners in fifteenth-century word lists (Griffiths, 'Book Production Terms', 51). For a recent discussion of pen-flourished initials in English manuscripts of this period, see Doyle, 'Pen-Work Flourishing'.

[13] For a useful discussion of the range of decorative motifs adopted in English borders and the development of borders over time, see Scott, *Dated and Datable English Manuscript Borders*; see also Rickert, 'Illumination', 561–605.

[14] Scott, 'Design, Decoration and Illustration', 48–51. No Middle English terms distinguishing between these border types have yet been found.

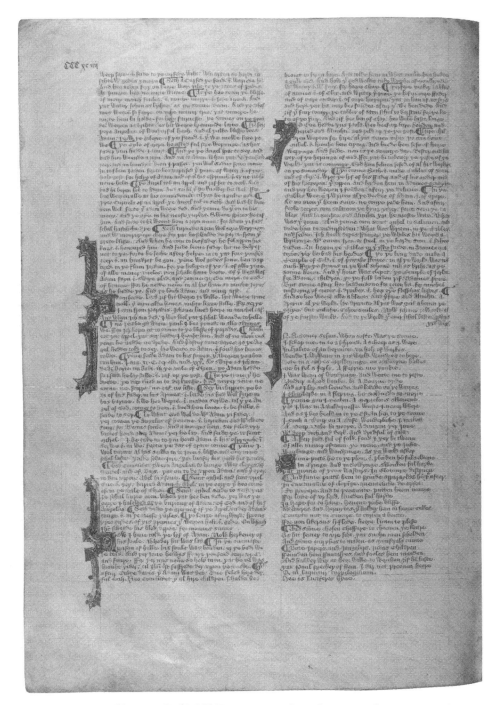

Figure 5.3 BodL, MS Eng. poet. a. 1, f. 2v: champ initials.

of surviving manuscripts, especially books with unfinished decorative programmes, supplemented with references to recipe books and treatises. The limner typically began by working in lead plummet, crayon or ink, sketching in the overall design and layout for the decoration or illustration and drawing any framing devices. If the preliminary sketching was in plummet or crayon, the illuminator might also sharpen up the design in pen and ink. Areas to be gilded would receive a layer of size (a glutinous wash) or gesso (gypsum) in preparation for the application of the gold leaf. Following the application and burnishing of the gold leaf, the limner began to apply pigments to the rest of the decoration or illustration.

The unfinished borders in a copy of John Trevisa's English translation of Higden's *Polychronicon*, HEHL, MS HM 28561, show that the first layer of pigment consisted of a flat wash of colour, with no attempt to provide modelling or other detail (Figure 5.4). A second layer of a darker or more saturated version of the same pigment could then be laid down to begin giving shape to the motifs. At this stage, the artist would typically sharpen the outlines with pen and ink and insert any pen-drawn flourishing or sprays. The final stage consisted of applying the modelling – usually a combination of darker body pigment and highlighting in white or yellow – along with any green being used to embellish the penned tendrils in the border sprays. The sequence of illumination, as observed in unfinished manuscripts such as this copy of Trevisa's *Polychronicon*, corresponds closely to the successive stages of illuminating described in the 1573 printed treatise *The Arte of Limning*.[15]

A surprising number of manuscripts from this period survive with incomplete decorative programmes. Unfinished manuscripts include those with decoration in varying states of completion, like the copy of *Polychronicon*, or with fully completed borders and secondary decoration but only blank spaces at all of the openings intended for miniatures, or with some completed miniatures but others left either completely blank or partially completed. The causes could be various: a reduction in funds during production; the death of the patron; difficulty in finding suitable pictorial models; error or oversight by the illuminator or coordinating craftsman; or the possibility that some books were produced on speculation with blanks left in order to permit a buyer to specify the desired level of illustration. Whatever the reasons for their existence, it is clear that book-buyers and readers were willing to accept books with incomplete decorative programmes.[16] The point here is one that recurs in several chapters of this volume: there is evidence of incompletion and disorder during this period of English book production, even in luxurious illustrated books.

[15] *STC* 24252; see also Gullick (ed.), *The Arte of Limming*, where this book is described as 'the earliest English printed book on painting' (1).

[16] Edwards and Pearsall, 'The Manuscripts of the Major English Poetic Texts', 266–7.

Figure 5.4 HEHL, MS HM 28561, f. 81r: unfinished initial and border with gilding, initial layers of pigment and ink outlining.

Nevertheless, people sought, at least, to plan and organize the illustration of books, and we can reconstruct their aspirations towards orderly, planned production from a few rare but valuable surviving documents, such as the contract between Robert Brekelyng, scribe, and John Forbor, probably a representative of the Dean and Chapter of York Minster. This document suggests book production and price scales of established complexity: for example, it differentiates between five-line initials and larger seven-line initials, whereas the account records for the production of the Lytlington Missal, Westminster Abbey, MS 37, separate the cost of the single full-page miniature in the book from the cost of the illumination of the rest of the manuscript.[17]

The relationship between Brekelyng and Forbor and the arrangements made to produce the Westminster Missal raise the question of agency in the planning of a book's decorative programme and the role of the limner or other book professionals in that process.[18] In this period, stationers may sometimes have acted as 'supervising entrepreneurs' in the making of manuscripts, overseeing the various stages of book production (as Erik Kwakkel argues here in Chapter 8), including arranging for the completion of illustration and decoration by specialist limners.[19] Their work anticipated that of later printers who oversaw not only the printing but also the illustration of books, both by commissioning or obtaining and making use of existing woodcut blocks, or by arranging for work by a limner (a practice which became less and less common in the decades after the advent of printing). Printers' houses may give us a clue as to the nature of the processes of manuscript production that preceded them. Some printers seem to have been involved in a variety of aspects of each edition's decoration – Caxton appears to have employed or worked closely with a binder (see Alexandra Gillespie's discussion here in Chapter 7), and the consistent presentation of initials in some of his books suggests he also had decorators at work in-house.[20] Other printers

---

[17] For Robert Brekelyng, see Scott (ed.), *The Mirroure of the World*, 35, n.6; Alexander, *Medieval Illuminators*, 179; Michael, 'English Illuminators', 77; Gee, 'Printers, Stationers and Bookbinders', 27. For the costing of the Lytlington Missal, see Alexander, *Medieval Illuminators*, 36; Tudor-Craig, 'The "Large Letters" of the Lytlington Missal'; Morgan, 'Technology of Production of the Manuscript Book', with earlier bibliography. For further discussion of the costings of book illumination in late medieval England, see Bell, 'The Price of Books'; Farquhar, 'The Manuscript as a Book'; Parkes and Salter (eds.), *Troilus and Criseyde*; Danbury, 'The Decoration and Illumination of Royal Charters'; Doyle, 'The English Provincial Book Trade'; De Hamel, *Medieval Craftsmen: Scribes and Illuminators*; Scott, 'Limning and Book-Producing Terms'; Morgan, 'Technology of Production of the Manuscript Book'.

[18] For an overview, see Alexander, *Medieval Illuminators*, and Alexander, 'Art History, Literary History'.

[19] It has been argued, for example, that costings in English manuscripts imply that a stationer arranged the subdivision of labour among different craftsmen, including the illuminator: see Doyle, 'The English Provincial Book Trade', 18. For the connection between stationers and bookbinders, see Griffiths, 'Book Production Terms', 51.

[20] Edwards, 'Decorated Caxtons'.

may have worked as Antoine Vérard did, who produced books for French and English readers by jobbing out the various aspects of book production, including their illustration. It is reasonable to assume that book producers worked in a similar variety of ways before printing – that in some cases a person like Forbor or an institution like Westminster Abbey may have employed limners directly; in other cases they may have worked through somebody who was involved full-time in the production of books, such as a stationer, who organized the labour on their behalf.

Knowledge of the personnel involved in illuminating books is principally derived from a variety of archival sources and the evidence provided by the manuscript books themselves. Christianson identified the names of over forty limners active in London between 1300 and 1500, and Michael subsequently added the names of approximately twenty-five limners active outside London between c.1350 and c.1450.[21] However, very few of these named individuals can be identified as having been responsible for the illumination of surviving manuscripts. Among them is the early fifteenth-century Dominican John Siferwas, who was employed as an illuminator by John, fifth Lord Lovell (d. 1408) and included his self-portrait in both a lectionary made for Salisbury Cathedral, BL, MS Harley 7026, and in the Sherborne Missal, BL, MS Add. 74236.[22] Another is Herman Scheerre, possibly a German or Fleming, who may have been trained as a panel painter, and who illuminated books in London.[23] Later in the fifteenth century, the London illuminator William Abell produced several manuscripts in conjunction with the scribe Ricardus Franciscus.[24] Abell was a limner and stationer who is first recorded at work

[21] Christianson, *A Directory of London Stationers*; Michael, 'English Illuminators'. As Michael points out, there can be uncertainty in distinguishing between multiple documentary references to the same individual over a period of time or to different illuminators with the same given name; see, for example, the name William Luminor/Luminour/Lymnour, which occurs six times in the Oxford archives between 1374 and 1412 (Michael, 'English Illuminators', 67).

[22] Christianson, *A Directory of London Stationers*, 160–1; Alexander, *Medieval Illuminators*, 30. The identification of the full-page miniature on f. 4v of the Lovell Lectionary as a self-portrait of the artist has been challenged by Scott, *Later Gothic Manuscripts*, no. 9. For the traditional identification, see Backhouse, 'The Lovel Lectionary', 116–17.

[23] Alexander, *Medieval Illuminators*, 124. Christianson, *A Directory of London Stationers*, 157–8, suggests that Herman Scheerre was a Herman Skereueyn who rented a shop in Paternoster Row in London. Scheerre signed BL, MS Add. 16998 (Offices and Prayers), and the name 'Herman' has been written in line endings of the Bedford Psalter and Hours (BL, MS Add. 42131). Other MSS have been attributed to Scheerre on stylistic grounds: see Scott, *Later Gothic Manuscripts*, nos. 16, 21, 23, and Orr, 'The Fitzherbert Hours', 239, n.30, for further bibliography.

[24] Ricardus Franciscus also collaborated with the Fastolf Master. See below for further discussion of their work, and also Wakelin, Chapter 2, p. 48, Kwakkel, Chapter 8, p. 180, Mooney, Chapter 9. p. 204 for Ricardus Franciscus. For manuscripts written by Ricardus Franciscus and illuminated by William Abell or the Fastolf Master, see Driver, ' "*Me fault faire*" ', and Kwakkel's chapter, p. 180 again. For the Fastolf Master, see also Alexander, 'A Lost Leaf from a Bodleian Book', 248–51; Alexander, 'Foreign Illuminators', 47; Farquhar, 'The Manuscript as a Book', 80, 82–8; Reynolds, 'English Patrons and

in 1446; he illuminated religious books as well as charters, ordinances, statutes and vernacular works such as the poetry of Geoffrey Chaucer and John Lydgate.[25] John Lacy, a Dominican recluse based in Newcastle, wrote and extensively illuminated a religious miscellany, Oxford, St John's College, MS 94, between 1420 and 1434, and even included a self-portrait.[26]

The identities of some artists are known only from inscriptions included in the manuscripts that they were responsible for illuminating. For example, in about 1380 the artist Alan Strayler supplied portraits of kings, popes and benefactors to the Catalogue of the Benefactors of St Albans Abbey, BL, MS Cotton Nero D.vii, and included a portrait of himself accompanied by the following inscriptions: 'Alanus Strayler circa depictionem presenti[s] libri plurimum laboravit & tres solidos & iiii or d. sibi debitos pro coloribus condonavit [Alan Strayler worked hard on the painting of the present book and has forgiven the three sous and four pence due to him for the colours]'; 'Nomine pictoris: Alanus Strailer habetur / Qui sum sive choris celestibus associetur [In the name of the painter: Alan Strayler is responsible – I am he; may he be placed with heavenly choirs]' (f. 108r – see Figure 5.5). The artist Johannes inscribed 'Iohannes me fecit [had me made]' in the background of a miniature in an extensively illustrated copy of Marco Polo's *Li livres du graunt caam* (BodL, MS Bodley 264, f. 220r).[27] According to an inscription, John Shippey was the scribe and illuminator of part of the Luton Guild Register, Luton Museum Service, MS 1984/127 ('This wrytten and lymmed by John Shrppey [*sic*]').[28] Another scribe and illuminator may have been Thomas Wygg, who signed the London Skinners' Company's Register of the Assumption of the Virgin.[29]

There are also other artists named in the records who may have illustrated books as well as working in other media, among them Thomas Daunt, citizen of London, who is known to have painted the arms of Henry V on banners and shields, William

French Artists', 311; Spencer, *The Sobieski Hours*, 19, 53, 69, nn.54–5; Reynolds, 'Masters, Anonymous', 664. König identifies the artist of *Le livre du chastel de labour* (Philadelphia, Free Library, MS Widener 1, datable *c*.1430–40) as the Fastolf Master, but Hindman ascribes the illumination to the Bedford workshop. König and Bartz, *Das Buch vom erfüllten Leben*; Hindman, '*La Voie de Povreté ou de Richesse*', 202–5, item 70. Three illuminations may show stylistic elements of the Fastolf Master, most notably sculpted facial features and starry night skies. See Tanis with Thompson (eds.), *Leaves of Gold*, 204, figs. 70–1.

[25] Alexander, 'A Lost Leaf from a Bodleian Book', 167, 168, cites BodL, MS Bodley 686 (Chaucer, *The Canterbury Tales* with eleven poems by Lydgate; described in Manly and Rickert (eds.), *The Text of The Canterbury Tales*, 1.64–70, 1.571–4, pl. 4), and BodL, MS Fairfax 16, containing Chaucer's minor poems, reproduced in Norton-Smith (ed.), *Bodleian Library MS Fairfax 16*; Christianson, *A Directory of London Stationers*, 59–60; see also Scott, *Later Gothic Manuscripts*, nos. 94, 95, 101.

[26] Friedman, *Northern English Books*, 52–3; Doyle, 'The English Provincial Book Trade', 22. The self-portrait occurs on Oxford, St John's College, MS 94, f. 16v.

[27] Scott, *Later Gothic Manuscripts*, no. 13; Christianson, *A Directory of London Stationers*, 124, hypothesizes that Johannes was John Hun, who rented premises in Paternoster Row in 1404.

[28] f. 121r; see Marks, 'Two Illuminated Guild Registers', 123 and 137, n.10.

[29] Marks, 'Two Illuminated Guild Registers', 137, n.10.

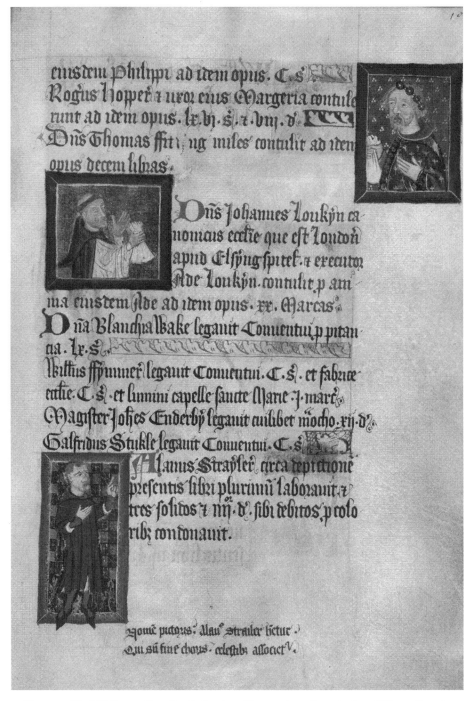

Figure 5.5 BL, MS Cotton Nero D.vii, f. 108r: self-portrait and inscription of Alanus Strayler.

Seyburgh, John Massingham and Christian Colborne, for example, although no books illuminated by these artists are mentioned.[30] Robert Pygot, a painter associated with a set of panels depicting St Etheldreda, may have been one of the illuminators of the presentation copy of Lydgate's *Lives of SS. Edmund and Fremund*, BL, MS Harley 2278.[31]

It has been possible to identify many anonymous artists on the basis of distinctive stylistic traits and to distinguish their work in multiple manuscripts.[32] An important example is the Fastolf Master, an anonymous French artist who worked for French and English patrons during the Hundred Years War. The style of the Fastolf Master has been detected in Sarum Hours as well as in French secular texts illuminated for English patrons, as in the prayer roll of Henry Beauchamp, Duke of Warwick, in Latin and French, made *c*.1440, and in a well-known manuscript of French secular prose copied for Sir John Fastolf in 1450.[33] Because some of these manuscripts contain border decoration entirely English in character, the Fastolf Master may have moved to England at some point in his career. Other anonymous artists to whom a body of work has been attributed include the Master of TCC, MS B.11.7, the Master of the *Troilus* frontispiece, the Master of the John Rylands *Troy Book*, the Caesar Master, the Abingdon Missal Master, the Placentius Master, the Owl Master, the Caxton Master and the Master of BL, MS Add. 48976. The large number of surviving illuminations attributed to an otherwise anonymous master (or of works that remain unascribed) is not unusual in an age when the artist was a craftsman working anonymously. As J. J. G. Alexander reminds us, the practice of assigning names or workshops is linked with 'the values ascribed in our present Western society to individualism, and consequently with the need to ascribe achievement to a single, individual talent. It does not reflect contemporary, that is, late medieval, preoccupations.'[34] A similar anonymity characterizes the designers and cutters of wood-blocks in the early days of printing in England;

---

[30] Thomas Daunt, who painted a shield and banners, among other items, for the funeral of Henry V, is cited in Monnas, 'Textiles from the Funerary Achievement', 135. Sutton, 'Christian Colborne', 56, n.9, describes the career of Colborne (d. 1496), who worked as a painter in London for about thirty years, supplying banners with coats-of-arms for the coronation of Richard III and cartoons for the royal embroiderer for the coronation of Henry VII. See also Driver, 'Inventing Visual History', 193–6.

[31] Marks and Williamson (eds.), *Gothic: Art for England*, no. 318.

[32] For a pioneering example of this approach, see Rickert, *The Reconstructed Carmelite Missal*. Many of Rickert's attributions have been subsequently revised in Scott, *Later Gothic Manuscripts*, no. 2.

[33] Utrecht, Museum Catharijneconvent, MS ABM h4a is described in Marks and Williamson (eds.), *Gothic: Art for England*, no. 92, and Wüstefeld, 'A Remarkable Prayer Roll', 243–4. BodL, MS Laud misc.570, is cited in Pächt and Alexander, *Illuminated Manuscripts in the Bodleian Library*, no. 695. *DMOL*, 1.100, comments on the discrepancy of date, misread in Bühler, 'Sir John Fastolf's Manuscripts', 123–8 as 1454. Driver, '"*Me fault faire*"', discusses this manuscript at some length. Wakelin, *Humanism, Reading, and English Literature*, 103, notes its texts and context, and Mooney notes its scribe in this volume, p. 204.

[34] Alexander, *Medieval Illuminators*, 140.

there are no self-portraits or images of English woodcut designers or block cutters in the early period of printing, and woodcuts produced in England, which draw closely on continental models, are not signed or initialled as they begin to be elsewhere in the fifteenth century.

The manuscripts themselves reveal that one of the most significant aspects of the working practices of the limners was collaboration, even in completing the illustration and decoration of individual books. This collaboration occurred between craftsmen within a limning shop, that is, between the master and assistants or apprentices, and between independent limners or workshops. Although there are relatively few documented references to the employment of assistants or apprentices by English limners of this period, apprenticeship was a well-established practice within book production in general in the guild-controlled urban setting of London.[35] In 1402, an apprentice limner, Thomas Hardynge, was involved in a legal suit because he had left his term of service to the London limner John White early.[36] In fact, the terms of apprentices could even be bequeathed to other artists, as for example in the case of the London limner John Fysshe, who bequeathed 'the termys of apprentishod þat I haue in Robert Ffitz John myn apprentice and William Buttler myn apprentice' to William Abell, the well-known London limner.[37] Members of religious orders who practised the craft of illumination also appear to have had assistants or trainee limners under their supervision, as is suggested by the example of the limner John Tye, an Austin friar, who received permission from his order in 1384 to train Henry Hood in the art of book illumination.[38] John Siferwas probably had as many as four assistants working under his direction while completing the ambitious decorative programme of the Sherborne Missal.

However, most of the evidence indicating the collaborative nature of manuscript illumination in this period is derived from manuscript books themselves and, in particular, from the way in which multiple styles or hands can be identified in the illustrations and decorations of individual volumes.[39] Our knowledge of much of the day-to-day organization of the late medieval illuminating workshop remains largely conjectural, but study of the distribution of hands among the texts within individual manuscripts in combination with the changing patterns of collaboration in illustration across manuscripts allows us to identify a variety of practices of collaboration among limners. This is especially possible in the late fourteenth and the fifteenth centuries, when arrangements for making, including decorating,

---

[35] Christianson, *A Directory of London Stationers*, 28.

[36] Ibid.

[37] Ibid., 110.

[38] Sandler, 'A Note on the Illuminators', 365. See also Pouzet, p. 222 below.

[39] Croenen, *Patrons, Authors and Workshops*, 18, makes a similar point about Parisian illuminators. For a case-study of different artists with similar styles and the idea of the 'workshop', see Reynolds, 'The Workshop of the Master of the Duke of Bedford'.

manuscripts seem to have become more commercial, organized, more often collaborative and – if the much greater number of surviving books is to be the measure – much more productive.

Although the arrangements whereby the illumination of a given manuscript was divided up in a coordinated fashion remain unclear, the analysis of hands suggests that limners might specialize either as border decorators or as miniaturists. The English-made prayer book of Charles d'Orléans, BN, MS Lat. 1196, offers a case in point, with its illumination having been attributed to four different miniature painters and eleven separate border hands. The work of many of these hands has been identified in other manuscripts, but the precise combination of hands in the Paris manuscript has not been found in any other manuscript. In a similar fashion, the two hands of the miniatures and the three border styles of Cambridge, Fitzwilliam Museum, MS 56, a Book of Hours made about fifty years later than Charles d'Orléans's manuscript, have been individually located in other manuscripts but appear to have collaborated in this one instance only. Collaboration on illumination seems to have extended occasionally to several artists working jointly on individual borders, with one artist being responsible for the decorative sprays and foliage, and another artist completing figurative elements inset within the border. Kathleen Scott argues that such a 'mixed stylistic group of illustrators working in kaleidoscopic combinations with each other and with other border artists is virtually certain to be evidence of independent workers in the same area collaborating rather than for the existence of one sizable shop'.[40] Christianson's studies of London book production and Stacey Gee's of York support this conclusion: where there is evidence of the rental of commercial space by book artisans, such 'shops' are always relatively modest in size, typically consisting of two small rooms not big enough for many people. The picture that emerges is of multiple small shops operated by individual stationers, scribes, bookbinders or limners, each with perhaps one or two apprentices or assistants.[41]

Yet the fact that the workshops of illuminators and other book artisans tended to be grouped together within the same locality or even street would have facilitated not only the subdivision of work among them, but also the provision of instructions and the borrowing and exchange of pictorial models.[42] Common sense suggests that people usually provided illuminators with spoken instructions, whether in person or through intermediaries, but obviously such spoken instruction is little documented. There is one example, however, of evidence showing that an illuminator might be required not only to arrive in person to receive work from a stationer,

[40] Scott, *Later Gothic Manuscripts*, II.328. See also Scott, 'A Mid-Fifteenth-Century English Illuminating Shop', 170–96.

[41] Gee, 'The Printers, Stationers and Bookbinders', 32–6. See also the arguments of Kwakkel, Chapter 8, and Mooney, Chapter 9, in this volume.

[42] Edwards and Pearsall, The 'Manuscripts of the Major English Poetic Texts', 263.

perhaps to receive spoken instructions, but also to accommodate ongoing personal supervision by the stationer. In the resolution to a legal dispute in 1445 in Oxford, the illuminator John Couley was required for the period of a year to come in person to the house of the University Stationer, John Godsond, to receive his assigned work and the required colours, and, while carrying out the work, to provide 'the aforesaid John Godsond … entrance to the place where the same John Couley illuminator stays and dwells and also works to supervise his work at any convenient time'.[43]

More evidence shows that written instructions were frequently provided to illuminators. The most common form of such instructions consists of tiny guide letters placed in the spaces for decorated initials, indicating which letter the artist should depict. Intended to be obscured by the painted initial, these guide letters can often be found in manuscripts with unfinished decorative programmes: they are visible, for example, in the copy of *Confessio Amantis* in CUL, MS Dd.8.19 (e.g., f. 8v). Moreover, a variety of other types of written instructions for limners appears in the margins of manuscripts. Written in either English or Latin, they may be placed in the upper or lower margin, in the side margins or in spaces left for decoration.[44] The surviving instructions are usually relatively terse, simply listing a subject title such as 'Cyrst befor pylate' or a standard textual reference such as 'domine ne in furore' ('Lord, do not in your fury').[45] On rare occasions, they are more extensive, as in a prayerbook of *c.*1410–15, BodL, MS Lat. liturg. e.17, with lengthy directions for miniatures such as the Last Judgement (f. 55v) or the Commendation of Souls (f. 95v).[46] A middle ground is the marginal instruction in a copy of Gower's *Confessio Amantis*, BodL, MS Bodley 902 (f. 8r – see Figure 5.6) in which the subject is identified, along with some basic information on figural poses: 'hic fiat confessor sedens *et* confess*us* cora*m* se genuflectendo [here let there be the Confessor sitting

---

[43] Michael, 'English Illuminators'; see also Scott (ed.), *The Mirroure of the World*.

[44] Such instructions may have been intended to be removed when the text block was trimmed following binding. See, for example, PML, MS M.893, the Beauchamp or Warwick Hours, with instructions for the illuminator in English in the upper margin, partially trimmed on some folios (e.g., f. 41r) and, presumably, completely trimmed from many others (e.g., ff. 12r, 17r, 26r).

[45] E.g., respectively, PML, MS M. 893, f. 29r; Edinburgh, University Library MS 308, f. 50v. For instructions in the Edinburgh Hours, see Scott, 'Limning and Book-Producing Terms', 153 and n.53, 168; Scott, *Later Gothic Manuscripts*, no. 113; Ker and Piper, *Medieval Manuscripts in British Libraries*, II.601. In BL, MS Royal 2.A.xviii, similar subject headings were inserted in the upper margin as guides for pasting in miniatures cut from another book (e.g., f. 7v, 'brydlingto' written above a pasted-in miniature of St John of Bridlington): see Marks and Morgan, *The Golden Age of English Manuscripts*, 101; Scott, *Later Gothic Manuscripts*, no. 37.

[46] Scott, 'Limning and Book-Producing Terms', 153 and 168, n.51. For examples of even more detail and specificity of symbolic meaning, see Jean Lebègue's instructions to illuminators for his French translation of Sallust in BodL, MS D'Orville 141, from early fifteenth-century Paris, described by Alexander, *Medieval Illuminators*, 57–9, and Hedeman, 'Making the Past Present', 173–96. For a later fourteenth-century English manuscript with unusually detailed instructions, see Sandler, 'Notes for the Illuminator', 551–64.

Figure 5.6 BodL, MS Bodley 902, f. 8r, close-up: marginal instructions to illuminator.

and the confessed in front of him kneeling]'.[47] Written instructions could also indicate the location of a miniature, whether a full or partial border was to be inserted on a particular folio or what type of decorated initial should be inserted into the

[47] Griffiths, '*Confessio Amantis*', 176, n.4.

space left by the scribe.[48] In the absence of explicit written instructions, illuminators may have occasionally used adjacent rubrics or titles as directions to indicate the subject matter to be represented.[49]

Besides these verbal instructions, the widespread repetition and re-use of compositions shows that pictorial models must also have been widely available to illuminators. In noting a tendency towards conformity in pictorial subject matter in English manuscripts of this period, Scott has suggested that both the Church and trade organizations such as the London Limners' Guild (later as part of the Stationers' Guild) may have encouraged standardization of iconography.[50] Much like written instructions, pictorial models were sometimes supplied in the margins, in the form of small sketches adjacent to the miniature space, as occurs in the copy of Lydgate's *Fall of Princes* in HEHL, MS HM 268.[51] Modelbooks may have also sometimes been employed; separate collections of models and designs existed in England, such as the so-called 'Pepysian' modelbook, Cambridge, Magdalene College, MS Pepys 1916, and the 'Sloane' sketchbook, BL, MS Sloane 1448A, and may have served as repositories of generic motifs, or maybe as instructional aids, experiments with compositions or even as advertisements.

Besides using models, and in keeping with their tendency to work anonymously, the illustrators of English manuscripts worked primarily to illustrate texts – the most extensive form of written 'instructions' perhaps – rather than to devise independent artwork of a more distinctively personal kind. Responding to these texts, they produced a wide variety of illustrations, but three genres – author portraits, allegorical scenes and pictures which illustrate narratives – are prominent. These genres could also be quite conventionalized, but not always so: a perceptible movement towards standardization in this period must be balanced by observation of inconsistencies and some disorganization. Author portraits, for example, were sometimes generic and sometimes specific. One of the earliest English author portraits is that of Bede, in BL, MS Yates Thompson 26, a manuscript of Bede's prose life of Cuthbert and extracts from his *Historia Ecclesiastica* made in England during the last quarter of the twelfth century. Figures representing Bede recur in English manuscripts of later centuries, perhaps because early examples provided models for later artisans. Notably, there is a kind of blurring between the role of the author and that of the maker of the book in many such depictions of Bede: for example,

---

[48] Scott, 'Limning and Book-Producing Terms'. Cf. Sandler, 'Notes for the Illuminator', 561, discussing *Omne Bonum* in BL, MS Royal 6.E.vii, who shows that the miniaturist might disregard or even correct written instructions, which suggests that 'sweeping conclusions about the primacy of written instructions … need to be modified to allow for a more active role on the part of manuscript illuminators'.

[49] Lawton, 'The Illustration of Late Medieval Secular Texts', 68–9; Hardman, 'Interpreting the Incomplete Scheme', 61; Sandler, 'Notes for the Illuminator', 553.

[50] Scott, *Later Gothic Manuscripts*, 1.52–9. See also Orr, 'Tradition and Innovation', 263–70.

[51] Alexander, *Medieval Illuminators*, 63–9, 184–6; Alexander, 'Preliminary Marginal Drawings'.

the drawing of the author at his desk with pen and scraper, like a scribe, in BL, MS Arundel 74, a manuscript probably from East Anglia and datable to the period between 1375 and 1406.[52] Among other authors illustrated in English manuscripts are Geoffrey Chaucer, Thomas Hoccleve, John Gower and Christine de Pizan;[53] religious writers such as Richard Rolle and John Wyclif are also sometimes represented.[54] Besides authors, portraits in some fifteenth-century manuscripts might represent a narrator as a kind of meta-fiction suggestive of the text's human maker, as in the portraits of pilgrims of *The Canterbury Tales*, which appear alongside those of the pilgrim-author, Chaucer.[55]

Allegorical texts also provided a basis for a popular genre of illustration in both manuscripts and printed books. Much recent discussion has focussed on the allegorical figures in the margins of BodL, MS Douce 104, a copy of Langland's poem *Piers Plowman*, but examples accompany other English literary and religious texts in the late fourteenth and fifteenth centuries.[56] Allegorical illustrations tied directly to the text often occur in works by John Lydgate, including *The Temple of Glass*, *The Fall of Princes*, *The Pilgrimage of the Soul* and *Troy Book*. BL, MS Cotton Tiberius A.vii, a translation of Guillaume de Guileville's *The Pilgrimage of the Life of Man* often ascribed to Lydgate, includes fifty-three coloured drawings that have been attributed to the limner William Abell (on whom, see discussion above) which are both allegorical and narrative, and remarkably reflective of the English poem.[57] The pilgrim, shown with his staff and scrip, confronts a:

> roche off harde ston
> And, At an eye, ther ran oute
> Dropes off water .al aboute:
> The dropys wer (to my semyng)

[52] BL, MS Yates Thompson 26, f. 2r, and BL, MS Arundel 74, f. 2v, reproduced on the 'British Library Digital Catalogue of Illuminated Manuscripts', www.bl.uk/catalogues/illuminatedmanuscripts.

[53] For portraits of Chaucer, see Pearsall, *The Life of Geoffrey Chaucer*, 285–305; McGregor, 'The Iconography of Chaucer', 338–50; Salter, 'The "Troilus Frontispiece"', 15–23; Krochalis, 'Hoccleve's Chaucer Portrait', 234–45; Seymour, 'Manuscript Portraits of Chaucer and Hoccleve'; Scott, *Later Gothic Manuscripts*, no. 51. For de Pizan, see Willard, *Christine de Pizan*, 50, 134, 172, 210; Laidlaw, 'Christine and the Manuscript Tradition', 231–50. For Gower, see BL, MS Egerton 1991, as the lover in *Confessio Amantis*; GUL, MS Hunter 59 (T.2.17) in *Vox Clamantis*; and BL, MS Add. 42131.

[54] Representations of Rolle occur in a fifteenth-century Carthusian miscellany (BL, MS Add. 37049) of texts and drawings, at least one of which is clearly labelled (cf. Brantley, *Reading in the Wilderness*, 151, who argues that they are representations of the imagined reader). Wycliffe may appear in BodL, MS Laud misc. 286.

[55] Gaylord, 'Portrait of a Poet'; Emmerson, 'Text and Image in the Ellesmere Portraits'; and Bowden, 'Visual Portraits'.

[56] Kerby-Fulton and Despres, *Iconography and the Professional Reader*; Pearsall, *The Life of Geoffrey Chaucer*; Scott, 'The Illustration of *Piers Plowman*'.

[57] Alexander, 'William Abell "Lymnour"', 167. Scott, *Later Gothic Manuscripts*, II.252, calls this artist 'the Cotton Master' and questions Alexander's attribution to Abell on the basis of the lively figural style, which contrasts with 'Abell's more stolid work'.

> Lych salte terys off wepyng;
> And in-ta cesterne ther besyde,
> The dropes gonne for to glyde.[58]

The image is rendered literally in the drawing of an eye, complete with an eyebrow, in a green craggy rock weeping tears into a trough that fills with blue water (Figure 5.7). On the next leaf, the pilgrim, in his drawers, bathes in the trough of water as the eye rains tears upon his head, just as is described in the text.

A manuscript of Lydgate's *Fall of Princes*, Philadelphia, Rosenbach Library, MS 439/16, also includes markedly literal renderings of the allegorical content. At the opening of Book VI, Boccaccio, the author of the source of the *Fall of Princes*, is shown 'pensiff' with head in hand as a vision of Fortune appears before him; rather than being shown conventionally with her wheel, she is depicted as a nude female figure made of roots and flowers:

> a monstruous ymage,
> Partid on tweyne of colour & corage,
> Hir riht[e] side ful of somer flours,
> The tothir oppressed with wyntris stormy shours.

Closely following Lydgate's description, the artist further supplies Fortune with 'An hundrid handis', or as many as he can fit in, a literal rendering of the allegorical vision.[59]

Narrative images, or pictures that tell a story, may accompany written stories, although not all images illustrating written narratives are in themselves narrative in their content. As Henrike Manuwald has recently pointed out in his analysis of images in the *Sachenspiegel* manuscript, some pictorial cycles can become very complex, and single images can also be termed narrative if they 'enable the viewer to construct underlying stories'. Early narrative cycles of the stories of Guy of Warwick and Bevis of Hampton which are unrelated to the texts they accompany occur in the Taymouth Hours, copied between 1325 and 1335, and in the somewhat later Smithfield Decretals.[60] On the other hand, narrative images that are very closely reflective of the text they illustrate may be found in the sole manuscript of the romance *Gawain and the Green Knight* and the three other poems now usually ascribed to the same poet, BL, MS Cotton Nero A.x, in which pictures outline the main actions of the story of *Gawain*. Narrative pictures of Noah's Ark and Daniel explaining to Belshazzar and his queen the writing on the wall illustrate the

---

[58] Furnivall and Locock (eds.), *The Pilgrimage of the Life of Man*, ll.21806–12.

[59] Philadelphia, Rosenbach Library, MS 439/16, f. 146v (Lydgate, *Fall of Princes*, VI, 15–35; III.675–78), datable *c*.1465–75, reproduced in Anderson, *Sixty Bokes Olde and Newe*, 106, and described in Tanis, *Leaves of Gold*, no. 72; Scott, *Later Gothic Manuscripts*, no. 119.

[60] BL, MS Yates Thompson 13; BL, MS Royal 10.E.iv, on which see Griffith, 'The Visual History of Guy of Warwick', 112.

Figure 5.7 BL, MS Cotton Tiberius A.vii, f. 83r: miniature showing rock with eye and tears.

moral homily *Cleanness*, while a drawing of Jonah and the whale introduces the text of *Patience*, both also found in the *Gawain* manuscript along with the text of the allegorical *Pearl*. The illustrations accompanying *Pearl* are primarily narrative, not symbolic, showing the dreamer asleep on his flowery mound and kneeling before the Pearl maiden, who wears the fashionable dress of the courts of Richard II and Henry IV; the images in this case function as chapter headings, introducing the main action of the text.[61]

The purpose of illustrations in the earliest printed books was as various as in manuscripts. Chaucer, Rolle, Christine and Gower are depicted in early printed editions too, just as they were in manuscripts.[62] Among allegorical figures, Fortune remained a popular subject of illustration for early producers of printed books, along with other figures inherited from manuscript illumination. The battling virtues and vices in the *psychomachia*, for example, appear in various printed books, sometimes far removed from their original context.[63] So the conventionality of images, but also the occasional disruptions of these patterns and conventions, continued in printed illustrations as in manuscript ones.

Moreover, in the first decades of printing, pictures sometimes moved from manuscript to print and then back again. Many of the printed images illustrating the *Kalender of Shepherds*, a work popular in manuscript and print from the 1480s through to 1600, derive from at least one manuscript source, Cambridge, Fitzwilliam Museum, MS 167, written in French, which provided an exemplar for the French printers Guy Marchant and Antoine Vérard, and thus indirectly for the English printers Richard Pynson, Wynkyn de Worde and others, who copied the French print models either in their editions of the *Kalender* or in other books printed for a literate laity. Some *Kalender* woodcuts then became models for the manuscript illuminator known as the Master of the Dresden Prayerbook.[64] Moreover, in print, pictures were sometimes copied from edition to edition even though the texts that they accompanied might vary, which suggests that readers were familiar with a world of visual images that functioned differently from texts alone. For instance,

---

[61] Gollancz, *Pearl, Cleanness, Patience and Sir Gawain*, 10 and *passim*. See also the brief discussion above and Hilmo, *Medieval Images*, 138–59.

[62] For Chaucer, see Driver, 'Mapping Chaucer', 228–49; Kelen, 'Climbing up the Family Tree', 109–23. For Rolle, see Driver, *The Image in Print*, 84, fig. 3.6. For Christine, see Driver, *The Image in Print*, 72–4, figs 2.50, 2.51; Driver, 'Christine de Pisan'. The earliest surviving woodcut portrait of Gower occurs much later, though, on the title-page of *The Painfull Adventures of Pericles Prince of Tyre* (London: T. P[urfoot] for Nat: Butter, 1608), *STC* 25638.5.

[63] The virtues and vices woodcuts in *The Castell of Labour* printed by Richard Pynson (1505? *STC* 12380) and Wynkyn de Worde (1506, *STC* 12381) are drawn directly from Antoine Vérard's English imprint of *c*.1503 (*STC* 12379). They appear as well in *The Boke Named the Royall*, the De Worde–Pynson collaboration of 1507 (*STC* 21430). See Hodnett, *English Woodcuts*, nos. 1198–204.

[64] Driver, 'When is a Miscellany not Miscellaneous?', 206–10; on the Dresden Prayerbook Master, see Brinkmann, *Die flämische Buchmalerei*.

a woodcut of Moses with the Ten Commandments illustrates several differently explicated versions of the Decalogue, in various editions of the *Kalender*. The same image of Moses found in the *Kalender* (or a copy) was then used to illustrate discussions of the Commandments or legal precedents or moral conduct more generally in other books.[65]

But because the same wood-block could be re-used, generic woodcut illustrations (scenes of battle, for example) are sometimes repeated in printed books without clear and direct reference to the text. A result is that in some early printed books – as in some manuscripts too – the pictures have no clear relation to the texts which they illustrate. It is even sometimes said that random woodcuts were used by printers to fill out the forme.[66] This repetition of stock scenes and sometimes of characters was adopted from manuscript illustration, where it also occurs. Lesley Lawton describes the illustrations in BL MS Harley 1766, a manuscript of John Lydgate's *Fall of Princes*, as derived from 'a few frequently repeated figure-types' and finds other picture cycles in secular manuscripts that employ 'time-honoured prototypes' and 'a stock of motifs involving undifferentiated figures and simple gestures that could be recombined at will'.[67]

In the earliest period of printing, filling the forme was also regularly achieved with blanks – blocks with no image, that left, in some cases, 'unfinished' spaces very similar to those sometimes seen in manuscripts (described earlier). It seems that such books were meant to have been illustrated later by hand or, more rarely, with copperplate or other types of illustration. Blanks occur, for example, in William Caxton's edition of Gower's *Confessio Amantis*, printed on 2 September 1483, which presumably were spaces left for woodcuts or another sort of illustration that was never supplied.[68] These blanks are similar not only to those found in manuscripts, but to spaces found in continental books which were then filled in with engravings, woodcuts or drawings, all methods employed by Caxton to illustrate books during his career. As has often been observed, starting with Gutenberg's bibles with their elaborate borders and initials, the decoration of printed books remained entirely consistent with the treatment of similar manuscripts for several decades after the introduction of the new technology.

Printing did, of course, bring change. Despite the continuing decoration of printed books by hand, much of the idiosyncratic detail of late medieval illustration was lost in mass reproduction, and so was colour: by *c.*1500 most books were not afforded the sort of hand-decoration that might add a rainbow of hues to borders or pick out paraphs or capitals in red. But pictures continued to illustrate texts. In

---

[65] Hodnett, *English Woodcuts*, nos. 470, 490, 1527, 2237.
[66] Scheller, *Exemplum*, 1–88.
[67] Lawton, 'The Illustration of Late Medieval Secular Texts', 46 nn.26, 48, 45.
[68] Driver, 'Printing the *Confessio Amantis*', 270–80, 273 n.11, 275–6, n.14.

England, books in print were illustrated by woodcuts very shortly after William Caxton's setting up shop in Westminster. Just as manuscripts before them had, books published in the early years of printing contained vital visual information that helped instruct readers, guided them through the written text and enhanced enjoyment of the written page.

6

Compiling the book

MARGARET CONNOLLY

Book production in a manuscript culture was a more laborious task than in the present day, involving more stages and more labour. It might be compared with medieval food preparation where the chef was often required to be both butcher and cook, as a contemporary recipe for 'signet roste' demonstrates:

Tak a swane and kute the rofe of his mowthe ynto the braynward endelongys withe a knyf and let hym blood to dethe or elys brek his neke and kute his nek ynto a knot and let hym blode and kepe the blode yn a faire vessele for the sawce and skald hym and draw hym and rost hym as a gose.[1]

A similar quest for raw ingredients was very much part of the task of producing a manuscript, and even supposing a convenient supply of physical materials (parchment, paper and ink, as discussed by Orietta da Rold in Chapter 1, above), there remained the problem of acquiring suitable textual material to fill the book. Scribes needed exemplars from which to work, and compilers, supervisors and traders needed booklets or other segments of ready-to-read text. Ralph Hanna has emphasized the important part played in fourteenth- and fifteenth-century English book production by 'exemplar poverty', with manuscript compilers never sure when, or even if, copy-texts for any given work might become available.[2] In response, he argues, compilers were constrained to make the fullest possible use of whatever exemplars they had, with consequences for the organization of particular volumes (as will be discussed below). It might therefore be assumed that scribes would tend to make repeated use of exemplars in their possession to produce multiple copies, but this does not seem to have been the case in the copying of vernacular literary texts. Where more than one copy of a text may be attributed to a particular scribe, it usually transpires that different copy-texts were employed for each production, as in the case of the two manuscripts of Hoccleve's *The Regiment of Princes* copied

[1] BL, MS Add. 5467, f. 48r.
[2] Hanna, 'Miscellaneity and Vernacularity', 47.

by the 'Hammond scribe', and the same scribe's production of two copies of *The Canterbury Tales*.[3] A notable exception is the 'Beryn scribe', who engaged in the production of five copies of the Middle English prose *Brut*, relying each time on a single imperfect exemplar.[4]

Problems of supply might be expected to be felt least keenly in a metropolitan context, and the majority of manuscripts of the works of Geoffrey Chaucer, John Gower and John Lydgate demonstrate the very real advantages of textual reproduction within the central location of London.[5] This was an environment in which, thanks to the supply of exemplars, collaboration could flourish, resulting in joint productions such as the Trinity Gower (TCC, MS R.3.2), written by five scribes, including the Privy Seal clerk, Thomas Hoccleve; an anonymous Gower specialist, who contributed to no fewer than eight copies of *Confessio Amantis*; and Adam Pinkhurst, who was responsible for two, possibly three, copies of *The Canterbury Tales*, as well as copies of *Boece* and *Troilus and Criseyde* (as explained more fully by Linne Mooney in Chapter 9).[6] This increasing scribal specialization was not confined to the capital: in Suffolk, the 'Edmund-Fremund scribe' was involved in making four copies of the *Lives of SS Edmund and Fremund*, three of the *Secrees of Old Philisoffres* and two of *The Fall of Princes*.[7] Nevertheless, finding exemplars of suitable quality remained a problem, especially for complex works such as *The Canterbury Tales*, whose manuscripts sometimes betray signs of scribal frustration in the form of gaps, blank leaves, notes and comments.[8] Raw textual materials were also needed by printers whose editorial endeavours and strategies are usefully understood as continuations of scribal working practices. The early printers made claims that they were not content to work from just any old text: William Caxton famously relates how he used a different and better ('very trewe') manuscript to prepare his second edition of *The Canterbury Tales*; and fifty years later William Thynne took pains to find 'trewe copies or exemplaries' for his 1532 edition, setting out, according to his son, to 'serche all the liberaries of Englande for Chaucers Workes'.[9]

---

[3] This scribe's work was first noticed by Eleanor Hammond: see Mooney, 'More Manuscripts Written by a Chaucer Scribe', and Mooney, 'A New Manuscript by the Hammond Scribe'.

[4] This anonymous scribe also copied the 'Tale of Beryn' in Alnwick Castle, MS 455; see Matheson and Mooney, 'The Beryn Scribe'.

[5] Although Hanna claims otherwise ('Miscellaneity and Vernacularity', 47).

[6] Doyle and Parkes, 'The Production of Copies', 177, list ten manuscripts copied by the Gower specialist, including seven copies of *Confessio*; Griffiths adds another in 'Confessio Amantis'; Mooney, 'Chaucer's Scribe', identifies Pinkhurst.

[7] Scott, 'Lydgate's *Lives of SS Edmund and Fremund*', 342–3, 355–7.

[8] See Partridge, 'Minding the Gaps'.

[9] Blake cites Caxton's prologue in 'Caxton's Second Edition of *The Canterbury Tales*', 136. For extracts from the preface to Thynne's edition and the quotation from Francis Thynne, see Blodgett, 'William Thynne', 36 and 39.

Caxton claims to have acquired his better exemplar by chance, stating in the prologue to the second edition that after the publication of the first he was approached by a gentleman well-wisher who 'sayd he knewe a book whyche hys fader had and moche louyd that was very trewe … and sayd more yf I wold enprynte it agayn he wold gete me the same book for a copye'.[10] The serendipitous nature of this encounter and its role in authorizing the volume's contents echo earlier descriptions of the process of assembling collections of literary works. In the verse preface which was almost certainly meant to precede TCC, MS R.3.20, the fifteenth-century scribe John Shirley, a member of the household of Richard Beauchamp, Earl of Warwick, records how he has included 'ye copyes' in his anthology 'as fortune hathe them brought to me', commenting also, not entirely consistently, that he has sought them out 'on this hallfe and beyond ye see', in 'sondry place', echoing his statement that for a previous anthology, BL, MS Add. 16165, he 'sought þe copie in many a place'.[11] Shirley's volumes, especially TCC, MS R.3.20, and other mid fifteenth-century literary anthologies such as BodL, MS Fairfax 16, BodL, MS Tanner 346, BodL, MS Bodley 638 and Longleat, MS 258 were important in preserving and transmitting secular courtly verse, especially poems by Chaucer and Lydgate, and in the process contributed to the formation of the canon of the works of these authors. Importantly, these manuscripts were produced in an environment where intimate details about particular texts and authors might still be remembered. Shirley's long headnotes are especially informative in this regard, often providing important clues about the origins of particular pieces and the circumstances of their composition; not all of them can be independently verified, but it is unwise to dismiss them as gossip.[12]

Shirley's selections of texts were intended for circulation within his own social milieu: the audience positioned by his prefaces is the 'company' of the noble household, comprising the different social categories of 'knight squyer or lady / or other estat'.[13] Another mid fifteenth-century poetic anthology which was designed both for and by household readers is CUL, MS Ff.1.6.[14] Names which occur among its leaves locate its production and reception within the familial and social networks of the Findern family, a prominent family in South Derbyshire in the later fifteenth and early sixteenth centuries. As many as thirty individuals from this circle contributed to the copying of the manuscript, and presumably decisions about what to include

---

[10] Blake, 'Caxton's Second Edition of *The Canterbury Tales*', 136.

[11] Connolly, *John Shirley*, 209 (lines 17–20) and 206 (line 15).

[12] The identification of Adam Pinkhurst as the copyist of the Hengwrt and Ellesmere manuscripts of *The Canterbury Tales* confirms the importance of Shirley's testimony: Shirley alone explains that the lines to 'Adam scriveyn' constitute 'Chauciers wordes a Geffrey vnto Adame (his owen scryveyne)', and this stanza survives uniquely in TCC, MS R.3.20, p. 367.

[13] Connolly, *John Shirley*, 209 (lines 23–4) and 211 (lines 92–3).

[14] See Beadle and Owen (eds.), *The Findern Anthology*, and Harris, 'The Origins and Make-Up'.

were similarly collaborative. Its generic mixture, which includes devotional poetry and historical prose as well as romances and courtly lyrics, cautions us against the temptation to impose unduly narrow definitions on such anthologies.[15] Shirley's volumes also include both prose and verse, and devotional as well as courtly poetry, a diversity which is especially marked in his last anthology, BodL, MS Ashmole 59. Similarly, although their contents are predominantly English, Shirley's collections contain texts in Latin and French, a fact which demonstrates the linguistic flexibility of his mid fifteenth-century readers.[16] Trilingual anthologies are more usually associated with earlier periods of book production in England: some good examples are BodL, MS Digby 86, copied in Worcestershire in the late thirteenth century, and BL, MS Harley 2253, produced at Ludlow before 1350. Shirley's later volumes are a reminder that familiarity with all three languages of England remained a feature of the audience for English books for longer than we might imagine.[17]

BL, MS Harley 2253 is a complex compilation of secular and devotional material in verse and prose which has no discernible principle of overall organization. Its hybrid quality distinguishes it from more homogeneous later fourteenth-century West Midlands anthologies such as the so-called Vernon manuscript, BodL, MS Eng. poet. a. 1.[18] The texts in this massive coucher book are all in English and all of a religious or didactic nature; together they form a coherent collection which was designed to provide a comprehensive programme of religious reading and instruction for the 'sowlehele' (health of the soul). The 'Vernon scribe' made an effort to organize the texts he had gathered into five broadly generic categories, grouping together legendary material, prayers and devotional works, general didactic material, mystical devotional works and short devotional lyrics.[19] These clusters, though of unequal size, were deliberately planned, as is evident from the volume's physical construction and the points at which the beginnings and endings of texts coincide with changes in quires. It is usually assumed that basic organizational strategies such as this were intended to aid the reader, but they might also be evidence of types of filing systems used by scribes during production; similarly, the volume's contemporary index might have been designed for the convenience of either readers or subsequent copyists.[20] An uneven supply of exemplars may also have influenced this

[15] On the dangers of this, see Pearsall, 'The Whole Book'.

[16] TCC, MS R.3.20 has a significant group of French poems; see Connolly and Plumley, 'Crossing the Channel'.

[17] See Tschann and Parkes (eds.), *Facsimile of Oxford ... MS Digby 86*, and Corrie, 'The Compilation of ... MS Digby 86'; Ker (ed.), *Facsimile of ... MS. Harley 2253*, and Fein (ed.), *Studies in the Harley Manuscript*.

[18] See Doyle (ed.), *The Vernon Manuscript*, Pearsall (ed.), *Studies in the Vernon Manuscript* and Scase (ed.), *A Facsimile Edition*.

[19] See Blake, 'Vernon Manuscript'.

[20] BodL, MS Eng. poet. a. 1, ff. i–viii, by a different scribe who entitles the volume 'Þe book þat is cald in latyn tonge Salus anime and in englyshs tonge sowlehele': see Serjeantson, 'The Index of the Vernon Manuscript'.

choice of format, as seems to have been the case where fifteenth-century compilations were assembled according to generic principles: both the Lincoln Thornton
manuscript (Lincoln, Cathedral, MS 91) and the Heege manuscript (NLS, MS
Advocates' 19.3.1) contain clusters of similar texts, such as romance narratives and
religious works, within discrete codicological units.[21] Although the procuring of
copy-texts for a collection as large as the Vernon manuscript must have been a for-
midable task, the texts it reproduces were popular ones, judging from their survival
in other manuscripts, and must have been in active circulation. Many are translations from originals in Latin or French, and most are fourteenth-century in date,
although a few are earlier. One such older work is *Ancrene Wisse*, or the 'Roule of
Reclous' as it is described in the list of contents, a title which the text also carries in
Cambridge, Magdalene College, MS Pepys 2498.[22] The latter is another large contemporary religious anthology from the East rather than the West Midlands, and its
scribal dialect has been located near to Waltham Abbey in Essex.[23] A. I. Doyle has
suggested that it may have been produced by secular clergy, perhaps at a religious
centre, but intended for lay readers.[24] It shares another text, 'The Pains of Sin and
the Joys of Heaven', with the Vernon manuscript and also contains a copy of a sermon cycle called *The Mirror*, the English prose translation of Robert de Gretham's
thirteenth-century Anglo-Norman verse text. This continued production and
re-presentation of texts whose origins were either much older or linguistically different is evidenced in a number of fourteenth-century anthologies, perhaps indicating that the products of earlier literary traditions were still valued and respected,
and/or that raw textual materials were in short supply. It may be that in this period
original writing in English could not keep pace with the demand for vernacular
reading material, forcing creative energies into the re-use of existing works through
translation, modernization, adaptation and sometimes revision.

The appetite for religious texts in particular seems to have been voracious. One
response to this in the first decade of the fifteenth century was the appearance of
longer works, such as Nicholas Love's *The Mirror of the Blessed Life of Jesus Christ*,
a translation of the pseudo-Bonaventuran *Meditationes vitae Christi* for 'hem þat
bene [of] symple vndirstondyng'.[25] Love selected and reordered the contents of his
source to render it more suitable for his predominantly lay audience: while maintaining its daily meditative scheme he allows an alternative, stating that the reader

[21] For Lincoln, Cathedral, MS 91, see Brewer and Owen (ed.), *The Thornton Manuscript* and Boffey
and Thompson, 'Anthologies and Miscellanies', 298–300; for NLS, MS Advocates' 19.3.1, see Hardman
(ed.), *The Heege Manuscript* and 'A Mediaeval "Library in Parvo"'.

[22] See Millett (ed.), *Ancrene Wisse*; for a discussion of the Pepys manuscript, see Hanna, *London
Literature*, 148–221.

[23] *LALME*, 1.64; by the same hand as BodL, MS Laud misc. 622 and BL, MS Harley 874.

[24] Doyle, 'A Survey', i, 106.

[25] Love, *The Mirror of the Blessed Life*, 10, lines 22–3.

may 'take þe partes þerof as it semeþ moste confortable & stirynge to his deuocion, sumtyme one & sumtyme an oþere'.[26] The directive to read selectively as an aid to meditation had ancient monastic origins, but in the fifteenth century this approach was offered to a different audience of less sophisticated readers who were likely to need help in successfully negotiating the text. The high degree of internal organization which characterizes such works as Love's *Mirror*, in particular the very visible structuring and division of material into discrete sections, was an authorial strategy which made selective consumption much more feasible.

Similar organizational techniques were adopted by compilers who put together collections of extracts from longer religious texts. CUL, MS Hh.1.12 brings together material from Richard Rolle's *Form of Living* (three extracts), *The Pricking of Love* (eight extracts) and *Pore Caitif* (fifteen extracts), along with two sections of Walter Hilton's *Eight Chapters* and some shorter texts such as *St Brendan's Confession* and the *Meditacio sancti Augustini*.[27] A degree of coherence is evident from the grouping of these extracts: those from *Pore Caitif* come first, followed by most of those from *The Prickynge of Love*, then Hilton and then Rolle. One extract from *The Prickynge of Love* appears detached from the main group towards the beginning of the manuscript and another is now the volume's final text; the penultimate item is an extract from *Pore Caitif*, similarly detached from the main body of borrowings from that text. These groupings and the departures from them may simply reflect the exigencies of the copying process and the availability of copy-texts, but they may also be evidence of a more thoughtful attempt to order material sympathetically and beneficially. The collection as a whole is arranged according to a familiar pedagogical hierarchy whereby the basic elements are covered first and more sophisticated ideas introduced later. The reader of CUL, MS Hh.1.12 is thus first offered expositions of the Pater Noster, Ave, Creed, Ten Commandments, seven deadly sins and five wits, before being confronted with the more abstract and challenging concept of spiritual love, aspects of which are demonstrated through a variety of works. Yet the reader is not restricted to negotiating the texts sequentially. The volume is preceded by a kalendar which 'maketh mencyoun of alle the chapettels þat ben in þe book' and which numbers each item; the equivalent numbers have been added to the margins at the start of each text, facilitating the finding of particular sections.[28] This exactly replicates the authorial strategy used in the devotional prose text *Contemplations of the Dread and Love of God*, where a table of contents precedes the work with the following advice to the user: 'And þat þou mowe sone finde what mater þe pleseþ, þese titles ben here and in þe pistil marked wiþ diuerse lettres in manere of a table.'[29] It

---

[26] Ibid., 220, lines 32–4.

[27] Hardwick and Luard, *A Catalogue*, iii.264–5; Connolly (ed.), *IMEP, XIX*, 191–200.

[28] The kalendar is on CUL, MS Hh.1.12, ff. 2r–3v; for a reproduction of ff. 2v–3r, see Connolly, 'Practical Reading for Body and Soul', 173.

[29] Connolly (ed.), *Contemplations of the Dread and Love of God*, 3 lines 2–4.

is even possible that this was the example which inspired the organization of CUL, MS Hh.1.12, since an extract from the final chapter of *Contemplations*, 'How a man or a woman of symple kunnynge shall make his preier to almyghty God', originally stood at the head of this anthology.[30] Although in CUL, MS Hh.1.12 the kalendar and marginal numbers were retrospective provisions which were contributed by a different scribal hand, in conjunction with the careful ordering of texts within the collection they reveal an awareness that features of compilation and layout could influence and encourage different approaches to the reading of the book.

The high degree of organization displayed in CUL, MS Hh.1.12 is by no means replicated in all fifteenth-century devotional anthologies; its provision of a sophisticated external *accessus* makes this manuscript the exception rather than the norm. Many other collections are less overtly organized. Nevertheless, the intentions which lie behind their construction may be revealed by close attention to the nature and arrangement of their contents. Elementary devotional compilations were produced in great numbers during the fourteenth and fifteenth centuries and were typically structured to allow the reader's progression from simple to more substantial texts.[31] A good example of this type of compilation may be found in the first gathering of TCC, MS R.3.21, which begins with line-by-line translations of the Pater Noster, Ave and Creed; these are followed by a series of short expositions of the Ten Commandments, five wits of the body and soul, seven virtues, seven sins, seven works of bodily and spiritual mercy and seven gifts of the Holy Spirit.[32] These basic texts were intended to teach the rudiments of the Christian faith and to provide the minimum level of theological knowledge which had been decreed desirable for both laity and clergy by the Council of Lambeth in 1281, but they were sometimes little more than simple lists, such as those found in CUL, MS Nn.4.12.[33] In CUL, MS Hh.3.13, the components have been reduced to seven elements (Commandments, sins, works of mercy, virtues, wits), each of which has been pared down to the bare minimum (see Figure 6.1).[34] Thus the 'vij bodyly dedes of mercy' are described as a series of imperatives: 'Fede þe hungry, Gyf drynke to þe thrysty, Clothe þe naked, herber þe howsles, vysett þe seeke, Delyuyr prisoners, And bery þe pour whan þey be deed'; even more reductively the 'vij princypal vertues' are listed merely as terms: 'Fayth, hop, Charyte, Righwysnesse, Wysdam, Strenght And mesur'. After

---

[30] Due to the loss of leaves, the manuscript now begins imperfectly mid-way through the second item mentioned in the list of contents and ends abruptly a few lines before the close of the thirty-fourth item listed.

[31] Raymo, 'Works of Religious and Philosophical Instruction', 2273–4 and B2495–501, lists eighty-five examples of these miscellaneous manuals.

[32] TCC, MS R.3.21, ff. 1–32. See Mooney (ed.), *IMEP, XI*, 23–8 and Chapter 9, pp. 207–10 below.

[33] CUL, MS Nn.4.12, ff. 39r–40r; see Hardwick and Luard, *A Catalogue*, IV.499 and Connolly (ed.), *IMEP, XIX*, 351.

[34] CUL, MS Hh.3.13, f. 109r; see Hardwick and Luard, *A Catalogue*, III.280–1 and Connolly (ed.), *IMEP, XIX*, 201–2.

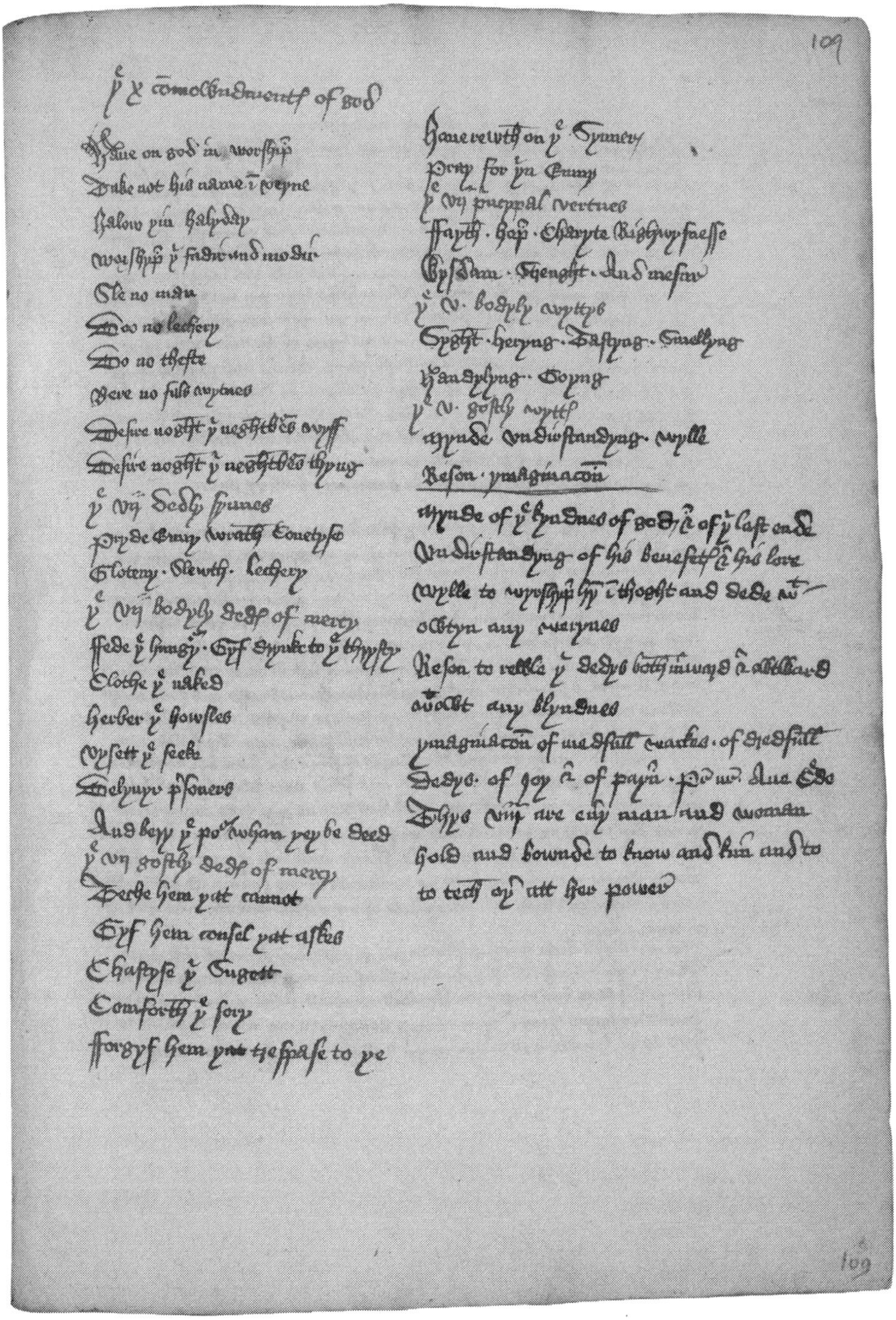

Figure 6.1 CUL, MS Hh.3.13, f. 109r: lists of commandments, works of mercy, virtues and so on, compiled for easy reading.

the final item the series concludes with a note: 'P*ater n*oster, Aue, Cr*e*de. Thys viij [*sic*] are eu*ery* man and woman hold and bownde to know and kun, and to to [*sic*] tech o*þer* att her power.' The brief mention of merely the titles of the key prayers, and the distilling of other elements into summaries and lists, coupled with the convenient presentation of this material on one side of a single leaf where it could be assimilated at a glance, suggests that this mini-manual was intended to function as a mnemonic device for prompting personal learning or the instruction of others. Such intentions were not necessarily mutually exclusive: both are expressed by John Lacy, the Dominican anchorite and scribe of Oxford, St John's College, MS 94, who states that he 'wrooth þis book and lymned hit to his awne vse and aftur to othur in exitynge hem to deuocion and preyers to god'.[35]

In other cases, devotional miscellanies were constructed with less limited expectations. The first self-contained section of JRL, MS Eng. 85 is a devotional manual which begins with the alphabet, Pater Noster, Ave, Creed and blessing, and a series of short expositions of the sins, wits and virtues.[36] The topics of prayer, faith and charity are then expounded in three more substantial texts: 'The Twelve Lettyngis of Prayer', 'A Short Declaration of Belief' and the 'Eight Points of Charity', which reappear together, though not always in sequence, in several other devotional miscellanies. The instructional intention which informs this conjunction of texts is explained most fully in JRL, MS Eng. 85, where a prologue describes their function as 'more declaracioun of þingis þat gone biforn'.[37] For example, while previously only the form ('but þe text', where 'but' means *only*) of the Pater Noster was offered, now more information will be given about prayer: 'wherþoruʒ men moun knowe þe beter whi men ben not herd in her preier of god alwei whanne þei preien'. The compiler of JRL, MS Eng. 85 is unusual in explaining his intentions so directly, but other anthologists used the same strategy, selecting from a wide range of short texts in order to provide the most appropriate degree of progression for their intended readers. Works such as *Foure Errours*, *The Sixteen Conditions of Charity* and *The Abbey of the Holy Ghost* occur frequently in this context where textual choice could influence both the pace and direction of devotional development; moral treatises such as *The VIII Tokenes of Mekenes* could encourage the reader towards a more harmonious Christian life on earth, whereas meditative texts such as *The Three Arrows of Doomsday* promoted the contemplation of death and the last judgement. C. A. Martin has proposed a broad classification scheme for manuals based on their

---

[35] Oxford, St John's College, MS 94, f. 101v; Lacy's injunction that the book's readers pray for his soul prefaces a series of Latin prayers and an English devotional manual; see Ogilvie-Thomson (ed.), *IMEP, VIII*, 87–9.

[36] JRL, MS Eng. 85, ff. 2–37. See Connolly, 'Books for the "helpe of euery persoone þat þenkiþ to be saued"', esp. 172–5.

[37] JRL, MS Eng. 85, f. 19v; the prologue is quoted fully in Connolly, 'Books for the "helpe of euery persoone þat þenkiþ to be saued"', 173–4.

codicological contexts, and more detailed investigation of this aspect might advance our knowledge of such collections.[38]

Compilers also quarried longer texts in their search for suitable progressive material. In CUL, MS Ii.4.9, a mid fifteenth-century devotional anthology produced in Norfolk, extracts from Love's *Mirror* follow copies of *The Six Masters* or *A Litil Schort Tretice* by Adam the Carthusian, *The Abbey of the Holy Ghost* and *The Charter of the Abbey of the Holy Ghost* at the end of a manual of instruction; a second hand has added extracts from John Gaytryge's *Sermon* (or 'Lay Folks' Catechism'), a note attributed to St Bridget and an extract from Rolle's *The Form of Living*.[39] The richest devotional seams were found in Rolle's and Hilton's writings which, along with anonymous works such as *Pore Caitif* and *Contemplations of the Dread and Love of God*, were the most frequently mined by compilers in order to create devotional anthologies where borrowings and sources were sometimes acknowledged but more often were not. CUL, MS Ff.5.40 is a collection of twenty devotional prose works including several by Hilton (Book I of *The Scale of Perfection*, *On the Mixed Life* and *Of Angel's Song*) and Rolle (*The Commandment*, a translation of *Emendatio vitae* and *The Form of Living*).[40] Extracts from both *The Form of Living* and *The Scale of Perfection* are given in addition to the full-text versions, and there are also extracts from John Gaytryge's *Sermon* and *Clennesse of Sowle* (the Middle English translation of Catherine of Siena's *Dialogo*); none of the authors is acknowledged by name, nor are the extracts related to their full-text sources. The parallel devotional volume CUL, MS Dd.5.55 offers a shorter collection of works by Hilton and Rolle; again, no ascriptions are offered, with the exception of the erased inscription in the bottom margin of f. 102v which reads 'Here endys þe tretys of Walter Hilton', although the text on this leaf is actually a medley of quotations from St Bonaventure, St Bernard and Rolle.[41] In CUL, MS Ii.6.40 a few lines from *The Form of Living* are joined onto a copy of *The Commandment*; neither text is identified as Rolle's, although the next item, a series of extracts, with considerable additions and omissions, from *The Mirror of Holy Church* or *The Mirror of St Edmund* (the English translation of the *Speculum ecclesiae* of Edmund of Abingdon), is introduced with the rubric: 'Her byginniþ a deuout meditacion of Ricard Hampol.'[42] Other anthologies take more care to provide correct attributions. The as yet unedited Middle English translation

---

[38] Martin, 'Middle English Manuals of Religious Instruction'.

[39] Hardwick and Luard, *A Catalogue*, III.448–50; *LALME*, I.68; Connolly (ed.), *IMEP, XIX*, 210–17.

[40] Hardwick and Luard, *A Catalogue*, II.498–500; *LALME*, I.67 (two entries); Connolly (ed.), *IMEP, XIX*, 135–41.

[41] Hardwick and Luard, *A Catalogue*, I.275–6; *LALME*, I.66; Connolly (ed.), *IMEP, XIX*, 21–3. MSS CUL, MS Ff.5.40 and CUL, MS Dd.5.55 are parallel volumes which partially duplicate BodL, MS Rawl. C.285.

[42] CUL, MS Ii.6.40, f. 207v. This anthology also has extracts from St Bridget's *Revelations* and *The Pore Caitif*, and copies of *Contemplations of the Dread and Love of God* and *The Pater Noster of Richard Ermyte*; see Hardwick and Luard, *A Catalogue*, III.538–9 and Connolly (ed.), *IMEP, XIX*, 233–7.

of Rolle's *Emendatio vitae* – which is given only a blandly anonymous introduction in BodL, MS Douce 322: 'Howe that a man shulde lyue in contemplacioun and meditacioun' – is carefully described as the work of Rolle in two other manuscripts.[43] In other cases we can clearly perceive efforts to assemble coherent collections of the works of particular writers. CUL, MS Dd.5.64 represents a 'collected works' of Richard Rolle, its first two sections preserving his Latin works, and the third containing copies of all his major English writings; evidently fifteenth-century concerns about canonicity were not confined to the transmission of courtly literature, nor was the impetus to prepare authorial anthologies one which arose only with print technology.

The practices of extraction and anthologization were so widespread in the production of devotional manuscripts that certain combinations of texts seem to have circulated together as a matter of course, a process that was greatly facilitated by their frequent copying in self-contained units or 'booklets', as Pamela Robinson terms them.[44] A booklet might contain a single work or a number of short works and could comprise either a single quire or several gatherings; the booklet's crucial distinguishing feature is that its physical boundaries are not transcended by the text or texts within it. The booklet was a useful format for both producers and consumers, as Linne Mooney has shown in her discussion of the work of the 'Trinity Anthologies scribe' and his associates in late fifteenth-century London.[45] Mooney notes that the contents of the second of the three booklets which make up BodL, MS Douce 322, a devotional collection which William Baron provided for his 'nece', Pernelle Wrattisley, a nun at Dartford Abbey, parallel those of the second booklet of TCC, MS R.3.21. The same scribal hand was responsible for both, but the unembellished nature of the Trinity booklet, where the historiated initials are mere pen-and-ink sketches, compared with the completed decorative scheme in Douce, suggests that the former was the exemplar for the latter. Mooney goes further: she suggests that some of the twenty-six booklets which now make up TCC, MS R.3.21 and its secular partner TCC, MS R.3.19 may have never left the environment where they were produced, functioning instead as display copies for prospective buyers to peruse. In this way a buyer might select whole collections of texts, or certain combinations, or even individual pieces, to create a bespoke anthology from scratch, or to add material to existing volumes. Fifteenth-century merchants such as Roger Thorney and William Middleton, both of whom left their names in TCC, MS R.3.21, may have been accustomed to this method of book acquisition,

---

[43] BodL, MS Douce 322, f. 78r. The text is identified as 'þe twelve chapitres of richard heremite of hampool' in CUL, MS Ff.5.30, f. 164v and as 'Duodecim capitula ricardi hampole heremite' in BodL MS Digby 18, f. 37v; see *IPMEP* 652 and Lagorio and Sargent, 'Mystical Writings', 3424 [15], version A.

[44] Robinson, 'The "Booklet"'.

[45] Mooney, 'Scribes and Booklets', and Chapter 9, pp. 207–10 below.

and reliance on booklets to create or augment one's library may have been a long-standing practice, judging from the earlier examples cited by Robinson.[46]

The booklet format had many practical benefits, and it is not surprising to find it employed in a wide range of fifteenth-century manuscript contexts and retained by compilers after printing in the form of *Sammelbände*.[47] It was a favoured method of book production in the transmission of secular poetry, as may be seen from TCC, MS R.3.19 and other collections such as BodL, MS Fairfax 16 and BodL, MS Tanner 346.[48] It was also the format preferred by producers of devotional anthologies such as those cited above. Another example is the fifteenth-century devotional collection, Oxford, Corpus Christi College, MS 220, which is in its original limp parchment binding.[49] Booklets frequently feature in the composition of later medieval medical and scientific manuscripts, perhaps because this was an easy way to combine older texts with more recent commentaries, and also because booklets tended to be small and easily portable, aspects obviously advantageous to anyone involved in practical medicine.[50] Differences in size, whether in the physical dimensions of leaves or the number of quires gathered together, indicate that sections of such volumes had separate origins, but it is often impossible to judge the point at which different segments were brought together to form a single book. Another feature which practical users found convenient was the tendency for blank leaves to occur at the end of a booklet where the written material had not quite filled the space allowed in the gathering. This constituted handy writing space where extra material, such as prognostications, charms and recipes, might be added; in this way the process of compilation could persist long after the main period of production had finished. However, such layers of use, and the contribution of material by many different hands, have complicated both the process of assembly and our understanding of it. In some contexts the presence of blank leaves may be one of the identifying features of booklet construction, along with the soiling and rubbing of the outer leaves of gatherings; but in medical manuscripts such as leechbooks and remedy-books, which were designed for practical use, these traces are much less noticeable, since blank spaces have frequently been filled and the books themselves are often dirtied by use.[51]

---

[46] Robinson, 'The "Booklet"', 56–61, notes collections formed from booklets by an anonymous thirteenth-century Berkshire lawyer and by William Rede, Bishop of Chichester (d. 1385).

[47] On the latter, see Gillespie, 'Poets, Printers and Early English *Sammelbände*', and Gillespie, *Print Culture and the Medieval Author*, 45–54.

[48] Boffey and Thompson, 'Anthologies and Miscellanies', 280–1.

[49] Robinson, 'The "Booklet"', 52–3, and Ogilvie-Thomson, *IMEP, VIII*, 25–6; on the binding of limp 'booklets', see discussion by Gillespie in Chapter 7, pp. 168–9 below.

[50] Voigts, 'Scientific and Medical Books', 353–6.

[51] Mooney, 'Manuscript Evidence', 193–6, notes two instances where verse instructions for bloodletting occur on folios apparently stained with blood.

A typical fifteenth-century leechbook, CUL, MS Ee.1.15, illustrates many of these points.[52] This small paper quarto is written by several different hands. Its principal contents are five substantial collections of Middle English medical recipes, but there is also a great deal of diagnostic material, including uroscopic texts and a lunary, and various useful items such as an explanation of weights and measures and a list of distances. What now constitutes the manuscript's first section was originally the last part of an alphabetical herbal index; its header letters P–Y are still visible. The 'P' category on f. 1r is relatively full, beginning with 'popie white, popye rede', and some entries have relevant additions: 'ys good for a man or a woman þat is in a francy' is noted alongside 'palma xpi' (*palma christi*), for example. Conversely, no herbs are recorded under 'Q' or 'Y' (f. 1v, f. 6v), and 'erbe xpofer' (*herb cristofre*) is the single entry under 'X' (f. 6r). The resulting blank spaces have not, however, been wasted. On f. 1v two items have been added: a recipe for a powder to be taken every morning and evening, benefits unspecified, and dietary advice on herbs to be used daily and foodstuffs to be avoided ('beware of mustye brede for any thynge'). On f. 6r–v the blank space now accommodates a list of perilous days, the inauspicious days for bloodletting and other medical treatment, and notes on the beneficial properties of various substances, including apples and butter. The addition of such notes and related texts is just what might be expected as the herbal knowledge from the original index was put into practical use. More surprising is the insertion of another bifolium, now constituting ff. 4–5, into this rump of a herbal; these leaves are of markedly smaller size than those which surround them and contain material in Latin, an English recipe for plague and a fragment of another medical recipe added by a rougher hand. Towards the end of the volume as we now have it the fifth and largest collection of recipes (ff. 101v–156v) has also suffered various disruptions. A leaf has been excised after f. 134, and the next gathering, ff. 135–42, has much smaller leaves; this contains Latin medical material, an English recipe for ague by a different hand and another recipe beginning 'And take sage and fetherfew' which is then continued by another hand; the same hand is responsible for two further recipes on f. 142r–v. These intrusions again demonstrate the open-ended and dynamic nature of textual acquisition and book compilation.

The contents of CUL, MS Ee.1.15 are mostly in English with a smattering of Latin texts: a herbal, legal writs, an indulgence.[53] Some works are macaronic, such as the charm 'Maria peperit cristum' for difficult childbirth (a Latin prose prayer with English instructions), and several others are translations from Latin, including the influential verse herbal attributed to 'Macer Floridus' and *The treatise of the oke tre*, translated from Arnald of Villanova's *De Virtute quercus*; additionally,

---

[52] Hardwick and Luard, *A Catalogue*, ii.15–16; Connolly (ed.), *IMEP, XIX*, 94–105; see also Connolly, 'When the Right Word *Really* Matters'.

[53] CUL, MS Ee.1.15, ff. 71r–72v, 127v, 128r.

the various uroscopic texts either derive from Latin or co-exist in both Latin and English. An incomplete recipe for a salve mixes French and English terms in the style of glosses ('floure de genesse þat is flowre of brome'), and is found elsewhere in both French and English versions.[54] It is clear from this linguistic diversity and increasing engagement in translation that compilers of practical collections faced issues similar to those experienced by producers of devotional anthologies: in both areas, textual supply struggled to match demand, and while initially a certain degree of linguistic flexibility could be taken for granted, over time older texts needed to be re-packaged through translation to remain accessible and relevant to different audiences.

Other aspects of assembly which have been noted with regard to the contents of religious manuscripts may be observed in the field of *Fachliteratur* (practical writing), in particular the use of similar strategies for the organization of materials. Enumeration, the favourite technique of compilers of devotional manuals, is much in evidence in practical anthologies which provide lists and short texts quantifying things by four (humours, complexions, seasons), seven (days of the week, planets), twelve (months, zodiacal signs) and twenty (colours/contents of urine, medicinal distillations).[55] Enumeration is also used to improve readerly access to large works. In the substantial culinary collection in BL, MS Add. 5467, each individual recipe has a number and centred heading, made prominent by large textura script, elements which are keyed to a two-column index at the end of the text.[56] The collection is also subdivided into sections which group similar foodstuffs or cooking methods together ('diuerses sauces pur diuerses vyaundes'; 'la maner pur roster et saucer diuerses viaundes'). It is not always clear whether indexes and contents lists are integral or additional features of the texts they accompany. In CUL, MS Dd.6.29, a different hand has supplied a table of contents to a collection of more than 200 medical recipes and charms (see Figures 6.2 and 6.3).[57] Although the last entries in the table correspond to the final five recipes in the collection, these recipes were added by a different hand. Page numbers in red ink have been added in the top margins throughout and are used in the table of contents to indicate where particular groups of recipes may be located. These types of feature helped the user to negotiate each collection quickly, although the intrinsic difficulty of achieving accuracy in indexing (still noticeable in modern books!), especially when using roman numerals, is reflected in both cases in discrepancies between the indexes and the recipes themselves.

[54] Ibid., f. 100v. See Connolly, 'When the Right Word *Really* Matters'.

[55] For examples of texts organized in this manner, see CUL, MSS Dd.6.29, Dd.10.44, Ee.1.13 and Ee.1.15; see Connolly, 'Practical Reading for Body and Soul', 156–7.

[56] The recipes themselves are on BL, MS Add. 5467, ff. 25r–64r, preceded by a partial index on f. 23r; a full index follows on ff. 65r–66v; see Griffin, 'The Culinary Collection'.

[57] CUL, MS Dd.6.29, ff. 20r–25r and 34r–106r; see Hardwick and Luard, *A Catalogue*, 1.300–2 and Connolly (ed.), *IMEP, XIX*, 31–7.

In terms of the assembly of contents, works of science and information were as subject to similar concerns, practices and restrictions as their better-known literary and religious cousins. If anything, the processes of selection, extraction and anthologization seem to have been even more complicated in the case of medical and scientific texts, as research into the intricate connections between uroscopic texts is starting to reveal.[58] Another context where evidence of complex inter-relations is just emerging is the neglected area of alchemical literature. Otherwise unconnected alchemical anthologies may be linked through shared textual contents, as may be seen in a group of later fifteenth- and sixteenth-century manuscripts: CUL, MS Kk.6.30, TCC, MS O.5.31, BodL, MS Ashmole 1486 and Copenhagen, RLC, MS 1727.[59] The correspondence between the two later volumes, BodL, MS Ashmole 1486 and Copenhagen RLC, MS 1727, is particularly strong: they share twelve English prose texts, copied in the same order with identical Latin headings. Ten of these are found in an earlier manuscript, TCC, MS O.5.31, but there the regular sequence is considerably disrupted: texts, sometimes duplicated, appear in a different order, and headings, where present, often take vernacular forms. The last member of this group, CUL, MS Kk.6.30, gives Latinate headings to its texts which are ordered and divided in a manner that resembles their treatment in TCC, MS O.5.31, but overall CUL, MS Kk.6.30 has the least material (only five texts) in common with the others. These textual connections may be traced through entries in the relevant volumes of *The Index of Middle English Prose (IMEP)*, but exclusive reliance upon this reference work is unsatisfactory, since its entries elide other aspects of manuscript contents, ignoring verse and works in other languages – a particular problem for practical anthologies, especially alchemical compendia whose contents are typically of a mixed linguistic nature. Nevertheless, the partial evidence assembled here demonstrates previously unperceived connections between these four alchemical anthologies in terms of their dependence on a common stock of texts. Evidently practical texts, just like their devotional counterparts, could and did circulate in sets and sequences. Yet these were not regarded as sacrosanct by scribes who, instead of slavishly following their exemplars, selected and shaped their contents to suit the circumstances of their particular commissions.

A different type of compilation which has not yet been considered in this discussion is the individual miscellany which was not composed from booklets but which grew organically over time, usually in an unorganized manner, in response to its compiler's particular interests. Such volumes can be tricky to comprehend but may be illuminated by biographical information. The combination of legal, technical

---

[58] Tavormina, 'The Twenty-Jordan Series' and 'The Middle English *Letter of Ipocras*'.

[59] Respectively, Hardwick and Luard, *A Catalogue*, iii.726–8 and Connolly (ed.), *IMEP, XIX*, 292–9; James, *The Western Manuscripts*, iii.331–2 (no. 1312) and Mooney (ed.), *IMEP, XI*, 121–5; Eldredge (ed.), *IMEP, IX*, 98–100; and Taavitsainen (ed.), *IMEP, X*, 7–11.

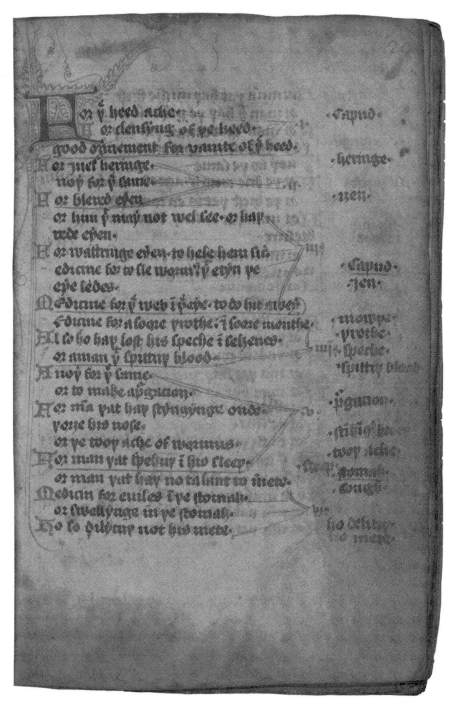

Figure 6.2 CUL, MS Dd.6.29, f. 20r: a table of contents.

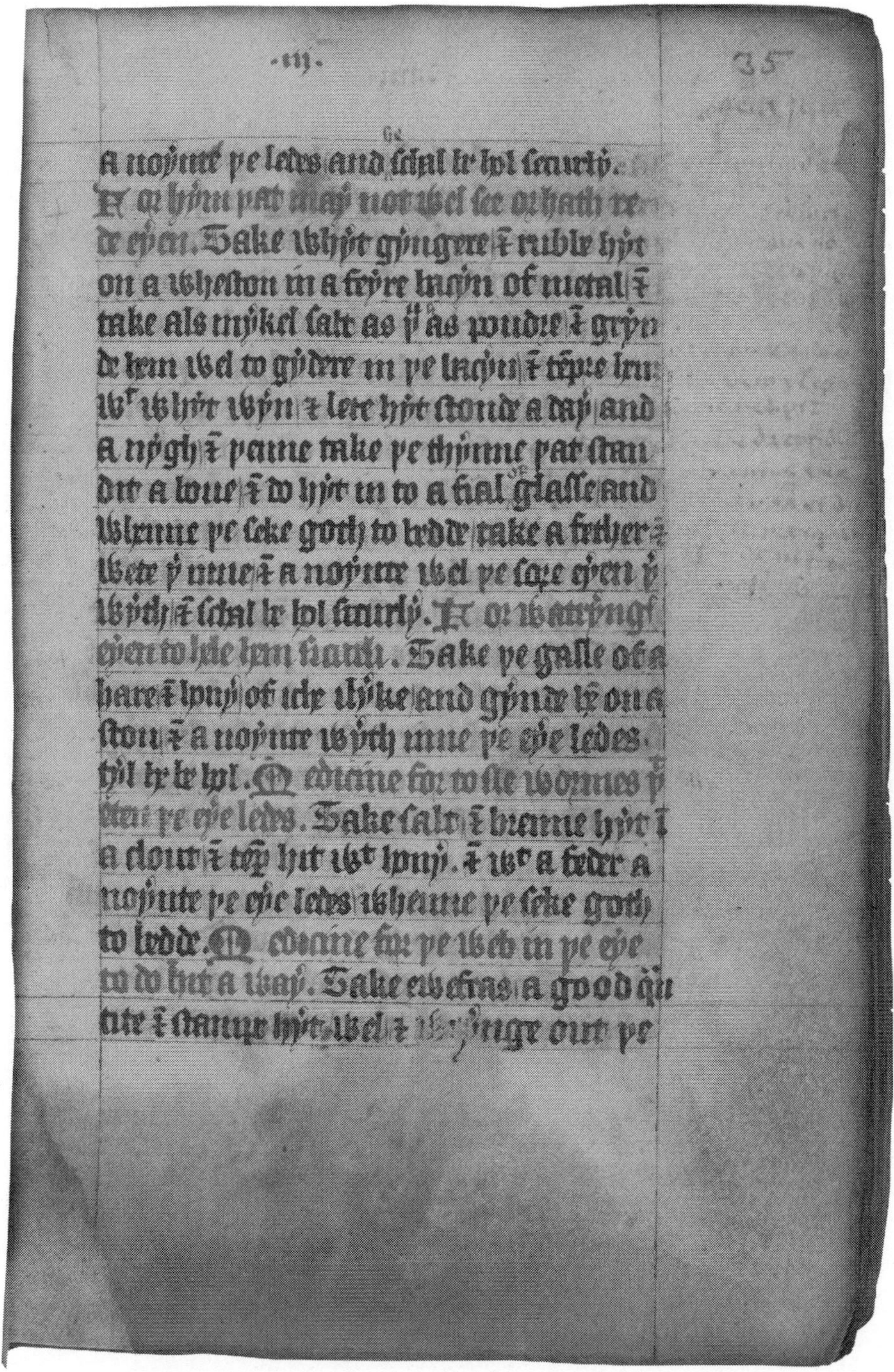

Figure 6.3 CUL, MS Dd.6.29, f. 35r: numbering in the running title and chapter headings which correspond to the table of contents.

and spiritual texts in the Wagstaff miscellany (Beinecke Library, MS 163), seems less surprising when connected with the figure of John Whittocksmead (1410–82), who was a prominent member of the West Country gentry; who served on royal commissions and as bailiff to the bishop of Salisbury; and whose activities brought him into contact with other local gentry and with various religious houses.[60] Naturally enough, volumes which may be associated with named individuals have attracted greater attention than the more numerous anonymous compilations, but over-reliance on a few such examples may skew understanding of this kind of book, and the partial availability of manuscript facsimiles compounds the problem. The term 'commonplace book', which has a precise meaning when applied to Renaissance manuscripts, is often used carelessly in this context 'as a catch-all to a variety of late Middle English manuscripts of a miscellaneous nature, regardless of how or why they were put together'.[61] The distinctive nature of the commonplace book is its very individuality; Pearsall emphasizes that its unique combination of contents could be imagined to be of interest to no one but its maker and offers as a typical example the collection of family records, lists of rents and copies of legal documents compiled by Robert Reynes of Acle in Norfolk.[62] However, another problem is that such miscellanies are sometimes dismissed as *too* individual, their circumstances of production judged too particular to be taken as characteristic of the general conditions of later medieval book production.

Most of the preceding discussion presupposes that the process of assembling the medieval book was an activity governed by a sense of purpose and a degree of intent, although we should be wary of assuming that all manuscript production was so purposeful.[63] We also suppose that what we now regard as medieval books were exactly that: books assembled in the Middle Ages. We sometimes forget that intervening historical events may have altered the picture and that what we now possess may actually be examples of post-medieval assembly, brought together in the sixteenth century or later. It is possible that the thirteen booklets which now make up TCC, MS R.3.21 were brought together by John Stow.[64] In his *Survey of London*, Stow acknowledged his acquaintance with John Shirley's manuscripts, saying 'I haue seene them, and partly do possesse them', and he may have been responsible for disassembling the second of Shirley's anthologies.[65] As

---

[60] Keiser, 'Practical Books for the Gentleman', 474–6.

[61] Pearsall, 'The Whole Book: Late Medieval English Manuscript Miscellanies', 23.

[62] BodL, MS Tanner 407, printed by Louis (ed.), *The Commonplace Book of Robert Reynes of Acle*.

[63] Pearsall, 'The Whole Book: Late Medieval English Manuscript Miscellanies', warns against supposing that all miscellanies necessarily contain 'hidden designs' (17) or that they were produced according to a 'guiding intelligence' (18).

[64] Mooney, 'Scribes and Booklets', 266.

[65] London, Lambeth Palace, MS Sion College, Arc. L.40.2/E.44, BL, MS Harley 78, ff. 80r–83v and TCC, MS R.3.20 originally comprised one codex; see Connolly, *John Shirley*, 95–6 and 182–5.

manuscripts found their way into collections and libraries in subsequent centuries they were typically re-bound, or perhaps bound for the first time, not always with material that they had circulated with previously. Another manuscript linked to Shirley is HEHL, MS Ellesmere 26.A.13: its parchment flyleaves carry his motto and inscription giving the names of his second wife and her sister Beatrice; another inscription later in the volume records his gift of that section to Avery Cornburgh, who was later Beatrice's husband. However, the easy assumption that Shirley owned the whole book as we now see it needs to be unpicked. This is a composite manuscript made up from two sections, and there is no evidence at all to link the second of these with Shirley. Furthermore, although the flyleaves are assumed to belong with the first section, there is little real evidence for this, and they could in fact have originally prefaced a different volume of Shirley's.[66] The two halves of the manuscript were not necessarily together in his time: its binding dates only from about the year 1840 when it was part of the Bridgewater library, and we cannot be sure what the volume looked like before then. In another nineteenth-century library the expense of binding was so great that its owner, the collector Sir Thomas Phillipps, economized by instructing his servants to sew together his manuscripts in soft covers.[67] Printed books were not immune to codicological disturbance either. At Althorp, George John, second Earl Spencer, built up an important collection of early printed books with the aid of his librarian, Thomas Dibdin, but their efforts to secure copies of all of Caxton's imprints involved the bibliographical practice of 'improving' imperfect copies by the addition of pages taken from duplicates. As a result the Althorp Caxtons (acquired by the John Rylands Library in 1892) have a mixed pedigree whose true bloodlines can rarely be fully established.[68]

There are many ways in which the appearance of the surviving end-product of centuries of bibliographical activity may falsely shape our sense of what fourteenth- and fifteenth-century manuscripts were like and how they were put together. The environment of the modern library is where most of us now encounter manuscripts, whether in the hallowed environs of the Cambridge Manuscripts Room or through virtual access by way of digitization.[69] Consequently, we see far more manuscripts than any medieval reader, a privilege which enables us to draw comparisons between books that never passed through the same hands or sat together on the same shelves

[66] A possibility discussed by Connolly, *John Shirley*, 104–6.

[67] As recalled by Sir Frederic Madden in his journal, 17 July 1862, quoted by Munby, *The Formation of the Phillipps Library*, 108.

[68] Lister, 'The Althrop Library', describes the cannibalization and facsimile restoration that were commonly accepted practices during the bibliomania of the early nineteenth century; see 69, 74, 79–80.

[69] For example, Corpus Christi College, Cambridge is making its collection available online through http://parkerweb.stanford.edu

before modern times. Understanding what these books were like in their own age and how they were perceived by their readers, as opposed to how they appear to us now, remains a challenge.

Book size is one of the issues here. As modern readers, our expectation is that, except for textbooks and anthologies, books will contain single texts, but what was the norm in medieval England once the textual production had passed out of the hands of the author? Was it for books which consisted of single texts, or for author-based collections, as in France, or collections of texts by several authors? Many of the manuscripts considered in this chapter are (or were) multi-text volumes, and it is often assumed that the issuing of single texts only became standard after printing because small volumes were cheaper to produce. Yet cost-effectiveness must surely have been important in a manuscript culture too, and the market for English books may have been moving towards the production of single texts before printing, as demand increased in the fifteenth century.

There is some evidence to suggest that the provision of single-text books might have been more usual in the later Middle Ages than has hitherto been supposed. Many references to books provide scant details of their contents, concentrating instead on their outer appearances; in wills and inventories descriptions such as 'a sauter couered in blew ... a book couered in grene with praiers therinne' are common, and literary texts also participate in this representation: in *The Canterbury Tales*, the Clerk's twenty philosophical books are 'clad in blak or reed'.[70] The inventory of Henry VIII's books at Greenwich records large numbers of books in this fashion: 'in one deske xxxi bookes couered with redde ... in an other deske xvi bookes couered with redde ... liii bookes couered with leather'.[71] Yet when indications are given of what lies between the covers, these are often couched in terms of single authors or works. Many of the books bequeathed by Henry Scrope, Lord of Masham, in 1415 are described as single-text volumes: to his mother-in-law he left 'unum parvum librum vocatum Virginal' (a little book called Virginal) and 'unum librum vocatum Apocalipsi' (a book named Apocalyse); to his cousin, Henry Fitzhugh, he left 'unum librum' containing Rolle's *Incendium amoris* and 'unum quaternum, parvum' (a small quire) containing Rolle's *Judica me*; to his sister Matilda, a nun at the Minoresses, he left a small book containing the Hours of the Cross, a roll with the Hours of St Anne and 'unum librum in Anglicis, qui vocatur Stimulus conscientiae' (a book in English, which is called *The Prick of Conscience*).[72] In 1481, Sir Richard Roos left his niece, Alianore Howte, 'my grete booke called saint Grall bounde in boordes couerde with rede leder and plated

---

[70] Cited from Meale, ' "... alle the bokes" ', 131; Benson (ed.), *The Riverside Chaucer, The Canterbury Tales*, I.294.

[71] Cited from Carley, 'The Royal Library', 278.

[72] Cited from Cavanaugh, 'A Study of Books Privately Owned in England', II.775.

with plates of laten' (metal).[73] Similarly, in a copy of a letter preserved in CUL, MS Dd.11.45, the writer begs a friend to help him retrieve 'ane inglische buke es cald mort arthur' which had been lent to 'Syr William Cuke preste of Byllesbe'.[74] The complex textual tradition of Arthurian romance, with its layers of translation and adaptation makes it impossible to be sure exactly what work is meant: it is not necessarily Malory's. What *is* clear, though, is that a book containing a single text (or perhaps a single important text?) is being described here. When testators and correspondents describe their books in these ways they betray their perceptions of them, perceptions which might then inform our own: contemporary evidence of how books were regarded by their makers, owners and readers can only enhance modern understanding of these medieval artefacts and the culture in which they were produced and consumed.

[73] Seaton, *Sir Richard Roos*, 547–8.
[74] CUL, MS Dd.11.45, f. 142r.

7

Bookbinding

ALEXANDRA GILLESPIE

Fourteenth- and early fifteenth-century English bindings have never been of as much interest to binding scholars as have twelfth- and thirteenth-century English Romanesque stamped bindings or the stamped, tanned leather covers that were placed on books from 1450 forward.[1] This is largely because, to quote Mirjam Foot, 'in the first three quarters of the [twentieth] century, the history of bookbinding was virtually synonymous with the history of binding decoration'. Very few treasure or embroidered bindings from the Middle Ages survive, and stamped bindings (covers impressed with hot metal stamps or rules) are as 'decorative' as most medieval bindings get.[2] Books of fourteenth- and early fifteenth-century England get short shrift because they are rarely stamped. They are often covered in plain, alum-tawed skin;[3] and the only decorative flourishes they bear that might interest a student of 'decoration' appear on metal clasps, catch-plates and catch-pins, and the silk stitching of compound endbands[4] which survive with even less frequency than old boards or

Thanks to Frederick Bearman, John McQuillen, Philip Oldfield and Rod Thomson for help, advice and correction. All remaining errors are my own.

[1] For a useful introduction to bookbinding to 1400 in England, see Gullick and Hadgraft, 'Bookbindings', 95–109; for more technical detail, see Szirmai, *Archaeology*.

[2] Foot, 'Bookbinding and the History of Books', 113. On English medieval treasure and textile bindings, see Nixon and Foot, *The History of Decorated Bookbinding in England*, 18–24.

[3] Alum-tawed (sometimes 'whittawed') skin describes skin treated using alum; even if stained, the whiteness produced by the process is apparent in cross section. Oil-tanning turns skins a yellowish brown; vegetable tanning produces the 'polished brown surface' preferred for stamping (Pollard, 'Describing Medieval Bookbindings', 58). Parchment is skin treated with lime and dried under tension (Vest, 'The Production and Use of Alum-Tawed Leather'; Reed, *Ancient Skins, Parchments and Leathers*). Skins used in medieval England included seal, deer, pig, calf/cow, ox, goat/hair sheep (difficult to distinguish) and wool sheep; in medieval England, wool sheep is very commonly used. Hadgraft, 'English Fifteenth-Century Bookbinding Structures', gives 15 per cent calf and 85 per cent sheep for his survey of fifteenth-century books but, like many specialists (e.g., Szirmai, *Archaeology*, 225–7), is cautious about species identification (242–3). See Federici, Di Majo and Palma, 'The Determination of Animal Species', on the need for high magnification for accurate identification.

[4] 'Endbands' are cores of skin or cord laced into the boards; the stitching over them is either integral to or 'tied down' into the spine folds of the text block. They may be single; compound endbands

covers. The prevailing view of late medieval English bookbinding is therefore still that of G. D. Hobson (in 1929): it 'left hardly anything of any interest to the student of bindings'.[5]

The purpose of this chapter is to offer an alternative view. The period 1350–1500 has a great deal to offer students of books who are interested in their covers as well as their contents. Even the paucity of evidence noted by Hobson deserves further thought. Consider, for example, the impact of sixteenth-century changes to library furnishings. English books had previously been chained flat on lecterns or stacked horizontally on shelves or in chests; now they were stored upright. One consequence was that there was no longer space for something which had previously been a perfectly normal feature of late medieval binding – a draped cover called a 'chemise'.[6]

The term 'chemise' first appears in bookbinding descriptions in English in the 1890s; the term was picked up from fourteenth- and fifteenth-century continental records of the *camisia* or *chemise*.[7] Fifteenth-century English record-keepers may have had a different word for this sort of binding. The Churchwardens' accounts of the Parish of St Mary, Thame, 1448–9, record sums paid for 'mendyng of ye bagge of ye grete leger' and the making of 'the bagke to a grete boke'.[8] Such bags could have been separate entities: medieval manuscripts are still sometimes kept free of dust and greasy fingerprints in cloth bags. But the Churchwardens of St Mary might equally have had their 'grete boke' and ledger sewn into a binding that took the shape of a bag.

Such 'bagged' books – chemise bindings – form an extended example at the beginning of this chapter because they serve as a salutary reminder of all the material that has been unstitched, unstuck, and sliced and torn off books that interest us. Chemise bindings are also useful because they suggest that even the most fragmentary evidence of binding practice can contribute much to a history of medieval books. To start with, the concept of a 'chemise' needs further explanation. The term describes a kind of primary or secondary book cover where soft textile or leather flaps extend past the boards or edge of the text block and over the fore-edge in order to 'wrap up' the book.[9] A useful example of such a binding is Beinecke,

---

have additional, decorative layers of stitching/braiding. Endbands are sometimes also stitched through 'tabs': pieces of the skin that serves as the primary cover. See Gast, 'A History of Endbands'.

[5] *English Binding before 1500*, 15.

[6] Szirmai, *Archaeology*, 268–71; on furnishing and binding generally, see Streeter, *The Chained Library*.

[7] *OED*, s.v. 'chemise'; Szirmai, *Archaeology*, 234.

[8] *MED*, s.v. 'bag'.

[9] For binding scholars, the term 'text block' describes the quires of paper or parchment that form the body of a book. I follow Bearman, 'The Origins and Significance,' and use 'chemise' rather than Szirmai's 'overcover' (*Archaeology*, 234–6), reserving the latter word for secondary covers without flaps. I use 'wrapper' to describe fully detached coverings.

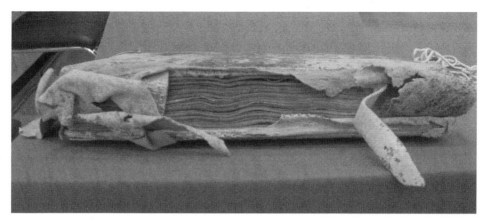

Figure 7.1 Beinecke, MS 27: chemise cover, wooden boards.

MS 27, an early fifteenth-century English copy of the *Speculum humanae salvatoris* – see Figure 7.1.[10] A red-stained, tawed primary cover has been affixed to its boards. A chemise has then been constructed from two skins. Two pieces of the first of these, a soft, white tawed skin, have been pasted on top of the turn-ins of the primary cover at the outer edge of the inner face of both boards. These 'pockets' have then been stitched at the boards' edge to a much heavier, red-stained tawed skin. This skin forms the flaps of the chemise; the flaps have been trimmed off at the tail, but they still extend about 25mm. at the head and 50mm. at the fore-edge of the book. Two red-stained, tawed fastening straps are fixed under the primary cover at the edge of the upper board. These pass through slits cut in the chemise, and close to catch-pins (now missing) on the lower board. The chemise is also held in place by two tackets that attach the fastening straps to the fore-edge flap of the chemise.[11]

Chemises could be the primary covering over a book's boards or be a secondary cover to an existing primary cover. In both cases, pockets could be used to secure the chemise to the boards. In the absence of pockets, the chemise was simply pasted directly onto the boards. They might be made of textile or of skin, and there was variation in style as well as materials. Some chemises simply wrap around the book with the aid of fastening devices, as is the case for Beinecke, MS 27. Some included a long tail-flap for carrying the book, and some are 'girdle books', where the chemise

---

[10] See Shailor, *Catalogue of … the Beinecke Rare Book and Manuscript Library.* She suggests that the binding may be 'Dutch or German?', but the rest of the book is English work and I see no reason not to locate the binding in England.

[11] A tacket is a length of skin, parchment, paper or string, used in much the way we might now use a 'twist-tie', as when tackets are threaded through two holes in the quire fold and then twisted or knotted at the back. See Gullick, 'From Scribe to Binder'; Pickwoad, 'Tacketed Bindings'; Szirmai, *Archaeology*, 142, 287, 287–90, 305–7.

flaps are drawn into a knot or hook, designed to hang the book upside-down from a belt or girdle.[12]

Chemises are a western development in bookbinding. They first appear on twelfth-century books from European monasteries. Christopher Clarkson argues that at English foundations such as Bury, Cirencester, Hereford and Worcester all twelfth-century 'monastic library books – "working" books – were meant to be protected by a chemise'.[13] This may be so, but, as J. A. Szirmai has noted, a great deal of the surviving evidence of chemise-bound books comes from later in the medieval period.[14] This evidence has largely been neglected, and yet it has much to contribute to the history of the book in England at the end of the Middle Ages.

The chemises – or rather, tiny fragments of them – that survive on books from the library of Bury St Edmunds monastery are a case in point. In 1599, a great many of Bury's books came to Pembroke College, Cambridge, in the gift of William Smart, an alderman of Ipswich. The medieval bindings on these manuscripts seem largely intact.[15] Their styles and dates vary. Some – for instance, Pembroke, Camb., MS 18 with writings of St John Chrysostom; and Pembroke, Camb., MS 44 with Amalarius of Metz's *Liber officialis* (both twelfth-century) – have flat spines with tab endbands. The boards are cut square, flat and flush to the text block; the sewing supports enter directly into the boards' edge and the lacing paths are straight.[16] These are features of twelfth- and thirteenth-century binding styles and thus of the foundational work to build Bury's library.[17] The edges of the boards on other Bury bindings are bevelled and the outer faces cushioned. The spines of these books are round, and the sewing supports enter the boards over the outer face. Lacing paths sometimes converge so that exposed channels on the inner face of the boards are *v*-shaped. Such features are characteristic of bookbinding in England in the century and a half before printing. Among the relevant examples in the Bury collection are Pembroke, Camb., MS 98, writings of Peter of Rouen, procured and then donated for the brothers' use by 'ffr. Rob. Ikelyngeham monachus' (f. ir) and Pembroke, Camb., MS 89, *Gregorius super Ezechielem*, gifted by 'fr. Will. Barwe' (f. 1r). Ikelyngeham and Barwe were respectively prior and sacrist of the monastery in the first quarter of the fifteenth century, and the manuscripts they donated date to roughly the same period.[18]

---

[12] This follows Bearman's taxonomy, 'The Origins and Significance'.

[13] Clarkson, 'English Monastic Bookbindings', 197; see also Szirmai, *Archaeology*, 164–5.

[14] Szirmai, *Archaeology*, 234–9.

[15] On some 1970s repairs, see Clarkson, 'English Monastic Bookbindings', 183, n.5.

[16] A sewing 'support' is a length of skin or cord (usually split/double) onto which the quires of the text-block are sewn: supports are attached to boards in channels in a variety of 'lacing' patterns.

[17] McLachlan, *The Scriptorium of Bury St Edmunds*; Webber, 'The Provision of Books for Bury St Edmunds Abbey'.

[18] On Iklingham, see Thomson, *The Archives of the Abbey of Bury St Edmunds*, 37; for Barwe and his scribal work, see Parkes, *Their Hands before Our Eyes*, 21.

As different as they are, however, all four of the manuscripts just described and most others in the Pembroke collection contain identically positioned traces of the pocket of a soft, white, tawed chemise that was once pasted onto the inner face of the boards and stitched at the boards' edge. Sometimes, these traces are no more than fibres clinging to a patch of paste or an impression left on an endleaf. But in a few cases a whole section of the inner pocket survives: see Figure 7.2 from Pembroke, Camb., MS 101, a thirteenth-century collection of sermons. Even fragments are telling. Pembroke, Camb., MS 59 is a glossed book of Isaiah from the Romanesque period. Its binding is also late twelfth-century and is notable for its pastedowns and endleaves, which were made from leaves from a Hebrew *Siddur* (prayer-book).[19] The leaves show that a twelfth- or thirteenth-century binder working in or for the Bury monastery had access to books that had been used by the Jews in Bury before their expulsion in 1290. They also prove that the book's chemise was added a good while after it was first bound: the fragments of the chemise are pasted *over* offsets of script from the *Siddur*. The book's original pastedowns must have lifted off the inner board by the time the chemise was added.

The addition of a chemise to this manuscript and the *terminus post quem* supplied by the bindings of MSS 89 and 98 suggest that the Bury chemises were not twelfth- but fifteenth-century additions to its books. In the late fourteenth and fifteenth centuries, following attacks on its buildings and its records by townsfolk and in response to the erosion of its privileges, the monastery of Bury St Edmunds' archives were consolidated and augmented. The monk Henry Kirkstede tidied up and catalogued the monastery's book collection; John Lydgate became a reader and then poet amid that collection; Barwe and Ikelyngeham donated to it. It seems that someone also saw to it that the books that lined Bury's shelves and lay on its lecterns – books both new and old – were dressed up in matching white drapery.[20]

Frederick Bearman's important study of English chemise bindings helps us to understand the significance of those at Bury. Chemise coverings, Bearman argues, reflect a practice dating to early Christian times 'of draping and covering the hands while holding, offering, or receiving sacred books and other precious objects'. In late medieval art, saints, angels and mourners often hold books encased in drapery.[21] In medieval images of the annunciation, Mary sometimes protects the prayerbook she carries in the folds of her dress, and Low Countries artists of the late Middle Ages – Robert Campin, Juan de Flandes and Joos Van Cleve, for instance – developed this iconographic tradition. Their paintings show the book itself folded into the fabric

[19] Abrahams, 'Leaf from an English *Siddur* of the Twelfth Century'.

[20] Rouse, 'Kirkstede, Henry'; Summit, *Memory's Library*, ch. 1. Many books were also re-bound at this time, as noted by Sheppard, 'The Census of Western Medieval Bookbinding Structures', 177, and Hadgraft, 'English Fifteenth-Century Bookbinding Structures', 14, 210–14. They date the programme of book refurbishment at Bury to the late 1300s and mid-1400s (respectively).

[21] 'The Origins and Significance', 167–78 (170).

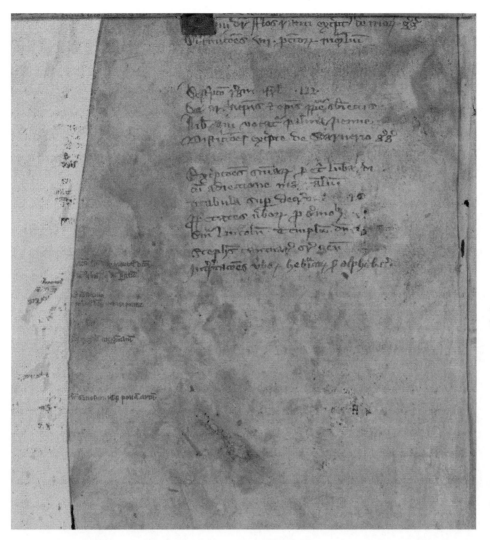

Figure 7.2 Pembroke, Camb., MS 101, close-up: inner face of upper board, remains of chemise.

or skin of a chemise so that the binding of the holy words of Scripture mirrors the draping of Mary's own sacred form. Like the book, she is the precious vessel in which – the observer is meant to recall – God's 'Word' is contained (John 1.1).[22] Bearman's work thus suggests that by supplying their newly arranged books with chemises, the monks at Bury St Edmunds not only protected the books' edges from dust or damage but deepened their association with all that was sacred, precious and authoritative.

[22] See Frey, 'Maria Legens – Maria Legere'.

The association of this style of binding and the veneration of certain texts may have implications for the way that we interpret other accounts of medieval English books. If it was normal to bind important or sacred books in chemises and sometimes to use the long flaps of those chemises as handles – to carry books about in their bindings as if in bags – then this might suggest a new way of approaching an important scene in the fifteenth-century poem *Mum and the Sothsegger*. In the scene, the narrator of the poem wakes from a dream. Rather than starting again on his frustrating search for a truth-teller amid all the corruption of fifteenth-century English society, he opens a bag a books:

> Now forto conseille the king vnknytte I a bagge
> Where many a pryue poyse [secret verse] is preyntid withynne
> Yn bokes vnbredid [unbound] in balade-wise made.

The detailed catalogue of the bag's contents that follows – with a 'penyworth of papir'; 'a volume … of viftene leves'; pamphlets, scrolls and writs – has often attracted comment from critics who have been interested in the poem's account of late medieval society, its forms of political counsel and the bookish cultures that sustained both.[23] However, no one has yet had much to say about the 'bagge' that is the container for all of this useful historical knowledge. 'Many a pryue poyse' is 'preyntid withynne' this bag. In the next line, the reader learns that these verses are printed (written) within the myriad 'bokes' that fill – are themselves 'printed' (pressed) into – the bag. But the first two lines here may suggest something else as well. Perhaps each 'poyse' is 'preyntid withynne' the bag itself. Perhaps there is a book actually bound into this bag, as were so many books in late medieval England. For just a moment the *Mum*-poet's 'bagge … preyntid withynne' could be chemise-bound book. For just a moment the bag could be suggestive of the Christian traditions and truths the narrator seeks 'forto conseille the king'. What he ultimately finds is something more and less than this hopeful possibility. As the third line of the quotation here makes clear, the singular becomes multiple. The sacred, draped book turns into a sack of scrappy 'bokes' – documents that contain as much evidence of corruption as they do good counsel against it – and the bag turns out to be just a bag after all. If the Bury chemises register a symbolic association between a binding technique and religious convention in the late medieval period, the bag of books in *Mum* registers something different. It describes a moment in the history of England when textual material seemed suddenly to proliferate in a wide variety of forms. The argument of this chapter is that we would better understand that moment – and all the other moments that made

---

[23] Cited from Barr (ed.), *The Piers Plowman Tradition*, lines 1343–5, 1350, 1353; see also Gillespie, 'Books'.

up late medieval English society and culture – by studying the bindings of books as well as the pages they bound.

As this last comment implies, medieval bookbinding is not widely studied. This is perhaps because it seems, of all the aspects of a book, the one at the furthest remove from textual content. Medieval manuscript studies owe much to an early focus on texts and the editorial problems they present. But even as the field of 'book history' has come to accommodate broader interest in the social contexts for the production and dissemination of books and in the unique formal properties and histories of those books, the study of binding has remained extremely specialized.[24]

This is not to suggest that the study of binding is itself static. Far from it: like Foot (cited above), Szirmai notes that while 'the majority of scholars of previous generations' avoided the structural aspects' of binding and focussed on decorative styles, a new generation considers 'old binding structures' as 'a rich source of knowledge and insight' into the past.[25] Since its publication in 1999, Szirmai's *The Archaeology of Medieval Bookbinding* has become an indispensable guide to the study of the medieval bindings of Coptic, Ethiopian, Islamic and Byzantine as well as European medieval manuscripts. In the narrower field of English binding, Foot, Nicholas Pickwood, Nicolas Barker, David Pearson and Stuart Bennett have shown that bindings can teach us about 'the purpose of the book, its use and readership ... form and construction' and about the 'binder and his role in society'.[26] Of these writers, only Foot, Barker and Pickwood deal with bindings before the advent of printing, and then only occasionally. But in the case of the medieval period, their work is supplemented extremely usefully by that of Bearman, Clarkson, Michael Gullick, Jennifer Sheppard and the late Nicholas Hadgraft.[27]

Nevertheless it is notable that Sheppard's 1995 'hope' that work on bindings 'will become a regular part of our general bibliographical skills' is still just a hope.[28] Most medieval manuscript scholars know how to describe something like a 'medieval binding of pink leather over wooden boards: four bands: central clasp' (which is roughly how Neil R. Ker describes London, Lambeth Palace, MS Sion College,

[24] Gillespie, 'Analytical Survey 9'; and on the effect of this on binding studies, see Foot, *Bookbinders at Work*, ch. 1.

[25] Szirmai, *Archaeology*, x.

[26] Foot, 'Bookbinding and the History of Books', 113; see, among their other publications, Foot's *Bookbinders at Work* and *Studies in the History of Bookbinding*; relevant chapters in Barker's *Form and Meaning in the History of the Book*; Pickwood's 'Onward and Downward'; Bennett's *Trade Bookbinding in the British Isles*; Pearson's *English Bookbinding Styles*.

[27] For example, Sheppard, 'Some Twelfth-Century Monastic Bindings' and 'The Census of Western Medieval Bookbinding Structures'; Gullick's contribution to Thomson, *A Descriptive Catalogue of ... Worcester Cathedral Library*; Gullick and Hadgraft, 'Bookbindings'; Hadgraft, 'English Fifteenth-Century Bookbinding Structures'; Bearman, 'The Origins and Significance'; Clarkson, 'English Monastic Bookbinding' and 'Further Studies in Anglo-Saxon and Norman Bookbinding'.

[28] Sheppard, 'Some Twelfth-Century Monastic Bindings', 118.

Ar. L.40.2/L.12, a fifteenth-century *Ars Moriendi*, and is typical of his descriptions in *Medieval Manuscripts in British Libraries*).[29] But broad-ranging discussions of medieval English book history simply do not incorporate detailed discussion of binding into their conclusions. The result is one that the scholars who notice it bewail: 'The low importance … attached to binding structures by scholars who use medieval books and by those who have had the care of them', writes Sheppard, creates 'a devastating spiral.' Bindings are neglected. Because they seem of little scholarly interest, until very recently they were rarely catalogued and routinely 'restored'. 'There is no such thing as restoring an old binding without obliterating its entire history', wrote E. P. Goldschmidt in 1928.[30] Much evidence is lost or made inaccessible, making it harder to study old bindings, which are neglected further.

The aim of the present chapter, then, is to contribute to an existing conversation about medieval bookbinding, a conversation of vital importance to the preservation as well as to an understanding of this aspect of our cultural heritage. It is to suggest that binding research should not be the preserve of specialists, and that this is an ideal moment to make new connections between binding and the broader history of the book. Expanding upon Bearman's exemplary interdisciplinary work on chemises, my discussion of the bindings at Bury and the 'preyntid' bag in *Mum and the Sothsegger* argues for the inclusion of formal work on bindings alongside other kinds of bookish study – palaeographic and iconographic analysis; library, institutional and economic history; and literary criticism. Few well-known vernacular manuscripts are in medieval bindings: only four of Chaucer's works survive in what may be pre-1500 covers, for instance.[31] But discussion of medieval binding practice still has much to contribute to our knowledge of late medieval texts and of the circumstances in which those texts were produced and disseminated. Focussing on bindings in collections in London, Oxford and Cambridge and at the Beinecke and Huntington libraries, this chapter will outline some neglected but promising areas of enquiry for late medieval bookbinding before turning briefly to binding in the early years of printing.

Binders turn up early in English records. A. I. Doyle finds men and women styled 'binder' in English provincial towns as early as the 1290s.[32] These binders herald the

---

[29] Ker's notice of bindings makes his catalogue an invaluable handlist of those that survive in smaller British Libraries: we lack such a handlist for the British Library, Cambridge University Library and the Bodleian. Recent catalogues with superb work on bindings include Thomson, Shailor and Dutschke, see e.g., nn. 10, 18, 37.

[30] *Gothic and Renaissance Bookbindings*, 1.123.

[31] From my survey of books and catalogues: see the discussion of two parchment-bound *Astrolable* manuscripts below; the others are BodL, MS Selden Supra 56 (*Troilus*) and BodL, MS Rawl. D. 3 (*Astrolabe*).

[32] Doyle, 'The English Provincial Book Trade', e.g. the bookbinder in Newcastle upon Tyne recorded in the 1292 and 1296 Northumberland Lay Subsidy Roll (n.59).

change described by Nigel J. Morgan and Rodney M. Thomson in the second volume of *The Cambridge History of the Book*: after 1200, 'the dominance of the monastic book gradually and almost completely gave way to town-based commercial production'.[33] More archival research on the first commercial artisan-binders might not be especially fruitful: the record for the early period is extremely thin. But such work could yield interesting results for the period of concern in this volume. C. Paul Christianson's meticulous collection of London records of the book trade is full of examples of binders. They include some women, like the Alice Drax 'bookbinder' who was paid 19s 2d out of the Wardrobe Account of Henry IV in 1408.[34] It was a group of London citizens who 'use to bind and sell books' who, together with the Textwriters and Limners (whose misteries had been established since at least the 1350s), formed the Stationers' Company in 1403.[35] The stationer Peter Bylton, described in his 1454 will, as in most other records of him, as a 'citizen and bokebynder', was also a warden of the company (then still called the Mistery of Textwriters and Limners) in 1426. He was still active in the 1450s, when he purchased a tenement; he first rented a shop in Paternoster Row in 1404. He seems to have flourished throughout his long career: by 1410 he had taken over the rental of three more shops – two from goldsmiths and one from a scrivener and stationer, John Boys. If London stationers such as Boys could also be scriveners, so could its binders be scribes. William Agell of Selby was appointed church binder and scribe to the Bishop of London, Robert de Braybroke, in 1391.[36] The general picture is – as Erik Kwakkel shows in Chapter 8 in this volume – that of a book trade becoming increasingly commercial and organized, but of artisans and tradesmen with multiple occupations within that trade. Binding was as integral to a burgeoning bookish culture in late medieval England as it is now peripheral to discussion of that culture.

The binding of a book might occur at several stages of its history – at the direction, and even by the hands, of the scribe who had fulfilled a commission; or some time after the book had been delivered, according to a patron's or institution's needs. For long-lived medieval books, binding often occurred more than once. Towards the end of the fifteenth century, Winchcombe Abbey had two of its twelfth-century manuscripts, now Oxford, Jesus College, MS 102 and HEHL, MS HM 52435, taken to Oxford, where they were re-bound in stamped calf and chemises by the so-called 'Fishtail' binder.[37] Many medieval books, especially those from smaller institutions

---

[33] *CHBB: II*, xvii.

[34] *A Directory of London Stationers*, where he also notices a 'Dionisia le Bokebyndere' who brought charges over a burglary at her property in 1312.

[35] Blayney, *The Stationers' Company before the Charter*, 9–18 (at 13).

[36] See entries in Christianson, *A Directory of London Stationers*.

[37] Dutschke, *Guide to ... Manuscripts in the Huntington Library*, 11.773–5; on Winchcombe's books, see *MLGB*, 198–9. For the Fishtail binder, who worked in Oxford from at least c.1473 until 1500, see Oldham, *English Blind-Stamped Bindings*, 22, and Foot, 'English Decorated Bookbindings of the

or households, may have been bound or re-bound in this way, after travelling with owners or servants to a distant centre such as Oxford or London where craftspeople and their shops were assembled.

Early rules for monastic life prescribe binding, along with copying, decorating and studying books, and some medieval books whose bindings survive must represent the work of those who lived under such rules.[38] Larger religious institutions may have made use of artisan-binders dwelling in major towns. They may also have retained lay binders in their houses or employed itinerant ones for a set period to work on selections of books needing binding or repair. Clarkson has examined surviving Anglo-Saxon manuscripts from Exeter Cathedral now in the Bodleian Library and described the refurbishment of these books in the fifteenth century.[39] The work was undertaken by a Mr William Hayford and 'Richard his servant' in 1411–12. The cathedral's accounts state that Hayford undertook some of the work in Exeter, and some in Ashburton, a town about 20 miles south, perhaps his home. During his sojourn in Exeter, Hayford charged for 'rushes for his own house' and 'straw for his own bed'. As Joanne Overty has recently noted, late medieval institutional records very often show in-kind payment of this sort to itinerant and lay book artisans of all stripes – scribes and limners as well as binders.[40]

A history of binding in medieval England might accommodate a variety of these sorts of archival records, but the surviving forms of medieval bindings themselves suggest even more fruitful topics for discussion. One such topic is movement and change in medieval manuscript culture. Medieval books did not sit still between their boards, in their skins or upon their shelves – as is suggested by Winchcombe Abbey's peripatetic manuscripts and the Bury and Exeter Cathedral books that were re-bound at the end of the Middle Ages. They wandered, and they acquired bindings at different points in their journeys. Most students of the fifteenth-century girdle book containing Boethius's *Consolation of Philosophy* in Beinecke, MS 84 have argued from the style of its chemise and clasps that it was bound by continental artisans. English features of the scribal hands and provenance notes nevertheless show that it was copied and owned in England.[41] English books were sometimes sent overseas for newfangled kinds of binding. The humanist Thomas Linacre sent copies of the books that he presented to his patrons, Henry VIII and

---

Fifteenth Century', 104–5. Remains of tawed chemises, not previously noted, are visible under the furnishings of the Huntington MS and on turn-ins of the Oxford, Jesus College MS.

[38] See the discussion by Jean-Pascal Pouzet, pp. 220–4, below.

[39] 'Further Studies in Anglo-Saxon and Norman Bookbinding'.

[40] Clark, 'On the Work Done to the Library of Exeter Cathedral in the Early 15th Century'; Overty, 'The Cost of Doing Scribal Business', 7.

[41] See Shailor, *Catalogue of … the Beinecke Rare Book and Manuscript Library*; Bearman, 'The Origins and Significance', identifies several English girdle books; none are in the style of the Beinecke *Boethius*, which Shailor argues resembles German/Low Countries work (see Bruckner, 'Das Beutelbuch und seine Verwandten').

Cardinal Wolsey, to Paris, where he could have their calf-skin bindings tooled in the new, gilded style he had probably first seen while an envoy in Italy.[42]

Medieval books not only moved, they also changed. One of the first tasks of the student of a binding is to consider whether the structure is the first or one of subsequent treatments of the book. This cannot always be done with certainty given the difficulty of dating bindings generally.[43] But it can sometimes be established by the evidence of sewing stations. A set of unused pierced or slit holes visible in the gutter or, where the spine is damaged, the spine fold of quires is evidence of at least one other binding of a manuscript.[44] Westminster Abbey, MS 34/11 comprises six rather scrappy pieces of unevenly sized parchment containing an incomplete, fourteenth-century Latin–French–English vocabulary. At its largest the little booklet is 175mm. tall. A clustering of pierced holes occupying an area of about 50mm. at the top and 50mm. at the bottom of the quire fold suggests that they were held together by different tackets at different times. Another example is Pembroke, Camb., MS 70, a twelfth-century glossed gospel of Matthew from the library of Bury St Edmunds. It was re-bound using its old boards later in the Middle Ages, perhaps at the time the Bury books were being supplied with chemises. The old channels and thongs are visible where the cover of the manuscript has been damaged, and sewing holes from the earlier binding are sometimes visible about 25mm. from the tail of a quire fold.

Other bindings speak of a dynamic history for medieval books in different ways. Scholars frequently associate the use of fragments of medieval manuscripts in the production of bindings on printed books with the Reformation's 'onslaught' on the medieval textual record.[45] But old books supplied handy material to binders long before the Reformation – as did the Hebrew prayerbook used to bind Pembroke, Camb., MS 59, noted above. An example from later in the Middle Ages is St John's, Camb., MS S. 35, a late fifteenth-century confessional manual. Four leaves from a discarded canon law manuscript serve as a cover for the book. These covering leaves are stitched together at the outer edge. The primary sewing passes directly through the quire folds and the cover. The whole structure was fastened by three ties stitched to the fore-edge of the upper cover, closing to horn buttons on the lower cover, one of which survives (Figure 7.3). To reinforce the area where the ties are attached, another piece of an old manuscript – the pricked edge of a leaf – has been stitched on (Figure 7.4).

---

[42] See David Rundle's discussion of continental–English traffic in books in Chapter 13 in this volume; Barber, 'The Advent of Gold Tooling in English Bookbinding'.

[43] On which, see Oldham, *English Blind-Stamped Bindings*, 2–5.

[44] The absence of such holes does not prove a binding is 'original', however: binders could re-sew using old holes.

[45] Hellinga, 'Fragments Found in Bindings', 13; Ker, *Fragments of Medieval Manuscripts*, supplemented by Pearson, *Oxford Bookbinding 1500–1640*, 139–200.

Figure 7.3 St John's, Camb., MS S. 35: outer face of lower cover with horn button.

Bits of old manuscripts were also used as guards and/or reinforcing strips of parchment were folded around the back (and sometimes in the centre fold) of quires. Strips fashioned from the leaves of old books are used, for instance, in HEHL, MS HM 144, a late fifteenth-century miscellany containing some of Lydgate's poems, and Westminster Abbey, MS 34/5, a mid fifteenth-century, limp-bound compilation of philosophical extracts and notes belonging to an Oxford student called Henry Muryell.[46]

The use of recycled materials and habits of restoration and repair show that the binding of late medieval books could be a frugal business. This suggests a second topic for discussion of medieval bindings – costs. In his discussion of the commercial book trade in Chapter 8 of this volume, Erik Kwakkel argues that in the late Middle Ages binders developed new and less expensive techniques to meet the needs of a diverse clientele. Limp covers of skin, for instance, were increasingly used in place of wooden boards, especially on the sort of 'cheap' books that were made out of paper and written in cursive hands in the same period.

[46] Ker, *MMBL*, transcribes parts of draft letters by Muryell describing his studies and a petition naming an Oxford 'magist[er] W. rath' (d. 1480, *BRUO*, 1548).

*Figure 7.4 St John's, Camb., MS S. 35: inner face of upper cover,
showing parchment strip and tie stitching.*

But binding a book between boards did not necessarily involve expensive materials or even careful, time-consuming work. Boards could be recycled, like those on Pembroke, Camb., MS 70. A book in the Huntington Library, MS HM 58, a late fifteenth-century copy of *Agnus Castus*, is a particularly striking example of recycling. Its binder not only re-used some old boards from another manuscript but tied the two broken pieces of the lower board together with a piece of thick thread. He or she then covered the mend and channels from the old binding (which still have fragments of the old tawed supports in them) with a second-hand tanned cover. The cover's earlier history is evident from the indentations that have been left upon it by a strap which are still visible on the turn-in on the lower board.

What made binding with boards costly – or at least more costly than other available options – was not the boards themselves but a combination of labour-intensive processes associated with hard rather than soft covers on medieval books. HEHL, MS HM 132 is a Latin *Polychronicon* in the hand of its author, Ranulph Higden. It was copied at his monastery of St Werburgh in Chester no later than 1363/4, but its present binding – red-stained skin over cushioned oak boards with red and green silk endbands, two fore-edge straps and two (missing) pins – is in a style more characteristic of the fifteenth century.[47] On the rear pastedown, in a fifteenth-century anglicana–secretary hybrid hand, someone has noted the cost of materials:

In leddur hongre [Hungarian leather] ii d; In whyte threde ii d; ii new bordes id; ii skynys of parchement viii d; A skyn of redlather ii d; In blac sylke and greyne I d ob [halfpenny]; In glw ob; ii claspys ii d; summa totalis xix d.[48]

HEHL, MS HM 132 gives us a sense of the sort of labour involved to turn these bits and pieces into a binding. The binder of this book suspended the text block on a frame and sewed it and its endleaves (here made from 'ii skynys of parchement') with 'whyte threde' to the supports. He or she attached a compound endband sewn in 'blac sylke and greyne'. The endband cores and the regular supports were laced into channels in the 'new bordes'. Another example of a surviving endband is GUL, MS Hunter 136 (T.6.18), the Middle English translation of the *Imitatio Christi* which William Darker, a brother of Sheen, gave to Elizabeth Gibbs, Abbess of Syon in 1502. It still has fragmentary remains of bands of blue and green silk to go with its red-stained cover.

Once the binder had finished with the endbands and board attachment, he or she pasted a 'skyn of redlather' over the boards. The process might then be further complicated by the addition of a chemise, or, as in the case of HEHL, MS HM 132, by the addition of metal furnishing – 'claspys', straps, catch-plates, pins, label-frames and/ or bosses. The clasps on Higden's book are attached to straps and close to pins on the lower cover, which is characteristic of English bindings from the Romanesque period forward. Around 1400, a new style of 'hook-clasp' also emerged. Clasps were attached by a very short strap (or directly) to the fore-edge of a board and fastened to catchplates on the opposite board. English books are distinctive in their fastenings: they mostly close to the lower board, where most continental books close to the upper.[49]

HEHL, MS HM 35300 is another interesting example of clasps on an English book. It is a composite manuscript: one booklet contains a late thirteenth-century copy of some of Bede's writings; another contains a fifteenth-century copy of Bede's *Historia*. The binding had a chemise, now removed. Its fore-edge brass hook-clasps survive. The catch-plates are decorated by a single turned circle and a tripartite 'tail', the centre piece of which is engraved to resemble the shaft and pins of a feather. A near identical design, but with two turned circles, is visible on the catch-plates on BodL, MS Laud misc. 128, a Latin commentary on Augustine's *De civitate Dei*, a binding stamped by the Fishtail binder, who was mentioned above.[50] The Fishtail

---

[47] Galbraith, 'An Autograph MS of Ranulph Higden's *Polychronicon*'.

[48] See Pollard, 'Describing Medieval Bookbindings', 51–2, n.2. '[L]eddur hongre' perhaps describes the thick skin used for straps (*MED*, s.v. 'lether' – the term 'hongre' used for leather for reigns/crops).

[49] For some statistics establishing this, see Szirmai, *Archaeology*, table 9.16.

[50] The book has a table of contents added s. xv[4] by Dom. Thomas Wason of Glastonbury, on whom see Parkes, *Their Hands before Our Eyes*, 21.

binder worked in Oxford *c*.1475–1500. It may be inferred that HEHL, MS HM 35300 was probably also bound in Oxford at this time, commissioned by its first owner, Robert Elyot, a fellow of All Souls. (Elyot donated the book to Syon Abbey in 1490.)[51] The binders of both books may have used clasps available locally, perhaps designed by an Oxford craftsman or – since similar clasps are seen on German and Netherlandish books – imported from the continent.[52]

The relative cheapness of limp bindings can be established by comparison of the labour that went into their preparation with the work involved in the elaborate processes just described. Most limp covers on medieval books are made from parchment and fastened (if at all) by ties.[53] Limp covers could be affixed to the text block without time-consuming sewing onto supports. Two of the four Chaucer manuscripts that survive in medieval bindings are fifteenth-century manuscripts of *A Treatise on the Astrolabe* in parchment covers. MS 1 of the Institute of Electrical Engineers contains Petrus Peregrinus's *Epistola de magnete* and other tracts as well as Chaucer's work; the primary sewing of the quires passes directly through the cover.[54] St John's, Camb., MS E. 2 also contains scientific tracts besides Chaucer's – *De Septem climatibus expositio* and some instructions for divination by numerology. Its collation suggests a certain carelessness on the part of its binder: a⁴ 1¹⁰ 2⁸ (+ ff. 30, 31 misplaced after f. 14) 3⁸ 4⁸ (– ff. 31, 32) 5⁴ (– 1 canc.) b⁴. Its quires have been stab-stitched – that is, sewn through holes pierced sideways through the quires, rather than through the middle of the quire fold. The text block is then attached to its parchment cover by stitching through the fold of the third quire. The binding on each of these Chaucerian books is serviceable and light, but in each case the structures represent nothing like the labour put into the board-based bindings just described.

There were even simpler processes for limp binding. Tacketing, already described, took no more time than was required to acquire some thread, parchment or tawed skin, make holes through the folds of each quire and a cover, push the tackets through and knot them at the back.[55] There is a tidy row of tacket knots

---

[51] Ker, 'Robert Elyot's Books', who notices other bindings on books that belonged to Elyot and localizes several of these to Oxford also (237). At Syon, the Huntington book was further furnished with a horn label.

[52] Szirmai, *Archaeology*, figures 9.50 and 9.52 dates such clasps to the sixteenth century; together the Oxford examples suggest a late fifteenth-century date. On clasps, see Dürrfeld, 'Terra Incognita'.

[53] The term 'vellum' is often used (see Pearson, *English Bookbinding Styles*, 20), but strictly it applies to calf-skin only. Limp covers are often sheep-skin: following medieval use (*MED*, s.v. 'parchemin'), 'parchment' here refers to any species. See similar discussion by Orietta da Rold above, n. 10.

[54] This MS has unused sewing holes at head and tail of each quire fold, perhaps for a temporary 'archive' sewing (simple threading of quires – see Szirmai, *Archaeology*, figure 10.15 [c]).

[55] See further examples below; English examples noted by other scholars are Durham, Cathedral Library, MS A.IV.34; Oxford, Corpus Christi College, MS 220; Oxford, Lincoln College, MS 62 (Szirmai, *Archaeology*, 289).

at the top and bottom of St John's, Camb., MS C. 22, a Latin–English *Medulla grammaticae* from 1468. A limp piece of leather might simply serve as a wrapper for a book. Another of the interesting collection of limp English bindings in St John's College in Cambridge is MS K. 49. The six quires sit loosely within a thick piece of stained raw-hide that was once lined by pieces from another parchment manuscript. The lining is now missing; even were it intact, it would be difficult to date such a structure.[56] It is not the only way that the text block within, a fifteenth-century Middle English *Kalendarium medicinarum*, was bound: a regular pattern of sewing holes appears in the spine fold of all quires. But it does suggest how a book whose binding had worn out or that had never been bound – like all those items 'in quarterno/quaternis' that appear in medieval library catalogues – might sometimes have been stored.[57]

But it is important not to reduce such observations to a too-simple dichotomy, with expensive board bindings on the one hand, and cheap, limp, wrapper-like structures on the other. Limp bindings might be very elaborate. Many that survive from late medieval England contain quires sewn onto supports, like the early fifteenth-century Middle English prose *Brut* in Beinecke, MS 494, where the supports are laced into a limp tanned cover. Binders working with limp covers sometimes aimed for decorative effects. The cover of St John's, Camb., MS F. 22 is made from stiff, doubled-over parchment. The manuscript is a fifteenth-century copy of *Fasciculus morum* with English texts and receipts from Foston on the Wolds in Yorkshire. The quires have been sewn directly through the spine, which is strengthened by a thick piece of tanned hide: the long vertical and chain stitches that attach the text block form an elegant pattern (see Figure 7.5). A similar back plate appears on Beinecke, MS 365, the fifteenth-century miscellany known as the Book of Brome (which includes dramatic texts). The cover on this manuscript has other kinds of decoration: a motto or prayer has been added in a formal *textualis* script to a scroll on the top cover (the wording now obscure). Wording on limp bindings might be very decorative. St John's, Camb., MS K. 31 is a beautifully illuminated music book made for Lancelot Wharton, the penultimate prior of Rumburgh, Suffolk, 1523–5. His name and musical part – 'launcelot prior bassus' – are added with professionally executed monograms and heraldic devices to the upper cover of the limp parchment binding.[58] Finally, the edges of limp bindings might extend to form protective fore-edge flaps, as does the one on Wharton's music book. The upper cover has an 80mm. flap that can be wrapped over the book's fore-edge.

So limp bindings might be elaborate structures. And where limp structures *were* abbreviated – designed for convenience and not elegance – they may have served to

[56] James, *A Descriptive Catalogue of the Manuscripts in ... St John's*, mentions the lining.
[57] See Robinson, 'The "Booklet"', 53; Gullick and Hadgraft, 'Bookbindings', 107.
[58] See Corder, *A Dictionary of Suffolk Arms*, 252.

Figure 7.5 St John's, Camb., MS F. 22: spine with elaborate stitching.

do more than just cheapen the books they held together. Michael Gullick has shown that English monastic scribes used tackets to hold quires together after or perhaps during the writing process and before binding: they are sometimes still visible in the gutter of sewn books.[59] Tackets were used by a different sort of book producer later in the medieval period for similar purposes – that is, to secure working materials. CUL, MS Add. 7318 is a notebook of legal formulae, dated 1399–1464, compiled from paper quires with parchment guards. Each quire is attached by stitching and/ or three parchment tackets passed directly through the limp parchment cover. The book is of particular interest because it is a personal production: a collection by a Bury scrivener of professional materials that he assembled over time.[60] On two occasions, the book's producer found that he wanted to add more to a particular folio on which he had run out of room. He did so by stitching triangles of paper onto the folio with blue thread.

Blue thread turns up in a number of other apparently 'home-made' English books of the fifteenth century. Blue and undyed thread tackets are used to attach two extra parchment guards to secure a singleton (f. 15) in the centre of the second quire of Westminster Abbey, MS 34/5 – the twenty-seven leaf, parchment-bound

[59] Gullick, 'From Scribe to Binder'.
[60] Owen, 'A Scrivener's Notebook from Bury St Edmunds'.

paper notebook of the Oxford student Henry Muryell, mentioned above. Blue thread is used for stab-stitching a parchment guard to the three bifolia making up Westminster Abbey, MS 34/2, a Latin commentary on the papal schism put together by Westminster monks around the end of the fourteenth century. Blue thread is used to sew quires onto the strip of tanned calf that was attached (by secondary tacketing) to the inside of the limp parchment cover of BL, Add. MS 41666, the only copy of the poem *Mum and the Sothsegger*, which was mentioned above (see Figure 7.6: the blue thread could not be photographed, but the primary parchment tackets, tanned calf strip and parchment cover are clearly shown). This book seems from heavy correction to have been some kind of working document. Blue thread attaches an extra 'booklet' containing a quire of text of an earlier date to the limp, tawed cover of Beinecke, MS 163, a fifteenth-century English scientific miscellany. One final example is the buttoned-up confessional manual described above, St John's, Camb., MS S. 35. When someone, perhaps the cleric who owned this book, wanted to add Latin notes to the Middle English confessional materials it contains, he did so by stitching new quires into the folds of original ones. He inserted one bifolium using blue thread.

Close observation of these books – right down to the thread used to stitch them – reveals a great deal about their structure, about changes made to them over time and even about thread used in the home, household or study. It was usually not dyed but 'natural', as most household thread is today, although some people seem also to have used a variety in blue. It tells us more besides: it builds upon what is known about the textual world inhabited by parsons, students, scriveners, monks and poets in the late Middle Ages. That world was, as it is often imagined, one of heavy tomes bound in boards and chained to lecterns. It was also one where small compilations of quires were wrapped, tacketed or roughly stitched. Such books were not always taken to a binder. They could be compiled in the book producer's own space – in a room like the one where the narrator of Chaucer's *House of Fame* labours on his 'rekenynges'.[61] The limp-bound and tacketed books with which a poet-bureaucrat like Chaucer must have been familiar may have proved as handy for drafting poems as for totting up accounts.[62]

The limp-bound manuscripts just described are also a reminder that medieval manuscripts need never be finished. An owner might tacket in a new quire to an existing parchment-bound book. He or she could readily disbind a loosely stitched or tacketed book and put it back together in a new order. Ralph Hanna writes that the sort of miscellaneous vernacular textual compilations familiar to us from the Middle Ages (such as *The Canterbury Tales*) are partly the product of codicizing

[61] Benson (ed.), *The Riverside Chaucer*, *The House of Fame*, 653.
[62] Surviving fourteenth-century English account books in limp tacketed structures include NA, MS E. 101/369/11 (accounts of 1306 of the Royal Household); and NA, MS E. 101/14/22 (from 1312): Szirmai, *Archaeology*, 289–90, pointed out to him by Gullick and Bearman.

Figure 7.6 BL, MS Add. 41666: inner face of detached parchment cover, showing backplate, stitching and remains of tackets.

habits associated with booklet production, whereby scribes – unsure where their next exemplar might come from – forestalled final decisions about the shape of a book by producing it in movable parts.[63] Joel Fredell describes the circulation of a great many late medieval vernacular texts in limp-bound booklet format; he suggests that poets such as John Lydgate as well as lollard and political polemicists wrote short works in anticipation of such late medieval 'pamphleteering'.[64] These scholars argue that medieval works were made as they were imagined – in bookish pieces, open-ended, in portable and scrappy forms. The study of medieval book-bindings helps to show us the minute workings of this dynamic textual culture.

The preceding discussion of fourteenth- and fifteenth-century bookbindings largely excludes those that survive on printed books. This is deliberate: by dealing with some neglected bindings, the chapter is meant to supplement many existing studies of binding in the era of printing. In particular, it supplements accounts of the tanned, blind-stamped bindings that have preoccupied scholars of the late medieval book. The development of pioneering work by G. D. Hobson and J. Basil Oldham means that we are able to identify the stamps and thus the work of many

[63] 'Miscellaneity and Vernacularity'.
[64] ' "Go litel quaier" ': Lydgate's Pamphlet Poetry'.

bineries – the Scales binder and Sheen binders at work in London before 1475; the binders Hokyns, More, Hunt and the Fishtail binder at work in Oxford from 1439 to *c*.1500; the bindery or perhaps the in-house binders who dealt with many of William Caxton and Wynkyn de Worde's printed books; and so on.[65]

The technique that was employed by these binders – covering boards in tanned skins and decorating these skins with stamped shaped and ruled lines – was already established by the time they set to work. It had an earlier highpoint during the twelfth century, as noted above, but stamps never dropped entirely out of use, at least on continental books.[66] And yet Nicholas Hadgraft records a rather extraordinary reversal of practice in England in favour not only of blind-stamping but also of tanning at the end of the fifteenth century. Less than 10 per cent of the fifteenth-century bindings he surveys that were made before *c*.1450 are bound in tanned skin; by the 1490s, the figure is more like 90 per cent (and most of these books are stamped).[67] The same change can be observed on continental books. The English blind-stamped style has been associated with continental fashions, especially Netherlandish craft: it was on Low Countries books that late fifteenth-century English binders based their own designs.[68]

But the reason for the refashioning of bookbinding style *c*.1450 has never been accounted for satisfactorily. The technique of blind-tooling was itself in a period of transition at the end of the fifteenth century. In that period, perhaps first in Germany, binders began to replace their stamps with rolls and panels. These could treat more space on a cover more quickly, and the introduction of the new tools has therefore been associated with a much more dramatic innovation: the advent of printing. New measures that sped up the decorative process matched the new speed with which books were being produced, ready for the binder.[69]

But the shift away from tawing to tanning of skin for covers and the widened use of stamps – which, unlike rolls and panels, did *not* represent an abbreviation of the production process – predated all but Johannes Gutenberg's earliest experiments with movable type.[70] Blind-stamped English bindings of the period 1450–75 or so survive on manuscripts, not printed books. Printing was not the – at least not the

---

[65] Hobson, *Blind-Stamped Panels*; Oldham, *English Blind-Stamped Bindings* and *Blind Panels of English Binders*. See also, among many studies, Foot, 'English Decorated Bookbindings of the Fifteenth Century' and 'Bookbinding 1400–1557', and Nixon, 'William Caxton and Bookbinding'.

[66] Szirmai, *Archaeology*, 140–2, 166–7, 243; Gullick and Hadgraft, 'Bookbindings', state that no confirmed examples of stamped English bindings date from the period *c*.1200–1450 (107).

[67] 'English Fifteenth-Century Bookbinding Structures', 245; see also Pearson, *English Bookbinding Styles*, 41.

[68] Foot, 'Influences from the Netherlands on Bookbinding', 150–61.

[69] Szirmai, *Archaeology*, 243–7.

[70] The earliest English bindings in the 'new' style date from the very early 1450s: Pollard, 'The Names of Some English Fifteenth-Century Binders', 198 (who gives 1457 as the earliest date); Nixon, 'A Register of Writs and the Scales Binder', 366–7.

only – catalyst for change. A more plausible way to account for the new technique – one that might seem, at first, to have very little to do with books – is medieval Christendom's war with Islam. The alum that was used to treat skins designed for late medieval books had to be imported. In the thirteenth and fourteenth centuries it came to Western Europe from the Eastern Mediterranean – the Greek Islands and Phocaea (now Foça in Aegean Turkey). When eastern trade routes were cut off in 1453 as Byzantium fell to the Turks, there was an 'alum famine' in Europe, which ended only when new supplies were located in Italy.[71] It seems possible that fifteenth-century binders were forced by the famine to use tanned skins rather than tawed ones at least for a time. By a custom dating back to the twelfth century that had never died out, they used stamps to decorate these bindings, and then the new style caught on, partly because it was spread quickly by an increasingly numerous trade in printed books. Necessity became mother to a long-lived fashion.

Printing was not the sole harbinger of change in the world of medieval bookbinding, but it did lead to new business for binders. There was probably some speculative production of school books and service-books before the advent of printing, and certainly mass production of Books of Hours. There was a significant market for ready-made second-hand books in the period. Binders themselves contributed to it. The 1454 will of Peter Bylton, the London binder and stationer described above, instructs his executors to 'selle all my bokes', which they did – two of his manuscripts were purchased by Richard Hopton, a fellow of Eton, and survive as Eton College, MSS 39 and 101.[72] These ready-made books aside, most production of manuscripts was bespoke. Commissioners had control over when, or how or whether each book was bound.[73] After printing, as other choices – about script, size and decoration of a book – were completely or increasingly circumscribed, the patrons of bookshops might still buy a book unbound and decide what to do with it next. In this respect, of all the artisans who inhabited the shops on Catte Street in Oxford or Paternoster Row in London, the binders' work was among the least changed.

Nevertheless, such work did increase. As the book trade shifted away from bespoke and second-hand volumes and towards new ones, there was much more material to be bound. From early on, editions or parts of them were sometimes bound before they were sold. Half of the books in Richard Pynson's 1494 edition of Lygdate's *Fall of Princes* were 'prynted and bound' at his expense.[74] Nicholas Pickwood has done important work to show the impact of the new pressure to bind more books faster.

---

[71] Cherry, 'Leather', 299.

[72] See the entry for Bylton in Christianson, *A Directory of London Stationers*.

[73] See Chapter 8 by Erik Kwakkel.

[74] Plomer, 'Two Lawsuits of Richard Pynson', 129; the book is London: Richard Pynson, 1492, *STC* 3175; see the discussion of this edition by Daniel Wakelin, pp. 56–8 above. For pre-1530s trade bindings, see Gillespie, 'Poets, Printers and Early English *Sammelbände*'; on the later period, Bennett, *Trade Bookbinding in the British Isles*.

He describes a variety of abbreviations of technique: less sewing on fewer supports, the replacement of endbands by purely decorative headbands and increased use of temporary structures.[75] The tone of his and others' accounts of the change is sometimes elegiac: bookbinding was once a skilled craft that produced high-quality, long-lasting handiwork; printing heralded its inexorable decline to the present day, when the glued covers of paperbacks are lucky to last a single reading.

However, the author of *Mum and the Sothsegger* is already alive to this decline in standards when, *c.*1409, he describes one kind of scrappy book bound in 'forelle [limp parchment]' after another.[76] Medieval binders, like later ones, knew how to use shortcuts and make do with inexpensive materials. Medieval writers knew how to tacket their own books and avoid the cost or hassle of the bindery altogether. The cheap paperback is neither the invention nor the fault of printing. As long as people have wanted to get their hands on textual materials there have been slap-dash as well as skilled ways of getting that material into a serviceable form. By the late Middle Ages, the growth in kinds of literacy that is sometimes associated with printing had already occurred: the press may have produced more new books in more hurriedly made bindings, but it supplied them to the same sort of readers. In late medieval England, a ploughman might need a copy of a grant or deed, and a merchant might keep records in an account roll. Churches wanted service-books; bailiffs had rent-books. Kings owned books of counsel and romance, and so did their ladies; and a tradeswoman-turned-visionary like Margery Kempe might hold her prayer 'boke in hir hand' like a talisman when the church roof fell in.[77] There were ways of binding manuscripts to match all the diverse demands of this richly textual age. A great deal of fruitful and absorbing work remains to be done on them.

[75] 'Onward and Downward'.

[76] Barr (ed.), *The Piers Plowman Tradition*, 1586.

[77] Staley, ed., *The Book of Margery Kempe*, 1.9, line 484. See Clanchy, *From Memory to Written Record*, and Musson, *Medieval Law in Context*, 120–4, on the functional literacy required of the lower estates by late medieval bureaucracy. Cf. De Hamel, 'Books and Society', who perhaps takes too little account of the wide range of formats – single leaves; unbound or limp-bound booklets; books chained for display at shrines and in churches; books shared by reading aloud – by which a great many more people than ever entered a university, noble household or monastery came into contact with the written word, not excepting words bound in books, even in the fourteenth century.

8

Commercial organization and economic innovation

ERIK KWAKKEL

Bread, meat and manuscripts: to Brunetto Latini these were all the same. They were the fruits of daily trades that involved hand and foot as opposed to mouth and tongue, and these 'mechanical arts', as the Italian author argued, after Aristotle, were bound together in that they were all 'necessary for the life of men'.[1] Latini expressed these views in his *The Book of the Treasure (Li Livres dou Tresor)*, and a miniature in an early manuscript (see Figure 8.1) illustrates the kind of mechanical trades he is referring to, including copying books ('escriture').[2] Thirteenth-century Aristotle commentaries echo the view that the mechanical arts, including those of scribes, are a vital necessity for civic culture, '[q]uia sine artibus mechanicis impossibile est hominem vivere ad votum [because without [them] it is impossible for men to live as they will]', as Albertus Magnus put it in his commentary on Aristotle's *Politics* of c.1260.[3] The vitality of technology was not just food for academic thought in the Middle Ages: it had a real world value as well. Economic historians have argued that technology was a crucial force in the formation of late medieval society.[4] The rise of markets, division of labour and emergence of coinage which followed in the wake of new interest in and emphasis on technology helped to foster an increasingly specialized economy, where guilds emerged and gained importance, and where the concepts of competition and specialization flourished.[5] In this mixed light of new technologies, growing markets and specialization we can place and understand the economy of the book in late medieval England.

---

[1] Latini, *The Book of the Treasure*, 4–5 (4). For the mechanical arts, see Whitney, 'Paradise Restored'; Sternagel, *Die artes mechanicae* (Latini at 114–15).

[2] For the miniature, see Evans, 'Allegorical Woman and Practical Men', 305–6; Alexander, 'The Butcher, the Baker, the Candlestick Maker', 92.

[3] For the relation to civic culture, see Feldges-Henning, 'The Pictorial Programme of the Sala della Pace', 154–8 (quotation at 157).

[4] White, 'Medieval Engineering', and the discussion and bibliography in Whitney, 'Paradise Restored', 1–4.

[5] Epstein, 'Urban Society', 29–31; see also Britnell, *The Commercialisation of English Society*, 155–227.

Figure 8.1 BL, MS Add. 30024, f. 1v, close-up of left column: illustration showing book production ('escriture') as a mechanical trade.

The inclusion of book production in a miniature of *c.*1300 depicting a selection of mechanical arts is telling, because it shows that by this time the activity had become part of urban economies. The present chapter will show that in the fourteenth and fifteenth centuries the practice of producing books for profit in England had not only become very organized, but also that it incorporated an increasing number of new technologies, including new types of writing support materials and scripts. Some recent publications provide excellent assessments of the trade's organization and its participants.[6] This chapter emphasizes some important tendencies; raises some new questions, in part by comparing Britain with the continent; and fills some gaps, especially by drawing attention to the commercial book as a material object. This chapter demonstrates implicitly that the commercial system for book production and the importance of technology to it were established well before printing.

Before turning to the technological side of the economy of the handwritten book and discussing how market principles influenced the object's physical appearance and cost, some general characteristics of the economy of the book in England and its organization will be examined. An important feature of the late medieval economy was an increase in commercialization and organization. Primary expressions of these were markets that catered to a clientele with diverse backgrounds and needs, a division of labour among the craftsmen that supplied these markets with commodities and the organization of these men and woman into guilds.[7] These are trends seen in English commercial book production as well as other commercial endeavours. In London, for example, around the middle of the fourteenth century, those who employed a Court Letter and wrote legal instruments were united in the Mistery of Writers of the Court Letter, later called the Scriveners' Guild, while Writers of the Text Letter joined in a Stationers' Guild with other artisans involved in book production.[8] By the early fifteenth century, a significant level of specialization is present in the book trade, as becomes quickly clear from Christianson's *A Directory of London Stationers and Book Artisans*. Among the eighty-six artisans listed in the A–D section, to take a random sample, sixty-four (or a little over 75 per cent) are associated with a single trade.

Specialization is also reflected by a revealing source for the study of the English book trade: itemized accounts in manuscripts, stating the objects' costs. The following information is found in the back of Cambridge, Peterhouse, MS 110, a fifteenth-century volume with Augustine's *Letters*:

> Pro pergamo 27 quat. precium quaterni iii *d.* Summa vi *s.* ix *d.*
> Pro scriptura eorundem viz. xvi *d.* pro quaterno. Summa xxxvi *s.*
> Pro luminacione *viii d.*
> Pro ligacione ii *s.*[9]

---

[6] Michael, 'Urban Production'; Christianson, 'The Rise of London's Book-Trade'; Parkes, *Their Hands before Our Eyes*, 39–53; Mooney, 'Locating Scribal Activity'.

[7] Britnell, *The Commercialisation of English Society*, 179–203; Britnell, 'The Proliferation of Markets in England'; and Dyer, 'The Consumer and the Market in the Later Middle Ages'. The extent of trade specialization is demonstrated in Swanson, *Medieval Artisans*. See also Dyer, *Making a Living in the Middle Ages*, 201–12 and 320–1.

[8] For the formation of guilds, see Christianson, *A Directory of London Stationers*, 22 and 'A Community of Book Artisans', 25–6. See also Blayney, *The Stationers' Company before the Charter*.

[9] James, *A Descriptive Catalogue of … Peterhouse*, 128.

This English itemized bill shows a division into four major cost categories, and, notably, these represent four significant professions that may be gathered under the umbrella term 'book production': writing support (parchment maker), writing (scribe), illumination (limner) and bookbinding (binder). A similar division is present in itemized bills found in five other manuscripts in Peterhouse, apparently all drawn up by the individual who jotted the bill on the flyleaf of MS 110.[10]

There were two important ways in which readers could acquire books, such as those in Peterhouse, by commercial means. Firstly, they could directly approach individuals who were trained to write, such as scriveners, schoolmasters, students and notaries, and put them under contract to copy a book. On completion, the patron would receive the text in loose quires, with which he could turn to other artisans for additional work, such as the limner or binder.[11] Examples of such arrangements are the scribe William Ebesham copying manuscripts for Westminster Abbey (eight surviving books) and for John Paston, who was apparently a slow payer (two manuscripts survive). Another example is the Middle English miscellany of medical treatises and recipes copied by the Cambridge student of Canon Law Symon Wysbech for Robert Taylor of Boxford, Suffolk (now HEHL, MS 1336).[12]

Alternatively, a reader could turn to a bookseller or 'stationer', a somewhat confusing term that was used in the period to denote an individual who sold writing supplies; a specialized artisan (binder, limner, textwriter); a book-contractor who acted as an 'intermediary between producer and the public' (as Pollard interpreted the terms 'stationer' and 'stationarius' that he encountered in records from early fourteenth-century London); and/or a member of the London Stationers' Company.[13] In this chapter, the term is exclusively used to denote individuals who sold books or arranged to have them made for sale, be they members of a guild or not, and no matter what other professions they may have had (inside or outside the book trade). Patrons who went to a stationer to acquire a book had two options. Some booksellers had second-hand books in stock, and a reader might find what he needed second-hand. Stationers' dealings in second-hand books are apparent, among other things, from stock inventories taken after their death. Two surviving manuscripts that were once part of such inventories from London stationers show

[10] MSS 88, 114, 142, 193 and 198; see James, *A Descriptive Catalogue of … Peterhouse*, 105, 133, 169, 226 and 234, respectively. I owe the observation that the inscriptions are probably from the same hand to Daniel Wakelin, who examined the books *in situ*.

[11] Loose quires are mentioned in the court case of the London stationer William Baker, as discussed in Christianson, *A Directory of London Stationers*, 66 ('lous queres').

[12] Parkes, *Their Hands before Our Eyes*, 39–53 includes examples of ad hoc arrangements (Wysbech at 46, Ebesham at 47). Ebesham reminds Paston that part of his bill is still unpaid (Savage, *Old English Libraries*, 178).

[13] Pollard, 'The Company of Stationers before 1557', 5. Gillespie, 'Books', 92, for the term 'stationer' (following Blayney, *The Stationers' Company before the Charter*). See also Michael, 'Urban Production', 171 and Christianson, *A Directory of London Stationers*, 24–5.

that stocked second-hand books could be well over a hundred years old.[14] Many were obtained from the estates of deceased readers, but not all; in 1419, a keeper of Henry IV's books, Ralph Bradfield, was accused along with a London stationer, Thomas Marleburgh, of misappropriating some of the royal collection, presumably for sale.[15]

The other scenario of acquisition involved new books. Studies from Paris and other continental cities show that there, the stationer (called 'libraire' or 'librarius') frequently acted as middle-man, taking orders from clients and subcontracting labour to scribes, illuminators and binders in their vicinity.[16] These hired hands did not work in scriptoria (as is sometimes assumed); instead, each had his own 'studio' where he worked by himself. Continental studies suggest the books that came out of these contracts were sometimes made by affiliations of five or more individuals (several scribes and illuminators, a binder and a stationer), and that stationers preferred to hire artisans they had worked with before. The latter is shown by recurring associations between stationers, scribes and illuminators in different manuscripts.[17] Did the British book trade include such highly organized schemes of commercial book production, with a stationer functioning as 'supervisor' of an association of craftsmen?[18] And if so, was it common? And what kind of books may have come out of these schemes? In what languages were they written, and what texts did they contain? It is important to address these queries, as they affect our understanding of how developed and organized the trade was, and how broad the spectrum of the stationer's tasks were.

Continental and British studies emphasize that stationers acting as book-contractors are notoriously 'elusive figures' who, 'in contrast to scribes and illuminators, leave little physical evidence of their activity', even when they frequently acted as supervisors, and when their activities encompassed important artists and patrons.[19] While the notion of stationers acting as supervisors does

---

[14] Christianson, *A Directory of London Stationers*, 82 (Eton College, MSS 39 and 101); see also the inventories he lists, 66 (William Barough) and 68 (William Barwe); and on second-hand books generally, 40 (on London); his 'The Rise of London's Book-Trade', 132–3; and Parkes, 'The Provisions of Books', 418–19 (Oxford).

[15] Stratford, 'The Early Royal Collections', 261.

[16] Detailed evidence, based on surviving manuscripts and documentary evidence, is presented in (for example) Rouse and Rouse, 'The Commercial Production of Manuscript Books' and *Manuscripts and their Makers*; and Croenen, Rouse and Rouse, 'Pierre de Liffol' (on Paris). Some examples from the Low Countries are presented in Kwakkel, *Die Dietsche boeke*, 170–2 (Brussels) and Brinkman, 'Het Comburgse handschrift' (Ghent).

[17] Rouse and Rouse, *Manuscripts and Their Makers*, II.182–90 (Appendix 7M) presents a case-study of such a large affiliation of artisans working on several occasions with the same stationer.

[18] I am using the term 'organized' in this chapter to denote a scheme of book production in which a professional bookseller (rather than the patron) is coordinating a book's production. The term does not imply that the booksellers involved were necessarily members of guilds, although many of them probably were.

[19] Croenen, Rouse and Rouse, 'Pierre de Liffol' (quotation at 261), and Christianson, *A Directory of London Stationers*, 32–3.

not broadly resonate in current scholarship on book production in England, certain evidence can be used to show it did occur – as indeed some authoritative studies have already suggested.[20] The most telling evidence are contracts between stationers and artisans, references to which survive in legal documents. Around 1487, for example, the London stationer Philip Wrenne owed 5 marks to the limner Thomas Greneherst for labour and materials. The latter case is known to us because the stationer who acted as middle-man did not have the money to pay the limner. He tried to satisfy the artisan by offering him new work to settle the bill, which the latter refused, after which the dispute was brought in front of the court.[21] The affiliation between Wrenne and Greneherst suggests, according to Christianson, that artisans in London worked under 'subcontracts' made by a 'stationer–entrepreneur who had originally accepted the book commission'.[22] Yet another legal dispute between a stationer and a limner, this time in Oxford, allows us to add some detail to the interaction between booksellers and the artisans they hired, for example that the limner would pick up the needed materials from the stationer's house (and return his work there when finished) and that the stationer regularly checked up on the artisan's progress during the duration of the contract.[23]

Sketchy as it may be, such evidence requires that we consider the significance of these middle-men in English commercial book production. While the circumstances of production differ significantly, it is very easy to confuse a scheme where a patron approaches artisans directly for one that involves a stationer–supervisor. If it is at all clear that an artisan worked commercially, for example because evidence of a financial transaction exists, it is usually impossible to know whether he was approached directly by the client or put under contract by a stationer. Even when a large body of manuscripts with the work of an individual artisan is identified it is difficult to opt for one scenario or the other. This is demonstrated, for example, by the case of William Abell, a London limner working in Paternoster Row recorded to have received £1 6s 8d for decoration of the Consolidation Charter

---

[20] Pollard, 'The Company of Stationers before 1557', 14 (employment of book artisans by stationer was common); Christianson, 'The Rise of London's Book-Trade', 131–2 (stationers coordinated the work of others, paying artisans for these services); Christianson, *A Directory of London Stationers*, 24 (a bookman could act as a 'business agent in the commission of books'); Parkes, *Their Hands before Our Eyes*, 51 (commercial scribes worked for both clients and stationers). In Chapter 9 in this volume and elsewhere, Mooney argues that vernacular books were often made by individuals whose work was not 'organized' but 'ad hoc': their time was not usually dedicated to book production and they did not belong to one of the book guilds.

[21] Christianson, 'The Rise of London's Book Trade', 131.

[22] Christianson, 'An Early Tudor Stationer', 261. Reference to another London contract survives in the court case of William Baker (Christianson, *A Directory of London Stationers*, 66). Reference to a contract between a London stationer and an artisan in Oxford is discussed in Christianson, 'The Rise of London's Book Trade', 131.

[23] Michael, 'English Illuminators *c.*1190–1450', 68.

of Eton College. While this individual has to date been connected to twenty-one surviving Latin and Middle English manuscripts, among which are a Latin Book of Hours, various charters, a prayer roll and a copy of *The Canterbury Tales*, none of them provide conclusive evidence as to the scheme of book production that created them.[24] Similar obscurity surrounds the professionals hired to copy the text in these manuscripts. The Statutes of the Archdeaconry of London in HEHL MS HM 932, for which Abell produced historiated initials depicting Bishop Roger Niger and Archbishop William Courtenay, were copied by the scribe Ricardus Franciscus or Richard Franceys, in 1447. While no fewer then fourteen manuscripts of this prolific London scribe of French origins have been identified, ranging from documentary to literary products in Latin, Middle English and French, none of the books reveal with certainty how the artisan became involved in their production – through dealings with the patron directly, or indirectly, through a stationer.[25]

While we may well understand the association between Franceys and Abell as the result of a patron visiting the London professional book scene and bringing together artisans for the duration of a book project, it is equally plausible that these affiliations were accommodated by a stationer, in accordance with continental practices. It is important to note that individual cases of a manuscript that can successfully be related to a commercial artisan or a combination of artisans do not exclude either option. Artisans were paid, after all, in both the organized scheme involving a stationer and the direct approach of a client taking care of all the coordination, and in both cases the patrons ultimately picked up the tab. If costs of writing, illuminating or binding happen to be mentioned in accounts (as in Abell's case), these entries may reflect payments made directly to individual artisans or indirectly through stationers. And if these costs ended up being tallied on a flyleaf (as in the case of the Peterhouse manuscripts), they may have been placed there by the patron, keeping track of his expenses, or by the stationer, adding up the total costs of the book for the client's convenience. Even when we know the identity of the patron, as in case of Abell and Franceys, it does not exclude the possibility that a stationer may have been involved in the form of a middle-man.[26]

---

[24] For the limner, see Alexander, 'William Abell "Lymnour"' (payment noted at 166), and Christianson, *A Directory of London Stationers*, 59–60.

[25] Alexander, 'William Abell "Lymnour"', 167, no. 8 (HEHL MS HM 932). For the scribe, see Jefferson, 'Two Fifteenth-Century Manuscripts', 22, no. 1, and Parkes, *Their Hands before Our Eyes*, 43 and 117–18. A description of the historiated initials is found in the entry in Dutschke, *A Guide to ... Manuscripts in the Huntington Library*. Among Franceys's manuscripts are a Latin Book of Hours (BL, MS Harley 2915); several Middle English works, among which are Lydgate's *Fall of Princes* (Philadelphia, Rosenbach Library, MS 439/16) and Jacobus de Voragine's *Golden Legends* (BL, MS Harley 4774); a Grant of Arms to the Tallow Chandlers' Company of the City of London; and entries in Cok's Cartulary of St Bartholomew's Hospital. See Driver and Orr, Chapter 5, p. 114, and Pouzet, Chapter 10, p. 226.

[26] Beadle, 'Fastolf's French Books', 98, and Nall, 'Ricardus Franciscus Writes for William Worcester' for some of Richard Franceys's patrons.

Bearing all this in mind, recurring associations between book artisans may help to identify and further explore the activities of stationers acting as supervisors.[27] Of particular significance in the case of William Abell is the observation that the limner worked together with Richard Franceys on not one but at least four occasions involving four different patrons: the pair are connected to the production of the statutes of the Archdeaconry of London (as discussed); a copy of Stephen Scrope's English translation of the *Epistle of Othea*, commissioned by Sir John Fastolf (St John's, Camb. MS H. 5); a Cartulary for the Hospital of St Bartholomew in London; and a Grant of Arms for the Tallow Chandlers' Company of the City of London.[28] Their frequent collaboration for such a variety of patrons seems almost too coincidental for an ad hoc scheme, and one wonders whether these associations may be connected to a stationer acting as a book-contractor on behalf of a client, as a striking parallel to the continent, where stationers are known to have worked with preferred artisans. This scenario may also fit the bill in other cases of recurring associations, such as the six Latin and Middle English manuscripts identified by Scott as having been illuminated by the same pair of artisans (two of these books are, moreover, copied by the same scribe).[29] Scott's explanation of these recurring associations is a limner's shop where patrons dropped off books they would like to have illuminated. However, the affiliation of the limners may also be explained as a client having approached a stationer (rather than the artisans directly), who subsequently subcontracted work to individuals he had worked with in the past. Indeed, the relatively high number of books these limners worked on together makes this scenario perhaps more plausible (see also the discussion along these lines by Martha Driver and Michael Orr, Chapter 5).[30]

While the clues provided here are limited to a relatively small number of cases, they demonstrate that we cannot exclude the possibility that stationers in England acted as supervisors, in ways that may, sometimes, be easy to overlook. Such an inference is strengthened by the existence of contracts between stationers and artisans, as discussed, but also by the increased formal organization of book artisans, who monopolized the production of books through guild membership, placing more emphasis on specialization and increasing their professional and personal ties. Other evidence, not commonly brought into play in this respect, could potentially

[27] For this approach, see Christianson, *A Directory of London Stationers*, 32–4; Croenen, Rouse and Rouse, 'Pierre de Liffol'; Rouse and Rouse, *Manuscripts and Their Makers*, II.182–90 (Appendix 7M).

[28] Alexander, 'William Abell "Lymnour"', 168, no. 19, and Jefferson, 'Two Fifteenth-Century Manuscripts', 22, no. 11 (*Epistle of Othea*); Alexander, 167, no. 14, and Jefferson, 22, no. 12 (Cartulary); Alexander, 167, no. 13, and Jefferson, 22, no. 3 (Grant of Arms).

[29] Scott, 'A Mid-Fifteenth-Century English Illuminating Shop'. The six manuscripts include a Book of Hours and a Psalter, both in Latin; Peter Idley, *Instructions to his Son*; *The Mirroure of the Worlde*; and Lydgate's *The Life of Our Lady* and *Troy Book* (the latter survives in fragmentary form).

[30] Christianson, *A Directory of London Stationers*, 29, also understands the associations in Scott's case-study as resulting from a stationer acting as a contractor.

be payments to one individual alone for the production of an entire manu-script: given the high level of specialization in the late medieval English book trade, it is unlikely that one individual would execute all stages in a book's production by himself. Evidence from London suggests that some stationers had one additional profession in the trade, but none are known to have undertaken all the activities necessary for a book's production.[31] Also telling may be that some commercially produced books contain instructions to multiple artisans working on different pro-duction stages of a manuscript, as in some Oxford cases, which may be understood as a communication from the supervisor–stationer to the various individuals he had hired for the job.[32]

Scribes, illuminators and binders involved in commercial book production were united not merely through the object they helped produce (the manuscript) or the individuals who brought their skills together (the patron or the stationer), but also by the close proximity of their workshops, which were usually located in the same neighbourhood, as was the case with other urban trades. These work-shops also served as their homes, as was common practice in the manufacturing and service industries of the later Middle Ages, which means that the artisans not only worked, but also lived, in each other's vicinity.[33] In London, for example, the majority of book-men were concentrated on London Bridge and in Paternoster Row, and in Oxford many of them were located in Catte Street. The observation that the tradesmen in these centres frequently served as each other's witnesses in legal transactions, such as wills, indicates that their dealings transcended the professional.[34] Evidently, by the end of the fourteenth century members of the book trade had not only become part of the urban economy at large, they had also formed a community of their own. Their close proximity had practical and economic benefits. Not only could artisans learn from each other, perhaps even borrow each other's equipment, but the clustering also made it easier to coordinate and undertake collaborative book projects.

[31] Some artisans in Christianson's *A Directory of London Stationers* can be connected to two trades, but none seem to have undertaken all three main stages in a book's production (copying, decor-ating, binding). Based on the A–D section in his *Directory*, the second trade of London stationers include: parchmener (91), limner (59, 66, 71), textwriter (62, 64, 76, 86, 88) and bookbinder (63, 65, 68, 74, 77, 79). For this count, I have taken Christianson's claim that an individual is a 'stationer' to mean that he was a bookseller. Pollard has also suggested that a book commission probably implies the involvement of a stationer as a book-contractor ('The Company of Stationers before 1557', 14).

[32] Michael, 'Oxford, Cambridge and London', 110.

[33] Christianson, 'Evidence for the Study of London's Late Medieval Manuscript Book-Trade', 89–90 (centralization) and 94–6 (workshops of tradesmen of the book; see for more detail also Christianson, *A Directory of London Stationers*, 31–2); and Swanson, 'Medieval Artisans', 126–8 (craftsmen's work-shops in general). Some scribes lived and worked elsewhere, even outside the city limits (see Mooney, Chapter 9, pp. 201–4, and Parkes, *Their Hands before Our Eyes*, 51).

[34] Christianson, 'A Community of Book Artisans' (London), and Michael, 'Urban Production', 176 (Oxford).

As just noted, some artisans occupied several professions, which made economic sense, because it increased the chances of employment – a similar trend is seen on the continent. In the London book scene, for example, we encounter examples of a limner–textwriter, a bookbinder–scribe and a haberdasher–parchmenter.[35] Sometimes, book artisans had a second occupation related to writing but not to the book trade as such. William Chaunt, stationer of London, and two stationers in Oxford's Catte Street also worked as notaries, while the second occupation of the London stationer John Barkeby was teacher at a grammar school, where he was most probably employed as the writing master. With a salary of as much as £5 *per annum*, teaching boys how to write may have given Barkeby the financial means to undertake risky book projects in the capacity of stationer.[36] Being a stationer who supervised book projects was not for everyone. It required entrepreneurial skills as well as sufficient funding for multiple long-term investments, needed because book-contractors might supply their subcontractors with the materials required to copy or illuminate a book, such as colours and metals, and writing support, and they might also pay up front for labour while the book was being produced (before the client had paid).[37]

What kinds of manuscript were produced in these commercial centres of book production, and how did their physical features relate to the patron's wallet? A client on Paternoster Row or Catte Street probably had very specific ideas concerning the physical make-up of the manuscript he wanted, ideas that were informed by the format of other books he owned, his cultural background, the occasion or function for which the object was purchased (personal use, institutional use, a gift) or simply by what he could afford.[38] Due to technological developments, patrons in late medieval Britain were presented with multiple options regarding nearly every physical component and production stage of the manuscript, effectively allowing them to pursue a wide variety of physical formats. While the costs of the individual features are not precisely known, the material book may still tell us something about the patron's budget, for example if he had set out to acquire an expensive or a cheap manuscript. The possibility that he could make a choice about expense is vital. As the remainder of this chapter will show, not all manuscripts in the Middle Ages were luxury items, and printing did not bring about a completely radical shift

[35] See for example Christianson, *A Directory of London Stationers*, 60, 84, 88 and 95. For the continent, see Kwakkel, *Die Dietsche boeke*, 170 (Brussels), and Rouse and Rouse, *Manuscripts and Their Makers*, II.10–142 (Paris).

[36] Christianson, *A Directory of London Stationers*, 41–2 (occupation outside book trade), 64 (Barkeby) and 85 (William Chaunt); Michael, 'Urban Production', 179 and 183 (Oxford); and Orme, *Medieval Schools*, 71–2 and 133–4 (grammar schools).

[37] Michael, 'Urban Production', 170 (materials), and Christianson, 'The Rise of London's Book Trade', 131 (labour).

[38] Some influences on the physical format are discussed in Kwakkel, 'The Cultural Dynamics of Medieval Book Production'.

in the accessibility of books. Long before the advent of printing, book producers had the means to make their wares for patrons more affordable.[39]

Research related to cost has traditionally focussed on expensive books, such as those produced by William Abell and Richard Franceys, with high-quality script and illumination. But what about the other side of the spectrum? Common sense suggests that commercial book-men, whether working in an organized scheme or not, also catered to individuals who were less affluent or who simply wished to own a book that was not so expensive. While we easily accept that a high-quality manuscript is made commercially, even when the artisans are not known by name and evidence of a financial transaction does not exist, we tend not to draw such conclusions in the case of mediocre manuscripts. However, documentary evidence, most notably the estimated value of books in wills, suggests that professional craftsmen in London were also 'employed for less ambitious and costly production, particularly for utilitarian copies of popular treatises, romances, and chronicles', as was the case on the continent.[40] It is also noteworthy, in this respect, that the most striking feature of the technological innovations observed in fourteenth- and fifteenth-century manuscript production is the increased opportunity to manufacture (and thus commission) cheaper objects, a development that continued into the age of the printed book. To demonstrate this, the last section of this chapter will present some strategies the patron could employ in order to limit the cost of a book, following three of the main cost categories listed in the itemized bills mentioned above: writing, writing support and binding. While the physical characteristics discussed below are not confined to commercial book production as such, they could reduce the cost of a book produced commercially.

Itemized bills suggest that payments to the scribe were by far the highest cost of a newly produced manuscript. The accounts found in the six manuscripts in Peterhouse, Cambridge indicate that payments towards writing could be five times as high as the writing support, the second-highest expense.[41] In other cases, the differences between these two are less steep (though still significant): the breakdown of the costs of two London Bridge antiphoners shows that writing accounted for 56 per cent of the total, compared with 20 per cent for parchment, while the writing expenses for a Gospel Book copied in 1379–85 were 37 per cent of the total cost, compared with 17 per cent for parchment.[42] In both cases the material costs come second to writing, and the latter cost is more than twice as high. Especially relevant

---

[39] Cf. Bell, 'The Price of Books', and as is also noted in Kwakkel, 'A New Type of Book'.

[40] Christianson, *A Directory of London Stationers*, 21–2 (22). Kwakkel and Mulder, 'Quidam sermones', discuss cheap Middle Dutch commercial products from Brussels.

[41] Cambridge, Peterhouse, MSS 110, 114, 142, 193 and 198 (support at 3d per quire, writing at 16d) and 88 (support at 6d per quire, writing at 20d). See also Overty, 'The Cost of Doing Scribal Business', 6, table 3. See also Parkes, *Their Hands before Our Eyes*, 48–9.

[42] Overty, 'The Cost of Doing Scribal Business', 6–8.

for this enquiry is the question of what choices a patron had when it came to the actual copying of the text: how could he limit the expenses for this activity? First and foremost, the choice for a particular type of script could influence costs.

At the beginning of the fourteenth century a hierarchy of scripts had emerged whereby different scripts were available, each with its own purpose. This system was expanded in the second half of the century.[43] The costs of these scripts will have differed, in some cases significantly. Scribes usually mastered more than one script, and it is likely that a patron would have agreed on a certain script and its cost. Surviving advertisement sheets show that some professionals were able to accommodate a very broad range of script requests. The sole-surviving advertisement sheet from England, made by an early fourteenth-century Oxford writing-master, provides as many as twelve script samples, all of them for use in liturgical books.[44] Advertisement sheets were intended to attract clientele to the store and were probably placed outside the shop for passers-by to see. The blank verso of the Oxford sheet suggests it was attached to a wall; especially telling is the remark that whoever is interested to learn how to read and write 'der kumm har in [should enter]' on a similar German sheet from 1516.[45] However, the sheets also served a more practical purpose: a client could point out the preferred script, or even call it by its proper name, which was sometimes written next to the sample. On his sheet, Herman Strepel, a writing-master in Münster, informs his clientele that he can copy texts in 'fracta', 'rotunda' and 'modus copiistarum', among other scripts.[46] The availability of a terminology specific to the line of business and the fact that such terms were used to engage with clientele shows yet again how specialized the book trade had become by the close of the Middle Ages.

How much a scribe charged for a chosen script depended on its speed: the slower the script, the longer it took to copy a given text and the more money was charged – an economic principle the book shares with other artefacts. Because of the strong correlation between a script's speed and its level of formality, a patron looking to purchase a cheap copy would probably have opted for a less formal script, which was faster to write. Such a script hit the book markets of Western Europe with the 'littera cursiva', which started to complement book script or 'littera textualis' around 1300. The terms for these scripts and their significance is discussed by Daniel Wakelin in Chapter 3. As he notes, and as surviving manuscripts suggest, the difference in speed achieved by using different book scripts

---

[43] Parkes, 'Handwriting in English Books', 132–5.

[44] Van Dijk, 'An Advertisement Sheet'. For advertising sheets, see Wehmer, 'Die Schreibmeister-blätter', and Derolez, *Palaeography*, 17–20.

[45] Van Dijk, 'An Advertisement Sheet', 48, and Wehmer, 'Die Schreibmeisterblätter', 154 n.20 (for quotation).

[46] Lieftinck, 'Pour une nomenclature de l'écriture', 25–7. For the names of scripts on advertisement sheets, see Wehmer, 'Die Schreibmeisterblätter', 150, and Derolez, *Palaeography*, 17–20.

was significant.[47] The introduction of cursive writing in book production marks the start of a period in which patrons in England aspiring to own a manuscript were actually able to make a choice again when it came to script, which had not been the case since the prolific insular scripts of the early medieval period. The choice increased further with the introduction of secretary, around 1400, which would grow into a particularly popular script for commercially produced books. Patrons were not only offered yet again more choice, but the features of this cursive also offered something new: while it was slower than other cursives, it had a more formal *ductus*. In other words, it was a cheaper script with a more pretentious appeal.[48]

While choosing a script was the most important decision a client had to make when negotiating the cost for writing, there was another matter that needed to be addressed: should a higher quality of writing be pursued or would a lower quality suffice? Palaeographical studies of an individual scribe's oeuvre suggest that copyists had a selection of specific 'registers' available in which to present a given script, each with its own palaeographical features.[49] Diversification within the presentation of a single type of script is the result of the precision with which letter shapes are drawn, and since writing with more or less care influenced the production time of the codex, different grades probably came with different price tags. The oeuvre of Richard Frampton is a good example of how a scribe adapted the presentation of a given script according to circumstances or demand: copying two working copies of the *Cowcher*, this individual switches to a basic-variety anglicana to save time and reduce costs (NA, DL 42/192–193), while the book he made in commission for the Receiver General of the Duchy of Lancaster, an important patron, was copied in a higher grade that included some archaic features, which may have given the script more prestige (NA, DL 41/1–2).[50] It is possible that a patron specified what grade he preferred, even though this matter may have been discussed in less specific terms than with the choice of a script (which could be called out by its proper name): 'slower and meticulous' or 'faster and more casual' may have been typical qualifiers heard in this stage of the negotiations; or perhaps even a plain and simple 'as cheap as possible'.

Having settled on script and writing style, a patron who commissioned a book had to choose a kind of writing support. At an elementary level this choice is one

---

[47] In addition to the discussion by Wakelin in this book, p. 42, see Gumbert, 'The Speed of Scribes', 62; Parkes, *Their Hands before Our Eyes*, 71–85, esp. 82–5; Gullick, 'How Fast Did Scribes Write?', 47 no. 9, on a codex from Norwich copied in 1337 in a notary cursive, produced 35 per cent faster than a contemporary book in *textualis*, no. 12.

[48] Derolez, *Palaeography*, 160–2, and Brown, *A Guide to Western Historical Scripts*, no. 40 at 106–7.

[49] See for example Parkes, 'Richard Frampton' (distinctive styles of anglicana); Doyle, 'Stephen Dodesham', 97 (textura quadrata); Kwakkel, 'A Meadow without Flowers', 196–8 (littera textualis).

[50] Parkes, 'Richard Frampton', 120 (higher grade), 121 (lower grade).

between parchment (used here as a generic term covering skins from all animals) and paper, which was significantly cheaper. At the end of the fourteenth century, a parchment skin roughly equalled the cost of a 'quire' of paper, and while the latter held twenty-five sheets (fifty folia, or one hundred pages), the former contained only one or two sheets when used for larger-size books (four to eight pages) or three to four sheets when the skin was cut up to be used for medium- to smaller-size books (twelve to sixteen pages).[51] But even when a patron opted for the more expensive material, parchment, he had several options to reduce his expenses. One was to ask the scribe or stationer to use sheep-skin rather than calf-skin. Evidence from the fourteenth and fifteenth centuries suggests it may have cut the costs for the second-highest expense in itemized bills in half.[52] The size of the animal was also a factor. The records of Old London Bridge show that larger skins were more expensive, probably because they were rarer. For example, in a 1484 account, a 'roll' of large sheep-skins (sixty hides) is valued at 20s, or 4.2d per sheet. In comparison, a year earlier, 14s 10d is recorded for a roll of regular-size skins, or 2.96d per sheet – significantly less.[53] Effectively, these price differences made larger books more expensive. In some cases, however, it was necessary to purchase such large sheets, as for example for the production of liturgical manuscripts (which frequently measured over 500mm. in height). Evidence shows that larger sheets were bought in smaller batches than the standard roll of sixty skins, suggesting that stationers and scribes tried to be economical and purchase just enough to produce the required book.[54]

Another qualitative consideration is the presence of imperfections, both natural (such as dark patches and pronounced dots left by the hair) and artificial (most notably the damage done by the parchment maker during his preparation of the hide). Since imperfections were present on the sheet when they were purchased, such 'imperfect' sheets will presumably have been cheaper. One deficiency in particular had a significant impact on the cost of the writing support. If the patron wanted to cut costs but did not want to resort to using paper, or if this was not available, he could ask that off-cuts be used, which must have been a very cheap type of parchment; it was quite possibly even cheaper than paper. Off-cuts were left over after the parchment maker had produced the regular sheet. When the skin had dried, the parchment maker would cut a large rectangular shape out of the prepared hide, which would become the basis for one or more bifolia, or in some cases for an unfolded (plano) sheet. All that remained of the original hide were long and narrow

[51] For the relative cost of paper compared with parchment, see Lyall, 'Materials: The Paper Revolution', 11.

[52] Cf. Christianson, *Memorials of the Book Trade*, 19–21; De Hamel, *Medieval Craftsmen: Scribes and Illuminators*, 13; Savage, *Old English Libraries*, 247.

[53] Christianson, *Memorials of the Book Trade*, 19.

[54] Ibid., 20.

strips (of unequal width) that fell outside the 'scope' of the rectangle.[55] The practice of using this (very cheap) discarded parchment for manuscripts is rooted in an old tradition, going back to at least the ninth century, in which the material was used for brief, informal and often personal textual compositions written on unbound singletons, such as letters, notes and drafts. Eventually, parchment scraps ended up being used for manuscripts as well, albeit for very small books only, with a page height of no more than 130–70mm. In preserved codices off-cuts can be recognized by a variety of features but in particular by an elongated lacuna at the lower corner of the page formed by the flank of the animal, often accompanied by 'stretch marks' and some other imperfections. Notably, a preliminary study suggests this practice was becoming popular in fourteenth-century book production; as new commercial practices were established, so were ways of making books at lower costs.[56]

A good example of a codex made of such very cheap parchment is BodL, MS Douce 25 (Figure 8.2). This fifteenth-century copy of the English translation of the *Speculum ecclesie* measures only 127 × 95mm. and contains the peculiar lacunae (and stretch marks) that are so typical of off-cuts.[57] MS Douce 25 is part of a group of 'common-profit' books that were compiled from the estates of London citizens and intended for circulation among a lay reading audience.[58] It is intriguing to see that for the production of the Douce manuscript, which was, according to its colophon, 'maad of the goodis of a certeyne persoone', the costs of the writing support were kept as low as possible.[59] Apparently, the person who had it made, quite possibly the will's executor, deemed the text of greater value than the materials.[60] In some cases a manuscript contains lacunae at the edge of the page, but the dimensions of the sheets are too large to have been constructed from off-cuts. These show a more subtle attempt to economize. Rather than constraining the size of the rectangular shape to the best part of the hide, which meant excluding the outer rim, in such larger books the rectangle was extended beyond the 'prime-cut'. As a result, the deficiencies at the edge were included in the sheet. While their inclusion might have been

---

[55] Bischoff, 'Pergamentdicke und Lagenordnung', 135, illustration 14, and Gumbert, 'Sizes and Formats', 231, fig. 2. Note the shape of the leftover material in these illustrations.

[56] Some imperfections are discussed in De Hamel, *Medieval Craftsmen: Scribes and Illuminators*, 11. I wish to thank Georgia Angelopoulos, a professional calligrapher in Victoria, British Columbia, for providing me with a set of off-cuts, allowing me to study their physical peculiarities and dimensions. I am preparing a broader study of off-cuts in medieval written culture to appear in *English Manuscript Studies 1100–1700*.

[57] Madan, *A Summary Catalogue*, no. 21599. I have not been able to assess whether all the leaves in the codex were made from off-cuts.

[58] Scase, 'Reginald Pecock, John Carpenter', and discussion by Pouzet in this volume, p. 228.

[59] Gillespie, 'Vernacular Books of Religion', 319.

[60] See the on-line facsimile at Dovey et al. (eds.), *Early Manuscripts at Oxford University*, http://image.ox.ac.uk and the manuscript description at Wynn Thomas et al. (eds.), *Welsh Prose 1350–1425*, www.rhyddiaithganoloesol.caerdydd.ac.uk

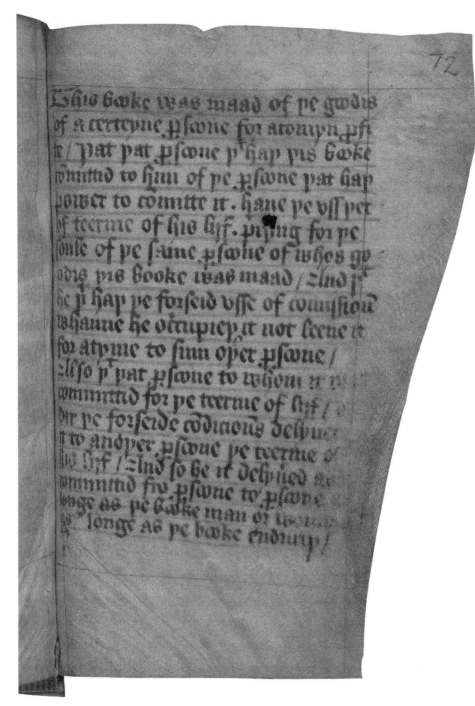

*Figure 8.2 BodL, MS Douce 25, f. 72r: parchment off-cuts in a common-profit book
(enlarged to 135% of the true size).*

perceived as aesthetically displeasing, it made the hide go further: it provided an extra 50–150mm. on all sides and would have helped to reduce the costs for parchment, if only slightly. The practice was applied, for example, in the production of Oxford, Merton College, MS 248, a fourteenth-century collection of sermons by John Sheppey, Bishop of Rochester. The codex measures 320mm. in height, and many leaves contain larger and smaller gaps at their edge.[61] Other examples are SJC, MS F. 7 (144), a Latin codex made in Oxford in 1432, measuring approx. 205 × 135mm.; and CUL, MS Dd.14.2, a volume with Middle English and Latin texts copied in 1381 in Bristol, measuring 171–83 × approx. 118mm.[62]

So scripts could be fast or slow, and thus more or less expensive; and there were significant innovations associated with writing support in the late Middle Ages. In the period of concern here, paper was introduced, and innovative ways of using parchment cheaply were developed. Binding practices may have kept pace with change. It is difficult to draw correlations between the physical features of bindings and their cost, primarily because few books still have their original binding, and if they do the manuscripts usually do not note how much was paid for the binding. We must turn again, therefore, to relative costs. The cheapest option for a patron, it would seem, was to have no binding at all – to leave a book in quires.[63] However, bookbindings were not necessarily expensive. The Peterhouse College manuscripts show, for example, that the binding costs (consisting of labour and materials) were only 4 per cent of the total, while the binding cost of two London Bridge Antiphoners was merely 6 per cent.[64] Logic suggests that if a patron could afford to have a manuscript made, he could probably afford the additional costs of having it bound.

Of particular significance for our investigation into how a commissioned book might be made more cheaply are bindings without wooden boards, or so-called limp bindings. Limp bindings were probably a very common way of binding books in England and throughout Europe, but they present a problematic object of study, because so few have survived.[65] While the sparse documentary evidence related to the commercial production of books usually does not provide much detail about the type of bindings, there is no reason to assume that limp bindings were not available in commercial centres such as London and Oxford. Agnes Scholla's doctoral research, one of the very few in-depth studies of this type of

---

[61] See the on-line facsimile at Dovey et al. (eds.), *Early Manuscripts at Oxford University*, http://image.ox.ac.uk

[62] *DMCL*, 1 nos. 17 and 301; 2, plates 222 and 167.

[63] A not infrequent choice, as noted by Gillespie above, p. 169.

[64] Overty, 'The Cost of Doing Scribal Business', 6.

[65] For limp bindings, see Szirmai, *Archaeology*, 285–319; Scholla, '*Libri sine asseribus*'; Scholla, 'Early Western Limp Bindings'. Their use and popularity in Britain is discussed in Gullick and Hadgraft, 'Bookbindings', 107 (fig. 5.2 provides an image).

binding, shows that limp bindings were in popular use among university students, as demonstrated by entries in library catalogues that remark on such bindings as 'ad modum scholarum' or 'libri ligati more studentium'. It is also quite possible that the very cheap books referred to in London wills were fitted with such bindings – some are even noted to have no binding at all, the very cheapest option.[66]

What made limp bindings cheap was the low cost of the cover material (which might be plain tawed or tanned leather, damaged parchment sheets or recycled manuscript leaves) and their short production time. The bindings essentially consist of a single parchment sheet wrapped around a manuscript and held in place by a limited number of stitches, usually two per quire – or, as Alexandra Gillespie shows in Chapter 7, by 'tackets' (loops of parchment or thread) in place of stitches. This made them easy and fast to produce.[67] Scholla's work shows that limp bindings were far more frequently used in combination with paper than with parchment: twenty-one of the twenty-nine manuscripts, or little over 70 per cent, from the period 1350–1400 in her corpus – to sample a period in which paper is in regular use in book production – are made of paper, suggesting that the cheapest kind of binding was predominantly used in combination with a cheap writing support.[68] Another indication of the low cost of these books is the observation that six of the eight parchment codices in the sample are made of medium- to poor-quality parchment: some are made from off-cuts, others contain leaves with holes and discolouration or folia that are recycled from other manuscripts.[69]

Limp bindings point at a significant trend in the production of inexpensive manuscripts: cheap books were often made that way in more than one respect. The cheapness of books with limp bindings is not only apparent through their binding and writing support, but also through the use of medium- to poor-quality script. When scribes used *textualis*, for example, they frequently included cursive features such as loops and connected letters, suggesting they wrote in a hasty (and thus

---

[66] Scholla, '*Libri sine asseribus*', 277–8. Thomas Giles left his son 'all his books, bound and unbound' (Christianson, *A Directory of London Stationers*, 21).

[67] For the low cost of limp bindings, see Pickwoad, 'The Interpretation of Bookbinding Structure', 213 and 217; Foot, 'Bookbinding 1400–1557', 111 ('limp structures were used … for cheap retail bindings'). For these and other inexpensive bindings, see also Gillespie, Chapter 7.

[68] Scholla, '*Libri sine asseribus*', 87–195 provides a detailed description of the eighty-nine manuscripts she used for her study. The parchment copies from 1350–1400 are found at 102, 115, 131, 140, 143, 161 and 173; paper copies at 91, 107, 108, 109, 111, 112, 113, 114, 117, 119, 120, 121, 122, 123, 125, 158, 159, 160, 162, 163 and 169. I have left out of my count those manuscripts that cannot be dated or that are not dated precisely enough.

[69] See Scholla, '*Libri sine asseribus*', 102–3, 131–2 and 173–4. Based on Scholla's detailed parchment description it can be extrapolated that off-cuts were used in Darmstadt, Hessische Landes- und Hochschulbibliothek, MS 1088 (Latin, Sermons and Saints' Lives, 150 × 110mm.), Hamburg, Staats- und Universitätsbibliothek, MS 2009c (German devotional miscellany, 127 × 90mm.) and Trier, Stadtbibliothek, MS 244/1382 (Latin theological miscellany, 130 × 90mm.).

cheaper) manner. The absence of illumination is also striking.[70] The practice of combining several cost-reducing features extends beyond books with limp bindings. To provide an example from paper codices, in the fourteenth century such books were nearly exclusively copied in cursive script, with the exception of some Italian specimens.[71] In other words, individuals who had these books made opted for cost-reducing measures in the two most expensive elements of book production, writing and writing support.

In the fourteenth and fifteenth centuries, the English book market had started to diversify and include budget-friendlier objects, allowing booksellers to tap into new markets and cater to new audiences. While many patrons in the manuscript age did not choose to cut costs, it is important to note they had the choice to do so over a century before the market started to provide cheaper books on a large scale through the printing press. An investigation of the lower end of the market shows that patrons had a lot of choice with regards to the materials used (such as writing support and binding) and the execution of the various production stages (speed and care being important parameters). Such diversification was not a novelty in English book production. Some of the options discussed above, such as the choice between sheep-skin and calf-skin, high- and low-quality handwriting, and expensive and cheap bindings, predate the period under investigation in this volume. However, by the end of the Middle Ages the selection had increased significantly. The growing demand for manuscripts is probably an important cause for this increased diversity, as is the desire for more choice that came with a growing market. This expansion, occurring in an age when books made in return for payment had become increasingly important among other schemes of manuscript production, emphasizes the close ties between commerce and the mechanical art of producing books. When the age of the handwritten book drew to a conclusion, the book trade had evolved into a business that gave both affluent readers and those on a budget a chance to lay their hands on a manuscript that matched their preferences and resources, and the professionals who took care of the business had become part of a highly specialized and organized trade.

---

[70] Scholla, 'Libri sine asseribus', 209–10 (script) and 212 (illumination). Only six of the fifty-eight codices with limp bindings in her corpus contain illumination: see the table at 202. For the hasty scribe, see Parkes, Their Hands before Our Eyes, 71–85.
[71] Kwakkel, 'A New Type of Book', 243 n.83.

9

Vernacular literary manuscripts and their scribes

LINNE R. MOONEY

This chapter will focus on production of vernacular literary manuscripts in the London area during the period after 1350 and to the early sixteenth century. Throughout this period, London seems to have been both origin and centre of secular vernacular literary book production, and many of the scribes we find copying the works of the poets William Langland, Geoffrey Chaucer, John Gower, Thomas Hoccleve, John Lydgate and others appear to have been doing so within the city or in its immediate environs.[1] This is not to say that they were all commercial producers of books: in fact there is only very limited evidence for commercial literary manuscript production before the third quarter of the fifteenth century, near the end of the period under question. One must be careful to draw distinctions between scribes copying vernacular literary texts (who seem to have done so in addition to other jobs involving writing), those copying other kinds of texts, principally in Latin, for high demand, such as school books, works studied at universities, bibles and liturgical manuscripts (who might make up the members of the Mistery or Guild of Textwriters) and those importing books from the continent or re-selling books produced in England.[2] Those producing copies of *literary* texts in London in the late fourteenth and first half of the fifteenth centuries were professional writers, in the Middle English sense of 'scribes', but they do not appear to have made their living principally by copying vernacular literary texts.

To explain what this distinction means in this chapter, it is necessary to begin with some definitions.[3] A 'professional' scribe here means a person (usually male)

---

[1] For evidence of scribes who were not freemen of the city of London within its environs, see Mooney, 'Locating Scribal Activity', 191–204.

[2] Ibid., 184–90. These distinctions do not hold fast: textwriters were among those who formed the Stationers' Company in 1403; and before and after the founding of the Stationers' Company, members of other London companies also imported books, notably the Mercers. See the discussion of the complexities of the 'trade' by Kwakkel, Chapter 8 above.

[3] See also Mooney, 'Professional Scribes?'.

who makes his living by writing, but he does not simply copy texts for his own or his family's or community's use. Such a person might make his living primarily by writing legal documents and/or keeping accounts. He might be a scrivener: a kind of accountant/legal notary and possibly, in London, a member of the Scriveners' Guild after it was formed in the late fourteenth century. He might be a royal or civic clerk, or serve as secretary or man of affairs to some wealthy person, whether noble or not. Those professional scribes considered here were copying vernacular literary writings in addition to their usual scribal activities. Such a person might copy literary texts for his principal employer, thus offering evidence of early audiences, or he might copy for another patron who resided or worked in the same locale or milieu. All of his work was for a bespoke trade, where patrons ordered books, and these professional scribes, singly or in ad hoc teams of men like themselves, fulfilled the commission.

By a 'commercial' scribe this chapter means a person, again, usually male, who made his living largely by copying books for a bespoke trade and perhaps, later in the fifteenth century, speculatively for sale in a shop. The London Textwriters, just mentioned, were a guild of such scribes: in 1403, they joined with others who 'use to bind and sell books' in London to form what came to be known as the Stationers' Company.[4] Their principal occupation was the copying of books, not documents, and they thus had to have some means to gain access to exemplars and means to publicize their skills and sell their wares, in a book stall or in a shop.

All commercial scribes are professional scribes – trained writers of some sort. But not all professional scribes are commercial scribes. The 'professional' scribes emerged first, as demand for books exceeded the ability of monasteries to produce them in sufficient numbers from about 1200 on. Other literate men in the community were already available to pick up the slack as demand grew;[5] or lay men might be trained by the monks for the purpose. The 'commercial' scribes emerged later, in the fourteenth and fifteenth centuries, as it became clear that one could make a living not just by taking on writing tasks, but by producing and selling books.

As Erik Kwakkel (Chapter 8) and Jean-Pascal Pouzet (Chapter 10) also note in this volume, none of the distinctions we can draw here are clear-cut: a 'commercial' stationer might contract a 'professional' scribe to complete a commission. 'Commercial' producers might have more than one occupation, just as 'professionals' did. All book work had a commercial aspect. But the more dedicated, more

---

[4] Blayney, *The Stationers' Company before the Charter*, 13.

[5] Doyle, 'The Work of a Late Fifteenth-Century Scribe', also makes this point in relation to the work William Ebesham for Westminster Abbey: 'The abbey was not without its own scribes but there must have been more than enough for them to do in a period when care of the conventual muniments and individual book-ownership were both well-developed' (321).

organized work associated with some scribes – the retention of exemplars and mass production of copies from them, for instance – made them the immediate precursors of the first commercial printers. It was the professionals – household secretaries, scriveners, notaries and others – who continued to thrive long after the advent of printing. The commercial producers' work was taken over by that of press; to think of it another way, it became their business.[6] The Stationers' Company in London, formed by manuscript producers and sellers in 1403, came eventually to monopolize the printed trade.

While the evidence suggests that London was the centre of vernacular book production, we certainly have evidence of book production outside metropolitan London. Besides the thriving trade in books written for the communities around England's universities and monasteries, non-metropolitan authors also attracted local scribes to copy their works. For instance, there are a number of manuscripts of the C text of William Langland's *Piers Plowman* with spellings that some have argued to demonstrate that the scribes originally came from the same Worcestershire–Shropshire area as Langland.[7] Likewise, some early copies of Nicholas Love's *The Mirror of the Blessed Life of Jesus Christ* are written by scribes using Yorkshire spellings: though himself a southerner, Love was prior of the North Yorkshire Carthusian house of Mount Grace.[8] A prolific scribe who copied works by John Lydgate, including four copies of his *Lives of SS Edmund and Fremund*, two each of his *Troy Book* and (with Benedict Burgh) his *Secrees of Old Philisoffres* and at least one of *The Fall of Princes*, lived in or near Bury St Edmunds, where Lydgate's Benedictine Abbey dedicated to St Edmund was located.[9] John Capgrave seems to have made his own copies of his writings in both Latin and English and also supervised the copying of other manuscripts of his works written using spellings typical of the area around King's Lynn in Norfolk where he was prior of the

[6] See Love's famous discussion of *Scribal Publication in Seventeenth-Century England*.

[7] Samuels, 'Langland's Dialect'; but see Horobin, 'In London and Opelond'.

[8] Sargent in the introduction to (ed.), *The Mirror of the Blessed Life*; Smith, 'Dialect and Standardization in the Waseda Manuscript'; Sargent, 'What Do the Numbers Mean?', 238, where he explains that only a few of the early manuscripts of Love's *Mirror* survive in northern dialects. He names BodL, MS Bodley 131 as an example, having been written by John Morton of York in a scribal dialect described by *LALME* as that of the West Riding (LP 473).

[9] Edwards, 'Stow and Lydgate's *St Edmund*'; Edwards, 'The McGill Fragment'; Scott, 'Lydgate's *Lives of SS Edmund and Fremund*'. Manuscripts attributed to him thus far are: 1) Arundel Castle, Duke of Norfolk, MS Edmund-Fremund (Lydgate, *SS Edmund and Fremund*; 2) BL, MS Arundel 99 (Lydgate, *Troy Book*); 3) BL, MS Harley 1766 (Lydgate, *Fall of Princes*); 4) BL, MS Harley 2255 (Lydgate anthology); 5) BL, MS Harley 4826, 4–81, 100–144v (Lydgate, *SS Edmund and Fremund* and Hoccleve, *The Regiment of Princes*); 6) BL, MS Sloane 2464 (Lydgate, *Secrees*); 7) BL, MS Yates Thompson 47 (Lydgate, *SS Edmund and Fremund*); 8) BodL, MS Ashmole 46 (Lydgate, *SS Edmund and Fremund* and Lydgate and Burgh, *Secrees*); 9) BodL, MS Laud misc. 673 (Lydgate and Burgh, *Secrees*); 10) Montréal, Quebec, McGill University, MS 143 (Lydgate, *Fall of Princes* (fragment)). Horobin has recently identified another manuscript by this scribe and has found his hand copying documents in Bury: see Horobin. 'The Edmund-Fremund Scribe'.

Augustinian friary.[10] Osbern Bokenham of the Augustinian priory at Clare, Suffolk, also served as scribe for copies of his *Legendys of Hooly Wummen* and complete *Legendary of Saints*.[11] Some early copies of John Trevisa's translations of Ranulph Higden's *Polychronicon* and Bartholomeus Anglicus's *De Proprietatibus rerum* are written with spellings typical of the south-west around Bristol and Berkeley Castle, Gloucestershire, the seat of Trevisa's patron, Sir Thomas Berkeley.[12] A number of manuscripts of Wycliffite writings originated in Oxford where their author lived, and later around Northamptonshire and Leicestershire, centres of lollard activity.[13] Many of the early copies of the *Speculum vitae* were copied in Yorkshire, where this anonymous prose didactic text originated.[14]

These early copies of important Middle English works associated with the place where the author lived demonstrate a 'big bang' theory of distribution of Middle English texts propounded by Michael Sargent among others. That is, they support the idea that earlier copies originated closest to the author and then spread further if the work attracted sufficient attention to warrant it.[15] While some works remained provincial, the most popular writings in Middle English spread throughout the country. For instance, although the earliest copies betray their London origins, Chaucer's *The Canterbury Tales* survives in manuscripts whose spellings may suggest scribes as far afield as Lincolnshire or Yorkshire (Paris, Bibliothèque Nationale, MS anglais 39), East Anglia (GUL, MS Hunter 197 (U.I.1) from Norfolk and CUL, MS Dd.4.24 from the area around Cambridge), and the West Midlands (BL, MS Lansdowne 851 from the north of the West Midlands or BL, MS Add. 25178 from the south of the West Midlands). Although, as Simon Horobin argues in Chapter 3 and as I note below, some of the scribes of works in provincial dialects may have been based in London, it seems likely this popular text was copied away from the metropolis too. Works such as *Pearl* and *Sir Gawain and the Green Knight* that

---

[10] Lucas, 'John Capgrave, O.S.A.'; and Lucas, 'A Fifteenth-Century Copyist at Work under Authorial Scrutiny'. Manuscripts attributed to him thus far are: 1) CCCC, MS 408 (Capgrave, *De Illustribus Henricis*); 2) CUL, MS Gg.4.12 (Capgrave, *Abbreviacion of Chronicles*); 3) BL, MS Add. 36704 (Capgrave, *Life of St Augustine, Life of St Gilbert, Tretis on the Orders*); 4) Oxford, Balliol College, MS 189 (Capgrave, *Commentarius in actus apostolorum*); 5) HEHL, MS HM 55 (Capgrave, *Life of St Norbert*); 6) BodL, MS Bodley 423, ff. 355–414 (Capgrave, *Solace of Pilgrimes*). Manuscripts thus far attributed to other scribes and corrected or annotated by him are: 1) Oxford, All Souls College, MS 17 (Capgrave, *De Fidei symbolis*); 2) Oxford, Balliol College, MS 190 (Capgrave, *De Fidei symbolis*); 3) BodL, MS Duke Humfrey b.1 (*Commentarius in exodum*, 1440); 4) Oxford, Oriel College 32 (*Commentarius in genesim*, 1438).

[11] Horobin, 'A Manuscript Found in the Library of Abbotsford'.

[12] Hanna, 'Sir Thomas Berkeley'.

[13] Contrary to the evidence for other vernacular writings of more secular content, there does appear to have been well-organized (and so perhaps 'commercial') production of Wycliffite Bibles and other Wycliffite writings earlier than the mid fifteenth century (Hudson, 'Lollard Book Production', esp. 128–32; Doyle, 'English Books in and out of Court', esp. 169; Sargent, 'What Do the Numbers Mean?', 214–16).

[14] Hanna, 'The Yorkshire Circulation of *Speculum Vitae*'.

[15] Sargent, 'What Do the Numbers Mean?' discusses this author-centred production.

survive only in one manuscript (BL, MS Cotton Nero A.x) reveal by their spelling, grammar and syntax the geographical district of their authors and do not seem to have reached beyond their limited provincial audience.[16]

Patrons requesting vernacular books outside London sometimes sought the services of the same men they employed for other written documents, that is, men of legal training whether of fixed abode or itinerant within a county district, who wrote out deeds, leases or contracts for them.[17] In the first half of the fourteenth century, the trilingual anthology of verse and prose, BL, MS Harley 2253, was copied by a scribe more accustomed to writing legal documents than literary texts, as Carter Revard has shown by having identified his hand in archives of documents produced around Ludlow.[18] Horobin's identification of the Edmund-Fremund scribe copying documents in Bury St Edmunds is evidence that some provincial scribes continued copying both literary texts and legal documents well into the fifteenth century.[19]

It is clear nevertheless that London was the centre for production of Middle English literature. As the largest city in England, London had the critical mass of readers to constitute an ample audience for English texts, and the largest concentration of wealthy merchants whose first (or only) language was English rather than French or Latin. It may be, too, that London was the literary capital because the presence of an intellectual stratum of society formed of the clerks who worked for royal and civic government gave rise to authors, scribes and audience for these vernacular writings.[20] All of these potential readers preferred their texts in London spellings, that is, copies written by London scribes, and this preference worked against the provincial authors. Geoffrey Chaucer and Thomas Hoccleve were based in London. And London's literate audience may be why Langland, and perhaps Gower, moved there, while other authors had patrons or supporters in London.[21] Love's *The Mirror of the Blessed Life of Jesus Christ* became a 'best seller' after Archbishop Arundel

---

[16] See Bowers, '*Pearl* in Its Royal Setting', for an alternative reading that this scribe had migrated to London. Nevertheless, Bowers's conclusion that the unpopularity of the work might be explained by its difficult dialect supports the 'big bang' theory of distribution in that the sole copy was apparently written in the Cheshire dialect of the author. This rule might apply even if early ownership of the manuscript is far afield from the author's origins, as is the case with the sole manuscript of *The Book of Margery Kempe* (BL, MS Add. 61823), written in a Norfolk dialect appropriate to Margery, a native of King's Lynn (and presumably also to her scribe, Salthows), but which belonged from an early date to the library of the Mount Grace Priory in North Yorkshire.

[17] For the same class of men employed for copying books in London, see Mooney, 'Locating Scribal Activity' and further discussion below.

[18] Revard, 'Scribe and Provenance'.

[19] Horobin, 'The Edmund-Fremund Scribe'.

[20] Kerby-Fulton, 'Professional Readers of Langland'; Kerby-Fulton and Justice, 'Langlandian Reading Circles'; Strohm, *Social Chaucer*.

[21] Langland came from the area around the Malvern Hills, while John Gower's English writing betrays his Kentish origins.

approved its text for reading by devout Christians in 1409.[22] John Trevisa, clerk and chaplain of Somerset-based Sir Thomas Berkeley, saw wider distribution of his translations of his *Polychronicon* and *De Proprietatibus rerum* after his patron had carried his manuscripts to the metropolis where copies could be made in London by London scribes, though using an exemplar written in Trevisa's own West Country language.[23]

The earliest copies of texts of the major late fourteenth-century writers Geoffrey Chaucer and John Gower, and of their early fifteenth-century successor Thomas Hoccleve, survive in manuscripts that betray the London origins of their earliest scribes. In the case of these three London-based authors, we have identified some of the scribes who copied the earliest and most authoritative manuscripts of their works as those closest to their authors. Thomas Hoccleve, like John Capgrave and Osbern Bokenham, himself made copies of his works, such that the most authoritative scribe is not only close to but in fact identical with the author. Hoccleve's holograph manuscripts have recently been reproduced in a facsimile volume edited by J. A. Burrow and A. I. Doyle; the editors only briefly discuss the reasons for his choosing to write these copies of his own works, but do comment that the three holograph manuscripts (like that illustrated in Figure 9.1) contain copies of 'all the poems currently attributed to him' except *The Regiment of Princes*.[24] We know that Hoccleve also wrote a holograph copy of *The Regiment* because a poem dedicating it survives in one of these manuscripts, HEHL, MS HM 111, on f. 37v; in this balade he makes it clear that he copied the poem in his own hand when he apologizes for his poor handwriting, blaming failing eyesight:

> Unto the rial egles excellence
> I humble Clerc, with al hertes humblesse,
> This book presente, and of your reverence
> Byseeche I pardon and foryevenesse
> That of myn ignorance and lewdnesse
> Nat have I write it in so goodly wyse
> As that me oght unto your worthynesse;
> Myn eyn hath custumed bysynesse
> So dawsed that I may no bet souffyse.[25]

Hoccleve's apologies for his ignorance are common matter for such dedications, but his apologies for his poor handwriting and eyesight are so distinctive that we

---

[22] See Sargent's introduction to (ed.), *The Mirror of the Blessed Life*, esp. 36–7.

[23] Hanna, 'Sir Thomas Berkeley', esp. 915–16, where Hanna summarizes the role of Berkeley's patronage in creating an audience for Trevisa's translations, first in the area around Berkeley Castle itself, then in the metropolis, as 'a concerted effort to extend his patronage and to make it nationally visible' (915).

[24] Burrow and Doyle (eds.), *Thomas Hoccleve*, xi.

[25] HEHL, MS HM 111, on f. 37v. This is my own transcription from the book; see also Robbins (ed.), *Secular Lyrics*, 92.

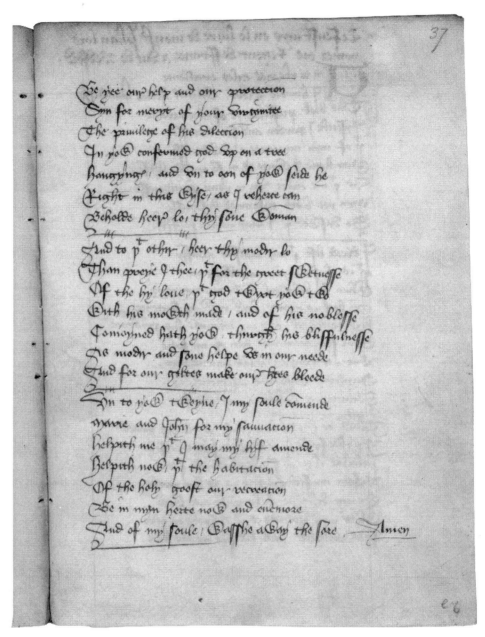

Figure 9.1 HEHL, MS HM 111, f. 37r: holograph manuscript of the poetry of Hoccleve.

can take them for autobiographical detail.[26] Thus we have evidence that Hoccleve copied out a complete set of his writings towards the end of his life, presumably to preserve an accurate series of texts as exemplars for posterity.

Chaucer's earliest scribes were associated with the city of London, where he lived from 1374 to 1385 or 1386 and with which he must have maintained contact throughout his life through family connections. Adam Pinkhurst, scrivener of London, copied several of the earliest manuscripts of his works: the Hengwrt and Ellesmere manuscripts of *The Canterbury Tales*, at least one copy of *Troilus and Criseyde* and at least one further copy of *The Canterbury Tales*, of which now only a single leaf survives.[27] By employing the same scribe to copy so many of his writings, Chaucer may have been attempting, like Hoccleve, to create a set of authorial copies as exemplars; he certainly betrays a keen awareness of the problems of scribal corruption and a desire to establish the canon of his works.[28] The man he chose to do this had a career profile that exactly illustrates the type of the 'professional' scribe defined above. Pinkhurst may have begun his career keeping accounts for a London merchant. He kept accounts and performed other copying services for the Mercers' Company of London; he was a member of the Scriveners' Company of London; and he worked directly for Geoffrey Chaucer in writing out the first copies of some of his works.[29] He copied other literary writings besides

[26] Besides this apology, I have detected from dated documents he wrote for the Office of the Privy Seal that Hoccleve's handwriting became larger in size and less controlled in appearance in later years: see Mooney, 'Some New Light on Thomas Hoccleve'. The three holograph manuscripts in the Burrow and Doyle facsimile, and much of his Formulary for the Office of the Privy Seal, are written in this larger, less controlled hand, contrasting with his smaller, tighter script and greater control in the portion of the TCC, MS R.3.2 manuscript of Gower's *Confessio Amantis* to which he contributed. See Doyle and Parkes, 'The Production of Copies', plate 53, in contrast to the handwriting in his holograph manuscript, Durham, University Library, MS Cosin V.iii.9, illustrated in plate 54 of the same article. I have recently identified a manuscript I believe to be this missing holograph copy of the *Regiment*, British Library, Royal 17D.xviii: see my forthcoming article, 'A Holograph Copy of Thomas Hoccleve's *Regiment of Princes*', *SAC*, 33 (2011).

[27] He wrote the fragment of *Troilus and Criseyde* now surviving as Hatfield House, Marquiss of Salisbury, Cecil Papers, Box S/1, and the fragment of *The Canterbury Tales* in CUL, MS Kk.1.3 part 20 and perhaps the fragment of *The Canterbury Tales* in NLW, MS 21972D. He embellished the copy of Chaucer's *Boece* in NLW, MS Peniarth 393D (see Stubbs, 'A New Manuscript?').

[28] For instance, he wrote his poem to 'Adam his own Scriveyn' to scold the scribe for carelessly miscopying his texts; and at the end of his *Troilus and Criseyde*, V, 1793–8, he prays that scribes will not miscopy his poem:

> And for ther is so gret diversite
> In Englissh and in writing of oure tonge,
> So prey I God that non myswrite the [*Troilus and Criseyde*],
> Ne the mysmetre for defaute of tonge;
> And red wherso thow be, or elles songe,
> That thow be understonde, God I biseche.

Gillespie, *Print Culture and the Medieval Author*, ch. 1, esp. 29–31, discusses Chaucer's awareness of scribal miscopying and his desire to establish a canon.

[29] Evidence of his working directly for Chaucer comes from the one-stanza poem by Chaucer addressed to 'Adam, his owen Scryveyne', which survives in TCC, MS R.3.20: see Mooney, 'Chaucer's Scribe', 101–3.

Chaucer's, including William Langland's *Piers Plowman* and part of a copy of John Gower's *Confessio Amantis*.[30] His manuscripts also illustrate contacts among the scribes of these works by London authors: Hoccleve corrected Pinkhurst's Hengwrt manuscript of *The Canterbury Tales*; and Pinkhurst, Hoccleve and the so-called 'Scribe D' all contributed to the copy of Gower's *Confessio Amantis* in TCC, MS R.3.2.[31]

Scribe D, so called because he is the fourth hand in that important copy of Gower's *Confessio Amantis*, was responsible for copying works by Langland and Chaucer (another two of the earliest manuscripts of *The Canterbury Tales*), besides his eight or ten copies of Gower's *Confessio Amantis*. He is also responsible for copying one manuscript of John Trevisa's translation of Bartholomeus Anglicus, *De Proprietatibus rerum*.[32] Scribe D also appears to have been a resident of London, both because of his collaboration with other scribes (including Pinkhurst) who were based there and because the artists who illustrated his copies of *Confessio Amantis* were London-based.[33]

Even in London, the centre for vernacular literary production throughout the period in question, there does not appear to have been 'commercial' production of literary texts before the mid fifteenth century. There is no evidence that late medieval secular book production took place in commercial 'scriptoria'. The work of C. Paul Christianson demonstrates that there were shops operated by various book producers in certain areas of London – notably in Paternoster Row and other streets around St Paul's Cathedral.[34] But before 1450, there is no evidence, at least not from vernacular books, of consistent collaborations between the artisans in those shops; of consistent supervision of their work by stationers;

---

[30] Pinkhurst's hand is also found in TCC, MS B.15.17 (Langland, *Piers Plowman*, B text); TCC, MS R.3.2, ff. 9r–32v (portion of Gower, *Confessio Amantis*).

[31] Doyle and Parkes, 'The Production of Copies'.

[32] Manuscripts attributed to him thus far are: 1) TCC, MS R.3.2, ff. 66r–73v, 113 (line 61)–154 (Gower, *Confessio Amantis*); 2) BL, MS Add. 27944, ff. 2r–7v, 196–335v (Trevisa, trans., *De Proprietatibus rerum*); 3) BL, MS Egerton 1991 (Gower, *Confessio Amantis*); 4) BL, MS Harley 7334 (Chaucer, *The Canterbury Tales*); 5) London, University Library, MS V.88 (the Ilchester manuscript of Langland, *Piers Plowman*); 6) New York, Columbia University Library, MS Plimpton 265 (Gower, *Confessio Amantis*); 7) BodL, MS Bodley 294 (Gower, *Confessio Amantis*); 8) BodL, MS Bodley 902, ff. 2r–16v (Gower, *Confessio Amantis*); 9) Oxford, Christ Church, MS 148 (Gower, *Confessio Amantis*); 10) Oxford, Corpus Christi College, MS 67 (Gower, *Confessio Amantis*); 11) Oxford, Corpus Christi College, MS 198 (Chaucer, *The Canterbury Tales*); 12) Princeton, University Library, MS Taylor 5, ff. 7r–190r (Gower, *Confessio Amantis*); and possibly also 13) GUL, MS Hunter S.1.7 (7) (Gower, *Confessio Amantis*); and 14) PML, MS M. 125 (Gower, *Confessio Amantis*).

[33] See Lawton, 'The Illustration of Late Medieval Secular Texts' and Griffiths, '*Confessio Amantis*'. See also further information on this scribe in forthcoming published works by Linne Mooney and Estelle Stubbs and also by Simon Horobin.

[34] Christianson, *A Directory of London Stationers* and *Memorials of the Book Trade*, and esp. 'Evidence for the Study of London's Late Medieval Manuscript Book-Trade'; and, for another view, Mooney, 'Locating Scribal Activity', esp. 183–91.

or of the retention of exemplars for the repeated, 'commercial' production of manuscripts.

Doyle and Parkes first made these points in 1978 with the example of the copy of Gower's *Confessio Amantis* in TCC, MS R.3.2, to which Pinkhurst, Hoccleve and Scribe D all contributed, and no evidence has been found since then to question it.[35] As they point out, even Pinkhurst (whom they call 'Scribe B') and Scribe D do not use the same exemplar for writing their two copies each of Chaucer's *The Canterbury Tales*; their surviving work collectively supports the argument against highly organized commercial production and in favour of more ad hoc arrangements.[36] They conclude that the lack of supervision that a single locale, a scriptorium, would have brought to the production of MS R.3.2 itself argues against the existence of single sites of commercial production.[37] (One should note, however, that they and others following them claim a lack of evidence for scriptoria for vernacular literary texts, not all texts, and for the first few decades of the fifteenth century, not the entire century.)

Besides these best-known London literary scribes, others have been identified who apparently did not work in commercial scriptoria and who did not only produce literary manuscripts but appear to have held day jobs as scribes or clerks (whether freelance or employed directly) in London or Westminster. One of these is William Ebesham, who apparently worked within the close of Westminster Abbey, though not as a member of its religious community. According to A. I. Doyle, he originally settled there to take sanctuary from debt and fulfilled commissions from the Abbey itself, its monks and laymen outside its precincts, including Sir John Paston the Elder.[38] Another such scribe is the London-based scribe who wrote a compilation of Middle English texts in HEHL, MS HM 114. He copied literary works, including Chaucer's *Troilus and Criseyde* and Langland's *Piers Plowman*, but

---

[35] Ibid., esp. 196–203.

[36] Ibid., 186, 192.

[37] Ibid., 196–203.

[38] Doyle, 'The Work of a Late Fifteenth-Century Scribe'. His hand has been found copying only one vernacular literary text (Lydgate and Burgh, *Secrees*), but he illustrates the freelance nature of much of London's book production in this period. Manuscripts attributed to him thus far are: 1) Boston, Harvard Medical School, Countway Library of Medicine, MS 19, written for Sir John Fastolf; 2) Durham, University Library, MS Cosin V.iii.7, ff. 1r–94r, ff. 99v–102 (*Mandeville's Travels*, story of Holy Cross, verse on Book of Judith, devotional pieces including on Henry VI, pieces on clerical life, all in Latin); 3) BL, MS Add. 10106 (chronicle up to the reign of Edward IV, texts related to Westminster Abbey); 4) BL, MS Lansdowne 285, ff. 1–43 (line 15), 48–56v, 82–140, 152–196v (Sir John Paston's *Great Book*, including Lydgate and Burgh's *Secrees*); 5) London, College of Arms, MS Young 72 (smaller copy of *Liber niger quaternus*); 6) Longleat, MS 38, ff. 9r–49v, ff. 53r–200v (privileges of Westminster Abbey); 7) JRL, MS Lat. 395 (Rolle's and other devotional works, saints' lives); 8) Oxford, St John's College, MS 147 (Rolle's and other devotional texts, saints' lives); 9) Westminster Abbey, Muniments Book I (*Liber niger quaternus*, that is, title deeds and documents about the property and privileges of the Abbey); 10) Westminster Abbey, MS 29 (William Fleet's Latin history of Westminster Abbey); 11) BL, MS Add. 43491, ff. 12r–13r (Letter and bill to Sir John Paston the elder, 1468).

also appears to have taken work from the Priory of St Bartholomew's in Smithfield and to have worked for the London Guildhall.[39]

Another prolific scribe, the so-called 'Petworth scribe', contributed to two copies of Chaucer's *The Canterbury Tales*, two of Love's *The Mirror of the Blessed Life of Jesus Christ*, and one each of Gower's *Confessio Amantis*, Lydgate's *The Siege of Thebes*, Walton's translation of Boethius's *De Consolatione philosophiae*, the anonymous *Master of Game*, *The South English Legendary* and the *Gilte Legende*, but he also kept accounts for the London Guild of Skinners for over twenty years, showing that like Pinkhurst and the HEHL, MS HM 114 scribe he combined employment in the city of London with the copying of vernacular literary manuscripts (Figure 9.2 shows a *Confessio Amantis* he copied).[40] Similarly, the author and scribe Thomas Usk both composed vernacular literature – *The Testament of Love* – and worked as scribe or clerk for the Goldsmiths' Company and for the draper John of Northampton.[41] Members of London's and Westminster's clerical intelligentsia provided both scribes and patrons of vernacular religious writings: Kathryn Kerby-Fulton and Stephen Justice offer evidence of scribes of royal government both copying and owning manuscripts of Langland's *Piers Plowman*, and A. I. Doyle points to ownership of vernacular religious texts by clerks of the Exchequer and members of their extended families.[42]

Clerks of city government, or members of the Textwriters', Scriveners' or other city guilds, might practise their trade freely anywhere in London or its environs, but others were more restricted by not having obtained the freedom of the city. As I note above and have argued elsewhere, many of the scribes copying vernacular literary texts in London appear by their regional spelling-preferences to have migrated to the city from other parts of the country, just as authors did; and others appear to have migrated from foreign countries to work as copyists

[39] Hanna, 'The Scribe of Huntington HM 114'. MSS attributed to him thus far are: 1) BL, MS Harley 3943, ff. 2r–7v, ff. 9r–56v, ff. 63r–67v (Chaucer, *Troilus and Criseyde*); 2) London, Corporation of London Record Office, Letterbook I, f. 223r (lines 9–37), f. 224v, f. 226v (last 6 lines), f. 227 (lines 2–bottom), f. 228r and probably ff. 229r–231v (line 25); 3) London, Corporation of London Record Office, Cust. 12 (*Liber albus*), ff. 44–55v, 202v–203v, 239–244v, 256–311v and rubric marginalia *passim*; 4) London, Lambeth Palace, MS 491 part 1, ff. 1r–290v (*Brut, The Siege of Jerusalem, Awntyrs of Arthure*); 5) HEHL, MS HM 114 (Chaucer, *Troilus and Criseyde*, Langland, *Piers Plowman* and *Susanna*).

[40] His manuscripts include portions of the Petworth House and Lichfield Cathedral copies of *The Canterbury Tales*; NLS, MS Advocates' 18.1.7 (Love, *The Mirror*); Tokyo, Waseda University, MS NE 3691 (Love, *The Mirror*); Pembroke, Camb., MS 307 (Gower, *Confessio Amantis*); BL, MS Arundel 119; BL, MS Sloane 3501 (Lydgate, *The Siege of Thebes*); Oslo, Schøyen collection, MS 615 (Walton, trans., *Boethius*); Tokyo, Takamiya collection, MS 45 (fragments); Tokyo, Takamiya collection, MS 54 (*South English Legendary*); London, Guildhall, MS 31692, ff. 2r–19r (the Register of the Skinners' Company, or *Book of the Fraternity of the Assumption of Our Lady*).

[41] Barron, 'New Light on Thomas Usk', 1; Barron, Review of Lisa Jefferson (ed.), *Wardens' Accounts*, 173–5. For parallels between Usk and Adam Pinkhurst, see Turner, 'Conflict'.

[42] Kerby-Fulton and Justice, 'Langlandian Reading Circles'; Doyle, 'Books Connected with the Vere Family'.

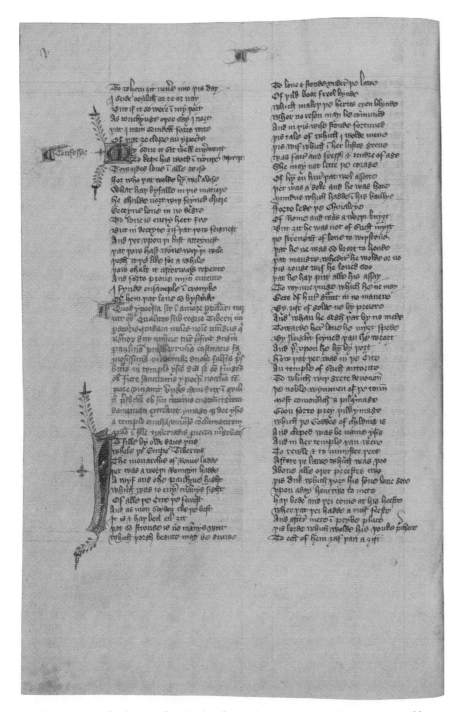

Figure 9.2 Pembroke, Camb., MS 307, f. 12v: Gower, Confessio Amantis, copied by the so-called 'Petworth scribe'.

in London.[43] Since licence to work in London involved becoming a member of one of London's Livery Companies through either a lengthy apprenticeship, an expensive payment for more immediate admission to a guild without apprenticeship, or a powerful patron, many of these scribes who had migrated to the city practised their trade either outside the city walls (outside the jurisdiction of the city) or in extra-parochial sites, called 'liberties', within the city itself. Liberties, so called because they were beyond the jurisdiction of the city, included the Hospital and Priory of St Bartholomew's, Smithfield (outside the walls but by the end of the fourteenth century within the city limits), for whom the scribe of HEHL, MS HM 114 did some work and where John Shirley lived during the latter part of his life while copying several of his literary anthologies. Other liberties were the Hospital of St Thomas of Acon, where Adam Pinkhurst may have worked for the Mercers (although, as a scrivener, he could practise his trade anywhere); Holy Trinity Aldgate, St Martin le Grand and other religious or monastic sites where we have localized scribes; and the convent of Blackfriars, where clerks for the Heralds may have kept office.[44] The scribe of HEHL, MS HM 114 uses spellings typical of south-eastern Essex;[45] the so-called 'Beryn scribe' too writes with Essex or southern Norfolk spellings;[46] and a scribe responsible for copying Chaucer's *The Canterbury Tales*, Gower's *Confessio Amantis* and Lydgate's *Fall of Princes* discloses underlying spellings typical of the West Midlands,[47] although all three were apparently working in London. Ricardus Franciscus, or Richard Franceys (fl. 1447–67), may have been a Frenchman working as a scribe in London, so his employment by the Garter King of Arms John Smert, possibly based in the liberty of Blackfriars, would have made it possible for him to work in London though a foreigner (see Figure 9.3 for an example of his work).[48]

---

[43] See Mooney, 'Locating Scribal Activity', where this phenomenon is more fully described and more specific examples offered.

[44] Mooney, 'A New Manuscript by the Hammond Scribe', esp. 119–21.

[45] *LALME*, LP 6030, grid 578/190 (I, 92).

[46] *LALME*, LP 6040, grid 567/185 (I, 59); for more on this scribe, see below.

[47] Manly and Rickert identify his manuscript of Chaucer's *The Canterbury Tales* as displaying spellings typical of Shropshire (Manly and Rickert (eds.), *The Text of The Canterbury Tales*, 1.202); see my article, 'A New Scribe of Chaucer and Gower', and Mooney and Mosser, 'The Belvoir Castle (Duke of Rutland) Manuscript'.

[48] Literary manuscripts attributed to him thus far are: St John's, Camb., MS H.5 (Scrope, trans. of de Pisan, *Epistre of d'Othea*); CUL, MS Add. 7870, ff. 34r–77v (Courtecuisse, trans., *Des quatre vertus cardinaulx*); BL, MS Harley 4775 (Jacobus de Voragine, *Legenda aurea*); BL, MS Harley 2915 (Book of Hours); PML, MS M. 126 (Gower, *Confessio Amantis*); BodL, MS Laud misc. 570 (French translation of John of Wales; de Pizan, *Epistre d'Othea*); Oxford, University College, MS 85 (Chartier, *Le quadrilogue invectif*); and Philadelphia, Rosenbach Library, MS 439/16 (Lydgate, *Fall of Princes*). Documents ascribed to him are London, Tallow Chandlers' Company, Grant of Arms; London, St Bartholomew's Hospital, Archives, Large Cartulary, ff. 326–65; Nancy, Archives Départementales de Meurthe et Moselle, MS H.80, membranes 1, 2 (Statutes of Order of the Garter); BodL, MS Ashmole 764 (miscellany of heraldic texts); BodL, MS Ashmole 789, ff. 1–5 (writing exercises in Latin and English and decorated

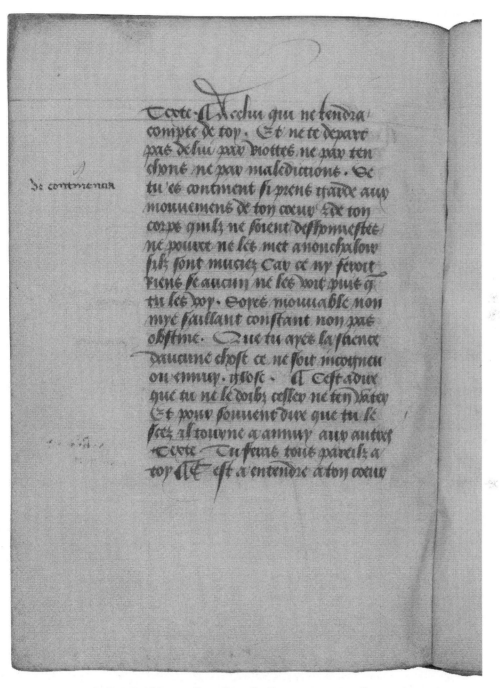

Figure 9.3 CUL, MS Add. 7870, f. 56v: Ricardus Franciscus copying Courtecuisse, trans.,
Des quatre vertus cardinaulx.

Until the mid fifteenth century, then, it appears that the scribes who produced copies of vernacular literary texts in London and its vicinity were either men who worked freelance outside the city's jurisdiction or in liberties within the city, or men who worked as clerks for various royal or civic offices, taking on copying in addition to their other jobs.[49] In the middle of the fifteenth century comes the first evidence for what might be more organized, commercial production of vernacular manuscripts in London, in the form of a scribe who makes several copies of the Middle English prose *Brut* from a single defective exemplar.[50] Even this example does not prove commercial production, however, since, as Lister Matheson and I have pointed out, it simply demonstrates that a single scribe held on to an exemplar and made several copies from it: he might do this in other settings besides a commercial scriptorium, such as a library or archive where he worked at another sort of job. Although he writes copies of several other literary texts, we find no other evidence of his keeping an exemplar for, or making multiple copies of, any of those texts.

Some London scribes in the second half of the fifteenth century apparently continued holding other jobs while copying vernacular literary texts. Ricardus Franciscus, or Richard Franceys, already mentioned, apparently took on copying work at times for John Smert, Garter King of Arms, for St Bartholomew's Hospital in Smithfield and for the Archdeaconry of London, besides producing English and French vernacular literary texts for various patrons, including Sir John Fastolf and Fastolf's secretary William Worcester.[51] Stephen Dodesham (d. 1482) produced three copies of Lydgate's *The Siege of Thebes*, one of Chaucer's *Treatise on the Astrolabe*, one of Burgh's translations of Cato's *Disticha*, three of Love's *The Mirror of the Blessed Life of Jesus Christ* and other vernacular translations of religious writings,

alphabet); and HEHL, MS HM 932 (*Statutes of Archdeaconry of London*). See Scott, 'A Mid-Fifteenth-Century English Illuminating Shop', 170, n.3; and Jefferson, 'Two Fifteenth-Century Manuscripts'; Hamer, 'Spellings of the Fifteenth-Century Scribe Ricardus Franciscus Writes for William Worcester'; Nall, 'Ricardus Franciscus'. Franceys is also discussed briefly by Parkes, *Their Hands before Our Eyes*, 43, 117–18, and by Kwakkel, Chapter 8 above.

[49] Royal and civic offices also constitute the main livelihood of some of the authors of this period, like Thomas Usk, Geoffrey Chaucer and Thomas Hoccleve.

[50] Matheson and Mooney, 'The Beryn Scribe'. Manuscripts attributed to him thus far are: 1) Alnwick Castle, Duke of Northumberland, MS 455 (Chaucer, *The Canterbury Tales*); 2) Ann Arbor, MI, University of Michigan Library, MS 225, ff. 1r–29r, f. 108r (line 22)–135r (prose *Brut*); 3) CUL, MS Kk.1.3 part 10 (Lydgate, *The Life of Our Lady*); 4) BL, MS Harley 1337 (prose *Brut*); 5) BL, MS Harley 6251 (prose *Brut*); 6) BodL, MS Hatton 50, ff. 2–17v, 84v (line 21)–107v, 119 (line 7)–130v (prose *Brut*); 7) BodL, MS Tanner 11, pages 1–116, 140 (line 19)–163, 164 (lines 27–31) 196 (corrected catchword), 205 (line 4)–209 (line 3) (prose *Brut*); 8) Oxford, St John's College, MS 57 (*Prick of Conscience*, London chronicle, *The Parliament of Fowls*, statutes and ordenances under Henry V); 9) Princeton, University Library, MS 100, ff. 1r–165r, 203r–215r (Chaucer, *The Canterbury Tales*); and possibly also 10) BodL, MS Rawl. B.190 (prose *Brut*); and 11) BL, MS Stowe 71 (prose *Brut*).

[51] See discussion above of his working in London, although a foreigner, with a list of the works ascribed to him in n.48.

besides Latin texts. Dodesham entered into a religious life at the Carthusian priory at Witham and later transferred to the priory at Sheen.[52] He thus illustrates the crossover between secular and monastic production of such literary texts, since it may be that some of his vernacular texts were written after entering into religious life (see further discussion of monastic scribes by Pouzet in Chapter 10). The so-called 'Hammond scribe' (fl. 1458–80) may have worked for the Garter King of Arms John Smert or for the draper Sir Thomas Cooke (Mayor of London, 1462–3), besides copying many vernacular literary manuscripts, only some of which seem to have belonged initially to Sir Thomas Cooke or members of his household.[53]

The 'Hammond scribe' is associated in one manuscript with another London-based scribe who does appear to have crossed the line to commercial production of vernacular literary manuscripts, whom I call the 'Trinity Anthologies scribe' because of his contributions to two manuscripts at Trinity College, Cambridge (TCC, MS R.3.19 and MS R.3.21) that strongly suggest organized, commercial production.[54]

[52] Doyle, 'Stephen Dodesham'. Manuscripts attributed to him thus far are: 1) TCC, MS B.14.54 (exposition of Creed, etc. in English); 2) Boston, Public Library, MS f.med.94 (Lydgate, *The Siege of Thebes*); 3) TCC, MS B.15.16 (Love, *The Mirror*); 4) CUL, MS Add. 3042, ff. 116–25 (prayers in English and Latin); 5) CUL, MS Add. 3137 (Lydgate, *The Siege of Thebes*); 6) CUL, MS Dd.7.7–10 (four-volume set of Nicholas de Lyra, on the bible); 7) CUL, MS Kk.6.41 (short Latin spiritual treatises); 8) Downside Abbey, MS 26542 (*The Pricking of Love, Pore Caitif,* three shorter didactic texts); 9) Dublin, Trinity College 678 (F.5.8) (trans. of Thomas à Kempis, *Imitatio Christi*); 10) GUL, MS Hunter T.3.15 (Love, *The Mirror*); 11) GUL, MS Hunter 258–9 (U.4.16–17) (two-volume set of an English translation of Richard of St Victor, *The Study of Wisdome*); 12) Karlsruhe, Badische Landesbibliothek, St Georgen 12 (*Sanctilogium salvatoris*: the first of two original volumes, the second lost); 13) BL, MS Add. 11305 (*Prick of Conscience*); 14) BL, MS Harley 630, f. 163r–v (one leaf of *Golden Legend*); 15) Beinecke, MS 661 (Lydgate, *The Siege of Thebes*); 16) New York, *olim* Cockerell/Dawson/Duschnes (pseudo-Augustine, *Sermones morales ad fratres suos in heremo*); 17) BodL, MS Bodley 423, ff. 128r–242r (religious and devotional texts); 18) BodL, MS Bodley 549, ff. 25r–198v, except ff. 77v–79r (Latin *Horologium sapientiae*, etc.); 19) BodL, MS Bodley 619 (Chaucer, *Treatise on the Astrolabe*); 20) BodL, MS Eng. poet. e. 15 (Burgh's trans. of Cato's *Disticha*); 21) BodL, MS Rawl. A.387B (Love, *The Mirror*); 22) Oxford, Trinity College, MS 46 (Latin choir Psalter, canticles, litanies and lessons for the dead, Carthusian liturgical calendar).

[53] Hammond, 'A Scribe of Chaucer'; Hammond, 'Two British Museum Manuscripts'; Doyle, 'An Unrecognized Piece of *Piers the Ploughman's Creed*'; Green, 'Notes on Some Manuscripts of Hoccleve's *Regiment*'; Doyle, 'English Books in and out of Court'; Mooney, 'More Manuscripts Written by a Chaucer Scribe'; Mooney, 'A New Manuscript by the Hammond Scribe'. Manuscripts attributed to him thus far are: 1) TCC, MS R.14.52 (medical miscellany); 2) TCC, MS R.3.21, ff. 34r–49v ('Parce michi Domine', *Pety Job*); 3) TCC, MS O.3.11 (London city and legal documents); 4) BL, MS Add. 29901 (heraldic precedents); 5) BL, MS Add. 34360 (literary miscellany); 6) BL, MS Arundel 59 (Hoccleve, *The Regiment of Princes*); 7) BL, MS Cotton Claudius A.viii, ff. 175r–197v (Fortescue, *Governance of England*); 8) BL, MS Harley 78, f. 3 (fragment of *Piers the Ploughman's Creed*); 9) BL, MS Harley 372, ff. 71r–112r (Hoccleve, *The Regiment of Princes*); 10) BL, MS Harley 2251 (literary miscellany); 11) BL, MS Harley 4999 (*Statutes of the Realm*, 1 Edw. III to 18 Hen. VI); 12) BL, MS Royal 17.D.xv, ff. 167r–301r (Chaucer, *The Canterbury Tales*); 13) London, Royal College of Physicians, MS 388 (Chaucer, *The Canterbury Tales*); 14) BodL, MS Rawl. D.913, f. 43 (fragment of English prose *Merlin*); 15) Worcester, Cathedral Library, F.172 (scriptural narratives, devotional texts).

[54] See my article, Mooney, 'Scribes and Booklets of Trinity College, Cambridge, MSS'.

These two manuscripts are made up of booklets that may have been produced, like printed quarto pamphlets, for commercial sale.[55] Texts copied into these booklets are duplicated in one booklet (booklet IX of MS R.3.21) and in another manuscript by the 'Trinity Anthologies scribe' (BodL, MS Douce 322), of which the second booklet duplicates the texts in the second booklet of TCC, MS R.3.21, except in reverse order.[56] This duplication suggests that exemplars, possibly some of these booklets themselves, were kept by the scribe and his colleague(s) for copying at the request of a patron. These scribes might still be copying for a bespoke trade, since some of the booklets of MS R.3.21 and MS Douce 322 were apparently made up of texts specifically requested by their owners from the scribes' stock. In TCC, MS R.3.21, the scribe clearly added a prayer for Edward IV to Lydgate's poem 'A Prayer for King, Queen and People'. The original version of the poem related to Henry VI. The prayer was requested, and perhaps composed, by the owner, Roger Thorney, so he must have asked the main scribe to add it to his booklet at the time of purchase. It is evident that the prayer for Edward IV was added, and not part of the original copying of the manuscript, because there is a change of ink for this added prayer. And this requesting an addition from the original scribe suggests, too, that Thorney purchased the booklet directly from the 'Trinity Anthologies scribe' and from a prepared booklet chosen from his stock.[57] If we follow Doyle and Parkes's definition of strictly commercial production as evidenced either by multiple copies produced (like print) without pre-arranged purchase, or by multiple copies produced from a single exemplar kept by the scribe for this purpose,[58] these booklets copied by the 'Trinity Anthologies scribe' offer us the first unambiguous example of commercial vernacular literary book production in England.

This group of manuscripts offers still more evidence of commercial production in what happened to them later in the fifteenth century, when they were apparently used as exemplars for further manuscript copies or for early printed books. The manuscript BodL, MS Douce 322, though destined for Dartford Nunnery, appears to have been made available for another round of copying, as evidenced by the duplication of its texts in the first part of another manuscript, BL, MS Harley 1706, and of some of its texts again in the second part of MS Harley 1706. Doyle argues that it could have served as an exemplar even if deposited in Dartford, as its frontispiece inscription suggests, for there were family relationships between nuns

---

[55] Among others, see Boffey and Thompson, 'Anthologies and Miscellanies', esp. 288–90.

[56] See Mooney, 'Scribes and Booklets'.

[57] Although we could argue that the scribe added the stanza at the bottom of f. 245v at the time of the purchase, that would have suggested that the booklet had been prepared with blank space at the bottom of this leaf; given that there were no other half-leaves left blank, this seems unlikely.

[58] Doyle and Parkes, 'The Production of Copies', 199–200; see also Matheson and Mooney, 'The Beryn Scribe', 362–4, 368–9.

at the houses of Dartford and Barking for which the Harley manuscript was destined.[59] But it could also have been delayed (or never delivered to Dartford) and remained in the London book-producing district around St Paul's long enough to serve as an exemplar for the Harley book. Another possibility would be that both MS Douce 322 and MS Harley 1706 were word-for-word copies of an exemplar retained by this group of scribes, as some of the booklets of TCC, MS R.3.19 and MS R.3.21 seem to have been.

At the same time, the other two manuscripts by the 'Trinity Anthologies scribe' (TCC, MS R.3.19 and MS R.3.21) demonstrate the close relationship between commercial book production and early printing. The brief period of commercial manuscript production of vernacular literary texts in London was soon eclipsed by the introduction of print, which could produce more copies, more accurately and faster than the scribes could. Gavin Bone first drew attention to the connection between the two Trinity manuscripts and texts produced by William Caxton and Wynkyn de Worde.[60] Texts from both the portion of MS R.3.19 copied by the main scribe (the 'Trinity Anthologies scribe') and the booklets written in the late fifteenth or first half of the sixteenth century with which they were bound appear to have served as exemplars for early editions by Caxton and de Worde.[61] For instance, the third scribe of TCC, MS R.3.19 wrote the anonymous *The Court of Love* (ff. 217–39) in a separate booklet later joined to those written by the 'Trinity Anthologies scribe', and the pages on which he wrote his copy of the poem are marked with printers' ink, showing that this copy was used as the exemplar for printing. This same scribe also wrote, in another manuscript, a copy of Lydgate's *The Siege of Thebes*, the format of which betrays that it was written to accompany Caxton's printed copies of *The Canterbury Tales*, *Troilus and Criseyde* and John Mirk's *Quattuor Sermones* with which it is now bound.[62] Other texts added in MS R.3.19 also served as copy-texts for printers, offering further proof that many of the booklets that make up the two volumes MS R.3.19 and MS R.3.21 remained in the London book trade up to the introduction of print.[63] The probable line of descent for these texts began

---

[59] Doyle, 'Books Connected with the Vere Family', 229, 232–9.

[60] Bone, 'Extant Manuscripts Printed from by W. De Worde', 297–8, 303–4. See also Fletcher (ed.), *Manuscript Trinity R.3.19*, xxviii–xxx.

[61] For a list of the booklets and their contents, see Mooney, 'Scribes and Booklets of Trinity College, Cambridge, MSS', table 1. The later booklets are V, written by Scribe B of this manuscript and giving information about the relationship between complexions and seasons; XI and XIII written by Scribe C, containing *The Court of Love* and *The Petigrew of England*, with copies of Lydgate's fables of 'The hound that bare the chese' and 'How the wolffe diseyvyd the crane' added to blank leaves by John Stow at the end of booklet IX; and XII written by Scribe D, containing a copy of *Piers of Fulham*.

[62] Bone, 'Extant Manuscripts Printed from by W. de Worde', 286–91, where he demonstrates that this copy of *The Siege* was later used as the copy text for de Worde's print of *c*.1500; this information updated in Gillespie, *Print Culture and the Medieval Author*, 77–88.

[63] Mooney, 'Scribes and Booklets', 263–6.

with copies made by John Shirley, when he settled into lodgings within the close of St Bartholomew's Priory in Smithfield after 'retirement' from a career as private secretary and man of affairs to Richard Beauchamp, Earl of Warwick.[64] Some of Shirley's books, or their exemplars, appear to have passed to the 'Hammond scribe' and his collaborator, the 'Trinity Anthologies scribe', and were copied into the booklets of MS R.3.19 and MS R.3.21 to serve as exemplars for their production of booklet manuscripts; and these booklets then became available to Caxton's, then de Worde's, printing houses as copy-texts.[65]

Professional and commercial manuscript production of vernacular literary manuscripts does continue after the introduction of print, but from the early sixteenth century it appears to be reserved for copies written by the authors themselves or for specialized texts appealing to a particular audience – an individual, a household or a family. Members of the household or those employed by the household produce these copies, which appear to have remained in the households for which they were written. Even before the turn of the sixteenth century we find collections of literary texts written for a household, sometimes by several members, like the so-called Findern manuscript (CUL, MS Ff.1.6).[66] Members of mercantile households also composed and copied texts specific to their patrons, households and cities. John Vale wrote a collection of copies of legal documents relating to London, historical accounts of events occurring in or near London, together with Sir John Fortescue's *The Governance of England* and John Lydgate's *The Serpent of Division* in the third quarter of the fifteenth century while in the service of Sir Thomas Cooke (draper, and mayor of London, 1462–3).[67] Robert Fabian, draper of London, wrote his *Chronicle* at the very end of the fifteenth and beginning of the sixteenth centuries.[68] In the sixteenth century, a professional scribe employed by the Percy family, earls of Northumberland, produced two manuscripts of vernacular literary texts

---

[64] Shirley's volumes, now BL, MS Add. 16165, TCC, MS R.3.20 and BodL, MS Ashmole 59, uniquely preserve a number of short texts of Chaucer, Lydgate and other vernacular writers. See Connolly, *John Shirley*, 172–85; and Mooney, 'John Shirley's Heirs', 196–7.

[65] For further examples of the transition from manuscript to print, see Gillespie, *Print Culture and the Medieval Author*, ch. 1, esp. 49–50 for these two scribes.

[66] Beadle and Owen (eds.), *The Findern Manuscript*, vii–xiv; Robbins, 'The Findern Anthology'; and numerous articles since then have built on the theory of various members of the Findern household and their guests adding to the manuscript.

[67] Kekewich et al., *The Politics of Fifteenth-Century England*, esp. ch. 3 and part 2.

[68] Robert Fabian, or Fabyan, was the author of *Fabian's Chronicle*, describing events of the second half of the fifteenth century, with particular emphasis on London. He writes in the prologue to his work that he will finish in 1507, having spent nine years in writing his *Chronicle*. While by then a successful draper and alderman in his own right, he had spent part of his youth in the household of Sir Thomas Cooke. As I have mentioned already, it is possible that the 'Hammond scribe' was also employed by Sir Thomas at some point during his career as scribe. See Kekewich et al., *The Politics of Fifteenth-Century England*, 94; and Mooney, 'More Manuscripts Written by a Chaucer Scribe', 404–5.

and histories specific to the family.[69] As print began to impinge on the marketability of more expensive manuscript books, commercial manuscript production fell off, but we still find professionals working – in households and elsewhere – as producers of vernacular literary manuscripts.

[69] His hand can be found in two manuscripts recording events in the history of the Percy family, BL, MS Royal 18.D.ii, ff. 1v–5r, ff. 165r–211v, and BodL, MS Selden B.10, ff. 200r–209v, datable to 1520. BL, MS Royal 18.D.ii also contains vernacular literary writings including works by Lydgate.

10

Book production outside commercial contexts

JEAN-PASCAL POUZET

On f. 98r of BodL, MS Lat. misc. c.66 the following inscription is found: 'Qui scripcit carmen Humffridus est sibi nomen' ('He who wrote the song, Humphrey is his own name'). The scribe was also the owner and compiler of this late fifteenth- and early sixteenth-century commonplace book: he was Humphrey Newton of Newton and Pownall in Cheshire (1466–1536). Although his note is like a colophon, it is in approximate Latin (note the idiosyncratic spelling of 'scripcit' and the contorted syntax), and there is no 'carmen' or song in the immediate vicinity. It appears amidst two alphabetic series of ornamented capital letters modelled on secretary script (ff. 95–103 and 104v) in a quire including a majority of courtly poems (ff. 92v–111v); those letters may be announced as 'De Exemplis scribendi *pro* scriptore' in the authorial table of contents (f. 92r) (Figure 10.1), and they may have been 'valuable' for the drafting of legal documents which they precede.[1] The model alphabets make it seem as if Humphrey was a full-time professional scrivener displaying some of his skills. But he was not (although he may have undertaken conveyancing for himself and neighbours), and his mock-colophon may simply serve as an oddly placed and elaborate pen-trial. At any rate, the inscription creates an effect of ingenious *trompe l'oeil*, as does much else in Humphrey's highly personal manuscript which was never intended to be a commercial artefact. The baroque candour of Humphrey's emulation of scribal expertise instead offers a flamboyant example of the non-professional scribe indulging in 'informal book production'[2] – one of the categories of non-commercial book producers considered in these pages.

As Humphrey Newton's scribal work implies, there is much in the manuscript culture of late medieval England to justify a chapter on manuscripts rather than

I thank Hugues Azérad, André Crépin, Ralph Hanna, Tony Hunt, Stephen Morrison, Nigel Ramsay, John J. Thompson, Rodney M. Thomson, James Willoughby and Jocelyn Wogan-Browne for thought-provoking conversations. In quotations from manuscripts the punctuation is editorial.

[1] Hanna, 'Humphrey Newton', 284.
[2] Boffey and Thompson, 'Anthologies and Miscellanies', 303.

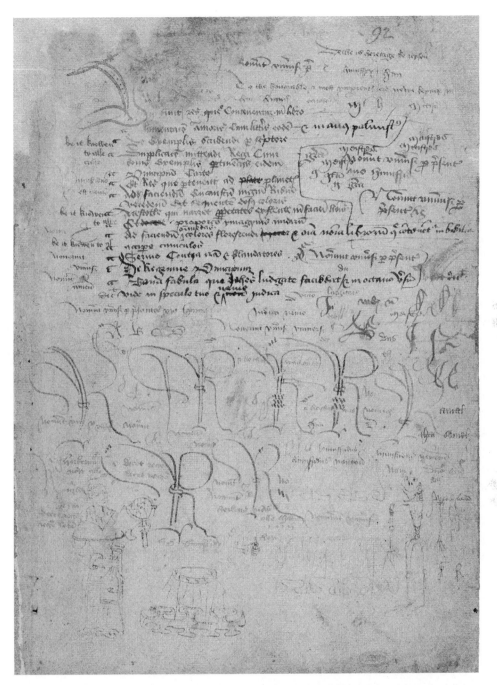

*Figure 10.1 BodL, MS Lat. misc. c.66, f. 92r: showing Humphrey Newton's heading
for a poem on a* Nightingale, *incorrectly ascribed to Lydgate.*

print. By contrast, almost all printed books and *Sammelbände* were meant, from the start, to be part of a commercial, profit-making scheme. Print involved a scheme of production and distribution which encouraged, as David McKitterick writes, 'an experiment … of what was to be acceptable and *saleable* to readers'.[3] Although limited in time and place, the active interest taken by some of the religious orders between *c.*1470 and *c.*1540 in the printing press might have distinguished them from secular entrepreneurs. J. G. Clark has recently argued that in the large Benedictine houses of St Albans, Abingdon and Tavistock such an interest succeeded in 'taking the technology outside the … commercial mainstream'. But there is no conclusive evidence that the religious were inclined to attenuate the thoroughly commercial aspects of print.[4] Of course, the entrepreneurial dimension of early printers' activities in England was tightly bound up with their cultural interests, political persuasions and technological developments; the latter were still influenced by the 'codicizing' procedures involved in late medieval manuscript book and booklet production.[5] Nevertheless, the connections maintained by William Caxton are exemplary: by original profession a mercer, Caxton's background suggests that, from the first, printers in England were committed to processes of book production predicated on principles of speculative development, remuneration and profit.[6]

The distinction between 'commercial' and 'non-commercial' production of manuscripts between *c.*1350 and *c.*1500, by contrast, is hedged in with a number of difficulties and ambiguities which this chapter will attempt to map out. In an important overview of 'The English Provincial Book Trade before Printing', A. I. Doyle points out 'significant non-commercial segments' for 'the whole of book-production and distribution' and advances that 'even by the fifteenth century it is doubtful if the majority of books were being made or changed hands for money'. He further proposes that the term 'book trade' may 'embrace three sorts of activity for remuneration': '(1) the practice of various handicrafts towards making the physical objects; (2) the provision of texts and the coordination of the crafts to produce copies; (3) the selling of books, old and new, and of the requisite materials'. He reminds us that 'none of these activities need be full-time occupations and one or more of them cannot give a living until the accessible market is large enough'.[7] All these statements are important, not only because they draw up a general pattern of interlocking book-producing activities, each of which implied the contracts and payment characteristic of a medieval 'market economy', but also because they are a salutary reminder that the procedures involved in making medieval books were

---

[3] McKitterick, *Print, Manuscript and the Search for Order*, 93 (my italics).
[4] Clark, 'Print and Pre-Reformation', 91.
[5] Gillespie, 'Balliol MS 354' and *Print Culture and the Medieval Author*.
[6] Blake, *William Caxton*; Sutton, 'Books Owned by Mercers'.
[7] Doyle, 'The English Provincial Book Trade', 13; examples of part-time scribes are discussed by Parkes, *Their Hands before Our Eyes*, 45–6.

precarious and versatile and cannot simply be divided between 'commercial' and 'non-commercial'. Nevertheless, this chapter is concerned with evidence of book production where economic parameters, particularly those of 'remuneration', at all three stages outlined by Doyle, were attenuated. It argues that the detection of the 'significant non-commercial segments' is essential to the study of book production in the period considered in this volume.

As it was on the continent, English book production was immersed in the pre-industrial craft economy. Each of its various stages fell into the province of distinct lines of trade, of which corporate institutions (guilds, misteries and companies) were a shrewd and effective embodiment, geared to certain local situations.[8] The provision of animal membrane (parchment and vellum) depended on the remunerated work of skinners,[9] and so an antecedent segment in the chain of 'handicrafts'. Until 1494, the availability of paper was almost entirely predicated on imports from continental paper-mills.[10] As to the procurement of quills of requisite quality – goose quills in particular, 'some to portraye, somme to noote and write', as the Goose herself reminds us in John Lydgate's *Horse, Goose and Sheep* – the profession of poulterer must have been very significant for book production on a local basis.[11] Much attention has been devoted recently to the London-based corporations, such as the Companies of Scriveners, Textwriters and Stationers, on account of their importance to several stages in the processes of the production, publication and distribution of commercial books,[12] but others, such as the Grocers – as Doyle reminds us – or the Haberdashers equally merit fresh consideration for their role as 'retailers of miscellaneous household supplies' in urban centres, which must have included parchment, paper, ink and probably other writing implements (pumice, for instance) and must have involved supply to those making books on a non-commercial basis.[13] Thus, ink was essentially a marketed – and enviable – commodity, as shown for instance in CUL, MS Dd.12.23, a legal *omnium-gatherum* of Latin and 'practical' French materials possibly derived from Oxford elementary courses on tenures, procedure

[8] Farr, *Artisans in Europe*, 45–94. Gillespie, 'Books', 100 describes book production as 'a matter of competing and localised concern' in London; this also applies elsewhere.

[9] Part of the omnipresent leather industry: see Cherry, 'Leather'.

[10] Lyall, 'Materials: The Paper Revolution'; Kwakkel, 'A New Type of Book'; Da Rold, 'Fingerprinting Paper' and Chapter 1 in this volume.

[11] *IMEV* 658; Lydgate, *Minor Poems*, II.547 (stanza 27, line 184).

[12] Christianson, 'Evidence for the Study of London's Late Medieval Manuscript Book-Trade'; Christianson, *A Directory of London Stationers*; Christianson, 'The Rise of London's Book-Trade'; Blayney, *The Stationers' Company before the Charter*; Michael, 'Urban Production'; Mooney, 'Locating Scribal Activity' and Chapter 9 in this volume.

[13] Doyle, 'The English Provincial Book Trade', 21 and n.45 and n.59 for evidence of Grocers at Lincoln and Durham around 1360. The London Haberdasher Walter Lucy regularly sold ink and red wax to the Privy Seal: see Burrow, *Thomas Hoccleve*, 43 (no. 43), 45 (no. 50), 46 (no. 56), 48 (no. 62), 49 (no. 68). Jurkowsky, 'Lollard Book Producers', makes a case for more studies of the parchmenters in London and other urban communities.

and pleading. One of the scribes, one J(ohn) Mershfeld, marked his copying of the first two units conspicuously: with formulaic colophons (at booklet boundaries, ff. 24v and 48v); with his exuberant monogram with elaborate cruciform flourishes (f. 24v); and with a barely legible two-line note in red ink to the effect that 'qui complevit <4 words> petit incaustum…' ('he who has completed <…> asks for ink…') (f. 24v).[14] When anthologized in Latin or English, recipes for making ink (chiefly black and red) occur with equal frequency in manuscripts from gentry households and manuscripts of religious provenance (notably the houses of the regular orders). Here such recipes may denote a greater correlation between cultural capital (invested in the keeping of records and the circulation of texts), economic resources and a keen sense of the need for good management – to which, notably in the case of the religious orders, traditions of book production and technical knowledge (whether internal or hired, as we shall see below) may be added. Perhaps except for economically viable, land-holding and cattle- and poultry-rearing establishments where the 'raw' materials were readily obtainable, the production of books outside commercial contexts may thus never have eluded forms of wage-based labour and remunerative transaction, when it came to prepared membrane, paper and other writing necessities.

Non-commercial book production most particularly needed the decisive impetus of regional and local circumstances and motivations. The local proximity of supply for most primary materials and the subsequent tangibility of regional styles of craftsmanship have been noticed for books as well as for other artefacts, as in East Anglia, Yorkshire or the West Midlands. The importance of cultural geographies is therefore emphasized in studies which reinstate book production within a continuum of local crafts for which 'the availability of the raw material often determined the place of production'[15] – while, of course, the medieval road network and such nodal points as markets and fairs, religious institutions or gentry households energized segmented localities with the inter-regional circulation of languages and texts.[16] For example, the importance of the influence of such patrons as Sir Thomas Berkeley, his daughter Elizabeth and her husband Richard Beauchamp, Earl of Warwick, is predicated on the size, situation and

---

[14] Baker and Ringrose, *A Catalogue of English Legal Manuscripts*, 125–8, ignore the monogram and the red note; for all non-legal items in Insular French, see Dean, *Anglo-Norman Literature*, entries 135, 190, 281, 282, 291, 293, 300. John Mershfeld may be identical with the individual documented in *BRUO*, II.1266.

[15] Rogers, 'Regional Production', 97.

[16] On roads, see Stenton, 'The Road System of Medieval England'. Cultural geographies of local book production are considered by Riddy, *Regionalism in Late Medieval Manuscripts and Texts*; Beadle, 'Middle English Texts and their Transmission'; Hanna, notably in 'Yorkshire Writers', *London Literature* and 'Some North Yorkshire Scribes'; Scase, *Essays in Manuscript Geography* and (ed.), *Manuscripts of the West Midlands*, www.mwm.bham.ac.uk; Edwards (ed.), 'Regional Manuscripts 1200–1700'; Pouzet, 'Lieux et présence'; see also Horobin, Chapter 3 in this volume.

wealth of their estates, whence to derive substantial, long-term sources of income to fund the making of books and the transmission of texts.[17] Noble and gentry households as well as religious institutions often constituted, in Shakespeare's words, the crucial sort of 'local habitation' which non-commercial book production necessitated.

However, among the religious, it seems that only such institutions as cathedral chapters or the largest, substantially endowed houses of the regular orders had the socio-economic conditions requisite for *in situ* provisioning of materials for book production, principally through the management of their manorial units. It has often been noted that, in absolute numbers, from the early to mid fourteenth century the need to produce books must have been reduced in religious establishments founded between the early twelfth and the early fourteenth centuries. Such institutions had accumulated many books already. Surviving evidence for the production of books at such places as the Cistercian abbey at Buildwas in Shropshire or the Augustinian priory at Llanthony Secunda in Gloucestershire suggest markedly more dispersed undertakings after *c.*1340 than before that date.[18] For the houses of the regular orders in general, however, archival and codicological evidence survives reflecting moments of activity, so that the 'comparative marginality' of 'local manufacture' from the 1200s diagnosed by R. M. Thomson is matched in some cases with a 'resurgence of monastic scribal activity in the second half of the fourteenth century'.[19] More recent foundations such as the Brigittine house at Syon or secular academic institutions needed to launch non-protracted campaigns of production or acquisition *ab initio*.[20] Although there are probably fewer eloquent testimonies than at the Cistercian abbey of Beaulieu or at the cathedral priory at Norwich in the late thirteenth and early fourteenth centuries,[21] a number of institutions offer crucial illustration of 'in-house' production in the fourteenth and fifteenth centuries too. At the monastic cathedral chapter of Durham in this period, for instance, monks including John Fishburn (librarian) and John Wessyngton (prior 1416–46) are associated with the transcription of several

---

[17] Meale, 'Patrons, Buyers and Owners'; Hanna, 'Sir Thomas Berkeley'; Briggs, 'MS Digby 233'; Ross, *The Estates and Finances of Richard Beauchamp*; Perry, 'The Clopton Manuscript'. Doyle, 'Publication by Members of the Religious Orders', 117, suggests that Berkeley sponsored a minority of the copies of John Walton's English translations of *De Re Militari* and *De Consolatione philosophiae*; the latter text was printed in 1525 at the Benedictine (not 'Austin', *pace* Doyle) Tavistock press mentioned above.

[18] Sheppard, *The Buildwas Books*; Bennett, 'The Book Collections'.

[19] Thomson, 'Monastic and Cathedral Book Production', 165–7 (which echoes Denholm-Young, *Handwriting in England and Wales*, 46); Bell, 'Monastic Libraries', 235.

[20] De Hamel, *Syon Abbey*, 49, writes that the Syon books 'make a remarkably good subject for investigating the mechanics of building up a monastic library in the fifteenth century'; see also Gillespie and Doyle (eds.), *Syon Abbey*.

[21] On Beaulieu, see Hockey (ed.), *The Account Book of Beaulieu Abbey*, 195–8 (the *percamenarius* was both parchment maker and bookbinder), and on Norwich, Ker, 'Medieval Manuscripts from Norwich Cathedral Priory', 248–51 and 266–71.

'substantial' volumes.[22] The attention which the Benedictine abbey of St Albans (mentioned above with reference to print culture) and the Augustinian abbey of St-Mary-in-the-Fields in Leicester have received has uncovered a sense of historical continuity in the domestic impulse there to provide and produce books.[23] At St Albans, a miscellaneous formulary was assembled, perhaps also bound, and written principally in a competent hand modelled on anglicana by William Wyntershulle, almoner of the abbey and the abbot's chaplain in 1382. A paragraph in his hand describes the equipment pertaining to the 'libraria siue studium [library or study]', including 'libri' 'in diuersis voliminibus [sic] et ydiomatibus … cum clapsulis bordoes et tissewes pro eisdem [books in various volumes and languages … with clasps, boards and tissue for their making]', and 'pergamenum, velym, motlyn abortif cum pellibus equum, cornuus [sic] et damarum … et vitulinis pro eisdem cooperiendum et ligandum, cum papiro pro his [parchment, vellum, uterine membrane with horse-skins, horns and doe-skins … and calf-skins to cover [their boards] and bind them, with paper for [covering and binding] them]'.[24] There is a wealth of information to be gleaned from such a modest description, not least the mention of the storage of the membrane of unborn sheep ('motlyn abortif'), also known generically as 'uterine' membrane, which yielded almost translucent membrane – suitable for repair patches, for instance. An example is the rectangular parchment patch glued onto one leaf of an all-paper codex, John Capgrave's *Life of Saint Katherine* (BL, MS Arundel 20, f. 8v), copied by R. Englysh; the patch makes good a tear caused by a scribal correction.[25]

Conversely, although dependencies and cells of larger establishments did produce some books,[26] smaller houses could not afford to dedicate activity to book production, and probably had to buy at least part of the parchment or vellum and writing materials to cover their needs, even if they owned some animals that might in theory have provided writing membrane. The account roll for 1377–8 of the Augustinian priory at Bolton (West Yorkshire) shows that the community sold, next to the hides of cows, oxen and bulls, 180 sheep-skins worth xxij s vj d, but that they bought an unspecified quantity of parchment at ij s. Perhaps the home-grown skins were not good enough to make 'good parchemyn / to write on bookes in quaiers many fold', as Lydgate's Sheep says; or perhaps no one at the priory was able

---

[22] Doyle, 'Book Production by the Monastic Orders', 8–9, 18 (nn.50–4); on Wessyngton, see also Piper, 'The Libraries of the Monks of Durham', 234–6.

[23] On St Albans, see Doyle, 'Book Production by the Monastic Orders', 3–7; on Leicester, see below.

[24] CUL, MS Ee.4.20, f. 274r (usual foliation); on the contents, see Baker and Ringrose, *A Catalogue of English Legal Manuscripts*, 200–6, and for the Insular French items Dean, *Anglo-Norman Literature*, entries 287, 291, 293, 298, 300, 308, 317, 318, 387, 390, 395.

[25] On doubts about the use of uterine membrane, see Thomson, 'Technology of Production of the Manuscript Book', 76.

[26] See Heale, 'Books and Learning in the Dependent Priories' and *The Dependent Priories*, 148–9, 166, 181–3.

to make parchment.[27] Bolton has been persuasively associated with a handful of early fourteenth- to early fifteenth-century manuscripts containing Insular French and English literary and religious texts, but it seems likely that not all of these books were domestic productions.[28]

The preceding evidence shows that sometimes there was 'commercial' and sometimes domestic supply of materials for book production (and for technical processes, like binding, related to these) in religious and other households. By implication, a survey of the conditions of medieval book production suggests that it is necessary to distinguish between inherently commercial books and books for which a commercial dimension intervenes, so to speak, as an indispensable yet peripheral corollary of their production. Yet since no book was totally immune from commercial logic, strictly speaking, there may have been no such thing as a book produced entirely outside commercial contexts in medieval England, whether this means liturgical books, library books or archival books (including all classes of 'business' volumes, such as cartularies or account books).[29] But there were widespread, scattered efforts to minimize or mitigate the costs of book production, and all these vital gestures compose the history of non-commercial production.

Eschewing the need to produce or acquire new sheets or new quires (especially of prepared membrane) commercially may have constituted a significant way of limiting costs. It seems that individuals or institutions devised policies of economy whereby 'in-house' production involved the recycling of parchment as palimpsests. The second booklet of BodL, MS Fairfax 27, ff. 7–25 (datable to the start of the fifteenth century) contains a treatise on the accentuation of biblical words and proper nouns, probably copied by a scribe named Bolton, whose name is next to an idiosyncratic colophon on f. 24v.[30] The manuscript has an untraced medieval history, but there is a strong probability of religious provenance. Underneath the fifteenth-century text is another, still discernible on ff. 20–5, in a one-column layout that looks close, for instance, to that in BodL, MS Auct. D. Inf. 2. 7 (*olim* Fairfax 15), a late twelfth-century glossed copy of the gospel of Luke from Bridlington Priory, an important house of Augustinian canons in East Yorkshire. The surviving flyleaf at the front of the manuscript also typically re-uses a dismembered fragment of a liturgical codex.

---

[27] Kershaw et al. (eds.), *The Bolton Priory Compotus*, 556, 568; Lydgate, *Minor Poems*, II.554 (stanza 52, lines 367–8).

[28] *MLGB*, II; Hanna and Lawton (eds.), *The Siege of Jerusalem*, xiv–xv, xxx; Pouzet, 'Augustinian Canons', 271–3; *pace* Pouzet, 'Quelques Aspects de l'influence des chanoines augustins', 200–3, the link between *this* Bolton and London, BL, MS Add. 32578 is moot: see Hanna, 'Yorkshire Writers', 97–8.

[29] Gullick and Hadgraft, 'Bookbindings', 95; on the latter class, see Ramsay, 'Archive Books'.

[30] Madan et al., *A Summary Catalogue*, 785–6 (who date it to the fourteenth century); *MLGB*, II (the link to Bolton Priory can be safely rejected).

It is equally likely that the traditional activities which stood at the further end of the book-producing chain (assembling quires and binding them) may not always have seemed important enough to warrant the sort of expense that was involved in procuring the 'raw' materials. Assembling and binding were desirable whenever one wanted to ensure a book's sustainability, but they were not indispensable. A quire or series of quires did not have to be bound to be written, read or circulated; assembling quires could have been achieved without resorting to the skills of a commercially contracted expert.[31] The writing of catchwords or the sewing of folded sheets were not in themselves beyond the grasp of monastic precentors or librarians, chaplains or the clerks employed in noble or ecclesiastical households, or even members of the gentry. Archival and codicological evidence shows that quires may have lain unbound for some time before they were built into books; this testifies to a significant form of protracted or 'continued' book production over time, both commercial and non-commercial.[32]

Wages for scribal labour took the lion's share of the book-producing budget, so that one of the most frequent, straightforward and efficient ways of reducing or just waiving the costs of production of books was for any individual who was sufficiently 'script-literate' to perform the copying himself. To produce a compilation principally for one's own use, it was customary to borrow a book which could serve as an exemplar to copy from. Exemplars could be lent by courtesy or borrowed against a pledge, or *cautio*. The latter scheme, originally monastic, may have been emulated and systematized in continental academic circles through the *pecia* system. If this onerous *pecia* system was ever practised in English Universities, which is now rather uncertain, then it was almost entirely defunct in England by *c*.1350, and some, no less typical university books, including 'personal compilations', were not principally commercial; this applies even to lawbooks, for instance.[33] There is evidence of Oxford and Cambridge scholars (masters or students) producing their own money-sparing copies of curricular texts in law, philosophy or theology from authoritative exemplars, and including some 'extra-curricular' materials.[34] Such procedures might have been ambivalent socio-economically: if scholars undertook this kind of work on behalf of an individual or an institution, it might acquire a commercial

---

[31] As argued by Gillespie, p. 160, in this volume.

[32] The time lapse may have been very long: BL, MS Royal 10.B.vii, a thirteenth-century copy of Richard Fishacre's Commentary on Peter Lombard's *Sentences*, was bound around 1450 thanks to William Redymer, an Augustinian canon at St Mary's Priory, Southwark and a Cambridge don.

[33] On the '*pecia*-system' for law-books and the relative emancipation from it as reflected in the virtually non-commercial production of 'personal compilations', see Ramsay, 'Law', 263–5 and 287; on the *pecia* generally, see Parkes, 'The Provision of Books', 462–70.

[34] See, for example, at Oxford, the scribal work of William Persson of New College, executed between 1428 and 1435 (now Oxford, New College, MS 127), or that of John Mabulthorpe of Lincoln College, between 1436 and 1445 (now Oxford, Lincoln College, MS lat. 101), both presented in [De la Mare and Gillam], *Duke Humfrey's Library*, 102–3.

dimension. On 6 April 1451, John Manyngham, the registrar ('secretarius') of the University of Oxford (1447–51), was granted the grace to employ an undergraduate as *amanuensis* in the common library of the University. Apparently this was motivated by Manyngham's personal need for humanistic texts – a need, however, he also saw to by doing some of the copying himself.[35] The massive *Tabula septem custodiarum* (the Franciscan index to patristic commentaries on the Bible) and concordance to the New Testament in BL, MS Harley 3858 (i) were copied by Robert Masham, of Durham Cathedral Priory, probably when he studied at Durham College, Oxford. It was common for student-monks to copy manuscripts which might subsequently pass into the communal collections of the mother institutions from which their college depended.[36] The book displays a hierarchical variety of scripts suggestive of skilful but non-commercial practice. Masham characterizes the concordance as 'bona et utilis [good and useful]' in its *explicit* (f. 154v) and insists on the usefulness of the *Tabula* 'ad predicandum [to preach]' (f. 62r).

Not surprisingly, it is from the diverse institutions of religion as well as from the more dispersed endeavours of secular households that most evidence of non-commercial or strongly attenuated commercial production emerges. With due consideration to statutory and local differences, much in the patterns of book production that can be reconstructed for the houses of the religious orders and the cathedral chapters holds, to some extent, for other institutions such as hospitals, secular colleges, chapels and parishes.[37] Over the course of their existence, religious establishments of different ages and traditions needed to replace or augment a proportion of their liturgical or otherwise communal collections. This they might do through buying or exchanging new or second-hand volumes or booklets, through receiving bequests, or through employing resources and procuring materials necessary for the writing or binding of new books or booklets. There is much evidence to suggest that the first two modes of expansion of the collections count for a good two-thirds of the whole new or replacement shelving.[38] The third mode of enlargement and enrichment of the communal stock, however, must have been particularly necessary whenever a specific work was needed. Under those circumstances the equation between needs and resources was particularly crucial, and would

[35] [De la Mare and Gillam], *Duke Humfrey's Library*, 88–9. One product of this collaborative work may survive as Dublin, Trinity College, MS D.4.24, a humanistic miscellany.

[36] Doyle, 'Book Production by the Monastic Orders', 8–9 and 18 (n.54). On the academic education of the regulars and the books in transit, see Clark, 'University Monks', and such specific studies as Forde, 'The Educational Organization of the Augustinian Canons'.

[37] On hospitals, see Rawcliffe, notably ' "Written in the Book of Life" ', 'Passports to Paradise' and below; on secular colleges Willoughby, 'The Provision of Books in the English Secular College'; on various beneficed clergy (such as chaplains) and parish priests as copyists, see relevant examples discussed by Parkes, *Their Hands before Our Eyes*, 33–53.

[38] Bell, 'The Libraries of Religious Houses'. Emden, *Donors of Books*, gives an impression of the volume of gifts or bequests in a major religious establishment before and after 1350.

require a balance between the resources and skills available and effectively mustered 'in house' and those acquired through necessarily external contacts.[39] The latter implied more or less direct commercial transactions with professional scribes or artists who could come to a house to perform paid work – no new thing, as the hiring of professional scribes is well attested before 1300.[40] Most of the peripatetic craftsmen may have been lay, but some may well have been professed religious and permitted to travel around, thanks to statutory dispensations or official leave, on account of their duties and skills. The Austin friars were among the orders lending the prerequisite institutional support, as is reflected in a permission granted in May 1384 by the chapter of the English province to brother John Tye (perhaps originally from the house at Stafford) to 'vocare et retinere fratrem Henricum Hood per annum tantum ipsum instruendo in arte illuminandi libros [summon and retain brother Henry Hood for as much as a year teaching him the art of illuminating books]'.[41] M. B. Parkes has noted that the Dominican order tended to favour external contracting over 'in-house' investment but also notes that there are significant local counterexamples, especially among preachers or anchorites of that order.[42] In the case of religious artisans, any remuneration might have enhanced personal *peculium*: such property, held by permission of a house or order, was analogous to but technically not a form of commercial remuneration.

Different categories of requisite books mobilized different resources. A sizeable proportion of library and archival books were predominantly 'in-house' products – although this may not have excluded a degree of collaboration with hired scribes. Conversely, certain tasks involving an amount of specialized expertise, such as elaborate illumination or the notation of music in liturgical manuscripts, seem to have remained the province of contracted experts and commercial work; such manuscripts may have been commissioned by influential lay or religious dignitaries for the use of communities or for personal devotion.[43] A number of books of polyphony, however, may have been distinctly less commercial. Fiona Kisby has remarked that books of polyphony in late fifteenth- and early sixteenth-century London

---

[39] On the balance in the larger establishments, see Clark, 'The Religious Orders in Pre-Reformation England', 23, and Lovatt, 'College and University Book Collections', 152 (quoting Clark).

[40] Gullick, 'Professional Scribes'; Michael, 'English Illuminators' and 'Urban Production'.

[41] On Tye and Hood, see Roth, 'Sources for a History of the English Austin Friars', 223, and Michael, 'English Illuminators', 91, within his 'preliminary survey'.

[42] Parkes, *Their Hands before Our Eyes*, 27. On the Dominican anchorite John Lacy who wrote and illuminated Oxford, St John's College, MS 94, see Connolly, Chapter 6 above. Typical pastoral (stridently non-commercial) compilations are represented by manuscripts such as Oxford, New College, MS 88 studied by Wenzel, 'A Dominican Preacher's Handbook'.

[43] Pfaff, *The Liturgy in Medieval England*; Wathey, 'The Production of Books of Liturgical Polyphony'; Bent, 'Music Seen and Music Heard'; Reames, 'Late Medieval Efforts at Standardization'; Parkes, *Their Hands before Our Eyes*, 46 (on 'pricking'). On commissions, see Alexander, 'Painting and Manuscript Illumination'; Stratford and Webber, 'Bishops and Kings'; Luxford, *The Art and Architecture of English Benedictine Monasteries*, 69–71 (examples of Benedictine book patronage).

parish churches were 'rarely purchased from external sources' such as stationers but 'more often copied piecemeal by the performers associated with a particular parish church', because they constituted 'unique anthologies representative of the repertories performed in particular institutions'.[44] Similarly, the writing (modelled on a very good textura quadrata) and musical notation of the fine late fourteenth-century antiphonal associated with the Augustinian priory at Westacre in Norfolk, now St John's, Camb., MS D. 21, may indicate quality and leisurely 'in-house' production, mainly by the canons themselves.

Both domestic and external resources were vitally dependent not only on the income or 'value' of an institution and on available internal expertise, but also on the institutional readiness to 'invest' time, energy and means in the making of books or in the accommodation or instruction of those who might make them. In establishments which were adequately endowed and staffed, forms of professional collaboration may have taken place in any degree of complexity between members of a house and external craftsmen. There was a tradition of 'in-house' scribal work at the Benedictine abbey of Bury St Edmunds, but collaboration with external and commercial scribes and artisans must have seemed perfectly natural to the abbey's librarian, Henry de Kirkestede (fl. 1360–78), and to the member and poet John Lydgate, whose works were often copied by the 'Edmund-Fremund scribe' who worked in the town, rather than the monastery (which commissioned at least one book of verse from him).[45] Similarly, at Leicester we may still capture something of a sense of long-term commitment to the making of books in various forms and circumstances. The second half of the fourteenth century, during and after William Cloune's abbacy (1345–78), seems to have been a felicitous period of book procurement and production.[46] A note in TCC, MS B.14.7 (f. 197r, bottom margin) implies that brother John Neuton of Leicester was associated with the earlier phases of fabrication of this manuscript, as it was still 'in quaternis [in quires]', and 'non illuminatum nec ligatum [neither illuminated nor bound]', when he delivered it ('liberavit') to Ralph Thurleston, a fellow canon, subsequently prior of Mottisfront (1352–66).[47] As Teresa Webber suggests, the content

---

[44] Kisby, 'Books in London Parish Churches', 314–15.

[45] On the earliest book production in house, see Webber, 'The Provision of Books for Bury St Edmunds Abbey', but on Kirkestede's itemized recording of the costs of producing manuscripts, see Gransden, 'Some Manuscripts in Cambridge from Bury St Edmunds', 238–9. The 'Edmund-Fremund scribe' also transcribed portions of a Bury Pittancers' Register, now London, BL, MS Harley 27; see Doyle, 'Book Production by the Monastic Orders', 7, 18 (n.37), and Horobin, 'The Edmund-Fremund Scribe'.

[46] Webber, 'The Books of Leicester Abbey', 139–45.

[47] Webber, 'Latin Devotional Texts', 33–4 and 40, nn.58–68; Webber, 'The Books of Leicester Abbey', 140; Gullick and Webber, 'Summary Catalogue … from Leicester Abbey', 178. James, *The Western Manuscripts*, 1.411, and Webber, 'Latin Devotional Texts', 40, n.58, transcribe the note (Webber misses the form of the last word, really the plural accusative 'quaternos'). TCC, MS B.14.7 is A20.436 in the Leicester catalogue edited by Webber and Watson (eds.), *The Libraries of the Augustinian Canons*, 201.

of this Latin spiritual anthology probably served as an archetype in the production of two volumes: a lost, apparently duplicate copy perhaps transcribed domestically by Geoffrey Sallow, another fellow canon,[48] and TCC, MS B.2.16 part 1, an illuminated *compendium* of devotion and moral instruction produced for Henry IV before he became king, possibly through the agency of his confessor, Philip Repyngdon, Abbot of Leicester (1394–1405). TCC, MS B.2.16 is not clearly, but not inconceivably, a Leicester book; Webber recognizes that 'the quality of the script and decoration indicate that it was the work of professional craftsmen', which of course would once more suggest a scenario of collaboration between Leicester canons, noted for their Lancastrian affinities, and hired scribes.[49] At the close of the next century, there is William Charyte's very comprehensive descriptive index of all classes of communal books of his house drawn up between 1477 and 1494, the fair copy of which is now BodL, MS Laud misc. 623. As a librarian with the 'listing gene' (as Richard Sharpe writes), Charyte scrutinized materials and recycled bibliographic data to prepare a list of titles of works in quires, booklets and books which existed before his own time. He also created four categories of various new books, including 'Libri quos propria manu scripsit et compilauit [Books which he wrote and compiled with his own hand]' (f. 50v) and 'Libri quos … emit et perquisiuit [Books which he bought and acquired]' (f. 51r).[50] All four categories exemplify the sort of balance of book-producing activities normal for a large house. The entries listed as A20.1905–1925 in the printed catalogue, together with the 'novum rentale' which he compiled and wrote (now BodL, MS Laud misc. 625), suggest that the scribal capacities of Charyte were employed in archival codices and rolls. But one of two exceptions, 'vnus liber de certis vocabilis biblie [one book of certain terms in the Bible]' (A20.1912), is specified as having been 'scriptus in papiro et postea in pergameno [written on paper and afterward on parchment]', presumably from 'draft' to 'fair'. This entry offers a valuable insight into hierarchical attitudes to materials – and, inferentially, into the way scribal time and resources were mobilized in the house to book production.

Some marginal annotations (e.g., ff. 109v, 110r, 163v, 164rv, 165r) are in the hand of this 'frater Johannes Neuton', who may also have written all the quires constituting this codex.

[48] Webber, 'The Books of Leicester Abbey', 144; this duplicate copy is A20.435 in the Leicester catalogue (bearing a different *secundo folio* indication compared to MS B. 14. 7).

[49] Webber, 'The Books of Leicester Abbey', 140, n.89, 142–3, 145; see also Gullick and Webber, 'Summary Catalogue … from Leicester Abbey', 178, n.11, and the descriptive comments in Binski and Panayotova (eds.), *The Cambridge Illuminations*, 258–9 (no. 118).

[50] Sharpe, 'The Medieval Librarian', 229. See further Doyle, 'Book Production by the Monastic Orders', 5–6, 12; Bell, 'Monastic Libraries', 231; Bell, 'The Libraries of Religious Houses', 140; Sharpe, 'Library Catalogues and Indexes', 212–13; Webber, 'The Books of Leicester Abbey', 143–4; Gullick and Webber, 'Summary Catalogue … from Leicester Abbey', 183–6. Charyte's catalogue is printed in Webber and Watson (eds.), *The Libraries of the Augustinian Canons*, 104–399. BodL, MS Laud misc. 623, ff. 49v, 50v and 51r are reproduced in the still valuable Thompson, *The Abbey of St Mary*, 204–30.

Having discussed both the acquisition and treatment of materials and the provision of books in non-commercial contexts, especially religious households, it is now appropriate to focus on the writing of books themselves – the central and most documented phase of production. An appreciation of non-commercial forms of scribal activity involves reconsideration of some of the ways scribes or their hands are described, most importantly as 'professional' or 'non-professional'. As Linne Mooney reminds us (Chapter 9), not all professional scribes were commercial scribes, because the categories of 'professional' and 'commercial' do not apply to the same dimension of text-writing.[51] 'Professional' scribes were writers who had received advanced formal training – which in principle guaranteed some degree of competence and proficiency. Mooney considers professional scribes as copyists of vernacular literary writings 'for the bespoke trade'; this chapter is concerned with the non-commercial activity of professional writers. The question of how all classes of professional scribes gained their education is central and problematic, and would require a study of its own. At least the rudimentary elements of literacy, letter formation and grammar must have been acquired in monastic and cathedral schools, or under the supervision of local lay scriveners 'at wryting scole' who taught practical subjects including grammar, letter-drafting, conveyancing and conversational-*cum*-legal French. They sometimes moved to the universities in order to integrate their teaching in some dedicated *syllabi*; William Kingsmill, William Sampson and John Le(y)land are typical examples of them. Distinctly non-commercial manuscripts that contain multi-lingual school exercises (Latin with Insular French or English translations for easier parsing), heterogeneously assembled and copied in a variety of unpractised hands, or that preserve series of short tracts on grammar topics (often derived from 'business-oriented' academic *syllabi*) thus survive in remarkable numbers.[52] For example, CUL, MS Hh.1.5, a densely written, squat but clear grammatical miscellany on paper and parchment,[53] compiled, copied and partly composed by William Forster probably shortly before 1400 may have been acquired in the second half of the fifteenth century by John Hull, canon at the Augustinian priory of Worksop (Nottinghamshire), perhaps for educational purposes.[54] More

---

[51] Mooney, pp. 192–4 above. There is currently a greater distinction between 'commercial' and 'professional', as reflected in Parkes, *Their Hands before Our Eyes*, ch. 3.

[52] Orme, *Medieval Schools*; and Orme, *Education and Society*; see also Thomson, *A Descriptive Catalogue of Middle English Grammatical Texts*, 6–7, 40–1; Wright, 'Late Middle English Parerga'; 'at wryting scole' comes from BL, MS Harley 5396, f. 274r, discussed below.

[53] Robinson, 'The Format of Books', 48, implies that the manuscript is made *only* of paper; in fact, the outer bifolia of all quires are parchment sheets.

[54] CUL, MS Hh.1.5 has 'W. Fforster' or 'W.Ff.' in several places (e.g., ff. 129rb, 171rb, 191v), but erased on f. 3v (originally f. 1v, displaced by misbinding). The note 'Wyllelmus dei gracia possit permoueri ad multa beneficia [That William by the grace of God may be promoted to many benefices]' (f. 3v/1v) also appears to have been written by one of the brethren of the house in a hand modelled on anglicana, but distinct from that which wrote 'Johannes Hull Canonicus de Wyrkesopp <4 letters> assidue [John Hull canon of Worksop <...> assiduously]' (f. 129va), an inscription itself subsequently erased. On

advanced scribal 'technology' and specialized skills were more generally obtainable 'on the job' in religious institutions, or when a young boy was apprenticed to a craftsman whose line of trade involved the command of secretarial expertise.

The career of John Cok (c.1392–1468), however, is one among those indicative of a degree of porosity between originally distinct branches of scribal training and activity, which may further complicate understanding of the interface between non-remunerative activity and commercial segments of book production. It is unclear how Cok received his earliest education as a writer of text, but since he was apprenticed to a goldsmith, he may have completed most of his scribal training before he was first employed as copyist for St Bartholomew's Hospital in Smithfield, London. Cok's long association with the hospital may owe something to the fact that it was one of the liberties within London, in legal and socio-economic terms an attractive location for scribes interested by prospects of pursuing 'mixed' careers, non-commercial and peripherally commercial. This may in turn explain how Cok's scribal work was connected at once with the *in situ* production of archival and library books as well as with the literary entrepreneur John Shirley (also associated with St Bartholomew's) and the stints of hired craftsmen, Ricardus Franciscus and William Abell who collaborated with Cok on the hospital's cartulary.[55] The facets of Cok's scribal oeuvre reflect different destinations, distinct intentions of formality and various scribal times in his life.

Whatever the origin of their scribal education, professional copyists might have been involved in a number of scribal situations over the course of their activities, with possibilities of mixed careers. Non-commercial professional scribes could be clerks in royal or ecclesiastical administration; secretaries or chaplains or physicians attached to the household of a secular or religious dignitary; members of the merchant class or of the gentry; or, of course, secular or regular members of the Church. Some physicians could apparently be self-supporting practitioners and scribes for their own needs. Thomas Fayreford practised around Barnstaple 'in diversis locis [in diverse places]' in Devon in the early fifteenth century, compiling all and writing some of BL, MS Harley 2558, perhaps for himself and future apprentices (the quotation is from f. 9r of his manuscript). His idiosyncratic assembly of booklets and texts constitutes a medical library of multi-lingual materials. Its essentially non-commercial, experiential, pragmatic contents are distinct from more intellectually speculative and systematically planned, commercial products typical of an academic medical education – such as the volumes commissioned by Gilbert Kymer

Worskop Priory, see Knowles and Hadcock, *Medieval Religious Houses*, 180. Doyle, 'Book Production by the Monastic Orders', 13, 19, n.66, implies that Forster was a canon of Worksop, but this is not clear.

[55] Doyle, 'A Survey', 2.201, 'More Light on John Shirley' and 'Book Production by the Monastic Orders', 13, 19 (n.69); Kerling, *Cartulary of St Bartholomew's Hospital*, 3, 175; Connolly, *John Shirley*, 57–9, 164–5; Parkes, *Their Hands before Our Eyes*, 38 and Mooney, Chapter 9 in this volume. On the hospital as a liberty and Franciscus, see Mooney, 'Locating Scribal Activity', 199 (and n.56).

at Oxford and thereafter at Salisbury Cathedral.[56] The utilitarian dimension, or value, of the texts that trained scribes copied is very significant, whether this meant transcribing *Fachliteratur* (technical writing) or texts reflecting religious or literary interests. Those who practised writing of a professional standard developed general expertise, some of which was derived from specialized procedures (accountancy or legal formularies, for example). But opportunities to make good use of one's professional skills may have arisen in contexts where the utilitarian nature of writing was discernibly more personal than collective. In this case, professional copyists might have rubbed shoulders with non-professional scribes, especially if they wrote at leisure to suit their own needs or inclinations.

To understand how the categories of 'professional' and 'non-professional' are both distinguishable, yet inscribable within a continuum characterized by varying degrees of proficiency, it is appropriate to sketch what might be termed a phenomenology of scribal perception and activity in contexts where the commercial dimension is not in the foreground. Whenever it is liberated from the constraints of remuneration or profit, the making of books is freer to depend on individual talent and craftsmanship and on the deployment of that talent in time and space. In such ways, the 'features of fashion' recently examined by M. B. Parkes emerge.[57] Each scribe might have developed his or her own methods and rhythms of writing and compiling books in intimate contact with his or her own physical, technological and linguistic environment which, in return, he or she shaped and influenced. It may be argued that the production of books is thus concomitant with a 'production of space', as proposed by Henri Lefèbvre, who defines the concept of space as the encounter between the 'sensory' and the 'social'. As Lefèbvre writes, 'a rhythm invests places … It embodies its own law, its own regularity, which it derives from space – from its own space – and from a relationship between space and time'. The interactive relationship which Lefèbvre posits between personal *habitus* and environing space (as both lived in and invested, in other words, 'produced') encourages 'a mediation of rhythms' through which 'an animated space comes into being which is an extension of the space of bodies'.[58]

---

[56] Jones, 'Harley MS 2558'. The re-used pamphlets are predominantly fourteenth century, but there is also a thirteenth-century bifolium (ff. 7ra–8vb) containing an extract of the *Novele cirurgerie*; f. 7 is much worn out, and the bottom half of its first column on the recto has two stains, perhaps like the blood spurts noticed by Mooney in manuscripts giving instructions for bloodletting (Mooney, 'Manuscript Evidence', 195, fig. 3 and 197, fig. 4). Those translating scientific writings might have been sensitive to the commercial potential of a 'rapidly extending market' evoked for instance by Rawcliffe, *Leprosy*, 165, or implied by Taavitsainen and Pahta, *Medical and Scientific Writing*. On Kymer, see [De la Mare and Gillam], *Duke Humfrey's Library*, 2, 22, 50–1, 58–64; Baxter, *Sarum Use*, 66; Parkes, *Their Hands before Our Eyes*, 47, 52.

[57] Parkes, *Their Hands before Our Eyes*, 101–45 and, from a different angle, Wakelin, Chapter 2, in this volume.

[58] Lefèbvre, *The Production of Space*, 206–7.

In all this there is much that relates fruitfully to the perception and practice of non-commercial scribes. Three particular issues emerge. Firstly, there is the vexed question of the existence of stable scriptoria in fourteenth- and fifteenth-century England.[59] This may be elucidated if we consider the scriptorium as not so much a fixed physical space but rather as a conjunction of 'scriptorial facilities', defined as the ad hoc resources which an individual or group of individuals undertake to invest in book production. These can be moveable and versatile, single-handed or cooperative, and may depend on institutional support or talent. The notion of scriptorial facilities involves the production of space, the 'multiple and shifting' sites essential to the perceptive and expressive mediation of book production.[60] This notion may serve to disentangle commercial from non-commercial work in contexts in which they go vertiginously cheek by jowl, as in religious houses (as discussed above) or, less palpably, in the production of common-profit books, for instance. Common-profit inscriptions record from whose 'goods' the manuscripts were made (typically, the chattels of a wealthy deceased merchant). But the logistic and financial circumstances attending production itself are eclipsed by the foregrounding of the spiritual 'reward' derived from the making and reading of books as 'post-mortem charity' and the conditions of transmission 'fro persoone to persoone man or womman as longe as þe booke endureth', as one such book famously stipulates.[61] Maureen Jurkowski has recently noted how the forms of these codices raise essential questions about their place in patterns of metropolitan and provincial book production, and more largely in late medieval religious and manuscript culture. Some parchmenters and members of charitable London fraternities were involved in making both common-profit books *and* some lollard codices; this, together with the juxtaposition of orthodox, Wycliffite and 'grey-area' texts in common-profit books, suggests that the choice and quality of material, layout of the written page, use of scripts and mode of binding run a complex gamut of compromise between 'non-commercial' and 'commercial' activity which presupposes a high degree of flexibility of scribal space.[62]

Secondly, if we think about scribal space in this way, as mobile and flexible, differences in scribal conception and execution between professional and non-professional copyists may come out more clearly. We may consider copyists as craftsmen *and* artists or 'creators' of scripts and books, and turn to what Hans-Georg Gadamer says of 'The Ontology of the Work of Art and its Hermeneutic Significance':

[59] Parkes, *Their Hands before Our Eyes*, 22–5, synthesizes the evidence for *scriptoria* in medieval England.

[60] Gillespie, 'Books', 101. This is consonant with Taavitsainen, 'Scriptorial "House-Styles"'.

[61] CUL, MS Ff.6.31, f. 100r, discussed, along with other 'common-profit' manuscripts, by Doyle, 'A Survey', 11.208–14 and Scase, 'Reginald Pecok, John Carpenter', 261, 263 (quoted).

[62] Hudson, 'Some Aspects of Lollard Book Production' and 'Lollard Book Production'; Jurkowski, 'Lollard Book Producers', 215–16.

It is a problem of a special kind whether the formative process itself should not be seen as already constituting an aesthetic reflection on the work. It is undeniable that when he considers the idea of his work the creator can ponder and critically compare and judge various possibilities of carrying it out. But this sober clarity which is part of creation itself seems to be something very different from the aesthetic reflection and aesthetic criticism, which the work itself is capable of stimulating. It may be that what was the object of the creator's reflection, i.e. the possibilities of form, can also be the starting point of aesthetic criticism.[63]

The applicability of these considerations to book production outside commercial contexts is this. Criticism that bears on what we would call the 'possibilities of scribal form' (the general layout of the page induced from a choice over sizes and hierarchies of scripts, for instance), and criticism that derives from the aesthetic effect produced by scribal work itself, are two different forms of critical experience and knowledge. The professional (whether working for remuneration or not) is a competent practitioner who maintains a high and balanced degree of perception of both forms throughout his work. The non-professional, because his formative training was incomplete for some reason, disturbs the balance between the two forms of experience: his critical reflection has not sufficiently anticipated the creative possibilities of form, and the result is that both the technology of writing and its aesthetic rendition and effect are somewhat flawed.

Two cautionary corollaries attach to such a distinction. Firstly, a *combination* of traits rather than isolated features (which are apt to have a complex aetiology) may suggest non-professionalism. A list of them may include ill-planned framing, irregular or no horizontal or vertical ruling, significant 'dislocations between the stints of the scribes' (in the case of collaboration),[64] only one matrix script employed, crudely or poorly executed decoration for initials, 'failure to lay ink uniformly',[65] shaky or distorted letter-forms, irregular size of compartments and loops, inconsistent spelling and blatant grammatical errors. Secondly, non-professional practitioners may display varying degrees of competence or incompetence. The best ones may be arguably close to, and sometimes virtually indistinguishable from, some professional scribes, while the worst, although they may be 'full of passionate intensity', accumulate the greater number of flaws. For example, BL, MS Royal 17.C.xxxiii preserves a copy of *Oon of Foure*, the Middle English translation of Clement of Llanthony's harmony of the gospels known as *Unum ex quattuor*, together with a substantial appended booklet of biblical passages. The mediocre quality of parchment, the

---

[63] Gadamer, *Truth and Method*, 118, n.218.

[64] Thomson, *A Descriptive Catalogue of . . . Merton College*, 107, in the description of Oxford, Merton College, MS 135 (L.1.7). When loosely coordinated for some spatial or temporal reason, professional scribes, even commercial ones, could also be incapable of seamless transitions; see Parkes, *Their Hands before Our Eyes*, 47–8.

[65] Fletcher and Harris, 'A Northampton Poetic Miscellany', 223.

irregularity in the shapes of the sheets and the idiosyncratic enactment of the writing space (especially by the main of two scribes) give it a distinct post-*Orrmulum* feel – as if it were one of that text's modest descendants (Figure 10.2).[66] One particularly striking example of misconceived copying – most probably on the part of a young, as yet inexpert practitioner – occurs on ff. 309r–310r in the fourth (and final) section of the now composite BL, MS Harley 5396 (ff. 272–311), where the last stanza of *The Tournament of Tottenham* is dismembered from the bulk of the poem by an intercalated conversion table probably for measures of wool, possibly but not necessarily copied before the literary text.[67]

Thirdly, the creative dimension of an aesthetics of scribal space suggests the fundamental precondition of a non-commercial scribal oeuvre: the chance to spend non-remunerated time in productive scribal leisure. After an ancient, biblical and patristic tradition of discursive ambivalence (traced admirably by Jean Leclercq), from the mid eleventh century onwards the notion of *otium*, or its Greek lexical counterpart, *hesychasm*, was almost decisively wrung away from its negative undertones (charged on *otiositas*) and accorded the positive sense which became predominant in monasticism all over Western Europe.[68] Monastic *otium* allowed for the conception of scribal work and secretarial skills as manual *and* spiritual labour (one of the 'comprehensive means of subjugating the body for the future benefit of the soul').[69] It suggested the ethical utility of writing books, which offered the intellectual or spiritual pleasures of scribal practice concerned with correct wording and 'good' writing (if not also with 'writing well').[70] Although some of the most articulate formulations of *otium* predate the period under consideration here and originally apply to cloistered religious book production, I argue that in later medieval England *otium* not only remains a useful paradigm for the making of books within the religious orders but may also be fruitfully extended to book production by all classes of non-commercial professional and non-professional practitioners – for at

---

[66] Some sheets lack a concave edge at the outer lower corners (such as on ff. 303–4, a large triangle, perhaps lost to flaying), and there are some repair patches (such as on f. 115v). Scribe 1, the main scribe, models his script on anglicana written in a 'rough ill-formed hand' (as the catalogue describes at 'British Library Manuscripts Catalogue', www.bl.uk/catalogues/manuscripts). The thickness of the nib of his quill, which may suggest either a preference of width or a negligence of sharpening, does not particularly serve to economize on membrane; ff. 221v–222r were not ruled at all and the text is in double-spacing for no obvious reason. Scribe 2 did fewer stints and probably also acted as corrector.

[67] Fletcher and Harris, 'A Northampton Poetic Miscellany', 232–3 (f. 310r is reproduced); as they note at 222, in terms of contents BL, MS Harley 5396 (iv) invites comparisons with other non-commercial books now CUL, MSS Ee.4.35, Ff.1.6 and Ff.5.48.

[68] Leclercq, *Otia monastica*, 27–41. I use the adjective *hesychasmic* (based on the Greek stem), where *otiose* would be too ambiguous.

[69] Ivy, 'The Bibliography of the Manuscript Book', 37.

[70] Such a concern is reflected, for instance, in Charles d'Orléans's scribal work: see Gros, 'L'Ecriture du prince'; Ouy, 'Charles d'Orléans' and *La Librairie des frères captifs*; Arn, 'Two Manuscripts, One Mind'; Arn, 'A Need for Books' (notably at 85).

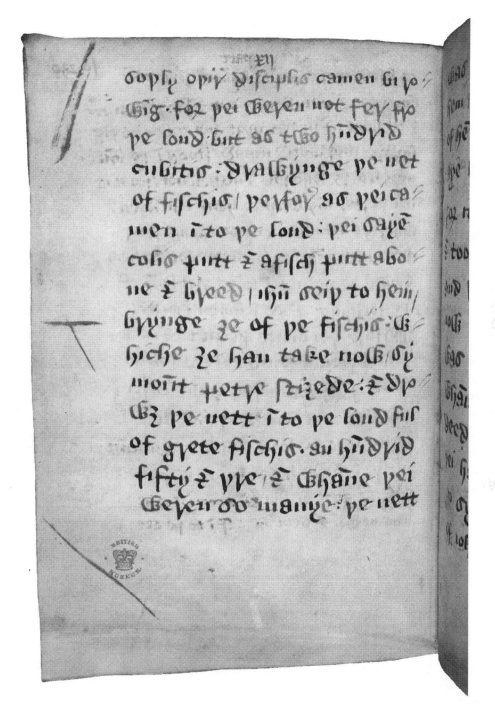

Figure 10.2 BL, MS Royal 17.C.xxxiii, f. 221v: thick letter-forms and double-spacing of the scribe's work.

least two related reasons.[71] Firstly, the capacity to engage in scribal leisure transcends the social or vocational stance of those who carry it out: it is an ethic which does not have to be limited to the religious orders, but may be extended to both religious and secular contexts of non-remunerative, useful and creative scribal work. Secondly, *otium* – however *studiosum* – has its roots firmly planted in a terrain of discursive 'negotiations' with its other, *negotium*. The requisite investment in time and resources permitting scribal *otium* was itself always constrained by several factors in religious and secular contexts alike. For the regular members of the Church, there was evidently a long tradition of constitutional dispositions in the rules of several orders, notably the Benedictines, the Augustinian canons and friars, the Carthusians and the Carmelites.[72] Thus Robert of Bridlington's influential exposition of the Augustinian rule known as the *Bridlington Dialogue* notes that all book-producing tasks – 'pergamenam scriptoribus preparare, libros scribere, illuminare, regulare, notare, emendare, atque ligare [to prepare parchment for the scribes, write, illuminate, rule books, score music, correct and bind books]' – are to be performed 'pro loco et tempore, pro sua possibilitate et prelate dispositione [depending on place and time, on personal capacities and the prelate's disposition]'. (The latter term probably has to be understood subjectively – whether or not the superior was *favourably* disposed to 'in-house' book production.)[73] In secular households, notably those of the gentry, book work might be constrained by the strictures of economic necessity and embroiled in local or national political factions which might involve members of such households in violence and angst that left little room for the free play of *otium*. That makes, for instance, the scribal work of Robert Thornton of East Newton, North Yorkshire, ill-poised as he was between the feuds of the Percy and Neville families, all the more remarkable.[74] All this returns us to scriptorial facilities and scribal mediation. The 'hesychasmic' impulse to copy books non-commercially continued unabated in a number of communities of fourteenth- and fifteenth-century England: it is worth thinking about how it was conditioned by local, potentially counteractive factors.

As implied above with respect to St Bartholomew's, religious institutions which were particularly apt to encourage scribal *otium* included hospitals, *leprosaria* and almshouses, which were under a form of statutory rule (often modelled on that of Augustinian canons). Carole Rawcliffe has drawn attention to fashions of

---

[71] Leclercq, '*Otium Monasticum*' can be extended beyond the religious context; consider Olson's discussion of the 'recreational justification' in *Literature as Recreation*, 90–127.

[72] On Carthusian scribes, see Gillespie, '*Cura Pastoralis in Deserto*', notably 172–3; Doyle, 'Book Production by the Monastic Orders', 13–15; on Carmelite scribes, see Parkes, *Their Hands before Our Eyes*, 28–31.

[73] Lawson (ed.), *The Bridlington Dialogue*, 152–156a (154–154a; 'dispositio' is translated as 'orders').

[74] On this hitherto understudied question, see Johnston, 'A New Document Relating to the Life of Robert Thornton'.

record-keeping evinced in manuscripts originating from these institutions, where meticulous accountancy and husbandry are allied to devotional and memorial dispositions. An example is the cartulary of the hospital of St Bartholomew in Dover, compiled in 1373, 'de munimentis, juribus, possessionibus et consuetudinibus fratrum et sororibus [*sic*] hospitalis [from the muniments, rights, possessions and customs of the brethren and sisters of the hospital]'. It also asserts that the members of this community were to be 'huius beneficii et laboris non immemores [not oblivious of this benefit and labour]'.[75] In this respect, it is perhaps not inconsequential that the early career of the Oxford-educated scribe Roger Walle (fl. 1436–88), of the diocese of Coventry and Lichfield, was spent in a hospital. From around 1436 until April 1449, Walle was Master of St Andrew's Hospital at Denhall or Denwall, Cheshire, a small institution for the poor, aged and infirm and for pilgrims. There, he might have acquired a scribal ethic favourable to *otium*-oriented copying.[76] Although 'the *negotium* of the diocese' was in some ways 'the opposite of the *otium* of the monk',[77] the hesychasmic penchant seems to have been compatible with Walle's subsequent voluminous ecclesiastical career, chiefly as a prebendary and canon of Lichfield Cathedral. Walle appears to have been a prolific professional copyist capable of 'versatility' (as noted by M. B. Parkes), with a scribal oeuvre of at least seven known manuscripts.[78] Their overall variety, hierarchy and quality of script and duct (principally modelled on anglicana but influenced by secretary, with various degrees of formality of textura for some rubrics) and the contents of some of them might lead one to wonder whether Walle wrote some of them for remuneration, but some scribal facts militate against this view. His labour in compiling the Calendar of Statutes of the chapter of Lichfield Cathedral (BL, MS Cotton Vitellius A.x, ff. 163r–166v) 'extractum ex industria' in 1454, and in writing many of the substantial marginalia to the Statutes themselves (ff. 168r–204r) may have earned him more esteem than stipend within his own corporate institution, the more so as the book was, unequivocally, not intended to be a marketable commodity, but of communal utility.[79] Signs of personal property and other scribal peculiarities generally recur in books with which he is connected. The rebus of his name and surname appears in a variety of

---

[75] BodL, MS Rawl. B.335, f. 1v; Rawcliffe, 'Passports to Paradise', 18–19.

[76] Knowles and Hadcock, *Medieval Religious Houses*, 319, 355 on St Andrew's and 325, 370 on the Hospital of St John the Baptist in Lichfield, to which St Andrew's was granted in 1496; both establishments probably lived under a variant of the rule of St Augustine.

[77] Parkes, *Their Hands before Our Eyes*, 11.

[78] *BRUO*, III.1966, Sharpe, *A Handlist of the Latin Writers*, 597–8 (no. 1594); Ker, 'Patrick Young's Catalogue', 274, n.3; Parkes, *English Cursive*, 22 and facing plates 22 (i) and 22 (ii); Parkes, 'Patterns of Scribal Activity', 100, n.22; Parkes, *Their Hands before Our Eyes*, 110, n.41 and plate 34; Pouzet, 'Southwark Gower'.

[79] BL, MS Cotton Vitellius A.x, f. 163r, top margin. The Calendar is found in a dismembered medieval quire; details of Cottonian meddling are summarized by Tite, *The Early Records of Sir Robert Cotton's Library*, 82, 159, 248.

recognizable configurations, whether the jocularly textual 'Claudatur muro constat Liber iste Rogero [Confined by the wall, this book belongs to Roger]' in his fine copy of Gower's *Vox Clamantis* (BodL, MS Digby 138, f. 145r, top right margin), or his copy of Thomas Elmham's *Liber metricus de Henrico quinto* (GUL, MS Hunter 263 (U.5.3), f. 41r, bottom), or the gracious image of a roe enclosed within a wall in his *Polychronicon* (TCC, MS O.5.12, f. 1r, see Figure 10.3), or in his copy of explanations of difficult words chiefly in liturgical books (BodL, MS e Musaeo 64 (i), f. 1rv).[80] If the claustral trope was trumped in various guises by Walle on account of the erudite paronomasia his English name triggered, its imaginative force may equally have been prompted by the hesychasmic scribal ethic which he could indulge as a canon (whether residentiary, that is, figuratively 'walled-in', or not).[81]

It is, finally, with instances of non-religious scribal work from provincial gentry households or metropolitan administrations that the creative importance of *otium* is evident. Many well-known manuscripts (often miscellanies) containing English vernacular works offer pertinent examples of 'codicizing' procedures in non-commercial settings.[82] Some of the scribes of these miscellanies may be professional, but a great many are non-professional. The latter perform their scribal work with the best competence possible, sometimes displaying inventive fashions not commonly found in the work of professional practitioners. Their hesychasmic energies are particularly mobilized in procuring exemplars and integrating eligible materials into 'processes of serendipitous contextualisation'.[83] These processes, also discussed in Margaret Connolly's chapter, account for important features of non-commercial medieval books; they were processes aided by the increasing development of scribal literacy in the later medieval period. Interested collectors of materials, such as the Findern family of South Derbyshire, John Shirley or Humphrey Newton, certainly did not have to be 'paid' to search for exemplars 'in many a place'.[84] Newton's transmission of an astounding array of different materials in a dizzying number of configurations, from the sophisticated to the catastrophically disordered, makes him a paragon of ebullient 'information-gathering'.[85] His transmission of material is distinctly affective and hesychasmic.

---

[80] BodL, MS e Musaeo 64 is no. 1022 in Pächt and Alexander, *Illuminated Manuscripts in the Bodleian Library*, III.88.

[81] On canons' residence in secular cathedrals, see Edwards, *The English Secular Cathedral*, ch. 1; Lepine, A *Brotherhood of Canons*, chs. 7 and 8.

[82] E.g., Blanchfield, 'The Romances in MS Ashmole 61'; Boffey, 'Short Texts in Manuscript Anthologies'; Boffey and Meale, 'Selecting the Text'; Connolly, 'Practical Reading for Body and Soul'; Gillespie, 'Vernacular Books of Religion'; Hanna, 'Miscellaneity and Vernacularity'; Hardman, 'Compiling the Nation'; Thompson, 'Collecting Middle English Romances'.

[83] Hanna, 'Notes toward a Future History', 284.

[84] Shirley's words in his verse preface in BL, MS Add. 16165, f. iir; Connolly, *John Shirley*, 206.

[85] Robbins, 'The Poems of Humphrey Newton'; Marsh, 'Humphrey Newton'; Marsh, 'The Late Medieval Commonplace Book'; Marsh, '"I see by siȝt of evidence"'; Hanna, 'Humphrey Newton'.

Figure 10.3 TCC, MS O.5.12, f. 1r, close-up: inscription by 'Roger Walle'.

A poem on a *Nightingale*, incorrectly ascribed to Lydgate, is announced in Humphrey's table of contents as 'Uana fabula que Joh*ann*es Ludgate faciebat [A vain tale which John Lydgate made]' (Figure 10.1).[86] When passion governs, the

---

[86] BodL, MS Lat. misc. c.66, f. 92r.

defrayment of expenses incurred by the scribe-compiler and his helpers does not count as 'commercial'.

Hesychasmic impulses are also discernible when non-professional scribes decided to turn their scribal stints into a book. Codicological evidence suggests that some books – for instance Richard Hill's volume (Oxford, Balliol College, MS 354) and Humphrey Welles's anthology (BodL, MS Rawl. C.813) – were objects conceptualized and fabricated rather late in the process of creation.[87] Idiosyncratic colophons and other commentaries serving to mark off stints seem particularly numerous in these manuscripts: they are extremely informative about how scribal practice was influenced by the configurations of personal devotion in England, especially in the fifteenth century and after. Another example is Robert Thornton, who demonstrates quasi-professional scribal expertise in his two anthologies, Lincoln, Cathedral Chapter, MS 91 and BL, MS Add. 31042. In them he was probably responsible for the decorated initials of minor quality; it seems reasonable to consider that experienced non-professional scribes like him were generally able to perform minor artistic penwork such as initials with no highly sophisticated palettes of colours or decorative patterns.[88] In BL, MS Add. 31042, a colophon ending with the phrase 'secundum fantasiam scriptoris et cetera [following the imagination of the scribe, etc.]' (f. 32v), at a doubly pivotal locus – that is, a change in textual source and a change of quire – may well testify to the form of control which Thornton wished to exercise on the various book-producing activities through which the volume was created.[89] One of the implications of this *fantasia* – a figure of empowered secretarial *otium* – may be reflected in his concern with improving on the presentation and practical legibility of the *Liber de diversis medicinis* in his own transcription, notably with marginal headings.[90] As George Keiser has shown, the deliberate development of text-aids for the *Liber de diversis medicinis* is mirrored in the work of John Reed, parson of Nether Broughton in Leicestershire and vicar of Melbourne in South Derbyshire, who copied the text in BodL, MS Rawl. A.393 for the Findern family.[91]

When scribal and authorial regimes are conjoined, the notion of *otium* may come into play in especially intimate ways. Many surviving autograph manuscripts are not very prestigious, and they have therefore attracted less attention than they deserve; their cheap materials and modest confection are worth considering, however, because

---

[87] Gillespie, 'Balliol MS 354'; Jansen and Jordan (eds.), *The Welles Anthology*. Compare John Audelay's work, on which see Fein, 'Death and the Colophon', notably at 302.

[88] Brewer and Owen (eds.), *The Thornton Manuscript*; Thompson, *Robert Thornton*, 56–63; and Fredell, 'Decorated Initials', who tends (notably at 81) to belittle Thornton's 'scribal talents' in the 'decorative hierarchy' of initials.

[89] Thompson, *Robert Thornton*, 52–3; Pouzet, ' "Space this werke to wirke" '.

[90] Lincoln, Cathedral Chapter, MS 91, ff. 280r–314v.

[91] Keiser, 'Serving the Needs of Readers', 208 and 226, n.3; Keiser, 'MS. Rawlinson A.393'; Watson, *Catalogue of Dated and Datable Manuscripts*, I.110 and II, plate 815. On the Findern family, see Jurkowski, 'The "Findern Manuscript" '.

they suggest that the original compiler and writer of the book was in command of most stages in the production process. Some more prestigious autographs of religious and literary works have enjoyed pride of place in scholarly discussions; for instance, a wealth of information has been collected from a close examination of John Capgrave's and Thomas Hoccleve's manuscripts.[92] The standard of production of such autograph books may have varied according to their destination and to the resources invested in their making. Some books were presentation copies, or at least were intended to be ones. If the dedicatee had borne the costs of production, the commercial dimension was somewhat deflected from the book itself, insofar as patronage was a form of contact or contract more easily located within the bounds of interpersonal loyalty than within those of commercial culture *per se*. But the presenters of such books may well have incurred considerable expense, for the production of an autograph manuscript generally necessitated the remunerated work of professional artisans (for binding or decoration, for instance). Such expenditure was curbed when the presenter undertook to write the book himself, as did Capgrave, for instance in copying his *Solace of Pilgrims,* in a manuscript not of deluxe standard but of good scribal execution.[93] In his three autograph manuscripts, Hoccleve may even have been obliged to make ends meet by resorting to relatively cheap materials. His manuscripts consist of rather poor membrane: HEHL, MS HM 744 has at least one leaf with 'a rough oval area with a repaired tear' which Burrow and Doyle deem to be 'probably a flaw arising during the preparation of the skin';[94] Durham, University Library, MS Cosin V.iii.9 has membrane sheets which 'are not of high quality and are of varying thickness', and to Burrow and Doyle the texture of some of them looks more like the cheaper goat-skin than that of the expected sheep.[95] In a sense, the drastic material diet of these manuscripts appears consistent with Hoccleve's famous characterization, in *The Regiment of Princes*, of the 'trauaillous stilnesse' holding sway over the Privy Seal. The apparent oxymoron matches the time-hallowed paradox of laborious *otium* and may be understood as the hesychasmic labour of scribal industriousness, which applies even to professional documentary records – as Hoccleve's formidably massive *Formulary* preserving Latin and Insular French documents attests – and to the writing of poetry.[96] The self-fashioning dimension of *otium* is contrasted explicitly with 'al [the] bysynesse' of 'artificers' or common craftsmen, as implicitly with Hoccleve's paid work on commercial copies of poems by Chaucer and Gower.[97]

[92] Beadle, 'English Autograph Writings'; Lucas, *From Author;* Burrow and Doyle (eds.), *Thomas Hoccleve.* On Capgrave, see also Chapter 9 by Mooney and Chapter 3 by Horobin in this volume.

[93] BodL, MS Laud misc. 423 (E), ff. 355–414, on which see Lucas, 'An Englishman in Rome'.

[94] HEHL, MS HM 744, f. 33; Burrow and Doyle (eds.), *Thomas Hoccleve,* xxiii–xxiv.

[95] Burrow and Doyle (eds.), *Thomas Hoccleve,* xxviii.

[96] BL, MS Add. 24062; Thompson, 'A Poet's Contacts', 79, 97–101.

[97] Hoccleve, *The Regiment of Princes,* lines 1009–15, discussed by Burrow, 'Autobiographical Poetry', 405–6; see also Thompson, 'Thomas Hoccleve and Manuscript Culture' and Mooney, 'Locating Scribal Activity', 194–7.

As this survey has shown, the idea of the non-commercial production of books leads us to reconsider a number of issues relative to the textual cultures of late medieval England in their spatial, material and social dimensions. Books as manufactured artefacts were caught within a nexus of remunerated handicrafts. Yet cost-cutting or money-saving procedures suggest that scribes working outside commercial contexts responded to this basic social condition as often as possible – just as often as they did, as Erik Kwakkel shows in Chapter 8 in this volume, in commercial contexts. Such circumstances of book production attenuate the economic dimension inherent in the making of any book, while an amount of porosity between 'non-commercial' and 'commercial' is an important way of considering the degree of necessary co-existence of the two paradigms. Sometimes these economizing procedures constituted unpredictable reservoirs of innovative possibilities. Whether religious or secular, single-handed or cooperative, professional or not, each non-commercial manuscript shows that cost and effort were never so great as to preclude the practice and pleasures of scribal *otium*. It would be worth exploring whether such affective investments in the making of books are in line with the textual 'instability' and discursive 'malleability' of the written medium,[98] compared with commercially produced manuscripts – forms of variance which the commercial logic of the printing press was to restrain to a considerable extent. Finally, an emphasis on the 'non-commercial segments' of book production confirms the extent to which late medieval England was still stridently multi-lingual. Significant proportions of books were still not produced in English, and it may be argued that non-commercial book production may have also contributed to prolong the resilient prestige and scribal life of Latin and Insular French.[99]

[98] Thompson, 'Textual Instability'; Marotti, 'Malleable and Fixed Texts'; Love and Marotti, 'Manuscript Transmission'.

[99] See for example a significant proportion of heraldic materials, such as CUL, MS Ee.4.20 (noted above), which preserves probably the earliest known short treatise on heraldry in Insular French verse and prose, *De heraudie* (ff. 160v–161v).

II

Censorship

FIONA SOMERSET

Histories of the book often seem to assume that there could be no censorship before print – or that only print culture's technologies of rapid reproduction made censorship necessary.[1] Yet this has not stopped scholars who focus on manuscript culture from claiming that the century or so before print was an era of 'draconian censorship'.[2] This chapter aims to survey the evidence for censorship in the century or so before print and suggest what larger questions it may pose to us. Even if the regulation of book-copying and ownership were more difficult before printing, still books before print and stories about these books do seem to show the effects of aspirations towards censorship. These aspirations were articulated in the late fourteenth and fifteenth centuries through secular and ecclesiastical legislation that proposes to regulate speech and writing in order to combat the twin, and sometimes overlapping, fears of heresy and treason. That these are aspirations, rather than accomplishments, is worth emphasizing, for legislation often tells us more about what was desired than what happened. Whatever effects censorship had were more complex and subtle than a simple shutting-down – or even an overall atmosphere of severe repression. This was an era in which book production burgeoned and diversified – in which printed books were at first a feature of this diversification, developing alongside continued manuscript production and not strictly separable from it. Who engaged in activities that could be described as censorship in this context – in response both to legislation and to the fear and suspicion that it reflected and engendered? What effects did this censorship produce? Are the examples we have representative or anomalous?

This chapter is in memory of Mary Dove, a generous interlocutor during its production.

[1] For example, the only chapter on censorship in *CHBB: III*, Pamela Neville-Sington's 'Press, Politics and Religion', begins with the invention of the press.

[2] Watson, 'Censorship and Cultural Change', 826, and Simpson, *Reform and Cultural Revolution*, 335. But see Watson, 'Cultural Changes' and Simpson, 'Confessing Literature'.

Not all of the period's aspirations towards censorship can receive full treatment here, let alone their further implications. For example, even though the regulation of the spoken word seems to have been of greater concern than the written word, speech can be our focus only as it is related to the censorship of written documents.[3] It is related, of course. Speech and writing blur and converge when dissident statements referred to as 'clamour' are circulated and posted in public as bills, schedules and broadsides.[4] And speech and writing can work closely in tandem in book production, as where an original composition or copy is dictated to a scribe or sermons are recorded by a witness to their oral delivery or performed from a written copy. The friar who wrote *Dives and Pauper* and the sermons in Longleat, MS 4 attempts to make, from this close relationship, a justification for writing sermons in English: he claims 'sitthe it is leful to prechin þe gospel in Englych, it is leful to wrytin it in Englych boþin to þe techere and to þe herere ʒif he conne writin, for be writinge is mest sekyr examynacion of mannys speche and be wrytinge Goddys lawe may best ben cowd and best kept in mende'.[5] The irony is that this author made this claim shortly after 1409, when spoken preaching, long subject to restrictions, came to be more closely regulated than ever before: his premise does not provide him solid ground.

If writing provides the 'mest sekyr examynacion of mannys speche' and the best path to knowledge and memory, then it also provides firm evidence of that speaking and learning. Most previous work on censorship in the fourteenth and fifteenth centuries has focussed on the effects it might have had on the authors of books by analogy to the speakers of words. The goal here, by contrast, will be to consider more broadly distributed effects on the production, subsequent modification, circulation and ownership of books. As we shall see, legislation concerned itself more with the copying or ownership of potentially suspicious books than with their composition. This is just what we should expect. Barbara Newman and Ian Forrest have both recently corrected the assumption, common among literary scholars in particular, that writing a book routinely exposed its author to potential charges of heresy in the Middle Ages. Defiance of Church authority was the core of heresy: it might be revealed to investigators by refusal of the sacraments, contempt for customary religious practice, the tendency to form sectarian religious groups or (among the more learned or schooled) unauthorized or incendiary preaching and teaching and perhaps polemical writing.[6] But heresy investigations typically began from observed

---

[3] Forrest, *The Detection of Heresy*, 60–8, 75, 115–22; Arnold, 'Comment', 751.

[4] On 'the book' as including all medieval written artefacts, see Gillespie, 'Books', 88; Scase, *Literature and Complaint*.

[5] Quoted in Hudson and Spencer, 'Old Author, New Work', 231; thanks to Cara Hersh for sharing her copy of the opening folios of Longleat, MS 4.

[6] Forrest, *The Detection of Heresy*, 11–76; Newman, *God and the Goddesses*, 305–9.

practice or preaching, not from a person's writings – even if they might end with writings providing proof of continued defiance.

Finally, although censorship's effects on book production before print were certainly broader, this investigation will centre around (without limiting itself to) the heresy that most concerned these legislators, one that they called lollardy – even if what they or others meant by that term is debatable.[7] Censorship of treason not associated with lollardy and of forms of heterodoxy that may not be adequately described by this term is discussed more thoroughly elsewhere than is possible here.[8]

The idea that books might be seized and examined in order to ascertain the views of their authors and owners was a long familiar one. Yet it is systematically developed in English legislation between the 1380s and the 1420s. Books are mentioned first in the aftermath of the Blackfriars Council of May 1382, at which twenty-four conclusions were condemned as heretical or erroneous, though without naming Wyclif or any of his associates.[9] A letter from the king to the chancellor of Oxford in July 1382 orders that all books containing writings by John Wyclif or Nicholas Hereford in all the colleges of Oxford should be sought out and, 'ubicunque contigerit inveniri [wherever they happen to be found]', should be handed over to the archbishop within a month, without any attempt to change their contents.[10] The insistence that the books may not be altered suggests that the goal of this seizure remains the evidence against Hereford and Wyclif that these writings might provide. In 1388 and 1401, however, the purview and the goals of book seizures are successively widened. In 1388, several commissions (first to laymen, then to mixed groups of laymen and clerics) are granted to seek out and seize heretical books by Wyclif and Hereford, sometimes Aston and Purvey too. These commissions are undertaken first in Nottingham, then York, and then in Leicester, Salisbury, Norwich, Lincoln and Nottingham again.[11] Now a newly sharpened concern about the circulation of such writings is evident: in future, any trade in such volumes will be punished as severely as any teaching or maintaining of the views held within.[12] In 1401, the statute *De Heretico comburendo* not only reaffirms the death penalty for heresy in England, as is well known, but also orders that all persons possessing books and

---

[7] Cole, *Literature and Heresy*, 25–74.

[8] Scase, *Literature and Complaint*; Kerby-Fulton, *Books under Suspicion*.

[9] Catto, 'Wyclif and Wycliffism', 214–19. See also Forrest, *The Detection of Heresy*, 64–5; Cole, *Literature and Heresy*, 3–22; and, for the report from Courtenay's register, Wilkins, *Concilia Magnae Britanniae et Hiberniae*, III.157–64.

[10] Wilkins, *Concilia Magnae Britanniae et Hiberniae*, III.166. See also Hudson, *The Premature Reformation*, 103, n.265; Cole, *Literature and Heresy*, 82 and n.32.

[11] Richardson, 'Heresy and the Lay Power', 11–12; see also Forrest, *The Detection of Heresy*, 40; Wilkins, *Concilia Magnae Britanniae et Hiberniae*, III.204.

[12] Wilkins, *Concilia Magnae Britanniae et Hiberniae*, III.204; see esp. col. 1.37–42, col. 2.17–24, on which see Hudson, *The Premature Reformation*, 178.

writing containing heresy or error must hand them over to their bishop within forty days.[13] Now, authorship is no longer specified: the owners and distributors of heretical books will be answerable for the views in them as much as their authors.

Archbishop Thomas Arundel's *Constitutions* of 1407/1409 take an unusually broad and comprehensive approach to the restriction of preaching, teaching and writing. Two articles in the *Constitutions* focus on the censorship of books, as opposed to preaching and teaching. Article six stipulates that all writings by Wyclif in Oxford should be examined by a committee of twelve and subsequently held for copying by the university stationers only if their content is unanimously considered acceptable.[14] And article seven, famously, prohibits the translation of sacred Scripture in any form or the reading of any such translation produced since the time of Wyclif, unless the translation is approved by the provincial council. While the article leaves ambiguous the range of vernacular writings treating the bible that it might intend to include, William Lyndwood's commentary on this article in his *Provinciale* (compiled *c.*1422–34, and on the basis of experience in the prosecution of lollards under Archbishop Henry Chichele) suggests that it covers any translation of the words of the bible in any kind of writing.[15] Although these aspirations could scarcely have been enforced, they aim towards stringent regulation of a remarkably wide range of books.

Two briefer references in statutes produced after Henry Chichele became archbishop also focus on the ownership of books. The articles sent to the king by Oxford in 1414 voice a now generalized anxiety about incorrect translations in the hands of the laity, insisting that all works produced since the beginning of the papal schism should be confiscated until their translation can be approved by persons who are not suspect.[16] And a statute issued in Convocation in 1416 lists the ownership of suspicious books written in English as one of the signs of heresy that reputable lay persons should be encouraged to report.[17] Meanwhile, another strand of legislation gives new attention to the production of heretical books. A parliamentary statute of 1414 issued in response to the Oldcastle revolt includes writers of suspect books and sermons and their supporters among those who should be sought out.[18] And an abjuration formula, apparently produced in 1428 out of some collaborative discussion designed to systematize the pursuit of heresy and distributed in the province's

---

[13] *Statutes of the Realm*, ii.125–8. See also McHardy, '*De Heretico comburendo*', 112–26; Forrest, *The Detection of Heresy*, 34; Simpson, 'The Constraints of Satire', 18.

[14] Wilkins, *Concilia Magnae Britanniae et Hiberniae*, iii.317.

[15] Ibid. First noted by Hudson, 'Lollardy: The English Heresy?', 148–9. On Lyndwood, see Helmholz, 'Lyndwood, William'.

[16] Wilkins, *Concilia Magnae Britanniae et Hiberniae*, iii.360–5, esp. 365; on their origins, see Gillespie, 'Vernacular Theology', 415–16.

[17] Forrest, *The Detection of Heresy*, 48, 74 and Jacob (ed.), *The Register of Henry Chichele*, iii.18–19.

[18] *Statutes of the Realm*, ii.182. See also Forrest, *The Detection of Heresy*, 45–6.

Convocation, specifies a number of roles that convicted persons may play.[19] The suspect is required to admit to writing, compiling and retaining books containing heresies and errors, as well as affirming their contents, and, as part of his abjuration, is asked to hand over or report all books, quires or rolls that he has written and either still has or knows to be in the possession of others, that he has received or knows others to have received, and that he knows were written or dictated.[20] We can perceive in this legislation a growing desire to restrict the ownership and circulation of books, especially among certain readers,[21] and a growing familiarity with how books might be written, compiled, copied, dictated, held in secret and passed from hand to hand among the laity, both by established and by newly developing means: the legislators refer at first only to established means of book production and circulation at the university, the setting with which they are initially most familiar and where their concerns begin.[22]

In what ways might all this have affected the production of books and other forms of writing? Manuscript production is harder to regulate than the operation of printing presses, even when manuscript books were produced by artisans and others organized in some way and paid for their work; multiple copies of texts in manuscript resemble each other less than multiple copies of printed books do, and they are thus less easy to monitor. Consider for example BodL, MS Bodley 953, a copy of Richard Rolle's English *Psalter* owned and probably commissioned by Thomas Berkeley, a lavish, lectern-size volume – but one in which lollard versions of five of the canticles have been included.[23] Only a close reading of the whole work would detect this material, and it is not clear that anyone ever did. Nor do the authorities seem to have made any concerted effort towards detection, as Anne Hudson has pointed out. Even though some of those suspected of lollardy admit involvement in book production, none of the legislation, and no extant records or accounts of investigations, reveals any attempt to regulate the commercial production of vernacular writings by the inspection of exemplars, oversight of the commissioning of books or inspection of the final products.[24] Instead, investigations focus mainly on whether persons already suspect for heresy own suspicious books, and perhaps secondarily on their roles in the production, dissemination and use of books. Even

---

[19] Hudson, 'The Examination of Lollards'; Jacob (ed.), *The Register of Henry Chichele*, III.190–3'; Forrest, *The Detection of Heresy*, 108–9; Thomson, *The Later Lollards*, 224–5.

[20] Hudson, 'The Examination of Lollards', 136.

[21] That not all readers and not all books were of equal concern is shown by the extent to which Wyclif's works continued to circulate in the fifteenth century: see Hudson, 'Wyclif Texts in Fifteenth-Century London' and 'The Survival of Wyclif's Works'.

[22] For a lollard treatise commenting on how it was to be circulated and discussed in its author's absence, see Hudson, *The Works of a Lollard Preacher*, 138/2940–139/2962, and the 'Introduction', lii–liii.

[23] Hudson, ' "Who is My Neighbour?" '. On these and other professionally produced lollard volumes, see Hudson, 'Lollard Book Production', 131–4, 136.

[24] Hudson, 'Lollard Book Production', 129 and n.23; Jurkowski, 'Lollard Book Producers'.

if books might play a prominent role in demonstrating a suspect's heresy, they were never the sole grounds for the initial suspicion that led to investigation.[25]

Further difficulties emerge in censoring less organized forms of book production – for example, circulating booklets and the miscellanies, copied in a variety of settings, that might be produced from them for clearly or less clearly defined purposes.[26] These difficulties register in legislation both in carefully specified methods for detection in which failed attempts sometimes seem to resonate, and in the form of broadly aspirational claims that focus more on principle than practicality. For lollard texts are not at all easy to pinpoint and identify. In a textual milieu where it was typical for manuscripts to be anonymous and undated, where biblical translation, paraphrase and interpretation proliferated in a wide variety of forms, where a dizzying array of vernacular works of religious instruction was available and where social satire involving criticisms of clerical abuses was widespread and by no means invariably associated with heresy, only readers attuned to the specific idiom and polemical talking points of lollard texts would have found them easy to detect.

This problem of identification was compounded by lollards' habit of producing interpolated copies of mainstream works.[27] One copy of the Rolle *Psalter* commentary provides a striking demonstration that readers did not always know what they had. BodL, MS Laud misc. 286 includes a unique metrical preface of sixty lines deploring (apparently oblivious to the affiliations of the copy it introduces) that Rolle's *Psalter* commentary has been grafted with heresy by lollards. The volume is copied in three to seven hands, five mapped by *LALME* as northern dialects, and the stints of scribes B and C (both in Staffordshire dialects), covering psalms 1–17.50, contain lollard interpolations. Subsequent to psalm 17.50 the manuscript is uninterpolated: the Old Testament canticles are included as well, with uninterpolated commentary.[28]

But even works composed by lollards and outspoken in their assertions might take considerable effort to locate, given that these works are typically found in miscellaneous manuscripts.[29] Miscellanies whose contents are predominantly mainstream include outspoken lollard works, and manuscripts with predominantly lollard content include mainstream works: intermediary texts and manuscripts that are not so easy to classify abound. Some predominantly mainstream miscellanies

---

[25] Hudson stresses the first point (see, e.g., 'Lollard Book Production', 125), McSheffrey the second ('Heresy, Orthodoxy', 59). See below on John Claydon.

[26] For examples, see Hudson, 'A Lollard Quaternion', and Hanna, 'Two Lollard Codices'.

[27] Brady, 'Lollard Interpolations and Omissions', esp. 202, n.31; Hudson, 'A New Look at the Lay Folks' Catechism', 'The Lay Folks' Catechism', 'The Variable Text' and '"Who is My Neighbour?"'; Hanna, *London Literature*, 202–12.

[28] Hudson, 'The Variable Text', 56–7; Hudson, 'Lollard Book Production', 135; e-mail of July, 2009; Ogilvie-Thomson (ed.), *IMEP, XVI.*

[29] Hudson, 'Some Problems of Identity and Identification'.

may include lollard writings by accident, inadvertently providing an example of the difficulties of identifying such works. But it seems unlikely that all miscellanies with mixed content can be explained in this way. It also seems clear that some mainstream items suited the tastes of many lollard readers and were sought out for inclusion, such as Thomas Wimbledon's sermon, Richard Rolle's *The Form of Living* or pseudo-Bonaventuran material on the life of Christ. TCC, MS B.14.38 contains all three: this is a hand-sized parchment book consistently, if not lavishly, decorated and written in the same hand throughout most of its length (the first six initials in gold, red and blue, thereafter in red and blue; red and blue paraphs; marginal corrections and annotations in the same hand). Its full contents are: 1) the *English Wycliffite Sermons*, Sunday Epistle sermons; 2) continuing without a break, Wimbledon's sermon, attributed in a Latin colophon at its end; 3) Rolle's *The Form of Living*, beginning on a new folio but with no heading; 4) a lollard treatise on the Pater Noster, following without a break, the first capital not executed, and breaking off in mid folio for no apparent reason. The final item, 5) a Middle English version of the passion section of pseudo-Bonaventure's *Meditations on the Life of Christ*, probably represents a shift in the volume's initial plan: it is copied by a different scribe beginning on the verso of this page, with no attempt to imitate the flourished initials or paraphs of the earlier section, no marginalia, heavy ruling in pen and without catchwords in subsequent – perhaps added – quires.[30] Both hands are dated to the end of the fourteenth century. Even if the final text was added, its inclusion indicates that somebody thought all these items belonged together; and the first four items were certainly conceived of as a unit.

Another complicating factor in determining which books to suspect was that lollard writings also proliferated far beyond a primarily sectarian readership. Expensive volumes such as copies of the bible remained in the hands of prominent owners never suspected of heresy, even in the hands of royalty, such as Thomas of Gloucester (younger son of Edward III), Henry IV, Thomas of Lancaster (son of Henry IV), Henry VI and Henry VII.[31] Other volumes were owned by religious houses, such as Syon, the nuns of Barking, Norwich Cathedral Priory, the Franciscan house at Shrewsbury and a house of Dominican recluses in Newcastle.[32] And even while many similarly expensive or humbler volumes now contain no marks of medieval ownership, some can be traced to specific medieval owners ranging from bishops to

---

[30] On lollard interest in Wimbledon's sermon, see Walsham, 'Inventing the Lollard Past'. On lollard interest in Rolle, see Somerset, 'Wycliffite Spirituality'. On TCC, MS B.14.38, see Mooney (ed.), *IMEP, XI*.

[31] Dove, *The First English Bible*, 44. These copies are respectively BL, MS Egerton 617/618; an unidentified bible in the possession of the London bookseller Thomas Marlborough in 1419; Wolfenbüttel, Herzog-August-Bibliothek, MS Cod. Guelf. Aug.A.2; BodL, MS Bodley 277; BL, MS Royal I.C.viii. See also Peikola, 'Aspects of *mise-en-page*', 60–1, n.19.

[32] Dove, *The First English Bible*, 53–4.

priests to servants – some of them opponents rather than suspects of heresy, others with no apparent links with lollardy.[33] For example, an early fifteenth-century compilation derived from the *Glossed Gospels* but rearranged for liturgical reading with further controversial content added (York Minster Library, MS XVI.D.2) was owned both by John Wakeryng, master of St Bartholomew's Smithfield from 1422 to 1466, and by Archbishop William Warham, who investigated lollardy in Kent in 1511–12.[34] And a bible, now CSJC, MS E.14, was owned by Clemens Ridley, servant to a priest who was buried in London.[35]

Individual lollard writings might also be re-copied beyond the movement, sometimes in ways that demonstrate a fine awareness of the bounds between heresy and orthodoxy and aim to expurgate potentially suspect statements, sometimes in indifference to or ignorance about (or even, perhaps, out of interest in) such content. The seven copies of the lollard 'Schort Reule' illustrate this range of responses. Four of the seven copies of this miniature rule for living, advising each of the three estates in turn, do not differ significantly and contain polemical statements relatively easy to identify as lollard. Yet only two of these copies appear in predominantly lollard manuscripts (BodL, MS Eng. th. f.39; CCCC, MS 296) while the other two appear in more mixed collections unified by an emphasis on lay instruction (BodL, MS Bodley 938; Westminster School, MS 3). Meanwhile, of the other three copies, one includes a strongly polemical conclusion about judgement, yet appears in a manuscript otherwise not polemical, but rather unified by the theme of judgement (BodL, MS Laud misc. 174). One softens the critique of the Church and eliminates a polemical digression, yet appears in a manuscript predominantly containing more outspoken lollard writings (BL, MS Harley 2398). The final copy (BodL, MS Bodley 9) modifies the text for inclusion in a small prayerbook apparently owned by a religious house for women, in the process meticulously removing all potentially suspect content. This textual history demonstrates strikingly that the collection of materials with a unifying theme, or the exigencies of exemplar poverty and, perhaps above all, the attractions that a text might hold for a broad range of readers regardless of its lollardy sometimes weighed more strongly for specific book producers than ideological coherence.[36]

On the other hand, censorship pursued through the examination of book contents could be frighteningly effective. Two well-known cases show us how, even if the fact that we have only two such cases suggests that their circumstances were

---

[33] See further Gillespie, 'The Mole in the Vineyard', 131–61; Hudson, 'Wyclif Texts in Fifteenth-Century London', 'The Survival of Wyclif's Works' and '"Who is My Neighbour?"'.

[34] Pickering and Powell (eds.), *IMEP, VI*, 35–6; Hudson, 'Wyclif Texts in Fifteenth-Century London', 16–17.

[35] Dove, *The First English Bible*, 54.

[36] See Raschko, 'Common Ground for Contrasting Ideologies', esp. 10–21, for more detailed analysis.

in some ways exceptional. The first is that of John Claydon, a lollard of relatively humble social status who was held responsible for the contents of his book.[37] Claydon was a London skinner who had previously been convicted of heresy by Bishop Braybrooke and who thus counted as a relapsed heretic. He was investigated by Archbishop Chichele in 1415. He was asked whether he thought the contents of one of the books that had been found in his possession, the *Lanterne of Liȝt*, were true: he had commissioned a copy of this book from the scribe John Gryme, who had worked on the book at his house, and he had subsequently had it bound. Claydon's role in the production of the book was apparently felt to compound his offence: he was said to have 'fatebatur se scribi et ligari fecisse [confessed that he had had it copied and bound]'. If any attempts were made to find Gryme, beyond asking Claydon if he knew where he was (and Claydon said no), they are unrecorded. When Claydon said that he did think the book contained much truth – an admission corroborated by his servants' testimony – four friars examined the book for heresy and found fifteen erroneous or heretical statements in it. He was accordingly convicted, handed over to the secular arm and burnt.[38]

The second case is that of Reginald Pecock, arraigned for heresy in 1457. Recent scholarship suggests that the reasons for Pecock's prosecution may have stemmed more from personal and political rivalries, both ecclesiastical and secular, than from his written views.[39] Nonetheless, the final resolution of proceedings against him suggests that the object of his punishment was to silence him and suppress his writings. Pecock abjured in 1457 and submitted to the burning of his books. Initially, orders were given for him to be absolved and restored as bishop of Chichester. However, apparently as the result of a power struggle between the king and archbishop, within two years he had been removed from office and sent to Thorney Abbey near Peterborough, imprisoned without visitors unless authorized by the king or archbishop, without books other than service-books, a Psalter, a legendary and a bible, and without writing materials.[40]

The unusual focus, in the verdict against Pecock, on the thorough-going censorship of an author, should be weighed against the far more common emphasis, in other heresy trials, on ownership, copying and circulation. But even if books are commonly mentioned in trial proceedings, there are no other extant cases in which a suspect's books lead to his burning quite as directly as John Claydon's.[41]

---

[37] Anne Hudson has often referred to this case (e.g., *The Premature Reformation*, 211–14; 'Lollard Book Production', 125–6).

[38] Jacob (ed.), *The Register of Henry Chichele*, iv.132–8. For the quotation, see 136/23.

[39] A full account and translations of key documents appear in Scase, *Reginald Pecock*. See also James, 'Revaluing Vernacular Theology'.

[40] Scase, *Reginald Pecock*, 139–40.

[41] For a selective survey of cases in which books form part of the evidence, see Hudson, *The Premature Reformation*, 166–8.

At other times when books are investigated in heresy trials, it sounds as though their contents – in other hands – might not have been suspicious or even identifiably lollard. In 1430, Robert Bert of Bury St Edmunds had his copy of *Dives and Pauper* confiscated: his ownership and loaning out of this volume were seen as key evidence in his trial for heresy before Bishop William Alnwick in Norwich. Yet Abbot Whethamstede commissioned a copy of this same book for the library at St Albans between 1420 and 1440, along with a copy of William Woodford's anti-Wycliffite writings.[42] Later in the fifteenth and early sixteenth centuries, the lollards in Coventry shared and read together many books of the bible, also a book 'de mandatis' (perhaps a commentary on the Ten Commandments), saints' lives, a book on the craft of dying, a primer, a book on the passion of Christ and Adam, and a book against the sacrament of the altar.[43] Even if any of these books could have contained identifiably lollard content, only the last seems unquestionably lollard on the basis of its description. It was perhaps more the use that was made of these materials, as Shannon McSheffrey has suggested, that made them evidence of heresy.[44] Certainly, there is no record that their contents were investigated in detail.

The censorship of books achieved by commissions and in heresy prosecutions plainly did not extend to scrutinizing every volume of vernacular religious writing in lay, clerical or religious hands between 1382 or even 1409 and 1530 as intensively as John Claydon's books were scrutinized. Nonetheless, we should consider whether censorship through the implementation of the legislation may be accompanied by broader, more indirect cultural effects: a kind of secondary censorship, engaged in by the authors, compilers, scribes and owners of books themselves.

Writers or owners might, for example, seek licence or authorization for their composition, copying or ownership of potentially suspect books. Examples where licensing appears to have been sought have seemed particularly compelling for scholars arguing for a broader cultural climate of fear, suspicion and consequent restraint.[45] But we should also consider whether the rarity of these examples is in itself significant.[46] As with the case of John Claydon, the examples here are familiar but nevertheless deserve review.

Two works composed after 1409 claim to have been licensed by Arundel: Nicholas Love's *The Mirror of the Blessed Life of Jesus Christ* and the anonymous text *The Myroure of Oure Ladye*. Love, in a memorandum present in twenty of the forty-two extant manuscripts of his *Mirror* that are not missing the folios where it should

---

[42] The example and the contrast are drawn from Hudson, *The Premature Reformation*, 418.

[43] McSheffrey, 'Heresy, Orthodoxy', 62, lists examples. For the full list, see McSheffrey and Tanner (eds.), *Lollards of Coventry*, 343–4.

[44] McSheffrey, 'Heresy, Orthodoxy', 49–50, 52; yet perhaps not all of these were printed volumes: see Somerset, Review of McSheffrey and Tanner (eds.), *Lollards of Coventry*.

[45] Watson, 'Censorship and Cultural Change', 852–5.

[46] As noted by Dove, *The First English Bible*, 46.

appear, claims that Arundel examined a copy about 1410, and after a few days Arundel approved it and decreed that it should be made publicly available.[47] In this case it appears that rather than submitting to an established procedure, Love spontaneously sought out Arundel's approval as part of an exercise in self-promotion. As for the anonymous *Myroure*, written for the nuns of Syon some time between 1415 and 1450, the author claims to have sought licence from the bishop in advance for his activity as a translator of the bible ('I asked and haue license of oure bysshope to drawe suche thinges in to Englysshe') and alludes to 'lysence' being granted to readers for the reading of English bibles ('ye may haue hem … out of englysshe bibles if ye haue lysence therto').[48] In both cases, but perhaps especially the second, *licence* may have its broader sense of 'permission' rather than referring to a specific, established legal procedure.[49] Certainly there is no hint that, as Love claimed, the bishop examined the text once produced. Rather, translator and reader are described as seeking permission in advance.[50]

In addition, three fifteenth-century copies of the *Speculum vitae* include a Latin note claiming that the work was examined for heresy in Cambridge in 1384 and cleared of all charges: 'ideo quicunque fueris, o lector, hanc noli contempnere, quia sine dubio si aliqui defectus in ea inventi fuissent, coram Universitate Cantabrigiae combusta fuisset [and so, whoever you may be, O reader, do not condemn it, for if any fault in it had been found, without doubt it would have been burnt in Cambridge]'.[51] Whether or not the claim is true, the final, defiant flourish demonstrates that its aim is to assert its acceptability to any possible reader ('quicunque fueris').[52] Not only authors and copyists, but owners, too, appear to have sought licences, although we have just one example, among the approximately 253 extant Wycliffite Bible manuscripts, of a copy that claims licence for its owner, in JRL, MS Eng. 77, a Later Version New Testament dated by Neil Ker to the end of the fourteenth or beginning of the fifteenth century.[53] This copy includes an informal note that the writer's mother sought approval of the book from doctors Thomas Eborall and William Ive, successive masters of Whittington College in London from 1444 to 1464 and 1464 to 1470, before buying it: Ralph Hanna suggests that this must

---

[47] Sargent, *The Mirror of the Blessed Life*, 36–7; Gillespie, 'Vernacular Books of Religion', 322–4; Dove, *The First English Bible*, 46.

[48] Quoted not from J. H. Blunt's EETS edition, but from a better text in Hargreaves, '*The Mirror of Our Lady*', 277–8. See also Dove, *The First English Bible*, 47.

[49] *MED*, s.v. 'licence', sense 1b. Even in references to licensing preachers, the word *licence* typically refers to the permission granted, not the document or procedure with which it is granted: see for example the *Lanterne of Liȝt*'s complaint: 'but if þat prest schewe þe mark of þe beest, þe which is turned in to a newe name and clepid a special lettir of lisence' (*Lanterne of Liȝt*, 18/2–3).

[50] Dove, *The First English Bible*, 47.

[51] Gillespie, 'Vernacular Books of Religion', 332–3. Quoted from Allen, 'The *Speculum Vitae*', 148.

[52] Hudson doubts the account is true, *The Premature Reformation*, 416.

[53] Dove, *The First English Bible*, 47–53.

have taken place in London in the 1460s, shortly after both men were involved in Pecock's trial.[54] Yet clearly Eborall and Ive, if they did in fact look at the manuscript, either did not examine it too closely or were not concerned that it contains not only a Wycliffite translation of the New Testament, but, as a prologue to Matthew, a rather inflammatory pro-translation tract that also appears in CUL, MS Ii.6.26.[55]

These few examples all recount different procedures of licensing. Two assert the examination and approval of a specific work – although one of those examples dates itself safely far before 1409, yet after 1382. One licenses its translator but also mentions 'licence' being given to readers, while one focusses on the persons involved in gaining approval of its contents as much as the translation itself. Together, in their rarity and variety, these examples suggest that there was no general system of licences to which all had to submit. They also suggest that licences were thought to authorize persons, rather than, or as often as, the books they produced or owned.[56]

Faced with the prospect of burning, however, writers and owners instead of seeking approval might simply refrain from composing, compiling or copying anything further, and destroy or hand over the books they already have.[57] Hudson's research on lollard book production has from its earliest stages given attention to the impact of such self-censorship on lollardy. But Nicholas Watson was the first to consider the issue more broadly, suggesting a sharp reduction in new, original and daringly innovative theological works like those of William Langland and Julian of Norwich after 1400 as a result of Arundel's *Constitutions* and the anti-intellectual climate they engendered.[58] Widespread initial acceptance of this claim was followed by vigorous questioning.[59] Watson's powerful negative claim about the effects of censorship on authors cannot finally be proven or disproven – nor can it be our main focus here. Yet an arguably far more significant innovation in his article was to consider the restrictions imposed by the *Constitutions* on an expansive corpus, rather than separating out genres and kinds (e.g., heretical from orthodox, parabiblia from bible, mystical effusion from pastoral instruction).[60] Subsequent respondents have expanded his purview even further, to include for example hagiography, drama,

---

[54] Hanna, 'English Biblical Texts before Lollardy', 150; Hudson, 'Wyclif Texts in Fifteenth-Century London', 3–4. Neither Dove, Hanna nor Hudson mentions that the note has been thoroughly inked over: for more on this, see below.

[55] Dove, *The First English Bible*, 52; Hudson ' "Who is My Neighbour?" '.

[56] Dove, *The First English Bible*, 55; McSheffrey, 'Heresy, Orthodoxy', 48–50.

[57] Hudson has often cited John Phip, who stated that he would rather burn his books than have them burn him (*The Premature Reformation*, 168; 'Lollard Book Production', 136).

[58] Watson, 'Censorship and Cultural Change'.

[59] Kelly, 'Lollard Inquisitions', esp. 288, n.38; Sargent (ed.), *The Mirror of the Blessed Life*, 74–96, and 'What do the Numbers Mean?'; Somerset, 'Professionalizing Translation'; Kerby-Fulton, *Books under Suspicion*, 397–401; Bose, 'Religious Authority and Dissent'; Hanna (ed.), *IMEP, XII*, xi–xxiii.

[60] Watson, 'Conference Response'.

music and writings in Latin as well as English and Anglo-Norman.[61] All the more so when we focus on book production and ownership rather than authorship, this broadened view makes visible just how much did not change – and that what does change cannot be characterized simply as the repression of some of these kinds and the cultivation of others.

Clearly, the effect of the *Constitutions* was not a uniform, sudden shutdown in book production of all kinds coupled with the destruction of all potentially suspect books. Instead, what we find is an efflorescence in the copying of books of vernacular religion that cannot, on the face of it, be easily accommodated to claims of overarching repression. This efflorescence was matched in several other areas of book production, as is well known.[62] Yet when we look beyond the relatively straightforward growth overall in the circulation of vernacular writing, we find other narratives, involving increasing diversification, modification and decreasing standardization, in which self-censorship may play a part.

For example, a rather different story could be told about lollard book production than about English book production more generally in this period. Anne Hudson has shown that many early lollard books seem to have been rapidly produced in multiple copies by a team of scribes working in similar dialects and similar, slightly dated anglicana hands. Most show signs of careful correction, and most have a layout that clearly differentiates between text, gloss and commentary. Most of this work had already been accomplished before 1409, or certainly before 1414.[63] After the second decade of the fifteenth century this form of lollard production seemingly comes to an end. This shift is surely one visible effect of persecution, although whether it is the result of the death of one patron and difficulty in finding another, the imprisonment of key figures following the Oldcastle revolt or primary or secondary censorship, is less certain. However, lollard books continue to be copied, if in less organized ways, and often in more miscellaneous volumes. While Helen Spencer finds greater (if rather uneven) reticence in the later sermon collections redacted from the *English Wycliffite Sermons*, her research nevertheless demonstrates ongoing engagement with this collection by compilers throughout the fifteenth century.[64] Ongoing engagement by compilers and copyists – some reticent, some unconcerned, some outspoken – can also be traced in the large corpus of miscellaneous manuscripts containing lollard works produced or preserved across the fifteenth century.

---

[61] See several articles in a forum in *English Language Notes* in 2006 as well as: Kerby-Fulton, *Books under Suspicion*, 397–401; Simpson, 'Saving Satire' and 'The Constraints of Satire'; Raschko, 'Common Ground for Contrasting Ideologies'; Morey, *Book and Verse*; Winstead, *John Capgrave's Fifteenth Century*; Minnis, *Translations of Authority*, 1–37.

[62] Edwards and Pearsall, 'The Manuscripts of the Major English Poetic Texts', 257–8; Sargent, 'What Do the Numbers Mean?' See also the discussion in the '"Introduction"' to this volume.

[63] Hudson, 'Lollard Literature'.

[64] Spencer, 'The Fortunes of a Lollard Sermon-Cycle', 356, and *English Preaching*, 278–311.

We need many more such stories about shifts in book production in the fifteenth century and their causes.[65] For example, we know that Mirk's *Festial* and Love's *The Mirror of the Blessed Life* each went through a phase of rapid, organized production that resembles early lollard book production. In each case it has been suggested that this form of production was a response to lollardy, designed to counteract its influence.[66] It would be fascinating to test the validity of these claims by examining cases of rapid, organized production more broadly, and considering them together with the less uniform copying of, for example, derivatives of the *English Wycliffite Sermons* and *Festial* or the large number of other Middle English pseudo-Bonaventuran materials extant in various sorts of copies that followed alongside and in their wake.[67] As another example, the Wycliffite Bible is extant in more copies than any other Middle English work: especially given that it is the one book named in Arundel's *Constitutions*, it makes an embarrassing poster-child for the success of censorship before print. But further investigation of variations among these copies is needed in order to evaluate Hanna's claim that this bible supplanted previous sorts of biblical writing available in the vernacular once it became available.[68] The continued and even burgeoning presence of parabiblia in Wycliffite Bible manuscripts needs more attention, as well as the proliferation of formats, contexts and redactions in which this bible was produced after an initial phase of greater uniformity.[69]

Rather than submitting books for official approval, ceasing to produce them or destroying them, authors, copyists and owners of books might instead attempt concealment. For owners of books, concealment might be most simply achieved by hiding their books. We know that some books were indeed concealed in this way, such as a bible whose flyleaf reports that it was found in a 'prests hawlle' in 1542 (Orlando, FL, MS Van Kampen 639); it is hard to be sure from this and other stories whether the practice was a common one.[70] There may have been other, more subtle methods of concealing books. For example, it has been suggested that bequeathing books to religious houses was a safe way to transfer them into corporate hands that need not fear investigation for heresy.[71] Yet, since any such bequest would create a durable record of previous ownership, it does not seem a particularly evasive manoeuvre.

[65] For examples, see Hanna's 'Introduction' to *IMEP, XII*, and Gillespie, 'The Haunted Text'.

[66] Sargent (ed.), *The Mirror of the Blessed Life*, 54–75, 153; Fletcher, 'John Mirk and the Lollards'.

[67] For sermons, see Spencer, *English Preaching*, 269–320. Pseudo-Bonaventuran materials were studied by the ' "Geographies of Orthodoxy" ' AHRC project.

[68] Hanna, 'English Biblical Texts before Lollardy', 153. On other forms of bibilical writing in English, see Morey, *Book and Verse*.

[69] See now Peikola, ' "First is written" ', 'Aspects of *mise-en-page*' and 'The Sanctorale'; Dove, *The First English Bible*.

[70] Dove, *The First English Bible*, 298/3–4; Hudson, *The Premature Reformation*, 168.

[71] Dove, *The First English Bible*, 54.

Anonymity might be a means for owners, authors and producers to conceal their involvement with a volume. However, it is difficult to provide firm evidence for this motivation in an era when many manuscripts bear on their face no firm evidence of authorship, no names of scribes or owners and no date. In many cases, flyleaves that included information of this kind may simply have been lost in later rebinding.[72]

The miscellaneous or interpolated character of some manuscripts and the partial reproduction of the Wycliffite Bible in others have also been attributed to an impulse towards concealment through camouflage.[73] Here the evidence is murkier still. There may indeed be cases where camouflage motivates the copying of a popular, mainstream work at the start of a manuscript, as in a book, now JRL, MS Eng. 85, which begins with the ABC and English copies of the Pater Noster, Ave Maria and Creed but then progresses through a variety of lollard-tinged pastoralia interspersed with polemic. Camouflage might also explain the inclusion of heterodox content within a recognized devotional compilation such as *Pore Caitif*, the pervasive interpolation of a widely read earlier work such as Rolle's *English Psalter*, or the inclusion of polemic within a standard reference format such as the biblical lectionary.[74] But if camouflage were the only motivation we were to attribute in all such instances, this would oversimplify the relationships and interchange between lollardy and other religious writings. Lollards probably incorporated heterodox material into works and compilations that they already valued highly but wanted to correct on some details, not into works they simply detested. Compilers and readers of less firm convictions may have been yet more catholic in their tastes.

Finally, a detailed investigation of the involvement in book production of four men prosecuted for their involvement in the 1414 Oldcastle revolt has revealed that all four operated in what might be interpreted as a concealed location, and by covert means. They worked in the Middlesex suburbs on the periphery of the city, rather than in Paternoster Row, where C. Paul Christianson has located most London book production, and in some cases parchmenters appear to have taken a leading role in the production of lollard books. But what this may show is not that lollard book producers were hiding on the fringes of London in a criminal area, but that the London book trade was in many ways less centralized than Christianson's reliance on Bridge House estate records led him to conclude.[75]

Where we can be fairly certain that concealment was the motivation for one or more of the practices discussed here, it suggests that the books in question were valued highly. After all, if an owner fears that his books may incriminate him, the more

---

[72] Spencer, *English Preaching*, 279, 318.

[73] Aston, 'Lollardy and Literacy', 211; Dove, *The First English Bible*, 52.

[74] See respectively Brady, 'Lollard Interpolations and Omissions' (*Pore Caitif*); n.28 (Rolle); Peikola, 'The Sanctorale' (lectionary in Thomas Woodstock's bible).

[75] Jurkowski, 'Lollard Book Producers', esp. 216–26; Jurkowski herself suggests this alternative interpretation (224–6); see also Mooney, 'Locating Scribal Activity', 183–204 and Chapter 9 in this volume.

obvious solution would be to destroy or not to write or make them. Especially at their more perfunctory, efforts at concealment might also be argued to suggest that authors, copyists and owners were aware that any inspection of books that might occur was likely to be cursory or inexpert.

Finally, we might consider ways in which people might make very local, specific alterations in response to the fear of censure. These might arise from circumspection by authors or translators, expurgation by compilers and copyists and erasure or excision by owners and other readers. This category of alteration is a hybrid one, and designedly so, juxtaposing forms of censorship before, during and after a book is produced in order to consider what they have in common, how their effects might be dissimilar, and in what ways these analytically distinct categories might converge when an author is also a copyist, a compiler is an owner, and so on. While circumspection by authors or translators has been the focus of most previous efforts to trace the effects of censorship in this sort of localized way, here we shall emphasize only what it has in common with the activities of copyists, compilers, owners and other readers: the difficulties that arise in locating changes whose motivations and circumstances are clear.[76]

For a compiler or copyist of available texts, censorship might take the form of leaving things out: a copyist might omit specific topics, or even specific words or turns of phrase, while a compiler might omit whole sermons or tracts, perhaps choosing others instead. This form of modification is relatively easy to trace. Granted, we need to make sure of the direction in which modifications are being made, for there are many examples of works in which new, inflammatory material is added, either as interpolations (as in the Rolle *Psalter* commentaries) or in the form of new bridge passages between selections placed in a compilation (as in JRL, MS Eng. 85). But where modifications have the effect of toning down a compilation or an individual work's assertions, we can be fairly sure of what a given copyist excised and what he retained – bearing in mind scribal error, or variations in a given exemplar that are now inaccessible to us. What is intriguing about each of the examples of expurgation that has received detailed study is how often such processes seem incoherent or partially executed – how difficult it is to discern a consistent ideological stance on the basis of changes in a given copy.

Consider, for example, the manuscripts of the English Wycliffite sermon cycle. Among those that have received special attention as unique cases are: BodL, MS Don. C.13; Cambridge, Sidney Sussex College, MS 74; and BodL, MS Bodley 95. Hudson finds that while BodL, MS Don. C.13 (hereafter Z) has been systematically expurgated, to the point where the strongly antifraternal *Vae Octuplex* has been reduced to little more than the biblical text that is the basis for original text's

---

[76] For a thoughtful analysis of these difficulties, see Hudson, 'The Variable Text', and on *Piers Plowman*, see Cole, *Literature and Heresy*, esp. 4.

exposition, still Z's views on what is offensive seem both idiosyncratic and inconsistent: for instance, some criticisms of both the theory and practice of confession are retained, while others are removed.[77] In contrast, Helen Spencer shows that BodL, MS Bodley 95, a later fifteenth-century adaptation of the derivative of the English Wycliffite sermons on the Sunday gospels also found in Sidney Sussex College, MS 74, while similarly inconsistent, is outspoken on friars and preaching but avoids any discussion of the sacraments.[78] It is also intriguing that expurgation is typically inconsistent not only within single copies, but between copies: while some copies of a given work bear changes, others are unaltered. This variation would seem unsurprising if it were clear that the unaltered copies are of earlier dates, or were plainly circulated only among lollards. But this is far from clearly the case, as the 'Short Rule' has already shown us.[79]

Erasure and excision should be considered separately from expurgation. Although we cannot always distinguish the two, the alteration of an existing copy of a text differs from alteration during copying. Some erasures seem fairly clearly to be aimed at deflecting an examination of the text for heresy, in that they eliminate obvious markings of heterodox provenance or content. For example, BodL, MS Fairfax 2 was originally dated to 1408, but the date has been altered by removing the fourth 'c' in 'm cccc viij' to make 1308, safely long before Wyclif.[80] The ascription of a short text by Wyclif to 'd. e.' in TCC, MS B.14.50 has been partly scraped away: only 'd' is now visible.[81] In Dublin, Trinity College, MS 245 the heading 'nota de sacramento altaris' has been inked over, though rather ineffectively.[82] These erasures seem to be motivated by a desire for concealment, rather than the wish to remove offensive material, which after all remains. The removal of a text containing heterodox materials from the beginning of a manuscript and its rebinding into the middle, as observed by Ralph Hanna in Oxford, Magdalen College, MS lat. 98 and MS lat. 99, suggests a similar motivation.[83]

In a wide variety of other cases, it is harder to be sure whether erasure or excision stems from the fear of censure or from affront, disgust or some other more personal motive. As already mentioned, nobody has yet addressed the fact that the 'licence' in the Wycliffite Bible in JRL, MS Eng. 77 has been quite thoroughly inked over (Figure 11.1).[84] But when this annotation was obscured, let alone why, is quite mysterious. Most forms of erasure are almost impossible to date: while inking

[77] Hudson, 'The Expurgation of a Lollard Sermon Cycle'.

[78] Spencer, 'The Fortunes of a Lollard Sermon-Cycle', 377–93.

[79] See above, n.36.

[80] Dove, The First English Bible, 257.

[81] TCC, MS B.14.50, f. 70r. See Von Nolcken, 'Notes on Lollard Citation', 417 and 430; Hudson, 'A Lollard Compilation', 26.

[82] Dublin, Trinity College, MS 245, f. 144r.

[83] Hanna, 'Dr Peter Partridge', 51–2.

[84] See fig. 2 in Dove, The First English Bible, 49.

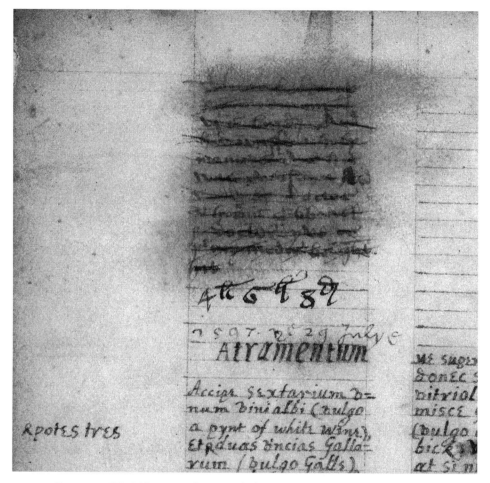

Figure 11.1 JRL, MS Eng. 77, f. 267v: inked-over note on the inspection of the book.

over leaves us the minimal evidence of the ink used, the scraping off of words or removal of leaves can be attributed to a specific time period only inferentially. As an example of a relatively probable inference, in Thomas Woodstock's household copy of Thomas Walsingham's *Short Chronicle* the names of the lollard knights have been thoroughly scraped away in the entry where they had previously been listed. Jill Havens has made a good case for why a member of Gloucester's household might have wished to expunge these names before his death in 1397: she is right that there would surely have been little motivation to do so later (even if her claim that the specific motivation for the change was that the eraser knew that the persons named were not in fact associated with lollardy seems to overburden the evidence).[85] A

---

[85] Havens, 'A Curious Erasure'.

more firmly datable case is that of BodL, MS Laud misc. 448, in which portions of the lollard commentary on the canticles have been first erased, then re-copied in a different fifteenth-century hand.[86] Some contestation over content has occurred, but it is unclear exactly what was at stake. Hanna discusses the excision from BodL, MS Digby 98 of two leaves on which Peter Partridge had copied letters by Wyclif, one of them probably his 'De Amore', a response to Rolle's *The Form of Living*. However, his suggestion that the person who removed the leaves was probably not Partridge, given that the index Partridge prepared still contains an entry for them, may appear less certain amidst the many examples of inconsistent or incomplete alteration that have been surveyed here.[87]

The examples surveyed here illustrate a difficulty that emerges in analysing any form of textual alteration. Alteration can be a form of secondary censorship in response to the threat of censure, but more generally it is a form of reader response (or authorial reconsideration) with a wider range of possible causes. An author, translator, compiler, copyist or reader may alter a text not only in order to eliminate content that might get himself or other owners of the text into trouble, but also to remove something offensive to himself, in an attempt to improve on the original, or out of error. How many of these causes, though, might adequately be described as censorship? While some critics might embrace all but the last one or two, my own sense is that primary censorship as implemented by ecclesiastical officials and secondary censorship as practised by those subject to them ought both to be quite narrowly defined.[88]

The narrowly defined forms of primary and secondary censorship developed here may, finally, be useful categories to describe some of the changes that take place between script and print and in the early years of printed book production before the Reformation. There were few restrictions on the texts English printers were allowed to print before 1515, when a decree of the fifth Lateran Council was issued stating that all books printed must first be approved by 'the bishops or competent persons appointed by them'.[89] The first moves against Lutheran printed books, including public burnings in St Paul's Churchyard, took place in the 1520s.[90] But as Sue Powell has argued, even before 1515, the list of English books printed has the appearance of being carefully constrained,[91] even though there is no evidence that Arundel's *Constitutions* (still technically in force) were utilized by the authorities in this period. The print market, or some sectors of it, may have been engaged in secondary censorship. Yet there are other possible explanations: earlier examples where

---

[86] Hudson, 'Who is My Neighbour?'
[87] Hanna, 'Dr Peter Partridge', 51.
[88] Hudson, 'Comment'.
[89] Schroeder (ed.), *Disciplinary Decrees*, 504–5.
[90] See Gleason, 'The Earliest Evidence for Ecclesiastical Censorship'.
[91] Sue Powell, plenary paper at 'After Arundel' conference, Oxford, April 2009.

works are mass produced in manuscript copies over a short period of time may give us new insights into why certain books were selected for production in printed form in the early years of print. And manuscript circulation may have complemented or even competed against print for some audiences.

By way of conclusion I would propose that book producers and owners would have been far less inconsistent and perfunctory in their efforts at censorship in this period (if that is what they are) if the terms of censorship had been clear to all and had been widely and systematically applied. What the evidence suggests is that censorship was very unevenly applied and that the grounds on which a book or tract might be considered suspect were clear to some but murky to the majority. What is more, lollard and other potentially suspect writings were of broad interest, and lollards and non-lollards read widely in each other's works, even if it seems likely that they did not always know what they were reading. Legislation that made persons accountable for the contents of the books they produced and owned did cast a long and chilly shadow across the late fourteenth and fifteenth centuries. We should be alert to the possibility that developments in the culture of book production may bear some relation to this climate change. To discount the effects of persecution is to forget those whom it damaged. But we should not overestimate them either. What we need, what we are now developing, is an increasingly layered picture of vibrancy and diversity in the culture of book production and use in England in this period.

12

Books beyond England

JOHN J. THOMPSON

It may initially seem odd that a chapter on books beyond England has been included in a volume of essays apparently dealing with the production of books in England. But English texts and manuscripts travelled widely in both geographical and social terms throughout this period, as, indeed, did their writers and later copyists, readers and hearers. The manuscripts that form the basis of this chapter are part of an under-investigated 'archipelagic' literary culture of book production, reception and reading that has been eclipsed by a larger and still imperfectly written English book history – larger, that is, because it deals with a much greater number of extant manuscripts and a greater population of Anglophone readers across a wider geographical area that includes London and Westminster – and imperfectly written (notwithstanding several modern team efforts), precisely because it is so metropolitan in focus.[1] Not unnaturally, this larger version of English book history has gained recent critical attention because of its focus on the production and distribution of works by major English authors, revealed through metropolitan and other strongly regional patterns of consumption in England in the period before printing. Nonetheless, 'Ireland', 'Scotland' and also 'Wales' have always occupied significant places in the Anglophone imagination and in the late medieval 'English' border cultures that manifested themselves as peripheral regional presences across these islands.[2] The English manuscripts and texts associated with these border cultures offer equally interesting but less easily characterized patterns of book production and use than those discussed elsewhere in this volume as part of the larger story of manuscript culture and publication in English book history. Such comparative studies seem particularly important if we are to resist imposing what might

---

[1] For the value of archipelagic viewpoints, see Smith, 'The British Isles in the Late Middle Ages', 7–19 and Kerrigan, *Archipelagic English*.

[2] Of these only Scotland gained a real toehold in this volume's predecessor: Lyall, 'Books and Book Owners in Fifteenth-Century Scotland'. The same general point might be made regarding *CHBB: III*, another successor volume to G&P.

be characterized as 'the print paradigm' on the story of fifteenth-century English manuscript culture before and after Caxton and the advent of commercial English printing.[3] As a result, codicologists must always remain alert to the possibility of locating 'English' manuscript production and book consumption through more complex socioliterary and geo-historical realities than have hitherto been the case in surveys of this kind. An analysis of books beyond England that were produced by or for writers and readers associated with Anglophone Ireland – the focus of this chapter – seems to offer just such an opportunity.

Mapping the English border cultures 'beyond England' is never going to be easy, since the surviving texts and manuscripts are often challenging to localize and contextualize in geographical, social, linguistic and textual terms. *The Linguistic Atlas of Late Mediaeval English* (*LALME*) remains an essential bibliographical tool in this respect, not only deploying linguistic analyses of phono-graphological features for dialectological identification in dot maps for England, Scotland and Wales, but also offering, in volume I, a convenient index of localizable written sources across both Britain and Ireland in a repository list.[4] Largely because the identifiable late medieval Scottish and Welsh writings in English are relatively few in number, the dot maps in *LALME* for these regions remain sparsely populated, as, indeed, do the dot maps for some English, particularly northern, geographical regions. Significantly, *LALME* has produced no dot maps at all for Ireland. This last detail offers a useful caution on at least two fronts. Firstly, and most obviously, it reveals much about the unsettled and often peripatetic nature of the literary and linguistic cultures in Ireland that sponsored Anglophone writings, about which more will be said below.[5] More generally, however, it confirms a point emphasized often by the editors of *LALME* themselves – and one that has become a truism for everyone seriously engaged in the codicological study of English manuscripts and texts from this period – namely, that the evidence of geo-historical variation on which *LALME* is based must also take into account a wide range of other possible variables. Relevant factors include not only the geographical and social movement of texts and scribes across English sociolinguistic and politico-historical borders of all kinds, but also the particular types of Middle English material being written and later copied (and re-copied) in these areas, and, related to this variety, availability and usage of exemplars, dialect translations and *Mischsprachen*.[6] As well as all of this, one also has to consider the personal, sometimes idiosyncratic, perceptions of language and dialect, identity and literary taste that are often implicit in the work of individual writers and later

[3] Kelly and Thompson, 'Imagined Histories of the Book', 13–14.

[4] For the repository list, see *LALME*, I.59–171.

[5] For a preliminary survey of the extant manuscripts and texts, see McIntosh and Samuels, 'Prolegomena to the Study of Mediaeval Anglo-Irish', and also the documents for Ireland in the county list in *LALME* I. 270–9.

[6] Benskin and Laing, 'Translations and *Mischsprachen*'.

copyists, and variation in their presumed attitudes to the wishes and requirements of other readers and hearers in the period.

Ireland is not included in the regional forms of Middle English dialectal variation charted by *LALME* largely because one is dealing in this case with an Anglophone culture that was embedded uncertainly through various attempted plantation processes.[7] That embedded settler culture was itself inherently competitive and unstable, but versions of it were then legislated for and maintained through the work of legal, administrative or religious institutions, frequently dominated by English newcomers, supported more often than not by military assistance. The native Middle English dialects of these successive waves of immigrant English speakers (some of whom stayed much longer in Ireland or were assimilated much more quickly to their new surroundings than others) have left significant traces in English writings localized to Ireland, but, unlike the situation in England, such traces cannot always be explained diachronically or plotted in terms of the geographical region in Ireland that can sometimes be associated with the writers of the relevant texts and manuscripts. One also has to consider the possible influence of the Celtic languages, in terms of both morphology and syntax, on certain English speakers in Ireland, but not others, in this period and beyond. That influence might be most apparent in the writings of second- and third-generation bilingual vernacular speakers, but it might also have influenced the English speech of relative newcomers to Ireland from other border areas such as the Anglo-Welsh Marches, or Cornwall and the West, or, to the north, the Anglo-Scottish borders. Related to this remarkably wide geo-historical distribution and linguistic spread among the English-speaking population, there are many unanswered questions with regard to the forms of social contact that may be said to have existed (or, at times, even flourished) among the different vernacular speech communities in Ireland. It was between and within such communities that certain late medieval linguistic norms were established and broader cultural attitudes to reading and writing in English formed to produce the relatively homogenized versions of Middle Hiberno English now detectable in the surviving texts and manuscripts localizable to the region.

Once these sociolinguistic variables and historical considerations have been taken into account, one can tentatively begin the task of mapping several different kinds of book-producing activity among the Anglophone communities in Ireland, insofar as these have been reflected in the extant manuscripts and texts.[8] BL, MS Harley 913 is a useful and challenging case-study in this respect, both because of its early date (*c.*1330) and also because of its modern status as a battered relic of a trilingual

---

[7] See sensible general discussion of these early processes in Frame, *Colonial Ireland*; Davies, 'Frontier Arrangements'; and for the consequences of these early Plantation attempts, see Smyth, *Map-Making, Landscapes and Memory*; Canny, *Making Ireland British*.

[8] A process already begun in Thompson, 'Mapping'.

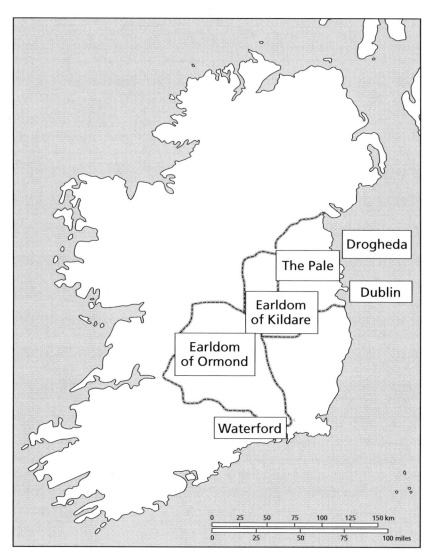

Figure 12.1 Map: Fifteenth-century Ireland: areas of Hiberno-English scribal activity.

literary culture that generally reflects an interest in Franciscan practices and Irish marcher culture, particularly in the Kildare and Waterford areas (see Figure 12.1).[9] The religious and didactic verse and other satirical and parodic items in the manuscript are nearly all written in either Latin or English, and there is only one French item (*The Walling of New Ross*).[10] While the occasional deployment of Irish language

[9] Benskin, 'The Hands of the Kildare Poems' Manuscript'; Lucas (ed.), *Anglo-Irish Poems*; Heuser (ed.), *Die Kildare-Gedichte*.

[10] For details of Anglo-Norman survivals, see Dolan, 'Writing in Ireland', 214–16.

loanwords for texts written in all three of the languages might easily be taken as set-tling questions of provenance and early readership for the collection as a whole, that evidence is sporadic and far from straightforward.[11] The items gathered in BL, MS Harley 913 frequently challenge the generic and tonal expectations of their read-ers and hearers, and appreciating the texts in the manuscript requires alertness to the subtleties of wordplay and translation. Such subtleties might well be taken as a 'Franciscan' trait, or as a feature of 'archipelagic' or 'marcher' literary culture – the three are not mutually exclusive – but quite for what purpose BL, MS Harley 913 was put together, where and by whom its items were copied, and the nature of the exemplars used, are all issues that remain open for debate.

On the other hand, the original production method deployed by the copyist of BL, MS Harley 913 seems clear enough.[12] Its items were transcribed into gather-ings of widely varying size, ranging from a series of single bifolia to quires of fours and eights, and even including one quire of ten. These once formed at least five unbound booklets. The items in some of these booklets had already proved sus-ceptible to damage by 1608, when Sir James Ware the elder (d. 1632) transcribed selected material incompletely from the manuscript into a small quire that even-tually formed part of BL, MS Lansdowne 418. Since Ware's time, the manuscript has suffered even further losses and disarrangement. By the time it was assembled for its current binding, some of the material Ware had found and was only able to copy with some difficulty had disappeared completely from BL, MS Harley 913. Moreover, the outer leaves of undamaged quires had been used as protective wrap-pers for their more vulnerable neighbours, thereby disturbing the sense order of the items copied and disguising the fascicular nature of the original production.

The reconstruction of the booklets of BL, MS Harley 913 offers a number of fur-ther clues as to the history of the material. Booklet four (ff. 54, 62, 63 and 49) was formed by just two bifolia. Folio 54r was left blank but the remaining space in the quire now preserves two Middle English poems with possible South-West Midlands associations, the first beginning 'Elde makiþ me geld' (*IMEV* 718), on ff. 54v, 62r, and the second beginning 'Whan erth haþ erþ iwonne wiþ wow' (*IMEV* 3939) on ff. 62r–63v, preserving both a Middle English and a Latin translated version of the 'earth upon earth' theme (the latter using *terra*, *vesta* and *humus* in place of the ME wordplay on 'erth'); these are followed by three short Latin items, namely: verse beginning 'Lolla, lolla parvule, cur fles tam amare' (f. 63v), apparently linked to 'Lollai lollai litil child, whi wepistou so sore' (*IMEV* 2025), on ff. 32r–v in booklet two; a text on the vices and virtues (ff. 49r–v); an incest riddle in the form of an *exor-dium* deploying women's names of Gaelic Irish origin ('nota de muliere que peperit puerum qui fuit filius eius …', f. 49v); and a short note by way of exemplum on an orchard-keeper who failed to share his apple crop with three gatekeepers ('nota de illo qui fuit in pomerio et parcavit poma …', f. 49v). A marginal note at the beginning of 'Lollai' on f. 32r in booklet two, underlined in red, reads 'require ista in latino xij folio [seek these things in Latin, the twelfth folio]'. The note is the only remaining hint that that booklet may have once been followed by booklet four in the unbound collection, since that further rearrangement would have resulted in the distance of just twelve folia between the English version and the Latin *Lolla* item that seems to have once been indicated by the scribe.

The two items on mortality in booklet four and the lullaby in booklet two are among the earliest examples of imaginative English vernacular writing in their respective genres. The copies in BL, MS Harley 913 have been described as 'Gedichte welche nachweisbar auf fremden Vorlagen von abweichendem Dialeckte beruhen [poems depending on foreign models in a different dialect]'.[13] Some hint that such material was accommodated in a receptive early home in BL, MS Harley 913 is given by the copyist's textual glosses for *Elde* and 'Whan erth haþ erþ'. On column b of f. 54v, in his copy of *Elde*, he writes in Latin 'id est puer [that is, a boy]' above the Middle English word 'schenlon [rascal]', at a point corresponding to line 40 in its modern edition, while 'bi schrew [(he) evokes a curse]' on the same line is glossed 'id est deuil [that is, sorrow]'. There is further explanatory marginal commentary by the copyist of BL, MS Harley 913 in 'Whan erth haþ erþ': 'frow [fragile]' is glossed 'festine' (line 3); 'muntid [(it) determines]' is glossed 'metitur' (line 12); 'all þat þou in erþ wonne [all your material gains]' is glossed 'lucrataris' (line 23); 'gethit [(it) achieves]' is glossed 'lucratur' (line 25); and over 'bilt [(it) builds]' the copyist writes, in red, in English 'biliþ' (line 46). Such unusually close attention to detail is striking because of the presumed early date of the copies in BL, MS Harley 913. Indeed, the text of 'Whan erth haþ erþ' can claim to be one of the two earliest surviving versions of this much-copied and revised English text; its only possible rival in this respect is a short extract copied (possibly from memory?) in BL, MS Harley 2253, a manuscript of about the same date, on this occasion from the Anglo-Welsh Marches, and copied by a scribe who shared with the copyist of BL, Harley 913 an occasionally scurrilous fascination with Latin, French and Middle English satire and parody, and also his general religious and didactic interests and his inclination to gather up and preserve locally produced material on near-contemporary historical and political topics.[14] Similar English and Latin religious and didactic material was also the stock in trade of later preachers' notebooks, and these texts from BL, MS Harley 913 bear particularly close comparison to items copied, *c.*1372, by the Norfolk Franciscan

---

[13] Heuser (ed.), *Die Kildare-Gedichte*, 167.

[14] Discussion and references in Thompson, 'Mapping', 124–6; see also Fein (ed.), *Studies in the Harley Manuscript*.

John of Grimestone in his manuscript (NLS, MS Advocates' 18.7.21).[15] More generally one might readily assume that the scribal copies of Latin and English texts based on 'foreign' models in BL, MS Harley 913 are derived from texts originally brought out of England by a new wave of fourteenth-century settlers well versed in the leisure-time and professional reading interests of English preacher poets. These texts presumably bear witness to the early and successful absorption of that inherited material into a polyglot 'Irish' context where similar Latin and vernacular writings were also already being produced and disseminated among sympathetic and scholarly Anglophone readers.

Other examples of such materials in Ireland enjoy less certain contexts. The survival of a fifteenth-century vellum strip preserving two stray lyrics, one a secular love lyric (*IMEV* 1010) and the other a macaronic poem warning against pride (*IMEV* 2774) in the so-called Ormond Manuscript, once held in Kilkenny Castle but now Dublin, National Library of Ireland, MS D1435, or of the slates excavated at Smarmore, Co. Louth (now Dublin, National Museum of Ireland, 1961/8–56 and 1963/89–91) that are inscribed with both Latin and English texts – the English mainly consisting of scraps of medical recipes – are poignant reminders of Anglophone Irish literary worlds that we have now almost irredeemably lost.[16] Of course, one can also only guess for the later medieval period as a whole at the number of Hiberno-English parodic and satiric works, secular, religious and didactic lyrics, preachers' notes, *aides-mémoires*, herbals and medical recipes, charms, epistolary items, written reports, polemical tracts, annals and family records, and basically all of the other kinds of written material that it is possible to think of, that have now disappeared from sight but might once have documented more fully the experience of reading and writing for leisure and for information in the period *c.*1350–*c.*1500 in the Lordship of Wexford, the Earldoms of Desmond, Ormond, Kildare and Ulster, or the other 'obedient shires' that eventually became known as the English Pale.

To demonstrate the obvious point that English texts preserved in Hiberno-English Latinate settings occasionally held enormous symbolic cultural value for their earliest readers, we can see the survival of BL, MS Harley 3724. The manuscript is dated *c.*1300, and its main item is a Latin copy of the first version of *Topographia Hibernica*, written *c.*1186–7 by Gerald of Wales (Giraldus Cambrensis), a work that Gerald publicized through a series of readings in Oxford (*c.*1188 or 1189?).[17] This item is accompanied in the manuscript by a number of short satires and goliardic

---

[15] Wilson, *A Descriptive Index of the English Lyrics in John of Grimestone's Preaching Book*; Wenzel, *Preachers, Poets*, esp. 101–73.

[16] For a useful codicological survey (although the Ormond lyrics are not mentioned), see Boffey, *Manuscripts of English Courtly Love Lyrics*, esp. 6–33. For the Smarmore survivals, see Britton and Fletcher, 'Medieval Hiberno-English Inscriptions'.

[17] Giraldus Cambrensis, *Opera v.*

items, including a liturgical parody based on the story of the Seven Sleepers of Ephesus and a fabliau-style account of a lecherous monk, versions of which are also found in BL, MS Harley 913. Such material is fitting company for the *Topographia Hibernica*, since, as well as demonstrating an ethnographic curiosity regarding Irish Gaelic culture and human and animal behaviour that was occasionally based on first-hand observation and often sensationalized, Gerald's writing was sometimes couched in the form of comfortable theological moralizations and allegories that would have been appreciated by most twelfth- and thirteenth-century Latin satirical writers and their readers. Not unnaturally, the Ireland of the *Topographia Hibernica* is seen from a Geraldine perspective, that is, from the point of view of half-victorious English conquerors of Gaelic Ireland after a sustained period of warfare and colonization. Partly because of his own self-promotional efforts, Gerald's writings on Ireland quickly seem to have become iconic works that were frequently revived, translated and exploited over the next 400 years for propaganda, especially during the century leading up to the strenuous Elizabethan efforts to justify renewed colonial ambitions in Ireland. As such, the *Topographia Hibernica* was sometimes preserved in carefully illuminated copies, such as the deluxe early text in BL, MS Royal 13.B.viii (*c*.1196–*c*.1223?). The survival of such copies makes the heavily drawn border work and skilfully executed illustrations accompanying the Hiberno-English copy in BL, MS Harley 3724 look relatively crude by comparison, but this later Latin copy seems important since its relatively early date means that it stands at the head of the vernacular processes of revival, translation and exploitation that were to mark Hiberno-English literary production and reading on the English conquest of Ireland for centuries.

The copyist of BL, MS Harley 3724 transcribed another Latin item of particular Hiberno-Irish interest on ff. 48r–49r. This is a version of the papal bull *Laudabiliter*, first recorded by Matthew Paris but also provided by Gerald of Wales, whereby the English Pope Adrian IV (Nicholas Breakspear, d. 1159) controversially granted Ireland to Henry II, thus endorsing the English military campaign that resulted in the submission of the Irish kings in 1171.[18] Immediately following *Laudabiliter*, on f. 49r, is recorded a Hiberno-English text of the Apostles' Creed beginning 'I bileue in god fadir almichty sshipper of heuene and of eorþe' (not identified in *IMEV* or its revision); it is followed on f. 49v by a twelve-line item headed 'Pater Noster in anglico', similar to the eighteen-line version (*IMEV* 2703) found in the fourteenth-century miscellany of mainly Latin theological material, prayers and devotions by various clerical hands in CUL, MS Gg.4.32 (not of Irish provenance). The expanded Pater Noster text in the latter manuscript is immediately followed by four lines in praise of the Virgin (*IMEV* 1064), then an unexceptional couplet

---

[18] Simms, 'The Norman Invasion'.

version of the Creed (*IMEV* 1282), all preceded by a set of three other short moral aphorisms in couplets on the same page (*IMEV* 476; 3201; 3248). In BL, MS Harley 3724, by contrast, the Anglophone versions of the Creed and Pater Noster in this predominantly Latin collection are placed in a far more exceptional and obviously meaningful Hiberno-English setting, at least insofar as they have been selected as items celebrating English vernacular associations with key texts conveying two of the most fundamental tenets of the Christian faith and located next to *Laudabiliter*, the Latin text that represents the origins of the justification for English governance of Ireland. The sequence of Latin and English vernacular items that is thus created obviously links issues of political power and control in Ireland to Anglophone versions of the basic principles of Christian belief.

The 'Geraldine' view of Irish history promulgated by Gerald of Wales was consolidated in the fifteenth century by the translation into Hiberno-English prose of the *Expugnacio Hibernica* (1189), his other seminal work on Ireland that explained and justified to its first readers and hearers how and why the establishment of English lordship in Ireland was necessary.[19] At least seven manuscripts of the translation of the *Expugnacio Hibernica* (now known to scholars as the *English Conquest of Ireland*) have survived: an early fifteenth-century text in BodL, MS Rawl. B.490, localized to Waterford in *LALME*; a linguistically and textually close copy also localized to Waterford made about fifty years later, now in London, Lambeth Palace, MS 598; a late fifteenth-century text with Meath associations, now in BL, MS Add. 40674; a mid fifteenth-century fragmentary extract, now forming the last leaf in BodL, MS Laud misc. 526, a manuscript also with early Meath associations; an unlocalized fifteenth-century copy in Dublin, Trinity College, MS 592, and another unlocalizable sixteenth-century copy, now Dublin, Trinity College, MS 593, that may have been derived from the text in Dublin, Trinity College, MS 592; and, finally, another sixteenth-century version transcribed for the 'Book of Howth', now London, Lambeth Palace, MS 623.

The fifteenth-century texts in BodL, MS Rawl. B.490 and London, Lambeth Palace, MS 598 are both localized by *LALME* in Waterford, and have been characterized as texts produced for 'communities whose book production was almost exclusively for local consumption … most of the exemplars would by hypothesis have been locally produced'.[20] The hypothesis itself might be applied to patterns of book production in many different geographical regions in England, so, in most important respects, it seems an oversimplification that may even distort the true nature of the limited available evidence. Waterford was an important trading port and gateway to Ireland, and, by the fifteenth century, some of its religious houses had long been associated with polyglot reading communities that shared Anglophone literary

[19] Furnivall (ed.), *The English Conquest of Ireland*.
[20] Benskin and Laing, 'Translations and *Mischsprachen*', 101, n.15.

interests with the rest of English-speaking Ireland and the scholarly world beyond. This view for the earlier period is supported by the likely Waterford provenance of some of the items in BL, MS Harley 913, or the survival of the few very early fourteenth-century English lyric scraps (*IMEV* 228.8; 1047; 2641), copied anonymously by some of the brethren of St John of Jerusalem, or their associates, in the Waterford house of the knights hospitaller, on what is now f. 22r in CCCC, MS 405.[21] In the later period, the city seems to have remained an important centre for the reading, writing, copying and distribution of Hiberno-English texts. For example, the copyist of BodL, MS Rawl. B.490 also transcribed in the same manuscript a text of James Yonge's *The Governance of Princes*, a Hiberno-English translation completed about 1422 and derived from a late thirteenth-century French version of the *Secreta Secretorum*.[22] Yonge's source was probably completed at the University of Paris with the assistance of a Walloon-speaking copyist by another Irishman originally from Waterford, the Dominican friar known as Jofroi de Waterford.[23] Similarly to the copyist of BodL, MS Rawl. B. 490, the copyist of Dublin, Trinity College, MS 592 also preserves copies of *The Conquest of Ireland* and *The Governance of Princes* within one collection, both probably unlocalizable, sadly, and the latter now a fragment. Finally, Yonge's text is extant in London, Lambeth Palace, MS 633, another manuscript that can be localized to Waterford but copied about a generation after Yonge's translation had first been made. The text in this manuscript is both linguistically and textually close to the earlier copy in BodL, MS Rawl. B.490.

The dedication in both these Waterford texts of *The Governance of Princes* is addressed 'to yow noble and gracious lord iamys de butler erle of ormound lyttenant of our lege lord king henry þe f<r>yfte in irland humely recomenddith hym your poer servant iamys yonge to your hey lordshippe …' (London, Lambeth Palace, MS 633, f. 1r). The gist of this information is also repeated by Sir James Ware Jr (1594–1666) in his *De Scriptoribus Hiberniae* (Dublin, 1639), where he describes how Yonge was commissioned to write a text described as 'Monita Politica de bono Regimine' for Ormond, the fourth Earl, when he was Lord Lieutenant of Ireland (a position he held in 1420, 1425 and 1442). Yonge's concluding lines, as reported by the copy in BodL, MS Rawl. B.490, apparently confirm that *The Governance of Princes* was a work completed on instruction, since his final address is to Butler as the patron 'whyche this boke to translate me comaundet' (f. 72r). The detail, though slight, is particularly interesting since Butler is also known to have patronized the Gaelic copyists who transcribed the *Martyrology of Óengus*, the *Acallam na Senórach* ('tales of the ancients', from the Fenian Cycle) and a *dindensenchus* (an onomastic census), all material in Irish now preserved on twelve leaves of vellum that have been inserted

---

[21] Sinclair, 'Anglo-Norman at Waterford'.
[22] Steele (ed.), *Three Prose Versions of the Secreta Secretorum*, 121–248.
[23] Hunt, 'Waterford, Jofroi of'.

in *Leabhar na Rátha* ('the book of the ringfort'), now BodL, MS Laud misc. 610.[24] As the fourth Earl of Ormond, Butler is also credited with being the first Hiberno-English governor to appoint a *brehon* (a judge for Irish Brehon law) to assist in civil law suits regulating property contracts and inheritance matters under his governance. If, indeed, it really was Butler's choice as Lord Lieutenant of Ireland to select James Yonge to translate the *Secreta Secretorum* into English, then this may indicate something of Butler's genuine scholarly and political interests in both Gaelic and Anglophone legal history and literary culture.

Yonge was presumably an obvious choice for the task of translation. He was a member of an English settler family residing in St John's parish, Dublin, and, although described as 'clerk, notary public' in documents dated March 1405, by 1422, he may well have already been in Butler's employ as a notary or private secretary.[25] As such (and true to form) *The Governance of Princes* exhorts Ormond to listen to wise counsel, just as Alexander, the ruler of the whole world in his time, heeded his teacher Aristotle's wisdom and thereby earned the obedience of his people. Yonge promises a version of Aristotle's wisdom in a book 'entremedelid with many good ensamplis of olde stories, And with the foure cardynale vertues, and dyuers othyr good matturis, and olde ensamplis and new'. Several of Yonge's interpolated anecdotes have been extracted from various scholarly sources, but the most interesting are derived, in quasi-journalistic fashion, from Yonge's understanding of the relatively recent history of the English conquest of Ireland: Sir Stephen Scrope's late change of heart in abandoning what Yonge characterizes as extortionate behaviour as Lord Deputy of Ireland under the lordship of Thomas, Duke of Clarence (whose charge Ormond was also under in his youth), is mentioned entirely favourably; so too is the success of Ormond's early military forays in Kildare, followed, later in the narrative, by reference to his recent armed exploits in Dundalk and Drogheda (that Yonge dates to 1422, practically the same date as his translation was completed). Also lauded is the wisdom of Henry II's much earlier twelfth-century military and diplomatic dealings with the Gaelic kings and princes that Yonge acknowledges he has found reported in Gerald. He inserts this material in his translation just before turning his attention to a chapter entitled 'of the Kynges tytles to the lande of Irland aftyr the cronycles' where information, again largely derived from Gerald, is used to illustrate the virtue of princely fortitude, basically following a line of argument that insists English might equals right.

Texts of either or both of *The Conquest of Ireland* and *The Governance of Princes* were read far beyond Waterford and well into the next century but probably never strayed far from local centres of English power and influence in Ireland. Perhaps BL, MS Add. 40674 is the best example of just how important continuing gentry

---

[24] O'Sullivan and O'Sullivan, 'Three Notes on Laud Misc. 610'.
[25] Dolan, 'Yonge, James'.

interest in the history of the English conquest in Ireland was for ensuring the survival of at least some part of the fifteenth-century Hiberno-English written record. The manuscript is in two parts that were bound together early, but no earlier than at some point in the first half of the sixteenth century, since part one preserves an abbreviated sixteenth-century version of Christopher Pembridge's *Annales Hiberniae*, covering the years 1162–1370 but expanded on ff. 44r–53v with additional material copied experimentally by an anonymous second hand in an inserted quire of ten, with many remaining blanks. On ff. 54v–55v, a passage outlining the right and title of the English kings is followed by *obits* of prominent sixteenth-century members of the Darcy, de Lacy and de Greville families. Intermarriage by members of these gentry households seems to have been a feature commonly recorded in the notices, which are usually in the hand of Philip Flattisbury from Johnstown, near Naas in Co. Kildare.[26] Flattisbury was a prominent landowner and indefatigable antiquary who occasionally roamed around Irish gentry households in peripatetic fashion, as annalist, copyist and secretary, often working on commission for the eighth and ninth Earls of Kildare, governors of Ireland under Henry VII and Henry VIII. The first part of BL, MS Add. 40674 contains a useful record of Flattisbury's engagement with local gentry culture, as well as with Irish annals and historical records, scholarly preoccupations that are also confirmed by the survival of an impressive number of other examples of his archival work in other extant manuscripts. His work in the first part of BL, MS Add. 40674 was eventually bound up with the fifteenth-century copy of the *Conquest of Ireland*, now commencing on f. 67r at the beginning of the second part of the manuscript. Near the end of the book, on f. 105r, the fifteenth-century *obit* of John Darcy of Platten, Co. Meath (d. 1 January 1482) has been recorded, followed, on the next leaf, by a roughly drawn version of the Darcy shield of arms that is at least a little more successfully drawn than the other attempt to draw the arms, also recorded on the same page (f. 106r). For a short time prior to this yoking of two versions of Irish history and English conquest, part two of BL, MS Add. 40674 had presumably enjoyed the status of being independently produced and probably unbound 'Darcy' quires.[27] That these quires have now avoided destruction seems down to a mixture of good fortune and a strong sixteenth-century scholarly interest in preserving the information that they contain.

The other manuscripts under discussion here seem to have enjoyed similarly fortunate later histories. BodL, MS Laud misc. 526 preserves a note on f. 41v 'Isto liber constat domino Willielmo preston Vicecomite De Gormanston' that indicates early ownership of the volume by the Preston family in Gormanstown, Co. Meath, prior to the book reaching William Camden, who gave it to Sir George Carew in

---

[26] Nicholls, 'Flattisbury, Philip'.
[27] Verduyn, 'Darcy family'.

1619, who then bequeathed it to his son Sir Thomas Stafford.[28] London, Lambeth Palace, MSS 598, 623 and 633 also all became 'Carew' manuscripts in due course.[29] The second part of BodL, MS Rawl. B.490 contains a note on a flyleaf that it was 'ex dono Willielmi Geraldi Cancellarii Hiberniae' (f. ir), presumably indicating that that manuscript eventually formed part of the personal archive of notes and manuscript materials on Ireland that the former Lord Chancellor, Sir William Gerard (d. 1581), bequeathed on his deathbed (along with 'the treasure of a true heart') to Arthur, Lord Grey of Wilton (1536–93).[30] Gray had become the new Lord Deputy of Ireland in the previous year, with Edmund Spenser, the English poet, appointed to be his secretary. Gerard's gift could hardly have come at a better time since, for better or worse, Gray's new secretary was about to become much better known among sixteenth-century and seventeenth-century political commentators in Ireland as the author of *A View of the Present State of Ireland*.[31]

In the final section of this chapter, I want to consider the general nature and extent of the incoming and outgoing traffic in Middle English texts and manuscripts, particularly where this can be associated with Edmund Spenser's fifteenth-century predecessors and their associates, among whom can be numbered the personnel charged with securing English forms of bureaucratic order and civic governance in Ireland. Such a task is no less daunting in codicological terms than what has gone before in this chapter, largely because the evidence of dialect and manuscript provenance remains an uncertain guide to the kinds of Anglocentric literary interests and frontier culture that may once have flourished in such largely colonial administrative and legal contexts. Nevertheless, it is still possible to sketch in broad outline the important role played by Hiberno-English speakers and newcomers alike in sponsoring certain types of Anglophone literary production beyond England in the period. The most obvious examples of such activity are provided by the circumstances in which records of dramatic entertainments were kept, particularly in the two copies of the Corpus Christi pageant lists, both for 1498, in the Great Chain Book of the Dublin Corporation (Dublin, City Archives, 1/2/1, ff. 56v–57v), or, perhaps, in the scrappily presented text of *The Pride of Life* copied from an unknown source and inserted by two early fifteenth-century scribes in the fourteenth-century account roll for the Priory of the Holy Trinity, Dublin, a manuscript that was destroyed in the explosion and fire at the Four Courts in 1922.[32] It is salutary to note that although the fourteenth-century provenance of the

---

[28] Coxe, *Bodleian Library Quarto Catalogues, 2, Laudian Manuscripts*, 380–1, 568.

[29] Pickering and O'Mara, *IMEP, XIII*, 58–9.

[30] Lock, 'Grey, Arthur, Fourteenth Baron Grey of Wilton'.

[31] First published after a delay of thirty-five years in Ware, *The Historie of Ireland*. See Richard McCabe, *Spenser's Monstrous Regiment*, 270–87.

[32] Fletcher, *Drama, Performance and Polity*, 90–125; Davis (ed.), *Non-Cycle Plays and Fragments*, lxxxv–c, 90–105.

manuscript is well established, neither the identity and dialect of these later scribes nor their intended purpose in copying this sole extant copy of *The Pride of Life* can be determined with any degree of certainty.

Similarly uncertain evidence is provided by the intelligently illustrated copy of the C text of *Piers Plowman* in BodL, MS Douce 104.[33] This Hiberno-English copy has obviously leaked from the relatively cohesive group in South-West Midlands dialect to which the extant complete or near-complete C text manuscripts generally belong.[34] Not only does this copy uniquely offer its readers a roughly contemporary, fully illustrated version of Langland's poem, that may well have absorbed local Hiberno-English iconographical motifs, but it also preserves idiosyncratic textual features and other contemporary annotations suggesting that this copy is more likely than not to have been produced in Ireland. The main text seems the work of a professionally trained scribe used to writing in a current hand based on anglicana that indicates he was presumably better practised in copying official documents emanating from Westminster or Dublin than transcribing literary material of this kind.[35] It is clear that he must have enjoyed sustained access to his Langland exemplar, all the same, and that this was a convenience he probably shared with the visual artist who worked alongside him in the practically simultaneous production and finishing of the manuscript. Equally intriguing is the evidence that the ornamental designs by the artist of BodL, MS Douce 104 reveal an understanding of how major fifteenth-century English centres handled decorative initials and borderwork, features of the finished book that have been said to betray 'a mixture of conventional knowledge and what may be either idiosyncrasy or provincial unease in their execution'.[36]

Some of the other fifteenth-century literary manuscripts known to have been copied by scribes who are associated with Anglophone Ireland raise new kinds of challenges regarding the textual transmission and afterlives of northern Middle English religious works, the scribes who copied them, and the books that now preserve them. Longleat, MS 29 and BodL, MS e Musaeo 232 are both excellent cases in point.[37] Both were largely copied by the same main scribe writing in a Hiberno-English dialect that (similarly to that of the much earlier copyist of BL, MS Harley 913) preserves underlying South-East Midlands forms. This scribe writes in a practised style of current handwriting modelled on anglicana that one might naturally

---

[33] Pearsall and Scott (eds.), *Piers Plowman, A Facsimile of Bodleian Library, Oxford, MS Douce 104*; Kerby-Fulton and Despres, *Iconography and the Professional Reader*.

[34] Samuels, 'Langland's Dialect', esp. 239–40. For idiosyncratic textual features of BodL, MS Douce 104, see also Pearsall (ed.), *Piers Plowman: A New Annotated Edition of the C-Text*, notes to VI, 3; VII, 164; XXII, 221.

[35] Kerby-Fulton and Justice, 'Langlandian Reading Circles'; also Kerby-Fulton and Justice, 'Reformist Intellectual Culture'.

[36] Pearsall and Scott (ed.), *Piers Plowman: A Facsimile of Bodleian Library, Oxford, MS Douce 104*, XXXV.

[37] See the manuscript descriptions in Ogilvie-Thomson (ed.), *Richard Rolle*, xvii–xxxv.

also associate with professionally trained government clerks. Both manuscripts he compiled can be classified as religious miscellanies likely to have had sufficiently broad appeal for a range of devout and literate audiences but with their items also showing signs of having once attracted the particular attention of female readers. Longleat, MS 29 is the larger and more varied of the two. Alongside its series of Latin and English epistles, visions, prayers, expositions and meditations on purgatory, Corpus Christi, the Signs of Death, the Lord's Prayer (accompanied by a litany naming several Irish saints), forms of confession, Marian laments and penitential items (including Chaucer's Parson's tale), it contains a series of verse and prose works associated with Richard Rolle, including his three English epistles, *The Form of Living*, *Ego Dormio* and *The Commandment*, and a series of shorter pieces in prose and verse. These are all apparently dedicated in a colophon to 'Margaretam reclusam de Kyrkby de amore dei [recluse of Kyrkeby for the love of God]' and may well have been derived ultimately from an autograph collection presented to Rolle's favourite female disciple. Copying of Longleat, MS 29 appears to have been completed at some date after 1422, with the signature 'Goldewell' on f. 168r supporting the view that the book soon passed into the ownership of John Goldwell, a fifteenth-century London mercer, upon whose death (1466) it probably then belonged to his daughter Elizabeth and, eventually, through the descendants of her second husband (who lived in the Warminster area), became the possession of Sir John Thynne, the sixteenth-century builder of Longleat House and founder of its library.[38] The litany naming Irish saints that is combined with the meditative exposition of the Lord's Prayer on ff. 19r–22r is certainly suggestive of an Irish provenance for this item, but it remains an open question how Goldwell obtained the manuscript so soon after it had first been copied and whether he or other metropolitan family members may have once had some closer connection to Irish affairs than is now apparent.

BodL, MS e Musaeo 232 was copied by the same Hiberno-English scribe and contains a meditation on the Passion, attributed to Rolle, a treatise on humility associated with St Bernard, *The Mirror of St Edmund*, and two short items also copied in Longleat, MS 29 on ff. 147r–149r, namely, a so-called 'devout prayere' on the Passion (*IMEV* 1761) and a short prose meditation and accompanying prayers inspired by the cult of the Five Wounds. The 'devout prayere' seems to offer a larger meditative model for a form of imaginative textual composition, linking author, scribe and audience in a celebration of 'the conceptual conjunction of text, page and reader, material culture and affective reflexivity'.[39] The repeated copying of both this item and the material on the Five Wounds following it by the same copyist is therefore interesting and suggestive, particularly since both manuscripts in which

[38] Ibid., xx–xxi.
[39] Kelly and Thompson, 'Imagined Histories of the Book', 2 and the extended analysis of this item, 2–5.

the short devotional sequence survives show signs of having caught the attention of two different sets of later readers. In the case of Longleat, MS 29, the signature 'Goldewell' was added, as indicated above, and the collection has also had new 'devout prayers' inserted by two anonymous but near-contemporary later fifteenth-century copyists where spaces still remained available in the assembled book.[40] On f. 69r in BodL, MS e Musaeo 232 are the signatures 'Annes hemperby', 'Annes helperby' (repeated) and 'Elyzabethe Stoughton', these names occurring together with the opening phrases of the Ave Maria, all written by late fifteenth-century hands that remain unidentified, while the text of *The Mirror of St Edmund* in the same manuscript is also signed at the end, in red, with the name 'Jon Flemmyn' in another roughly contemporary hand (f. 62r). The manuscript rubrication ends at this point, indicating that Flemmyn may well have been the manuscript rubricator, but quite how this or any of the other possible evidence of reader engagement links back to the original Hiberno-English copyist, or the specific types of devotional enthusiasm encouraged by the items he copied – some of which Flemmyn probably once rubricated – remains an open question.

By coincidence, the name of John Fleming ('Johannes Fleming hunc librum composuit [composed this book]') is also found copied by a seventeenth-century hand in Dublin, Trinity College, MS 156 containing a fifteenth-century Hiberno-English copy of *The Prick of Conscience* (*IMEV* 1193, 3428, 3429), copied in current hand modelled on anglicana by two Dublin scribes, followed by the second scribe's text of Richard Maidestone's *Seven Penitential Psalms* (*IMEV* 1961).[41] It seems unlikely that the John Fleming referred to in the note was a seventeenth-century reader claiming to have composed the fifteenth-century book, although the heavily stained opening leaf of the manuscript was evidently subject to some later scribal repair, perhaps around the same time as the note was added on f. 1r. On the other hand, the Fleming ascription is found on the same page as the opening of a seventeenth-century Dublin deed dated 1618 that mentions the name of James Ware as a beneficiary (ff. 1r–v). This may be a reference to one of the two Irish antiquarians of that name, father and son, both of whom were active at the time of the reported Dublin property transaction.[42] Ware Jr, who first printed Spenser's *View*, was apparently just as fascinated as his father with establishing the identities and achievements of even earlier writers in Ireland, and the note may well have been added by a legal associate of the family who shared their antiquarian interests and had identified Fleming as the book's original compiler. One would like some further corroborating evidence that this was indeed the case, but there is at least a reasonably strong possibility that the note in Dublin, Trinity College, MS 156 refers to the same fifteenth-century

[40] Ogilvie-Thomson (ed.), *Richard Rolle*, xviii–xix.
[41] Lewis and McIntosh, *A Descriptive Guide*, 51–2.
[42] Parry, 'Ware, Sir James'.

Dublin book producer whose name survives in the rubricated colophon in BodL, MS Bodley e Musaeo 232.

The text in Dublin, Trinity College, MS 156 is one of three extant manuscripts of *The Prick of Conscience* that can be localized to Ireland, the other two being Cambridge, Magdalene College, MS F.4.18 and Manchester, Chetham's Library, MS Mun. A.4.103, both associated on dialect evidence with the area of Co. Louth.[43] These last two manuscripts are characterized as Group II manuscripts of the Main Version of *The Prick of Conscience* and are not only textually closely related to each other but also to three other Group II manuscripts, including Dublin, Trinity College, MS 158.[44] This manuscript was originally copied in the early years of the fifteenth century in a North Lancashire dialect but now has later fifteenth-century associations that link it to the Preston family of Gormanstown, Co. Meath (whose ownership of the fragment in BodL, MS Laud misc. 526 of James Yonge's *Conquest of Ireland* was mentioned earlier) and other names associated with the area of Killeen, Co. Meath. This coincidence brings the discussion full circle, since it is evident from the limited remaining codicological evidence that the religio-didactic and historico-political reading interests of fifteenth-century English settler households in the Pale area north of Dublin were satisfied in a number of different ways by books 'beyond' England. As such, the 'obedient shires' of Meath and Louth emerge alongside Dublin and Kildare as an important geographical region in the history of English manuscript production, book ownership, reception and reading for the period *c*.1350–*c*.1500. The vernacular literary writings that can now be associated with the area, or with regions just beyond the Pale, not unnaturally mediated a localized Anglocentric belief system that has now been largely obliterated from view but may once have represented a significant cultural intervention in Anglo-Irish cultural affairs. Such writings were sponsored by some of the most influential stakeholders responsible for the development and consolidation of English models of civic, administrative and legal governance and security, or the even earlier processes of subinfeudation, motte construction and manorialization in Irish frontier society. In sum, the socioliterary milieux in which books beyond England were written and transmitted in Anglophone Ireland presumably provided, through the books themselves, significant markers of identity and ownership.

[43] Lewis and McIntosh, *A Descriptive Guide*, 39–40 (Cambridge) and 87 (Manchester).
[44] Ibid., 53–4.

13

English books and the continent

DAVID RUNDLE

When the Holy Roman Emperor, Charles V, entered London in June 1522, lavish entertainments were arranged to welcome and impress the imperial entourage.[1] One of that number, however, took at least some hours away from the festivities to wander through the bookshops that congregated around St Paul's. The courtier was best known for his parentage: Hernan Colón's father was Christopher Columbus.[2] While the father expanded knowledge of the world, the son wanted to gather learning together in his own book collection; the explorer's offspring was a librarian manqué, using his travels with the emperor to buy up books wherever he went, which he then catalogued time and again.[3] During his brief visit to London, Colón added to his library by purchasing over 200 books.[4] These included volumes from England's earliest printing presses: among them, an Aristotelian commentary by Alexander of Hales printed by Oxford's first printer, Theoderic Rood; two books, including a work of John Fisher's printed the previous year in Cambridge, by John Siberch; at least half a dozen printings for which Wynkyn de Worde was responsible, including

---

[1] Anglo, *Spectacle, Pageantry and Early Tudor Policy*, 182–206; Kipling, '"A Horse Designed by Committee"'; Robertson, 'L'Entrée de Charles Quint à Londres'.

[2] On Colón, see the full introduction to Marín Martínez et al., *Catálogo Concordado*, 1.19–309, and McDonald, *The Print Collection of Ferdinand Columbus*, 1.18–57. I would like to record my thanks to the late Klaus Wagner for his kindness when I visited Seville and the Colombina in 1994.

[3] The two most significant catalogues that Colón produced of his library are available in facsimile: Huntingdon (ed.), *Catalogue of the Library of Ferdinand Columbus*; Colón, *Abecedarium B*. The recent volumes of the *Catálogo Concordado* follow the numbering of *Registrum B* (only up to no. 1200), gathering together Colón's various descriptions of his books, and they should be used alongside the *Registrum* itself, which I cite below. For more on Colón's library, we can look forward to William Sherman's work on Renaissance libraries.

[4] Rhodes, 'Don Fernando Colón', lists eighty volumes because he confined himself to discussion of those that are now extant. As he himself noted, there were previously more; the full list can be compiled by a search of *Registrum B*. Christianson, 'The Rise of London's Book-Trade', 144, talks of Colón buying eighty books and suggests that the stationer John Taverner might have been the Spaniard's supplier, but there is no certainty that Colón bought his manuscripts all in one purchase, and the high number of books bought might militate against there having been a single supplier.

Robert Whittington's epigrams; and about double that number from the press of Richard Pynson.[5]

Rood of Cologne, de Worde *de ducatu Lothoringie*, Siberch of Siegburg and Pynson from Normandy: their names are a reminder that the pioneers of printing in England were primarily foreigners. England may have been unusual in the wider European context inasmuch as its first printer was one of its own nation, albeit one whose trading activities had seen him resident on the continent for more than a decade and a half. It was more typical in that Germans dominated the spread of this specifically teutonic invention in its earliest decades. The efforts of those continental printers who established themselves in London or in Oxford or, later, Cambridge were not enough, however, to sate the English taste for printed books. When Colón went in search of books in London, he was able to buy a short address to the new pope, Adrian VI, printed in Cologne earlier the same year, as well as older volumes from presses in the German lands, the Low Countries, France and Italy.[6] His ability to buy such a range reflected established practice. The first imports of printed books were by individual English travellers wishing to supplement their manuscript collections, but a speculative trade in shipping books to England developed before the first printing press crossed the Channel.[7] It may be that the earliest import of printed books for sale was transacted by the Cologne merchant Gerhard von Wesel, in 1466 or 1467.[8] It was soon commonplace for barrels of books to find space in a ship's hold alongside other commodities. To cite just one example, in June 1481, a Venetian galley docked in London with a small quantity of presumably (from their low value) unbound books to supplement its cargo of spices, sugar, soap and sponges, wax and silk, plus, in this veritable ark, two hens and two monkeys.[9] In that instance, the importer was a Florentine recorded as John de Barde, a member of the long-established Bardi family who had had the honour of being bankrupted by Edward III. John de Barde can stand as an example – alongside, say, Peter Actoris

---

[5] On Rood: Rhodes, 'Don Fernando Colón', no. 2; Siberch: Colón's copies do not survive but are noted at *Registrum B*, nos. 408 and 701 (*STC* 10898 and 16896); de Worde: Rhodes, 'Don Fernando Colón', nos. 57, 78, with, in addition, *Registrum B*, nos. 682, 827, 953 and 1069 (*STC* 268.3, 4601, 15579.4–8 and 25540.5); Pynson: Rhodes, 'Don Fernando Colón', nos. 18, 38, 39, 47, 49, with, in addition, *Registrum B*, nos. 10, 447, 693, 702, 738 and 914 (*STC* 14789, 25585, 13807, 4659 and 5639, with no exact match for *Registrum B*, no. 914 which Colón says was printed by Pynson in 1516: see *STC* 23156 etc). Note that this list is by no means exhaustive, relying mainly on Colón's own identification of editions.

[6] Rhodes, 'Don Fernando Colón', no. 26, which is *Registrum B*, no. 768. For the older volumes, see Rhodes, 'Don Fernando Colón', *passim* and further discussion below.

[7] Examples of individual purchases are provided by Armstrong, 'English Purchases'; Lowry, 'The Arrival and Use of Continental Printed Books in Yorkist England'.

[8] Pollard and Ehrman, *The Distribution of Books by Catalogue*, 10. On the subject in general, I have found particularly useful Hellinga, 'Importation of Books', supplemented by Ford, 'Importation of Printed Books into England and Scotland', and Needham, 'The Customs Rolls'.

[9] Cobb (ed.), *The Overseas Trade of London*, 46–51.

of Savoy – for the fact that the import of books, like the wider trade patterns, linked together the British Isles with the Mediterranean.[10] For their printed reading matter, the English were most often indebted to a cosmopolitan web of continental merchants.

Yet even those early printed books that we might consider 'home-grown', because their place of publication was in England, owed more to foreigners than just the probability that their printer was German. Those who sold the books were often those who bound them, and, in the first decades of print, many stationer-bookbinders were immigrants like Nicholas Spierinck (perhaps of Antwerp) or, in Cambridge, Garrat Godfrey from Limburg, and, in the other university town, William Howbergh from Antwerp, or the native of Alstadt known by his anglicized name, John Dorne.[11] And if it was not unusual for readers to hold in their hands an 'English' book bound by an immigrant craftsman, it was an everyday occurrence for their fingers and thumbs, when turning a book's leaves, to be touching continental paper. Print's preference for paper over parchment necessarily increased English book production's reliance on imported materials. There was only one fifteenth-century attempt at setting up an English paper-mill (and that seemingly reliant on Italian know-how); it proved short-lived.[12] Far into the sixteenth century, printers in England found it made better commercial sense to use paper produced abroad – most often from Normandy or Piedmont – and imported.[13] The fabric of the early English printed book was unEnglish.

It might be thought that the dominance of continental materials and artisans was the function of the novelty of the technology of print, a passing phase which naturally declined as the skills became domesticated. It may, indeed, be that in absolute terms the proportion of foreigners involved in the book trade eventually declined, but equally significant was the relative shift in nationalities engaged in the trade, as the religious turmoil that began in the late 1510s came to alter the traffic in both books and people: where Germanic names had been most frequent and had been supplemented by characters who, like Pynson, hailed from Normandy, later in the century Frenchmen from a variety of regions were more prominent, in part because of the displacement of Huguenots from their homeland.

But it is not with the later period that I wish to make a comparison. Instead, I want to place the evidence from the first half-century of print in England with the decades preceding. Just as the roll-call of foreign printers is well-known, so it is generally recognized that there were many continental scribes and artists active

---

[10] On Actoris, see now Needham, 'Continental Printed Books Sold in Oxford'.

[11] Duff, *A Century of the English Book Trade*, 41, 56–7, 77, 151; Leedham-Green, Rhodes and Stubbings (eds.), *Garrett Godfrey's Accounts*; Pearson, *Oxford Bookbinding 1500–1640*, esp. 130–1, 133, 201–10.

[12] Stevenson, 'Tudor Roses'.

[13] Shorter, *Paper Mills and Paper Makers*, 27–8; Hellinga, 'Printing', 95–7.

in England earlier in the fifteenth century, and that many manuscripts of English provenance were imported products.[14] What has less often been done is to gather together these pieces of evidence from across the manuscript–print divide and to enquire of them whether there are any detectable patterns. The international nature of the English book is a phenomenon more acknowledged than analysed. Scattered through recent scholarship are instances of England's debt to the continent; this chapter will add only modestly to that store of vignettes. At the same time, it will question how far the map of continental involvement in English books altered over the chronological span covered by this volume; it will enquire how far the traffic was one way, from the mainland to the British Isles; it will ask what cachet might have accrued to foreign book producers and their work. It will ask such questions – but it will not pretend full answers can yet be given.

There are three caveats to pre-empt our discussion. The first concerns the physical limits of England and the implications for books of the shifting boundaries and changeable relations between the countries of the British Isles.[15] Equally relevant is the fact that, throughout the period from 1350 to the early sixteenth century, there was more than just a corner of a foreign field that was under the jurisdiction of the English crown. Even after the mid fifteenth-century loss of the Gascon inheritance and occupied Normandy, Calais remained as a residue (with attempts – admittedly lacklustre – at further expansion made at the end of our period, in the 1510s). Such continental settings could themselves provide loci for both the composition and the circulation of texts: consider, for example, the presence of John Lydgate and John Shirley in Lancastrian Paris, or the book-owners of late medieval Calais.[16] Despite the apparent promise in the title of this chapter of a strict dichotomy, a distinction between England and the continent was more a geographical than a political or intellectual reality.

Even the physical fact of British separation from the European mainland could be experienced in different ways. For many, the sea acted as a barrier, but for others it was a channel of contact. In terms of international trade, for all the cloth and wool exported from England, the country was subordinate in importance to the northern European entrepôt, the Low Countries. Merchant companies might set up a branch in London, but usually these were satellites to those in Bruges. Ships sailing from the Mediterranean might call at Bristol or Southampton, en route to the Low Countries. The patterns of trade were continually in flux, with the beginning of the sixteenth century seeing the rise of Antwerp at the expense of Bruges and the beginnings of London's development into a metropolis, but the methods of

---

[14] Note, in particular, the comments of Parkes, 'The Provision of Books', 415–17, and Parkes, *Their Hands before Our Eyes*, e.g., 41–2.

[15] On some of which, see Thompson, Chapter 12 above.

[16] Schirmer, *John Lydgate*, esp. 113–19; Connolly and Plumley, 'Crossing the Channel'; Boffey, 'Books and Readers in Calais'.

communication remained the same. So, when Erasmus's favourite scribe, the one-eyed Pieter Meghen of Brabant, criss-crossed the Channel finding employment on both sides of it, his activities reflected established practice.[17] In terms of trade, the seas that lapped around the English coast connected the island people with the continent.

The second caveat is related to the first; it concerns the languages of the English. During our period, there was movement in the constellation of England's three tongues: the use of French declining (but not disappearing); the English vernacular rising, if not to prestige, then to acceptance as a literary language; and Latin, even if it did not shine as brightly, remaining the lodestar of learned communication. There was movement, but the constellation – the combination of languages – remained a constant.[18] This chapter would cut itself short if it concentrated on books in Middle English. Some such volumes did travel abroad with their English owners and remain there: for instance, the poetic miscellany, including works of John Lydgate, that emigrated to Rome early in its life and settled at the English Hospice (now the English College).[19] Others reached foreign hands, like the copy of John Gower in the collection of Jaquette of Luxemburg, wife to John, Duke of Bedford, or the unspecified English books owned by her sister-in-law, Jacqueline of Bavaria.[20] But, unsurprisingly, the vast majority of transactions between the English and other Europeans was in the languages they had in common. When a visitor like Hernan Colón visited the book stalls of London, he could find enough to buy without having to venture too far beyond the confines of the *lingua franca* of Latin. He certainly bought one imported 'book in the French language in prose and verse'.[21] He also showed an interest in English subjects, picking up, for instance, a volume in Latin on the tenure of hundreds.[22] His only forays into the English vernacular were the rudimentary grammatical texts that he bought, in Latin and English, works by

---

[17] Trapp, 'Notes on Manuscripts written by Peter Meghen'; Trapp, 'Pieter Meghen'; Brown, 'The Date of Erasmus' Latin Translation of the New Testament'.

[18] For a stimulating study with ramifications far beyond its specific focus, see Catto, 'Written English', 24–59; see also, esp. on the continuing presence of French, Pearsall, 'The Idea of Englishness'.

[19] Rome, Venerabile Collegio Inglese, MS Liber 1405, on which see Robbins, 'A Middle English Diatribe', citing it incorrectly as MS 1306. Note that in *IMEV*, this manuscript is cited as MS A. 347.

[20] On Jaquette's copy of John Gower's *Confessio Amantis*, now Pembroke, Camb., MS 307, see Harris, 'Patrons, Buyers and Owners', 170–1. On the six books 'in Engelssche sprake' of Jacqueline of Bavaria (or Hainault), wife of Humfrey, Duke of Gloucester, see Wijsman, 'Gebonden weelde', 175–8, and his description of Bruxelles, Bibliothèque Royale, MS 9627–28 in Bousmanne, Van Hemelryck and Van Hoorebeeck (eds.), *La Librairie des ducs de Bourgogne*, III.125–32.

[21] The 'Liber in gallica lingua prosa & versa', a copy of Pierre Gringore, *Les Fantasies de mere sote* (Paris: Jean Petit, s.a.) is recorded at *Registrum B*, no. 1014. Note also the work of Gui Jouenneaux Colón bought for 3d and recorded at *Registrum B*, no. 1420: 'Guidonis Iuvenalis epistola de suo ingressu religionis latine et galice'.

[22] *Registrum B*, no. 683 (*STC* 7726.7, and re-dating it). Cf. *Registrum B*, no. 1392 (*STC* 7709), which Colón describes as being in Latin and English.

schoolmasters like John Stanbridge.[23] As with the cosmopolitan Colón, so too with us: the paragraphs that follow will concentrate not on the minority of books in the English vernacular but on volumes mainly in Latin and occasionally in French.

The final caveat is the obligatory historian's warning about the nature of our evidence. Books often lead secret lives which they hide from latter-day scrutiny. We will encounter cases when manuscripts go so far as to deceive: their script can don a national costume, only for us to discover that it is a guise. The tradition of palaeography tends to define scripts by nationality, but some bookhands achieved an international popularity that makes confident localization a specialism for risk-takers. Or the books can sit in supercilious silence, refusing to confirm or deny the provenance that probability or speculation suggest to us. Our sources are all too rarely pliable witnesses. That being the case, the judicious course is to provide a minimal interpretation, presenting examples only where the evidence is overwhelming. Even then, our subject is capacious.

The state of the evidence is particularly pertinent to identifying foreign artisans of the book at work in England. There has been significant attention recently paid to continental artists illuminating manuscripts in England, like Herman Scheerre or the so-called 'Caesar Master', although even in that area the best scholars warn that our knowledge is incomplete.[24] Here the focus is instead on foreign scribes. While their presence in England certainly has a prehistory before our period, the evidence becomes more plentiful from early in the fifteenth century, but whether this reflects simply an increase in their number at that point or a shift in scribal habit is open to question.[25] The definite proof of a scribe's location comes from colophons and those, as is well known, varied in popularity across Europe.[26] Some scribes' origins will be hidden by their preference for anonymity, and the balance between nationalities might thus be skewed. That said, for the two English university towns, where the information is greatest, it is undeniable that a cosmopolitan range of scribes left evidence of their presence, hailing from Sweden to Moravia, from Milan to León.[27]

[23] *Registrum B*, nos. 13, 14, 684 and 1015: *STC* 13835, 20438 (Rhodes, 'Don Fernando Colón', no. 57), one of *STC* 18872–18875, and one of *STC* 23178–23181.5. On the first of these, see also n.59 below.

[24] On Scheerre: Spriggs, 'Unnoticed Bodleian Manuscripts', and Spriggs, 'The Nevill Hours and the School of Hermann Scheere'; 'Caesar Master': Scott (ed.), *The Mirroure of the Worlde*, 41–4. For comment on the state of research, see Scott, *Later Gothic Manuscripts*, esp. 1.62–4, and Alexander, 'Foreign Illuminators'.

[25] Parkes, *Their Hands before Our Eyes*, 28 (with special reference to friars).

[26] On colophons generally, see Condello and De Gregorio (eds.), *Scribi e colofoni*, particularly the essay in that volume by Derolez, 'Pourquoi les copistes signaient-ils leurs manuscrits?'

[27] Tydemannus of Narken (Sweden) was in Cambridge in 1450, where he copied Cambridge, Peterhouse, MS 188 ([Bénédictins da Bouveret], *Colophons*, no. 18047; *DMCL*, no. 286); on Matheus de Moravia, see n.31 below; an unsigned manuscript by Stefano Surigone of Milan and localizable to Oxford on the basis of its illumination, survives as TCC, MS B.14.47, on which see Rundle, 'Of Republics and Tyrants', 331, 333. On Surigone more generally, see Rundle, *England and the Identity of*

The overwhelming majority, however, identified themselves as 'alamannus', a term covering both the German-speaking lands and the Low Countries. Teutonic dominance in the early decades of print was a pattern that certainly had precedents.[28] Occasionally, a scribe identified himself as a student, presumably supplementing his income with copying work, which, in some instances, may have become a career. Nicholaus de Bodelswerdia may be a case in point, if the scribe of that name who had mastered a humanist script by mid century is the same as the Oxford student who was compiling manuscripts in the late 1420s.[29] There also occurred a small diaspora of foreign scribes away from the universities into the employ of institutions and individuals, with the likes of Henry Mere moving, it seems, from Oxford to Christ Church, Canterbury, while Herman Zurke of Griefswald followed his master, Gilbert Kymer, sometime Chancellor of Oxford University, to the cathedral precinct of Salisbury.[30]

We might wonder whether the alien nationality of a scribe mattered to an employer: was it merely incidental or was it at times itself a selling-point? Some commissioners perhaps did have a preference for alien scribes: Richard Broune, alias Cordone, appears to have been such a person, mentioning in his will two scribes, one being 'Mattheus scriptor meus' (identified as Matheus de Moravia), the other 'Iacobus de Selerhalle Teutonicus'.[31] If there were a cachet to being a foreign scribe, was this because they brought a quality of penmanship judged unavailable locally? Or was it precisely that they were foreign that created the attraction, with their employer in some small way aping the cosmopolitan eclecticism which was the vogue of princely courts?

The cosmopolitan or hybrid nature of a court was expressed in terms of artefacts and of humans (as well as other animals).[32] Employing foreigners for book-related

---

Italian Renaissance Humanism; William Salamon of the diocese of León is known for his work on the set of Hugo de S. Cher which is Oxford, Exeter College, MSS 51–68, on which see Watson, *A Descriptive Catalogue … of Exeter College Oxford*, 85–7 and *sub numeris* (noting also that 'scribe 3' also appears to be continental, and was a colleague of Henry Mere, on whom see n.30 below; see [De la Mare and Gillam], *Duke Humfrey's Library*, 105). Salamon also copied a *Confessio Amantis* for Sir Edmund Rede, now BL, MS Harley 3490; see Pearsall, 'The Rede (Boarstall) Gower'.

[28] To cite only some examples of extant dated manuscripts: *DMOL*, nos. 716 ('Albertus de Geldrop nacione brabantie'), 723 ('Tielmannus filii Reyneri alamani', also from Brabant), 743 ('Johannes Reynboldus Almanicus', from Hesse), 828 ('Johannes Jacobi Spaen de amsterdammis'); *DMCL*, no. 128 ('Tielmannus filius Clewardi').

[29] For the evidence, see [De la Mare and Gillam], *Duke Humfrey's Library*, nos. 97–9.

[30] On Mere, see Parkes, 'A Fifteenth-Century Scribe: Henry Mere'; on Zurke, see [De la Mare and Gillam], *Duke Humfrey's Library*, nos. 44–7.

[31] Salter (ed.), *Registrum cancellarii oxoniensis*, 99–311, at 308. Matheus is identified as Matheus de Moravia, by *BLR*, 5 (1956), 282–3, discussing BodL, MS Lat. th. b.5, which is signed by a scribe of that name and dated to 1455/6; on this manuscript, see [De la Mare and Gillam], *Duke Humfrey's Library*, no. 100. Of Jacobus de Selerhalle, who may be identifiable as Jacobus Frys (in Salter (ed.), *Registrum cancellarii oxoniensis*, 136), no signed manuscripts survive.

[32] See Vale, *The Princely Court*, esp. 297.

duties could be one small part of this greater ostentation. Henry VII looked to continental book artisans who were already settled in his realm to act as his librarian – first, the scribe Quentin Poulet from Lille (1492–1506), then the printer William Faques (d. 1508), a native of Normandy.[33] Earlier in the fifteenth century, Henry IV's youngest son, Humfrey, Duke of Gloucester, who already had an Italian surgeon at his court, appointed in quick succession two further Italians as secretary: both Tito Livio Frulovisi, from Ferrara, and Antonio Beccaria, from Verona, produced manuscripts for the duke, and also seem to have taken charge of his book collection, on occasions adding contents lists or annotations to the volumes.[34] If Gloucester's was an unusual (if not unprecedented) choice, all the more exotic in fifteenth-century Britain was the move beyond the Latin alphabet promoted by George Neville, Archbishop of York, in his support for Greek scribes.[35]

Cosmopolitan habits of patronage could slip or slide several rungs down the social ladder. When William Gray, the future bishop of Ely, travelled through Germany and to Italy with such a lavish entourage that the suggestion he was of royal blood was given credence, he picked up extra followers on his tours.[36] One was a Dutch scribe whom he encountered in Cologne: Theodore Werken of Appenbroeck (South Holland).[37] Werken travelled with Gray and his retinue to Italy, where he learnt the fashionable bookhand the humanists called *littera antiqua*. However, Werken did not remain with Gray during his time as English royal procurator at the papal curia; instead, he came to England, seemingly employed by one of Gray's more modest companions, Richard Bole, who was to become Gray's archdeacon at Ely. Werken provides a case both of cosmopolitan patronage by the relatively lowly and of a foreign scribe's career which did not fall within the ambit of either university. There is an irony to this: the majority of manuscripts copied by Werken are now in Oxford, in the collection of Balliol College, thanks to the generosity of Gray and Bole. In his own lifetime, however, we can trace Werken's presence in London, presumably Ely, and, late in his career, Canterbury (where he made transcriptions of printed books),

[33] For both Poulet and Faques, see Kipling, 'Henry VII and the Origins of Tudor Patronage', 121–31, and for a summary of Poulet's career, see Kren and McKendrick, *Illuminating the Renaissance*, 520. On the royal library under the early Tudors, see Backhouse, 'The Royal Library from Edward IV to Henry VII'; Stratford and Webber, 'Bishops and Kings', esp. 209–17; Carley (ed.), *The Libraries of King Henry VIII*, xxv–xxvi.

[34] For the surgeon Giovanni Signorelli, see Vickers, *Humphrey Duke of Gloucester*, 381; on Gloucester's secretaries and their manuscripts, see Sammut, *Unfredo duca di Gloucester*, 17–22; De la Mare, 'Manuscripts Given to the University of Oxford by Humfrey', 115–18; Rundle, 'Tito Livio Frulovisi', and Rundle, 'From Greenwich to Verona'.

[35] Weiss, *Humanism in England*, 141–8 (in the new on-line edition, 216–27); Lowry, 'John Rous'.

[36] On Gray's royal pretensions, see Rundle, *England and the Identity of Italian Renaissance Humanism*. Still seminal on his book-collecting is Mynors, *Catalogue of the Manuscripts of Balliol*, xxiv–xlv and *passim*.

[37] Mynors, 'A Fifteenth-Century Scribe'; [De la Mare and Hunt], *Duke Humfrey and English Humanism*, nos. 43, 51–2; De la Mare, 'A Fragment of Augustine'; *DMCL*, no. 16.

but not in Oxford. While the university towns, as I have suggested, were epicentres of continental scribal activity, they did not have a monopoly.

The characters mentioned so far have been men who settled in England for extended periods. There were others, of course, who crossed the Channel for only a few weeks or months. The best remembered among them are those sent on embassies – Jean Froissart, for instance, in the mid 1390s or, a century later, John Michael Nagonius – when diplomatic courtesies could be enhanced by the gift of a book of the visitor's own works, produced under their supervision or written in their own hand.[38] There were others, however, who travelled for more personal reasons. The Paduan scribe, Milo da Carraria, can stand as an example of this: the colophons of his manuscripts suggest that he went on a sort of reverse Grand Tour, travelling across the Alps, through Germany to Bruges and then arriving in London by 1447.[39] He produced about half a dozen manuscripts while in England, presumably paying his way by his scribal activities; but he did not stay for long, since he is next known to have been in Naples in 1450.[40] About a decade before Milo arrived, another scribe similarly made an apparently short stay in England: a German, Petrus Lomer 'de Colorna' (presumably Cologne), adopted an idiosyncratic style of *littera antiqua* which can be seen in two extant manuscripts.[41] If the scribe had not signed himself, it would have been difficult to identify him as German; and, if each of his manuscripts had not been provided with distinctive English illumination, their origins would not have been obvious – a salutary reminder that the provenance of a manuscript can be more complex than hasty assumptions suggest.

If those who were scribes or who became scribes travelled to the British Isles either to visit or to stay, the traffic was not all in one direction. Let me confine myself to one set of examples drawn from the middle of our period. The reassertion of Rome as home of the papacy, first attempted in 1376 and finally achieving durable success from the 1440s, eventually made that city a cultural capital where scribes of a wide

---

[38] Paris, Bibliothèque Nationale, MS fr. 831 may be the manuscript of Froissart's poems made under his supervision and given to Richard II: Froissart, *L'Espinette amoureuse*, 9–11; Croenen, Figg and Taylor, 'Authorship, Patronage, and Literary Gifts'. On Nagonius, see Gwynne, 'The Frontispiece to an Illuminated Panegyric'. See also Roberts, 'Importing Books for Oxford, 1500–1640'.

[39] For Milo's signed manuscripts, see *Colophons*, nos. 13834–7; De Robertis and Miriello (ed.), *I manoscritti*, I, no. 93; Milazzo et al., *I manoscritti*, no. 24; Kristeller, *Iter Italicum*, III.406a.

[40] On Milo in England, see [De la Mare and Hunt], *Duke Humfrey and English Humanism*, nos. 24–6, and *BLR*, 13 (1991), 501–2.

[41] The two manuscripts are Padua, Biblioteca Capitolare, MS C 78 and Verona, Biblioteca Capitolare, MS CCXXXIV (221). The latter is datable to the late 1430s because it includes some rubricated chapter headings written by Tito Livio Frulovisi (who was in England *c*.1436–*c*.1438). For an illustration of the latter manuscript (including images of Frulovisi's script and the English illumination), see the reproduction of f. 127r at Piazzi, *Biblioteca Capitolare Verona*, 147. The former manuscript is mentioned by Derolez, *Codicologie des manuscrits en écriture humanistique*, I, no. 352, and II, no. 611, where it is assumed, presumably on the basis of present location of the codex, that its scribe was active in the Veneto.

array of nationalities could find employment, in or around the curia.[42] In the mid fifteenth century, those people included a Scotsman, George of Kynninmond, who appears to have worked in the household of Cardinal Filippo Calandrini, and an Englishman, Thomas Candour, who was a chamberlain to Nicholas V.[43] Both these men – and others – mastered the new humanist style of bookhand, but Candour, whose career saw him move back and forth between his homeland and Italy, did not just adopt it, he adapted it into his own archaizing script.[44] An equally striking instance of palaeographical mimicry is provided by a scribe who by his name, John Bateman, would appear to be English and by the parchment he used would appear to have been at work in Italy: he signed two manuscripts, one in an Italian-style gothic cursive, the other in humanist cursive, with which Bateman experiments as his copying progresses.[45] In the case of all the codices just mentioned, we know their British connections either because the scribe signed himself or because it has been possible to reconstruct his identity. We can only wonder how many other manuscripts might appear to us continental but actually be the product of an anonymous Englishman or a Scot.

Not only did scribes from north of the English Channel work in other parts of Europe, manuscripts produced in England also travelled to the continent. It was not just those who had endured long-term, if genteel, captivity, like Charles duc d'Orléans and his brother, Jean d'Angoulême, who could return with books made during their enforced sojourn.[46] Briefer visits could also provide opportunities for both book creation and book purchase. Louis de Gruthuyse, the man sometimes credited with encouraging Edward IV's taste in Burgundian manuscripts, himself bought manuscripts in England on his journeys to London in the 1460s as an ambassador; his interest concentrated on French books but also included a copy of *Modus tenendi parlamentum*.[47] Three decades earlier, the papal collector, Pietro del Monte, spent some of his spare time in England transcribing texts and having them illuminated in the local style before he took them back with him to Italy in 1440.[48] A further example comes from the same period: the codices already mentioned which were written by Petrus Lomer may have travelled to Italy soon after

---

[42] Caldelli, *Copisti a Roma*, esp. 25–32, although her list of *stranieri* includes only two from Britain, both Scots, Robert Pringil (140) and George of Kynninmond (106–7).

[43] For an image of Kynninmond's script, see Caldelli, *I codici datati nei vaticani latini*, tav. 121 (of Vatican City, Biblioteca Apostolica Vaticana, MS Vat. lat. 200, produced for Calandrini in 1456). On Candour, see Rundle, 'The Scribe Thomas Candour', with full bibliography.

[44] On archaizing scripts generally, see Parkes, 'Archaizing Hands'.

[45] The two manuscripts are Vatican City, Biblioteca Apostolica Vaticana, MS Vat. lat. 11493 and MS Reg. lat. 1469.

[46] Ouy, 'Charles d'Orléans' and other essays in Arn (ed.), *Charles d'Orléans in England 1415–1440*.

[47] On Gruthuyse, see Lafitte, 'Les Manuscrits de Louis de Bruges'. The copy of *Modus tenendi parlamentum* is now Paris, Bibliothèque Nationale, MS fr. 6049.

[48] Rundle, 'A Renaissance Bishop and his Books', nos. 8, 12.

their production.[49] Although there was nothing in this period to compare with the migration of manuscripts to the continent that occurred during the Reformation era, there was at least some informal exporting of books.

Even taking the examples just cited into account, it is undeniable that, throughout the period covered by this volume, England was a net importer of books, as well as of book artisans.[50] England had a reputation for some other cultural products – its music and its musicians, say – but its books, for the most part, were not sought-after artefacts. The English may have been little prized for their mastery of book-arts, but it may be that, in the generations between, say, Walter Burley and Thomas More, there were few authors who gained an international reputation, unless it was for their engagement (*pro* or *contra*) with lollard heresy.[51] On occasion, an Englishman abroad might ask for a manuscript to be compiled and sent to him from his homeland, as Adam Easton did when he wrote to London during his long-term sojourn at the papal court in Avignon. He asked for a copy to be made of Wyclif's writings because 'I cannot obtain a copy of his statements [here]'.[52] More often, such an émigré would buy books or have them written for him in his place of residence – Easton's copy of John of Salisbury appears to be a case in point.[53] Easton died in Rome, but his manuscripts did reach England; they were sent back after his demise as a bequest to Norwich Cathedral Priory. Other books arrived in England along with their owner: it is said that, in the 1440s, the curialist, Andrew Holes, had bought so many manuscripts a ship was required to carry them all back from Italy.[54] Over twenty of Holes's books are now identifiable, with several of them the work of the same Germanic scribe, Johannes Baerts, at work in Florence.[55] Other volumes that Holes came to own were not commissioned by him but instead bore the marks of former owners; he seems to have had a particular interest in those that had belonged in the previous generation to the Florentine Chancellor, Coluccio

[49] The Veronese location of one of the manuscripts (see above n.41), and the presence in it of Frulovisi's script, suggests a possible route to Italy: Antonio Beccaria, Frulovisi's successor as secretary to Humfrey, Duke of Gloucester, returned to his hometown of Verona at the end of the 1440s.

[50] For a recent statement of 'the failure of English book producers to satisfy [local] demand', see Reynolds, 'England and the Continent', 76–85.

[51] For examples of European dissemination, see Genet, 'The Dissemination of Manuscripts'; Hudson, *The Premature Reformation*, esp. 8, 104, 514–15; Harvey, 'The Diffusion of the Doctrinale'.

[52] Pantin, *Documents Illustrating … the English Black Monks*, III.77, discussed Sharpe, Carley, Thomson and Watson (eds.), *English Benedictine Libraries*, 291, 610. On Easton, see Harvey, *The English in Rome*, 188–237.

[53] Oxford, Balliol College, MS. 300B, on which see Mynors, *Catalogue of the Manuscripts of Balliol*, 320–1.

[54] The story originates with Vespasiano da Bisticci, *Le Vite*, 1.313. On Holes generally, see Harvey, 'An Englishman at the Roman Curia'.

[55] Manuscripts made for Holes by Baerts include: BodL, MS Bodley 339; BodL, MS Rawl. G.48; Oxford, Magdalen College, MS lat. 191; Oxford, New College, MS 219; he also corrected Oxford, New College, MS 201. On the first three of these manuscripts, see *DMOL*, no. 78.

Salutati.[56] They stand as witness to a phenomenon critical to the book trade before print: the informal market in second-hand manuscripts.

There were some types of manuscript, from certain locales, for which there was an international fashion. The thirteenth-century copies of legal texts made in the Bolognese style would be one such case from before our period.[57] Within our time-span, the outstanding example of this was the vogue for Books of Hours from the Low Countries, the popularity of which made speculative production commercially viable.[58] They can stand as a precursor to the instances of continental printing aimed specifically at the English market.[59] But, in the context of manuscript culture, they were exceptional. Most new manuscripts were made on commission. The stationers who would arrange for books to be made to order would usually also have in their shops older manuscripts ready to sell. John Gunthorp, well-travelled cleric and diplomat for both Edward IV and Henry VII, had a penchant for book-buying – he was one of the first generation to be able to collect both printed volumes and manuscripts; he was, like Colón, a man given to providing revelatory notes about when and where he bought his books.[60] On at least one occasion, he visited the London stationer, David Lyonhill.[61] A couple of decades earlier, Gunthorp bought 'at Westminster' a manuscript which must have filled him with nostalgia (see Figure 13.1). It was a Latin translation of Homer, written in Italy in a script which he would have instantly recognized: the scribe (so well known to him but mysterious to us) had been employed by John Tiptoft, Earl of Worcester, when both he and Gunthorp were in Ferrara; Gunthorp, as he parted with his money, might also have recalled how Tiptoft now lay dead, his head asunder from his body, having been executed during the Readeption.[62] This example can remind us that the trade in second-hand books could itself be highly international.

[56] Those formerly owned by Salutati include: Oxford, New College, MSS 155, 272; Vatican City, Biblioteca Apostolica Vaticana, MS Urb. lat. 694. On the first of these, see Kohl, 'Readers and Owners of an Early Work'.

[57] For the subject generally, see L'Engle and Gibbs, *Illuminating the Law*, 41–8 and *passim*; for some examples which reached Cambridge early in their lives, see Rogers, 'From Alan the Illuminator to John Scott the Younger', 290; for ones of Oxford provenance, see Alexander and Temple, *Illuminated Manuscripts*, nos. 884, 885, 888, 891, 896, 907.

[58] Colledge, 'South Netherlands Books of Hours'; De Hamel, 'Reflexions on the Trade'; Rogers, 'The Miniature of St John the Baptist'; Kren and McKendrick, *Illuminating the Renaissance*, nos. 25, 41, 88, etc. For examples of Books of Hours made or adapted in France for English users, see Reynolds, 'English Patrons and French Artists'.

[59] Colón bought at least one example of this phenomenon: an 'Ortus Vocabulorum' (including English text) printed by Petrus Olivier in 1520 at Rouen (*STC* 13835): *Registrum B*, no. 13.

[60] For his biography, see *BRUC*.

[61] He bought from him, in 1491, CCCC, MS 164 part 1, a fourteenth-century copy of Ranulph Higden. On Lyonhill, see Christianson, *A Directory of London Stationers*, 130.

[62] CUL, MS Mm.3.4. The manuscript's scribe was a 'V f I', about whom little is known – our ignorance extends even to uncertainty about his nationality. For much of what we can surmise, see [De la Mare and Hunt], *Duke Humfrey and English Humanism*, nos. 72, 76–9.

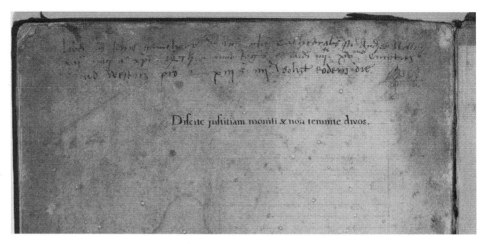

Figure 13.1 CUL, MS Mm.3.4, f. 189v, close-up: ownership inscription of John Gunthorp.

It has been suggested that the trade in second-hand books developed in the four-teenth century in the wake of the hooves of two of the horses of the Apocalypse: war and pestilence.[63] The dislocation both of these caused played its part but is not a sufficient explanation for the activity of this market. Acts of war were preceded and followed by the arts of diplomacy, when an emissary's mind might wander from menacing mayhem to consider buying a book, as when Richard Courtenay, Bishop of Norwich, in Paris in 1414 and 1415, haggled over the possible purchase of manuscripts from Pietro di Sacco, the Veronese librarian of Jean, duc de Berry.[64] Another factor was institutional de-accessioning: religious foundations grew and, as they did, their book stock could become too large for its physical home. Books might be disposed of by sale or sent to a dependent priory or college, as clearly happened with volumes from the great collection of Christ Church, Canterbury.[65] The medieval library was organic, contracting as well as expanding. This was especially true for monastic establishments; private collections, if they were not donated to an institution, were more likely to undergo piecemeal dispersal. That a library might die with its owner, however, was not necessarily a sign it was unvalued – on the contrary, its dispersal could reflect a culture of respect for the dead, with the late owner's betters and peers taking the effort to buy a book from his executors as a memento of their now-past relationship.[66] Perhaps some such impulse explains why Thomas of Woodstock, Duke of Gloucester, bought a French manuscript of the *Roman de la Rose* from the executors of Sir Richard Stury, a well-known figure at court; some of

[63] Parkes, *Their Hands before Our Eyes*, 42.
[64] The story is re-told by Rouse and Rouse, *Manuscripts and their Makers*, 1.297–300.
[65] De Hamel, 'The Dispersal of the Library of Christ Church'.
[66] I discuss this practice in Rundle, 'Habits of Manuscript-Collecting'.

the duke's books in turn were bought after his death by Edmund Stafford, Bishop of Exeter.[67]

All that said, some manuscripts certainly did travel as, in effect, booty of war. By far the most significant example of this in the period covered by this volume was the purchase by John, Duke of Bedford, of the French royal library that had been originally collected under Charles V. It is thought that Bedford had the manuscripts transported to England.[68] A few, certainly, the duke gave away as gifts: for example, an outsize copy of Bersuire's French translation of Livy which was 'sent from the parts of France' for his brother, Humfrey, Duke of Gloucester.[69] We know that others were available for sale in the following decades: thus, Jean d'Angoulême could purchase in London in 1441 a French Durandus which had been made in Paris for his grandfather, and twenty years later Louis de Gruthuyse was able to buy several manuscripts which had once been in the French royal collection.[70] What, though, is remarkable is the number of manuscripts which were among those bought by Bedford which reveal no evidence of having passed some time north of the Channel. There are over fifty manuscripts extant from the collection apparently bought by Bedford; the number of those which provide definite evidence of a presence in fifteenth-century England is in single figures.[71] Even the statement that Louis de Gruthuyse bought his manuscripts in London is rarely corroborated by internal evidence. My purpose is not to throw doubt on the claim that Charles V's library passed from France to England and slowly returned to the continent in later decades. What I wish to emphasize, instead, is the limitations of our knowledge – the sedate lives now led by old manuscripts in the shelter of air-conditioned

[67] The *Roman* manuscript is now BL, MS Royal 19.B.xiii; on Stury, whose name was blackened after his death by suggestions of heresy, see McFarlane, *Lancastrian Kings*, esp. 148–76; on Stafford's buying Gloucester's books, Cavanaugh, 'A Study of Books privately Owned in England', II.805–6.

[68] On the duke's library, see Stratford, *The Bedford Inventories*, 91–6, 119–23.

[69] The Livy is now Paris, Bibliothèque Sainte-Geneviève, MS 777; Humfrey also came to own BL, MS Royal 19.C.iv, which had been owned by Charles V and which may, therefore, have also been a gift to Humfrey from his brother.

[70] The Durandus, in Golein's translation, is now Paris, Bibliothèque Nationale, MS fr. 437, on which see Bibliothèque Nationale, *La Librairie de Charles V*, no. 176. On Louis de Gruthuyse's purchases, see Lafitte, 'Les Manuscrits de Louis de Bruges'.

[71] It can be assumed that Bedford bought those manuscripts listed in the 1424 inventory of the French royal library: Delisle, *Recherches sur la librairie de Charles V*, with the relevant inventory signified as 'F'. Our main sources for knowledge of extant codices mentioned in that inventory are Delisle himself and Bibliothèque Nationale, *La Librairie de Charles V*. In addition to those manuscripts mentioned above, see Cambridge, Jesus College, MS Q.B.9 (26), on which, see Briggs, *Giles of Rome's De Regimine Principum*, 175–9; CUL, MS Kk.4.7, with an earlier provenance identified by Williman, 'Some Additional Provenances', 446; BL, MS Royal 20.B.i, with an English script adding a contents list at f. 31v. All contain evidence of having been in England in the fifteenth century. If we extend our chronological range to sixteenth-century marks of English ownership, we can add CCCC, MS 243 part 1, with an earlier provenance identified by Williman, 'Some Additional Provenances', 431, and TCC, MS O.9.35; but, of course, the later the evidence, the less certainty that it demonstrates that the manuscript originally arrived in England as part of Bedford's purchase.

repositories can hide all too well their adventurous pasts, when they could travel with scant regard for national boundaries.

The circulation of manuscripts, imported to and then exported again from England, tended to be informal and to be driven as much by provenance as by content. In this period, the re-selling and re-use of books were not an adjunct to the production of books – quite the opposite. Even a library built up over a generation could be formed mainly from second-hand volumes. Of the identified extant manuscripts from the collection of Humfrey, Duke of Gloucester, now often celebrated for its new humanist texts, just under half the books were made before he was born. Moreover, for those that date from his lifetime, well over one-third came to him from a previous owner. In sum, nearly two-thirds of the duke's manuscripts were second-hand when they reached the princely library. For much of the period covered by this volume, book culture was a gerontocratic society, in which young manuscripts had to find their place alongside more venerable volumes. The provision of books was only in small part about the production of new codices.

The intervention of print transformed this dynamic – formalizing a market which traded in new books.[72] But the second-hand and the not-so-new, of course, still played a part in this changing structure. As was mentioned at the start of this chapter, Hernan Colón bought a product of Rood's Oxford press (for 16d); it had been printed in 1481.[73] Rooting among the stationers' wares, Colón found a number of other books we would define as incunables: the oldest seems to have been a large devotional work printed at Venice in 1476 (highly priced at 53d).[74] Nor was it only printed books that the stationers could sell him. He had no prejudice against the older form of books, and he bought three fifteenth-century codices while he was in England: a copy of William Woodford's anti-Wycliffite *De Sacramentis altaris* (for 10d), a manuscript of Burley on Porphyry (for 6d) and an English collection of humanist texts (for 16d).[75] Manuscripts could still compete in the market-place with the parvenus of print, even if some of them sat at its lower end.

All of the three manuscripts Colón took back with him to Spain from London appear to have previously been in private hands; none was an escapee from an institutional library. We do not see in his purchases the feature which was to become the keynote of the following decades: the shedding of old books from institutions, with the subsequent export of some of them to the continent. Some Protestant scholars saw this as an unfortunate by-product of the Henrician cleansing of the

[72] For important comment, see Pollard, 'The English Market for Printed Books'.
[73] Rhodes, 'Don Fernando Colón', no. 2, which is *Registrum B*, no. 4 (Alexander de Hales, Oxford, 1481).
[74] Rhodes, 'Don Fernando Colón', no. 50, which is *Registrum B*, no. 1 (Albertus de Padua, Venice: De Corona, 1476).
[75] Seville, Biblioteca Colombina, MS 5/3/8, MS 5/2/41 and MS 5/5/28. On all of these, see Guillén and Francisco, *Catálogo... de la Biblioteca Colombina de Sevilla, sub numeris.*

Church of corrupt monasticism, and there is no doubt that the early Reformation provided the opportunity for some books to travel abroad, like the manuscripts from the Cambridge friaries that found safe haven in Rome.[76] Yet this is not a complete explanation. As has already been mentioned, the migration of manuscripts was not a new phenomenon; it was one, though, that gained extra impetus in the early sixteenth century, ahead of the impact of religious turmoil. The example of the University Library of Oxford is informative. Endowed with the donations of Humfrey, Duke of Gloucester, and other fifteenth-century donors, it fell into decline in the early years of the sixteenth century, with its opening hours decreasing. By the time of the royal visitation of 1535 – usually taken as the first onslaught against the old institution – books were already disappearing from the library. The reasons for its decline are nowhere stated, but we can guess that in an age of collegiate printed book collections, a university manuscript library could be written off as old-fashioned and out-dated. The consequence was certainly the eventual destruction – more through mishap than through malice – of many manuscripts, but while those came to the end of their lives, others began a new itinerant career. It was the start of a long-lasting era of the travel of manuscripts from the British Isles to the European mainland.

I would not wish to close this chapter allowing the impression to develop that an international life was the lot of every book: there were also those which were more parochial, and it was natural for them to be weighted towards the English vernacular. Some insular books may, in fact, display a conscious, even obdurate, eschewing of the cosmopolitanism that marked intellectual life. Yet, for others, foreign influences – in script, in illumination, in materials, in structure – moulded their existence, even when it was unacknowledged. Cosmopolitanism had multifarious aspects and, as this chapter has attempted to suggest, it had its own history, with influences and their intensity – the balance of cultural trade – shifting from generation to generation. The most basic point I want to urge, however, is that, when we sit before manuscripts and incunables in their well-appointed modern archives, the very stability of their setting can make us liable to forget the fluidity that marked their earlier lives. We inhabit a world of national libraries, but the books they contain are often poor advocates for any patriotic cause. Indeed, given the information that has been touched on here and that could be amassed in richer detail, we are left with one insistent question: leaving aside the minority of volumes that were solely in the English language, and on English parchment, and throughout their lives only in England, how many 'English books' can justly be bounded by such a confining name?

---

[76] Ker, 'Cardinal Cervini's Manuscripts'; Fossier, 'Premières recherches sur les manuscrits latins'; Crook, 'Manuscripts Surviving from the Austin Friars'. On the issue more generally, see Carley, 'The Dispersal of the Monastic Libraries'; Watson, *Medieval Manuscripts in Post-Medieval England*.

Afterword: the book in culture

WENDY SCASE

The Production of Books in England 1350–1500 analyses its subject in starkly material terms. Problems addressed in this volume range from the material constituents of books, through the physical processes involved in their deployment, to the economic relations and ideologies that enabled and constrained production. What materials were books made from, how were they supplied and what did they cost? What kinds of people wrote the texts and decorated the pages, and what processes – linguistic, intellectual, physical – were involved in copying and decorating? What scripts, page layouts, decoration and illustration are used, how are the varieties to be explained, and what costs were involved? Where did scribes and decorators obtain exemplars? What materials and methods were used for binding books, who carried out this work, where and at what cost? How did all of these processes inter-relate on a practical basis: did someone serve as coordinator – as a kind of 'project manager' – or was it necessary for the person paying for the work to organize these processes? How did print culture relate to patterns of manuscript production? The purpose of this afterword is to reflect on the significance of the ideas and information in the foregoing chapters for the study of literature and history in the period *c.*1350–*c.*1500, to ask how it may help us to think about the medieval book in relation to culture. I shall begin and end this piece with reflections on the relations of the volume with disciplinary traditions and research methodologies, examining the place of this book in contemporary academic culture.

The fact that scholars can be asked to write chapters that address book production in these terms indicates how far the subject has come in the twenty or so years since the publication of this volume's acknowledged predecessor: Jeremy Griffiths's and Derek Pearsall's *Book Production and Publishing in Britain 1375–1475*. As the chapters in the present volume demonstrate, it is now becoming feasible to generalize about book production, to synthesize many individual studies rather than to have to offer the specific to serve for the general (for example, where the present volume is organized around materials and processes, the section on production in Griffiths and Pearsall has chapters on books of lollards and religious orders, the

London book trade and liturgical music books). Furthermore, drawing its primary categories of analysis from the physical materiality of the book, this volume resonates with the new sense of the centrality of the history of the book as an endeavour in cultural and literary study. It is also significant that these chapters address a set of questions which could, in principle, be answered definitively. Pursuing a research programme organized around questions to which answers can be right or wrong reflects renewed confidence in empirical research and a sense that adding definitively to our knowledge and understanding of the objects we have inherited from the past is a use of time and resources that will have many beneficiaries and many enduring benefits. Such work also offers a robust response to a chilling alternative. If we cease to cultivate these scholarly activities, our knowledge and understanding of medieval codices will soon be as limited as our access to Linear A tablets.

Perhaps to a greater extent even than those of its predecessor, however, the research agenda and the choice of primary source materials of *The Production of Books in England 1350–1500* are shaped by the traditions of Middle English literary studies. There is frequent recourse to the manuscripts of the major Middle English poets: Langland, Chaucer, Hoccleve, Gower and Lydgate. Orietta da Rold's discussion of ink-colour is illustrated from studies of *Canterbury Tales* manuscripts; Daniel Wakelin examines choices of script in relation to Lydgate manuscripts, and double-copying in relation to Chaucer, Hoccleve and Lydgate manuscripts; Simon Horobin discusses the dialects and localization of manuscripts of Chaucer, Gower and Langland; Stephen Partridge relies explicitly on 'the manuscript traditions of major English literary texts by Chaucer, Gower, Langland, Hoccleve and Lydgate'; Martha Driver and Michael Orr discuss decoration and illustration in similar sources. This focus on manuscripts of the authors that are to us 'canonical' reflects the fact that much of the manuscript scholarship drawn on in these chapters has been informed by and produced within the disciplinary frameworks and agendas of medieval English literary studies, historically often driven by editorial imperatives, for example, to establish Chaucer's own order for *The Canterbury Tales*, and by linguistic problems, for example, to distinguish Chaucer's usage from that of his scribes.

Undoubtedly, the essays in this volume provide scholars of medieval English literature after 1350 – and particularly those specially interested in the major Middle English poets – with an immensely valuable resource. These chapters synthesize a huge volume of recent work and add new examples and discussion. Students coming into manuscript studies and early book history from literary backgrounds are offered here an analysis of the *status quaestionis*, while those wanting information about the material conditions of authorship and reading in the period will find the material presented in ways readily applicable to curriculum authors. But what of the implications of this focus for studies beyond the Middle English curriculum? To what extent are the manuscripts of the major medieval English poets likely to be representative of books produced in England, or even in English, as a whole? And what areas of book history, and of medieval culture and history more broadly, are most likely to be illuminated by work with this focus?

While this volume may be shaped by English literary studies, contributors range far beyond the curriculum authors, extending into the broad domain of vernacular manuscripts and related materials. And the implications of this work extend significantly beyond those traditionally associated with the discipline. There is space here to notice only some of the contributions that these studies of English literary manuscripts and related visual and print culture may make to our knowledge of medieval book production and of medieval cultural history more broadly. It is clear from the evidence presented by David Rundle, Erik Kwakkel and others in this volume, and elsewhere, that old and perhaps second-hand books were highly important in medieval culture. Books were bequeathed, used and then handed over to libraries, mended, patched, bound and perhaps re-bound in several configurations (as Alexandra Gillespie points out) before eventually some of them wore out. The vernacular London 'common-profit' manuscripts were made with this intention explicitly in mind; an inscription in CUL, MS Ff.6.31, for example, states that this book is to be passed from person to person for safe-keeping during their lifetimes 'as longe as þe booke endureth'.[1] A wealth of evidence corroborates what the common-profit books imply: Middle English manuscripts readily entered the 'second-hand' or 'pre-owned' economy alongside volumes of Latin and/or Anglo-Norman works. But it is equally obvious that the newest literary works could not have been obtained second-hand. A demand for original Middle English poetry and newly available English translations of Latin and French texts must have stimulated book production. Collectively, the essays in this volume help us to think about responses to this stimulus.

Print culture, several of these essays suggest, appropriated in many ways the systems and conventions of manuscript culture. Just so, as these essays also demonstrate, the production of English literary manuscripts in many ways appropriated traditional methods and conventions of book production. The page layouts of books of vernacular literature were modelled on those in university books, as Stephen Partridge shows. Decorative elements were sometimes based on pattern books or made use of recycled woodcuts, while infrastructures and personnel used to decorate Latin books were also employed for English books, as is discussed in the chapter by Martha Driver and Michael Orr. The methods and symbols used by scribes to abbreviate words, save space and speed up the copying process, described by Daniel Wakelin, were adopted from systems developed in the copying of Latin.

Yet it is clear that in many ways vernacular manuscript production did not fit seamlessly into the structures and processes used for the production of Latin books.

---

[1] CUL, MS Ff.6.31, f. 100r, cf. Scase, 'Reginald Pecock, John Carpenter'.

The nature of the 'market' for vernacular manuscripts seems to have provided a stimulus for technological innovation rather than simple continuation of existing practices. English texts in principle had a larger audience than Latin (and French) ones, for English was accessible to almost everyone (albeit that illiterates would have to access vernacular texts by hearing them read aloud), while knowledge of Latin and French was confined to elites of one kind or another. This audience in principle, therefore, included those of limited means. Thus there was a stimulus for technological innovation to meet demand quickly and cheaply.

Some aspects of technological innovation seem to have been driven by the special demands of vernacular book production. The 'translation' of spelling in an exemplar text into the scribe's own system is a feature associated with and generated by the copying of English because, unlike Latin, the vernacular was not standardized in this period. We can infer from this translation something about the ways different scribes worked, as Simon Horobin and Daniel Wakelin do in their chapters. Scribes who reproduce the spellings of difficult or unfamiliar names and words, or write a word twice or miss out a phrase, were very probably copying from an exemplar rather than writing to dictation. Scribes who reproduce spelling, punctuation and word-division exactly were probably copying one letter at a time. Scribes who get difficult words 'right' but 'translate' the spellings of common words were very probably reading and copying phrase by phrase.

Thus points where the traditional processes did not work for books with English content can sometimes offer opportunities for insight into the special processes involved in their production. Further extensions of this kind of investigation of the special demands of vernacular book-making are possible. I offer just one suggestion. The decoration and illumination of initials in vernacular books could not entirely follow the patterns used for the decoration of Latin and French texts. The characters thorn and yogh were of course not found in Latin or French. Where these letters are marked for decorative treatment different responses can sometimes be observed even among decorators who worked on the same manuscript. The Vernon manuscript, BodL, MS Eng. poet. a. 1 offers very revealing examples. Some decorators respond to the guide letter yogh by painting an initial <Z> (which could have been modelled on conventions in French and Latin manuscripts), while others attempt the yogh, for which French and Latin manuscripts offered no models. Some decorators paint initial thorn with a <Y>, while others provide the thorn. This last distinction might perhaps indicate the regional origins of the decorators (<y> being used for both letters in the north and east, while <y> was distinguished from thorn in the south and Midlands),[2] and the first could even suggest that such decorators were

---

[2] For an example of decorated initial <Z> where the guide letter is yogh, see f. 246r, top of col. c, and for examples of decorated initial thorns that are indistinguishable from <Y>, see f. 353v, col. b; for regional distinctions in the distribution of thorn, see Benskin, 'The Letters <þ> and <y>'. Detailed

not literate in English (perhaps they numbered among the immigrant decorators discussed by Driver and Orr and Rundle).

These are just two examples of how studying vernacular books in the period 1350–1500 might shed new light on innovation in book-production processes as well as on the social and cultural dynamics behind them. When we ask where the enabling innovations and skills for making vernacular books came from, these essays seem to suggest that we should be prepared to look beyond existing infrastructure and processes used in making books that were in high demand, such as service-books and primers. There are many respects in which the existing capacity and infrastructure for other production processes – the copying of texts, the provision of material, the technologies, even the binding of books – do not seem to have met the demands generated by the making of the vernacular book. To take binding first, if it is reasonable to assume that the kinds of limp bindings and soft covers described by Alexandra Gillespie could have been produced by informal means, perhaps taking place in households, religious institutions, students' lodgings and so on, then much book production must have gone on without use of the services of a binder. The copying of the texts presents us with even more interesting possibilities concerning the relation of vernacular book production with existing infrastructure. Linne Mooney emphasizes that many of the scribes of the major English poetic texts were people whose employment involved writing, such as clerks in households or government or civic service, or scriveners who wrote legal documents. She terms such people 'professional' scribes, distinguishing them from 'commercial' scribes, such as the 'Textwriters' – the persons who copied Latin texts needed in high numbers, such as service-books. Daniel Wakelin's evidence that the scripts of vernacular books are mostly modelled on those used for document writing shows that the technologies of bureaucracy, as well as its personnel, were exploited for vernacular book production. Orietta da Rold's chapter shows that the material supplies associated with documentary culture – especially paper and inks – also supplied vernacular book production. We have been aware of various aspects of the evidence for the role of documentary or bureaucratic culture in book production for some time.[3] Now we can start to see the evidence coalescing to form a larger picture. Materials, technology and skilled labour provided by bureaucracy seem to have been adapted to meet the needs of vernacular book production, rather than – as we might have expected – those of existing book-production infrastructure used for high-demand Latin books (as described by Erik Kwakkel).

analyses of the Vernon manuscript are in Scase (ed.), *A Facsimile Edition*; Scase (ed.), *The Making of the Vernon Manuscript*.

[3] Recent monographs that explore aspects of the interface between bureaucracy, law and vernacular literature include Knapp, *The Bureaucratic Muse*, Steiner, *Documentary Culture and the Making of English Literature*, Giancarlo, *Parliament and Literature in Late Medieval England* and Scase, *Literature and Complaint*.

The patterns gradually accumulating from research and now confirmed and reinforced by this volume present scholars – not only historians of the book, but also
scholars of other disciplines – with intriguing research problems. Why was it that
bureaucratic infrastructure, material and personnel met the needs of vernacular
book production? Was it that there was spare capacity in this craft, and spare supply
of its materials, rather than in that of the 'commercial' scribes, to use the language
of Linne Mooney and Jean-Pascal Pouzet? Or was vernacular copying so insignifi-
cant, chancy (Margaret Connolly demonstrates the difficulties that attended access
to exemplars of vernacular material) and unlucrative that 'commercial' scribes did
not risk involvement? Or was it demanding in special ways that these scribes could
not satisfy but clerks and scriveners could? Was there something in the education,
training or professional practices of clerks and scriveners that gave them skills that
transferred readily to the copying of vernacular texts for books? Or was there something special about the class of 'professional' writers – scriveners and the like – that
put them in a position to be offered work of this kind? Was their involvement a
function of the social and economic relations of the scribes with the audiences of
the books they copied? As professionals who already often entered directly into
business or working relations with members of the vernacular book-owning classes
and vernacular authors (for example, providing services as will-writers or serving
as household clerks), were they perhaps in a readier position to pick up copying
commissions from this new class of book-owners than commercial scribes? (It is
not quite analogous, admittedly, but it is tempting to wonder whether we might
liken the relation of the patron of the scrivener with the patron of the commercial producer to that of the supermarket book-buyer – picking up a book along
with other purchases, price-sensitive, satisfied with limited choice of title, genre
and production quality – with the customer of today's specialist bookseller.) Or was
it that the scrivener class overlapped significantly with the audiences for vernacular
literature, and even perhaps with that of the authors, so that copying literature was
somehow of a piece with reading and writing it? Or was it that informal methods
of production and access to production services somehow enabled evasion of ecclesiastical censorship, as suggested by Fiona Somerset in relation to Wycliffite books
(although a problem here is that the lollard bibles and some other books look like
'commercial' products)?[4]

Questions such as these remind us that the materiality of book production is
always part of, and cannot be understood independently from, larger cultural processes and trends. The new insights that the foregoing essays provide on how books
were made have their fullest significance in relation to histories of literacy, education
and reading, of consumer culture, of the organization, division and remuneration

---

[4] See Doyle, 'English Books in and out of Court', 163–81 (169) and the excellent discussion by
Jurkowski, 'Lollard Book Producers'.

of labour, of technology, and of faiths and ideologies. Recent years have seen much exploration of the relations between vernacular literary culture and its social, cultural and economic contexts.[5] The ideas and information presented in this volume have much to contribute to further investigation of this kind.

Investigation of the problems outlined above should, however, keep firmly in mind that any conclusions about the distinctive features of the production of vernacular book production must in our present state of knowledge be extremely tentative. John Thompson issues a salutary reminder that we should not unthinkingly assume that the metropolitan patterns which have occupied many scholars applied uniformly across all regions of England and beyond. And obviously, we can only speculate on the degree of representativeness of those manuscripts that survive. It is equally obvious that assessments of the contribution of the scrivener classes to innovation and of the degree to which production of manuscripts of the major poets was an engine of technological and cultural change need to be made in the light of the whole picture. Despite the milestone of this volume, and the recent appearance of other landmarks such as volumes II (2008) and III (1999) of *The Cambridge History of the Book in Britain*, we still know very little about the total extant corpus of manuscripts of English provenance that survive from the period 1350–1500. The research infrastructure for study of the early printed book (notably *Early English Books Online*) is vastly superior to that available for manuscripts. We do not even know how many manuscripts survive from the period. Even more astonishingly, perhaps, we have no comprehensive list of manuscripts containing vernacular materials. The present volume offers a step change in the study of English book production by synthesizing and reflecting on the wealth of research germane to the topic. It will underpin the further work on manuscripts and early books that is so badly needed, and, it is to be hoped, it will stimulate multi-disciplinary, quantitative and corpus approaches that will transform the subject once again.

---

[5] Much of this work has been informed by new historicist and cultural materialist approaches to literature; key topics are the politics of language, multi-lingualism and the relations of vernacular writing to social and economic power and to dissent. The bibliography is immense. The essays in Wallace (ed.), *The Cambridge History of Medieval English Literature* offer useful orientations and bibliography. Recent significant contributions include – to select more or less at random – Minnis, *Translations of Authority*; Rice, *Lay Piety and Religious Discipline in Middle English Literature*; and Wogan-Browne et al. (eds.), *Language and Culture in Medieval Britain*.

Bibliography

A Catalogue of the Harleian Manuscripts in the British Museum, 3 vols. (London: House of Commons, 1808).

Abrahams, Moses, 'Leaf from an English *Siddur* of the Twelfth Century', in *Jews College Jubilee Volume* (London: Luzac, 1906), 109–13.

Alexander, J. J. G., 'A Lost Leaf from a Bodleian Book of Hours', *BLR*, 8 (1971), 248–51.

'Art History, Literary History and the Study of Medieval Illuminated Manuscripts', *Studies in Iconography*, 18 (1997), 51–66.

'Facing the Middle Ages: Concluding Remarks', *Gesta*, 46 (2007), 193–7.

'Foreign Illuminators and Illuminated Manuscripts', in *CHBB: III*, 47–64.

'Painting and Manuscript Illumination for Royal Patrons in the Later Middle Ages', in *English Court Culture in the Later Middle Ages*, ed. V. J. Scattergood and J. W. Sherborne (London: Duckworth, 1983), 141–62.

'Preliminary Marginal Drawings in Medieval Manuscripts', *Artistes, artisans et production artistique au Moyen Âge: Volume III*, ed. Xavier Barral i Altet (Paris: Picard, 1990), 307–19.

'The Butcher, the Baker, the Candlestick Maker: Images of Urban Labor, Manufacture and Shopkeeping from the Middle Ages', in *Material Culture and Cultural Materialisms in the Middle Ages and Renaissance*, ed. Chris Perry (Turnhout: Brepols, 2001), 89–110.

'William Abell "Lymnour" and 15th-Century English Illumination', in *Kunsthistorische Forschungen Otto Pächt zu seinem 70. Geburtstag*, ed. Artus Rosenauer and Gerold Weber (Salzburg: Residenz Verlag, 1972), 166–72.

Medieval Illuminators and Their Methods of Work (New Haven: Yale University Press, 1992).

Alexander, J. J. G. and Binski, Paul, *Age of Chivalry: Art in Plantagenet England, 1200–1400* (London: Royal Academy of Arts, 1987).

Alexander, J. J. G., Marrow, James H. and Sandler, Lucy Freeman (eds.), *The Splendor of the Word: Medieval and Renaissance Illuminated Manuscripts at the New York Public Library* (New York Public Library, 2005).

Alexander, J. J. G. and Temple, Elzbieta, *Illuminated Manuscripts*, in *Oxford College Libraries, the University Archives and the Taylor Institution* (Oxford: Clarendon Press, 1985).

Allen, Hope Emily, 'The *Speculum Vitae*: Addendum', *PMLA*, 32 (1917), 133–62.

Anderson, David (ed.), *Sixty Bokes Olde and Newe: Manuscripts and Early Printed Books from Libraries in and near Philadelphia Illustrating Chaucer's Sources, His Works and Their Influence* (Knoxville: University of Tennessee Press with the New Chaucer Society, 1986).

Anglo, Sydney, *Spectacle, Pageantry and Early Tudor Policy*, 2nd edn (Oxford: Clarendon Press, 1997).

Appadurai, Arjun (ed.), *The Social Life of Things: Commodities in Cultural Perspective* (Cambridge University Press, 1986).

Armstrong, Elizabeth, 'English Purchases of Printed Books from the Continent 1465–1526', *EHR*, 94 (1979), 268–90.

Arn, Mary-Jo, 'A Need for Books: Charles d'Orléans and His Travelling Libraries in England and France', *JEBS*, 12 (2009), 77–98.

(ed.), *Charles d'Orléans in England 1415–1440* (Cambridge: Brewer, 2000).

The Poet's Notebook: The Personal Manuscript of Charles d'Orléans (Paris BnF MS Fr. 25458) (Turnhout: Brepols, 2008).

'Two Manuscripts, One Mind: Charles d'Orléans and the Production of Manuscripts in Two Languages (Paris, BN MS Fr. 25458 and London, BL MS Harley 682)', in *Charles d'Orléans in England (1415–1440)*, ed. Mary-Jo Arn (Cambridge: Brewer, 2000), 61–78.

Arnold, John H., 'Comment: Social Contexts of Censorship and Power', *Journal of British Studies*, 46 (2007), 748–52.

Aston, Margaret, 'Lollardy and Literacy' (1977), in Margaret Aston, *Lollards and Reformers: Images and Literacy in Late Medieval Religion* (London: Hambledon, 1984), 193–218.

Auerbach, Erna, *Tudor Artists* (London: Athlone, 1954).

Backhouse, Janet, 'An Illuminator's Sketchbook', *British Library Journal*, 1 (1975), 3–14.

'The Lovel Lectionary: A Memorial Offering to Salisbury Cathedral', in *The English Medieval Cathedral: Papers in Honour of Pamela Tudor-Craig*, ed. Janet Backhouse (Donington: Paul Watkins, 2003), 112–25.

'The Royal Library from Edward IV to Henry VII', in *CHBB: III*, 267–73.

The Sherborne Missal (London: British Library, 1999).

Baker, J. H., 'The Books of the Common Law', in *CHBB: III*, 411–32.

Baker, J. H. and Ringrose, J. S., *A Catalogue of English Legal Manuscripts in Cambridge University Library* (Woodbridge: Boydell, 1996).

Barber, Giles, 'The Advent of Gold Tooling in English Bookbinding and the Intermediary Role of Thomas Linacre', in *'For the love of the binding': Studies in Bookbinding History Presented to Mirjam Foot*, ed. David Pearson (London: British Library, 2000), 53–66.

Barker, Nicolas J., 'A Register of Writs and the Scales Binder: II The Scales Binder', *Book Collector*, 21 (1972), 356–79.

Form and Meaning in the History of the Book: Selected Essays (London: British Library, 2003).

(ed.), *Two East Anglian Picture Books: A Facsimile of the Helmingham Herbal and Bestiary and Bodleian MS. Ashmole 1504* (London: Roxburghe Club, 1988).

Barr, Helen (ed.), *The Piers Plowman Tradition* (London: Everyman's Library, 1993).

Barr, Helen and Hutchinson, Ann M. (eds.), *Text and Controversy from Wyclif to Bale: Essays in Honour of Anne Hudson* (Turnhout: Brepols, 2005).

Barron, Caroline M., 'New Light on Thomas Usk', *Chaucer Newsletter*, 26.2 (2004), 1.

Review of Lisa Jefferson (ed.), *Wardens' Accounts and Court Minute Books of the Goldsmiths' Mistery of London 1334–1446*, *Urban History*, 32 (2005), 173–5.

Bat-Yehouda-Zerdoun, Monique, 'La Fabrication des encres noires d'après les textes', in *Codicologica: Les matériaux du livre manuscrit*, ed. J. P. Gumbert and Albert Gruys (Leiden: Brill, 1980), 52–8.

Baxter, Philip, *Sarum Use: The Development of a Medieval Code of Liturgy and Customs* (Salisbury: Sarum Script, 1994).

Beadle, Richard, 'English Autograph Writings of the Later Middle Ages: Some Preliminaries', in *Gli autografi medievali: Problemi paleografici e filologici; Atti del convegno di studio della Fondazione Ezio Franceschini, Erice, 25 settembre–2 ottobre 1990*, ed. Paolo Chiesa and Lucia Pinelli (Spoleto: Centro Italiano di Studi sull'Alto Medioevo, 1994), 249–68.

'Geoffrey Spirleng (c.1426–c.1494): A Scribe of *The Canterbury Tales* in His Time', in *Of the Making of Books: Medieval Manuscripts, Their Scribes and Readers: Essays Presented to M. B. Parkes*, ed. Pamela R. Robinson and Rivkah Zim (Aldershot: Scolar, 1997), 116–46.

'Middle English Texts and Their Transmission, 1350–1500: Some Geographical Criteria', in *Speaking in Our Tongues: Medieval Dialectology and Related Disciplines*, ed. Margaret Laing and Keith Williamson (Cambridge: Brewer, 1994), 69–91.

'Prolegomena to a Literary Geography of Later Medieval Norfolk', in *Regionalism in Late Medieval Manuscripts and Texts: Essays Celebrating the Publication of a Linguistic Atlas of Medieval English*, ed. Felicity Riddy (Cambridge: Brewer, 1991), 89–108.

'Sir John Fastolf's French Books', in *Medieval Texts in Context*, ed. Graham D. Caie and Denis Renevey (London and New York: Routledge, 2008), 96–112.

Beadle, Richard and Owen, A. E. B. (eds.), *The Findern Anthology, Cambridge University Library MS. Ff.1.6* (London: Scolar, 1977).

Bearman, F., 'The Origins and Significance of Two Late Medieval Textile Chemise Bookbindings in the Walters Art Gallery', *Journal of the Walters Art Gallery*, 54 (1996), 163–87.

Bell, David N., 'Monastic Libraries: 1400–1557', in *CHBB: III*, 229–54.

'The Libraries of Religious Houses in the Late Middle Ages', in *The Cambridge History of Libraries in Britain and Ireland, Volume I: To 1640*, ed. Elisabeth Leedham-Green and Teresa Webber (Cambridge University Press, 2006), 126–51.

Bell, H. E., 'The Price of Books in Medieval England', *Library*, 4th ser., 17 (1936–7), 312–32.

Bell, Maureen (ed.), *The British Book Trade Index* (University of Birmingham, 2005), www.bbti.bham.ac.uk

[Bénédictins du Bouveret] *Colophons des manuscrits occidentaux des origins au XVIe siècle*, 6 vols. (Fribourg: Editions Universitaires, 1965–82).

Benjamin, Walter, 'Das Kunstwerk im Zeitalter seiner technischen Reproduzierbarkeit', in *Illuminationen: Augewählte Schriften*, ed. S. Unseld (Frankfurt am Main: Suhrkamp, 1955; repr. 1961), 148–84.

Bennett, H. S., *English Books and Readers 1475 to 1557: Being a Study in the History of the Book Trade from Caxton to the Incorporation of the Stationers' Company* (Cambridge University Press, 1952).

Bennett, Kirsty, 'The Book Collections of Llanthony Priory from Foundation until Dissolution (c.1100–1538)', unpub. PhD thesis (University of Kent, 2007).

Bennett, Stuart, *Trade Bookbinding in the British Isles, 1660–1800* (New Castle: Oak Knoll, 2004).

Benskin, Michael, 'Chancery Standard', in *New Perspectives on English Historical Linguistics: Volume II: Lexis and Transmission*, ed. Christian J. Kay, Carole Hough and Irené Wotherspoon (Amsterdam: Benjamins, 2004), 1–40.

'The Fit-Technique Explained', in *Regionalism in Late Medieval Manuscripts and Texts: Essays Celebrating the Publication of a Linguistic Atlas of Mediaeval English*, ed. Felicity Riddy (Cambridge: Brewer, 1991), 9–26.

'The Hands of the Kildare Poems' Manuscript', *Irish University Review*, 20 (1990), 163–93.

'The Letters <þ> and <y> in Later Middle English, and Some Related Matters', *Journal of the Society of Archivists*, 7 (1982), 13–30.

Benskin, Michael and Laing, Margaret, 'Translations and *Mischsprachen* in Middle English Manuscripts', in *So Meny People, Longages and Tonges: Philological Essays in Scots and Mediaeval English Presented to Angus McIntosh*, ed. Michael Benskin and M. L. Samuels (Edinburgh: Middle English Dialect Project, 1981), 55–106.

Benson, David C. and Blanchfield, Lynne S., *The Manuscripts of Piers Plowman: The B Version* (Cambridge: Brewer, 1997).

Benson, Larry D., 'The Order of *The Canterbury Tales*', *SAC*, 3 (1981), 77–120.

(ed.), *The Riverside Chaucer*, 3rd edn (Oxford University Press, 1987).

Bent, Margaret, 'Music Seen and Music Heard: Music in England *c.*1400–1547', in *Gothic: Art for England 1400–1547*, ed. Richard Marks and Paul Williamson (London: Victoria and Albert Publications, 2003), 120–7.

Bibliothèque Nationale [de France], *La Librairie de Charles V* (Paris: Bibliothèque Nationale, 1968).

Binski, Paul and Panayatova, Stella (eds.), *The Cambridge Illuminations: Ten Centuries of Book Production in the Medieval West* (London and Turnhout: Harvey Miller/Brepols, 2005).

Bischoff, Bernhard, *Latin Paleography: Antiquity and the Middle Ages*, trans. Dáibhí Ó Cróinín and David Ganz (Cambridge University Press, 1990).

Bischoff, Frank M., 'Pergamentdicke und Lagenordnung', in *Pergament: Geschichte, Struktur, Restaurierung, Herstellung*, ed. Peter Rück (Sigmaringen: Jan Thorbecke Verlag, 1991), 99–144.

Blades, William, 'On Paper and Paper-Marks', *Library*, 1 (1889), 217–23.

Blake, N. F., 'Caxton's Second Edition of *The Canterbury Tales*', in *The English Medieval Book: Studies in Memory of Jeremy Griffiths*, ed. A. S. G. Edwards, Vincent Gillespie and Ralph Hanna III (London: British Library, 2000), 135–53.

'Editorial Assumptions and Problems of *The Canterbury Tales*', *Poetica*, 20 (1984), 1–19.

'Manuscript to Print', in *G&P*, 403–32.

The Textual Tradition of The Canterbury Tales (London: Arnold, 1985).

'Vernon Manuscript: Contents and Organisation', in *Studies in the Vernon Manuscript*, ed. Derek Pearsall (Cambridge: Brewer, 1990), 45–59.

William Caxton and English Literary Culture (London and Rio Grande: Hambledon, 1991).

Blanchfield, L. S., 'The Romances in MS Ashmole 61: An Idiosyncratic Scribe', in *Romance in Medieval England*, ed. M. Mills, J. Fellows and Carol M. Meale (Cambridge: Brewer, 1991), 65–87.

Blayney, Peter W. M., *The Stationers' Company before the Charter: 1403–1557* (London: Worshipful Company of Stationers and Newspapermakers, 2003).

Blodgett, James E., 'William Thynne (d. 1546)', in *Editing Chaucer: The Great Tradition*, ed. Paul G. Ruggiers (Norman, OK: Pilgrim Books, 1984), 35–52.

Boase, T. S. R. (intro.), *English Illumination of the Thirteenth and Fourteenth Centuries*, Bodleian Library Picture Book, no. 10 (Oxford: Bodleian Library, 1954).

Boffey, Julia, 'Books and Readers in Calais: Some Notes', *The Ricardian*, 13 (2002), 67–74.

Manuscripts of English Courtly Love Lyrics in the Later Middle Ages (Woodbridge: Brewer, 1985).

'Short Texts in Manuscript Anthologies: The Minor Poems of John Lydgate in Two Fifteenth-Century Collections', in *The Whole Book: Cultural Perspectives on the Medieval Miscellany*, ed. Stephen G. Nichols and Siegfried Wenzel (Ann Arbor: University of Michigan Press, 1996), 69–82.

Boffey, Julia and Edwards, A. S. G., *A New Index of Middle English Verse* (London: British Library, 2005).

'Literary Texts', in *CHBB: III*, 555–75.

'Middle English Literary Writings, 1150–1400', in *CHBB: II*, 380–90.

Boffey, Julia and Meale, Carol M., 'Selecting the Text: Rawlinson C. 86 and Some Other Books for London Readers', in *Regionalism in Late Medieval Manuscripts and Texts: Essays Celebrating the Publication of a Linguistic Atlas of Late Mediaeval English*, ed. Felicity Riddy (Cambridge: Brewer, 1991), 143–69.

Boffey, Julia and Thompson, John J., 'Anthologies and Miscellanies: Production and Choice of Texts', in G&P, 279–315.

Boffey, Julia and Edwards, A. S. G., with Barker-Benfield, B. C. (eds.), *The Works of Geoffrey Chaucer and The Kingis Quair: A Facsimile of Bodleian Library, Oxford, MS Arch. Selden. B. 24* (Cambridge: Brewer, 1997).

Bone, Gavin, 'Extant Manuscripts Printed from by W. De Worde with Notes on the Owner, Roger Thorney', *Library*, 4th ser., 12 (1931–2), 284–309.

Bornstein, Diane (ed.), *The Middle English Translation of Christine de Pisan's Livre du Corps de Policie* (Heidelberg: Carl Winter Universitätsverlag, 1978).

Bose, Mishtooni, 'Religious Authority and Dissent', in *A Companion to Medieval English Literature and Culture c.1350–c.1500*, ed. Peter Brown (Blackwell Reference Online, 2007), www.blackwellreference.com

Bose, Mishtooni and Hornbeck. J. Patrick, II (eds.), *Wycliffite Controversies* (Turnhout: Brepols, forthcoming).

Bousmanne, Bernard, Van Hemelryck, Tania and Van Hoorebeeck, Celine (eds.), *La Librairie des ducs de Bourgogne, Volume III* (Turnhout: Brepols, 2007).

Bowden, Betsy, 'Visual Portraits of the Canterbury Pilgrims, 1484(?) to 1809', in *The Ellesmere Chaucer: Essays in Interpretation*, ed. Martin Stevens and Daniel Woodward (San Marino: Huntington Library, 1995), 171–204.

Bower, Peter, 'The White Art: The Importance of Interpretation in the Analysis of Paper', in *Looking at Paper: Evidence and Interpretation: Symposium Proceedings, Toronto 1999*, ed. John Slavin et al. (Ottawa: Canadian Conservation Institute, 2001), 5–16.

Bowers, John M., *Chaucer and Langland: The Antagonistic Tradition* (Notre Dame, IN: University of Notre Dame Press, 2007).

'*Pearl* in Its Royal Setting: Ricardian Poetry Revisited', *SAC*, 17 (1995), 111–55.

'Two Professional Readers of Chaucer and Langland: Scribe D and the Hm 114 Scribe', *SAC*, 26 (2004), 113–46.

Brady, Sr Mary Teresa, 'Lollard Interpolations and Omissions in Manuscripts of *The Pore Caitif*', in *De Cella in Seculum: Religious and Secular Life and Devotion in Late Medieval England*', ed. Michael Sargent (Cambridge: Brewer, 1989), 183–203.

Brantley, Jessica, *Reading in the Wilderness: Private Devotion and Public Performance in Late Medieval England* (University of Chicago Press, 2007).

Brewer, D. S. and Owen, A. E. B. (eds.), *The Thornton Manuscript: Lincoln Cathedral MS 91*, (London: Scolar, 1975; 2nd edn, 1977).

Brewer, J. S., Dimock, James F. and Warner, G. F. (eds.), *Giraldi Cambrensis Opera*, Rolls Series 21, 8 vols. (London: Longmans, Green, Reader and Dyer, 1861–91).

Briggs, Charles F., 'MS Digby 233 and the Patronage of John Trevisa's *De regimine principum*', *EMS*, 7 (1998), 249–63.

Giles of Rome's De Regimine Principum: Reading and Writing Politics at Court and University, c.1275–c.1525 (Cambridge University Press, 1999).

Brinkman, Herman, 'Het Comburgse handschrift en de Gentse boekproductie omstreeks 1400', *Queeste: Tijdschrift over middeleeuwse letterkunde in de Nederlanden*, 5 (1998), 98–113.

Brinkmann, Bodo, *Die flämische Buchmalerei am Ende des Burgunderreichs: Der Meister des dresdener Gebetbuchs und die Miniaturisten seiner Zeit* (Turnhout: Brepols, 1996).

'British Library Digital Catalogue of Illuminated Manuscripts' (British Library, n.d.), www. bl.uk/catalogues/illuminatedmanuscripts

'British Library Manuscripts Catalogue' (British Library, n.d.), http://www.bl.uk/catalogues/ manuscripts

Britnell, Richard H., *The Commercialisation of English Society, 1000–1500* (Cambridge University Press, 1993).

'The Proliferation of Markets in England, 1200–1349', *Economic History Review*, 2nd ser., 34 (1981), 209–21.

Britton, Derek and Fletcher, Alan J., 'Medieval Hiberno-English Inscriptions on the Inscribed Slates of Smarmore: Some Reconsiderations and Additions', *Irish University Review*, 20 (1990), 55–72.

Broekhuijsen, Klara H., *The Masters of the Dark Eyes: Late Medieval Manuscript Painting in Holland* (Turnhout: Brepols, 2009).

Brown, A. J., 'The Date of Erasmus' Latin Translation of the New Testament', *Transactions of the Cambridge Bibliographical Society*, 8 (1984), 351–80.

Brown, Carleton and Robbins, Rossell Hope, *The Index of Middle English Verse* (New York: Columbia University Press, 1943).

Brown, Michelle P., *A Guide to Western Historical Scripts from Antiquity to 1600* (London: British Library, 1990).

'Continental Symptoms in Insular Codicology: Historical Perspectives', in *Pergament: Geschichte, Struktur, Restaurierung, Herstellung*, ed. Peter Rück (Sigmaringen: Jan Thorbecke Verlag, 1991), 57–62.

Brown, T. Julian, *Palaeographer's View: Selected Papers of Julian Brown*, ed. Janet M. Bately, Michelle Brown and Jane Roberts (London: Harvey Miller, 1993).

Brownrigg, Linda L. (ed.), *Making the Medieval Book: Techniques of Production* (Los Altos Hills, CA: Anderson-Lovelace, 1995).

Bruckner, Ursula, 'Das Beutelbuch und seine Verwandten – der Hülleneinband, das Faltbuch und der Buchbeutel', *Gutenberg-Jahrbuch*, 72 (1997), 307–24.

Bühler, Curt F., 'Sir John Fastolf's Manuscripts of the "Epître d'Othéa"', *Scriptorium*, 3 (1949), 123–8.

Burns, Robert I., SJ, 'Paper Comes to the West, 800–1400', in *Europäische Technik im Mittelalter: 800 bis 1400, Tradition und Innovation*, ed. Uta Lindgren (Berlin: Mann, 1996), 413–22.

Burrow, J. A., 'Autobiographical Poetry in the Middle Ages: The Case of Thomas Hoccleve', *Proceedings of the British Academy*, 68 (1982), 389–412.

Thomas Hoccleve (Aldershot: Variorum, 1994).

Burrow, J. A. and Doyle, A. I. (eds.), *Thomas Hoccleve: A Facsimile of the Autograph Verse Manuscripts*, EETS ss 19 (Oxford University Press, 2002).

Busonero, Paola, Mazzoli, Maria Antoinetta, Casagrande Devoti, Luciana and Ornato, Ezio, *La fabbrica del codice: Materiali per la storia del libro nel tardo medioevo* (Rome: Viella, 1999).

Butcher, Andrew, 'The Functions of Script in the Speech Community of a Medieval Town, c.1300–1550', in *The Uses of Script and Print, 1300–1700*, ed. Julia Crick and Alexandra Walsham (Cambridge University Press, 2004), 157–70.

Butterfield, Ardis, 'Articulating the Author: Gower and the French Vernacular Codex', *Yearbook of English Studies*, 33 (2003), 80–96.

Caldelli, Elisabetta, *Copisti a Roma nel quattrocento* (Rome: Viella, 2006).

I codici datati nei vaticani latini 1–2100 (Città del Vaticano: Biblioteca Apostolica Vaticana 2007).

Calkins, Robert G., 'Stages of Execution: Procedures of Illumination as Revealed in an Unfinished Book of Hours', *Gesta*, 17 (1978), 61–70.

Campbell, Lorne and Foister, Susan, 'Gerard, Lucas and Susanna Horenbout', *The Burlington Magazine*, 128 (1986), 719–27.

Canart, Paul, 'La Paléographie est-elle un art ou une science?', *Scriptorium*, 60 (2006), 159–85.

Cannon, Christopher, *The Making of Chaucer's English: A Study of Words*, Cambridge Studies in Medieval Literature, 39 (Cambridge University Press, 1998).

Canny, Nicholas, *Making Ireland British, 1580–1650* (Oxford University Press, 2001).

Carley, James, 'The Dispersal of the Monastic Libraries and the Salvaging of the Spoils', in *The Cambridge History of Libraries Britain and Ireland: Volume I: To 1640*, ed. Elisabeth Leedham-Green (Cambridge University Press, 2006), 292–321.

The Libraries of King Henry VIII, CBMLC 7 (London: British Library in association with British Academy, 2000).

'The Royal Library under Henry VIII', in *CHBB: III*, 274–81.

Carlson, David R., 'The Woodcut Illustrations in Early Printed Editions of Chaucer's Canterbury Tales', in *Chaucer Illustrated: Five Hundred Years of The Canterbury Tales in Pictures*, ed. William Finley and Joseph Rosenblum (New Castle: Oak Knoll, 2003), 73–120.

Carter, Harry, *A View of Early Typography up to about 1600* (Oxford: Clarendon, 1969).

Catto, J. I. 'Wyclif and Wycliffism at Oxford, 1356–1430', in *The History of the University of Oxford, Volume II: Late Medieval Oxford*, ed. J. I. Catto and Ralph Evans (Oxford: Clarendon Press, 1992), 175–261.

Catto, Jeremy, 'Written English: The Making of the Language 1370–1400', *Past and Present*, 179 (2003), 24–59.

Cavanaugh, Susan H., 'A Study of Books Privately Owned in England, 1300–1450', 2 vols., unpub. PhD thesis (Philadelphia: University of Pennsylvania, 1980).

Cawley, A. C. and Stevens, Martin (eds.), *The Towneley Cycle: A Facsimile of Huntington MS HM 1* (Leeds: University of Leeds, School of English, 1976).

Cerquiglini, Bernard, *In Praise of the Variant: A Critical History of Philology*, trans. Betsy Wing (Baltimore: Johns Hopkins University Press, 1999).

Chaplais, Pierre, *English Royal Documents King John–Henry VI 1199–1461* (Oxford: Clarendon Press, 1971).

Chapman, R. G. (intr.), *Scenes from the Life of Christ in English Manuscripts* (Oxford: Bodleian Library, 1951).

Cherry, J., 'Leather', in *English Medieval Industries: Craftsmen, Techniques, Products*, ed. John Blair and Nigel Ramsay (London: Hambledon, 1991), 295–318.

Chesney, K., 'Two MSS of Christine de Pisan', *MÆ*, 1 (1932), 35–41.

Christianson, C. Paul, 'A Century of the Manuscript-Book Trade in Late Medieval London', *Medievalia et Humanistica*, 12 (1984), 143–65.

'A Community of Book Artisans in Chaucer's London', *Viator*, 20 (1989), 207–18.

A Directory of London Stationers and Book Artisans 1300–1500 (New York: Bibliographical Society of America, 1990).

'An Early Tudor Stationer and the "Prynters of Bokes"', *Library*, 6th ser., 9 (1987), 259–62.

'Evidence for the Study of London's Late Medieval Manuscript Book-Trade', in *G&P*, 87–108.

Memorials of the Book Trade in Medieval London: The Archives of Old London Bridge (Cambridge: Brewer, 1987).

'The Rise of London's Book-Trade', in *CHBB: II*, 128–47.

Clanchy, M. T., *From Memory to Written Record: England 1066–1307*, 2nd edn (Oxford: Blackwell, 1993).

Clark, J. G., 'Print and Pre-Reformation Religion: The Benedictines and the Press, *c*.1470–*c*. 1550', in *The Uses of Script and Print, 1300–1700*, ed. J. Crick and A. Walsham (Cambridge University Press, 2004), 71–92.

'The Religious Orders in Pre-Reformation England', in *The Religious Orders in Pre-Reformation England*, ed. J. G. Clark (Woodbridge: Boydell, 2002), 3–33.

'University Monks in Late Medieval England', in *Medieval Monastic Education*, ed. George Ferzoco and Carolyn Muessig (London and New York: Leicester University Press, 2000), 56–71.

Clark, J. W., 'On the Work Done to the Library of the Exeter Cathedral in the Early 15th Century', *Cambridge Antiquarian Society Proceedings*, x (XLIV of New Series) (1904), 294–306.

Clark, R. J. H., 'Raman Microscopy Application to the Identification of Pigments on Medieval Manuscripts', *Chemical Society Reviews*, 24 (1995), 187–96.

Clarke, Mark, *The Art of All Colours: Medieval Recipe Books for Painters and Illuminators* (London: Archetype Publications, 2001).

Clarke, Peter D. with Lovatt, R. (eds.), *The University and College Libraries of Cambridge*, CBMLC, 10 (London: British Academy, 2002).

Clarkson, Christopher, 'English Monastic Bookbinding in the Twelfth Century', in *Ancient and Medieval Book Materials and Techniques: Erice, 18–25 September 1992*, ed. Marilena Maniaci and Paola F. Munafò (Città del Vaticano: Biblioteca Apostolica Vaticana, 1993), 181–200.

'Further Studies in Anglo-Saxon and Norman Bookbinding: Board Attachment Methods Re-Examined', in *Roger Powell: The Compleat Binder*, ed. J. L. Sharpe (Turnhout: Brepols, 1996), 154–214.

'Rediscovering Parchment: The Nature of the Beast', in *Conservation and Preservation in Small Libraries*, ed. N. Hadgraft and K. Swift (Cambridge: The Parker Library, 1994), 75–96.

Clemens, Raymond and Timothy Graham, *Introduction to Manuscript Studies* (Ithaca: Cornell University Press, 2007).

Coates, Alan, *English Medieval Books: The Reading Abbey Collections from Foundation to Dispersal* (Oxford: Clarendon Press, 1999).

Cobb, H. S. (ed.), *The Overseas Trade of London: Exchequer Customs Accounts 1480–1*, London Record Society Publications 27 (London Record Society, 1990).

Cobban, Alan, *English University Life in the Middle Ages* (University College London Press, 1999).

Cole, Andrew, *Literature and Heresy in the Age of Chaucer* (Cambridge University Press, 2008).

Colledge, Edmund, 'South Netherlands Books of Hours Made for England', *Scriptorium*, 32 (1978), 55–7.

Colón, Fernando, *Abecedarium B: Y Supplementum*, intr. T. Marín Martínez (Madrid: Fundacion Mapfre America, 1992).

    Catalogue of the Library of Ferdinand Columbus. Reproduced in Facsimile from the Unique Manuscript in the Colombine Library of Seville, ed. A. M. Huntington (New York: Huntington, 1905).

Condello, Emma and De Gregorio, Giuseppe (eds.), *Scribi e colofoni: Le sottoscrizioni di copisti dalle origini all'avento della stampa* (Spoleto: Centro Italiano di Studi sull'Alto Medioevo, 1995).

Connolly, Margaret, 'Books for the "helpe of euery persoone þat þenkiþ to be saued": Six Devotional Anthologies from Fifteenth-Century London', *Yearbook of English Studies*, 33 (2003), 170–81.

    (ed.), *Contemplations of the Dread and Love of God*, EETS os 303 (Oxford University Press, 1994).

    John Shirley: Book Production and the Noble Household in Fifteenth-Century England (Aldershot and Brookfield, VT: Ashgate, 1998).

    'Practical Reading for Body and Soul in Some Later Medieval Manuscript Miscellanies', *JEBS*, 10 (2007), 151–74.

    (ed.), *IMEP, XIX: Manuscripts in the University Library, Cambridge (Dd–Oo)* (Cambridge: Brewer, 2009).

    'When the Right Word *Really* Matters: Practical Translation in a Fifteenth-Century Leechbook', in *The Medieval Translator* 12, ed. Denis Renevey and Christiania Whitehead (Turnhout: Brepols, 2009), 147–56.

Connolly, Margaret and Mooney, Linne R. (eds.), *Design and Distribution of Late Medieval Manuscripts in England* (York Medieval Press, 2008).

Connolly, Margaret and Plumley, Yolanda, 'Crossing the Channel: John Shirley and the Circulation of French Lyric Poetry in England in the Early Fifteenth Century', in *Patrons, Authors and Workshops: Books and Book Production in Paris around 1400*, ed. Godfried Croenen and Peter Ainsworth (Leuven: Peeters, 2006), 311–32.

Corder, Joan, *A Dictionary of Suffolk Arms* (Ipswich: Suffolk Record Society, 1965).

Corrie, Marilyn, 'The Compilation of Oxford, Bodleian Library, MS Digby 86', *MÆ*, 66 (1997), 236–49.

Courthope, W. (ed.), *Thys rol was laburd and finished by Master John Rows of Warrewyk* (London, 1859; repr. Gloucester: Alan Sutton, 1980).

Coxe, H. O., *Bodleian Library Quarto Catalogues, 2, Laudian Manuscripts (1858–85)*, rev. R. W. Hunt (Oxford: Bodleian Library, 1973).

Craigie, W., ' "Champ" and "Vynet" ', *Notes and Queries*, 148 (1925), 171.

Croenen, Godfried and Ainsworth, Peter (eds.), *Patrons, Authors and Workshops: Books and Book Production in Paris around 1400* (Leuven: Peeters, 2006).

Croenen, G., Figg, K. and Taylor, A., 'Authorship, Patronage, and Literary Gifts: The Books Froissart Brought to England in 1395', *JEBS*, 11 (2008), 1–42.

Croenen, Godfried, Rouse, Mary and Rouse, Richard, 'Pierre de Liffol and the Manuscripts of Froissart's *Chronicles*', *Viator*, 33 (2002), 261–93.

Crook, E. J., 'Manuscripts Surviving from the Austin Friars at Cambridge', *Manuscripta*, 27 (1983), 82–90.

Cutler, John L. and Robbins, Rossell Hope, *Supplement to the Index of Middle English Verse* (Lexington: University of Kentucky Press, 1965).

D'Haenens, Albert, 'Pour une sémiologie paléographique et une histoire de l'écriture', *Scriptorium*, 29 (1975), 175–98.

Da Bisticci, Vespasiano, *Le vite*, ed. A. Greco, 2 vols. (Florence: Istituto Nazionale di Studi sul Rinascimento, 1970–6).

Da Rold, Orietta, 'A Study of Cambridge University Library MS Dd.4.24 of Chaucer's *Canterbury Tales*', unpub. PhD thesis (De Montfort University, 2002).

'Fingerprinting Paper in West Midlands Medieval Manuscripts', in *Essays in Manuscript Geography: Vernacular Manuscripts of the English West Midlands from the Conquest to the Sixteenth Century*, ed. Wendy Scase (Turnhout: Brepols, 2007), 257–71.

'Textual Copying and Transmission', in *The Oxford Handbook of Medieval English Literature*, ed. Elaine Treharne and Greg Walker (Oxford University Press, 2009), 33–56.

'The Quiring System in Cambridge University Library MS Dd.4.24 of Chaucer's *Canterbury Tales*', *Library*, 7th ser., 4 (2003), 107–28.

'The Significance of Scribal Corrections in Cambridge University Library, MS Dd.4.24.', *Chaucer Review*, 41 (2007), 393–436.

Dain, Alphonse, *Les manuscrits*, 3rd edn (Paris: Belles Lettres, 1975).

Danbury, E., 'The Decoration and Illumination of Royal Charters in England, 1250–1509: An Introduction', in *England and Her Neighbours, 1066–1453: Essays in Honour of Pierre Chaplais*, ed. M. Jones and M. Vale (London: Hambledon, 1989), 157–79.

Davies, R. R., 'Frontier Arrangements in Fragmented Societies: Ireland and Wales', in *Medieval Frontier Societies*, ed. Robert Bartlett and Angus MacKay (Oxford: Clarendon Press, 1989), 77–100.

Davis, G. R. C., *Medieval Cartularies of Great Britain: A Short Catalogue* (London: Longmans, 1958).

Davis, Norman (ed.), *Non-Cycle Plays and Fragments*, EETS ss 1 (London: Oxford University Press, 1970).

'The Language of Two Brothers in the Fifteenth Century', in *Five Hundred Years of Words and Sounds: A Festschrift for Eric Dobson*, ed. Eric G. Stanley and Douglas Gray (Cambridge: Brewer, 1983), 23–8.

De Hamel, Christopher, 'Books and Society', in *CHBB: II*, 3–21.

Medieval Craftsmen: Scribes and Illuminators (London: British Library, 1992).

'Reflexions on the Trade in Books of Hours at Ghent and Bruges', in *Manuscripts in the Fifty Years after the Invention of Printing*, ed. J. B. Trapp (London: Warburg Institute, 1983), 29–34.

Syon Abbey: The Library of the Bridgettine Nuns and Their Peregrinations after the Reformation (Otley: The Roxburghe Club, 1991).

The British Library Guide to Manuscript Illumination: History and Techniques (London: British Library, 2001).

'The Dispersal of the Library of Christ Church, Canterbury from the Fourteenth to the Sixteenth Century', in *Books and Collectors 1200 –1700: Essays Presented to Andrew Watson*, ed. James P. Carley and Colin G. C. Tite (London: British Library, 1997), 263–79.

De la Mare, Albinia C., 'A Fragment of Augustine in the Hand of Theoderic Werken', *TCBS*, 6 (1972–6), 285–90.

'Manuscripts Given to the University of Oxford by Humfrey, Duke of Gloucester', *BLR*, 13 (1989), 112–21.

[De la Mare, Albinia C., and Gillam, Stanley], *Duke Humfrey's Library and the Divinity School 1488–1988* (Oxford: Bodleian Library, 1988).

[De la Mare, Albinia C., and Hunt, Richard], *Duke Humfrey and English Humanism in the Fifteenth Century* (Oxford: Bodleian Library, 1970).

De Ricci, Seymour and Faye, Christopher Urdahl, *Supplement to the Census of Medieval and Renaissance Manuscripts in the United States and Canada* (New York: Bibliographical Society of America, 1962).

De Ricci, Seymour and Wilson, W. J., *Census of Medieval and Renaissance Manuscripts in the United States and Canada*, 3 vols. (New York: Bibliographical Society of America, 1935–40, 1961).

De Robertis, Teresa and Miriello, Rosanna (eds.), *I manoscritti datati della Biblioteca Riccardiana di Firenze*, 1 (Florence: SISMEL Edizioni del Galluzzo, 1997).

Dean, Ruth J and Boulton, Maureen B. M., *Anglo-Norman Literature: A Guide to Texts and Manuscripts* (London: ANTS, 1999).

Delaissé, L. M. J., 'The Importance of Books of Hours for the History of the Medieval Book', in *Gatherings in Honor of Dorothy Miner*, ed. Ursula E. McCracken et al. (Baltimore: Walters Art Gallery, 1974), 203–25.

Delaney, Sheila, *The Naked Text: Chaucer's 'Legend of Good Women'* (Berkeley: University of California Press, 1994).

Delisle, Leopold V., *Recherches sur la librairie de Charles V*, 2 vols. (Paris: H. Champion, 1907).

DeMarrais, Elizabeth, Gosden, Chris and Renfrew, Colin (eds.), *Rethinking Materiality: The Engagement of Mind with the Material World* (Cambridge: McDonald Institute for Archaeological Research, 2004).

Denholm-Young, N., *Handwriting in England and Wales*, 2nd edn (Cardiff: University of Wales Press, 1964).

Denne, Samuel, 'Observations on Paper-Marks', *Archaeologia*, 12 (1796), 114–31.

Dennison, Lynda and Rogers, Nicholas, 'A Medieval Best-Seller: Some Examples of Decorated Copies of Higden's *Polychronicon*', in *The Church and Learning in Later Medieval Society: Essays in Honour of R. B. Dobson*, ed. C. M. Barron and Jenny Stratford (Donington: Shaun Tyas, 2002), 80–99.

Derenzini, Giovanna, 'La produzione della carta a Fabriano agli inizi del' 400', *Contributi italiani alla diffusione della Carta in occidente tra XIV e XV Secolo*, ed. Giancarlo Castagnari (Fabriano: Pia Università dei cartai, 1990), 137–46.

Derolez, Albert, *Codicologie des manuscrits en écriture humanistique sur parchemin*, 2 vols. (Turnhout: Brepols, 1984).

'Pourquoi les copistes signaient-ils leurs manuscrits?', in *Scribi e colofoni: Le sottoscrizioni di copisti dalle origini all'avento della stampa*, ed. Emma Condello and Giuseppe de Gregorio (Spoleto: Centro Italiano di Studi sull'Alto Medioevo, 1995), 37–56.

'The Aesthetics of the Gothic Manuscript', *Scriptorium*, 50 (1996), 3–12.

The Palaeography of Gothic Manuscript Books from the Twelfth to the Early Sixteenth Century (Cambridge University Press, 2003).

Dolan, Terence P., 'Writing in Ireland', in *The Cambridge History of Medieval English Literature*, ed. David Wallace (Cambridge University Press, 1999), 208–28.

'Yonge, James (fl. 1405–1434)', *ODNB*.

Dove, Mary, *The First English Bible: The Text and Context of the Wycliffite Versions* (Cambridge University Press, 2007).

Dovey, Matthew J. et al. (eds.), *Early Manuscripts at Oxford University* (2000; repub. Oxford Digital Library, 2003), http://image.ox.ac.uk/

Doyle, A. I., 'A Survey of the Origins and Circulation of Theological Writings in English in the Fourteenth, Fifteenth and Early Sixteenth Centuries with Special Consideration of the Part of the Clergy Therein', unpub. PhD thesis, 2 vols. (Cambridge University, 1953).

'A Text Attributed to Ruusbroec Circulating in England', in *Dr. L. Reypens-Album, Studien on Tekstuitgaven von Ous Geestelijk*, erf. 16 (1964), 153–71.

'An Unrecognized Piece of *Piers the Ploughman's Creed* and Other Work by Its Scribe', *Speculum*, 34 (1959), 428–36.

'Book Production by the Monastic Orders in England (1375–1530)', in *Medieval Book Production: Assessing the Evidence*, ed. Linda Brownrigg (Los Altos Hills: Anderson-Lovelace, 1990), 1–19.

'Books Connected with the Vere Family and Barking Abbey', *Transactions of the Essex Archaeological Society*, 25 (1958), 222–43.

'English Books in and out of Court from Edward III to Henry VII', in *English Court Culture in the Later Middle Ages*, ed. V. J. Scattergood and J. W. Sherborne (London: Duckworth, 1983), 163–81.

'More Light on John Shirley', *MÆ*, 30 (1961), 93–101.

'Pen-Work Flourishing of Initials in England from *c*.1380', in *Tributes to Kathleen L. Scott: English Medieval Manuscripts and Their Readers*, ed. Marlene Villalobos Hennessy (London and Turnhout: Harvey Miller, 2009).

'Publication by Members of the Religious Orders', in G&P, 109–123.

'Recent Directions in Medieval Manuscript Study', in *New Directions in Later Medieval Manuscript Studies*, ed. Derek Pearsall (York Medieval Press, 2000), 1–14.

'Stephen Dodesham of Witham and Sheen', in *Of the Making of Books: Medieval Manuscripts, Their Scribes and Readers, Essays Presented to M. B. Parkes*, ed. Pamela R. Robinson and Rivkah Zim (Aldershot and Brookfield, VT: Ashgate Publishing, 1997), 94–115.

'The Copyist of MSS Bodley 283 and Durham Cosin V.ii.15', *JEBS*, 9 (2006), 125–9.

'The English Provincial Book Trade before Printing', in *Six Centuries of the Provincial Book Trade in Britain*, ed. Peter Isaac (Winchester: St Paul's Bibliographies, 1990), 13–29.

(ed.), *The Vernon Manuscript: A Facsimile of Bodleian Library, Oxford, MS Eng.Poet.a.1* (Cambridge: Brewer, 1987).

'The Work of a Late Fifteenth-Century Scribe, William Ebesham', *BJRL*, 39 (1957), 298–325.

Doyle, A. I. and Parkes, M. B., 'The Production of Copies of *The Canterbury Tales* and the *Confessio Amantis* in the Early Fifteenth Century', in *Medieval Scribes, Manuscripts, and Libraries: Essays Presented to N. R. Ker*, ed. M. B. Parkes and Andrew G. Watson (London: Scolar, 1978), 163–210.

Dresvina, J., 'A Note on a Hitherto Unpublished Life of St Margaret of Antioch from MS Eng. th.e.18: Its Scribe and Its Source', *JEBS*, 10 (2007), 217–31.

Driver, Martha W., 'Christine de Pisan and Robert Wyer: *The C. Hystoryes of Troye*, or *L'Epistre d'Othea* Englished', *Gutenberg-Jahrbuch*, 72 (1997), 125–39.

"In her owne persone semly and bewteus': Representing Women in Stories of Guy of Warwick', in *Guy of Warwick: Icon and Ancestor*, ed. Alison Wiggins and Rosalind Field (Cambridge: Brewer, 2007), 133–53.

'Inventing Visual History: Re-presenting the Legends of Warwickshire', in *Essays in Manuscript Geography: Vernacular Manuscripts of the English West Midlands from the Conquest to the Sixteenth Century*, ed. Wendy Scase (Turnhout: Brepols, 2007), 161–202.

'Mapping Chaucer: John Speed and the Later Portraits', *Chaucer Review*, 36 (2002), 228–49.

'"*Me fault faire*": French Makers of Manuscripts for English Patrons', in *Language and Culture in Medieval Britain: The French of England, 1100–c. 1500* ed. Jocelyn Wogan-Browne (Woodbridge: Boydell and Brewer, 2009).

'Medievalizing the Classical Past in Pierpont Morgan MS M 876', in *Middle English Poetry: Texts and Traditions, Essays in Honour of Derek Pearsall*, ed. A. J. Minnis (York Medieval Press, 2001), 211–39.

'Printing the *Confessio Amantis*: Caxton's Edition in Context', in *Re-visioning Gower*, ed. R. F. Yeager (Asheville, NC: Pegasus, 1998), 269–303.

The Image in Print: Book Illustration in Late Medieval England (London and Toronto: British Library, 2004).

'When is a Miscellany not Miscellaneous? Making Sense of the *Kalender of Shepherds*', *Yearbook of English Studies*, 33 (2003), 199–214.

Drogin, Marc, *Medieval Calligraphy: Its History and Technique* (Montclair: Allanheld and Schram, 1980).

Duff, Edward G., *A Century of the English Book Trade* (London: Bibliographical Society, 1948).

Duffy, Eamon, *Marking the Hours: English People and Their Prayers 1240–1570* (New Haven: Yale University Press, 2006).

Dugdale, William, *Antiquities of Warwickshire* (London, 1656).

Dunlop, Louisa, 'Pigments and Painting Materials in Fourteenth- and Early Fifteenth-Century Parisian Manuscript Illumination', in *Artistes, artisans et production artistique au Moyen Âge: Volume III*, ed. Xavier Barral i Altet (Paris: Picard, 1990), 271–93.

Dürrfeld, Eike Barbara, 'Terra Incognita: Toward a Historiography of Book Fastenings and Book Furniture', *Book History*, 3 (2000), 305–13.

Dutschke, C. W., *Guide to Medieval and Renaissance Manuscripts in the Huntington Library*, 2 vols. (San Marino: Huntington Library, 1989).

Dyer, Christopher, *Making a Living in the Middle Ages: The People of Britain 850–1520* (New Haven: Yale University Press, 2002).

'The Consumer and the Market in the Later Middle Ages', *Economic History Review*, 2nd ser., 42 (1989), 305–27.

Echard, Siân, 'Dialogues and Monologues: Manuscript Representations of the Conversation of the *Confessio Amantis*', in *Middle English Poetry: Texts and Traditions: Essays in Honour of Derek Pearsall*, ed. Alistair J. Minnis (York Medieval Press, 2001), 57–75.

'Glossing Gower: In Latin, in English, and *in absentia*: The Case of Bodleian Ashmole 35', in *Re-visioning Gower*, ed. R. F. Yeager (Asheville: Pegasus, 1998), 237–56.

Edwards, A. S. G., 'Decorated Caxtons', in *Incunabula: Studies in Fifteenth-Century Printed Books Presented to Lotte Hellinga*, ed. Martin Davies (London: British Library, 1999), 493–506.

'Fifteenth-Century Middle English Verse Author Collections', in *The English Medieval Book: Studies in Memory of Jeremy Griffiths*, ed. A. S. G. Edwards, Vincent Gillespie and Ralph Hanna III (London: British Library, 2000), 101–12.

'Manuscripts and Readers', in *A Companion to Medieval English Literature and Culture, c.1350–c.1500*, ed. Peter Brown (Oxford: Blackwell, 2007), 91–106.

(ed.), 'Regional Manuscripts 1200–1700', *English Manuscript Studies* 14 (2008).

'Stow and Lydgate's 'St Edmund', *Notes and Queries*, 218 (1973), 365–9.

'The McGill Fragment of Lydgate's *Fall of Princes*', *Scriptorium*, 28 (1974), 75–7.

Edwards, A. S. G. and Pearsall, Derek, 'The Manuscripts of the Major English Poetic Texts', in G&P, 257–78.

Edwards, A. S. G. and Hanna, Ralph III, 'Rotheley, the De Vere Circle, and the Ellesmere Chaucer', *Huntington Library Quarterly*, 58 (1996), 11–35.

Edwards, Kathleen, *The English Secular Cathedral in the Middle Ages: A Constitutional Study with Special Reference to the Fourteenth Century*, 2nd edn (Manchester and New York: Manchester University Press and Barnes and Noble, 1967).

Eisenstein, Elizabeth L., *The Printing Press as an Agent of Change: Communications and Cultural Transformations in Early Modern Europe*, 2 vols. (Cambridge University Press, 1979).

Eldredge, L. M. (ed.), *IMEP, IX: Manuscripts in the Ashmole Collection, Bodleian Library, Oxford* (Cambridge: Brewer, 1992).

Emden, A. B., *A Biographical Register of the University of Cambridge to 1500* (Cambridge University Press, 1963).

A Biographical Register of the University of Oxford to A.D. 1500, 3 vols. (Oxford: Clarendon Press, 1957–9).

Donors of Books to S. Augustine's Abbey Canterbury (Oxford Bibliographical Society and Bodleian Library, 1968).

Emmerson, Richard K., 'Reading Gower in a Manuscript Culture: Latin and English in Illustrated Manuscripts of the *Confessio Amantis*', SAC, 21 (1999), 143–86.

'Text and Image in the Ellesmere Portraits of the Tale-Tellers', in *The Ellesmere Chaucer: Essays in Interpretation*, ed. Martin Stevens and Daniel Woodward (San Marino: Huntington Library, 1995), 143–70.

Early English Books Online (ProQuest LLC, 2003–2010), http://eebo.chadwyck.com/home

Epstein, Steven, 'Urban Society', in *The New Cambridge Medieval History: V, c.1198–c.1300*, ed. David Abulafia (Cambridge University Press, 1999), 26–37.

Evans, Michael, 'Allegorical Woman and Practical Men: The Iconography of the Artes Reconsidered', in *Medieval Woman: Dedicated and Presented to Professor Rosalind M. T. Hill on the Occasion of her Seventieth Birthday*, ed. Derek Baker (Oxford: Blackwell, 1978), 305–29.

Farber, Allan S., 'Considering a Marginal Master: The Work of an Early Fifteenth-Century, Parisian Manuscript Decorator', *Gesta*, 32 (1993), 21–39.

Farquhar, James D., *Creation and Imitation: The Work of a Fifteenth-Century Manuscript Illuminator* (Fort Lauderdale: Nova University Press, 1976).

'Identity in an Anonymous Age: Bruges Manuscript Illuminators and Their Signs', *Viator*, 11 (1980), 371–84.

'Making Connections in the Irregular Web of Manuscript Production of the Southern Netherlands', *Journal of the Walters Art Gallery*, 54 (1996), 135–46.

'Manuscript Production and Evidence for Localizing and Dating Fifteenth-Century Books of Hours: Walters Ms. 239', *Journal of the Walters Art Gallery*, 45 (1987), 44–57.

'The Manuscript as a Book', in *Pen to Press: Illustrated Manuscripts and Printed Books in the First Century of Printing*, ed. Sandra Hindman and James D. Farquhar (College Park: Art Department, University of Maryland, 1977), 11–99.

Farr, J. R., *Artisans in Europe, 1300–1914* (Cambridge University Press, 2000).

Federici, Carlo, Di Majo, Anna and Palma, Marco, 'The Determination of Animal Species Used in Medieval Parchment-Making: Non-Destructive Identification Techniques', in *Roger Powell: The Compleat Binder*, ed. J. L. Sharpe (Turnhout: Brepols, 1996), 146–53.

Fein, Susanna, 'Death and the Colophon in the Audelay Manuscript', in *My Wyl and My Wrytyng: Essays on John the Blind Audelay*, ed. Susanna Fein (Kalamazoo: Western Michigan University Press, 2009), 294–306.

'Good Ends in the Audelay Manuscript', *Yearbook of English Studies*, 33 (2003), 97–119.

(ed.), *Studies in the Harley Manuscript: The Scribes, Contents, and Social Contexts of British Library MS Harley 2253* (Kalamazoo: Western Michigan University Press, 2000).

Feldges-Henning, Uta, 'The Pictorial Programme of the Sala della Pace: A New Interpretation', *JWCI*, 35 (1972), 145–62.

Fenn, John (ed.), *Original Letters Written during the Reign of Henry VI, Edward IV and Richard III*, 5 vols. (London: Robinson, 1787).

Firth Green, Richard, *A Crisis of Truth: Literature and Law in Ricardian England* (Philadelphia: University of Pennsylvania Press, 1999).

'Lydgate and Deguileville Once More', *Notes & Queries*, 223 (1978), 105–6.

'Notes on Some Manuscripts of Hoccleve's *Regiment of Princes*', *British Library Journal*, 4 (1978), 37–41.

Fisher, J. H., *The Emergence of Standard English* (Lexington: University of Kentucky Press, 1996).

Fletcher, Alan J., *Drama, Performance and Polity in Pre-Cromwellian Ireland* (Cork University Press, 2000).

'John Mirk and the Lollards', *MÆ*, 56 (1987), 217–24.

Fletcher, Alan J. and Hudson, Anne, 'Compilations for Preaching and Lollard Literature', in *CHBB: II*, 317–39.

Fletcher, Bradford Y. (ed. and intr.), *Manuscript Trinity R.3.19: A Facsimile*, (Norman, OK: Pilgrim Books, 1987).

Fletcher, Bradford Y. and Harris, A. L., 'A Northampton Poetic Miscellany of 1455–1456', *EMS*, 7 (1998), 216–35.

Foot, Mirjam M., 'Bookbinding 1400–1557', in *CHBB: III*, 109–27.

Bookbinders at Work: Their Roles and Methods (London: British Library, 2006).

'Bookbinding and the History of Books', in *A Potencie of Life: Books in Society: The Clark Lectures, 1986–1987*, ed. Nicholas J. Barker (London: British Library, 1993), 113–26.

'English Decorated Bookbindings of the Fifteenth Century' (1989), in *Studies in the History of Bookbinding* (Aldershot: Scolar, 1993), 98–120.

'Influences from the Netherlands on Bookbinding in England during the Late Fifteenth and Early Sixteenth Centuries' (1979), in *Studies in the History of Bookbinding* (Aldershot: Scolar, 1993), 146–63.

Studies in the History of Bookbinding (Aldershot: Scolar, 1993).

'The Future of Bookbinding Research', in *The Book Encompassed: Studies in Twentieth-Century Bibliography*, ed. Peter Davison (Cambridge University Press, 1992), 99–106.

Ford, Judy Ann, *John Mirk's Festial: Orthodoxy, Lollardy, and the Common People in Fourteenth-Century England* (Woodbridge: Boydell and Brewer, 2006).

Ford, Margaret Lane, 'Importation of Printed Books into England and Scotland', *CHBB: III*, 179–201.

Forde, S., 'The Educational Organization of the Augustinian Canons in England and Wales, and Their University Life at Oxford, 1325–1448', *History of Universities*, 13 (1994), 21–60.

Forrest, Ian, *The Detection of Heresy in Late Medieval England* (Oxford: Clarendon Press, 2005).

Fossier, F., 'Premières Recherches sur les manuscrits latins du Cardinal Marcello Cervini (1501–1555)', *Mélanges de l'École Française de Rome. Moyen Âge–Temps Modernes*, 91 (1979), 381–456.

Frame, Robin, *Colonial Ireland: 1169–1369* (Dublin: Helicon, 1981).

Fredell, Joel, 'Decorated Initials in the Lincoln Thornton Manuscript', *SB*, 47 (1994), 78–88.

'"Go litel quaier": Lydgate's Pamphlet Poetry', *JEBS*, 9 (2006), 51–73.

'The Lowly Paraf: Transmitting Manuscript Design in *The Canterbury Tales*', *SAC*, 22 (2000), 213–80.

Frey, Winifred, 'Maria Legens – Maria Legere: St Mary as an Ideal Reader and St Mary as a Textbook', in *The Book and the Magic of Reading in the Middle Ages*, ed. Albrecht Classen (New York: Garland, 1998), 277–93.

Friedman, John B., *Northern English Books, Owners, and Makers in the Late Middle Ages* (Syracuse University Press, 1995).

Froissart, Jean, *L'Espinette amoureuse*, ed. A. Fourrier, 2nd edn (Paris: Klincksieck, 1972).

Fuchs, Robert, Meinert, Christiane and Schrempf, Johannes, *Pergament: Geschichte – Material – Konservierung – Restaurierung*, Kölner Beiträge zur Restaurierung und Konservierung von Kunst- und Kulturgut, 12 (Munich: Siegl, 2001).

Furnivall, Frederick J. (ed.), *The English Conquest of Ireland AD 1166–1185, Mainly from the 'Expugnatio Hibernica' of Giraldus Cambrensis*, EETS os 107 (London: Oxford University Press, 1896).

Furnivall, F. J. and Locock, K. B. (eds.), *The Pilgrimage of the Life of Man*, EETS es 77, 83, 92 (1899, 1901, 1904; repr. in one vol., 1973).

Gadamer, Hans Georg, *Truth and Method* (1986), trans. J. Weinsheimer and D. G. Marshall, 2nd edn rev. (New York and London: Continuum, 2003).

Galbraith, V. H., 'An Autograph MS of Ranulph Higden's *Polychronicon*', *Huntington Library Quarterly*, 23 (1959–60), 1–18.

Garand, Monique-Cécile, 'Manuscrits monastiques et scriptoria aux XIe et XIIe siècles', *Codicologica*, 3(1980), 8–33.

Garbaty, T. J., 'A Description of the Confession Miniatures for Gower's *Confessio Amantis* with Special Reference to the Illustrator's Role as Reader and Critic', *Mediaevalia*, 19 (1996), 319–43.

Gasparinetti, A. F. (ed.), *Zonghi's Watermarks* (Hilversum: Paper Publications Society, 1953).

Gast, Monica, 'A History of Endbands Based on a Study by Karl Jäckel', *New Bookbinder*, 3 (1983), 42–58.

Gaylord, Alan, 'Portrait of a Poet', in *The Ellesmere Chaucer: Essays in Interpretation*, ed. Martin Stevens and Daniel Woodward (San Marino: Huntington Library, 1995), 121–42.

Gee, Stacey, 'The Printers, Stationers and Bookbinders of York before 1557', *TCBS*, 12 (2000), 27–54.

Géhin, Paul, *Lire le manuscrit médiéval: Observer et décrire* (Paris: Colin, 2005).

Genet, Jean-Philippe, 'The Dissemination of Manuscripts Relating to English Political Thought in the Fourteenth Century', in *England and Her Neighbours 1066–1453: Essays in Honour of Pierre Chaplais*, ed. M. Jones and M. Vale (London: Hambledon Press, 1989), 217–37.

Giancarlo, Matthew, *Parliament and Literature in Late Medieval England* (Cambridge University Press, 2007).

Gillespie, Alexandra, 'Analytical Survey 9: The History of the Book', *New Medieval Literatures*, 9 (2007), 245–86.

'Balliol MS 354: Histories of the Book at the End of the Middle Ages', *Poetica*, 60 (2003), 47–63.

'Books', in *Oxford Twenty-First Century Approaches to Literature: Middle English*, ed. Paul Strohm (Oxford University Press, 2007), 86–103.

'Poets, Printers, and Early English *Sammelbände*', *Huntington Library Quarterly*, 67 (2004), 189–214.

Print Culture and the Medieval Author: Chaucer, Lydgate, and their Books, 1473–1557 (Oxford University Press, 2006).

'Review of Hellinga and Trapp (eds.), *The History of the Book in Britain, 1400–1557*', *Notes & Queries*, ns, 246 (2001), 11–14.

Gillespie, Vincent, '*Cura Pastoralis in Deserto*', in *De Cella in Seculum: Religious and Secular Life and Devotion in Late Medieval England*, ed. Michael G. Sargent (Cambridge: Brewer, 1989), 161–81.

'The Haunted Text: Reflections in *The Mirror to Devout People*', in *Medieval Texts in Context*, ed. Denis Renevey and Graham D. Caie (London and New York: Routledge, 2008), 129–72.

'The Mole in the Vineyard: Wyclif at Syon in the Fifteenth Century', in *Text and Controversy from Wylclif to Bale: Essays in Honour of Anne Hudson*, ed. Helen Barr and Ann M. Hutchinson (Turnhout: Brepols, 2005), 131–61.

'Vernacular Books of Religion', in G&P, 317–44.

'Vernacular Theology', in *Oxford Twenty-First Century Approaches to Literature: Middle English*, ed. Paul Strohm (Oxford University Press, 2007), 401–20.

Gillespie, Vincent and Doyle, A. I. (eds.), *Syon Abbey with the Libraries of the Carthusians*, CBMLC, 9 (London: British Library in association with British Academy, 2001).

Giraldus Cambrensis [Gerald of Wales], *Opera omnia*, ed. James F. Dimock, 8 vols. (London: Longman, 1861–91).

Glauning, Otto (ed.), *Lydgate's Minor Poems. The Two Nightingale Poems (A.D. 1446)*, EETS es 80 (London: Kegan Paul, Trench, Trübner and Co., 1900).

Gleason, J. B., 'The Earliest Evidence for Ecclesiastical Censorship of Printed Books in England', *Library*, 6th ser., 4 (1982), 135–41.

Gobbitt, Thomas, 'Law in English Manuscripts 1060 to 1220', unpub. PhD thesis (University of Leeds, 2010).

Goering, Joseph and Rosenfeld, Randall (eds.), 'The Tongue is a Pen: Robert Grosseteste's *Dictum 54* and Scribal Technology with Edition and Translations of the Text from MS. Oxford, Bodleian Library, Bodley 798', *Journal of Medieval Latin*, 12 (2002), 114–40.

Goldschmidt, E. P., *Gothic and Renaissance Bookbindings, Exemplified and Illustrated from the Author's Collection*, 2nd edn, 2 vols. (London: Benn, 1928).

Gollancz, Israel, *Pearl, Cleanness, Patience and Sir Gawain, Reproduced in Facsimile from the Unique MS Cotton Nero A.x in the British Museum*, EETS os 162 (London: Oxford University Press, 1923).

Gould, Karen, 'Terms for Book Production in a Fifteenth-Century Latin–English Nominale (Harvard Law School Library Ms. 43)', *Papers of the Bibliographical Society of America*, 79 (1985), 75–99.

Gransden, Antonia, 'Some Manuscripts in Cambridge from Bury St Edmunds Abbey: Exhibition Catalogue', in *Bury St Edmunds: Medieval Art, Architecture, Archaeology and Economy*, ed. Antonia Gransden (Leeds: Maney, 1998), 228–85.

Griffin, Carrie, 'The Culinary Collection of British Library MS Additional 5467: An Edition and Commentary', unpub. MA thesis (University College, Cork, 1999).

Griffith, David, 'Owners and Copyists of John Rous's Armorial Rolls', in *Essays in Manuscript Geography: Vernacular Manuscripts of the English West Midlands from the Conquest to the Sixteenth Century*, ed. Wendy Scase (Turnhout: Brepols, 2007), 203–28.

'The Visual History of Guy of Warwick', in *Guy of Warwick: Icon and Ancestor*, ed. Alison Wiggins and Rosalind Field (Cambridge: Brewer, 2007), 110–32.

Griffiths, Jeremy, 'Book Production Terms in Nicholas Munshull's Nominale', in *Art into Life: Collected Papers from the Kresge Art Museum Medieval Symposia*, ed. Carol G. Fisher and Kathleen L. Scott (East Lansing: Michigan State University Press, 1995), 49–71.

'*Confessio Amantis*: The Poem and Its Pictures', in *Gower's Confessio Amantis: Responses and Reassessments*, ed. A. J. Minnis (Cambridge: Brewer, 1983), 163–78.

Griffiths, Jeremy and Pearsall, Derek (eds.), *Book Production and Publishing in Britain 1375–1475* (Cambridge University Press, 1989).

Gringore, Pierre, *Les Fantasies de mere sote* (Paris: Jean Petit, s.a.).

Gros, Gérard, 'L'Écriture du prince: Étude sur le souci graphique de Charles d'Orléans dans son manuscrit personnel (Paris, Bibl. Nat. Fr. 25458)', in *L'Hostellerie de pensée: Études sur l'art littéraire au Moyen Âge offertes à Daniel Poirion par ses anciens élèves*, ed. Michel Zink, Danielle Bohler, Eric Hicks and Manuela Python (Paris: Presses de l'Université de Paris-Sorbonne, 1995), 195–204.

Guillén, Sáez and Francisco, Jose, *Catálogo de manuscritos de la Biblioteca Colombina de Sevilla*, 2 vols. (Seville: Cabildo de la S. M. y P. I., 2002).

Guineau, B., Dulin L., Vezin J. and Gousset M.-T., 'Analyse, à l'aide de méthodes spectropho-tométriques, des couleurs de deux manuscrits du xve siècle enluminés par Francesco Di

Antonio Del Chierico', in *Ancient and Medieval Book Materials and Techniques: Erice, 18–25 September 1992*, ed. Marilena Maniaci and Paola F. Munafò (Città del Vaticano: Biblioteca Apostolica Vaticana, 1993), 121–55.

Gullick, Michael, 'A Bibliography of Medieval Painting Treatises', in *Making the Medieval Book: Techniques of Production*, ed. Linda L. Brownrigg (Los Altos Hills, CA: Anderson-Lovelace, 1995), 241–4.

(ed.), *Extracts from the Precentors' Accounts Concerning Books and Bookmaking of Ely Cathedral Priory* (Hitchin: Red Gull, 1985).

'From Parchmenter to Scribe: Some Observations on the Manufacture and Preparation of Medieval Parchment Based upon a Review of Literary Evidence', in *Pergament: Geschichte, Struktur, Restaurierung, Herstellung*, ed. Peter Rück (Sigmaringen: Jan Thorbecke Verlag, 1991), 145–57.

'From Scribe to Binder: Quire Tackets in Twelfth-Century European Manuscripts', in *Roger Powell: The Compleat Binder*, ed. J. L. Sharpe (Turnhout: Brepols, 1996), 240–59.

'How Fast Did Scribes Write? Evidence from Romanesque Manuscripts', in *Making the Medieval Book: Techniques of Production*, ed. Linda L. Brownrigg (Los Altos Hills, CA: Anderson-Lovelace, 1995), 39–58.

'Professional Scribes in Eleventh- and Twelfth-Century England', *EMS*, 7 (1998), 1–24.

The Arte of Limming: A Reproduction of the 1573 Edition Newly Imprinted (London: Society of Scribes and Illuminators, 1979).

'The Binding Descriptions in the Library Catalogue from Leicester Abbey', in *Leicester Abbey: Medieval History, Archaeology and Manuscript Studies*, ed. Joanna Story, Jill Bourne and Richard Buckley (Leicester: The Leicestershire Archaeological and Historical Society, 2006), 147–72.

Gullick, Michael and Hadgraft, Nicholas, 'Bookbindings', in *CHBB: II*, 95–109.

Gullick, Michael and Webber, Teresa, 'Summary Catalogue of Surviving Manuscripts from Leicester Abbey', in *Leicester Abbey: Medieval History, Archaeology and Manuscript Studies*, ed. Joanna Story, Jill Bourne and Richard Buckley (Leicester: The Leicestershire Archaeological and Historical Society, 2006), 173–92.

Gumbert, J. P., 'Sizes and Formats', in *Ancient and Medieval Book Materials and Techniques: Erice, 18–25 September 1992*, ed. Marilena Maniaci and Paola F. Munafò (Città del Vaticano: Biblioteca Apostolica Vaticana, 1993), 227–63.

'The Speed of Scribes', in *Scribi e colofoni: Le sottoscrizioni di copisti dalle origini all'avvento della stampa, atti del seminario di Erice X Colloquio del Comité International de Palaeographie Latine (23–8 ottobre 1993)*, ed. Emma Condello and Giuseppe De Gregorio (Spoleto: Centro Italiano di Studi sull'Alto Medioevo, 1995), 57–69.

Gwynne, P., 'The Frontispiece to an Illuminated Panegyric of Henry VII: A Note on the Sources', *JWCI*, 55 (1992), 266–70.

Hadgraft, Nicholas, 'English Fifteenth-Century Bookbinding Structures', unpub. PhD thesis (University College, London, 1998).

Halliwell, J. O. (ed.), 'The crafte of lymnynge of bokys', in *Early English Miscellanies in Prose and Verse* (London: Warton Club, 1855), 72–91.

Hamburger, Jeffrey, 'The Casanatense and Carmelite Missals: Continental Sources for English Manuscript Illumination of the Early 15th Century', in *Masters and Miniatures – Proceedings of the Congress on Medieval Manuscript Illumination in the Northern Netherlands*

(Utrecht, 10–13 December 1989), ed. Koert van der Horst and Johann-Christian Klamt (Doornspijk: Davaco, 1991), 161–73.

Hamer, Richard F. S., 'Spellings of the Fifteenth-Century Scribe Ricardus Franciscus', in *Five Hundred Years of Words and Sounds: A Festschrift for Eric Dobson*, ed. Eric G. Stanley and Douglas Gray (Cambridge: Brewer, 1983), 63–73.

Hammond, Eleanor Prescott, 'A Scribe of Chaucer', *Modern Philology*, 27 (1929–30), 27–30.

'Two British Museum Manuscripts (Harley 2251 and Adds. 34360): A Contribution to the Bibliography of John Lydgate', *Anglia*, 28 (1905), 1–28.

Hanna, Ralph III, 'Analytical Survey 4: Middle English Manuscripts and the Study of Literature', in *New Medieval Literatures*, 4 (2001), 243–64.

'Booklets in Medieval Manuscripts: Further Considerations', *SB*, 39 (1986), 100–11.

'Dr Peter Partridge and MS Digby 98', in *Text and Controversy from Wyclif to Bale: Essays in Honour of Anne Hudson*, ed. Helen Barr and Ann M. Hutchinson (Turnhout: Brepols, 2005), 41–65.

'English Biblical Texts before Lollardy and their Fate', in *Lollards and Their Influence in Late Medieval England*, ed. Fiona Somerset, Jill C. Havens and Derrick G. Pitard (Woodbridge: Boydell and Brewer, 2003), 141–53.

'Humphrey Newton and Bodleian Library, MS Lat. misc. c. 66', *MÆ*, 69 (2000), 279–91.

'Introduction', in *IMEP, XII: Manuscripts in Smaller Bodleian Collections*, ed. Ralph Hanna III (Woodbridge: Boydell and Brewer, 1997), xi–xxiii.

London Literature, 1300–1380 (Cambridge University Press, 2005).

'Middle English Books and Middle English Literary History', *Modern Philology*, 102 (2004), 157–78.

'Miscellaneity and Vernacularity: Conditions of Literary Production in Later Medieval England', in *The Whole Book: Cultural Perspectives of the Medieval Miscellany*, ed. Stephen G. Nichols and Siegfried Wenzel (Ann Arbor: University of Michigan Press, 1996), 37–51.

'Notes toward a Future History of Middle English Literature: Two Copies of Richard Rolle's *Form of Living*', in *Chaucer in Perspective: Middle English Essays in Honour of Norman Blake*, ed. Geoffrey Lester (Sheffield Academic, 1999), 279–300.

Pursuing History: Middle English Manuscripts and Their Texts (Stanford University Press, 1996).

'Sir Thomas Berkeley and His Patronage', *Speculum*, 64 (1989), 878–916.

'Some North Yorkshire Scribes and Their Context', in *Medieval Texts in Context*, ed. Denis Renevey and Graham D. Caie (London and New York: Routledge, 2008), 167–91.

(ed.), *Speculum Vitae: A Reading Edition*, EETS os 331–2, 2 vols. (Oxford University Press, 2008).

(ed.), *IMEP, XII: Manuscripts in Smaller Bodleian Collections*, ed. Ralph Hanna III (Woodbridge: Boydell and Brewer, 1997).

'The Scribe of Huntington HM 114', *SB*, 42 (1989), 120–33.

'The Yorkshire Circulation of *Speculum Vitae*', in *Design and Distribution of Late Medieval Manuscripts in England*, ed. Margaret Connolly and Linne R. Mooney (York Medieval Press, 2008), 279–91.

'Two Lollard Codices and Lollard Book Production', in *Pursuing History: Middle English Manuscripts and their Texts* (Stanford University Press, 1996), 48–59.

William Langland (Aldershot: Variorum, 1993).

'Yorkshire Writers', *Proceedings of the British Academy*, 121 (2003), 91–109.

Hanna, Ralph, III with Griffiths, Jeremy, *A Descriptive Catalogue of the Western Medieval Manuscripts of St John's College, Oxford* (Oxford University Press, 2002).

Hanna, Ralph, III and Lawton, David (eds.), *The Siege of Jerusalem*, EETS os 320 (Oxford University Press, 2003).

Hardman, Phillipa, 'A Mediaeval "Library in Parvo"', *MÆ*, 47 (1978), 262–73.

'Compiling the Nation: Fifteenth-Century Miscellany Manuscripts', in *Nation, Court and Culture: New Essays on Fifteenth-Century English Poetry*, ed. Helen Cooney (Dublin: Four Courts, 2001), 50–69.

'Interpreting the Incomplete Scheme of Illustration in Cambridge, Corpus Christi College MS 61', *English Manuscript Studies 1100–1700*, 6 (1997), 52–69.

'Presenting the Text: Pictorial Tradition in Fifteenth-Century Manuscripts of *The Canterbury Tales*', in *Chaucer Illustrated: Five Hundred Years of The Canterbury Tales in Pictures*, ed. William K. Finley and Joseph Rosenblum (New Castle: Oak Knoll, 2003), 37–72.

(ed.), *The Heege Manuscript: A Facsimile of National Library of Scotland MS Advocates 19.3.1* (Leeds Studies in English, 2000).

Hardwick, C. and Luard, H. R., *A Catalogue of Manuscripts Preserved in the Library of the University of Cambridge*, 5 vols. (Cambridge University Press, 1856–67).

Hargreaves, Henry, '*The Mirror of Our Lady*: Aberdeen University Library MS 134', *Aberdeen University Review*, 42 (1968), 267–80.

Harris, Kate, 'Patrons, Buyers and Owners: The Evidence for Ownership and the Role of Book Owners in Book Production and the Book Trade', in G&P, 163–200.

'The Origins and Make-Up of Cambridge, University Library MS Ff.i.6', *TCBS*, 8 (1983), 299–333.

'The Patronage and Dating of Longleat House MS. 24, a Prestige Copy of the *Pupilla Oculi* Illuminated by the Master of the *Troilus* Frontispiece', in *Prestige, Authority and Power in Late Medieval Manuscripts and Texts*, ed. Felicity Riddy (Woodbridge: York Medieval Press, 2000), 35–54.

Harvey, Margaret, 'An Englishman at the Roman Curia during the Council of Basle: Andrew Holes, His Sermon of 1433 and His Books', *Journal of Ecclesiastical History*, 42 (1991), 19–38.

'The Diffusion of the Doctrinale of Thomas Netter in the Fifteenth and Sixteenth Centuries', in *Intellectual Life in the Middle Ages: Essays Presented to Margaret Gibson*, ed. Lesley Smith and Benedict Ward (London: Hambledon, 1992), 281–94.

The English in Rome 1362–1420 (Cambridge University Press, 1999).

Hatfield-Moore, Deborah, 'Paying the Minstrel: A Cultural Study of BL. Harley 913', unpub. PhD thesis (Queen's University, Belfast, 2001).

Havens, Jill C., 'A Curious Erasure in Walsingham's *Short Chronicle* and the Politics of Heresy', in *Fourteenth-Century England II*, ed. Chris Given-Wilson (Woodbridge: Boydell, 2002), 95–106.

'Shading the Grey Area: Determining Heresy in Middle English Texts', in *Text and Controversy from Wyclif to Bale: Essays in Honour of Anne Hudson*, ed. Helen Barr and Ann M. Hutchinson (Turnhout: Brepols, 2005), 337–52.

Heale, Martin, 'Books and Learning in the Dependent Priories of the Monasteries of Medieval England', in *The Church and Learning in Later Medieval Society: Essays in Honour of R. B.*

Dobson, ed. Caroline M. Barron and Jenny Stratford (Donington: Shaun Tyas, 2002), 64–79.

The Dependent Priories of Medieval English Monasteries, Studies in the History of Medieval Religion 22 (Woodbridge: Boydell, 2004).

Heawood, E., 'Sources of Early English Paper-Supply', *Library*, 4th ser., 10 (1929–30), 282–307.

Hector, L. C., *The Handwriting of English Documents* (London: Arnold, 1966).

Hector, L. C. and Harvey, Barbara (eds.), *The Westminster Chronicle: 1381–1394* (Oxford: Clarendon Press, 1982).

Hedeman, Anne D., 'Making the Past Present: Visual Translation in Jean Lebègue's "Twin" Manuscripts of Sallust', in *Patrons, Authors and Workshops: Books and Book Production in Paris around 1400*, ed. Godfried Croenen and Peter Ainsworth (Leuven: Peeters, 2006), 173–96.

Hellinga, Lotte, 'Fragments Found in Bindings and Their Role as Bibliographical Evidence', in *'For the love of the binding': Studies in Bookbinding History Presented to Mirjam Foot*, ed. David Pearson (London: British Library, 2000), 13–33.

'Importation of Books Printed on the Continent into England and Scotland before *c.*1520', in *Printing the Written Word: The Social History of Books, circa 1450–1520*, ed. Sandra Hindman (Ithaca: Cornell University Press, 1991), 205–24.

'Printing', in *CHBB: III*, 65–108.

Hellinga, Lotte and Kelliher, Hilton, 'The Malory Manuscript', *British Library Journal*, 3 (1977), 91–113.

Hellinga, Lotte and Trapp, J. B. (eds.), *The Cambridge History of the Book in Britain: Volume III, 1400–1557* (Cambridge University Press, 1999).

Helmholz, R. H., 'Lyndwood, William (*c.*1375–1446)', in *ODNB*.

Henderson, Aitken, 'A Preliminary Note on 15th-Century Watermarks', *Transactions of the Glasgow Archaeological Society*, 1 (1890), 89–110.

Heuser, Wilhelm (ed.), *Die Kildare-Gedichte: Die ältesten mittelenglischen Denkmäler in anglo-irischen Überlieferung* (Bonn: P. Hanstein, 1904; repr. Darmstadt: Wissenschaftliche Buchgesellschaft, 1967).

Hills, R. L., 'A Technical Revolution in Papermaking, 1250–1350', in *Looking at Paper: Evidence and Interpretation: Symposium Proceedings, Toronto 1999*, ed. John Slavin et al. (Ottawa: Canadian Conservation Institute, 2001), 105–11.

'Early Italian Papermaking, a Crucial Technical Revolution', in *Produzione e commercio della carta e del libro secc. XIII–XVIII*, ed. Simonetta Cavaciocchi (Florence: Le Monnier, 1992), 72–97.

Hilmo, Maidie, *Medieval Images, Icons, and Illustrated English Literary Texts from the Ruthwell Cross to the Ellesmere Chaucer* (Aldershot and Burlington, VT: Ashgate, 2004).

'The Clerk's "Unscholarly Bow": Seeing and Reading Chaucer's Clerk from the Ellesmere MS to Caxton', *JEBS*, 10 (2007), 71–105.

Hindman, S., 'La Voie de Povreté ou de Richesse (Le Livre du Chastel de Labour)', in *Leaves of Gold: Manuscript Illumination from Philadelphia Collections*, ed. James R. Tanis with Jennifer A. Thompson (Philadelphia Museum of Art, 2001), 202–5.

Hobson, G. D., *Blind-Stamped Panels in the English Book-Trade c.1485–1555* (London: Bibliographical Society, 1944).

English Binding before 1500 (Cambridge University Press, 1929).

Hoccleve, Thomas, *The Regiment of Princes*, ed. Charles R. Blyth (Kalamazoo: Medieval Institute Publications, 1999).

Hockey, Stanley F. (ed.), *The Account Book of Beaulieu Abbey*, Camden Society, 4th ser., 16 (London: Royal Historical Society, 1975).

Hodnett, Edward, *English Woodcuts, 1480–1535* (1935; repr. Oxford University Press, 1973).

Horobin, Simon, 'A Manuscript Found in the Library of Abbotsford House and the Lost Legendary of Osbern Bokenham', *EMS*, 14 (2007), 132–64.

' "In London and opelond": The Dialect and Circulation of the C Version of *Piers Plowman*', *MÆ*, 74 (2005), 248–69.

'The Edmund-Fremund Scribe Copying Chaucer', *JEBS*, 12 (2009), 195–203.

The Language of the Chaucer Tradition (Cambridge: Brewer, 2003).

'The Scribe of Rawlinson Poetry 137 and the Copying and Circulation of *Piers Plowman*', *Yearbook of Langland Studies*, 19 (2005), 3–26.

'The Scribe of the Helmingham and Northumberland Manuscripts of *The Canterbury Tales*', *Neophilologus*, 84 (2000), 457–65.

Horobin, Simon and Mooney, Linne R., 'A *Piers Plowman* Manuscript by the Hengwrt/Ellesmere Scribe and Its Implications for London Standard English', *SAC*, 26 (2004), 65–112.

Horobin, Simon and Wiggins, Alison, 'Reconsidering Lincoln's Inn MS 150', *MÆ*, 77 (2008), 30–53.

Hudson, Anne, 'A Lollard Compilation and the Dissemination of Wycliffite Thought', in *Lollards and Their Books*, ed. Anne Hudson (London: Hambledon, 2003), 13–29.

'A Lollard Quaternion', in *Lollards and Their Books, ed. Anne Hudson* (London: Hambledon, 2003), 193–200.

'A New Look at the Lay Folks' Catechism', *Viator*, 16 (1985), 243–58.

'Comment: Senses of Censorship', *Journal of British Studies*, 46 (2007), 758–61.

(ed.), *English Wycliffite Sermons: Volume I* (Oxford: Clarendon Press, 1983).

'Lollard Book Production', in *G&P*, 125–42.

'Lollard Literature', in *CHBB: II*, 329–39.

Lollards and Their Books (London: Hambledon, 2003).

'Lollardy: The English Heresy?', in *Lollards and Their Books*, ed. Anne Hudson (London: Hambledon, 2003), 141–63.

'Some Aspects of Lollard Book Production' (1972), in *Lollards and Their Books*, ed. Anne Hudson (London: Hambledon, 1985), 181–91.

'Some Problems of Identity and Identification in Wycliffite Writings', in *Middle English Prose: Essays in Bibliographical Problems*, ed. A. S. G. Edwards and Derek Pearsall (New York: Garland, 1981), 81–90.

Studies in the Transmission of Wyclif's Writings (Brookfield, VT: Ashgate Variorum, 2008).

'The Examination of Lollards', in *Lollards and Their Books*, ed. Anne Hudson (London: Hambledon, 2003), 125–40.

'The Expurgation of a Lollard Sermon Cycle', in *Lollards and Their Books*, ed. Anne Hudson (London: Hambledon, 2003), 201–15.

'The Lay Folks' Catechism: A Postscript', *Viator*, 18 (1988), 307–9.

The Premature Reformation: Wycliffite Texts and Lollard History (Oxford: Clarendon Press, 1988).

'The Survival of Wyclif's Works in England and Bohemia', in *Studies in the Transmission of Wyclif's Writings* (Brookfield, VT: Ashgate Variorum, 2008), 1–43 (items individually paginated).

'The Variable Text', in *Crux and Controversy in Middle English Textual Criticism*, ed. A. J. Minnis and Charlotte Brewer (Cambridge: Brewer, 1992), 49–60.

The Works of a Lollard Preacher, EETS os 317 (Oxford: Oxford University Press, 2001).

'Wyclif Texts in Fifteenth-Century London', in *Studies in the Transmission of Wyclif's Writings* (Brookfield, VT: Ashgate Variorum, 2008), 1–18 (items individually paginated).

'"Who is My Neighbour?" Some Problems of Definition on the Borders of Orthodoxy and Heresy', in *Wycliffite Controversies*, ed. Mishtooni Bose and Patrick Hornbeck (Turnhout: Brepols, forthcoming).

Hudson, Anne and Spencer, H. L., 'Old Author, New Work: The Sermons of MS Longleat 4', *MÆ*, 53 (1984), 220–38.

Hughes, Andrew, *Medieval Manuscripts for Mass and Office: A Guide to Their Organization and Terminology* (University of Toronto Press, 1982).

Hull, Eleanor, *The Seven Psalms: A Commentary on the Penitential Psalms*, ed. Alexandra Barratt, EETS os 307 (Oxford University Press, 1995).

Humphreys, K. W., *The Book Provisions of the Medieval Friars, 1215–1400* (Amsterdam: Erasmus Booksellers, 1964).

Hunt, Tony (ed.), 'The "Novele cirurgerie" in MS London, British Library Harley 2558', *Zeitschrift für romanische Philologie*, 103 (1987), 271–99.

'Waterford, Jofroi of (fl. late 13th cent.)', *ODNB*.

Hunter, J., 'Specimens of Marks Used by the Early Manufacturers of Paper, as Exhibited in Documents in the Public Archives of England', *Archaeologia*, 37 (1857), 447–54.

Huntington, Archer M. (ed.), *Catalogue of the Library of Ferdinand Columbus* (New York: Huntington, 1905).

Isidore of Seville, *Etymologiarum Sive Originum Libri XX*, ed. W. M. Lindsay, 2 vols. (Oxford: Clarendon Press, 1911).

Etymologies, trans. Stephen A. Barney et al. (Cambridge University Press, 2006).

Ivy, G. S., 'The Bibliography of the Manuscript Book', in *The English Library before 1700: Studies in Its History*, ed. Francis Wormald and Cyril Ernest Wright (London: Athlone, 1958), 32–65.

Jacob, E. F. (ed.), *The Register of Henry Chichele*, 4 vols. (Oxford: Clarendon Press, 1938–47).

Jacquot, Jean (ed.), *Fêtes et cérémonies au temps de Charles Quint* (Paris: Centre National de la Recherche, 1960).

James, M. R., *A Descriptive Catalogue of the Manuscripts in the Library of Peterhouse* (Cambridge University Press, 1899).

A Descriptive Catalogue of the Manuscripts in the Library of St John's College, Cambridge (Cambridge University Press, 1913).

The Apocalypse in Art (Oxford University Press, 1931).

The Western Manuscripts in the Library of Trinity College, Cambridge: A Descriptive Catalogue, 4 vols. (Cambridge University Press, 1900–4).

James, Sarah, 'Revaluing Vernacular Theology: The Case of Reginald Pecock', *Leeds Studies in English*, 33 (2002), 135–69.

Jansen, S. L. and Jordan, K. H. (eds.), *The Welles Anthology MS. Rawlinson C.813: A Critical Edition* (Binghamton: Medieval And Renaissance Texts and Studies, 1991).

Jefferson, Lisa, 'Two Fifteenth-Century Manuscripts of the Statutes of the Order of the Garter', *EMS*, 5 (1997), 18–35.

Wardens' Accounts and Court Minute Books of the Goldsmith's Mistery of London, 1334–1446 (Woodbridge: Boydell, 2003).

Johns, Adrian, *The Nature of the Book: Print and Knowledge in the Making* (Chicago University Press, 1998).

Johnston, M., 'A New Document Relating to the Life of Robert Thornton', *Library*, 7th ser., 8 (2007), 304–13.

Jurkowski, Maureen, 'Lollard Book Producers in London in 1414', in *Text and Controversy from Wyclif to Bale: Essays in Honour of Anne Hudson*, ed. Helen Barr and Ann M. Hutchinson (Turnhout: Brepols, 2005), 201–26.

'The "Findern Manuscript" and the History of the Fynderne Family in the Fifteenth Century', in *Texts and Their Contexts: Papers from the Early Book Society*, ed. John Scattergood and Julia Boffey (Dublin: Four Courts, 1997), 196–222.

Kane, H. (ed.), *The Prickynge of Love*, 2 vols. (Salzburg: Institut für Anglistik und Amerikanistik, Universität Salzburg, 1983).

Kato, Takako, *Caxton's Morte Darthur: The Printing Process and the Authenticity of the Text*, *MÆ* Monographs ns 22 (Oxford: Society for the Study of Medieval Languages and Literature, 2002).

'Corrected Mistakes in Cambridge University Library MS Gg.4.27', in *Design and Distribution of Late Medieval Manuscripts in England*, ed. Margaret Connolly and Linne R. Mooney (York Medieval Press, 2008), 61–87.

Keiser, George R., 'MS. Rawlinson A.393: Another Findern Manuscript', *TCBS*, 7 (1980), 445–8.

'Practical Books for the Gentleman', in *CHBB: III*, 470–94.

'Serving the Needs of Readers: Textual Division in Some Late Medieval English Texts', in *New Science out of Old Books: Studies in Manuscripts and Early Printed Books in Honour of A. I. Doyle*, ed. Richard Beadle and A. J. Piper (Aldershot: Scolar, 1995), 207–26.

Kekewich, Margaret Lucille, Richmond, Colin, Sutton, Anne F., Visser-Fuchs, Livia and Watts, John L., *The Politics of Fifteenth-Century England: John Vale's Book* (Stroud: Sutton, 1995).

Kelen, Sarah A., 'Climbing up the Family Tree: Chaucer's Tudor Progeny', *JEBS*, 6 (2003), 109–23.

Kelliher, Hilton, 'The Early History of the Malory Manuscript', in *Aspects of Malory*, ed. Toshiyuki Takamiya and Derek Brewer (Cambridge: Brewer, 1981), 143–58, 222–5.

Kelly, H. A., 'Lollard Inquisitions: Due and Undue Process', in *The Devil, Heresy and Witchcraft in the Middle Ages: Essays in Honor of Jeffrey B. Russell*, ed. Alberto Ferreiro (Leiden: Brill, 1998), 279–303.

Kelly, Stephen and Thompson, John J., 'Imagined Histories of the Book: Current Paradigms and Future Directions', in *Imagining the Book*, ed. Stephen Kelly and John J. Thompson (Turnhout: Brepols, 2005), 1–14.

Kendrick, Laura, *Animating the Letter: The Figurative Embodiment of Writing from Late Antiquity to the Renaissance* (Columbus: Ohio State University Press, 1999).

'Linking *The Canterbury Tales*: Monkey-Business in the Margins', in *Drama, Narrative and Poetry in The Canterbury Tales*, ed. Wendy Harding (Toulouse: Presses Universitaires du Mirail, 2003), 83–98.

Ker, Neil R., 'Cardinal Cervini's Manuscripts from the Cambridge Friars', in *Books, Collectors and Libraries: Studies in the Medieval Heritage*, ed. A. G. Watson (London: Hambledon, 1985), 437–58.

Fragments of Medieval Manuscripts Used as Pastedowns in Oxford Bindings, with a Survey of Oxford Binding c.1515–1620 (Oxford Bibliographical Society, 1954).

Medieval Libraries of Great Britain: A List of Surviving Books (London: Royal Historical Society, 1964).

'Medieval Manuscripts from Norwich Cathedral Priory' (1949–53), in *Books, Collectors and Libraries: Studies in the Medieval Heritage*, ed. A. G. Watson (London: Hambledon, 1985), 243–72.

'Patrick Young's Catalogue of the Manuscripts of Lichfield Cathedral' (1950), in *Books, Collectors and Libraries: Studies in the Medieval Heritage*, ed. A. G. Watson (London and Ronceverte: Hambledon, 1985), 273–91.

'Robert Elyot's Books and Annotations', *Library*, 5th ser., 30 (1975), 233–7.

(ed.), *The Winchester Malory: A Facsimile*, EETS ss 4 (Oxford University Press, 1976).

Ker, Neil R. and Piper, A. J., *Medieval Manuscripts in British Libraries*, 5 vols. (Oxford, Clarendon Press, 1969–2002).

Kerby-Fulton, Kathryn, *Books under Suspicion: Censorship and Tolerance of Revelatory Writing in Late Medieval England* (University of Notre Dame Press, 2006).

'Professional Readers of Langland at Home and Abroad: New Directions in the Political and Bureaucratic Codicology of *Piers Plowman*', in *New Directions in Later Medieval Manuscript Studies: Essays from the 1998 Harvard Conference*, ed. Derek Pearsall (York Medieval Press, 2000), 103–29.

Kerby-Fulton, Kathryn and Despres, Denise L., *Iconography and the Professional Reader: The Politics of Book Production in the Douce Piers Plowman* (Minneapolis: University of Minnesota Press, 1999).

Kerby-Fulton, Kathryn and Hilmo, Maidie, *The Medieval Professional Reader at Work* (Victoria: English Literacy Studies, 2002).

Kerby-Fulton, Kathryn and Justice, Stephen, 'Langlandian Reading Circles and the Civil Service in London and Dublin, 1380–1427', *New Medieval Literatures*, 1 (1998), 59–83.

'Reformist Intellectual Culture in the English and Irish Civil Service: The *Modus Tenendi Parliamentum* and Its Literary Relations', *Traditio*, 53 (1998), 149–202.

Kerling, Nellie J. M. (ed.), *Cartulary of St Bartholomew's Hospital, Founded 1123: A Calendar* (London: St Bartholomew's Hospital, 1973).

Kerrigan, John, *Archipelagic English: Literature, History, and Politics 1603–1707* (Oxford University Press, 2008).

Kershaw, Ian and Smith, David M. (with Cooper, T. N.) (eds.), *The Bolton Priory Compotus 1286–1325, together with a Priory Account Roll for 1377–1378* (York: Yorkshire Archaeological Society with Boydell, 2000).

Kipling, Gordon, '"A Horse Designed by Committee": The Bureaucratics of the London Civic Triumph in the 1520s', *Research Opportunities in Renaissance Drama*, 31 (1992), 79–89.

'Henry VII and the Origins of Tudor Patronage', in *Patronage in the Renaissance*, ed. Guy F. Lytle and Stephen Orgel (Princeton University Press, 1981), 117–64.

Kisby, Fiona, 'Books in London Parish Churches before 1603: Some Preliminary Observations', in *The Church and Learning in Later Medieval Society: Essays in Honour of R. B. Dobson*, ed. Caroline M. Barron and Jenny Stratford (Donington: Shaun Tyas, 2002), 305–26.

Knapp, Ethan, *The Bureaucratic Muse: Thomas Hoccleve and the Literature of Late Medieval England* (University Park: Pennsylvania State University Press, 2001).

Knowles, David, *The Religious Orders in England, Volume III: The Tudor Age* (Cambridge University Press, 1959, repr. with corr. 1971).

Knowles, David and Hadcock, R. N., *Medieval Religious Houses, England and Wales*, 2nd edn rev. (London: Longman, 1971).

Kohl, Benjamin G., 'Readers and Owners of an Early Work of Giovanni Conversini da Ravenna: Oxford, New College, MS. D. 155', *Scriptorium*, 40 (1986), 95–100.

König, Eberhard, 'A Leaf from a Gutenberg Bible Illuminated in England', *British Library Journal*, 9 (1983), 32–50.

König, Eberhard and Bartz, G., *Das Buch vom erfüllten Leben*, 2 vols. (Lucerne: Faksimile Verlag Luzern, 2005).

Kren, Thomas and McKendrick, Scot, *Illuminating the Renaissance: The Triumph of Flemish Manuscript Painting in Europe* (London: J. Paul Getty Museum, 2003).

Kristeller, Paul Oskar, *Iter Italicum: A Finding List of Uncatalogues or Incompletely Catalogued Humanistic Manuscripts of the Renaissance in Italian and Other Libraries*, 6 vols. (London: Warburg Institute and Leiden: Brill, 1963–92).

Kristensson, Gillis, 'Another Piece of Evidence for the Study of Middle English Spelling', *Neuphilologische Mitteilungen*, 82 (1981), 159–61.

Krochalis, Jeanne, 'Hoccleve's Chaucer Portrait', *Chaucer Review*, 21 (1986), 234–45.

Kuczynski, Michael P., 'The Earliest English Wyclif Portraits?: Political Caricatures in Bodleian Library, Oxford, MS Laud Misc. 286', *JEBS*, 5 (2002), 121–39.

Kuskin, William, *Symbolic Caxton: Literary Culture and Print Capitalism* (University of Notre Dame Press, 2008).

Kwakkel, Erik, 'A Meadow without Flowers: What Happened to the Middle Dutch Manuscripts from the Charterhouse Herne?', *Quaerendo: A Quarterly Journal from the Low Countries Devoted to Manuscripts and Printed Books*, 33 (2003), 191–211.

'A New Type of Book for a New Type of Reader: The Emergence of Paper in Vernacular Book Production', *Library*, 7th ser., 4 (2003), 219–48.

Die Dietsche boeke die ons toebehoeren: De kartuizers van Herne en de productie van Middelnederlandse handschriften in de regio Brussel (1350–1400) (Leuven: Peeters, 2002).

'The Cultural Dynamics of Medieval Book Production', in *Manuscripten en miniaturen: Studies aangeboden aan Anne S. Korteweg bij haar afscheid van de Koninklijke Bibliotheek*, ed. Jos Biemans, Klaas van der Hoek, Kathryn M. Rudy and Ed van der Vlist (Zutphen: Walburg Pers, 2007), 243–52.

Kwakkel, Erik and Mulder, Herman, 'Quidam sermones: Mystiek proza van de Ferguut-kopiist (Brussel, Koninklijke Bibliotheek, hs. 3067–73)', *Tijdschrift voor Nederlandse Taal- en Letterkunde*, 117 (2001), 151–65.

L'Engle, Susan and Gibbs, Robert, *Illuminating the Law: Legal Manuscripts in Cambridge Collections* (London: Harvey Miller, 2001).

Labarre, E. J., 'The Study of Watermarks in Great Britain', in *The Briquet Album, a Miscellany on Watermarks, Supplementing Dr Briquet's Les Filigranes by Various Paper Scholars*, ed. E. J. Labarre (Hilversum: Paper Publications Society, 1952), 99–106.

Lafitte, M.-P., 'Les Manuscrits de Louis de Bruges, chevalier de la Toison d'or', in *Le Banquet du Faisan, 1454: L'Occident face au défit de l'empire ottoman*, ed. Marie-Therese Caron and Denis Clauzel (Arras: Artois Presses Université, 1997), 243–55.

Lagorio, Valerie M. and Sargent, Michael G., 'English Mystical Writings', in *A Manual of the Writings in Middle English 1050–1500: VII*, gen. ed. J. B. Severs and Albert E. Hartung (New Haven: Connecticut Academy of Arts and Sciences, 1993), 3049–137 and B3405–71.

Laidlaw, James, 'Christine and the Manuscript Tradition', in *Christine de Pizan: A Casebook*, ed. Barbara K. Altmann and Deborah L. McGrady (New York: Routledge, 2003).

Laing, Margaret and Lass, Roger (eds.), *A Linguistic Atlas of Early Middle English, 1150–1325* (University of Edinburgh, 2007), www.lel.ed.ac.uk/ihd/laeme1/laeme1.html

Latini, Brunetto, *The Book of the Treasure (Li Livres dou Tresor)*, trans. Paul Barrette and Spurgeon Baldwin (New York and London: Garland, 1993).

Lawson, R. P. (ed.), *The Bridlington Dialogue: An Exposition of the Rule of St Augustine for the Life of the Clergy, Given through a Dialogue between Master and Disciple, Translated and Edited by a Religious of C. S. M. V.* (London: A. R. Mowbray, 1960).

Lawton, Lesley, 'The Illustration of Late Medieval Secular Texts, with Special Reference to Lydgate's "Troy Book"', in *Manuscripts and Readers in Fifteenth-Century England: The Literary Implications of Manuscript Study*, ed. Derek Pearsall (Cambridge: Brewer, 1983), 41–69.

Le Goff, Jacques, *Time, Work and Culture in the Middle Ages*, trans. Arthur Goldhammer (University of Chicago Press, 1980).

Leclercq, Jean, '*Otium Monasticum* as a Context for Artistic Creativity', in *Monasticism and the Arts*, ed. Timothy G. Verdon and John Dally (Syracuse University Press, 1984), 63–80.

Otia monastica: Études sur le vocabulaire de la contemplation au Moyen Âge (Rome: Pontificium Institutum S. Anselmi and Herder, 1963).

Leedham-Green, Elisabeth, 'University Libraries and Book-Sellers', in *CHBB: III*, 316–53.

Leedham-Green, Elisabeth and Webber, Teresa (eds.), *The Cambridge History of Libraries in Britain and Ireland, Volume I: To 1640* (Cambridge University Press, 2006).

Leedham-Green, Elisabeth, Rhodes, D. E. and Stubbings, F. H. (eds.), *Garrett Godfrey's Accounts c.1527–1533* (Cambridge Bibliographical Society, 1992).

Lefèbvre, Henri, *The Production of Space* (1974), trans. D. Nicholson-Smith (Oxford: Blackwell, 1991; repr. 2001).

Lemon, R., 'A Collection of Water Marks by the Late Mr R. Lemon of the Record Office', in *Guide to the Collector of Historical Documents*, ed. Scott Davey and Samuel Davey (London: Davey, 1891).

Lepine, David, *A Brotherhood of Canons Serving God: English Secular Cathedrals in the Later Middle Ages* (Woodbridge: Boydell, 1995).

Lewis, Robert (gen. ed.), *The Middle English Dictionary* (1953–2001), from *The Middle English Compendium* (University of Michigan Digital Library Production Service, 2001), http://quod.lib.umich.edu/m/med/

Lewis, Robert E. and Angus McIntosh, *A Descriptive Guide to the Manuscripts of the 'Prick of Conscience'*, *MÆ* Monographs, ns, 12 (Oxford: Society for the Study of Mediaeval Languages and Literature, 1982).

Lewis, Robert E., Blake, N. F. and Edwards, A. S. G., *Index of Printed Middle English Prose* (New York: Garland, 1985).

Lieftinck, M. G. I., 'Pour une nomenclature de l'écriture livresque de la période dite gothique', in *Nomenclature des écritures livresques du IXe au XVIe siècles: Premier Colloque international de paléographie latine, Paris, 28–30 avril 1953*, ed. Bernhard Bischoff, G. I. Lieftinck and B. Battelli (Paris: Centre National de la Recherche Scientifique, 1954), 15–34.

Lister, Anthony, 'The Althop Library of Second Earl Spencer, now in the John Rylands University Library of Manchester: Its Formation and Growth', *BJRL*, 71.2 (1989), 67–86.

Lock, Julian, 'Grey, Arthur, Fourteenth Baron Grey of Wilton (1536–1593)', *ODNB*.

Loomis, Laura Hibbard, 'The Auchinleck Manuscript and a Possible London Bookshop of 1330–1340', *PMLA*, 57 (1942), 595–627.

Louis, Cameron (ed.), *The Commonplace Book of Robert Reynes of Acle: An Edition of Tanner MS 407* (New York: Garland, 1980).

Lovatt, Roger, 'College and University Book Collections and Libraries', in *The Cambridge History of Libraries in Britain and Ireland, Volume I: To 1640*, ed. Elisabeth Leedham-Green and Teresa Webber (Cambridge University Press, 2006), 152–77.

Love, Harold, *The Culture and Commerce of Texts: Scribal Publication in Seventeenth-Century England* (Oxford: Clarendon Press, 1993; repr. Amherst: University of Massachusetts Press, 1998).

Love, Harold and Marotti, Arthur F., 'Manuscript Transmission and Circulation', in *The Cambridge History of Early Modern English Literature*, ed. David Loewenstein and Janel Mueller (Cambridge University Press, 2002), 55–80.

Love, Nicholas, *The Mirror of the Blessed Life of Jesus Christ: A Full Critical Edition, Based on Cambridge University Library MSS 6578 and 6686, with Introduction, Notes and Glossary*, ed. Michael G. Sargent (University of Exeter Press, 2005).

Lovett, Patricia, *The British Library Companion to Calligraphy, Illumination and Heraldry: A History and Practical Guide* (London: British Library, 2000).

Lowry, Martin, 'John Rous and the Survival of the Neville Circle', *Viator*, 19 (1988), 327–38.

'The Arrival and Use of Continental Printed Books in Yorkist England', in *Le Livre dans L'Europe de la Renaissance*, ed. Pierre Aquilon and Henri-Jean Martin (Paris: Promodis, 1988), 449–59.

Lucas, Angela M. and Lucas, Peter J., 'Reconstructing a Disarranged Manuscript: The Case of MS Harley 913, a Medieval Hiberno-English Miscellany', *Scriptorium*, 44 (1990), 286–99.

Lucas, Angela M. (ed.), *Anglo-Irish Poems of the Middle Ages* (Blackrock: Columba, 1995).

Lucas, Peter J., 'A Fifteenth-Century Copyist at Work under Authorial Scrutiny: An Incident from John Capgrave's Scriptorium', *SB*, 34 (1981), 66–95.

'An Englishman in Rome: Capgrave's 1450 Jubilee Guide, *The Solace of Pilgrimes*', in *Studies in Late Medieval and Early Renaissance Texts in Honour of John Scattergood: 'The key of all good remembrance'*, ed. Anne Marie D'Arcy and Alan J. Fletcher (Dublin: Four Courts, 2005), 201–17.

From Author to Audience: John Capgrave and Medieval Publication (University College Dublin Press, 1997).

'John Capgrave, O. S. A. (1393–1464), Scribe and "Publisher"', *TCBS*, 5 (1969), 1–35.

Luders, Alexander, et al. (eds.), *Statutes of the Realm*, 11 vols. (London: Record Commission, 1810–28).

Luxford, Julian M., *The Art and Architecture of English Benedictine Monasteries, 1300–1540: A Patronage History* (Woodbridge: Boydell, 2005).

Lyall, R. J., 'Books and Book Owners in Fifteenth-Century Scotland', in G&P, 239–56.

'Materials: The Paper Revolution', in G&P, 11–29.

Lydgate, John, *Fall of Princes*, ed. Henry Bergen, 4 vols., EETS es 121, 122, 123, 124 (London: Oxford University Press, 1924–7; repr. 1967).

Minor Poems, ed. Henry Noble MacCracken, 2 vols., EETS es 107, os 192 (London: Kegan Paul, Trench, Trübner, 1911–34).

Madan, Falconer, *A Summary Catalogue of Western Manuscripts in the Bodleian Library at Oxford: Volume IV* (Oxford: Clarendon Press, 1897).

Madan, Falconer, Craster, Herbert Henry Edmund and Denholm-Young, N., *A Summary Catalogue of Western Manuscripts in the Bodleian Library at Oxford, Volume II, Part 2* (Oxford: Clarendon Press, 1937).

Maniaci, Marilena, *Archeologia del manoscritto: Metodi, problemi, bibliografia recente* (Rome: Viella, 2002).

Maniaci, Marilena and Munafò, Paola F. (eds.), *Ancient and Medieval Book Materials and Techniques: Erice, 18–25 September 1992* (Città del Vaticano: Biblioteca Apostolica Vaticana, 1993).

Manly, John Matthews and Rickert, Edith (eds.), *The Text of The Canterbury Tales: Studied on the Basis of All Known Manuscripts*, 8 vols. (University of Chicago Press, 1940).

Manuwald, Henrike, 'Pictorial Narrative in Legal Manuscripts? The *Sachsenspiegel* Manuscript in Wolfenbüttel', *Word and Image*, 23 (2007), 275–89.

Marín Martínez, Tomas, Asencio, Jose Manuel R. and Wagner, Klaus, *Catálogo concordado de la biblioteca de Hernando Colón*, 2 vols. (Madrid: Fundacion Mapfre America, 1993–5).

Marks, Richard, 'Two Illuminated Guild Registers from Bedfordshire', in *Illuminating the Book: Makers and Interpreters. Essays in Honor of Janet Backhouse*, ed. Michelle Brown and Scot McKendrick (London: British Library, 1998), 121–41.

Marks, Richard and Morgan, Nigel, *The Golden Age of English Manuscripts Painting 1200–1500* (London: Chatto and Windus, 1981).

Marks, Richard and Williamson, Paul (eds.), *Gothic: Art for England 1400–1547* (London: Victoria and Albert Publications, 2003).

Marotti, Arthur F., 'Malleable and Fixed Texts: Manuscript and Printed Miscellanies and the Transmission of Lyric Poetry in the English Renaissance', in *New Ways of Looking at Old Texts: Papers of the Renaissance English Text Society, 1985–1991*, ed. William Speed Hill (Binghamton: Medieval and Renaissance Text and Studies, 1993), 159–73.

Marsh, Deborah, 'Humphrey Newton of Newton and Pownall (1466–1536): A Gentleman of Cheshire and His Commonplace Book', unpub. PhD thesis (University of Keele, 1995).

'"I see by sivt of evidence": Information-Gathering in Late Medieval Cheshire', in *Courts, Counties and the Capital in the Later Middle Ages*, ed. Diana E. S. Dunn (Stroud and New York: Sutton, 1996), 71–92.

'The Late Medieval Commonplace Book: The Example of the Commonplace Book of Humphrey Newton of Newton and Pownall, Cheshire (1466–1536)', *Archives*, 25 (2002), 58–73.

Martin, C. A., 'Middle English Manuals of Religious Instruction', in *So Meny People, Longages and Tonges: Philological Essays in Scots and Mediaeval English Presented to Angus McIntosh*, ed. Michael Benskin and M. L. Samuels (Edinburgh: Middle English Dialect Project, 1981), 283–98.

Marzec, Marcia Smith, 'The Latin Marginalia of the *Regiment of Princes* as an Aid to Stemmatic Analysis', *Text*, 3 (1987), 269–84.

Mason Bradbury, Nancy and Collette, Carolyn P., 'Changing Times: The Mechanical Clock in Late Medieval Literature', *Chaucer Review*, 43 (2009), 351–75.

Matheson, Lister M. (ed.), *Death and Dissent: Two Fifteenth-Century Chronicles* (Woodbridge: Boydell, 1999).

  The Prose 'Brut': The Development of a Middle English Chronicle (Tempe, AZ: Medieval and Renaissance Texts and Studies, 1998).

Matthew, Colin, Harrison, Brian and Goldman, Lawrence (eds.), *Oxford Dictionary of National Biography* (Oxford University Press, 2004–10), www.oxforddnb.com/public/index.html

McCabe, Richard, *Spenser's Monstrous Regiment, Elizabethan Ireland and the Poetics of Difference* (Oxford University Press, 2002).

McDonald, Mark P., *The Print Collection of Ferdinand Columbus 1488–1539*, 2 vols. (London: British Museum Press, 2004).

McFarlane, K. B., *Lancastrian Kings and Lollard Knights* (Oxford: Clarendon Press, 1972).

McGann, Jerome J., *The Textual Condition* (Princeton University Press, 1991).

McGregor, James H., 'The Iconography of Chaucer in Hoccleve's De *Regimine Principum* and in the *Troilus* Frontispiece', *Chaucer Review*, 11 (1976–7), 338–50.

McHardy, A. K., '*De Heretico Comburendo*, 1401', in *Lollardy and the Gentry in the Later Middle Ages*, ed. Margaret Aston and Colin Richmond (Stroud: Sutton, 1997), 112–26.

McIntosh, A. I., 'A New Approach to Middle English Dialectology' (1963), in *Middle English Dialectology: Essays on Some Principles and Problems*, ed. Margaret Laing (Aberdeen University Press, 1989), 22–31.

  'Towards an Inventory of Middle English Scribes' (1974), in *Middle English Dialectology: Essays on Some Principles and Problems*, ed. Margaret Laing (Aberdeen University Press, 1989), 46–63.

  'Word Geography in the Lexicography of Middle English' (1973), in *Middle English Dialectology: Essays on Some Principles and Problems*, ed. Margaret Laing (Aberdeen University Press, 1989), 86–97.

McIntosh, Angus and Samuels, M. L., 'Prolegomena to the Study of Mediaeval Anglo-Irish', *MÆ*, 37 (1968), 1–11.

McIntosh, Angus, Samuels, M. L. and Benskin, M. (eds.), *A Linguistic Atlas of Late Mediaeval English 1350–1450*, 4 vols. (Aberdeen University Press, 1986).

McKenzie, D. F., *Bibliography and the Sociology of Texts* (Cambridge University Press, 1999).

  Making Meaning: 'Printers of the Mind' and Other Essays, ed. Peter D. McDonald and Michael F. Suarez, SJ (Amherst: University of Massachusetts Press, 2002).

McKitterick, David, *Print, Manuscript and the Search for Order 1450–1830* (Cambridge University Press, 2003).

McLachlan, Elizabeth Parker, *The Scriptorium of Bury St Edmunds in the Twelfth Century* (New York: Garland, 1986).

McSheffrey, Shannon, 'Heresy, Orthodoxy, and English Vernacular Religion, 1480–1525', *Past and Present*, 186 (2005), 47–80.

McSheffrey, Shannon and Tanner, Norman (eds.), *Lollards of Coventry, 1486–1522* (Cambridge University Press, 2003).

Meale, Carol M., ' "…alle the bokes that I haue of latyn, englisch, and frensch": Laywomen and Their Books in Late Medieval England', in *Women and Literature in Britain 1150–1500*, ed. Carol M. Meale (Cambridge University Press, 1993), 128–58.

'Patrons, Buyers and Owners: Book Production and Social Status', in G&P, 201–38.

Meyre Lee, Robert J., 'Manuscript Studies, Literacy Value, and the Object of Chaucer Studies', *Studies in the Age of Chaucer*, 30 (2008), 1–37.

Michael, M. A., 'A Manuscript Wedding Gift from Philippa of Hainault to Edward III', *Burlington Magazine*, 127 (1985): 582–98.

'English Illuminators *c.*1190–1450: A Survey from Documentary Sources', *EMS*, 4 (1993), 62–113.

'Oxford, Cambridge and London: Towards a Theory for "Grouping" Gothic Manuscripts', *The Burlington Magazine*, 130 (1988), 107–15.

'Urban Production of Manuscript Books and the Role of University Towns', in *CHBB: II*, 168–94.

Milazzo, M. M. et al. (eds.), *I manoscritti datati della Sicilia* (Florence: SISMEL Edizioni del Galluzzo, 2003).

Millar, Eric G., *English Illuminated Manuscripts from the XIVth to the XVth Centuries* (Paris: Van Oest, 1928).

Miller, Daniel, *Material Cultures: Why Some Things Matter* (University of Chicago Press, 1998).

(ed.), *Materiality* (Durham: Duke University Press, 2005).

Millett, Bella (ed.), *Ancrene Wisse: A Corrected Edition of the Text in Cambridge, Corpus Christi College, MS 402*, EETS os 325, 326 (Oxford University Press, 2005–6).

Minnis, Alastair, *Translations of Authority in Medieval English Literature: Valuing the Vernacular* (Cambridge University Press, 2009).

Mitchner, Robert W., 'Wynkyn de Worde's Use of the Plimpton Manuscript of *De Proprietatibus rerum*', *Library*, 5th ser., 6 (1951), 7–18.

Monnas, Lisa, 'Textiles from the Funerary Achievement of Henry V', in *The Lancastrian Court: Proceedings of the 2001 Harlaxton Symposium*, Harlaxton Medieval Studies III, ed. Jenny Stratford (Donington: Shaun Tyas, 2003), 125–46.

Mooney, Linne R., 'A New Manuscript by the Hammond Scribe: Discovered by Jeremy Griffiths', in *The English Medieval Book: Studies in Memory of Jeremy Griffiths*, ed. A. S. G. Edwards, Vincent Gillespie and Ralph Hanna III (London: British Library, 2000), 113–23.

'A New Scribe of Chaucer and Gower', *JEBS*, 7 (2004), 131–40.

'Chaucer's Scribe', *Speculum*, 81 (2006), 97–138.

(ed.), *IMEP, XI: Manuscripts in the Library of Trinity College, Cambridge* (Cambridge: Brewer, 1995).

'John Shirley's Heirs: The Scribes of Manuscript Literary Miscellanies Produced in London in the Second Half of the Fifteenth Century', *Yearbook of English Studies*, 33 (2003), 182–98.

'Locating Scribal Activity in Late Medieval London', in *Design and Distribution of Later Medieval Manuscripts in England*, ed. Margaret Connolly and Linne R. Mooney (York Medieval Press, 2008), 183–204.

'Manuscript Evidence for the Use of Medieval English Scientific and Utilitarian Texts', in *Interstices: Studies in Middle English and Anglo-Latin Texts in Honour of A. G. Rigg*, ed. Richard Firth Green and Linne R. Mooney (University of Toronto Press, 2004), 184–202.

'More Manuscripts Written by a Chaucer Scribe', *Chaucer Review*, 30 (1996), 401–7.

'Professional Scribes?: Identifying English Scribes Who Had a Hand in More Than One Manuscript', in *New Directions in Later Medieval Manuscript Studies: Essays from the 1998 Harvard Conference*, ed. Derek Pearsall (York Medieval Press, 2000), 131–41.

'Scribes and Booklets of Trinity College, Cambridge, MSS R.3.19 and R.3.21', in *Middle English Poetry: Texts and Traditions: Essays in Honour of Derek Pearsall*, ed. Alistair J. Minnis (Woodbridge: Boydell and Brewer, 2001), 241–66.

'Some New Light on Thomas Hoccleve', *SAC*, 29 (2007), 293–340.

Mooney, Linne R. and Matheson, Lister M. 'The Beryn Scribe and His Texts: Evidence for Multiple-Copy Production of Manuscripts in Fifteenth-Century England', *Library*, 7th ser., 4 (2003), 347–70.

Mooney, Linne R. and Mosser, Daniel W., 'The Belvoir Castle (Duke of Rutland) Manuscript of John Lydgate's Fall of Princes', *JEBS*, 12 (2009), 161–72.

Moore, Samuel, Meech, S. B. and Harold Whitehall, *Middle English Dialect Characteristics and Dialect Boundaries: Preliminary Report of an Investigation Based Exclusively on Localized Texts and Documents* (Ann Arbor: University of Michigan Press, 1935).

Morey, James H., *Book and Verse: A Guide to Middle English Biblical Literature* (Urbana: University of Illinois Press, 2000).

Morgan, Margery M., 'A Specimen of Early Printer's Copy: Rylands English MS. 2', *BJRL*, 33 (1951), 194–6.

'Pynson's Manuscript of *Dives and Pauper*', *Library*, 5th ser., 8 (1953), 217–28.

Morgan, Nigel J., 'Technology of Production of the Manuscript Book: Illumination – Pigments, Drawing and Gilding', in *CHBB: II*, 84–95.

Morgan, Nigel J. and Thomson, Rodney M. (eds.), *The Cambridge History of the Book in Britain: Volume II, 1100–1400* (Cambridge University Press, 2008).

Mosser, D. W., 'Dating the Manuscripts of "The Hammond Scribe": What the Paper Evidence Tells Us', *JEBS*, 10 (2007), 31–70.

Munby, A. N. L. with Popham, A. E, *The Formation of the Phillipps Library 1841–1872, with an Account of the Phillipps Art Collection* (Cambridge University Press, 1956).

Murray Jones, Peter, 'Harley MS 2558: A Fifteenth-Century Medical Commonplace Book', in *Manuscript Sources of Medieval Medicine: A Book of Essays*, ed. Margaret R. Schleissner (New York: Garland, 1995), 35–54.

'"Sicut hic depingitur …": John of Arderne and English Medical Illustration in the Fourteenth and Fifteenth Centuries', in *Die Kunst und das Studium der Natur von 14. zum 16. Jahrhundert*, ed. Wolfram Prinz, Andreas Beyer and Gerhard Baader (Weinheim: Acta Humaniora/VCH, 1987), 103–26.

'Staying with the Programme: Illustrated Manuscripts of John of Arderne, c.380–c.1550', *EMS*, 10 (2002), 204–27.

'The *Tabula medicine*: An Evolving Encyclopaedia', *EMS*, 14 (2008), 60–85.

Musson, Anthony, *Medieval Law in Context: The Growth of Legal Consciousness from Magna Carta to the Peasants' Revolt* (Manchester University Press, 2001).

Mynors, R. A. B., 'A Fifteenth-Century Scribe: T. Werken', *TCBS*, 1 (1950), 97–104.

Catalogue of the Manuscripts of Balliol College, Oxford (Oxford: Clarendon Press, 1963).

Nall, Catherine, 'Ricardus Franciscus Writes for William Worcester', *JEBS*, 11 (2008), 207–12.

Needham, Paul, 'Allan H. Stevenson and the Bibliographical Use of Paper', *SB*, 47 (1994), 24–64.

'Continental Printed Books Sold in Oxford, *c*.1480–3: Two Trade Records', in *Incunabula: Studies in Fifteenth-Century Printed Books Presented to Lotte Hellinga*, ed. Martin Davies (London: British Library, 1999), 243–70.

'The Customs Rolls as Documents for the Printed-Book Trade in England', in *CHBB: III*, 148–63.

Neville-Sington, Pamela, 'Press, Politics and Religion', in *CHBB: III*, 576–607.

Newman, Barbara, *God and the Goddesses: Vision, Poetry, and Belief in the Middle Ages* (Philadelphia: University of Pennsylvania Press, 2003).

Nicholls, K. W., 'Flattisbury, Philip (fl. 1503–1526)', *ODNB*.

Nightingale, Pamela, *A Medieval Mercantile Community: The Grocers' Company and the Politics and Trade of London, 1000–1485* (New Haven and London: Yale University Press, 1995).

Nixon, Howard M., 'A Register of Writs and the Scales Binder', *Book Collector*, 21 (1972), 227–44, 356–79.

Five Centuries of English Bookbinding (Aldershot: Scolar, 1978).

'William Caxton and Bookbinding', *Journal of the Printing Historical Society*, 11 (1976–7), 92–113.

Nixon, Howard M. and Foot, Mirjam M., *The History of Decorated Bookbinding in England* (Oxford: Clarendon Press, 1992).

Norton-Smith, John (ed.), *Bodleian Library MS. Fairfax 16* (London: Scolar Press, 1979).

O'Sullivan, Anne and O'Sullivan, William, 'Three Notes on Laud Misc. 610 (or the Book of Pottlerath)', *Celtica*, 9 (1971), 135–51.

Ogilvie-Thomson, S. J. (ed.), *IMEP, VIII: Manuscripts Containing Middle English Prose in Oxford College Libraries* (Cambridge: Brewer, 1991).

(ed.), *IMEP, XVI: Manuscripts in the Laudian Collection, Bodleian Library, Oxford* (Cambridge: Brewer, 2000).

Richard Rolle: Prose and Verse, EETS os 293 (Oxford University Press, 1988).

Oldham, J. Basil, *Blind Panels of English Binders* (Cambridge University Press, 1958).

English Blind-Stamped Bindings (Cambridge University Press, 1952).

Olson, Glending, *Literature as Recreation in the Later Middle Ages* (Ithaca: Cornell University Press, 1982).

Orme, Nicholas, *Education and Society in Medieval and Renaissance England* (London and Ronceverte: Hambledon, 1989).

Medieval Schools: From Roman Britain to Renaissance England (New Haven and London: Yale University Press, 2006).

Ornato, Ezio, 'Les Conditions de production et de diffusion du livre médiéval (xiiie–xve siècles). Quelques considerations générales', in *La Face cachée du livre médiéval: L'Histoire du livre vue par Ezio Ornato, ses amis et ses collègues*, ed. Ezio Ornato (Rome: Viella, 1997), 97–116.

Orr, Michael T., 'Hierarchies of Decoration in Early Fifteenth-Century English Books of Hours', in *Tributes to Kathleen L. Scott: English Medieval Manuscripts and Their Readers*, ed. Marlene Villalobos Hennessy (London and Turnhout: Harvey Miller, 2009).

'Illustration as Preface and Postscript in the Hours of the Virgin of Trinity College MS. B. 11. 7', *Gesta*, 34.2 (1995), 162–76.

'The Fitzherbert Hours (Dunedin Public Libraries, Reed MS 5) and the Iconography of St Anne Teaching the Virgin to Read in Early Fifteenth-Century England', in *Migrations: Medieval Manuscripts in New Zealand Collections*, ed. Stephanie Hollis and Alexandra Barratt (Cambridge Scholars, 2008), 216–46.

'The Hours of Elizabeth the Queen: Evidence for Collaboration between English Illuminators and an Artist from the Gold Scrolls Group', in *Flanders in a European Perspective: Manuscript Illumination around 1400 in Flanders and Abroad*, ed. Maurits Smeyers and Bert Cardon (Leuven: Peeters, 1995), 619–33.

'Tradition and Innovation in the Cycles of Miniatures Accompanying the Hours of the Virgin in Early Fifteenth-Century English Books of Hours', in *Manuscripts in Transition: Recycling Manuscripts, Texts and Images*, ed. Brigitte Dekeyzer and Jan Van der Stock (Leuven: Peeters, 2005), 263–70.

Oschinsky, Dorothea, *Walter of Henley and Other Treatises on Estate Management and Accounting* (Oxford: Clarendon Press, 1971).

Ouy, Gilbert, 'Charles d'Orléans and his Brother Jean d'Angoulême in England: What Their Manuscripts Have to Tell', in *Charles d'Orléans in England 1415–1440*, ed. Mary-Jo Arn (Cambridge: Brewer, 2000), 47–60.

La Librairie des frères captifs: Les manuscrits de Charles d'Orléans et Jean d'Angoulême (Turnhout: Brepols, 2007).

'Une Maquette de manuscrit à peintures', in *Mélanges d'histoire du livre et des bibliothèques offerts à Monsieur Frantz Calot* (Paris: Librairie d'Argences, 1960), 43–51.

Overgaauw, E. A., 'Fast or Slow, Professional or Monastic: The Writing Speed of Some Late Medieval Scribes', *Scriptorium*, 49 (1995), 211–27.

Overty, Joanne Filippone, 'The Cost of Doing Scribal Business: Prices of Manuscript Books in England, 1300–1483', *Book History*, 11 (2008), 1–32.

Owen, A. E. B., 'A Scrivener's Notebook from Bury St Edmunds', *Archives*, 14 (1979), 16–22.

Owen, Charles A. Jr, 'A Note on the Ink in Some Chaucer Manuscripts', *Chaucer Newsletter*, 2 (1980), 14.

The Manuscripts of The Canterbury Tales (Cambridge: Brewer, 1991).

Oxford English Dictionary (2nd edn, 1994), *Oxford English Dictionary Online* (Oxford University Press, 2009), http://www.oed.com/

Pächt, Otto. and Alexander, J. J. G., *Illuminated Manuscripts in the Bodleian Library*, Oxford, vol. III (Oxford: Clarendon Press, 1973).

Panayotova, Stella and Webber, Teresa, 'Making an Illuminated Manuscript', in *The Cambridge Illuminations: Ten Centuries of Book Production in the Medieval West*, ed. Paul Binski and Stella Panayotova (London and Turnhout: Harvey Miller/Brepols, 2005), 23–36.

Pantin, W. A., *Documents Illustrating the Activities of the General and Provincial Chapters of the English Black Monks 1215–1540* (London: Royal Historical Society, 1931–3).

Parkes, M. B., 'A Fifteenth-Century Scribe: Henry Mere', in *Scribes, Scripts and Readers* (London: Hambledon, 1991), 249–56.

'Archaizing Hands in English Manuscripts', in *Books and Collectors 1200–1700: Essays Presented to Andrew Watson*, ed. James P. Carley and Colin G. C. Tite (London: British Library, 1997), 101–41.

English Cursive Book Hands, 1250–1500 (Oxford: Clarendon Press, 1969).

'Handwriting in English Books', in *CHBB: II*, 110–35.

'Layout and Presentation of the Text', in *CHBB: II*, 55–74.

'Patterns of Scribal Activity and Revisions of the Text in Early Copies of Works by John Gower', in *New Science Out of Old Books: Studies in Manuscripts and Early Printed Books in Honour of A. I. Doyle*, ed. Richard Beadle and A. J. Piper (Aldershot: Scolar, 1995), 81–121.

Pause and Effect: An Introduction to the History of Punctuation in the West (Aldershot: Scolar, 1992).

'Richard Frampton: A Commercial Scribe *c.*1390–*c.*1420', in *The Medieval Book and a Modern Collector: Essays in Honour of Toshiyuki Takamiya*, ed. Takami Matsuda, Richard A. Linenthal and John Scahill (Cambridge: Brewer, 2004), 113–24.

'The Influence of the Concepts of *Ordinatio* and *Compilatio* on the Development of the Book', in *Scribes, Scripts and Readers: Studies in the Communication, Presentation and Dissemination of Medieval Texts*, ed. M. B. Parkes (London: Hambledon, 1991), 35–70.

'The Provision of Books', in *The History of the University of Oxford, Volume* II: *Late Medieval Oxford*, ed. J. I. Catto and Ralph Evans (Oxford: Clarendon Press, 1992), 407–83.

Their Hands before Our Eyes: A Closer Look at Scribes. The Lyell Lectures Delivered in the University of Oxford 1999 (Aldershot: Ashgate, 2008).

Parkes, M. B. and Beadle, Richard (eds.), *Poetical Works, Geoffrey Chaucer: A Facsimile of Cambridge University Library MS Gg.4.27*, 3 vols. (Cambridge: Brewer, 1979–80).

Parkes, M. B. and Salter, Elizabeth (eds.), *Troilus and Criseyde: A Facsimile of Corpus Christi College Cambridge MS 61* (Cambridge: Brewer, 1978).

Parry, Graham, 'Ware, Sir James (1594–1666)', *ODNB*.

Partridge, Stephen, 'Minding the Gaps: Interpreting the Manuscript Evidence of the *Cook's Tale* and the *Squire's Tale*', in *The English Medieval Book: Studies in Memory of Jeremy Griffiths*, ed. A. S. G. Edwards, Vincent Gillespie and Ralph Hanna III (London: British Library, 2000), 51–85.

'The *Canterbury Tales* Glosses and the Manuscript Groups', in *The Canterbury Tales Project Occasional Papers Volume 1*, ed. N. F. Blake and Peter Robinson (Oxford: Office for Humanities Communication, 1993), 85–94.

Pearsall, Derek, 'Appendix I: The Chaucer Portraits', in *The Life of Geoffrey Chaucer: A Critical Biography*, Derek Pearsall (Cambridge, MA: Blackwell, 1992), 285–305.

'"If heaven be on this earth, it is in cloister or in school": The Monastic Ideal in Later Medieval English Literature', in *Pragmatic Utopias: Ideals and Communities, 1200–1630*, ed. Rosemary Horrox and Sarah Rees Jones (Cambridge University Press, 2001), 11–25.

(ed.), *Piers Plowman: A New Annotated Edition of the C-Text* (University of Exeter Press, 2008).

(ed.), *Studies in the Vernon Manuscript* (Cambridge: Brewer, 1990).

'The Idea of Englishness in the Fifteenth Century', in *Nation, Court and Culture: New Essays on Fifteenth-Century English Poetry*, ed. Helen Cooney (Dublin: Four Courts, 2001), 15–27.

The Life of Geoffrey Chaucer: A Critical Biography (Cambridge, MA: Blackwell, 1992).

'The Manuscripts and Illustrations of Gower's Works', in *A Companion to Gower*, ed. Siân Echard (Cambridge: Brewer, 2004), 73–97.

'The Ellesmere Chaucer and Contemporary English Literary Manuscripts', in *The Ellesmere Chaucer: Essays in Interpretation*, ed. Martin Stevens and Daniel Woodward (San Marino, CA: Huntington Library and Tokyo: Yushodo, 1995), 263–80.

'The Rede (Boarstall) Gower: British Library, MS Harley 3490', in *The English Medieval Book: Studies in Memory of Jeremy Griffiths*, ed. A. S. G. Edwards, Vincent Gillespie and Ralph Hanna III (London: British Library, 2000), 87–99.

'The Whole Book: Late Medieval English Manuscript Miscellanies and their Modern Interpreters', in *Imagining the Book*, ed. Stephen Kelly and John J. Thompson (Turnhout: Brepols, 2005), 17–29.

Pearsall, Derek and Scott, Kathleen (eds.), *Piers Plowman: A Facsimile of Bodleian Library, Oxford, MS Douce 104* (Cambridge: Brewer, 1992).

Pearson, David, *English Bookbinding Styles 1450–1800: A Handbook* (London: British Library, 2004).

Oxford Bookbinding 1500–1640, Including a Supplement to Neil Ker's 'Fragments of Medieval Manuscripts Used as Pastedowns in Oxford Bindings' (Oxford Bibliographical Society, 2000).

Peikola, Matti, 'Aspects of *mise-en-page* in Manuscripts of the *Wycliffite Bible*', in *Medieval Texts in Context*, ed. Graham D. Caie and Denis Renevey (London and New York: Routledge, 2008), 28–67.

' "First is writen a clause of the bigynnynge therof": The Table of Lections in Manuscripts of the Wycliffite Bible', *Boletin Millares Carlo*, 24–5 (2005–6), 343–78.

'The Sanctorale, Thomas of Woodstock's English Bible, and the Orthodox Appropriation of Wycliffite Tables of Lessons', in *Wycliffite Controversies*, ed. Mishtooni Bose and Patrick J. Hornbeck II (Turnhout: Brepols, 2009).

Perry, R., 'The Clopton Manuscript and the Beauchamp Affinity: Patronage and Reception Issues in a West Midlands Reading Community', in *Essays in Manuscript Geography: Vernacular Manuscripts of the English West Midlands from the Conquest to the Sixteenth Century*, ed. Wendy Scase (Turnhout: Brepols, 2007), 131–59.

Petrucci, Armando, *Writers and Readers in Medieval Italy: Studies in the History of Written Culture*, trans. Charles Radding (New Haven and London: Yale University Press, 1995).

Pfaff, Richard W., *The Liturgy in Medieval England: A History* (Cambridge University Press, 2009).

Piazzi, A., *La Biblioteca Capitolare, Verona* (Florence: Nardini, 1994).

Pickering, O. S and O'Mara, V. M., *IMEP, XIII: Manuscripts in Lambeth Palace Library* (Cambridge: Brewer, 1999).

Pickering. O. S. and Powell, Susan (eds.), *IMEP, VI: A Handlist of Manuscripts Containing Middle English Prose in Yorkshire Libraries and Archives* (Cambridge: Brewer, 1989).

Pickwood, Nicholas, 'Onward and Downward: How Bookbinders Coped with the Printing Press 1500–1800', in *A Millennium of the Book: Production, Design and Illustration in Manuscript and Print, 900–1900*, ed. Robin Myers and Michael Harris (Winchester: St Paul's Bibliographies, 1994), 61–106.

'Tacketed Bindings: A Hundred Years of European Bookbinding', in *'For the love of the binding': Studies in Bookbinding History Presented to Mirjam Foot*, ed. David Pearson (London: British Library, 2000), 119–67.

'The Interpretation of Bookbinding Structure: An Examination of Sixteenth-Century Bindings in the Ramey Collection in the Pierpont Morgan Library', *Library*, 6th ser., 17 (1995), 209–49.

Piper, A. J., 'The Libraries of the Monks of Durham', in *Medieval Scribes, Manuscripts and Libraries: Essays Presented to N. R. Ker*, ed. M. B. Parkes and Andrew G. Watson (Aldershot: Scolar, 1978), 213–49.

Pirani, F., *I maestri cartari*, ed. G. Pinto (Florence: Chiari, 2000).

Plomer, Henry R., 'Two Lawsuits of Richard Pynson', *Library*, 2nd ser., 10 (1909), 115–33.

Pollard, Alfred W. and Redgrave, G. R., *A Short-Title Catalogue of Books Printed in England, Scotland, and Ireland and of English Books Printed Abroad, 1475–1640*, 2nd edn rev and enlarged by W. A. Jackson, F. S. Ferguson and Katharine F. Pantzer, 3 vols. (London: Bibliographical Society, 1986–91).

Pollard, Graham, 'Describing Medieval Bookbindings', in *Medieval Scribes, Manuscripts and Libraries: Essays Presented to N. R. Ker*, ed. M. B. Parkes and Andrew G. Watson (Aldershot: Scolar, 1978), 50–65.

'The Company of Stationers before 1557', *Library*, 4th ser., 18 (1937), 235–60.

'The English Market for Printed Books', *Publishing History*, 4 (1978), 7–48.

'The Names of Some English Fifteenth-Century Binders', *Library*, 5th ser., 25 (1970), 193–218.

Pollard, Graham and Ehrman, Albert, *The Distribution of Books by Catalogue from the Invention of Printing to A.D. 1800* (Cambridge: The Roxburghe Club, 1965).

Pouzet, Jean-Pascal, 'Augustinian Canons and Their Insular French Books in Medieval England: Towards an Assessment', in *Language and Culture in Medieval Britain: The French of England c.1100–c.1500*, ed. Jocelyn Wogan-Browne et al. (York Medieval Press, 2009), 266–77.

'Lieux et présence de l'anglo-français insulaire dans l'écriture religieuse anglaise (fin XIIe – fin XIVe siècle)', in *Journée d'études anglo-normandes organisée par l'Académie des Inscriptions et Belles-Lettres: Palais de l'Institute, 20 juin 2008: Actes*, ed. A. Crépin and J. Leclant (Paris: De Boccard, 2009), 39–80.

'"Pieces of Pye": Books Connected with John Pye, "Stacioner" of London, and his circle', unpub. conference paper (Eleventh Biennial Congress of the Early Book Society, University of Exeter, July 2009).

'Quelques Aspects de l'influence des chanoines augustins sur la production et la transmission littéraire vernaculaire en Angleterre (XIIIe–XVe siècles)', *Comptes Rendus de l'Académie des Inscriptions et Belles-Lettres* (janvier–mars 2004), 169–213.

'Southwark Gower – Augustinian Agencies in Gower's Manuscripts and Texts', *Proceedings of the First International Conference of the John Gower Society*, ed. E. Dutton et al. (Cambridge: Brewer, 2010), 11–24.

'"Space this werke to wirke": Quelques Figures de la complémentarité dans les manuscrits de Robert Thornton', in *La complémentarité: Mélanes offerts: Josseline Bidard et Arlette Sancery à l'occasion de leur départ en retraite*, ed. M.-F. Alamichel (Paris: AMAES, 2005), 27–43.

Putnam, George Haven, *Books and Their Makers during the Middle Ages: A Study of the Conditions of the Production and Distribution of Literature from the Fall of the Roman Empire to the Close of the Seventeenth Century*, 2 vols. (1896–7; repr. as one vol., New York: Hilary House, 1962).

Quandt, Abigail B. and Noel, William G., 'From Calf to Codex', in *Leaves of Gold: Manuscript Illumination from Philadelphia Collections*, ed. James R. Tanis with Jennifer A. Thompson (Philadelphia Museum of Art, 2001), 14–20.

Ramsay, Nigel, 'Archive Books', in *CHBB: II*, 416–45.

'Law', in *CHBB: II*, 250–90.

Ramsay, Nigel and Willoughby, James (eds.), *Secular Colleges*, CBMLC (London: British Library, 2009).

Raschko, Mary, 'Common Ground for Contrasting Ideologies: The Texts and Contexts of "A Schort Reule of Lif" ', *Viator*, 40 (2009), 387–410.

Raven, James, *The Business of Books: Booksellers and the English Book Trade, 1450–1850* (New Haven: Yale University Press, 2008).

Rawcliffe, Carole, *Leprosy in Medieval England* (Woodbridge: Boydell, 2006).

'Passports to Paradise: How English Medieval Hospitals and Almshouses Kept Their Archives', *Archives*, 27 (2002), 2–22.

' "Written in the Book of Life": Building the Libraries of Medieval English Hospitals and Almshouses', *Library*, 7th ser., 3 (2002), 127–62.

Raymo, Robert R., 'Works of Religious and Philosophical Instruction', in *A Manual of the Writings in Middle English 1050–1500: VII*, gen. ed. J. B. Severs and Albert E. Hartung (New Haven: Connecticut Academy of Arts and Sciences, 1986), 2255–378 and B2467–582.

Reames, Sherry L., 'Late Medieval Efforts at Standardization and Reform in the Sarum Lessons for Saints' Days', in *Design and Distribution of Late Medieval Manuscripts in England*, ed. Margaret Connolly and Linne R. Mooney (York Medieval Press, 2008), 91–117.

Reed, Ronald, *Ancient Skins, Parchments and Leathers* (London and New York: Seminar, 1972).

Revard, Carter, 'Scribe and Provenance', in *Studies in the Harley Manuscript: The Scribes, Contents, and Social Contexts of British Library MS Harley 2253*, ed. Susanna Fein (Kalamazoo, MI: Western Michigan University Press, 2000), 21–109.

Reynolds, Catherine, 'England and the Continent: Artistic Relations', in *Gothic: Art for England 1400–1547*, ed. Richards Marks and Paul Williamson (London: Victoria and Albert Publications, 2003), 76–85.

'English Patrons and French Artists in Fifteenth-Century Normandy', in *England and Normandy in the Middle Ages*, ed. David Bates and Anne Curry (London and Rio Grande: Hambledon, 1994), 299–313.

'Masters, Anonymous, and Monogrammists, Fastolf Master [Master of Sir John Fastolf]', in *The Dictionary of Art*, ed. Jane Turner et al., 34 vols. (New York: Grove's Dictionaries, 1996), xx.664.

'The Workshop of the Master of the Duke of Bedford: Definitions and Identities', in *Patrons, Authors and Workshops: Books and Book Production in Paris around 1400*, ed. Godfried Croenen and Peter Ainsworth (Leuven: Peeters, 2006), 437–72.

Rhodes, Dennis E., 'Don Fernando Colón and His London Book Purchases, June 1522', *Papers of the Bibliographical Society of America*, 52 (1958), 231–48.

Rice, Nicole R., *Lay Piety and Religious Discipline in Middle English Literature* (Cambridge University Press, 2009).

Richardson, H. G., 'Heresy and the Lay Power under Richard II', *EHR*, 51 (1936), 1–28.

Rickert, Margaret, 'Illumination', in *The Text of the Canterbury Tales: Studied on the Basis of All Known Manuscripts*, ed. John M. Manly and Edith Rickert (University of Chicago Press, 1940), 1.561–605.

La miniatura inglese, 2 vols. (Milan: Electa Editrice, 1959–61).

Painting in Britain: The Middle Ages, 2nd edn (Harmondsworth: Penguin, 1965).

The Reconstructed Carmelite Missal (London: Faber, 1952).

Riddy, Felicity (ed.), *Regionalism in Late Medieval Manuscripts and Texts: Essays Celebrating the Publication of a Linguistic Atlas of Medieval English* (Cambridge: Brewer, 1991).

Rigg, A. G. (ed.), *A Glastonbury Miscellany of the Fifteenth Century: A Descriptive Index of Trinity College, Cambridge, MS o.9.38* (Oxford: Clarendon Press, 1968).

Robbins, Rossell Hope, 'A Middle English Diatribe against Philip of Burgundy', *Neophilologus*, 39 (1955), 131–46.

(ed.), *Secular Lyrics of the xivth and xvth Centuries*, 2nd edn (Oxford: Clarendon Press, 1955).

'The Findern Anthology', *PMLA*, 69 (1954), 610–42.

'The Poems of Humphrey Newton, Esquire, 1466–1536', *PMLA*, 65 (1950), 249–81.

Roberts, Julian, 'Importing Books for Oxford, 1500–1640', in *Books and Collectors 1200–1700: Essays Presented to Andrew Watson*, ed. James Carley and Colin G. Tite (London: British Library, 1997), 317–33.

Robertson, Jean, 'L'Entrée de Charles Quint à Londres, en 1522', in *Fêtes et Cérémonies au Temps de Charles Quint*, ed. Jean Jacquot (Paris: Centre National de la Recherche Scientifique, 1960), 169–81.

Robinson, Pamela R., *Catalogue of Dated and Datable Manuscripts c.737–1600 in Cambridge Libraries*, 2 vols. (Cambridge: Brewer, 1988).

Catalogue of Dated and Datable Manuscripts c.888–1600 in London Libraries, 2 vols. (London: British Library, 2003).

'The "Booklet": A Self-Contained Unit in Composite Manuscripts', *Codicologica/Litterae Textuales*, 3 (1980), 46–69.

'The Format of Books: Books, Booklets and Rolls', in *CHBB: II*, 41–54.

Roest, Bert, *A History of Franciscan Education (1210–1517)* (Leiden: Brill, 2000).

Rogers, Nicholas J., 'Fitzwilliam Museum MS. 3–1979: A Bury St Edmunds Book of Hours and the Origins of the Bury Style', in *England in the Fifteenth Century: Proceedings of the 1986 Harlaxton Symposium*, ed. Daniel Williams (Woodbridge: Boydell and Brewer, 1987), 229–43.

'From Alan the Illuminator to John Scott the Younger: Evidence for Illumination in Cambridge', in *The Cambridge Illuminations: The Conference Papers*, ed. Stella Panayotova (London: Harvey Miller, 2007), 287–99.

'Regional Production', in *Gothic: Art for England 1400–1547*, ed. R. Marks and P. Williamson (London: Victoria and Albert Publications, 2003), 94–7.

'The Bury Artists of Harley 2278 and the Origins of Topographical Awareness in English Art', in *Bury St Edmunds: Medieval Art, Architecture, Archaeology and Economy*, ed. Antonia Gransden (Leeds: Maney, 1998), 217–28.

'The Miniature of St John the Baptist in Gonville and Caius MS 241/127 and Its Context', *TCBS*, 10 (1992), 125–38.

Root, Robert Kilburn (ed.), *The Book of Troilus and Criseyde* (Princeton University Press, 1926).

The Textual Tradition of Chaucer's Troilus (London: Kegan Paul, Trench, Trübner, 1916).

Rose, Mark, *Authors and Owners: The Invention of Copyright* (Cambridge, MA: Harvard University Press, 1993).

Ross, C., *The Estates and Finances of Richard Beauchamp, Earl of Warwick* (Oxford: Dugdale Society, 1956).

Roth, Francis, 'Sources for a History of the English Austin Friars', *Augustiniana*, 9 (1959), 109*–294*.

Rouse, Mary A., 'Archives in the Service of Manuscript Study: The Well-Known Nicolas Flamel', in *Patrons, Authors and Workshops: Books and Book Production in Paris around 1400*, ed. Godfried Croenen and Peter Ainsworth (Leuven: Peeters, 2006), 69–89.

Rouse, Richard H., 'Kirkstede, Henry (b. *c.*1313, d. in or after 1378)', *ODNB*.

Rouse, Richard H. and Rouse, Mary A., 'The Commercial Production of Manuscript Books in Late Thirteenth-Century and Early Fourteenth-Century Paris', in *Medieval Book Production: Assessing the Evidence*, ed. Linda L. Brownrigg (Los Altos Hills, CA: Anderson-Lovelace, 1990), 103–15.

Manuscripts and Their Makers: Commercial Book Producers in Medieval Paris 1200–1500, 2 vols. (London: Harvey Miller, 2000).

Roy, Ashok and Smith, Perry (eds.), *Painting Techniques: History, Materials and Studio Practice* (London: International Institute for Conservation of Historic and Artistic Works, 1998).

Royce-Roll, Donald, 'Materials, Preparations and Recipes of the Medieval Illuminator', *AVISTA Forum Journal*, 18 (2008), 31–49.

Rück, Peter (ed.), *Pergament: Geschichte, Struktur, Restaurierung, Herstellung* (Sigmaringen Jan: Thorbecke Verlag, 1991).

Rundle, David, 'A Renaissance Bishop and His Books: A Preliminary Survey of the Manuscript Collection of Pietro del Monte (*c.*1400–57)', *Papers of the British School at Rome*, 69 (2001), 245–72.

England and the Identity of Italian Renaissance Humanism, forthcoming.

'From Greenwich to Verona: Antonio Beccaria, St Athanasius and the Translation of Orthodoxy', *Humanistica*, forthcoming.

'Habits of Manuscript-Collecting and the Dispersals of the Library of Humfrey, Duke of Gloucester', in *Lost Libraries: The Destruction of Great Book Collections since Antiquity*, ed. James Raven (Basingstoke: Palgrave Macmillan, 2004), 106–24.

'Of Republics and Tyrants: Aspects of Quattrocento Humanist Writings and Their Reception in England, *c.*1400–*c.*1460', unpub. DPhil. thesis (University of Oxford, 1997).

'The Scribe Thomas Candour and the Making of Poggio Bracciolini's English Reputation', *EMS*, 12 (2005), 1–25.

'Tito Livio Frulovisi and the Place of Comedies in the Formation of a Humanist Career', *Studi Umanistici Piceni*, 24 (2004), 193–202.

Rust, Martha Dana, *Imaginary Worlds in Medieval Books: Exploring the Manuscript Matrix* (Basingstoke: Palgrave Macmillan, 2007).

Ryder, Michael L., 'The Biology and History of Parchment', in *Pergament: Geschichte, Struktur, Restaurierung, Herstellung*, ed. Peter Rück (Sigmaringen Jan: Thorbecke Verlag, 1991), 25–33.

Salter, Elizabeth, 'The "Troilus Frontispiece"', in *Troilus and Criseyde: A Facsimile of Corpus Christi College Cambridge MS 61*, ed. M. B. Parkes and Elizabeth Salter (Cambridge: Brewer, 1978), 15–23.

Salter, H. E. (ed.), *Registrum cancellarii oxoniensis, 1434–69*, 2 vols. (Oxford Historical Society, 1932).

Sammut, Alfonso, *Unfredo duca di Gloucester e gli umanisti italiani* (Padua: Antenore, 1980).

Samuels, M. L., 'Langland's Dialect' (1985), in *The English of Chaucer and His Contemporaries*, ed. Jeremy J. Smith and M. L. Samuels (Aberdeen University Press, 1988), 70–85.

'Some Applications of Middle English Dialectology' (1963), in *Middle English Dialectology: Essays on Some Principles and Problems*, ed. Margaret Laing (Aberdeen University Press, 1989), 64–80.

'The Scribe of the Hengwrt and Ellesmere Manuscripts of *The Canterbury Tales*' (1983), in *The English of Chaucer and His Contemporaries*, ed. Jeremy J. Smith and M. L. Samuels (Aberdeen University Press, 1988), 38–50.

Samuels, M. L. and Smith, Jeremy J. 'The Language of Gower' (1981), in *The English of Chaucer and His Contemporaries*, ed. Jeremy J. Smith and M. L. Samuels (Aberdeen University Press, 1988), 13–22.

Sandler, Lucy Freeman, 'A Note on the Illuminators of the Bohun Manuscripts', *Speculum*, 60 (1985), 364–72.

Gothic Manuscripts 1285–1385, 2 vols., A Survey of Manuscripts Illuminated in the British Isles, 5 (Oxford: Harvey Miller and Oxford University Press, 1986).

'Jean Pucelle and the Lost Miniatures of the Belleville Breviary', *Art Bulletin*, 66 (1984), 73–96.

'Notes for the Illuminator: The Case of the Omne Bonum', *Art Bulletin*, 71 (1989), 551–64.

Sargent, Michael G. (ed.), 'Introduction', in Love, Nicholas, *The Mirror of the Blessed Life of Jesus Christ: A Full Critical Edition, Based on Cambridge University Library MSS 6578 and 6686, with Introduction, Notes and Glossary*, ed. Michael G. Sargent (University of Exeter Press, 2005).

'What Do the Numbers Mean? Observations on Some Patterns of Middle English Manuscript Transmission', in *Design and Distribution of Late Medieval Manuscripts in England*, ed. Margaret Connolly and Linne R. Mooney (York Medieval Press, 2008), 205–44.

Savage, Ernest A., *Old English Libraries: The Making, Collection, and Use of Books during the Middle Ages* (Chicago: McClurg and London: Methuen, 1912).

Scase, Wendy (ed.), *Essays in Manuscript Geography: Vernacular Manuscripts of the English West Midlands from the Conquest to the Sixteenth Century* (Turnhout: Brepols, 2007).

Literature and Complaint in England 1272–1553 (Oxford University Press, 2007).

(ed.), *Manuscripts of the West Midlands: A Catalogue of Vernacular Manuscript Books of the English West Midlands, c.1300–c.1475* (University of Birmingham, 2006), www.mwm.bham.ac.uk

Reginald Pecock (Aldershot: Ashgate, 1996).

'Reginald Pecock, John Carpenter and John Colop's "Common-Profit" Books: Aspects of Book Ownership and Circulation in Fifteenth-Century London', *MÆ*, 61 (1992), 261–74.

(ed.), *The Making of the Vernon Manuscript: The Production and Contexts of Oxford, Bodleian Library, MS Eng. poet.a.1* (Turnhout: Brepols, forthcoming).

(ed.), *A Facsimile Edition of the Vernon Manuscript: A Literary Hoard from Medieval England* (Oxford: Bodleian Library, 2010).

Schaap, Barbara, '*Scribere pulchre potes, si posteriora notes* … On Writing-Masters, Sheets and Tracts', *Scriptorium*, 59 (2005), 51–73.

Scheller, Robert W., *Exemplum: Model-Book Drawings and the Practice of Artistic Transmission in the Middle Ages (c.900 – c.1470)*, trans. M. Hoyle (Amsterdam University Press, 1995).

Schibanoff, Susan, 'The New Reader and Female Textuality in Two Early Commentaries on Chaucer', *SAC*, 10 (1988), 71–108.

Schirmer, Walter F., *John Lydgate*, trans. Ann E. Keep (London: Methuen, 1961).

Schmidt, Gerhard, 'Chaucer in Italy: Some Remarks on the "Chaucer Frontispiece" in MS. 61, Corpus Christi College, Cambridge', in *New Offerings, Ancient Treasures: Studies in Medieval Art for George Henderson*, ed. Paul Binski and William Noel (Stroud: Sutton, 2001), 478–91.

Scholla, Agnes B. H., 'Early Western Limp Bindings: Report on a Study', in *Care and Conservation of Manuscripts 7: Proceedings of the Seventh International Seminar Held at The Royal Library Copenhagen 18–19 April 2002*, ed. Gillian Fellows-Jensen and Peter Springborg (Copenhagen: Museum Tusculanum, 2003), 132–58.

'*Libri sine asseribus*: Zur Eindbandtechnik, Form und Inhalt mitteleuropäischer Koperte des 8. bis 14. Jahrhunderts', unpub. PhD thesis (University of Leiden, 2002).

Schroeder, H. J., *Disciplinary Decrees of the General Councils: Text, Translation and Commentary* (St Louis, MO: Herder, 1937).

Schulz, H. C., 'Middle English Texts from the "Bement" Manuscript', *Huntington Library Quarterly*, 3 (1939–40), 451–7.

Scott, Kathleen L., 'A Mid-Fifteenth-Century English Illuminating Shop and Its Customers', *JWCI*, 31 (1968), 170–96.

'Caveat lector: Ownership and Standardization in the Illustrations of Fifteenth-Century English Manuscripts', *EMS*, 1 (1989), 19–63.

Dated and Datable English Manuscript Borders c.1395–1499 (London: Bibliographical Society and British Library, 2002).

'Design, Decoration and Illustration', in G&P, 31–64.

'*Fall of Princes* by John Lydgate', in *Leaves of Gold: Manuscript Illumination from Philadelphia Collections*, ed. by James R. Tanis with Jennifer A. Thompson (Philadelphia Museum of Art, 2001), 208–10.

'Four Early Fifteenth-Century English Manuscripts of the *Speculum humanae salvationis* and a Fourteenth-Century Exemplar', *EMS*, 10 (2002), 177–203.

'Instructions to a Limner in Beinecke MS. 223', *Yale University Library Gazette*, 72.1–2 (1997), 13–16.

Later Gothic Manuscripts 1390–1490, A Survey of Manuscripts Illuminated in the British Isles 6, 2 vols. (London: Harvey Miller, 1996).

'Limner-Power: A Book Artist in England c.1420', in *Prestige, Authority and Power in Late Medieval Manuscripts and Texts*, ed. Felicity Riddy (Woodbridge: York Medieval Press, 2000), 55–75.

'Limning and Book-Producing Terms and Signs *in situ* in Late Medieval English Manuscripts: A First Listing', in *New Science out of Old Books: Studies in Manuscripts and Early Printed Books in Honor of A. I. Doyle*, ed. Richard Beadle and A. J. Piper (Aldershot: Scolar, 1995), 142–88.

'*Lydgate's Lives of SS Edmund and Fremund*: A Newly Located Manuscript in Arundel Castle', *Viator*, 13 (1982), 335–66.

'Representations of Scribal Activity in English Manuscripts c.1400–c.1490: A Mirror of the Craft?', in *Pen in Hand: Medieval Scribal Portraits, Colophons and Tools*, ed. Michael Gullick (Walkern: Red Gull, 2006), 115–49.

The Caxton Master and His Patrons (Cambridge Bibliographical Society, 1976).

'The Illustration and Decoration of Manuscripts of Nicholas Love's Mirror of the Blessed Life of Jesus Christ', in *Nicholas Love: Waseda, 1995*, ed. Shoichi Oguro, Richard Beadle and Michael G. Sargent (Cambridge: Brewer, 1997), 61–86.

'The Illustration and Decoration of the Register of the Fraternity of the Holy Trinity at Luton Church, 1475–1546', in *The English Medieval Book: Studies in Memory of Jeremy Griffiths*, ed. A. S. G. Edwards, Vincent Gillespie and Ralph Hanna III (London: British Library, 2000) 155–83.

'The Illustration of *Piers Plowman* in Bodleian Library MS. Douce 104', *Yearbook of Langland Studies*, 4 (1990), 1–86.

(ed.), *The Mirroure of the Worlde: MS Bodley 283 (England, c.1470–1480): The Physical Composition, Decoration and Illustration* (Oxford: Roxburghe Club, 1980).

Tradition and Innovation in Later Medieval English Manuscripts (London: British Library, 2007).

'Two Sequences of Dated Illuminated Manuscripts Made in Oxford, 1450–64', in *Books and Collectors, 1200–1700: Essays Presented to Andrew Watson*, ed. James P. Carley and Colin G. C. Tite (London: British Library, 1997), 43–69.

Seaton, Ethel, *Sir Richard Roos, c.1410–1482: Lancastrian Poet* (London: Rupert Hart-Davis, 1961).

Senocak, N., 'Book Acquisition in the Medieval Franciscan Order', *Journal of Religious History*, 27 (2003), 14–28.

Serjeantson, Mary S., 'The Index of the Vernon Manuscript', *Modern Language Review*, 32 (1937), 222–61.

Seymour, M. C., 'A Literatim Trevisa Abstract', *Neuphilologische Mitteilungen*, 93 (1992), 185–91.

A Catalogue of Chaucer Manuscripts, 2 vols. (Aldershot: Scolar, 1995–7).

'Manuscript Pictures of Duke Humfrey', *BLR*, 12 (1986), 95–105.

'Manuscript Portraits of Chaucer and Hoccleve', *Burlington Magazine*, 124 (1982), 618–23.

Shailor, Barbara A., *Catalogue of Medieval and Renaissance Manuscripts in the Beinecke Rare Book and Manuscript Library at Yale University* (Turnhout: Brepols, 2004).

Sharpe, Richard, *A Handlist of the Latin Writers of Great Britain and Ireland before 1540*, 2nd edn (Turnhout: Brepols, 2001).

'Library Catalogues and Indexes', in *CHBB: II*, 197–218.

'The Medieval Librarian', in *The Cambridge History of Libraries in Britain and Ireland, Volume 1: To 1640*, ed. Elisabeth Leedham-Green and Teresa Webber (Cambridge University Press, 2006), 218–41.

Sharpe, Richard, Carley, James P., Thomson, Rodney M. and Watson, Andrew G. (eds.), *English Benedictine Libraries: The Shorter Catalogues*, CBMLC, 4 (London: British Library, 1995).

Sheppard, Jennifer M., 'Reading the Binding, Reading the Record: The Census of Western Medieval Bookbinding Structures to 1500 in British Libraries', in *Care and Conservation of Manuscripts 5: Proceedings of the Fifth International Seminar Held at the University of Copenhagen 19–20 April 1999*, ed. Gillian Fellows-Jensen and Peter Springborg (Copenhagen: Royal Library, 2000), 48–62.

'Some Twelfth-Century Monastic Bindings and the Question of Localization', in *Making the Medieval Book: Techniques of Production*, ed. Linda Brownrigg (Los Altos Hills, CA: Anderson-Lovelace, 1995), 181–98.

The Buildwas Books: Book Production, Acquisition and Use at an English Cistercian Monastery, 1165–c.1400 (Oxford Bibliographical Society, 1997).

'The Census of Western Medieval Bookbinding Structures to 1500 in British Libraries, Stage 1: Cambridge. A Final Report – and a Glimpse of Some "Treasures"', in *Care and Conservation of Manuscripts 8: Proceedings of the Eighth International Seminar Held at the University of Copenhagen 16–17 October 2003*, ed. Gillian Fellows-Jensen and Peter Springborg (Copenhagen: Royal Library, 2003), 175–89.

Shorter, Alfred H., *Paper Mills and Paper Makers in England 1495–1800* (Hilversum: Paper Publications Society, 1957).

Simms, Katharine, 'The Norman Invasion and the Gaelic Recovery', in *The Oxford Illustrated History of Ireland*, ed. R. F. Foster (Oxford University Press, 1989), 53–103.

Simpson, James, 'Confessing Literature', *ELN*, 44 (2006), 121–6.

Reform and Cultural Revolution: The Oxford English Literary History, Volume II, 1350–1547 (Oxford University Press, 2002).

'Saving Satire after Arundel's Constitutions: John Audelay's "Marcol and Solomon"', in *Text and Controversy from Wyclif to Bale: Essays in Honour of Anne Hudson*, ed. Helen Barr and Ann M. Hutchinson (Turnhout: Brepols, 2005), 387–404.

'The Constraints of Satire in *Piers Plowman* and *Mum and the Sothsegger*', in *Langland, the Mystics, and the Medieval English Religious Tradition: Essays in Honour of S. S. Hussey*, ed. Helen Phillips (Cambridge: Brewer, 1990), 11–30.

Sinclair, Alexandra, *The Beauchamp Pageant* (Donington: Paul Watkins, 2003).

Sinclair, K. V., 'Anglo-Norman at Waterford: The Mute Testimony of MS Cambridge, Corpus Christi College 405', in *Medieval French Textual Studies in Memory of T. B. W. Reid*, ed. Ian Short (London: ANTS, 1984), 219–38.

Smallwood, T. M., 'Another Example of the Double-Copying of a Passage of Middle English', *Neuphilologische Mitteilungen*, 87 (1986), 550–4.

Smith, Brendan, 'The British Isles in the Late Middle Ages: Shaping the Regions', in *Ireland and the English World in the Late Middle Ages*, ed. Brendan Smith (Houndmills: Palgrave Macmillan, 2009), 7–19.

Smith, Jeremy J., *An Historical Study of English: Function, Form and Change* (London: Routledge, 1996).

'Dialect and Standardization in the Waseda Manuscript of Nicholas Love's *Mirror of the Blessed Life of Jesus Christ*', in *Nicholas Love: Waseda, 1995*, ed. Shoichi Oguro, Richard Beadle and Michael G. Sargent (Woodbridge: Boydell and Brewer, 1997), 129–41.

'Spelling and Tradition in Fifteenth-Century Copies of Gower's *Confessio Amantis*', in *The English of Chaucer and His Contemporaries*, ed. Jeremy J. Smith and M. L. Samuels (Aberdeen University Press, 1988), 96–113.

'The Trinity Gower D-Scribe and His Work on Two Early *Canterbury Tales* Manuscripts', in *The English of Chaucer and His Contemporaries*, ed. Jeremy J. Smith and M. L. Samuels (Aberdeen University Press, 1988), 51–69.

Smyth, William J., *Map-Making, Landscapes and Memory: A Geography of Colonial and Early Modern Ireland, c.1530–1750* (Cork University Press in association with Field Day, 2006).

Somerset, Fiona, *Clerical Discourse and Lay Audience in Late Medieval England* (Cambridge University Press, 1998).

'Professionalizing Translation at the Turn of the Fifteenth Century: Ullerston's Determinacio, Arundel's Constitutiones', in *The Vulgar Tongue: Medieval and Postmedieval Vernacularity*, ed. Fiona Somerset and Nicholas Watson (University Park: Pennsylvania State University Press, 2003), 145–57.

Review of Shannon McSheffrey and Norman Tanner (eds.), *Lollards of Coventry, 1486–1522*, *The Medieval Review*, 2004 (Indiana University Scholar Works Repository, 2004), https://scholarworks.iu.edu/dspace/handle/2022/3631

'Wycliffite Spirituality', in *Text and Controversy from Wyclif to Bale: Essays in Honour of Anne Hudson*, ed. Helen Barr and Ann M. Hutchinson (Turnhout: Brepols, 2005), 375–86.

Somerville, Sam, 'Parchment and Vellum', in *The Calligrapher's Handbook*, ed. Heather Child (London: A&C Black, 1985), 59–83.

Sotheby, Samuel Leight, *Principia Typographica*, 3 vols. (London: McDowall, 1858).

Spencer, Eleanor P., *The Sobieski Hours: A Manuscript in the Royal Library at Windsor Castle* (London: Academic, 1977).

Spencer, Helen Leith, *English Preaching in the Late Middle Ages* (Oxford: Clarendon Press, 1993).

'The Fortunes of a Lollard Sermon-Cycle in the Later Fifteenth Century', *Mediaeval Studies*, 48 (1986), 352–96.

Spriggs, G. M., 'The Nevill Hours and the School of Herman Scheere', *JWCI*, 37 (1974), 104–30.

'Unnoticed Bodleian Manuscripts, Illuminated by Herman Scheerre and His school', *BLR*, 7 (1964), 193–203.

Staley, Lynn (ed.), *The Book of Margery Kempe* (Kalamazoo, MI: Medieval Institute Publications, 1996).

Statutes of the Realm, 12 vols. (London: Record Commission, 1810–28).

Steele, Robert (ed.), *Three Prose Versions of the Secreta Secretorum*, EETS es 74 (London: Kegan Paul, Trench, Trübner, 1898).

Steer, F. W. (ed.), *Scriveners' Company Common Paper*, London Record Society, 4 (London Record Society, 1968).

Steiner, Emily, *Documentary Culture and the Making of English Literature* (Cambridge University Press, 2003).

Stenton, F. M., 'The Road System of Medieval England', *Economic History Review*, 7 (1936), 1–21.

Sternagel, Peter, *Die artes mechanicae im Mittelalter: Begriffs- und Bedeutungsgeschichte bis zum Ende des 13. Jahrhunderts* (Kallmünz über Regensburg: Verlag Michael Lassleben, 1966).

Stevens, Martin and Woodward, Daniel, *The Ellesmere Chaucer: Essays in Interpretation* (San Marino: Huntington Library, 1995).

Stevenson, Allan H., 'Tudor Roses from John Tate', *SB*, 20 (1967), 15–34.

Strang, Barbara M. H., *A History of English* (London: Methuen, 1970).

Stratford, Jenny, *The Bedford Inventories: The Worldly Goods of John, Duke of Bedford, Regent of France (1389–1435)* (London: Society of Antiquaries of London, 1993).

'The Early Royal Collections and the Royal Library to 1461', in *CHBB: III*, 255–66.

(ed.), *The Lancastrian Court: Proceedings of the 2001 Harlaxton Symposium*, Harlaxton Medieval Studies XIII (Donington: Shaun Tyas, 2003).

Stratford, Jenny and Webber, Teresa, 'Bishops and Kings: Private Book Collections in Medieval England', in *The Cambridge History of Libraries in Britain and Ireland: Volume I: To 1640*, ed. Elisabeth Leedham-Green and Teresa Webber (Cambridge University Press, 2006), 178–217.

Streeter, B. H., *The Chained Library: A Survey of Four Centuries in the Evolution of the English Library* (London: Macmillan, 1931).

Social Chaucer (Cambridge, MA: Harvard University Press, 1989).

(ed.), *Oxford Twenty-First Century Approaches to Literature: Middle English* (Oxford University Press, 2007).

Theory and the Premodern Text (Minneapolis: University of Minnesota Press, 2000).

Stubbs, Estelle, 'A New Manuscript by the Hengwrt/Ellesmere Scribe? Aberystwyth, National Library of Wales, MS. Peniarth 393D', *JEBS*, 5 (2002), 161–8.

'A Study of the Codicology of Four Early Manuscripts of *The Canterbury Tales*: Aberystwyth, National Library of Wales MS. Peniarth 392d (Hengwrt), Oxford, Corpus Christi College, MS. 198 (Corpus), London, British Library MS. Harley 7334 (Harley 4), and California, San Marino, Huntington Library MS. El. 26 C 9 (Ellesmere)', unpub. PhD thesis (University of Sheffield, 2006).

' "Here's One I Prepared Earlier": The Work of Scribe D on Oxford, Corpus Christi College, MS 198', *Review of English Studies*, 58 (2007), 133–53.

(ed.), *The Hengwrt Chaucer Digital Facsimile* (Leicester: Scholarly Digital Editions, 2000).

Summit, Jennifer, *Memory's Library: Medieval Books in Modern England* (University of Chicago Press, 2008).

Supino Martini, Paula, 'Il libro e il tempo', in *Scribi e colofoni: Le sottoscrizioni di copisti dalle origini all'avvento della stampa*, ed. Emma Condello and Giuseppe de Gregorio (Spoleto: Centro Italiano di Studi sull'Alto Medioevo, 1995), 3–33.

Sutton, Anne F., 'Books Owned by Mercers of London 1400–1540', unpub. conference paper (Eleventh Biennial Congress of the Early Book Society, University of Exeter, July 2009).

'Christian Colborne, Painter of Germany and London, Died 1486', *Journal of the British Archaeological Association*, 135 (1982), 55–61.

The Mercery of London: Trade, Goods and People, 1130–1578 (Aldershot: Ashgate, 2005).

'The Mercery Trade and the Mercers' Company of London: From the 1130s to 1348', unpub. PhD thesis (University of London, 1995).

Sutton, Anne F. and Visser-Fuchs, Livia, 'British Library Manuscript Additional 48031A: The Manuscript, Its Later Ownership and Its Contents', in *The Politics of Fifteenth-Century England: John Vale's Book*, ed. Margaret Lucille Kekewich, Colin Richmond, Anne F. Sutton, Livia Visser-Fuchs and John L. Watts (Stroud: Sutton, 1995), 127–268.

Sutton, Anne F., and Visser-Fuchs, Livia, 'The Provenance of the Manuscript: The Lives and Archive of Sir Thomas Cooke and His Man of Affairs, John Vale', in *The Politics of Fifteenth-Century England: John Vale's Book*, ed. Margaret Lucille Kekewich, Colin Richmond, Anne F. Sutton, Livia Visser-Fuchs and John L. Watts (Stroud: Sutton, 1995), 73–123.

Swanson, Heather, *Medieval Artisans: An Urban Class in Late Medieval England* (Oxford: Blackwell, 1989).

Swanson, R. N., *Indulgences in Late Medieval England: Passports to Paradise?* (Cambridge University Press, 2007).

Swinburn, L. M. (ed.), *Lanterne of Liȝt*, EETS os 151 (1917; repr. London: Brewer, 1999).

Szirmai, J. A., *The Archaeology of Medieval Bookbinding* (Aldershot: Scolar, 1999).

Taavitsainen, Irma (ed.), *IMEP, X: Manuscripts in Scandinavian Collections* (Cambridge: Brewer, 1994).

'Scriptorial "House-Styles" and Discourse Communities', in *Medical and Scientific Writing in Late Medieval English*, ed. Irma Taavitsainen and Päivi Pahta (Cambridge University Press, 2004), 209–40.

Taavitsainen, Irma and Pahta, Päivi (eds.), *Medical and Scientific Writing in Late Medieval English* (Cambridge University Press, 2004).

Tanis, James R. with Thompson, Jennifer A. (eds.), *Leaves of Gold: Manuscript Illumination from Philadelphia Collections* (Philadelphia Museum of Art, 2001).

Tanselle, G. Thomas, *Bibliographical Analysis: A Historical Introduction* (Cambridge University Press, 2009).

Tavormina, M. Teresa, 'The Middle English Letter of Ipocras', *English Studies*, 88 (2007), 632–52.

'The Twenty-Jordan Series: An Illustrated Middle English Uroscopy Text', *American Notes and Queries*, 18 (2005), 40–64.

Thomas, Arthur H. (ed.), *Calendar of the Plea and Memoranda Rolls of the City of London: Volume III, 1381–1412* (Cambridge University Press, 1932).

Thompson, A. H., *The Abbey of St Mary of the Meadows Leicester* (Leicester: Leicestershire Archaeological Society, 1949).

Thompson, John J., 'A Poet's Contacts with the Great and the Good: Further Consideration of Thomas Hoccleve's Texts and Manuscripts', in *Prestige, Authority and Power in Late Medieval Manuscripts and Texts*, ed. Felicity Riddy (York Medieval Press, 2000), 77–101.

'Collecting Middle English Romances and Some Related Book-Production Activities in the Later Middle Ages', in *Romance in Medieval England*, ed. Maldwyn Mills, Jennifer Fellows and Carol M. Meale (Cambridge: Brewer, 1991), 17–38.

'Mapping Points West of West Midlands Manuscripts and Texts: Irishness(es) and Middle English Literary Culture', in *Essays in Manuscript Geography: Vernacular Manuscripts of the English West Midlands from the Conquest to the Sixteenth Century*, ed. Wendy Scase (Turnhout: Brepols, 2007), 113–28.

Robert Thornton and the London Thornton Manuscript: British Library MS Additional 31042 (Cambridge: Brewer, 1987).

'Textual Instability and the Late Medieval Reputation of Some Middle English Religious Literature', *Transactions of the Society for Textual Scholarship*, 5 (1991), 175–94.

'The Middle English Prose *Brut* and the Possibilities of Cultural Mapping', in *Design and Distribution of Late Medieval Manuscripts in England*, ed. Margaret Connolly and Linne R. Mooney (York Medieval Press, 2008), 245–60.

'Thomas Hoccleve and Manuscript Culture', in *Nation, Court and Culture: New Essays on Fifteenth-Century English Poetry*, ed. Helen Cooney (Dublin: Four Courts Press, 2001), 81–94.

Thomson, David, *A Descriptive Catalogue of Middle English Grammatical Texts* (New York: Garland, 1979).

Thomson, John A. F., *The Later Lollards, 1414–1520* (Oxford University Press, 1965).

Thomson, Rodney M., *A Descriptive Catalogue of the Medieval Manuscripts in Worcester Cathedral Library* (Cambridge: Brewer, 2001).

A Descriptive Catalogue of the Medieval Manuscripts of Merton College, Oxford (Cambridge: Brewer, 2009).

Books and Learning in Twelfth-Century England: The Ending of 'Alter Orbis', Lyell Lectures for 2000–1 (Walkern: Red Gull, 2006).

'Monastic and Cathedral Book Production', in *CHBB: II*, 136–67.

The Archives of the Abbey of Bury St Edmunds (Woodbridge: Boydell and Brewer, 1980).

Morgan, Nigel, Gullick, Michael, and Hadgraft, Nicholas, 'Technology of Production of the Manuscript Book: Parchment and Paper, Ruling and Ink', in *CHBB: II*, 75–84.

Tilley, Christopher Y. Keane, Webb, Kuechler-Fogden, Susanne, Spyer, Patricia, Rowlands, Michael, *Handbook of Material Culture* (London: Sage, 2006).

Tite, Colin G. C., *The Early Records of Sir Robert Cotton's Library. Formation, Cataloguing, Use* (London: British Library, 2003).

Trapp, J. B., 'Notes on Manuscripts Written by Pieter Meghen', *Book Collector*, 24 (1975), 80–96.

'Pieter Meghen 1466/7–1540: Scribe and Courier', *Erasmus in English*, 11 (1981–2), 28–35.

Tschann, Judith and Parkes, M. B. (eds.), *Facsimile of Oxford, Bodleian Library, MS Digby 86*, EETS ss 16 (Oxford University Press, 1996).

Tudor-Craig, Pamela, 'The "Large Letters" of the Lytlington Missal and Westminster Abbey in 1383–84', in *Illuminating the Book: Makers and Interpreters. Essays in Honor of Janet Backhouse*, ed. Michelle P. Brown and Scot McKendrick (London and Toronto: British Library and University of Toronto Press, 1998), 102–19.

Turner, Marion, 'Conflict', in *Oxford Twenty-First Century Approaches to Literature: Middle English*, ed. Paul Strohm (Oxford University Press, 2007), 258–73.

Turville-Petre, Thorlac, 'Some Medieval English Manuscripts of the North-West Midlands', in *Manuscripts and Readers in Fifteenth-Century England: The Literary Implications of Manuscript Study*, ed. Derek Pearsall (Cambridge: Brewer, 1983), 125–41.

Vale, Malcolm, *The Princely Court: Medieval Courts and Culture in North-West Europe 1270–1380* (Oxford University Press, 2001).

Van Buren, Anne H. and Edmunds, Sheila, 'Playing Cards and Manuscripts: Some Widely Disseminated Fifteenth-Century Model Sheets', *Art Bulletin*, 56 (1974), 12–30.

Van der Velden, H., 'Prayer Roll of Henry Beauchamp, Duke of Warwick', in *Gothic: Art for England 1400–1547*, ed. Richard Marks and Paul Williamson (London: Victoria and Albert Publications, 2003), 228.

Van Dijk, S. J. P., 'An Advertisement Sheet of an Early Fourteenth-Century Writing Master at Oxford', *Scriptorium*, 10 (1956), 47–64.

Verduyn, Anthony, 'Darcy family (per. *c.*1284–1488)', *ODNB*.

Vespasiano da Bisticci, *Le vite*, ed. Aulo Greco, 2 vols. (Florence: Nella Sede dell'Istituto, 1970–6).

Vest, Marie, 'The Production and Use of Alum-Tawed Leather in the Middle Ages and Later', in *Care and Conservation of Manuscripts 5: Proceedings of the Fifth International Seminar Held at the University of Copenhagen 19–20 April 1999*, ed. Gillian Fellows-Jensen and Peter Springborg (Copenhagen: The Royal Library, 2000), 16–20.

Vickers, Kenneth Hotham, *Humphrey Duke of Gloucester* (London: Constable, 1907).

Vinaver, Eugène (ed.), *Malory: Complete Works* (Oxford: Clarendon Press, 1967).

'Principles of Textual Emendation', in *Studies in French Language and Medieval Literature Presented to Professor Mildred K. Pope* (Manchester University Press, 1939), 351–69.

Voigts, Linda Ehrsam, 'Scientific and Medical Books', in G&P, 345–402.

Von Nolcken, Christina, 'Notes on Lollard Citation of John Wyclif's Writings', *Journal of Theological Studies* ns 39 (1988), 411–37.

Wagner, Sir Anthony, *Aspilogia, Being Materials of Heraldry: A Catalogue of English Medieval Rolls of Arms*, 2 vols. (Oxford: Society of Antiquaries, 1940).

Wakelin, Daniel, *Humanism, Reading, and English Literature 1430–1530* (Oxford University Press, 2007).

    'Scholarly Scribes and the Creation of *Knyghthode and Bataile*', *EMS*, 12 (2005), 26–45.

    'The Carol in Writing: Three Anthologies from Fifteenth-Century Norfolk', *JEBS*, 9 (2006), 25–49.

    'William Worcester Writes a History of His Reading', *New Medieval Literatures*, 7 (2005), 53–71.

Wallace, David (ed.), *The Cambridge History of Medieval English Literature* (Cambridge University Press, 1999).

Walsham, Alexandra, 'Inventing the Lollard Past: The Afterlife of a Medieval Sermon in Early Modern England', *Journal of Ecclesiastical History*, 58 (2007), 628–56.

Ware, Sir James, *The Historie of Ireland, collected by Three Learned Authors viz. Meredith Hanmer, Doctor in Divinitie: Edmund Campion, sometime Fellow of St Johns Colledge in Oxford: and Edmund Spenser Esq.* (Dublin, 1633).

Wathey, Andrew, 'The Production of Books of Liturgical Polyphony', in G&P, 143–61.

Watson, Andrew G., *A Descriptive Catalogue of the Medieval Manuscripts of Exeter College Oxford* (Oxford University Press, 2000).

    Catalogue of Dated and Datable Manuscripts c.435–1600 in Oxford Libraries, 2 vols. (Oxford: Clarendon Press, 1984).

    Catalogue of Dated and Datable Manuscripts c.700–1600 in the Department of Manuscripts in the British Library, 2 vols. (London: British Library, 1979).

    Medieval Libraries of Great Britain: Supplement to the Second Edition (London: Royal Historical Society, 1987).

    Medieval Manuscripts in Post-Medieval England (Aldershot: Ashgate, 2004).

Watson, Nicholas, 'Censorship and Cultural Change in Late Medieval England: Vernacular Theology, the Oxford Translation Debate, and Arundel's Constitutions of 1409', *Speculum*, 70 (1995), 822–64.

    'Conference Response', unpub. conference paper (After Arundel Conference, St John's College, Oxford, April 2009).

    'Cultural Changes', *ELN*, 44 (2006), 127–37.

Watson, Rowan, *Illuminated Manuscripts and Their Makers* (London: Victoria and Albert Publications, 2003).

Webber, Teresa, 'Latin Devotional Texts and the Books of the Augustinian Canons of Thurgarton Priory and Leicester Abbey in the Late Middle Ages', in *Books and Collectors 1200–1700: Essays Presented to Andrew Watson*, ed. James P. Carley and Colin G. C. Tite (London: British Library, 1997), 27–41.

    'The Books of Leicester Abbey', in *Leicester Abbey. Medieval History, Archaeology and Manuscript Studies*, ed. Joanna Story, Jill Bourne and Richard Buckley (Leicester: Leicestershire Archaeological and Historical Society, 2006), 127–46.

    'The Provision of Books for Bury St Edmunds Abbey in the 11th and the 12th Centuries', in *Bury St Edmunds: Medieval Art, Architecture, Archaeology and Economy*, ed. Antonia Gransden (Leeds: British Archaeological Association, 1998), 186–93.

Webber, Teresa and Watson, Andrew G. (eds.), *The Libraries of the Augustinian Canons*, CBMLC, 6 (London: British Library with British Academy, 1998).

Wehmer, Carl, 'Die Schreibmeisterblätter des späten Mittelalters', in *Miscellanea Giovanni Mercati: Vol. VI Paleografia, Bibliografia, Varia* (Città del Vaticano: Biblioteca Apostolica Vaticana, 1946), 147–61.

Weiss, Roberto, *Humanism in England during the Fifteenth Century*, 3rd edn (Oxford: Blackwell, 1967).

Wenzel, Siegfried, 'A Dominican Preacher's Handbook from Oxford', *Archivum Fratrum Prædicatorum*, 68 (1998), 177–203.

Preachers, Poets, and the Early English Lyric (Princeton University Press, 1986).

White Jr., Lynn, 'Medieval Engineering and the Sociology of Knowledge', *Pacific Historical Review*, 44 (1975), 1–21.

Whitney, Elspeth, 'Paradise Restored: The Mechanical Arts from Antiquity through the Thirteenth Century', *Transactions of the American Philosophical Society* ns 80 (1990), 1–169.

Wijsman, H., 'Gebonden weelde: Productie van geïllustreerde handschriften en adellijk boekenbezit in de Bourgondische Nederlanden (1400–1550)', unpub. PhD thesis (University of Leiden, 2003).

Wilkins, David, *Concilia Magnae Britanniae et Hiberniae*, 4 vols. (London, 1737).

Willard, Charity Cannon, *Christine de Pizan: Her Life and Works* (New York: Persea Books, 1984).

Williman, D., 'Some Additional Provenances of Cambridge Latin Manuscripts', *TCBS*, 11 (1999), 427–48.

Willoughby, J., 'The Provision of Books in the English Secular College', in *The Late Medieval English College and Its Context*, ed. Clive Burgess and Martin Heale (York Medieval Press, 2008), 154–79.

Wilson, Edward, *A Descriptive Index of the English Lyrics in John of Grimestone's Preaching Book* (Oxford: *MÆ* Monographs, 1973).

Windeatt, B.A. (ed.), *Troilus and Criseyde: A New Edition of 'The Book of Troilus'* (London: Longman, 1984).

Winstead, Karen A., *John Capgrave's Fifteenth Century* (Philadelphia: University of Pennsylvania Press, 2007).

Wogan-Browne, Jocelyn, et al. (eds.), *Language and Culture in Medieval Britain: The French of England, c.1100–c.1500* (York Medieval Press, 2009).

Wogan-Browne, Jocelyn, Watson, Nicholas, Taylor, Andrew and Evans, Ruth (eds.), *The Idea of the Vernacular: An Anthology of Late Middle English Literary Theory, 1280–1520* (University Park: Pennsylvania State University Press, 1999).

Wormald, Francis and Wright, Cyril Ernest, *The English Library before 1700: Studies in Its History* (London: Athlone, 1958).

Wright, Cyril Ernest, 'Late Middle English Parerga in a School Collection', *Review of English Studies*, ns 2, 6 (1951), 114–20.

Wright, Sylvia, 'Bruges Artists in London', in *Flanders in a European Perspective. Manuscript Illumination around 1400 in Flanders and Abroad*, ed. Maurits Smeyers and Bert Cardon (Leuven: Peeters, 1995), 93–109.

'The Author Portraits in the Bedford Psalter-Hours: Gower, Chaucer and Hoccleve', *British Library Journal*, 18 (1992), 190–202.

Wüstefeld, W. C. M., 'A Remarkable Prayer Roll Attributed to the Master of Sir John Fastolf', *Quaerendo*, 33 (2003), 233–46.

Wynn Thomas, Peter et al. (eds.), *Welsh Prose 1350–1425* (Cardiff University, 2007), www.rhyd-diaithganoloesol.caerdydd.ac.uk

Young, John and Aitken, P. Henderson, *A Catalogue of the Manuscripts in the Library of the Hunterian Museum in the University of Glasgow* (Glasgow: Maclehose, 1908).

Zerdoun Bat-Yehouda, Monique, *Les Encres noires au Moyen Âge (jusqu'à l'âge 1600)* (Paris: Editions du Centre National de la Recherche Scientifique, 1983).

Zumthor, Paul, *Toward a Medieval Poetics*, trans. Philip Bennett (Minneapolis: University of Minnesota Press, 1992).

Index of manuscripts

General index

Printed in Great Britain
by Amazon